RELIGIONS OF JAPAN IN PRACTICE

PRINCETON READINGS IN RELIGIONS

————

Donald S. Lopez, Jr., Editor

TITLES IN THE SERIES

————

Religions of India in Practice edited by Donald S. Lopez, Jr.

Buddhism in Practice edited by Donald S. Lopez, Jr.

Religions of China in Practice edited by Donald S. Lopez, Jr.

Religions of Tibet in Practice edited by Donald S. Lopez, Jr.

Religions of Japan in Practice edited by George J. Tanabe, Jr.

RELIGIONS OF

JAPAN

IN PRACTICE

George J. Tanabe, Jr., Editor

PRINCETON READINGS IN RELIGIONS

PRINCETON UNIVERSITY PRESS

PRINCETON, NEW JERSEY

Library of Congress Cataloging-in-Publication Data
Religions of Japan in practice / edited by George J. Tanabe, Jr.
p.   cm. — (Princeton readings in religions)
Includes bibliographical references and index.
ISBN 0-691-05788-5 (cl. : alk. paper). — ISBN 0-691-05789-3 (pbk.
: alk. paper)
1. Japan—Religion.   I. Tanabe, George Joji.   II. Series.
BL2202.R48   1999
200′.952—dc21   98-44252

This book has been composed in Berkeley

The paper used in this publication meets the minimum requirements
of ANSI/NISO Z39.48-1992 (R 1997) (*Permanence of Paper*)

http://pup.princeton.edu

Printed in the United States of America

1 3 5 7 9 10 8 6 4 2

1 3 5 7 9 10 8 6 4 2
(pbk.)

PRINCETON READINGS

IN RELIGIONS

———

Princeton Readings in Religions is a series of anthologies on the religions of the world, representing the significant advances that have been made in the study of religions in the last thirty years. The sourcebooks used by previous generations of students, whether for Judaism and Christianity or for the religions of Asia and the Middle East, placed a heavy emphasis on "canonical works." Princeton Readings in Religions provides a different configuration of texts in an attempt better to represent the range of religious practices, placing particular emphasis on the ways in which texts have been used in diverse contexts. The volumes in the series therefore include ritual manuals, hagiographical and autobiographical works, popular commentaries, and folktales, as well as some ethnographic material. Many works are drawn from vernacular sources. The readings in the series are new in two senses. First, very few of the works contained in the volumes have ever have made available in an anthology before; in the case of the volumes on Asia, few have even been translated into a Western language. Second, the readings are new in the sense that each volume provides new ways to read and understand the religions of the world, breaking down the sometimes misleading stereotypes inherited from the past in an effort to provide both more expansive and more focused perspectives on the richness and diversity of religious expressions. The series is designed for use by a wide range of readers, with key terms translated and technical notes omitted. Each volume also contains an introduction by a distinguished scholar in which the histories of the traditions are outlined and the significance of each of the works is explored.

Religions of Japan in Practice is the fifth volume in the series. It brings together the work of thirty-eight leading scholars, each of whom has provided one or more translations of key works, most of which are translated here for the first time. Each chapter in the volume begins with a substantial introduction in which the translator discusses the history and influence of the work, identifying points of particular difficulty or interest. The volume as a whole offers both new materials and fresh insights for the study of the religions of Japan, providing an opportunity to reconsider the sometimes overly rigid dividing lines between religious sects and historical periods that heretofore have served as the framework within which Japanese religions have been understood.

I had initially planned to edit this volume myself but quickly determined that the task was beyond my capabilities. Robert Morrell played a central role in the initial stages of assembling and editing many of the chapters in the volume, and I gratefully acknowledge the crucial contribution of his time, energy, and insight. George Tanabe has used his rich knowledge of the entire range of Japanese religions to edit and organize the wealth of materials provided by the contributors into the present volume. He has also written a clear and accessible introduction that sets the forty-five chapters both in context and in conversation.

Several other volumes of Princeton Readings in Religion are in process, including volumes on tantra, medieval Judaism, Islamic mysticism, and the religions of Latin America, with a dozen more volumes planned.

Donald S. Lopez, Jr.
Series Editor

NOTE ON
TRANSLITERATION
NAMES, AND
ABBREVIATIONS

———

Japanese, Chinese, and Sanskrit words in the original appear with diacritical marks except for those that are in common English usage. Since most scholars of Japanese religions, at least as represented in this volume, prefer the Wade-Giles system of transliterating Chinese, it is used here, as in *pinyin* by the few who prefer that method. A conversion table is provided in the appendix. When Chinese, Japanese, and Sanskrit equivalent terms are provided in parentheses, they are indicated by the letters C., J., and S., respectively.

Japanese personal names are given according to the Japanese custom of listing the last name first, except for instances in which Japanese scholars write in English and use the convention of placing surname last.

References to standard collections of Buddhist texts are abbreviated as follows:

DNBZ Bussho kankō kai, ed., *Dai Nihon Bukkyō zenshō*.
T   Takakusu Junjirō and Watanabe Kaikyoku, ed., *Taishō shinshū daizōkyō*.

CONTENTS

Ethical Practices

SOCIAL VALUES

CLERICAL PRECEPTS

LAY PRECEPTS

Ritual Practices

GODS

Institutional Practices

CONTENTS BY CHRONOLOGY

CONTENTS BY TRADITION

Christianity

CONTRIBUTORS

Allan A. Andrews was professor of religion at the University of Vermont.

Michiko Y. Aoki is associate professor of Japanese at Clark University and a research fellow at Harvard Law School.

Carl Bielefeldt teaches in the Department of Religious Studies at Stanford University.

William M. Bodiford is associate professor in the Department of East Asian Languages and Cultures at the University of California, Los Angeles.

William E. Deal is Severance Associate Professor of the History of Religion and director of the Asian Studies Program at Case Western Reserve University.

James C. Dobbins is professor in the Religion Department and East Asian Studies Program at Oberlin College.

Yoshiko Kurata Dykstra teaches in the English Department at Kansai Gaidai University in Osaka.

H. Byron Earhart is professor of comparative religion at Western Michigan University.

Gary L. Ebersole is professor of history and religious studies at the University of Missouri, Kansas City.

David L. Gardiner is assistant professor in the Department of Religion at Colorado College.

Richard A. Gardner teaches at Sophia University in Tokyo.

Suzanne Gay is associate professor in the East Asian Studies Program at Oberlin College.

Ward Geddes is an academic *rōnin*.

Dennis Hirota is head translator of *The Collected Works of Shinran* and teaches at Ryūkoku University, Kyoto.

Charles Holcombe is associate professor in the Department of History at the University of Northern Iowa.

Richard Jaffe is assistant professor of religion at North Carolina State University.

Linda Klepinger Keenan is an independent scholar and translator of Minoru Kiyota, *Beyond Loyalty: The Story of a Kibei* (University of Hawaii Press, 1977).

William R. LaFleur is professor of Japanese at the University of Pennsylvania.

Jane Marie Law is assistant professor of Japanese religion and ritual studies in the Asian Studies Department at Cornell University.

Etsuko Mita is instructor of Japanese at Western Michigan University.

Robert E. Morrell is professor in the Department of Asian and Near Eastern Languages and Literatures, Washington University, St. Louis.

Sachiko Kaneko Morrell is the East Asian and Near Eastern Studies librarian at Washington University, St. Louis.

Joseph Parker is associate professor of East Asian thought in the International and Intercultural Studies Department at Pitzer College.

Richard K. Payne is dean and associate professor of Japanese Buddhism at the Institute of Buddhist Studies, Graduate Theological Union, Berkeley.

Cherish Pratt holds an M.A. in religion from the University of Hawaii and is assistant to the president of Catalyst for Women in New York City.

Ian Reader is a member of the Department of Japanese Studies at the University of Stirling in Scotland, U.K.

Janine Anderson Sawada is assistant professor in the School of Religion at the University of Iowa.

Miwa Stevenson is lecturer in the Department of East Asian Languages and Cultures at the University of Kansas.

Jacqueline I. Stone is associate professor in the Department of Religion, Princeton University.

Paul L. Swanson is a permanent fellow at the Nanzan Institute for Religion and Culture and teaches at Nanzan University in Nagoya, Japan.

George J. Tanabe, Jr., is professor in the Department of Religion at the University of Hawaii.

Mark Teeuwen is lecturer in the Department for Religious and Theological Studies, University of Wales, Cardiff.

Sybil Thornton is assistant professor of history at Arizona State University.

Mary Evelyn Tucker is associate professor in the departments of Religion and East Asian Studies at Bucknell University.

Jan Van Bragt is retired director of the Nanzan Institute for Religion and Culture at Nanzan University in Nagoya, Japan.

Hendrik van der Veere is lecturer in the Centre for Japanese and Korean Studies at Leiden University.

Paul B. Watt teaches in the Department of Religious Studies and is director of Asian Studies at DePauw University.

Albert Welter is associate professor of religious studies at the University of Winnipeg.

RELIGIONS OF JAPAN IN PRACTICE

INTRODUCTION

_____

George J. Tanabe, Jr.

The forty-five chapters in this anthology have no apparent master by which they may be ordered. This is, in part, by deliberate design, the attempt here being to present Japanese religions in their complex diversity rather than as neatly ordered systems of thought. It is also a reflection of recent methodological approaches that call into question essentialist readings of texts and highlight the manner in which their meanings are influenced not only by how they are placed in context but also by how researchers, according to their predilections, read them. Our knowledge has been enriched by recent scholars who have looked into these complex relationships and offered insights about the invention of traditions, the history of changing interpretations, the uses of power defended as legitimate mandates, and the impact of ideology on scholarship itself. What this anthology attempts to do is present documents, most of which have been translated for the first time here, that illustrate some of these lessons about the complexities of Japanese religions as practiced.

As every teacher knows, the classroom, especially at the undergraduate level, requires more order in its textbooks than is needed by scholars delving into complexities and testing received knowledge. As a textbook this anthology would largely be useless if in the interests of new knowledge and diversity it failed to give conceptual direction to the material. While it was inspired and produced with an awareness of the inadequacies of the old categories of chronology (Nara, Heian, Kamakura, etc.), religious traditions (Shintō, Buddhism, Confucianism, etc.), and sects (Tendai, Shingon, Zen, etc.) as organizing principles for a reader about Japanese religions, it is not the case that a solution is to be found in a destabilization of an old order faulted for assuming that facts exist and meanings are fixed. While it is true that texts are malleable, they still bend only within a certain range, the boundaries of which define a discernible integrity. The diversity of the texts presented in this volume is matched by the diversity of their introductions which were written by the translators themselves rather than by a single editor who would otherwise have given the book a greater coherence and homogeneity. Despite the vagaries of reading and understanding texts, each translator presents an introductory explanation of the essence of the text and assumes that his or her remarks are in accord with the integrity of the original document itself. Having fairly clear meanings thus exposed, the texts can be placed in some kind of conceptual order according to what they say. In moving away from the old categories of chronology and traditions, this volume has not lost confidence that facts and meanings can be discerned, and, in fact, it brings both to bear on the elucidation of the complexities of religious practices.

In choosing to emphasize practice, we do not assume that it is always antagonistic to or can be freed from abstract theory. While theory can be distinguished from practice and sometimes has nothing to do with it, a strict dichotomy between the two is mostly false. Thinking, after all, is a practical activity, and, as the Buddhist cleric Eison (1201–1290) says in chapter 7, scholarship and study are forms of practice for rectifying the mind. What we do hope to gain in our focus on practice is not liberation from theory but a greater understanding of the different ways in which theory and practice work on each other. We wish to call attention to interrelationships: as the meaning of a text can be shaped by a reader, so too can readers be shaped by texts, or at least that is the hope of writers.

The mutual relationship between writers and readers, texts and contexts, and theory and practice can be described as an association between hard rocks and shifting tides. The rocks—writers, texts, and theory—are fairly fixed in definite persons, set documents, and (for the most part) clear ideas. The shiftings tides—the flow of different readers, changing contexts, and diverse practices—wash over the rocks and even change their shape, though the rocks remain recognizable for a long time. This interaction of rocks and tides takes place in discernible patterns that are not entirely chaotic because the rocks are fixed points, nor are they rigid because the tides do shift. The unique circumstances of each writer and reader, text and context, and theory and practice are important to understand, and this anthology goes a long way toward adding interesting new details of this kind, but to avoid the risk of being inundated with information, it does so within a structure of thematic patterns.

In imposing categorical order onto these forty-five chapters, I recognize that the themes I have chosen allow for much overlap and interchangability such that a selection placed in one category can just as easily be put in another. Instructors and students should feel free to use this anthology as a flexible text, and, to assist in possible reorderings, I include two alternative schemes that list the readings according to chronology and religious tradition, which are still widely used in the teaching of courses. These alternative formats for teaching and learning are not mutually exclusive, and, while the old structures are not used for the overall organization of these readings, they are not abandoned entirely.

In ordering the readings under the part titles of Ethical Practices, Ritual Practices, and Institutional Practices, I propose a typology for the sake of approximating as best we can the actual orientation of real people who engage in religious practices without giving much thought to whether or not they are Shintoists or Buddhists or Confucians, and certainly without having much of an awareness of being Nara or Heian or Kamakura persons. It does not matter to the pilgrims visiting Kannon in the puppet play translated in chapter 11 that they recite the "wrong" chant, the nembutsu, which is dedicated to Amida rather than Kannon;

or that non-Shingon members go on a pilgrimage to worship Kōbō Daishi, the founder of Shingon (see chapter 34). While some of the readings express an uncompromising sectarianism, other works speak of a willingness and desirability to cross sectarian and religious boundaries, and the categories I have chosen fortunately allow for both exclusive and inclusive viewpoints to be expressed with a coherence that would be difficult to maintain if the selections were organized according to religious or sectarian traditions. Each of the three broad categories are further divided into subthemes.

Ethical Practices

The theme of ethical practices is treated very broadly, covering matters ranging from individual behavior to institutional codifications. By dividing this broad theme into subparts on social values, clerical precepts, and lay precepts, we see the levels at which formal rules and informal advice define preferred action for different groups and communities. Most of the chapters in the volume deal with prescribed behavior, that is, morality in the broadest sense of word, but the chapters included in this part address themselves primarily and specifically to the determination of moral responsibility in their respective ways.

Social Values

The volume begins with a work that mixes Confucian, Shintō, Taoist, and Buddhist elements to retell and create short anecdotes illustrating the maxims of good behavior. An easy connection is made between the Buddhist idea of karma, in which one reaps what one sows, and Confucian imperatives for right action such as being filial to parents and showing mercy to people. One of the highest values promoted in the stories is the display of good literary skills, and here too there is no clash between Buddhism and Confucianism. While Confucianism clearly lends itself more readily to maxims of good behavior, it is interesting to note how Buddhism is presented less as a means toward enlightenment and more as a moral teaching. The moral quality of Buddhism is a theme encountered in many of the selections on Buddhism, and in chapter 1 we see how in practical terms Buddhism was used for its ethical teachings.

In Kaibara Ekken (chapter 2) we find a more exclusively Confucian teaching on family values based on self-discipline, etiquette, mutual respect, "hidden virtue" whereby acts of kindness need not be publicly recognized, and, most importantly, the joy of doing good. Like the anecdotes about the maxims of good behavior, the Shingaku teaching as interpreted by Nakazawa Dōni (1725–1803) (chapter 3) is comfortably syncretic in its conviction that no single tradition has a monopoly on truth. Since the true mind is universal, Confucianism, Shintō, and Buddhism all have wise teachings that uphold, among other things, the importance of a naturalness that does not interfere with nature.

Clerical Precepts

Naturalness is a value often associated with Buddhism and its counsel against contrivance and too much involvement with society, but the Zen master Eisai (1141–1215) argued that the truths and powers of Buddhism have a direct impact on society by protecting the nation (chapter 4). The welfare of society thus being at stake, the ruler should support Buddhism, in particular Zen Buddhism. For their part monks have a critical role to play in the upholding of society through Zen: they must maintain a strict monasticism, for the power of Zen is dependent on the purity of its monks, and any lapse in discipline damages the character of Zen and, in turn, the health of the nation is put at risk. Eisai's call for monastic purity was also in response to the deterioration of discipline in the monasteries, a condition that pure monks in every age had occasion to decry.

In the mid-eighteenth century, the Shingon monk Jiun Sonja (1718–1804), similarly concerned about the fallen state of discipline, worked diligently to revive the monastic precepts, arguing that to follow those strict rules was to emulate the lifestyle of Śākyamuni himself, and that failure to do so was the death of Buddhism. As a young man, Jiun had received a good Confucian education, which emphasized morality as a matter of inner character, and it is not surprising that he regarded the Buddhist precepts as prescriptions to be internalized into one's mind and being, and not just left as external rules. As a Buddhist monk, Jiun also advocated meditation and sutra study, but far from being merely rules of conduct, the precepts defined, no less than meditation and the scriptural teachings, attitudes and actions essential for becoming a buddha (chapter 5).

Maintaining monastic discipline was a daunting task subject to constant failure, and if Eisai argued that Buddhism was important for the well-being of the state, by the Tokugawa period it was also true that the government was instrumental in the maintenance of the sangha (the Buddhist community) by adopting laws making it a crime, for instance, for monks to marry. When the government in the early Meiji period rescinded the law forbidding monks to eat meat and marry, Buddhist leaders of the time vigorously protested that action in what would seem to be an admission that the temples and monasteries were not capable of enforcing their own rules. Written by a monk using the pseudonym of Uan Dōnin, the tract translated in chapter 6 argues that the government must legally support and enforce the bans against meat-eating and marriage, and it further counters the Shintō and Confucian criticism of celibacy with arguments about how the Buddhist injunctions are actually consistent with nativist and Confucian ways. The government remained unmoved by these pleas and held that celibacy should be enforced internally, and that the new law decriminalizing clerical marriage still left monks free not to marry. In modern Japan, the struggle to maintain vegetarianism, celibacy, and other traditional requirements of the monastic life has for the most part been abandoned, and the life of a lay householder is all but universal for Buddhist priests.

Lay Precepts

The Buddhist precepts are not limited to the monastic code, which proscribes the lay life, but includes rules specifically applicable to lay persons. It is not even the case that commitment to the strict life of the monastery meant that monks had nothing to do with society. Aware of the perennial problem of maintaining strict monastic discipline, Eison (1201–1290) vigorously reaffirmed the monastic code (chapter 7), but putting it into practice necessarily meant service to others. Renouncing the world meant working for it, and Eison provided relief for outcastes and prisoners, arranged public works projects like repairing bridges, counseled forbearance and forgiveness, and constantly taught that one must shift one's focus from self-interest to the welfare of others. His disciple Ninshō was even more active in his social work, which was extended to the sick, orphans, and even animals.

Though a monk of the Shingon Ritsu (Precepts) school, Eison drew widely from all forms of Buddhist teachings. In a similar fashion, Kokan Shiren (1278–1346), a Rinzai Zen monk, placed Zen within the matrix of other types of Japanese Buddhism (chapter 8). At the same time, Shiren had a very narrow view by which he regarded the bodhisattva Zen precepts to be superior to the Hīnayāna rules. One must, furthermore, believe in the efficacy of ordination and, by extension, have faith in the Zen line of masters leading back to Śākyamuni himself. Yet this sectarian view contained a broad understanding that the significance of the precepts exceeds Zen itself since those rules were means for knowing the human heart, and what distinguishes human beings from beasts. For those who fail to live up to its demands of being truly human, there is a remedy in the form of repentance. As such, the precepts applied to lay persons as well as monks and nuns.

Ritual Practices

Included in this part are not only the chapters that deal with the formalized performances that are rituals in the strict sense, but also materials expressing views and beliefs having to do with the unseen worlds with which rituals are the means for establishing a relationship or making contact. These unseen worlds, which can be seen through ritual performance, simply described with a mythic imagination, or assumed to exist as places with familiar characteristics long accepted from the past, are treated in two subparts, one for gods, the other for spirits. The objective of making the unseen seen or the unrealized realized is an ambitious one, and in the third subpart on rituals of realization, all of the chapters deal with that most ambitious project of realizing that one is already a buddha, already inherently enlightened. The pursuit of this idea, which is also referred to by the term original enlightenment (*hongaku*), is so pervasive that it cuts across many Buddhist sectarian lines and crosses over into areas of Shintō and Shugendō practice as well. But ritual does not always work. Some practitioners, after years of effort, lost confidence in the power of ritual to produce insight and realization and proposed alternatives. Their recommendations can still be thought of as rituals in the broadest sense, but because they reject traditionally defined ritual action, they are treated in the fourth subpart entitled "Faith."

Gods

The *Records of the Customs and Land of Izumo* (*Izumo fudoki,* 733) (chapter 9) is an early text that is regarded as one of the scriptures for the IzumoTaisha sect of Shintō. It does not describe a specific ritual but tells of the intimate relationship among the gods (*kami*), the land, and its inhabitants. Neither is an entirely separate mythic world described as the abode of the gods, but the ordinary world is explained as an arena of divine activity. The signs of the link between the land and the gods are the words used to name places, and in the prayers (*norito*) that were ritually offered to the gods we see the use of words as a magical, potent medium linking people to the gods. As much as the gods, what is celebrated in norito is language itself, a verbal feast presented with sonorous richness, for it is primarily through a banquet of words that the gods can be induced to grant blessings, protection, and even the purification of sins (see Donald L. Philippi, tr., *Norito: A Translation of the Ancient Japanese Ritual Prayers* [Princeton: Princeton University Press, 1990]). As it is with the Buddhist precepts, there is an element of repentance that depends on words, for it is in the *saying* of one's sins that their existence is recognized and laid open to expiation.

The Buddhist deities are also sources of blessings and sometimes curses. There is an entire genre of Buddhist literature that tells stories about the marvelous workings of the buddhas and bodhisattvas, and in chapter 10 we read about the miracles granted by Kannon, the bodhisattva of mercy. Here too the catalyst is prayer, supplication made to Kannon, who otherwise does not act. Certainly the extraodinary power of Kannon is lauded in these tales, but the underlying moral is the need for piety and, therefrom, prayer. Morality is an important element in the nineteenth-century puppet play (chapter 11), also about Kannon, but the virtue of a blind man and his wife must be augmented by prayer and pilgrimage before Kannon restores sight to the blind man, who had taken his own life. Morality and magic take center stage in this puppet play, which presents the old lesson of the Buddhist miracle tales in which good is rewarded and evil punished by divine powers. In chapter 12 we return to the divine power of the kami, who are asked to bless a couple entering into marriage in a modern ritual using the ancient form of *norito* and its celebration through sumptuous words.

Spirits

The world of the gods is also the realm of the spirits of the dead, the existence of which is affirmed by all religious traditions in Japan. Along with morality and magic, the beliefs and practices associated with the spirits or souls of the departed form an enduring theme cutting across boundaries of time and sect. Drawing materials from the *Man'yōshū*, the earliest of the poetry anthologies, chapter 13 presents details of *tama* (spirit) belief, and how words, again, in poetic form rather than prayer, are deployed to try to recall, bind, or pacify the spirits of the dead. While prayer is addressed to the gods, poetry speaks to people, who, when they are gone, elicit strong feelings of love, longing, and loss. There is more to poetic function, however, than just the evocation of human sentiment and personal attachment; politics, too, is sometimes part of the poetry. The public elegy (*banka*) on the occasion of Prince Takechi's temporary enshrinement was used to legitimate Emperor Temmu's violent assumption of power in the Jinshin War by rhetorically transforming the events surrounding it into what Gary Ebersole calls a "mythistory."

That the votive document (*gammon*) by Kūkai (774–835) was dedicated to the deceased mother of a government official is an indication that politics may also have played an ancillary role in this ritual text (chapter 14). Kūkai wrote several votive documents for well-placed individuals and their families, and serving their ritual needs with new ceremonies featuring elaborate colors, smells, sounds, and resounding words aided his work in establishing a new form of Buddhism in Japan. The votive text presents an alternative to recalling or binding the spirit of a loved one and suggests a letting go, a release that is nevertheless comforting since the departed soul is to be received by the compassionate Buddha.

Life after death is not to be feared, especially when the spirit is placed in the care of a priest who has the sacerdotal knowledge for managing its fate through ritual. Even if something goes wrong in the afterlife, usually through ritual negligence on the part of surviving relatives, and the spirit turns out to be agitated and hungry rather than satisfied, the priest can perform a ritual to remedy the problem. The ritual for feeding the hungry ghosts (*segaki*) (chapter 15) is one example of this kind of spiritual technology for correcting such shortcomings, but it does require a specialist who knows how to form the hand gestures (*mudra*) and recite the mantras in a greatly Japanized form of Sanskrit. In these mantras, we see again the magical power of words.

Related to the idea that words have power to manipulate matters of the spirit is the intriguing notion that one's final thoughts at the moment of death condition one's rebirth. Genshin's (942–1017) deathbed rituals (chapter 16) prescribe the details for right consciousness at the critical moment of death, and while one's lifetime of actions and their karmic consequences cannot be totally ignored, negative karma can be offset by holding in mind images of Amida Buddha and chanting the *nembutsu* "Namu Amida Butsu" (Praise be to Amida Buddha). Perhaps no other phrase has been uttered by so many people with the belief in the power of those words to assure if not effect rebirth in the pure land than the *nembutsu*. Mind and voice, thought and word work together toward the end of having Amida come to greet the dying person and provide escort to the pure land. Even women, whose nature and abilities for gaining salvation have been seriously questioned in Buddhism, can gain rebirth through *nembutsu* piety (chapter 17), as can warriors, who, in taking human life, commit the deadliest sin of all. Priests belonging to the Jishū, the Time Sect founded by Ippen (1239–1289), typically borrowed ideas and practices from other forms of Buddhism but basically promoted the *nembutsu* practice, especially among warriors and commoners. In the war tale translated in chapter 18, the horrors of clashing armies shock those who experience bloody battle into a religious awakening centered on the *nembutsu*, the recitation of which is the simplest of rituals for dealing with the terrors of this world and for ensuring peace in the next life.

The taking of life takes many forms, and in modern Japan abortions are carried out in significant numbers. Out of fear that the spirits of the aborted fetuses will curse their parents, or out of a deep sense of guilt, or out of a concern for the well-being of the fetus now in the spirit world, rites (*kuyō*) for a "child of the waters" (*mizuko*) have been carried out in recent times. The abortion rituals also tell us much about the role that religious institutions play in promoting and even creating the need for these services, and in the pamphlet translated in chapter 19, we see how a temple promotes its abortion ritual by playing on fear, guilt, and a concern for well-being. The pamphlet is a lesson in the realities of institutional religion, and while advertising is a powerful creator of need, or at least felt needs, a pamphlet such as this would not have much effect if it did not resonate with preexisting beliefs about ritual and its capacity for handling the spirits of the dead.

Rituals of Realization

Like a challenge thrust forth daring anyone to meet it, the assertion that ordinary persons are already buddhas presents a paradox or perhaps a contradiction that has invited many to resolve. The idea is found in a constellation of other notions variously identified as nonduality, buddha nature, the womb matrix, original enlightenment, inherent enlightenment, enlightenment in this very body, passion equals enlightenment, and any number of other related claims, including the Pure Land equivalent that rebirth takes place at the moment of faith or that everyone is already saved by Amida. The truth of these claims is not immediately apparent since human experience still seems to lie at a great distance from this ideal state that purports nevertheless to be immediately close by. If these claims are true and one is already a buddha, then the obvious question arises: why practice? The answer, equally obvious, is that one has to practice in order to realize the truth that obviates practice.

Suchness is another term for the identity of the imperfect with the perfect, and in the *Contemplation of Suchness* (chapter 20) the paradoxical claim is put forth with startling simplicity. The text addresses lay persons primarily, and the level of clarity required for such an audience is achieved through a literalism that valorizes the world: even pigs and dogs are Suchness, and to feed them is to make offerings to the buddhas. In adopting yin-yang rituals and especially the idea of inherent enlightenment from Shingon Esoteric Buddhism, the Shintō purification rite radically transformed the practice of ritual purity. According to the idea of inherent enlightenment, all beings are naturally endowed with the qualities of enlightenment, that is, perfect purity as well, and purification was therefore no longer limited to the purging of impurity but came to include the realization of one's inherent enlightenment (chapter 21). The rituals of realization are more familiar to us in the context of Zen than in Shintō, and in Dōgen's (1200–1253) treatment (chapter 22), the practice of zazen (seated meditation) itself becomes the actualization of ultimate truth, and the practitioner, just as he or she is, becomes the incarnation of perfect enlightenment. The Zen master Chidō (13th c.) adopted the less paradoxical view in which a distinction is made between ordinary reality, which is like a dream, and the ultimate reality of Buddhist insight, which results from being awakened from the dream (chapter 23). Aimed at lay persons, Chidō's work is an exhortation about how expansive the mind can be, how grand one's vision can be, if only people were to wake up from their dreams. While Chidō does not engage in the literalism of asserting pigs to be Suchness, he does hold up a very ordinary experience, that of being awake rather than sleeping and dreaming, as the closest approximation of Buddhist enlightenment. It is a simile, but it evokes the language of valorizing the mundane. While he is critical of the Pure Land rejection of disciplined practice, he does express a point that is often mistakenly credited only to Pure Land innovations, namely, that the power of faith can overcome the karmic effects of sin.

The idea that one is already a buddha invites everyone to be his or her own authority. Such an authority is assumed when a writer composes a sutra purporting to be a record of the Buddha's preaching. The text translated in chapter 24 is apocryphal because it was clearly composed in Japan and could not have come from India by way of China and Korea, the route of so-called authentic sutras. Belonging to the Shugendō tradition of mountain asceticism, the text argues that authority and meaning rest in one's own experience and not on some teaching transmitted through an institution. And yet it cannot rest easy with the prospect that the truth it proposes is individually or personally derived, for that would reduce truth to opinion. There must be an external authority, but since it cannot be an institution, it is located in the original Buddha of no mind and no thought, the highest buddha. No mind and no thought are terms from the language of original enlightenment and its logic: the reason we can claim authority in ourselves is that it is the authority of the original Buddha.

Faith

In its criticism of traditional ritual practices, Pure Land Buddhism can be seen as a contrast to the other forms of Buddhism that place discipline and practice at their core. In another sense, however, the Pure Land conviction that salvation is not secured by the self-power of practice but only by reliance through faith on the other power of Amida leads to an immediate fulfillment that resonates with the rituals of realizing one is already a buddha. The rhetoric is different—being a buddha in this life versus being identified with Amida through the nembutsu in this life—but what is the difference between being a buddha and being Amida? The nonduality between the believer and Amida is the contention of *On Attaining the Settled Mind* (chapter 25), as is the claim that birth in the pure land has already been accomplished through the compassionate vow of Amida, and hence one can have a settled mind. To the question raised earlier as to why practice is necessary if one is already a buddha, the Pure Land answer, at least in this text, is that practices are not necessary as long as one trusts in Amida. The anecdotes in *Plain Words on the Pure Land Way* (chapter 26) depict monks who have thrown off concerns for status, fame, doctrinal learning, and intellectual calculation in favor of the simplicity of the *nembutsu*, the sole ritual, if it still is a ritual, that makes all other rituals unnecessary.

The letters of Shinran (1173–1263) in chapter 27 suggest that even true faith (*shinjin*) is a gift of Amida and not the result of human volition. There is nothing to do—no ritual, no practice, no contrivance. Faith puts an end to contrivance and becomes the moment of birth into the pure land. Without removing evil, faith bypasses it and allows sinners (as well as saints) to be reborn in the pure land. This does not mean that people can justifiably commit evil, for compassion requires people to be good though goodness is not a means to rebirth. Shinran, whose faith allowed him to ignore the clerical precepts and marry openly, occupied a position diametrically opposite to that of the traditional practitioners, but the line separating both can also be bent into a full circle such that his sense of immediate fulfillment meets the end point at which we find the rituals of realizing one is a buddha, perhaps Amida.

Institutional Practices

The rejection of ritual structure on the grounds of the immediacy of faith does not entail a repudiation of institutional structure. Indeed the Jōdoshinshū, the sect of True Pure Land Buddhism, which developed in the wake of Shinran's teachings, became one of the most formidable of institutions that could defend itself by force of arms when necessary. Religion and politics often clashed, but they also met on the common ground in which religious truth claims could be used to legitimize or enhance political institutions. The making of institutions requires founders, most of whom have been sanctified as great men, wizards, and even gods. Great efforts were also expended in defining the identity of sectarian institutions in terms of right practice or orthopraxis, and right thought or orthodoxy. In the arena of institutional life we see clearly what is appropriately called sectarianism, that is, the strict definition of exclusive zones of thought and practice. This does not controvert the repeated cases of syncretism across sectarian lines, but neither should such assimilative fluidity obscure the instances of rigidity. Balancing the tensions of sectarianism are the ordinary administration of buildings and furnishings, and the special social functions that some religious institutions play. Another lesson of the realities of organization is found in the gap between actual practices and stated ideals, and a view of these discrepancies is essential if we are to avoid the mistake of thinking that principles are always put into practice.

Court and Emperor

While we normally think that practice follows theory, there were times when actual practice preceded and then required the subsequent creation and support of principles. When one clan emerged in ancient Japan as more powerful than others, it could have ruled by brute force alone without concern for whether its rule was justified. The idea of legitimacy, however, made its appearance with some of the earliest writings in Japan, and the *Record of Ancient Matters* (*Kojiki*, 712) is a definitive text in establishing the principles that justified the practice of supremacy by the imperial clan. Departing from the Chinese principle that the ruler governed by divine right in the form of the mandate of Heaven, which could be lost through excess vice and claimed by another of greater virtue, the imperial clan established the principle of divine birth as the basis of legitimate rulership. The *Kojiki* asserts that the imperial house descends from the deity Amaterasu, and the emperor rules by virtue of having been born divine (see Donald L. Philippi, tr., *Kojiki* [Tokyo: University of Tokyo Press, 1968]).

Despite its divine origins, the imperial family functioned in a bureaucratic organization that was eminently human. The *Continued Chronicles of Japan* (*Nihon shoki*, 797) (chapter 28) provides a glimpse into the everyday workings of the court, some of which sounds remarkably familiar: new bureaucratic rules devised to correct certain abuses, sanctioning a crown prince for his debauchery, and the difficulty of finding suitable princes of acceptable moral behavior. While the dominant values are identifiable as Confucian, it is also clear that there was an easy coexistence with and mutual use of Buddhism and (what we now call) Shintō. There was no need for a theory of syncretism since the assimilation of ideas and practices did not always follow deliberate design but was carried out as direct practice. Though we can identify Shintō, Buddhist, and Confucian elements in the *Continued Chronicles of Japan*, it is clear that they melded into a single worldview, not three, in which spiritual forces, however they might be identified, were integrated parts of the temporal order.

This is not to say that there were no other circumstances in which religious traditions did appear differently and clash. The *Circumstances Leading to the Founding of the Monastery Complex of Gangōji* (*Gangōji engi*, 747) (chapter 29) is an important document not only for the founding of the temple but for the official introduction of Buddhism itself. The account is one of contention, strife, and even violence, as two political factions include in their opposing stances different religious understandings of the spiritual forces that affect worldly events. The deities are identified in opposition to each other, the one "Buddhist" and the other, for lack of a better term, "Shintō." Since the temporal world is directly affected by powerful, unseen forces identified as deities, the violent struggle between the two factions was also a battle of the gods, and the Buddhist deities proved themselves to be the greater masters of war.

Emerging victorious, Prince Shōtoku (574–622), grateful for the support of the buddhas and bodhisattvas, became an influential supporter of Buddhism. The biographies of Prince Shōtoku (chapter 30) are even more explicit about the relationship between Buddhism and power, and we read once again of how the war was won with the backing of the Buddhist deities. In his political uses of Buddhism, Prince Shōtoku is portrayed not just as a pragmatic warrior-politician petitioning the deities to be on his side, but also as a pious believer. Both stances go together, sincerity being an important element in the process of asking the buddhas to answer one's prayers for victory. Although Prince Shōtoku is reputed to have studied the philosophical teachings of Buddhism and gained an admirable mastery of them, in the account of his struggles with his opponents little is said about those teachings, but much is reported about the divine powers of the buddhas to help determine the course of history.

Spiritual beings can affect the outcome of wars, and, in turn, those who lose their lives fighting a war can become special spiritual beings. The Yasukuni Shrine pamphlet translated in chapter 31 explains that the shrine is a burial place for all those who died in service to the country, including the schoolchildren on Okinawa and the female telephone operators on Sakhalin who lost their lives in the Great Pacific War. The pamphlet provides an important lesson about how the war dead become spirits of the nation, a nation that is still symbolized by the emperor. All of these wars, civil and foreign, happened unfortunately but were fought for the sake of the nation and the emperor by contributing to "the important mission of creating a marvelous Japan with the emperor at its center." Published in 1992, the pamphlet is a good reminder of the intimate connection among citizens, spirits, the nation, and the emperor in modern Japan.

Sectarian Founders, Wizards, and Heroes

In turning from the imperial institution to sectarian ones, we find, as we might expect, intimate connections between divinity and humanity, especially in the founders of sects. Shrouded in so much legend that it is difficult to discern the real man, En the Ascetic (late 7th c.) has become a paradigmatic holy man and wizard of supernatural powers revered widely even outside of the Shugendō sect, of which he is the reputed founder. The account of him (chapter 32) tells of the importance of mountains as places to acquire spiritual powers through strict discipline, but even this supernatural wizard is also described in very human and moral terms as being filial to his parents. Mountains are also the setting for the story about how Kūkai (774–835), the founder of the Shingon sect, established a monastery on Mount Kōya and eventually died there, except that his death was only a seeming one, for he remains alive, sitting in eternal meditation in his mausoleum (chapter 33). Even today thousands of pilgrims flock to Mount Kōya to visit and pray to Kūkai, posthumously and popularly known as Kōbō Daishi, their living savior. The divinization of Kūkai was not the product of popular piety, but the construction by high-ranking monks developing the Shingon institution.

The telling of tales is an important part of the process of instilling faith in the buddhas and bodhisattvas, as we have already seen with the tales and puppet play about Kannon, and it continued to be instrumental in the later development of Kōbō Daishi as savior. While the story about Kōbō Daishi's eternal meditation was a creation by a monk at the top of the institution and was then disseminated to believers below, the stories about the encounters with Kōbō Daishi on the Shikoku pilgrimage were told by ordinary pilgrims making the journey. The seventeenth-century stories translated in chapter 34 are the first record of the voices and stories of pilgrims themselves. They were collected by a monk who had ties with the Shingon headquarters, and they tell of pilgrimage as a means of having direct encounters with the holy. They praise the virtue of doing the pilgrimage and offering alms to the pilgrims. Taken together, the stories of Kōbō Daishi's eternal meditation and the Shikoku pilgrimage show that in the making of belief through the telling of tales, stories can be told from the top down as well as the bottom up.

If, as scholars surmise, the *Personal Account of the Life of the Venerable Genkū* (*Genkū Shōnin shinikki*, chapter 35) was written by Shinkū (1145–1228), then it is another example of a founder having been divinized by those at the top of the sect. Genkū, or Hōnen (1133–1212), was the founder of the Pure Land sect (Jōdoshū), and Shinkū was one of his earliest disciples. The account transforms Hōnen into a divine savior, like Kūkai, and identifies him as a manifestation of the bodhisattva Seishi, who is often depicted, along with Kannon, as an attendant of Amida. Responding to criticisms that his master was a heretic for rejecting traditional practices, Shinkū defends Hōnen as a scholar as well as saint. History and myth are mixed to depict Hōnen as both human and divine, and the text, like the *Kojiki*, is another example of "mythistory" designed to make something human more divine.

The Nichiren priest Nisshin (1407–1488) was not the founder of his sect, but he became a hero within his organization and the center of a personality cult (chapter 36). What is interesting about his story is that he is not portrayed as a supernatural or divine figure, but as a resolute man who withstood government censure and torture for the sake of his sect and belief in the *Lotus Sutra*. A similar case of intense faith can be seen in Teshima Ikurō (1910–1973), who had a conversion experience in the midst of his own personal suffering. The founder of a small Christian organization, Kirisuto no Makuya (Tabernacle of Christ), Teshima emphasized individual faith and developed close relations with his followers, three of whom wrote testimonies that are translated along with a biograhical account of Teshima in chapter 37. While his followers report cases of healing (in one instance by Teshima's wife), they do not regard him as anything other than a remarkable teacher whom they came to love and respect dearly. Personal commitment to each other as well as the gospel of Jesus Christ is the story told of a man remarkable for his humanity and faith.

Orthopraxis and Orthodoxy

Nisshin and Teshima were heroes to their causes because of their exclusive commitment to the truths they found, respectively, in the *Lotus Sutra* and the Bible. They were fundamentalists, unable to recognize other forms of truth. In contrast to this restrictive view, Mujū Ichien (1226–1312), ostensibly a Rinzai Zen priest, held that the Buddhist truth takes on various forms, and that no single way can be upheld over others (chapter 38). While Mujū also presents the idea of how Buddhism is compatible with the other religious traditions, it is important to note that the non-Buddhist teachings "softened people's hearts," as he states it, to make them more amenable to accepting Buddhism. Buddhism therefore enjoys a privileged position over the rest, and it is primarily within the Buddhist fold that pluralism and diversity are celebrated equally. The Buddha taught different teachings to suit different people, and in making such accommodations he expressed his compassion. There is, in short, no single meaning to Buddhism, no orthodoxy.

It was not always the case that when institutions found themselves at odds with each other, the issues were free of concerns about the right articulation of truth. For Nisshin, the conflicts he experienced were directly related to his strict orthodoxy. The connection between conflicting orthodoxies and competing institutional (and personal) interests is not difficult to find, even within single traditions. Intrasectarian tension, for example, is the subject of chapter 39, this time within the world of Zen, and again it is a story of the interrelationship between doctrinal understandings and institutional well-being. The competition between Shūhō Myōchō (National Teacher Daitō, 1282–1337) and the monk Musō Soseki (1275–1351) was a debate over not just the philosophical truth of Zen but political correctness as well. The definition of doctrinal correctness or orthodoxy in this situation was a pressing issue even in a time of political stability; it is not just a change of rulers or the conduct of war that requires religious support and justification. Cultural and even aesthetic realignments also affect the articulation of right religion, and a judgment of heterodoxy in one situation may be beneficial to the gaining of orthodoxy in another circumstance.

The influence of social pressures on the determination of truth can also be seen in the argument between the Inner and Outer Shrines at Ise, which waged their theological debate mindful of the economic consequences of their theoretical formulations. The Outer Shrine priests claimed that their deity, Toyouke, was equal to and identical with Amaterasu, the *kami* of the Inner Shrine. But the Inner Shrine priests rejected this formulation, saying that Amaterasu was superior. The theological arguments in form were about the *kami* but in function concerned donations from pilgrims who flocked to Ise, pilgrims who would, if Toyouke were inferior, bypass the Outer Shrine and go directly to the Inner Shrine and pray to the superior Amaterasu. The debate spilled into the streets as Outer Shrine priests set up barricades to block entry to the Inner Shrine. The text translated in chapter 40 is by the great scholar Motoori Norinaga (1730–1801), who seemed to have a split mind on the matter and managed not to provide any clear resolution.

Motoori referred to the controversy with the image of split bamboo, but the fracturing of relations between the Inner and Outer Shrines did not elicit cries of dismay about the loss of harmony within Shintō. When Buddhists denounced each other, they sometimes lamented the loss of the "single flavor of the dharma" or the breakup of the harmony of the sangha, the fault for which, of course, could be laid on their opponents. But little is said about the single flavor of Shintō: what, after all, is Shintō? A scholar of our own time, the late Kuroda Toshio, has been influential with his analysis of the nature and function of religion in Japanese history, and in his essay on the subject (chapter 41), he criticizes the widespread treatment of Shintō as an independent indigenous religion. Arguing that an autonomous Shintō is a modern construction, Kuroda sees that the beliefs and practices surrounding the *kami* are so integrated into Buddhist and secular affairs that they cannot be separated out to form an independent "Shintō."

The inextricable integration of Shintō beliefs and practices into the religious views of Buddhists has caused enormous problems for the True Pure Land (Jōdoshin) sect, which officially rejects the magical rituals aimed at acquiring this-worldly benefits. Concerned about field studies that show Jōdoshin members patronizing temples and shrines offering this-worldly benefits, Sasaki Shōten, a contemporary Jōdoshin priest and scholar, calls for a reconsideration of the official teaching banning such practices (chapter 42). Sasaki recognizes that "the primitive mentality with Shintōism as its core" is an undeniable part of the Japanese religious view, including that of Buddhists, and it is useless to deny by doctrine what exists in fact. While sounding at times as if he is willing to accept those practices fully, Sasaki fundamentally cannot do so. His proposal is not to accept but to tolerate such folk practices so that people can be drawn in, or more importantly so that members do not have to be kicked out. The final goal, however, is to transform such primitive practices into true Jōdoshin faith, which, even in Sasaki's version, cannot tolerate magic as true religion. His willingness to accept the primitive mentality in order to transform it is reminiscent of Mujū's attitude toward the non-Buddhist religions that function to soften people's hearts so that they can embrace the Buddhist dharma.

Sasaki's article takes us well into the area in which we see the discrepancies between official doctrine and actual practice. In the Sōtō Zen pamphlet of chapter 43 we see a similar hiatus between precept and practice, except that in this case the presentation of Zen as a religion for peace of mind and general well-being rather than a path of meditation is made by the institution itself. An overt clash between theory and practice is avoided simply by not mentioning the doctrines for which Zen is philosophically famous. Sōtō Zen and Jōdoshin purists often point out that funeral rites and ancestor veneration are not Buddhist teachings, and yet we find in this official pamphlet positive, nostalgic affirmations of rites for memorializing the ancestors. This pamphlet Zen bears little resemblance to Dōgen Zen, though both are identified as Sōtō. The fact that this sentimental Zen of general well-being is promoted by the sect itself without any mention of seated meditation as the means to dropping off mind and body to reveal an originally existing buddha is extremely significant in its indication that instead of a conflict between doctrine and practice there is dropping off of classical doctrine in favor of de facto practice. Or, to put it in other terms, practice prescribes precept.

Special Places

The priority of practice over doctrine is not limited to modern developments but is also seen in the writings of Keizan (1264–1325), who stands second in importance to Dōgen himself in the line of Sōtō Zen partriarchs. Keizan, displaying a pragmatism for what works rather than what is doctrinally prescribed, easily adopted ritual practices that Dōgen would not have considered. The institutional development of Sōtō Zen would have been significantly retarded if Dōgen's successors had confined themselves to the limits of his demanding teachings and not adopted mortuary rites and rituals for this-worldly benefits. In Keizan's records selected for chapter 44, there is only one instance mentioned of him sitting in meditation; the other descriptions are about rituals for warding off evil and inviting blessings, and about the more mundane matters of institutional administration. Women play an important role (as they do in most temples today) in the life of his temple, and Keizan has much to say about his grandmother, mother, and Sonin, the woman who donated the land for his temple Yōkōji.

Keizan's records are about Yōkōji in a valley he named Tōkoku. Both names were chosen for their associations with Chinese Zen masters in whose lineage he was a dharma descendant. In his sermons, Keizan uses the language of original enlightenment to speak generically about every place being one's own self, one's radiant wisdom, the site of practice, and the practice of Buddha activity; but when he speaks specifically of Tōkoku Yōkōji—its buildings, its activities, its people, his relatives, and how he selected the site in a dream—it becomes apparent that the place is one of belonging, his home, the locus of his everyday spiritual life. Like the *Records of the Customs and Land of Izumo* (chapter 9) and its naming of places in association with the actions of the *kami*, Keizan's *Records of Tōkoku* explains the naming of that place in association with his spiritual tradition and describes it as the venue of Buddha activity as well as his everyday routine. Yōkōji is at once an ordinary and a special place.

Tōkeiji in Kamakura is a special place for women, specifically women who seek divorce from their husbands (chapter 45). The temple was founded as a convent in 1285 by Kakusan Shidō (1252–1305), widow of Hōjō Tokimune (1251–1284), the Kamakura military ruler who repelled the Mongol invasions in 1274 and 1281; and its name, Eastern Temple for Rejoicing (Tōkeiji), was appropriate for a woman who seems to have enjoyed a happy married life. By the Tokugawa period, the temple had acquired other names: Enkiridera, Divorce Temple; and Kakekomidera, Temple into Which One Runs for Refuge. The popular verse known as *senryū* speaks poignantly about the unhappy experiences of women seeking refuge from their husbands. In a time when divorce was uncommon and difficult to obtain since it could only be granted by the husband, Tōkeiji was a very special place, but its unique function was possible because of the theoretically normal role any temple plays as a place for the renunciation of the householder's life. Monasticism had its secular use, and though it was not easy being a nun ("how difficult / breaking the relationship / with vegetarian food"), it was a temporary status to be endured until the husband could be convinced of sending a letter of divorce.

Monasticism and divorce are not usually associated in texts on Japanese religion, but the case of Tōkeiji illustrates how natural and practical an alliance it was. Dealing with the world by withdrawing from it was also practiced by Eison, whose monastic vows made it imperative that he work with outcastes and prisoners. On a more ambitious scale, Eisai argued that monasticism was necessary for the welfare and protection of the nation itself. We can see a pattern in this association between monasticism and society, and to that degree we can state a generalization, a small one to be sure, but a generalization nevertheless: monasticism can perform social services. Opposed to this is the more usual pattern of monasticism performing services only for monastics; Uan Dōnin's call for a continued ban against clerical marriage was not couched in the interests of society at large, though he tried to demonstrate that celibacy was not inimical to society. Herein lies another pattern: monasticism is self-serving. The patterns vary: monasticism is a hard rock, but it is used in shifting tides.

The readings in this volume are filled with double-edged interrelationships that cut both ways. Religion, for instance, legitimates rulership, and the ruler, in turn, legitimates religion by legislating it. Sometimes the government intervenes in religious matters to the dismay of religious communities, and at other times the community complains that the government does not intervene enough. There are patterns of tolerant pluralism that stand in contrast to clear instances of sectarianism and censure. And then there is the kind of sectarian triumphalism that presents itself in the mask of pluralistic tolerance. Morality is a prevalent theme about reaping what we sow; but so is magic equally present with its promises of reaping even if we do not sow. Repeatedly we encounter the conundrum of being a buddha but having to become one nevertheless. This is attended by voices calling for strict practice in order to realize that there is no need to practice— voices that find counterpoints in those who said that there is no need to practice, period. At times the world is a defiled place worthy only of leaving for the perfect pure land, and at other times it is the very abode of the gods where pigs are buddhas. Rules are external and need to be internalized, but internal realization makes external rules unnecessary. There are living spirits of the dead to be bound, recalled, pacified, or conversely let go; there are also dead masters whose spirits never leave and stay to bless and protect. Divinized men and anthropomorphic gods grant miracles induced from them through performing rituals, reciting chants, uttering prayers, going on pilgrimage, being good, or just having faith. Myth is not to be confused with fact, but it can be blended with history to produce "mythistory" or with biography to create hagiography. For some, human institutions can never be sources of authority, especially when one is a buddha unto oneself, but institutions can also be the only source for defining what is true. Doctrine defines rituals and right conduct, but so can practice determine theory. And then there are times when neither is the cause of the other, when one side, usually theory, is simply ignored. Shintō is a recognizable religion but sometimes becomes invisible in its integration into Buddhist practice. Buddhism also has its own character, but it too can be hidden in a Shintō purification rite. Both Buddhism and Shintō can join together with Confucianism and other systems to form a single worldview, or they can clash even to the point of violence. Buddhism is for peace but also helps wins wars. Orthodoxies have definite consequences in society, and social conditions can help determine orthodoxies. The list of these double- or multiple-edged relationships can continue on and on, and surely readers will detect others.

All of the above are patterns that can be seen in repeated instances and therefore can be stated as generalizations, the making of which is essential to teaching and understanding, but by showing that patterns have opposing counterparts, we see the limits of any generalization and that countergeneralizations, equally valid, also need to be made. The resulting mosaic, seemingly on the verge of conceptual chaos, is what we are after, a kind of ordered disorder, a patterned confusion. If this anthology allows students and teachers to see this ordered confusion, then it will have succeeded in its original intent of challenging the artificial neatness of customary classroom knowledge by presenting in forty-five chapters the uniformities and disarray that actually exist in the religions of Japan in practice.

Ethical Practices

SOCIAL VALUES

─ 1 ─

Selected Anecdotes to Illustrate Ten Maxims

Ward Geddes

> In the winter of the fourth year of the reign period Kenchō (1252), I made some free
> time and wrote in that period when my mind was at repose. An old man, . . . retiring
> to a grass hermitage at the foot of Higashiyama, I have completed this book in the
> time free from my prayers.

So states the compiler/author at the end of the preface to the *Selected Anecdotes
to Illustrate Ten Maxims* (*Jikkinshō*). Most scholars have accepted these words as a
true record of the date of composition and the conditions under which the work
was created. Comparison of its contents with other literary works supports the
dating; no definite identification of the author has been made. The most likely
suggestion appeared in a postscript to a no longer extant manuscript that said,
"Some people say this is the work of Rokuhara Jirōzaemon Nyūdō, in the service
of Nagatoki, Tokishige, and others." The term Jirōzaemon Nyūdō signifies a position something like "lay priest, second gate guard of the left of Rokuhara," and
the actual identity of this person remains unclear. Because Nagatoki and Tokishige
were administrators in Kyoto's Northern Rokuhara District during the appropriate
period and the text that contained the attribution is one of the older manuscripts,
most scholars have accepted its reliability. The Japanese scholar Nagai Yoshinori
discovered records of a man, Yuasa Munenari, who may have been a gate guard
and lay priest during the time of *Selected Anecdotes'* compilation. However, the
supporting evidence is not conclusive, and the best one may say is that, of various
suggestions, this is the best supported, and it is possible that Yuasa Munenari did
in fact compile the work.

    Selected Anecdotes is a collection of short stories belonging to the genre known
as tale literature (*setsuwa bungaku*). Such anecdotes are generally short, are not
written with great attention to artistic or literary effect, are frequently received
rather than original tales, and usually include a moral for the reader. Since works
of this genre are composed mainly of tales taken from other sources, oral or
written, the creators of the tale collections are often referred to as compilers rather

than authors. However, an argument may be made that, as the collections are built on fairly consistent principles of organization and are structured in such a way as to further a philosophical or moral aim, use of the term "author" rather than "compiler" may be justified.

The earliest tale literature is represented in collections of Buddhist tales treating the early history of Buddhism, origins of temples, incidents in lives of holy men, miracles, and so forth. The suggestion is that these tales were first delivered orally by Buddhist monks and were set down in outline form to serve as mnemonic devices for the monks to refer to as they preached. Over time the collections come to include more and more secular material, and they may be seen as falling into two types: religious (i.e., Buddhist) and secular. *Selected Anecdotes*, while including many tales concerned with incidents related to Buddhism, is clearly a member of the secular group of *setsuwa* collections. In the preface the compiler tells his reader that the purpose of the collection is "to serve as an aid in forming the moral character of youth as yet untutored in the ways of the world." Here the emphasis is on preparation for entry into the everyday world of social encounters rather than the other-worldly concerns of religious enlightenment. Although Buddhist influences are found in many tales, generally such stories are used to demonstrate that many of the virtues demanded of Buddhists are also helpful in day-to-day conduct.

But Confucianism is the major argument of *Selected Anecdotes*. Much of the compiler's view of proper conduct is based on Confucian ideas of natural order, which are seen as determining social order. Thus tale 18 in chapter 5 cites *The Classic of Documents* (*Shu ching*), "The crowing of the hen is the finish of the family," to support the idea that women properly remain subordinate to men. To illustrate the harmoniously integrated relationship required in a well-run state, the preface to chapter 1 uses the organic metaphor of the sea as representing the ruler or state and its currents as signifying the people.

Other reflections of the influence of Confucian values are seen in *Selected Anecdotes*' stress on recognition of authority, observation of conduct appropriate to one's position, prudent and proper conduct in all situations, and the need for a balanced reaction to adversity or good fortune. Confucian concern for education and learning is expressed mainly in an emphasis on knowledge of Chinese classics and Japanese poetic works and the ability to compose and appreciate both Chinese and Japanese poetry.

In accordance with its generally authoritarian approach to relations between people, *Selected Anecdotes* is consistent in advocating conduct appropriate to one's station and the situations one encounters. However, this approach does not urge blind obedience to superiors or condone arbitrary actions by leaders. Although people serving those of higher rank generally are expected to follow orders, they are also instructed that superiors must be informed when they are unreasonable or in error. Conversely, those in high position are also admonished that they must listen to and heed wise advice and treat their subordinates fairly.

Two areas of human interaction are held to transcend the usual hierarchy of relationships: friendship and marriage. Both are viewed as originating from the heart and breaking the normal strictures of reason and society. Friendship originates in a kind of mystical communication of mind and emotion, particularly found in shared reactions to nature and poetry. However, a major concern is that friends are chosen carefully. Friends selected unwisely for the wrong reasons may lead one to disaster. Love, like friendship, transcends normal social strictures. Again, love may lead to unwise actions and result in loss of face. The *Selected Anecdotes* counsels that men of lower status may follow their hearts in the choice of a wife, but men of higher status must consider social standing. Thus, in a number of the tales, as in many works of Japanese literature, there is tension between human nature expressed in pursuit of love and Confucian tenets dictating well-governed actions and strict social organization.

Like most tale literature, *Selected Anecdotes* is a potpourri of clerical and secular, serious and comical, ancient and contemporary, mundane and fabulous tales of wisdom and folly intended to improve its readers. The one consistent guiding principle in the selection of the stories appears to have been the belief of the compiler/author that the tales derive from actual experience. Although some of the stories recounting religious or supernatural experiences may raise doubts in the modern reader, it seems that in their time they were regarded by their tellers and audiences as narrations of experience that might be encountered in daily life.

Fujiwara no Sukezane (dates unknown), whose misadventures are related in tale 3 below, exemplifies unacceptable behavior. The Confucian hero does not brag; he is learned but does not show off his abilities. Sukezane's loss of his topknot and the embarrassing outcome of his meddling in Lord Hanazono's poetry study both result from pride. The proper Confucian gentleman underplays his abilities and earns the admiration of others through exercising his skill unostentatiously.

The act by the retainer who cuts off Sukezane's topknot is an example of action unsuited to time and place. To lose one's topknot, a symbol of rank, was a major disgrace. The punishment inflicted by the country soldier outweighs the seriousness of Sukezane's offense. That the story has a person from the provinces commit this act reflects the usual Japanese attitude of the time that people from areas outside the capital are unrefined or, as the story says of the soldier, lack "either compassion or understanding."

The end of the tale presents Atsumasa as a model for conduct. Sukezane's verse poking fun at Atsumasa's nose is clever but shallow and in poor taste. Atsumasa uses the art of verse-capping both to repay Sukezane's insult and to display his much greater poetic ability. In contrasting the bare "Sukezane Garden" and the mountain with its nosegay, the verse implies the fertile creativity of Atsumasa's verse as opposed to the barren emptiness of Sukezane's. There is also an adroit use of puns involving the birds (*tori*) of the verse and the topknot (*motodori*) of Sukezane. Other possible allusions may include a reference to the saying "*tori naki sato no komori*" ("a bat from a village without birds"—i.e., "in the land of the blind, the one-eyed man is king"). The implication here is that where there are no learned people the ignorant try to make their influence felt. Additionally, the birdless garden with its apparently trackless snow may further hint at lack of literacy. The invention of Chinese characters is said in folklore to have been inspired by imitation of bird tracks (*tori no ato*).

Another element that runs through the tale is the tension between martial and literary accomplishment. Sukezane sees the possible rivalry for the court beauty, Sakin, as a contest between himself, a military man of sorts, and Nakamasa, a poet of high repute. As its author/compiler states, *Selected Anecdotes* is intended to present examples for young men hoping to advance in the world, that is, attain prominence in courtly society. The court continues to value literary ability above martial skill. As most of the young men for whom the tales are intended would belong to the military class, which was rising to power when the *Selected Anecdotes* was composed in the mid-thirteenth century, a stress on the importance of literary accomplishment in conducting oneself at court is to be expected. Thus, while some stories, like tale 55 of chapter 10, emphasize the importance of mastering both martial and literary skills, in general, as in the story of Sukezane, literary ability is more important.

The translation is based on Nagazumi Yasuaki, ed., *Jikkinshō* (Tokyo: Iwanami Shoten, 1958), with reference to Ishibashi Shōhō, *Jikkinshō shōkai*, rev. ed. (Tokyo: Meiji Shoin, 1927).

Further Reading

John Brownlee, "*Jikkinshō*, a Miscellany of Ten Maxims," *Monumenta Nipponica* 29, 2 (1974); Robert H. Brower and Earl Miner, *Japanese Court Poetry* (Stanford: Stanford University Press, 1961); Ward Geddes, "The Buddhist Monk in the *Jikkinshō*," *Japanese Journal of Religious Studies* 9, 2–3 (June–September 1982): 199–212; Ward Geddes, "The Courtly Model, Chōmei and Kiyomori in *Jikkinshō*," *Monumenta Nipponica* 42, 2 (Summer 1987): 157–166; Ward Geddes, "Takamura Monogatari," *Monumenta Nipponica* 30, 2 (Autumn 1991): 275–291; Ward Geddes, tr., *Kara monogatari: Tales of China*, in Center for Asian Studies Occasional Paper no. 16 (Tempe: Arizona State University, 1984); D. E. Mills, tr., *A Collection of Tales from Uji* (London: Cambridge University Press, 1970); Robert E. Morrell, tr., *Sand and Pebbles (Shasekishū): The Tales of Mujū Ichien, A Voice for Pluralism in Kamakura Buddhism* (Albany: State University of New York Press, 1985); Arthur Waley, *Translations from the Chinese* (New York: Alfred A. Knopf, 1919).

Selected Anecdotes to Illustrate Ten Maxims

CHAPTER 4: TALE 3

The Beauty, Sakin; Sukezane's Proud Words and His Argument with Nakamasa; Kebiishi Morishige; The Scholar Atsumasa

In the mid-eleventh century there was a lady-in-waiting of incomparable beauty called Sakin who served in the palace of ex-Emperor Horikawa's (r. 1087–

1107) mother, Queen Takako (d. 1084). Minamoto no Nakamasa (d. 1156), the supervisor of the military storehouses, was in love with her.

One day some men from the palace home guard gathered at the Kamoi Hall, one-time home of Horikawa. After they had drunk some sake, they began to discuss this Sakin.

"Her demeanor as she walked serenely in the palace grounds was more graceful than an angel's. If she is truly a creature of this world, I want something like her as a souvenir of life here."

Someone else answered, "A warrior for whom neither devils nor witches hold fear is fearsome indeed; yet, even your love is sure to come to nothing. Let's speak no more of her."

The governor of Ise, Fujiwara no Sukezane, who was given to putting on airs, said, "Even a warrior may fall in love. If I felt inclined to steal her, no matter how much Nakamasa tried to prevent it, I doubt that he could stop me." After this he seemed to be considering some kind of troublemaking and self-complacently spoke of Nakamasa in a scornful way. His companions had little to say and stopped talking.

Somebody apparently spread tales about this conversation. These rumors soon came to the ears of Nakamasa, who consulted with his men, saying, "This is not a situation easily ignored. My fellows, what am I to do? Sukezane doesn't know the bottom of a bow from its top. He would make no kind of an opponent in a fight, but he said these things and I cannot just let the matter lie. I think we should look into the situation and give him a scare."

His retainers replied, "That is easily done." That evening they awaited Sukezane's return from the palace and forced him to get down from his carriage. They made him write an apology pledging that he would not say such things again and then let him go.

However, there was a man among Nakamasa's retainers who, being a rough country soldier, lacked either compassion or understanding. He arrived late, just as Sukezane was about to cover his shame by taking refuge in a farmer's house, and, riding up to him without a word, cut off his topknot. The retainer then returned to Nakamasa's residence and presented the topknot to him.

"I never thought things would go this far. This is shocking," said Nakamasa. But, since there was no way to remedy the situation, he decided to leave it at that. Although for the sake of his reputation Sukezane could not speak openly about the incident, could one expect such a matter to be simply dropped?

Hearing what had happened, the ex-emperor summoned the perpetrators of this deed and cross-examined them closely. He decided that the cutting off of the topknot was not a serious offense. However, he ascertained the name of the man who had actually cut off the topknot and summoned him, but the culprit had fled without a trace.

Since Nakamasa did not have the resources to find the man, the ex-emperor, in concern, summoned [a certain] Morishige of the Department of Criminal Justice and ordered him to apprehend without fail the man who had cut off Sukezane's topknot.

On receiving this charge, Morishige made inquiries of the man's friends and relations and kept a secret watch, morning and night, on the house of his mother, a Buddhist nun. While the house was under surveillance, a monk disguised as a woman came knocking at the gate early one morning. Realizing that the monk's visit was not a casual occurrence, Morishige seized him on the spot for questioning.

The monk, excited and flustered, protested, "I have done nothing wrong. He is staying up in the hills at some place near Kiyomizu Temple. I have come merely as his messenger."

"My good monk, we have no business with you. You will serve as our guide in finding the place." And then saying, "You will hear more of this in a while when the matter has been settled," Morishige immediately set out to apprehend the culprit.

Since the arrival of Morishige and his men was completely unexpected, they had no trouble arresting the wanted man and taking him away. However, it occurred to Morishige that the minister of justice, Lord Taira no Tadamori, was located in the area of Kyoto known as Rokuhara, and if they passed through his estate, their prisoner would surely be taken from them. Feeling that such a development would truly make him look like a fool, Morishige seized a vagrant monk he happened upon and, fitting him out in eye-catching fashion, had him taken by way of Rokuhara. The real culprit he stealthily escorted by way of a little-frequented route. However, Tadamori, clearly thinking it a matter of little importance, simply let them pass.

Then the monks of Kiyomizu Temple arose in throngs, crying, "The act of seizing a man within the precincts of this temple for no apparent cause is unprecedented from olden times. Even if the man were a criminal, the abbot should surely have been contacted by the government before the arrest," and they appeared unwilling to let Morishige and his prisoner pass.

Perplexed, Morishige composed a letter on some paper he had in the breast of his kimono. Displaying it to the crowd, he called, "How could I arrest this man without consulting the abbot? Since we did not want talk circulating about the matter, we have not made our consultation public. Here is a document, which is proof that I contacted the abbot this morning."

"In that case there is no problem," said the monks, and they let him pass.

When he heard the details of Morishige's actions, the ex-emperor was extremely impressed by his resourcefulness.

The prisoner, summoned by the ex-emperor, said straightforwardly that he had cut off the topknot. Since at that time Sukezane remained concealed at home, Horikawa felt he would like to ask a few more questions. He said to Morishige, "Do you suppose you could go and confirm whether in fact this topknot was actually cut off?"

Morishige left, saying, "That will be easy." As he left he saw Yasutada of the palace guards and called, "Come along with me. I'm on my way to someone's for a drink. Join me."

Since Morishige was much in favor with the ex-emperor these days, Yasutada was happy to accompany him. Before he had time to wonder where they might be going, they had arrived at Sukezane's house. Morishige spent a full two hours in small talk, making conversation about various matters in order to disguise the purpose of his visit.

When their host brought out the sake and bade them drink, everyone relaxed and began to enjoy themselves. While exchanging cups with his host, Morishige feigned nervousness and, as if in great deference to Sukezane, reached for the sake bottle. In some apparent confusion he knocked off Sukezane's hat. While pretending to be deeply upset by his gaffe, Morishige raised a great fuss to create a diversion and managed to get a look at the top of Sukezane's head. He could see that the cap had been worn over the spot where Sukezane's remaining hair had been meticulously done up to cover the area where the top-knot had been cut off. Morishige signaled Yasutada with a look, and at this point the guard realized for the first time that he had been asked along to serve as a witness. Morishige apologized profusely for his blunder.

Since the enjoyment had gone out of the party, Morishige and Yasutada returned to the palace. Morishige reported what had happened, adding that he had taken along a witness.

"Even had you gone alone, I would not have doubted your word, but taking along a witness has doubly secured your statement," the ex-emperor said, deeply impressed.

Thus Nakamasa's retribution took on added significance. Even so, Sukezane remained argumentative as ever. Although people laughed when he made his appearances for duty at the palace, things continued pretty much unchanged.

About that time Lord Hanazono (1103–1147), who was later to become a high official and a well-known poet and musician, was still of low office and a certain doctor of letters, Atsumasa, was tutoring him. Although it may be easily imagined how lacking Sukezane was in intellectual qualities, he went to the Hanazono residence and during a conversation said, "When you are reading the classics you must call on me, for I expect I am not outdone by Atsumasa."

Although he had trouble knowing just what to make of this shallow remark, Hanazono, perhaps believing it true, responded politely.

Sukezane continued, "Knowing I was coming here, I have prepared a particularly witty Chinese verse."

"How interesting. What is it?"

"Nosegay, nosegay
The mists of spring
Around Atsumasa mountain
Are tinged in red."

His host laughed and said, "A most witty jingle." Thus praised, Sukezane left, feeling quite proud of himself. In his poem Sukezane had made a point of the fact that Atsumasa's nose was rather red. In spite of the truth of this, Lord

Hanazono began to feel bad about the verse and, when Atsumasa came again, told him what had happened.

Enraged, Atsumasa said, "If I were a fighting man, I should show him the same sort of calamity as Nakamasa did. However, even as deeply angered as I am, that sort of thing is not an action befitting one of my profession. Just let me add these final lines to his verse.

"No birds, no feathers—
The winter in Sukezane Garden
White with snow."

Lord Hanazono was most impressed. People of those times used to amuse themselves telling this story.

The following story derives from one appearing in a second-century B.C. Chinese work, *Writings from Huai-nan* (*Huai-nan tzu*). This well-known anecdote illustrates the Taoist principles of avoiding extremes of any kind and practicing inaction, which relies on the self-regulation of nature to solve human problems, since the good or bad effects of any action or event cannot be predicted with certainty. Thus, in the Taoist view one who understands the world does not attempt to impose one's will upon it but succeeds by acting in accordance with nature.

The old man of Hsin Feng referred to in the final paragraph is immortalized in a poem by the famous poet Po Chü-i (772–846) satirizing militarism. Versions of this tale found in variant manuscript copies differ slightly, but not significantly. Tales of this type preserved from the beginnings of Japanese history through the present, together with the Buddhist concept of "karmic reversal" (*gyakuen*), emphasize the importance of a stoic refusal to get upset at things since good can turn into bad, and bad into good.

CHAPTER 6 : TALE 31

The Old Man Po Sou's Horse; The Fu on the Old Man of Hsin Feng

Here is an example that proves that one should not give oneself over too deeply either to joy or sorrow. In ancient times there was an old man in China called Po Sou. He was fortunate to own a strong horse. Although he depended on the horse for his livelihood by renting it out to people and using it himself, it disappeared somewhere or other. Those who heard about his loss felt it was terribly unfortunate. But when they consoled the old man, he said, "Why get so excited? It may or may not be a good thing."

People found this attitude strange, but the horse came home, bringing along another horse of equal quality. Since this was a very fortunate development, the old man's friends and even casual acquaintances rejoiced.

Again, the old man said, "Why get excited? It may or may not be a good thing." Shortly after this, the old man's son mounted the horse, fell off, and broke his arm. Hearing about this, people came to pay their condolences, but again the old man said, "Why get excited? It may or may not be a good thing."

People again found this strange. A year later there was a great war throughout the country. When soldiers were drafted for this conflict, men were also called up from the old man's area. All went to war, and all died. Because the old man's son had only one good arm, he escaped this fate. Thus, although he had only one arm, he had his life. This story has been handed down from the past as an example of wisdom.

Even in these days wise people do not allow themselves to become flustered and flighty, resembling closely the spirit of the old man.

The old man of Hsin Feng, too, was able to avoid becoming a soldier in Yunnan because he broke his elbow. These incidents were in accordance with the law of nature and were very good things.

The next two tales treat events occurring at Shintō shrines. The Shintō gods are seen as responding to poetry and music. The most famous statement of this effect of poety is seen in Ki no Tsurayuki's (884–946) preface to the seminal collection of Japanese poetry, *Collection of Japanese Poetry of the Present and Past (Kokinwakashū)*. Tsurayuki says that "poetry moves heaven and earth, stirs the feelings of gods and spirits invisible to the eye, softens the relations between men and women, and calms the hearts of warriors."

In *Selected Anecdotes* poetry often "softens the relations between men and women," but even more frequently it is seen as a kind of social or political tool that, skillfully used, demonstrates one's intellectual superiority and qualifications for advancement in official rank or social recognition. Musical skill— ability to sing or play the biwa or flute—while also establishing one's reputation, at the same time often influences natural phenomena, which are generally understood as manifestations of the activity of Shintō gods. In the first tale recorded below, Genshō (unidentified), a man who held the title of Master of Music at the Iwashimizu Shrine in Kyoto, incurs the anger of the gods while visiting an outpost in present-day Okayama Prefecture. He then expiates this anger through skilled musicianship.

In the second tale, although the main theme remains the appeal of music to the Shintō gods, the objective of the biwa player is mastery of literary skill, an essentially Confucian ideal. The mention of the Decline of the Buddhhist Law/ Dharma (*mappō*) refers to the Buddhist concept holding that the ability of sentient beings to practice, or even understand, the Buddhhist prescription for attaining Enlightenment degenerated over time. The Decline of the Law/ Dharma is the final stage of this degeneration.

The mixture of Confucian, Shintō, and Buddhist ideas is striking. The final complication of belief patterns is found in the fact that Moronaga's words are taken from a prayer by Po Chü-i asking Buddha to bestow writing ability.

CHAPTER 10: TALE 21

The Master of Music of Iwashimizu Shrine; Genshō's Flute

The Master of Music, Genshō, who directed the music for festivals and ceremonies at Iwashimizu Shrine south of Kyoto, went to visit the shrine's holdings
at Yoshikawa in Bitchu Province. On his return to the capital he stopped at
Muro. While there he seemed about to die from a derangement of the spirit.
Half the hair on his head turned as white as snow. Thinking this was something
supernatural, he sought the help of a shaman. Speaking through this woman,
the god of the Kibitsu Shrine said, "Although you frequently pass through this
area, you never play your music for me. Therefore you are suffering in this
way." Genshō quickly paid a visit to that shrine, and as he played the tunes
secret to all but the emperor, his white hair returned to its normal color. One
must say that he was a wonderful credit to his calling.

CHAPTER 10: TALE 23

Prime Minister Moronaga's Biwa Playing

When Prime Minister Moronaga (1137–1192) was in Owari Province [modern
Gifu Prefecture], he made his way to the Atsuta Shrine night after night. On
the night of the seventh day, in the clear moonlight, he played his biwa. When
he recited, "My wish during life in this world is to master the writing of popular
works," the shrine shook violently. Even at the end of the law, mastery of an
art is a highly desirable accomplishment.

The next tale is a clear statement of the desirability of combining literary and
martial capabilities. For the young men who were to read *Selected Anecdotes,*
this accomplishment was essential. Although military families now held power
and governed, the emperor, despite holding little political power, continued to
reign and remained the symbol of state. The culture of the court, with its
emphasis on refinement of taste, literary skill, and aesthetic sensibility, continued to hold sway as the measure of a truly civilized man. To offset the rough
and ready aspects of character associated with military (and generally provincial) origins, young men from military families must add a finish of literary
skill. This was vital if one desired to obtain official position at court, the persistent center of culture. The preferences and tastes of the emperor and the
members of his court were approved and aspired to by all.

  Selected Anecdotes, like all works of its time, assumes that its audience
shares a common store of knowledge. In this tale what appear to the modern
reader as references to obscure figures of Chinese history or folklore, the arch-

ers Yang Yu and Li Kuang, were probably as familiar to readers as contemporary citations of the exploits of Robin Hood or William Tell are to a Western audience.

Again, allusion to *Chuang-tzu,* a Chinese classic surely familiar to most readers in the thirteenth century, must certainly have called to their minds the incident in which a young man attempts to imitate the way in which a prominent man walks, forgets how he himself walks, and ends up crawling home on his belly.

Another allusion to Chinese literature is seen in Shigefuji's (dates unknown) recitation of the poem about the lamps and the bells. *Ekirei* were bells brought by an imperial commissioner and put out in front of the inns. Their ringing signaled the raising of a levy of men and horses for travel or war. The poem is found in the *Collected Poetry of the T'ang Period (Ch'uan T'ang shih)* and appears in various Japanese works, including *Godanshō, Fukurosōshi,* and *Wakan rō-eishu.* Shigefuji obviously had literary knowledge, and his dismissal of his dual military and literary accomplishments is not to be taken seriously. In fact, this typically Japanese denial of ability is the standard method of acknowledging a compliment. In present-day Japan, also, compliments on one's accomplishments or abilities are invariably answered with disclaimers and self-effacement.

CHAPTER 10: TALE 54

Kiyowara no Shigefuji's Chinese Poem on the Study of Literary and Military Arts; His Chinese Poem on the Fishing Boats' Lights

Now, although one might wonder why those born into military families should attempt to master anything other than the art of archery like Yang Yu of the Spring and Autumn period or to follow in the footsteps of Li Kuang, the Han era master bowman, those who also study literature and love poetry are excellent indeed. Although Kiyowara no Shigefuji's military prowess enabled him to become inspector of the army, he was skilled in literary composition. Once, as the final couplet to a Chinese poem, he wrote:

> Confusing the study of literary and martial arts,
> Like an impersonator lacking self-identity,
> I am undone.

Modestly dismissing his dual accomplishments, Shigefuji alludes to the famous incident in *Chuang-tzu* that tells of a young man who, imitating another, ends up capable of doing nothing on his own.

Shigefuji accompanied the minister of the Home Bureau, Fujiwara no Tadabumi (873–947), when he was appointed shogun in 940 to quell the revolt of Taira no Masakado (d. 940). When they lodged overnight at the seaside by the Kiyomi Barrier in Suruga [present Shizuoka Prefecture], Shigefuji recited the following old poem, and the shogun in purity of soul was reduced to tears at its aptness.

> The shadows of the fishing boats' lamps burn the waves coldly;
> The sounds of the bells along the inn road echo through the
> mountains.

This poem was made by Tu Hsun-ho (9th c.) when he stayed at Lin chiang yi. It is indeed awesome to think that reflection during a night's lodging inspired these same thoughts in both men.

The final tale presented here, which is also the final tale in *Selected Anecdotes,* is an interesting example of the mixing of Buddhist, Taoist, and Confucian elements. The sincere performance of Taoist rites by Sukemichi's son moves Emma, the king of Buddhist hell, to spare Sukemichi's life. Although the son, Arikuni, has offended Buddhist principles, he has done so in good faith, following the ideal of filial piety, a cardinal Confucian precept. The character of Emma also has Confucian overtones: exemplifying the wise Confucian leader, he gives "precedence to mercy, encouraging rewards and reducing punishment."

Selected Anecdotes mixes, picks, and chooses models of conduct from Shintō, Taoist, Buddhist, and Confucian sources, but, even while invoking images such as the Taoist "will of heaven" found in the last sentence of this tale, it remains an essentially Confucian work emphasizing practical moral conduct in the world of here and now.

CHAPTER 10: TALE 79

The Sudden Death of Fujiwara no Sukemichi; His Son Arikuni's Handling of the Death Rites; The Debate at Emma's Palace

When the provincial inspector, Councillor Lord Fujiwara no Arikuni (943–1011), was young, he was in Kyushu with his father, Sukemichi, the governor of Buzen, when Sukemichi became sick and died. In accordance with the rules of worship, Arikuni prayed with all his soul to Taizan Fukun, the mountain god worshiped by Taoists in China. In three hours his father returned to life and said, "Although I was called to Emma's Palace, because of the beautiful offerings you made, the decision was made to send me back.

"During the discussion of my fate, one of Emma's servants said, 'Although it may be decided to send Sukemichi back to the world of the living, Arikuni should be summoned here. Because, although he is not a Taoist, he has practiced their worship rites, and that surely must be a sin.'

"When he said this, another of the men present said, 'Arikuni has committed no sin. He is located in the countryside, in a province far from access to any man versed in Buddhist ways, and his heart was unable to resist the call of filial piety. The fact that he took it upon himself to carry out such rites should result in no adverse judgment.'

"On hearing these words, all those present agreed, and I was sent back." Although he has countless matters to supervise, even in a case such as this, Emma deeply considers the accumulated karma of each individual case. How much more then should human beings exercise care? Therefore, to give precedence to mercy, encouraging rewards and reducing punishments, will ensure that in the world beyond your actions will touch upon the will of heaven and in the mundane world will meet the approval of men.

— 2 —

Kaibara Ekken's Precepts on the Family

Mary Evelyn Tucker

The Tokugawa period in Japanese history (1603–1868) is a significant era in the development of Confucian thought in East Asia. It was during this period that various schools and scholars of Confucianism flourished. As the Tokugawa Bakufu began to establish peace and to unify the country after several decades of civil war, new philosophies were encouraged to assist in the political, educational, and social realms. Confucianism in particular seemed suited to the new situation of internal peace presided over by the shogun in Edo (Tokyo). While it is now clear that the shogunate did not simply appropriate Confucian ideas as a means of establishing ideological control, it is true that Confucianism, often in collaboration with Shintoism and Buddhism, became the leading discourse of the period. How this discourse was used and by whom is a matter of some interpretation.

In a figure such as Kaibara Ekken (1630–1714) we have a fascinating example of a Confucian scholar who was interested in far more than political or ideological control. One of the leading intellectuals of his day, he was committed to making Confucian ideas more widely understood and appreciated. He saw that a philosophy with a vitalist metaphysics, a practical learning, and a comprehensive ethics was urgently needed to maintain a peaceful civil society in Tokugawa Japan. For Ekken this philosophy was most fully developed by Chu Hsi (1130–1200), who was the great twelfth-century synthesizer of Chinese neo-Confucianism. After studying Buddhism and Wang Yang-ming neo-Confucianism, Ekken decided that it was Chu Hsi who had articulated a comprehensive yet practical philosophy with definite educational implications.

Ekken set out in his studies, writing, and teaching to spread Chu Hsi neo-Confucianism in Japan. As an adviser and tutor of the ruling lord (*daimyō*) of Kuroda Province (*han*) in Kyūshū, he was well placed to have influence within the han and beyond. For nearly half a century he assisted the understanding of Chu Hsi's writings in Japan by punctuating the texts and writing commentaries on them. He also contributed to the practical learning of his day and wrote popular moral treatises for educational purposes.

In Ekken's life work he strove to articulate his own form of Chu Hsi neo-Confucianism. This might be described as an anthropocosmic philosophy of a vitalistic naturalism. By anthropocosmic I am suggesting that Ekken drew on the Confucian framework of Heaven, Earth, and Human to suggest that humans are a special and indispensable part of the universe. Humans are part of this framework because of the vital material force (ch'i) that flows through everything. Human ethical actions affect the universe; as we cultivate ourselves morally and spiritually we are able to form one body with all things.

In all of these discussions we are suggesting that Ekken's philosophy and his ethics have very real implications in the contemporary search for a more viable ecological philosophy and a more functional environmental ethics. Ekken's anthropocosmic worldview may be helpful in our own search for a new cosmological understanding of human-earth relations. His naturalistic ethics may, likewise, be significant in our own contemporary efforts to include nature in our sphere of moral concern, compassion, and protection.

The Creative Principles of Filiality and Humaneness

Ekken's anthropocosmic worldview and his interest in practical learning were inspired by his doctrine of filial piety and humaneness as extended to the natural world. From Chang Tsai's (1020–1077) doctrine in the *Western Inscription* of forming one body with all things, Ekken elaborated his unique understanding of assisting in the transforming and nourishing powers of heaven and earth. While his contemporary Nakae Tōju (1608–1648) saw filiality as having a counterpart in the human and natural worlds, Ekken took this understanding a step further by stressing the need for humans to activate a filial reverence for the whole natural world.

A primary motive in this activation of filiality was a sense of the debt (on) to heaven and earth as the parents of things. Ekken recognized the importance of loyalty and reverence to one's parents as the source of life, and he carried this feeling of respect to the cosmic order. He maintained that since nature is the source and sustainer of life, one should respond to it as to one's parents, with care, reverence, and consideration. Indeed, people must serve nature as they would their parents in order to repay their debt for the gift of life.

In this regard, Ekken urged people to cherish living things and to avoid carelessly killing plants or animals. He wrote: "No living creatures such as birds, beasts, insects, and fish should be killed wantonly. Not even grass and trees should be cut down out of season" (de Bary et al. 1958, p. 367). The reason for this care, he maintained, was that "All of these are objects of nature's love, having been brought forth by her and nurtured by her. To cherish them and keep them is therefore the way to serve nature in accordance with the great heart of nature" (ibid.). This care for nature was a key motivating force behind Ekken's own studies of the natural world, for he saw it as connected with filiality.

Central to his anthropocosmic worldview based on filial relationships was an all-embracing humaneness, which he defined as "having a sense of sympathy within and bringing blessings to man and things" (ibid.). His spiritual pursuits and his studies of nature are further linked by his understanding of a direct correspondence between humaneness in persons (C. *jen*; J. *jin*) and the origination principle (C. *yuan*; J. *moto*) in nature.

Indeed, Ekken recognized that the operation of principle in the Supreme Ultimate (C. *t'ai chi*, J. *daikyoku*) had the unique purpose of creating the myriad things and thus can be termed "the heart of nature" (*tenchi no kokoro*). Just as birth or origination are the supreme attributes of the natural world, so is humaneness the supreme attribute of the human. Thus origination is the counterpart in nature of humaneness in persons. In other words, what gives rise to life in the natural and human worlds is analogous.

In this way the creative dynamics of the universe find their richest expression in the creative reciprocity of human beings. The fecundity of nature and the well springs of the human heart are seen as two aspects of the all-embracing process of change and transformation in the universe. Ekken asserted that humans have a harmonious energy granted by nature, and this principle governs their lives. Extending to others is the creative virtue of humaneness.

For Ekken, then, the human was the "soul of the universe" and thus had both great privileges and awesome responsibilities in the hierarchy of the natural world. He wrote, "It is a great fortune to be born a human; let us not fritter away our lives meaninglessly." One can do this through studying the classics, investigating principle, developing practical learning, and activating humaneness. He also added the significant directive to "follow the example of nature" in achieving inner wisdom and contentment. With great detail he described the seasonal changes with which one should harmonize one's own moods and activities. He saw this as participating in the process of transformation, which for the human is the key to both knowledge and practice.

As part of his understanding of the human as the soul of the universe, Ekken adopted Chu Hsi's doctrine of total substance and great functioning (C. *ti-yung*; J. *taiyō*). To achieve this unique balance of theory and practice meant both an exploration of principle and an activation of humaneness.

Briefly stated, then, these are some of the central ideas in Ekken's anthropocosmic worldview, namely, that filial piety should be extended to the whole cosmic order, humaneness is the principle of creativity corresponding to origination in nature, and humans are the soul of the universe and participate through great substance and total functioning in the transformation of heaven and earth. This becomes a driving motivation for the pursuit of practical learning and the investigation of things.

With Ekken the understanding of the cosmic dimensions of reverence that were hinted at in earlier Japanese neo-Confucian thinkers was now transformed into a reverent investigation of nature. Similarly, the cosmic filiality of Nakae Tōju and other earlier neo-Confucians was seen as a reason for both protecting and studying nature through practical learning. All of this was underscored by Ekken's emphasis on *ch'i* as the dynamic unifying element of the universe.

Practical Learning: Content and Methods

Ekken's practical learning was of a broad and comprehensive nature, spanning both the humanities and natural sciences with an end toward personal moral cultivation and alleviation of larger social ills. Ekken's motivation in undertaking practical learning was to participate in the great transforming and nourishing processes of nature by carrying out Chu Hsi's injunction to investigate things and examine their principles. To facilitate this process he advocated a method of investigation that was adapted from Chu Hsi's directives to his students at the White Deer Grotto. He suggested that a correct methodology should be marked by characteristics that may be seen as elaborations of Chu Hsi's instructions, namely, study widely, question thoroughly, think carefully, judge clearly, and act seriously.

With regard to the first principle of the need for broad knowledge, Ekken felt that one must not eliminate either traditional learning or practical contemporary concerns. What is particularly striking about Ekken's breadth is his conscious effort to include knowledge pertinent to the ordinary Japanese of his day. Indeed, he felt it was his mission to study useful popular customs and agricultural techniques as well as to transmit Confucian moral values to the ordinary person.

Yet Ekken was aware of the need to maintain objectivity and rationality in the analysis of principles. He was not interested in simply collecting data or in becoming a specialist or a technician of knowledge. He wanted to be able to bring together specialized research and popular education and to see empirical investigation and ethical practice as part of a single continuum.

Like many Confucians before him, Ekken warned against the limitations of methods used by both the humanist scholar and the scientific researcher. For him, Confucian learning as an essentially ethical path must be distinguished from textual studies or technical skills, which may become ends in themselves. He urged scholars to maintain a reflective and contemplative posture when reading the classics so as not to fall into the traps of linguistic analysis and empty exegesis. Similarly, he rebuked the scholarly specialists who were interested only in personal recognition and the technicians who were obsessed with manipulative processes.

Yet in terms of the content of education he sought to bring together the study of both classical texts and the natural world. He advocated a practical learning that would foster self-cultivation while also assisting others. He urged that learning should be "preserved in the heart and carried out in action" (*juyo no gaku*). Traditional humanistic values and specific technical skills should be used for the benefit of both self and society. In this way the scholar would be assisting in the Confucian aspiration to participate in the transformation of Heaven and Earth.

Kaibara Ekken wrote numerous moral treatises (*kunmono*) for instructing various groups and individuals in Japanese society. In his eagerness to make Confucian moral teachings understood by a large number of people, he wrote these treatises in a simplified Japanese rather than in classical Chinese. This use of the vernacular meant the teachings could become more widespread and better understood. This popularization of Confucian ideas was an important element of Ekken's work as well as a dominant feature of Tokugawa thought. During this era Confucianism was gradually moving from the medieval period confines of the Buddhist monasteries and the province of elite families. Numerous samurai who were attracted to Confucianism for a variety of reasons helped in this spread of Confucian ethics. This occurred through their writings, through their acting as advisers to local lords (*daimyō*), and through the establishment of schools both public and private throughout Japan.

Clearly the samurai class, in particular, was attracted to Confucianism for its humane teachings, embracing a philosophy of education, a means of social ordering, and a pragmatic political program. It is also evident that many of the merchants found Confucianism to be a sound economic philosophy encouraging frugality, hard work, loyalty, and good business practices. All of this meant that during the Tokugawa period there was a significant growth in Confucian texts, schools, and ethical teachings. A major part of this growth was due to the writings of samurai-scholars such as Ekken.

Indeed, it has been suggested that Ekken was "responsible for one of the most systematic accounts" of the rationale of moral education in the Tokugawa period (Dore 1965, 35). This is especially due to his attempts to codify Confucian ethics in more than a dozen moral treatises. These were addressed to a broad spectrum of Tokugawa society, including the samurai, the family, women, and children. They covered topics as wide ranging as ethical practices for individuals and for families, educational curriculum and methods of study, advice on a successful business, caring for one's health, and attaining contentment. An underlying theme of these treatises was self-cultivation to benefit the family and the larger society. This key teaching from the *Great Learning* on the importance of self-cultivation was channeled into the techniques of the learning of the mind-and-heart (*shingaku*). Essentially a means of moral and spiritual discipline, this learning of the mind-and-heart became a vehicle for the transmission and spread of Confucianism across various classes and groups in Japan. Ekken's moral treatises were instrumental in this process.

Ekken's *Precepts on the Way of the Family* (*Kadōkun*) is part of a larger genre of house codes or family precepts (*kakun*). The custom of writing instructions for the family came to Japan from China during the Nara period and continued to be written by court families during the Heian period. In the Kamakura era the samurai wrote *kakun,* and in the Tokugawa period this custom was adopted by merchants as well as samurai. In his *Precepts on the Way of the Family*, Ekken expanded the theme of the *Great Learning* that order in the family will influence the larger society. This can be achieved through self-discipline and the practice of mutual reciprocity with others. The striking feature of Ekken's *Precepts on the Way of the Family* is his integration of instructions for moral cultivation with practical business advice. He stressed the need for ritual and reciprocity in family relations along with effort and diligence in the family business. He continually emphasized the need for restraint and frugality within the household as well as in running a business. He urged careful education of the children, servants, and employees.

Ekken outlined five stages in a person's life that relate to obligations to the family: attending to one's parental education until age twenty, studying the classics and arts from twenty to thirty, supporting one's family and managing its financial affairs between thirty and forty, planning for one's descendants until age fifty, and finally preparing things for after one's death.

For Ekken the external ordering of a person's life should reflect an internal ordering through self-cultivation. He suggested that people should try and harmonize with nature to encourage this cultivation. Specifically he noted that gardening may be most helpful in establishing this reciprocity with nature. Ultimately, for Ekken, self-cultivation reflected the larger patterns of heaven and earth in its ceaseless transformations. For him, the cultivation of oneself and the extension outward to one's family, the society, and the cosmos as a whole are part of one continual process of harmonization.

Thus in typical Confucian tradition, Ekken suggested that the natural biological bonds of the family are the model for other forms of reciprocal morality in the society at large. The patterns of mutual affection and obligations are extended outward from the family and relatives to friends and acquaintances, to all those in need. In several striking passages Ekken urged people to care for the hungry, the sick, the orphaned, and the widowed. In the spirit of Chang Tsai's *Western Inscription*, he suggested that the sense of obligation should move from a primary concern for one's family ever outward toward others.

The following is a translation of one chapter and the beginning of the second from Kaibara Ekken's *Kadōkun*. The entire text of six chapters appears in *Ekken zenshū* (The collected works of Kaibara Ekken) 3 (Tokyo: Ekken Zenshū Kankōbu, 1910–1911), 421–475. Ekken also wrote a shorter *Kakun*, which is less concerned with economic matters than is his *Kadōkun*.

Further Reading

Irene Bloom, *Knowledge Painfully Acquired* (New York: Columbia University Press, 1987); Wm. Theodore de Bary et al., eds., *Sources of Japanese Tradition* (New York: Columbia University Press, 1958); Wm. Theodore de Bary and Irene Bloom, eds., *Principle and Practicality* (New York: Columbia University Press, 1979); Ronald Dore, *Education in Tokugawa Japan* (Berkeley: University of California Press, 1965); Tetsuo Najita, *Visions of Virtue in Tokugawa Japan: The Kaitokudo Merchant Academy of Osaka* (Chicago: University of Chicago Press, 1987); Peter Nosco, ed., *Confucianism and Tokugawa Culture* (Princeton: Princeton University Press, 1984); Okada Takehiko, "Practical Learning in the Chu Hsi School: Yamazaki Ansai and Kaibara Ekken," in de Bary and Bloom 1979; Herman Ooms, *Toku-*

gawa Ideology: Early Constructs, 1570–1680 (Princeton: Princeton University Press, 1985); Janine Anderson Sawada, *Confucian Values and Popular Zen: Sekimon Shingaku in Eighteenth-Century Japan* (Honolulu: University of Hawaii Press, 1993); Tu Wei-ming, *Centrality and Commonality* (Albany: State University of New York Press, 1989); Tu Wei-ming, *Confucian Thought: Selfhood as Creative Transformation* (Albany: State University of New York Press, 1985); Mary Evelyn Tucker, *Moral and Spiritual Cultivation in Japanese Neo-Confucianism: The Life and Thought of Kaibara Ekken (1630–1714)* (Albany: State University of New York Press, 1989).

CHAPTER 1

REGULATING THE FAMILY BY DISCIPLINING ONESELF

Our duty in living in this world, whether we are of high or low rank, is to regulate the family by disciplining oneself. The root of [order in] the family lies in oneself. Therefore, the master who regulates the family must first discipline himself. Without disciplining oneself, regulating the family will be difficult. When one does not regulate the family, it will be difficult to have harmony. The noble person is always mindful of himself and worries about [the consequences of] future deeds. Thus he is at peace with himself and preserves the family. When the head of the house is honest, he can teach and lead the other family members. When the head is not honest, he cannot be a model for the family. To foster the good it will be difficult to eradicate evil. He cannot practice the family code. Thus, the deeds of the head of the house should be a model for the family's learning. He should behave carefully.

PRACTICING RITUAL

To regulate oneself and discipline the family requires ritual. Ritual means propriety in human relations [namely, ethics]. Ritual is being mindful in one's heart and having a model for oneself. Without mindfulness and without a model, the human heart may be lost and one's actions may degenerate; when such people interact with others, the Way of human relations disappears. Because of ritual people are different from birds and animals; without ritual we are the same as birds and animals. Practicing ritual is not difficult or painful. When many deeds are done according to the code we ought to follow, our heart will be tranquil and our actions will be temperate. Practicing ritual is like following a straight and level road. Consequently, when people have ritual they are peaceful, but without ritual they are anxious. Therefore, we should practice ritual.

We should constantly preserve ritual and be correct within [the household]. When we are not correct within, although we practice the good externally, all will become false. This is the beginning of preserving ritual. Being correct within means being affectionate and encouraging mutual respect between fathers and sons, brothers and sisters, and husbands and wives; taking care of things used in the house; managing employees without haste or negligence; using money without extravagance or waste; controlling lust and desires, knowing shame, and not acting foolishly.

SERVING PARENTS

In serving parents you should devote yourself, always asking about their health and tending to their needs with diligence. You should act according to an ancient saying: "Deliberate in the evening and reflect on it the next morning." Even if you have very little free time, make an effort to visit and serve your parents sometime during the day. Pay close attention to the conditions of their household, making the taste of food and drink good, checking the temperature yourself and then serving it, and making parents warm in the winter and cool in the summer. When you go out of the house you should first take leave of your parents, and when you return to the house you should again greet your parents. In interacting with your parents, you should be gentle in expression and not rude in speech. We must not lose these two practices, namely, seeing to one's parents' happiness and caring for their health. These are practices that are appropriate for all people's children, and we should not undermine these practices. Filiality means always thinking of one's parents and never forgetting them.

FAMILY RELATIONS

There is love between brother and sister and harmony between husband and wife, but in these relations there are also distinctions. A husband treats his wife with propriety. Teach and discipline your children and do not indulge them. Love them and do not despise them. Do not be negligent in guiding children, in practicing propriety, in having them read books, and in making them learn the arts. Their education should definitely be strict.

A person who rules the family as the master of the house tries first to serve his parents well. Next, guiding his wife and educating his children are essential. Finally, he should be considerate in his treatment of servants and have a correct display of propriety. He should not harm nor ridicule nor tyrannize them.

RAISING CHILDREN

In raising children, from an early age we must restrain any excesses and indulgences. The clothes, the belongings, and the way you raise your children should be appropriate to your income and not extravagant. Being too affectionate and being extravagant with things are not good for they teach extravagance to the child. Experiencing luxuries in childhood results in nothing but harm in later life. It is unwise to let children enjoy luxuries and then later try to control them. By being strict in the beginning, gradually one can become more indulgent. From childhood one must be taught the importance of being truthful and sincere. We should encourage frugality in many ways. From early childhood we should admonish children to avoid laziness and selfishness as well as to be humble and conciliatory.

A Chinese minister of the former Han dynasty, Jiayi, had a wise saying regarding raising children: "Teach them from an early age and choose their associates." We should pay attention to these two things. When we do not teach them from an early age, they will easily be steeped in vice. When people near us are evil, by looking at and hearing evil things, evil can become our own bad habit. From childhood if we see and hear evil things, the words that enter become contaminated, and later, although we hear and see good things, we cannot change. When bad habits stick, they become ingrained and we cannot change them.

We should respect ancestors and not neglect seasonal ceremonies. We should be close to our relatives. Being distant from relatives and close to strangers is unnatural. Revering and preserving national law, we must not speak ill of the government or the actions of officials above us.

Slandering those above us, speaking evil of the national government, is the greatest disloyalty and disrespect. We should be careful. Although there are people who slander others, we should not blindly follow the crowd. We should not be careless or garrulous in speaking. Always examining and disciplining ourselves, we should criticize our own faults. We must not blame others and point to their shortcomings.

PEACE IN THE THREE RELATIONS

In ruling the family it is essential not to have abrasiveness with the three relations: namely, between father and son, between brothers and sisters, and between husband and wife. An ancient saying tells us: "Intimacy between father and son; harmony between brothers and sisters; and correctness between husband and wife will enrich the home." When the relations between these three are bad, even though the family has wealth, they are impoverished.

PRACTICING GOODNESS BASED ON LOVE AND RESPECT

In associating with other members of the family, we must warn against evil and practice good. When we do not practice good, the Way of humans is not correct. In practicing good we must take love and respect as the basis. Love is having sympathy for people and avoiding cruelty. Respect is honoring people and not ridiculing them. These two are the method of the heart for practicing the good in human relations. In doing good there is nothing other than respect and love. With respect and love for one's parents as the basis, we must not slander brothers and sisters, husbands and wives, relatives or servants. We must love and respect people according to their rank. Even though we are not close, we must not be negligent. This is love. Even if a person is poor, we must not despise them. This is respect.

THINGS TO DO IN THE MORNING

Every day we should get up early, wash our hands and face, and first inquire about the health of our parents. We should ask what food and drink they would like, and we should prepare these things. If one's parents request a certain thing, we should seek it diligently and try to please them. We should instruct the children carefully in the tasks they should perform that day and order clearly and diligently what the servants should do that day. If there are duties to be done outside the house, have the servants do them. If there are requests from people, we should respond punctually and in an orderly manner. We should have the servants rise early and open the gate. We should make everything clean by sweeping within the house, in the garden, and inside and outside the gate. Rising late in the morning signals the decline of the family and it should be avoided. There is an ancient saying: "The status of a family can be seen according to the hour of their rising."

HOUSEHOLD MATTERS

The usual care with respect to household matters should be done expeditiously: first, taking care of the food and rice supply to have enough for the following autumn; next, storing up salt and soy sauce, making dried fish and salted fish, and gathering and stacking firewood, charcoal, and oil. When we do not have these supplies, we cannot meet our household needs. We should be kind to servants and look after their clothes, their food, and the condition of their rooms. We need to make them feel content and free from hunger or severe cold.

Correct distinctions should be made between men and women and between those who are within the household and those who are without. The samurai should always place instruments (such as spears, long swords, bows and arrows, cannons, staffs, and clubs) in appropriate places. One should always keep the necessary utensils in good shape, fix broken things, and promptly repair things that are damaged, such as houses, storerooms, walls, and fences. One should seek and store wood, bamboo, soil, and stones, feed the horses well, care for the domestic animals, and carefully nurture the plants and vegetables according to the season.

We should pay attention to the opening and closing of the storehouse when we put things in and take them out. We should be careful of thieves and watchful for fires. We should not be negligent. We should have fire prevention tools ready. In this way we should always be mindful and not careless in domestic things.

Each of [the four classes of] samurai, farmers, artisans, and merchants should constantly be diligent and not neglect the family business. In addition, we should be frugal and modest in various things and not act carelessly in domestic matters. Being diligent and frugal are two necessary elements in ruling the family. We should always practice these two things: diligence and frugality.

PRACTICING HIDDEN VIRTUE

Within the household we must practice hidden virtue. Preserving humaneness in the heart, practicing goodness in oneself, and not letting others know is hidden virtue. Even those who are less fortunate can practice goodness within their means. It is good to practice hidden virtue by giving food to those who are hungry, providing warmth for those who are cold, giving water to those who are thirsty, caring for the elderly, loving children, consoling the sick, exhorting younger people to have filiality and faithful service toward others, praising the talent and goodness of others, not blaming others' mistakes, concealing other people's evils yet admonishing the faults and mistakes of others [when appropriate], picking up things that may harm people such as posts, oranges with thorns, or stakes that fall on the road, returning to the owner things found on the road, and not killing living things recklessly just because they are small.

When we practice this for a long time the good will grow and we will be content. Even poor people can do this; how much more so should rich people! People who have wealth to spare should follow the principle that says the heavenly Way blesses those who give away excess. If one does not give alms to people and simply accumulates lots of material goods for oneself, later evil will surely arise, material goods will be lost, and little will remain for their children. People who have material wealth should practice goodness by first caring for their parents, then financially assisting relatives and friends, helping the poor, providing for those who are hungry and cold, and thus loving people broadly. Heaven will be deeply pleased with those who help others. Because of the principle that the heavenly Way rewards goodness with happiness, if we continue for a long time to love people broadly, Heaven will be deeply pleased and there is no doubt that we will receive happiness. There is a saying that "The heavenly Way likes the idea of reciprocity." If we practice goodness we will receive happiness from heaven; if we practice evil we will receive misfortune from heaven. The saying concerning "liking reciprocity" means that there is retribution for evil deeds and reward for good deeds. This principle is certain. This is the sincerity of the heavenly Way. When we practice goodness for a long time, it is worth a hundred times more than the prayers of those who do not practice the human Way and just pray and flatter the gods and buddhas to avoid misfortune.

Foolish people lack respect for the heavenly Way and question it because they do not know the principle that the heavenly Way rewards goodness with happiness. In both China and Japan there have been many such examples throughout the ages of the principle that the heavenly Way rewards goodness with happiness and rewards evil with misfortune. This principle is clear. At first there are no signs [of recompense], but later definitely there will be recompense. There is no doubt. When people practice evil and do not help by giving to others so that they too can have material wealth, they will be despised by heaven. This principle is inescapable. We should respect the heavenly Way.

THE MIND-AND-HEART OF THE SAMURAI

Those who are samurai should put their mind carefully toward military preparations. They should arrange soldiers' equipment, repair anything broken, and from time to time should wipe and polish the large and small swords they usually wear in their belts as well as other swords, bows, arrows, spears, and long swords. They should wipe away the dirt and make them shine. They should store up gold, silver, rice, and money for military armaments. When there is insufficient gold to meet all demands, they should not take out and use what they have stored for military use. Soldiers' armaments, even more than other equipment, should be clean for emergencies. If supplies are low they must stock up in times of peace. They should not be negligent. By this preparation of military equipment they will avoid confusion, and even though war breaks out, they will be able to enter the battle calmly. Furthermore, soldiers' armaments should not be unnecessarily decorative.

MAKING THE PRACTICE OF GOODNESS PLEASURABLE

The master of the house should always show love and make the practice of goodness enjoyable. If he has extra goods, he should give them to family members or poor relatives, help friends who are without money, alleviate the hunger and cold of the farmers of his own fief, assist poor and troubled people who come to his house, and help destitute people in appropriate ways. Among beggars there are old people, sick people, deformed people (especially blind, disabled, and deaf people), old people without children, orphans, and those who cannot obtain food because they have no relatives to care for them and thus have no choice but to become beggars. These are destitute people, and when we see these troubled people we should extend our assistance and compassion as much as possible. It is easy to care for the hungry. Doing good by helping others is the most enjoyable thing in the world. We need to think seriously about this. The Chinese Ming emperor asked his brother, Dong Ping Wang, when he came to see him in the capital, "What is pleasure in your country?" His brother answered, "In my country my highest pleasure is doing good." Both rich and poor should do good according to their rank. If they really mean it, even though they are poor, every day they can practice the good. There is nothing more enjoyable than doing good. If they make an effort to practice the good, they should know this pleasure well. An ancient saying notes: "It is hard to do good if you are unwilling to give." It is foolish to spend money on trifling matters. Such spenders do not intend to practice goodness or to help people.

ENDURANCE IN RULING THE FAMILY

We should use endurance in ruling the family. This means persevering and bearing with certain things. Perservering means avoiding extravagance and suppressing selfish desires. Moreover, it is bearing [the burden of] being poor and not desiring other people's things recklessly. Since most people are not sages, there are many things not suitable for our well-being. If we do not have endurance, relationships with people will not go smoothly. Thus, parents and older siblings rebuke children when the child's behavior toward them is inadequate and they are dissatisfied. When the love of parents or older siblings is inadequate, the children resent them. Moreover, the same problem arises between husbands and wives and between relatives. When people are not mutually patient and when they show anger and resentment, human relations worsen. If we are mutually patient with regard to the unsatisfactory deeds of others, if we are not angry and resentful, we will maintain harmony within the family. This is the Way of regulating the family. Moreover, we should exhaust the human Way in enduring and forgiving the misdeeds of others. We should not do anything that needs to be forgiven by others.

When we employ people in the house we must be empathetic toward them, sympathetic toward their hardships, and we should not cause them suffering. Servants are those who live by relying on their masters. We should sympathize with them and not cause them suffering by cruelty or lack of compassion. Those who employ people should reflect deeply on the hardships of servants.

There are four things necessary to govern a household:

1. Managing a livelihood by diligence in the family business
2. Being thrifty in order not to deplete family funds
3. Preserving oneself by self-restraint
4. Having tolerance, namely, love for people

This was said by Wang Ning, a Chinese historian in the Sui dynasty. Tolerance means understanding the heart of others by means of our own heart, giving people what they like and not giving them what they dislike. In order to rule the family, we must observe these four things.

It is important to choose a good teacher for children from an early age and make them read the books of the sages. Teaching them goodness and warning against evil, they should know and practice the way of filiality, loyalty, propriety, and honor. They should not be allowed to associate with evil people. We should warn against this most of all. They should not be allowed to listen to or hear bad things. In childhood it is especially easy to be infected with evil things. What is first learned as good and evil soon becomes ingrained. Children should be made to seek and mingle with good friends and to learn what is good. Because good and evil can become a habit, we must be mindful of our habits.

To preserve the household by self-discipline we must encourage frugality. Frugality means being thrifty and not being greedy or extravagant. Guarding one's desires and being moderate in family expenses is the way to preserve the family by disciplining oneself. In the *Analects* it says, "Little is lost by frugality." When we have frugality our mistakes are few.

If we become the lord of a house, we should have good relations with three families, namely, the father's family, the mother's family, and the wife's family. The father's family is the principal family. The blood that is passed from the ancestors is the same. There are differences of closeness and distance, but since they have the same material force (*ch'i*) as us, we should be on good terms. Being on good terms with the father's family is the way to serve ancestors. After the father's family, we should be on good terms with the mother's family. The wife's family comes next after the mother's family. Such is the order and importance of having good relations with these three families. This is an ancient custom. Nowadays people are only intimate with the wife's family, and they are distant from the father's and the mother's family. This is not knowing the importance [of relationships]. It is unfilial to parents and it is foolish. This is not to say one should not have good relations with one's wife's family. However, it is good to observe relationships in an appropriate manner.

EXERCISING THE BODY

Make both the cost and intake of daily food and drink moderate and exercise the body. Indulging in good food and drink and being idle is deleterious to the body. We should not be extravagant and lazy. If we follow this teaching we will receive three benefits: first you nurture virtue, then you strengthen the body, and finally you increase your wealth. When we eat and drink simply and exercise the body, we can enjoy good health since there will be no food stagnation. The blood will circulate well and the stomach stays healthy. If you exercise the body you can endure suffering and hard work and can practice loyalty and filiality, and thus it will be beneficial for teaming and for the arts. If one does not exercise, then idleness becomes a habit; one cannot endure hardship nor make continual efforts of loyalty and filiality, and one neglects scholarship and the arts. Samurai especially will lose their disciplined training; they cannot endure the hardships of the army; they will become sick and their body will deteriorate and become useless, and as a result they cannot exercise their duty. We must make the heart peaceful and the body active.

CHAPTER 2

When we put forth effort in the family business we can earn profit even if we do not seek it. The samurai should make an effort for his lord without flattery.

The farrmer should apply himself in the fields; he should revere authority, work hard as a public duty. The artisan should make good things and should not deceive people by making inferior things. The merchant should avoid fraud and usury in his trade. If the four classes act together like this without forcing themselves to be greedy for profit, they will enjoy happiness and fortune naturally. Those who fail to do their duty correctly and are greedy for profit and do evil things may be happy for a while; however, because it is a principle that heaven will despise them, later they will surely suffer misfortune. Foolish people try to make profits quickly and never anticipate later misfortune. The four classes must not be deceptive in performing their family work correctly and revering the Way of heaven. This is the way to escape misfortune and ensure happiness.

NOT BEING GREEDY FOR PROFIT

The family's misfortune arises, in most cases, from seeking profit. When we are greedy for profit, it often happens that instead misfortune comes and we lose assets. Rather than seeking profit, if you make an effort not to neglect the family business and not use family funds carelessly and not seek profit more than is suitable, there will be no misfortune and you will not lose property. Generally speaking, greed for profit is the origin of misfortune. We should avoid that.

EFFORT AND MINDFULNESS ARE THE WAY OF HEAVEN AND EARTH

It is an ancient saying that "If we make an effort we will overcome poverty; if we are mindful we will overcome misfortune." These words are very beneficial. People who diligently make an effort in the family business inevitably become rich. If we are mindful of ourselves there will be no misfortune. These two words [effort and mindfulness] we should always protect and practice. By actualizing these ourselves, our family members will do likewise. Making an effort is the Way of heaven; heaven revolves without ceasing. Being mindful is the way of Earth; earth is quiet and does not move. Making an effort and being mindful is basing our model on the Way of heaven and earth. This is the Way that humans ought to practice, for these are profound principles.

— 3 —

The Shingaku of Nakazawa Dōni

Janine Anderson Sawada

Neo-Confucian notions of self-cultivation came to have widespread influence in Tokugawa Japan (1600–1868), not only on the educated elite, but also among the less privileged sectors of society. The popularization of neo-Confucian ideas was largely due to the efforts of such movements as Sekimon Shingaku, a religious group founded in the early eighteenth century by a dry goods clerk named Ishida Baigan (1685–1744). Shingaku, the "learning of the mind," traced its roots to Mencius's belief that all human beings possess an "original mind" (C. *pen hsin*, J. *honshin*) naturally endowed with moral goodness. Mencius (372–289 B.C.E.?), the traditional successor to Confucius, taught that one could preserve the original mind by cultivating such universal values as humaneness and rightness. This positive view of human nature was developed into a system of religious discipline by neo-Confucian thinkers in Sung China (960–1279). The Sung masters considered the pursuit of the mind in its pure, unselfish state to be the cornerstone of moral education. They advocated a discipline of regular self-examination and reflection guided by the values enunciated in the Confucian canon. But in Tokugawa Japan, this regimen, which required literacy in Chinese, was impractical for all but an educated minority.

Ishida Baigan and his successor, Teshima Toan (1718–1786), rendered the neo-Confucian system of self-cultivation accessible to ordinary Tokugawa citizens. They reformulated the ideas of the Sung masters in a manner that could be understood even by semiliterate townsfolk and villagers. By the end of the eighteenth century, the Shingaku movement had generated a cadre of preachers who traveled throughout rural and urban areas of Japan explaining the importance of "knowing the original mind" (*honshin o shiru*). Teshima Toan's most famous disciple, Nakazawa Dōni (1725–1803), was responsible for the expansion of the Shingaku movement in the Edo (Tokyo) area. Dōni is said to have attracted large crowds of listeners, samurai as well as commoners. The following excerpts from Dōni's "talks on the Way" (*dōwa*) help explain this success. He skillfully conveys abstract notions by means of concrete metaphors—a talent that served him well as he traversed the country preaching to people of all classes.

The Shingaku teaching of knowing the original mind drew not only on the Mencian understanding of human nature, but also on the Mahāyāna Buddhist doctrine of the enlightened Buddha-nature that dwells in all sentient beings. Shingaku teachers were particularly influenced by popular forms of Zen that circulated in the Tokugawa period. Teshima Toan frequently elaborated his sermons by referring to Zen master Bankei Yōtaku (or Eitaku, 1622–1693), who taught the importance of dwelling in the "unborn Buddha-mind" (fushō no busshin). Similarly, in the first passage below, Dōni relies for inspiration on Ikkyū Sōjun (1394–1481), whose image as a humorous, paradoxical Zen teacher was by now widespread in Japan. Both Toan and Dōni understood the original mind to be free of all dualistic discriminations or "calculations" (shian). The true mind was a source of pure goodness within each human being that one could "discover" in a profound moment of insight (hatsumei)—a pivotal religious experience comparable to the enlightenment event in Zen. As Dōni points out, dualities such as form and emptiness, dark and light are transcended by the wisdom of the original mind, which he equates with the intangible realm of "heaven." He notes that though the world of the mind, or heaven, is not itself visible, it is the ultimate power that sustains all phenomena.

According to Dōni, once one knew the original mind, its wisdom would naturally manifest in moral behavior: one would embody filial piety, loyalty, diligence, and frugality. Instead of "calculating," one would simply follow the spontaneous, good impulses of the original mind; one would remain "without a (selfish) mind of one's own" (mushin) and allow everything to develop naturally. Here we can detect a note of the Taoist value of naturalness or spontaneity—an idea that not only played a part in the original formulation of Zen in China but also directly influenced Shingaku teachers in Japan.

Although raised in a strict Nichiren Buddhist family, Dōni was particularly sensitive to religious intolerance and sectarianism. In our last two excerpts, he admonishes his listeners that no single school has a monopoly on the truth, for knowing the original mind is the ultimate aim of all teachings. This all-inclusive attitude, typical of Shingaku preachers, exemplifies the long-standing East Asian tradition of the "Unity of the Three Teachings" (sankyō itchi). Indeed, Sekimon Shingaku succeeded in early modern Japan largely because it effectively synthesized Confucian, Shintō, and Buddhist ideas into a palatable, practical religion that met the needs of busy town dwellers and rural villagers.

The translations are from Ishikawa Ken, ed., Dōni-ō dōwa (Tokyo: Iwanami Shoten, 1935); and Shibata Minoru, ed., Sekimon Shingaku, in Nihon shisō taikei 42 (Tokyo: Iwanami Shoten, 1971).

Further Reading

Robert N. Bellah, Tokugawa Religion: the Cultural Roots of Modern Japan (New York: Free Press, 1985) [originally published in 1957 under the title Tokugawa Religion: The Values of Pre-Industrial Japan];

Wm. Theodore de Bary, *The Neo-Confucian Orthodoxy and the Learning of the Mind-and-Heart* (New York: Columbia University Press, 1981); Janine Anderson Sawada, *Confucian Values and Popular Zen: Sekimon Shingaku in Eighteenth-Century Japan* (Honolulu: University of Hawaii Press, 1993).

Old Man Dōni's Talks on the Way

[A] Now, in the dying days of Ikkyū's disciple Ninakawa Shin'uemon, when Ikkyū was about to pronounce the last words over him, Shin'uemon rose abruptly:

> I arrived alone, and will return alone, too;
> To say you'll teach me the Way is odd, indeed!

Ikkyū replied with the poem:

> Arriving alone and returning alone are both illusions.
> I'll teach you the Way of neither coming nor going.

This concerns the problem of karma; it is the one great matter of birth and death. It is a critical point. If you cannot grasp it, Ikkyū's death poem will also be difficult for you to comprehend:

> I will not die. I will not go anywhere; I'll stay here.
> Don't ask—I won't say anything.

Where is "here"? It is the heaven of empty space, invisible to the eye, which "neither comes nor goes." It is a wonderful realm; everything is completely sustained by it.

This cup, too—the form is earth, while the empty space inside and outside of it is heaven. This empty heaven is indispensable. If this cup were just a solid form, a cut-off cylindrical object, like the counterweight on a beam balance, it would not be able to fulfill the function of a cup. Precisely because it is hollow and there is empty heaven inside, it can scoop up tea and serve the function of a cup. People manage their needs with the help of the cup. One wouldn't be able to drink hot tea by scooping it up in one's hands.

People have their obdurate points, but the cup obediently says, "Yes! Yes! Yes!" and completely fulfills the Way of a cup all day long. On the other hand, at night in the cupboard it says, "Zzz, zzz, zzz," without the slightest hitch. It's a clever thing! At that time, even the name "cup" is utterly forgotten. But if there is a fire or something at night, the cup gets up again and runs around saying "Hey! Hey! Hey!" Even if you carelessly drop it and it breaks instantly, it doesn't become angry. At that moment, even though the form of the cup is broken, the name "cup" doesn't even get a crack. At that point, the cup's death poem is:

> Now I will break. I will not go anywhere; I'll stay here.
> Don't ask—you can't drink any tea.

So, Mr. Cup is able to grasp this realm of "neither coming nor going." And it is the same with a candle. When it is lit, there is the evanescent world of the candle; when the flame is extinguished, there is true darkness. Then the candle's death poem is:

> Now I will be extinguished. I will not go anywhere; I'll stay here.
> Don't ask—I won't give any light.

According to an old poem,

> The candle goes out—where does it go?
> Darkness is its original home.

"Dark" is the mind of darkness, which is heaven; "light" is the mind of the flame, which is also heaven. The mind has neither shadow nor shape; it is neither light nor dark. What sort of thing is this mind that "has no sound, no scent"? Please meditate on this.

[B] I, too, have had the experience of realizing for myself that this "I" is no match for nature. I'll tell you about that now. It was something that happened recently, in the summer. The midsummer heat was something terrible; each day was hotter than the day before. Hoping to cool off a bit from the muggy heat, I went out back. Fortunately there was a chair by the edge of the dugout pond, and I stayed there a while in the blessed coolness, putting the heat out of my mind. At one point, a gutter-worm crawled up onto my chair and seemed to be struggling painfully for some reason; then a needlelike thing emerged from its back. While I was watching, this thing divided into two parts and became wings: the gutter-worm became a kind of dragonfly and, somehow or other, flew off.

While I was marveling over nature's handiwork, another gutter-worm crawled up. This one, too, had winglike forms on its back. It also struggled to open up the wings into two parts, but they didn't separate. Then I had an idea. Thinking, "No fear, I'll spread your wings for you in an instant," I took a toothpick out of my wallet and divided its wings for it. Then it appeared to fly up about a fathom, but suddenly it fell down into the water and died. All that trouble for nothing; it would have been better to leave things up to the will of the Buddha. I had simply been overeager and needlessly destroyed life.

Please think about everything from this perspective. None of us is able to wait for the right season. We force things because of our impatience. As a result, we often end up bungling things in midcourse.

[C] Formerly there was an exceedingly filial son in a place called Nishi-no-zaki, and there was also a filial son of high repute in a place called Okazaki Village. Now, the filial son of Nishi-no-zaki was reflecting on what he had heard about the filial son of Okazaki Village. He felt that by all means he would like to hear what that filial son had to say and then serve his own parents with even greater care. One day he went out of his way to visit Okazaki Village. The filial son was out working the fields at the time and only his mother was home. She said, "My son will return shortly, so for the moment, please have a smoke of tobacco and wait for him."

So he waited, just as she suggested, and as evening approached, the filial son promptly returned, bearing a basketlike thing on his shoulders. He put it down by the side of the door and seated himself in a leisurely manner at the edge of the vestibule. His mother exclaimed, "Ah! You came back early!" while she poured hot water into a basin. She adjusted the temperature of the water, brought the basin over to one side, and said, "All right, put your feet out."

"Right!" he replied, and he put his legs, full of mud, straight out in front of his mother. Then his mother peeled off his straw sandals for him and, grasping the tips of his feet, splashed water on them and washed them for him; without a word, the son held out both his feet and let her wash them. At length she dried them with a towel; he went on upstairs just as he was, immediately sprawled out on his stomach, and began puffing away at his pipe.

His mother busied herself rinsing and drying his straw sandals and even tidied up his basket. After that, she set out the dinner trays and announced, "All right, eat your meal!" To which he replied,

"Yes!"—and while his mother waited on him, he ate his food. When he pushed away his tray, his mother busily cleaned up once again.

The filial son who had come to visit had been watching in amazement, thinking: "This is really too much. Still, there must be some particular reason why he is renowned for his filial piety." He said, "Well, I am from Nishi-no-zaki. I heard that you are a person who should be esteemed for your tremendous filial piety. Therefore, I felt I should go out of my way to make your acquaintance and have come to visit you. I have been watching your behavior, bit by bit, for some time, and I feel it is exceedingly rude. To thrust your muddy feet at your parent and make her wash them, even to have her wait on you as you eat your food—there must be some special reason for this." Whereupon the son replied,

"No, no. I do not perform any special deeds of filial piety–none at all. To bustle about like that and take care of me is my mother's deepest joy; she looks forward to doing it, day after day. What my mother enjoys is my joy. I just do exactly as my mother tells me, whatever that may be. If I assume that the work is a burden for an old person, and say that I'll do it myself, she feels bad. When my mother feels bad, somehow I do not feel right, either. For this reason, no matter what sort of thing it may be, I just do whatever my mother tells me. I have never done any special deeds of filial piety. I do not violate my mother's desire in regard to anything. If I violate it even a bit, I inflict that much anxiety on her; therefore, I just act like a small child, dependent on my parent. No matter how old I become, my mother thinks of me as a small child; so I act like a small child, dependent on my mother for everything."

This is sincere filial piety, free of selfish calculation. That filial son who went to visit was impressed as well and thought, "Yes, I see now that he is indeed an estimable person." And it is said that from then on, his own filial piety became more and more genuine. To be utterly without a mind of one's own and to leave everything up to one's parent, is, after all, what we call the proper conduct for a child. Even though externally such behavior may appear to be deeply improper, in one's mind one has a sense of what is proper, so the parent and child are completely united.

[D] In the comic interlude of a recent play, just as a fellow called Gen'uemon the Butcher is engaged in all sorts of evil schemes, a messenger brings a letter and asks: "Pardon me, but isn't there someone called Gen'uemon the Butcher around here?"

"No, there is no such person in these parts." Then the messenger says that he was definitely told that this was the place where he could find Gen'uemon. Whereupon Gen'uemon says, "Wait! Somehow, that name sounds familiar," and tilting his head to the side, "Oh, yes—I remember! No wonder it sounds familiar: it is I!"

This seems like nonsense when we see it in the play, but generally speaking, everyone is deluded to this extent. Pulled along by human desires day after day, we imagine our essential mind of faith to be somewhere else. That is a dreadful thing. Because of this delusion, love suicides, people drowning or hanging themselves—various disasters and calamities are likely to happen. Disturbed by this, our teachers thought long and hard in order to present us with a basic method for knowing the original mind, a method we can manage easily. Please, all of you, know the original mind. For to know your original mind is to know that you have no self.

[E]   There are all kinds of teachings, but there is no path
          Other than quitting evil and doing good.

But if you "do good" with a particular design in mind, it is useless. Enacting goodness is simply striving wholeheartedly to perfect your own path today.

          Do not be misled by the word "path"—
          It is the deeds you do day and night.

Everyone is misled by the names and forms of the path. People read only books and, without experiencing the path themselves, claim: "Confucius said, 'Such-and-such, so-and-so, such-and-such, so-and-so.'" This is of no benefit at all.

All scriptures, all books are about knowing one's original mind. They are ladders to help us "illuminate bright virtue." You cannot climb up to the roof unless you have a ladder. Once you have climbed to the top of the roof, you don't need the ladder anymore. But if someone dangles a long ladder from the rooftop and swings it around, that is a dangerous matter. Such people do not even listen when others tell them that someone could be hurt—they just raise their noses higher and say, "Confucius said, 'Such-and-such, so-and-so, such-and-such, so-and-so.'" They merely read books. Alongside them, other people boast that "Śākyamuni is powerful," or "Amida will conquer." When Shintō followers hear this, they ring their bells and rouse themselves to action: "Why, that's sacrilegious! That barbarian law [Buddhism] which pollutes our country of the gods–drive it out! Exorcise it!" In the meantime, others quarrel with each other about names only: the Lotus followers are beaten, the Gate followers are shut in, the Pure Land followers are locked up.[1] But the main house [of truth] is unaffected: what is there to fight about?

> Delusion is not being able to settle
> In a world that is completely settled.

To abandon useless disputation and simply strive scrupulously to carry out heaven's will for today is what is meant by the saying "Following one's nature is called the Way" [*Doctrine of the Mean* 1]. A certain book says, "If you preserve the Buddhist precepts by means of Shintō honesty, you will abide by the Confucian Five Relations and Five Constants."

[F] What is there outside the mind? As long as one has no desires, "this very mind is Buddha." As soon as one removes delusion, one is instantly a perfect Buddha. All of the sutras are about the mind. The *Amida Sutra*, the *Sutra on the Great Sun Buddha*, the *Lotus Sutra*, and the *Nirvana Sutra* are not at all different from each other. They all teach that the mind is the most important thing.

What is called the Confucian Way is also about the mind; its books are a map of the mind. The true, living Confucian Way is expressed in the saying "A single principle penetrates my Way" [*Analects* 4:15]. What does it penetrate? The marvelously illuminating thought of the original mind, the mind of no evil, penetrates the Three Thousand Worlds [the entire cosmos]. In other words, this saying is about the mind. Not even one word in all these books means anything else. They are all about the mind.

In Shintō, too, the *Chronicles of Japan*, the *Record of Former Events*, the *Essential Meaning of the Record of Old Things*, and various mystical writings, are all books that record matters of the gods. True Shintō is about the mind. This is not just my opinion—"Primal Shintō" and "Unity of Heaven and Humankind" [Shintō] are the gods' teachings that the mind is most important. There is no Shintō other than this. Or, to express the meaning of the unity of three teachings in verse:

> Many are the paths to climb up the mountain,
> But we see the same moon on the lofty peak.

Numerous paths originate at the foot of a great mountain. No matter what path one climbs to view the moon, it is always the same moon. We enjoy the same moon, here and there, under various kinds of names: the Lake Moon, the

Rice-Field Moon, the Sarashina Moon, the Musashi-Field Moon, the Fountain-Water Moon, the Lavatory-Pot Moon, the Puddle Moon, the Dog-Dish Moon, even the Urine-Pail Moon. People stretch out a sacred straw festoon and insist, "This is it! This one is the true one!" They fight over the light of the very same moon. Well, it's better to look upward [at the moon itself]. In his poems, Master Nichiren says,

> I lowered my head to reflect, but could not sleep;
> I exchanged the moon with Minobu Mountain.

. . . "Moon" here means the mind. Whether it be Buddha, Confucius, the infamous thief Ishikawa Goemon, an outcast, a beggar, or even the birds, the beasts, the grass, and trees—all things exemplify the mind that brims with heaven's virtue.

Note

1. This remark involves a series of untranslatable puns: The Lotus (Hokke) followers are beaten down with brooms (*hōki*), the Gate followers (*Monto*) have had their gate (*mon*) shut, the Pure Land (Jōdo) followers have had their lock (*jō*) fastened. Lotus refers to followers of Nichiren (1222–1282), who advocated devotion to the *Lotus Sutra*. Gate followers are the True Pure Land sect founded by Shinran (1173–1262), while Pure Land refers to followers of the Pure Land sect of Hōnen (1133–1212).

CLERICAL PRECEPTS

— 4 —

Eisai's Promotion of Zen for the
Protection of the Country

Albert Welter

The Buddhist tradition is not generally known for treatises associated with overt political aims. This is due, in part, to the Buddhist reputation for eschewing society and avoiding political involvement. This reputation, however, does little to explain the actual development of Buddhism as an ideology supporting political regimes. In the process of this development, Buddhism became, in fact, a strong force promoting political as well as religious ideology.

The impact of Buddhist political ideology in Japan was particularly strong. Early religious and political theory in Japan was heavily influenced by developments in China during the Sui (518–617) and T'ang (618–907) dynasties, an era when Buddhism was the dominant ideological force. As a result, the Japanese state was conceived in terms of a common East Asian Buddhist model. This model was based on Mahāyāna scriptures which recognized the complementary authority provided by Imperial Law (*ōbō*) and Buddhist Law (*buppō*). According to this model, the Buddhist clergy actively participated in affairs of state, and the ruler of the state was responsible for overseeing the affairs of the Buddhist clergy. No distinction between religious and secular aims was ultimately recognized. This model of the Buddhist state was based on the premise that religious and government institutions were united in a common purpose, drawn directly from Buddhist teaching. In this model, Buddhist religious aspirations were regarded as essential components of a civilized society, pillars necessary for the definition and preservation of the secular state. According to Buddhist theories relating to the social and political role of the state, the purpose of state authority and government institutions was to foster Buddhist righteousness. Both religious and secular establishments in the Buddhist state were united in this moral and spiritual aim.

By the late twelfth century, at the end of the Heian period (794–1185), the religious and political climate in Japan had deteriorated to the point that the existence of Buddhist teaching and the model of the Japanese Buddhist state were placed in jeopardy. Furthermore, belief in the ultimate demise of Buddhism was substantiated by the Buddhist teaching of Final Dharma age (*mappō*), believed to have begun in C.E. 1052. The social chaos and moral depravity among members of the Buddhist clergy were signs confirming the Buddhist prognosis that the current age was one of social and moral decay. This climate produced a series of Buddhist reformers, one of the most prominent of whom was the monk Eisai (or Yōsai, 1141–1215).

Eisai was trained in the practices of Tendai Buddhism, which included an Exoteric scriptural tradition based mainly on the *Lotus Sutra*, and an Esoteric (tantric) tradition similar to that of the Shingon school. Tendai was religiously and politically perhaps the dominant form of Buddhism in Japan during the Heian period. Supported by the leaders of Japan, the court aristocrats living in the Japanese capital of Heian (present-day Kyoto), the teachings of this school provided the rationale supporting the existence of the Japanese Buddhist state. Tendai also had a long tradition of meditation practice based on the procedures prescribed in the *Great Calming and Contemplation* (*Maka shikan, T* 1911). But during a pilgrimage to China, Eisai became absorbed in the practices of the Zen (Ch'an, "meditation") school. We can only imagine Eisai's reaction when he discovered that the monastic complexes on Mount T'ien-t'ai (Tendai), the inspiration for the nucleus of Tendai school temples on Mount Hiei in Japan, had been turned into centers for Zen training! Zen Buddhism, particularly the Rinzai (Lin-chi) branch, dominated the religious life of China at that time and was heavily supported by the Chinese state. In Japan, Zen was a little known and largely misunderstood form of Buddhism. Its presence, particularly in Eisai's promotion of it, represented a challenge to the long-standing role played by Tendai Buddhist teaching in Japanese political and social affairs.

In Eisai's view, Zen represented a remedy for the degenerate state into which Buddhist moral discipline had fallen in Japan. While Eisai's proposal for religious reform was quickly rejected by the old leaders of the Heian government and the Tendai Buddhist establishment, it was adopted by the newly established rulers of Japan, the military warlords of Kamakura.

Eisai's proposals for reforming Buddhism and the moral fiber of Japan were written down in his *Treatise on Promoting Zen for the Protection of the Country* (*Kōzen gokokuron*). In effect, the *Treatise* called for replacing Tendai teaching as the spiritual and moral focus of the country with the superior teaching of Zen. As a result, Zen came to serve as the new ideology supporting the new rulers of Japan, the military rulers based in Kamakura. Together, these military rulers and the monks of the Zen school came to define the new character of the Japanese state, replacing the positions formerly held by Heian court nobles and the monks of the Tendai school. This new definition of the Japanese state, combining the military power of the samurai rulers with the ideological backing of the Zen school, dominated Japan for several centuries from the Kamakura period to the beginning of the Edo period (c. 1600).

What was it about Zen, in Eisai's opinion, that recommended it as a reform doctrine for Japan? In the first place, Eisai was impressed with Zen practice. Of all the schools of Buddhism, Eisai credited Zen with best preserving the legitimate teaching of the Buddha. This teaching, according to Eisai, was contained in the wisdom literature (*prajñāpāramitā, hannya-haramitsu*) of the Buddhist tradition. The patriarchs and masters of the Zen school in China had, in Eisai's view, successfully preserved the essence of the Buddhist teaching on wisdom, passing it down from master to disciple through successive generations.

In addition, Eisai was impressed with the uncompromising attitude of the Zen school on the importance of Buddhist moral training and discipline. For Eisai, the ability of Buddhism to serve the social and public good was directly connected to the moral behavior of Buddhists, especially members of the Buddhist clergy. The preservation of Buddhism and the Buddhist religiopolitical order from moral and social decay was dependent on this behavior. According to Buddhist theory, it was not only the duty of the ruler to ensure that Buddhist discipline be upheld in his domain, it was in the ruler's own self-interest to do so. The preservation of a ruler's authority, according to Buddhism, depended on the cooperation of divine forces. Buddhist as well as native Japanese deities served to protect and defend Buddhist countries from disaster. These deities were summoned through rituals and prayers conducted by members of the Buddhist clergy. The willingness of deities to intervene on a country's behalf was believed to be determined by the moral character of those who summoned them. In short, the moral character of the country was directly reflected in the behavior of the Buddhist clergy. As a result, the Buddhist clergy were believed to play an active part in Japan's fate as a nation.

In the final analysis, the Zen school represented for Eisai the repository of true Buddhist teaching and moral discipline. As such, it deserved to be recognized as the legitimate ideology of the true Buddhist country. Using Buddhist scriptures as his authority, Eisai argued to the rulers of Japan that the promotion of Zen teaching assured the revival of Buddhist ideology. In this way, Zen teaching became the basis for reasserting the traditional complement of Buddhist law (*buppō*) and political authority (*ōbō*) in Japan.

A few comments must be made about the style that Eisai adopted in his *Treatise*. Following a style that was popular among Buddhist monks, who believed that what they had to say was unimportant alongside the words of the Buddha himself, Eisai preferred to make his case through examples cited from Buddhist scriptures. The understanding of Eisai's own points must thus be filtered through the materials he chose to include in his *Treatise*. The following selections are drawn from the beginning sections of Eisai's *Treatise*.

The translation is based primarily on Yanagida Seizan, ed. and tr., *Kōzen gokokuron* in *Chūsei zenka no shisō*, in Nihon shisō taikei 16, ed. Ichikawa Hakugen and Yanagida Seizan (Tokyo: Iwanami Shoten, 1972).

Further Reading

Martin Collcutt, *Five Mountains: The Rinzai Monastic Institution in Medieval Japan* (Cambridge: Harvard University Press, 1981); Heinrich Dumoulin, *Zen Buddhism: A History, Volume 2: Japan*, tr. James W. Heisig and Paul Knitter (New York: Macmillan Press, 1990); Albert Welter, "Zen Buddhism as the Ideology of the Japanese State: Eisai and the *Kōzen gokoku ron*," in *Creating the World of Zen: Song Dynasty Chan and Its Spread throughout East Asia*, ed. John McRae and Albert Welter (Honolulu: University of Hawaii Press/Kuroda Institute, 1996).

Treatise on Promoting Zen for the Protection of the Country

PREFACE

Great indeed is Mind! Heaven's height is immeasurable, but Mind rises above Heaven; the earth's depth is also unfathomable, but Mind reaches below the earth. The light of the sun and moon cannot be outdistanced, yet Mind passes beyond the light of sun and moon. The universe is limitless, yet Mind travels beyond the universe. Though referred to as Space, or the Primal Energy that gives rise to myriad existence, it is Mind that encompasses Space and generates the Primal Energy. Because of it, the sky shelters from above and the earth supports from below. Because of it, the sun and moon rotate, the four seasons change, and all things are generated. Great indeed is Mind! . . .

The great hero Śākyamuni Buddha transmitted the Mind teaching (the essence of enlightenment and the essential teaching of all the Buddhas) to the golden-haired ascetic, Kaśyapa, calling it "a special transmission outside the scriptures" (*kyōge betsuden*). . . . Knowledge of the Mind teaching has been made possible through the combined efforts of several generations of patriarchs in India and the followers of the teaching in China. It represents the actual teaching propagated by former Buddhas, transmitted from master to disciple via the robe of authentic transmission. In matters of religious discipline, it represents the genuine methods of the sages of old. The substance of the Mind teaching and the form that it takes are fully evident in the masters and disciples [that have adhered to it]. The stipulations for practicing the Mind teaching and the regulations governing its practices leave no confusion regarding its orthodoxy.

After the Great Master who came from the West (India), Bodhidharma, sailed by way of the South Seas and planted his staff on the banks of the East River in Loyang (the capital of China), the Mind teaching spread to Korea through Fa-yen Wen-i (885–958), and to Japan through Niu-t'ou Fa-jung (594–657) (whose teachings were brought back by Saichō). By studying it, one discovers the key for understanding all forms of Buddhism. By practicing it, one attains enlightenment in the span of this life. Externally, the Mind teaching conforms to the position taken in Tendai teaching that the Buddha-nature, through the aid of the precepts, is always present. Internally, it joins to this the view of *prajñā* that awakening is attained through wisdom. This in the final analysis, is the teaching of the Zen school.

In our country, the Divine Sovereign, the Japanese emperor, shines in splendor, and the influence of his virtuous wisdom spreads far and wide. Emissaries from the distant countries of Korea, India, and Southeast and Central Asia pay their respects at his palace. Government ministers carry on the business of governing the world, and Buddhist monks spread the religion of those who have renounced lay life in search of enlightenment. Even the sacred teaching of the Indian Brahmins, the Vedas, are included in the teachings [spread by these monks]. It is utterly impossible to consider that the teachings of the Five Houses of Zen (the five main branches of Zen that developed in China) be omitted from it.

Nevertheless, there are those who malign Zen teaching, calling it "the Zen of obscure realization," and those who harbor doubts about it, calling it "the false view of emptiness." Still others claim that it is ill-suited to this degenerate age, or that it is not what our country needs. . . . These people, while ostensibly upholding the Buddhist Law, are actually destroying the treasure that this law contains. They reject my position outright, without knowing what I have in mind. Not only are they blocking the entryway to Zen teaching, they are also ruining the work of our great forbear at Mount Hiei, the Tendai master Saichō. It is sad and distressing that my position be so dismissed before ascertaining whether it is correct or not.

As a result, I have gathered here representative materials from the three branches of the Buddhist canon (scriptures, monastic rules, and treatises) to inform the philosophically minded of our age about Zen teaching, and to record the essential teachings of the one true school of Buddhism for posterity. . . . The reason this is called the *Treatise on Promoting Zen for the Protection of the Country* is that it is consistent with the ideas originally taught in the *Benevolent Kings Sutra* (*Ninnōkyō, T* 246). . . . In the hope that Rinzai Zen will flourish far into the future, [I have taken up the brush,] undeterred by my violation [against proscriptions for indulging] in literary artifices. My hope is that the flame of succession in the transmission of the lamp will not be extinguished but will continue to burn brightly in the three assemblies at which Miroku (the future Buddha) is destined to preach; that the fountain from which Buddhist teaching sprang will not be exhausted but will continue to flow in the future age of a thousand Buddhas.

SECTION I: ENSURING THE LASTING PRESENCE OF BUDDHIST TEACHING

According to the *Scripture on the Six Perfections* (*Rokuharamitsukyō, T* 261), "The Buddha said, 'I preached the rules governing moral training (*vinaya*) so as to ensure the lasting presence of Buddhist teaching (in the world).'"

According to the *Treatise on the Great Perfection of Wisdom* (*Daichidoron, T*

1509), "There are seven divisions of Buddhist disciples. The first five are for different ranks of male and female clergy who have renounced lay life. The last two are for male and female members of the laity." When the conduct of these seven congregations of the Buddhist assembly is pure, Buddhist teaching will have a lasting presence (in the world).

As a result of this, the *Regulations for Pure Conduct at Zen Monasteries (Zen'on shingi)* of the Zen school says,

> The ability to spread Buddhist teaching throughout the world of unenlightened people most assuredly rests on strict purity in one's moral training. As a result, observing the Buddhist rules governing moral behavior (*kairitsu*) takes precedence in the practice of Zen and the investigation of the Way. Without the insulation and protection from transgressions and errors [provided by the monastic rules], how will one ever become a Buddha or a Patriarch? . . . Through reading and reciting the monastic rules and understanding the benefit they provide, one is well-versed in the differences between upholding the rules for moral behavior and violating them, and on what behavior is permissible and impermissible. . . . [Monks of the Zen school] rely completely on the sacred utterances issued from the mouth of the golden one, the Buddha; they do not indulge their fancies to follow ordinary fellows.

According to another scripture (the *Net of Brahma Sutra, Bommōkyō, T* 1484),

> Those who violate the legitimate rules of moral behavior in the Buddhist order are not allowed to receive any of the gifts provided to the monastery by lay donors. Nor are they allowed to set foot in the land of a righteous monarch who upholds Buddhist teaching within his kingdom, or allowed to drink the water in the land of a righteous monarch. The five thousand great deities who protect the land of the righteous monarch constantly obstruct the path that these people proceed along, rebuking them as 'terrible thieves . . . .'

According to the *Benevolent Kings Sutra*,

> Oh Great Monarch, when Buddhist teaching has degenerated to the state where its doctrines alone survive but it is no longer practiced (*masse*) . . . the king and his chief ministers of state will frequently carry out activities unwarranted by Buddhist teaching. They will only support Buddhist teaching and the community of monks for their own selfish interests, causing great injustices and all sorts of crimes. In opposition to Buddhist teaching and in opposition to the rules governing moral behavior, they will restrain Buddhist monks as if they were prisoners. When such a time arrives, it will not be long before Buddhist teaching disappears.

According to the *Great Perfection of Wisdom Sutra (Dai hannya-kyō, T* 220),

> Śariputra, five hundred years after my passing into nirvana, at the beginning of the age when Buddhist teaching has degenerated, this scripture on the

most profound teaching of Buddhist wisdom (*hannya*) will be found in a land to the northeast (i.e., Japan), where it will greatly enhance the practice of Buddhism. How is it so? All the Buddhas, the Thus Come Ones, together value this land and regard it as important, and together concentrate on protecting it. They ensure that Buddhist teaching will always endure in that land and will not perish.

The passages cited here make it clear how to "ensure the lasting presence of Buddhist teaching" by following the teaching of the Zen school that insists that the eternal presence of the Buddha and the potential for enlightenment are predicated on upholding the rules for moral behavior that the Buddha set forth.

SECTION II: PROTECTING THE COUNTRY (THROUGH ZEN)

According to the *Benevolent Kings Sutra*, "The Buddha has entrusted the Buddhist teaching on wisdom to all present and future rulers of petty kingdoms; it is considered a secret treasure for protecting their countries." The Buddhist teaching on wisdom referred to here is the teaching of the Zen school. In other words, if people within a country uphold the Buddhist rules governing moral behavior, the various heavenly beings will protect that country.

The Scripture on the *Perfection of Wisdom of the Victorious Ruler* (*Shō-tennō hannya-kyō*, T 231) says,

Suppose a Buddhist disciple (bodhisattva) on the way to enlightenment who had studied the Buddhist teaching on wisdom became the ruler of a country. When mean despicable sorts of people came to slander and insult him, this ruler defended himself without making a show of his majesty and authority, saying, 'I am the ruler of the country. I shall rule exclusively by the authority vested in me in the Buddhist teaching on wisdom. This is none other than the intention that I developed in the distant past when, in front of the Buddhas and World Honored Ones, I uttered the great vow to save all living beings without excepting any, by causing them to obtain the unsurpassable enlightenment of the Buddhas.

According to the *Scripture in Forty-Two Sections* (*Shijūnishōkyō*, T 784), "It is better for donors to donate food to one person who has attained 'no-thought' and 'nonabiding,' and 'freedom from cultivation' and 'freedom from realization,' than to donate food to a hundred billion Buddhas of the past, present, or future." What is here referred to as "no-thought" and "nonabiding," and "freedom from cultivation" and "freedom from realization," are the aims of the Zen school.

According to the *Surangama Sutra* (*Ryōgonkyō*, T 945),

The Buddha said, "Ananda, [the condition for] single-minded recitation of my 'white-umbrella' *mantra* [to invoke divine assistance and protection] is firm adherence to the prohibitions against the four grave offenses—unchastity, stealing, destruction of life, and false statements—on the part of Buddhist monks. To carry this out, it is necessary to designate someone, selected for their purity in abiding by the rules for moral behavior, as the Master [in charge of moral training]. The monks should put on clean new robes for the occasion and, while burning incense and secluding themselves inside, recite 108 times the 'white-umbrella' mantra that was taught by the Mind Buddha (the eternal essence of Buddhahood). After this is done, they should decide on a place to build a practice hall (dōjō) in accordance with the restrictions on the location of such buildings in the Buddhist rules for moral training. The possibility of enlightenment will present itself as quickly as it is sought. In the practice hall, the monks voice aloud their vows as bodhisattvas to save all living beings. They cleanse themselves with water whenever they return from going out. They perform worship services to the Buddha at the six designated times throughout the day and night, and as a result of this, do not lie down [during the training period]. If they continue this for the three-week training period, the Buddha will appear in person to them, pat them on the head and console them, and cause their awakening (i.e., enlightenment). Any living being who supports this 'white-umbrella' mantra through recitation [will be protected as follows]: fire will be unable to burn them, and water will be unable to drown them. . . . For those realizing the advanced state of mental absorption (samādhi), no curse or foreboding heavenly body will be able to harm them.

"Ananda, you should know that the 'white-umbrella' mantra has at its constant disposal a race of incalculably numerable Diamond Treasure-King Bodhisattvas, each of whom has the various members of a Diamond association under their command that accompanies them day and night. If there are any living beings who, though their minds are flustered or distraught, call to mind and recite aloud the 'white-umbrella' mantra, these Diamond Treasure-King Bodhisattvas will always be on hand to protect them. Imagine how much more divine assistance and protection can be commanded when the 'white-umbrella' mantra is recited by those whose minds are enlightened!

"Ananda, in this world which humanity inhabits there are eighty-four thousand heavenly bodies and twenty-eight great configurations of stars that may portend calamity. When evil portents appear in the world, they are able to cause calamities and disasters. In the places protected by the 'white-umbrella' mantra, [however,] . . . the portents of impending doom will never be able to appear . . ."

The "white-umbrella" mantra [invoking divine assistance and protection] is constantly performed in Zen monasteries. It is clear from this that the Zen school maintains the principle of "protecting the country."

5

Shingon's Jiun Sonja and His "Vinaya of the True Dharma" Movement

Paul B. Watt

Buddhism in the Tokugawa period (1600–1868) found itself in a new and, in many respects, hostile political and intellectual environment. The Tokugawa government, or *bakufu*, having come to power after decades of civil war and eager to extend its authority over all segments of society, issued ordinances designed to regulate the Buddhist community as well. Among the various demands it made of the religion was the requirement that each sect organize its temples so that a relatively few "main temples" controlled a large number of "branches." At both the *bakufu* and feudal-domain levels, officials were then put in place to watch over these temple hierarchies. The government also employed the temple system to help suppress another religion active in the late sixteenth and early seventeenth centuries, Christianity, and to further exert its control over the general populace. In theory, to ensure that no Japanese person had a Christian affiliation, the bakufu required all subjects to register at Buddhist temples; not to do so had serious consequences, for even if one were not a Christian, without a registration certificate, one could not travel, divorce, or receive a proper burial. Having become in effect an extension of government and enjoying the economic benefits that could come from having access to a large and captive audience, the Buddhist leadership appears to have suffered a marked decline in vitality and discipline during the Tokugawa centuries.

Buddhism also faced challenges from rival religious and intellectual movements. Chief among these rivals was Confucianism, whose fortunes steadily rose with bakufu support and whose ethical teachings gradually spread throughout the society. Criticisms of Buddhism that Confucian writers had advanced elsewhere in East Asia (e.g., that Buddhism's teaching about the illusory nature of ordinary experience and its recommendation of the monastic life undercut the values of filial piety and of loyalty to the state) were repeatedly voiced in Tokugawa Japan. But in the late seventeenth and eighteenth centuries Buddhism also had to respond to criticisms advanced by leaders of a Shintō and nativist revival, who argued that Buddhism was a foreign religion not suited to the Japanese, as well as to the charges of a small but influential rationalist movement, which was skeptical of all religious authority.

Active during the mid-Tokugawa period, the Shingon monk Jiun Sonja (1718–1804) was concerned about both the declining discipline of the clergy and the criticisms directed at the religion from contemporary schools of thought. The son of a masterless samurai, or *rōnin*, and a devoutly Buddhist mother, Jiun was born and raised in the large commercial city of Osaka. He received a Confucian education as a boy and initially held Buddhism in disdain. However, as a result of his father's dying wish, Jiun was forced at the age of thirteen to enter the care of the Shingon Vinaya master Ninkō Teiki (1671–1750), abbot of Hōrakuji, a temple located to southeast of the city. Under Teiki's guidance, Jiun soon abandoned his childhood Confucianism and devoted himself to his Buddhist training.

The education that Jiun received under Teiki's direction set the broad parameters of his later development as a Buddhist scholar and practitioner. As a member of the Shingon Vinaya (Shingon Ritsu) sect, a movement founded by Eison in the thirteenth century, Teiki saw to it that Jiun received instruction in the rules that govern the lives of the monks and nuns—the vinaya—as well as the teachings of Shingon or Esoteric Buddhism. Indeed, at the Shingon Vinaya center of Yachūji, where Jiun trained as a young monk, so great was the stress on monastic discipline and so little on Shingon that the temple attracted monks from a variety of sectarian backgrounds. Teiki also required that Jiun become thoroughly schooled in Confucianism. When Jiun was sixteen, Teiki sent him to Itō Jinsai's (1627–1705) School for the Study of Ancient Meanings in Kyoto, where Jiun studied the Confucian classics. Jiun's later writings give ample evidence of his broad knowledge of Chinese and Japanese Confucian sources, and in *his Sermons on the Ten Good Precepts (Jūzen hōgo*, 1774), his most influential collection of sermons, and elsewhere, Jiun took pains to reply to Confucian criticisms of Buddhism. Further, Teiki instructed Jiun in *Ryōbu* or "Dual" Shintō, the form of Buddhist-Shintō syncretism handed down within the Shingon sect. In the last decades of his life, Jiun advanced his own interpretation of Shintō, known as *Unden Shintō* (the Shintō transmitted by Jiun), in response to the Shintō revival of the mid- and late eighteenth century. Finally, Teiki gave Jiun rudimentary instruction in Sanskrit. Jiun later developed a self-taught mastery of the language and, with the aid of his disciples, compiled the thousand-chapter *Guide to Sanskrit Studies (Bongaku shinryo)*. This work stands as the high water mark of premodern studies of Sanskrit in Japan.

Informing all of these activities was a conception of Buddhism that Jiun seems to have forged in his late teens and twenties. After following in Teiki's footsteps at Hōrakuji for a short time, and after more than two years of intensive meditative practice under a Sōtō Zen master, Jiun commenced a movement in his late twenties which came to be known as the *Shōbōritsu* or "Vinaya of the True Dharma." At its core was Jiun's wish to reinvigorate Tokugawa Buddhism with the spirit and discipline that he believed existed in the Buddha's own day. He consciously downplayed sectarian interpretations and stressed what he judged to be the basics of Buddhist thought and practice: morality, meditation, and the study of the sutras. Especially important for Jiun was the revival of monastic discipline within the clergy and the dissemination of the precepts among the laity. In his view, the way of life set down for the clergy in the vinaya and summarized in shorter lists of precepts for the laity was a direct reflection of the insight attained by all Buddhas into the true, "empty" nature of reality. For Jiun, insight and ethical conduct were inextricably linked.

The following short sermons (hōgo) have been selected to illustrate Jiun's view of the precepts. They are recorded talks originally presented to his followers in the early 1760s during a period when Jiun was living in retreat.

The translations are based on Hase Hōshū, ed., *Jiun Sonja zenshū* 14 (Kyoto: Shibunkaku, 1974): 474–476, 425–428, and 392–395, respectively.

Further Reading

Joseph M. Kitagawa, *Religion in Japanese History* (New York: Columbia University Press, 1966): 131–176; Paul B. Watt, "Jiun Sonja (1718–1804): A Response to Confucianism within the Context of Buddhist Reform," in *Confucianism and Tokugawa Culture*, ed. Peter Nosco (Princeton: Princeton University Press, 1984):188–214; Paul B. Watt, "Sermons on the Precepts and Monastic Life by the Shingon Vinaya Master Jiun (1718–1804)," *The Eastern Buddhist* 25, 2 (Autumn 1992): 119–128.

Sermons on the Precepts

THE UPOSATHA REPENTANCE RETREAT

At the time the Buddha, the World-Honored One, entered nirvana, all within the great assembly mourned, but the Venerable Ananda, in particular, was racked with grief. Therefore, the Venerable Anuruddha rebuked him, saying, "At this late date, you should not wail like a small child. As an [eternal] principle, this is the way it must be. Why not [instead] ask the Buddha, the World-Honored One, how we should protect the Dharma after his death?"

The Venerable Ananda then suppressed his weeping and asked the World-Honored One about [the protection of the Dharma] after his death. As his parting injunction, the World-Honored One said, "As long as monks who observe the precepts in purity do not cease to hold the Uposatha in conformity with the Dharma at half-month intervals, we may refer to that period as one in which the true Dharma long abides." The Uposatha, therefore, is important. Further, in [another] sutra, the Buddha has said, "I will come once every half month." He was referring to the Uposatha.

The Buddha has explained that there are two kinds of [observers of] the precepts. First, there is the person who from the moment he or she receives the precepts is completely pure and does not violate them even in the slightest; the person is referred to as a "pure observer of the precepts." Second, there is the person of middling or inferior capacities who, though he or she may not commit any serious offense, nevertheless easily commits errors as a result of contact with the objects of the senses. However, if every half month the person reflects upon [his or her errors] and keeps them in mind, and in accordance with the Dharma repents before a vinaya master or his or her fellow followers of the precepts, refrains [from error] in the future, and participates in the Uposatha, then this person too may be referred to as a pure observer of the precepts.

If you constantly observe the precepts in this way, then to that degree we may refer to the true Dharma as long abiding. Of course, in such sutras as the *Mahāmāyā* (*Makamayakyō*), it is explained that the true Dharma lasts for one thousand years, the imitation Dharma for one thousand years, and the latter-day Dharma for ten thousand years. Or, according to a different version in [another] sutra, it is said that the true Dharma has continued down to the present. However, these are all provisional explanations directed at [people of varying] capacities. In fact, as I have said above, as long as there are people who observe the precepts in purity, who every half-month call them to mind and hold an Uposatha, and who practice faithfully, then to that degree the true Dharma will long abide.

We translate the word "Uposatha" (*fusatsu*) as *jōjū*; it means "to abide in purity." We also translate it as *chōyō*, by which we mean "to nourish the Dharmakaya." Those of you in the assembly who are receiving the precepts for the first time should keep [the Uposatha] in mind in this way.

THE PRECEPTS ARE THE TRUE CHARACTER OF YOUR OWN MIND

The precepts are explained as the ten major and forty-eight minor precepts in the *Sutra of Brahma's Net* (*Bonmōkyō*) and as the four major and forty-three [minor] precepts in the *Yoga* (*Yuga*) [*Sutra*]. Beyond these, there are different versions of the bodhisattva precepts in the *Śrīmālā Sutra* (*Shōmangyō*) and the *Good Precept Sutra* (*Zenkaikyō*). Should we expound [the precepts] in brief, there are the three thousand rules of dignified conduct and the eighty thousand fine points of decorum. Should we expound them in detail, the precepts are innumerable and without limit. If we speak of them in their entirety, there are the three collections of pure precepts.

Further, in the *Sutra of Brahma's Net* mention is made of the "One Precept of Light." The "One Precept" refers to the true character of your own mind. All of the various precepts are encompassed within it. How can the true character of your own mind be equated with the precepts? It is because, though the true character of all things does not obstruct [the expression of either] good or evil, good always accords with it. Evil is always contrary to it. Though the true character of all things does not have the attributes of quiescence or agitation, quiescence always accords with it. Agitation is always contrary to it. Though the true character of all things does not have the attributes of wisdom and ignorance, wisdom always accords with it. Ignorance is always contrary to it. This being the case, whether you recognize it or not, the precepts that prevent wrong and stop evil are naturally fully endowed within the true character of your own mind.

If you believe and understand this, you are a person worthy of receiving the bodhisattva precepts. You do not obstruct the fact that you [already] are a bodhisattva. If you think that outside of your own mind there is some established essence of the precepts, that is entirely a heterodox view. [If this is what you think,] it can hardly be said that you have the capacity of even a *śrāvaka*.

If you believe and understand this and keep it in mind, when you have reached a state of constant purity, there will be no object [of your mind]— including even mountains, rivers, and earth—that does not constitute a precept for you. You may know this through examples near at hand. When your mind becomes defiled by desire, there is no part of you, from the tip of your head to the bottom of your feet, that does not become an object of defilement. Men, women, mountains, rivers, the earth—all become objects of that defilement. When your mind becomes angry, all objects [of your mind] become objects of your anger. [Indeed,] there are some people who become angry merely at the sight of warped wooden clogs (*geta*). When you suffer from illness, from the top of your head to the bottom of your feet, everything becomes an object of suffering. Through these [examples], know that should you conform to the precepts within your own mind, all objects become precepts for you, and from the top of your head to the bottom of your feet, your body will naturally manifest the precepts. Should you conform to the meditation within your own mind, all objects become the attributes of your meditation, and its attributes will be manifest throughout your whole body. Should your mind conform to the wisdom of the undefiled nature of reality, there will be no objects or conditions that are not [a part of that] undefiled nature of reality.

Long ago, when the bodhisattva Aśvaghoṣa was still a follower of heterodox teachings, Parsva met him in a debate. At first, Aśvaghoṣa regarded him as a harmless old monk, but the next day, when he saw him on the debating platform, the points of Parsva's argument were manifest throughout his body. If it were not this way, it could not be said that he was a true master of debate. It is the same with the precepts. Unless your entire body becomes the precepts, so that you naturally manifest the precepts from the top of your head to the bottom of your feet, it cannot be said that you are a true observer of the precepts. It is best that you constantly keep this in mind in this way.

THE BODHISATTVA PRECEPTS AND THOSE WITH THE CAPACITY TO RECEIVE THEM

By the "precepts" we mean the precepts within your own mind, that is, the precepts of your Buddha-nature. By "meditation" and "wisdom" we mean the meditation and wisdom within your own mind, that is, the meditation and wisdom of your Buddha-nature. The teaching on the precepts that I pass on to you today is simply that which the Buddha, the World-Honored One, alone expounded after he had realized unsurpassed enlightenment and had seen that originally all sentient beings fully possess these precepts within their own minds. The text under consideration is that one expounded [by the Buddha] after he realized that originally all sentient beings fully possess this meditation and wisdom within their own minds.

In the case of the teachings on the precepts, we differentiate between the Great and Small Vehicles according to the capacities of the sentient beings [who receive them]. If a person has not yet set aside attachment to the form and mind of the five aggregates [of forms, sensations, perceptions, psychic constructions, and consciousness that constitute experience] and receives the precepts out of a desire to liberate himself or herself from this form and mind, any precepts that person receives are śrāvaka precepts. [However,] if there is a person who, from the start, has realized that the phenomena of form of the five aggregates are like clouds in the sky and that the phenomena of the mind are like [the reflections of] the moon in water; who has comprehended that all sentient beings and himself or herself are originally the same in their self-nature, that they can be said to be neither identical nor different; and who has aroused the four great [bodhisattva] vows to [save all sentient beings, put an end to all passions and delusions, study all the gates to the Dharma, and realize the unsurpassed Buddha way—[when that person] receives the precepts, the precepts he or she receives are all bodhisattva precepts.

Because the precepts of the śrāvaka are received before [the individual] has set aside attachments to form and mind, when his or her [own] form and mind disintegrate, the essence of the precepts likewise departs. Because the precepts of the bodhisattva are received with an impartial and all-encompassing mind, [the individual] having [already] set aside attachments to the five aggregates, the essence of the precepts extends infinitely into the future.

In the sutras, the meaning of the distinctive qualities of the five natures [that indicate different capacities for becoming a buddha] is explained. Though they expound upon five natures, there is just the one true nature of reality. Though there is the one true nature of reality, that does not prevent [the sutras] from expounding upon the five natures. Today there are people who are attached to worldly fame and profit, are addicted to [the satisfaction of] the five desires and licentious behavior, and who do not, even for a moment, set their mind on the true Dharma. In addition to their deep attachments and addictions, they further give rise to a worldly wisdom and cleverness and to false views and wrong thinking; aggravating their errors and compounding their mistakes, they know nothing of repentance. Though they may have the chance to hear the true Dharma and see the sutras of the Buddha, they do not believe in them. This kind [of person] is referred to as "a sentient being without nature"; [that is,] it must be said that for the moment he has no Buddha-nature. Today there are a great many of these people in the world. Even if such people should have an opportunity to receive the precepts, the connection [with the Dharma that they establish] is only a minor one. Surely they do not have the capacity to receive the bodhisattva precepts.

But there is another kind of sentient being who has realized the transience of the five desires, who knows that birth and death should be feared, who understands that one must practice the precepts, meditation, and wisdom, and who eagerly seeks the Dharma of nirvana and quiescence. When these people are compared with those of the first-mentioned capacity, the two are as far apart as heaven and earth; nevertheless, [people of the second type] have yet to raise up an all-encompassing mind. They do not understand that all sentient beings and themselves are originally the same in their self-nature. Because they desire liberation only for themselves, these [people], too, do not have the capacity to receive the bodhisattva precepts. They are called people with the seed-nature of śrāvakas.

Further, there are people with the capacity of great intelligence who, on their own, without waiting for instruction from others, meditate deeply upon the causes of birth and death, practice and attain the Way. Though they are superior to the people mentioned above, they are still overly concerned with their own minds and do not arouse the true thought of enlightenment. Therefore, they too do not have the capacity to receive the bodhisattva precepts. They are called people with the seed-nature of *pratyekabuddhas*.

Still further, there are people who comprehend that the form and mind of the five aggregates are like clouds in the sky and like the moon's reflection in water, and that the primary and secondary retribution [experienced] within the ten realms is entirely [dependent] on the transformations of their own minds; who give rise to a mind of impartiality and unconditional compassion in regard to all sentient beings; who transfer [the merit of] all of the myriad acts they undertake to the beings of the phenomenal realm; and who, sacrificing their lives, eagerly seek the unsurpassed Way. People of this kind of capacity are truly worthy of receiving the bodhisattva precepts.

Keeping this in mind and pondering it, participate in the ceremony [for the reception of the precepts] with utmost sincerity.

6

A Refutation of Clerical Marriage

Richard Jaffe

One of the most remarkable changes in Japanese Buddhism in the Meiji period (1868–1911) was the spread of open clerical marriage among the Buddhist clergy. Since the early Edo period (1603–1867), clerical marriage had been banned by state law for all Buddhist clerics except for those affiliated with denominations that traditionally had allowed marriage—Shugendō and Jōdo Shinshū. Although the prohibition against marriage had been frequently and flagrantly violated by many clerics, the regulation was also sporadically enforced with a vengeance by the Tokugawa authorities. At least superficially the leaders of the "celibate" denominations and the state demanded that their clerics adhere to the stricture against sexual relations and marriage.

In the wake of the violence triggered by the harsh anti-Buddhist measures enacted by the officials of the new Meiji regime from 1868 to 1872, bureaucrats at the Kyōbushō (Ministry of Religious Doctrine), the Ōkurashō (Ministry of Finance), and the Shihōshō (Ministry of Justice) worked toward the complete disestablishment of Buddhism. As part of their efforts, the officials at these ministries steadily dismantled the remaining Edo period regulations governing clerical life and eliminated any perquisites that had previously been granted the clergy by virtue of their status as "home-leavers" (*shukke*). Despite opposition from the Buddhist leadership, in short order the clerics were ordered to assume surnames, to register in the ordinary household registration system (*koseki*), and to serve in the military. These changes reduced the Buddhist clergy to subjects like all other Japanese and rendered the clerical estate an occupation that was no different from any other career in the eyes of the state .

Without doubt the decriminalization of clerical marriage was the most contested of all the changes in clerical regulations. With the support of such Buddhists as Ōtori Sessō (1804–1904), an ex-Sōtō cleric who had been appointed to the Kyōbushō, and the Tendai cleric Ugawa Shōchō, on Meiji 5/4/25 the officials at the Kyōbushō issued a regulation that stated, "From now on Buddhist clerics shall be free to eat meat, marry, grow their hair, and so on. Furthermore, there will be no penalty if they wear ordinary clothing when not engaged in religious activities." Although all aspects of the new regulation, referred to as the *nikujiki saitai* law because it decriminalized meat eating and clerical marriage, were resisted by the leaders of the Buddhist denominations, the most prominent and vexatious feature of the regulation for the Buddhist leadership was the end to state penalties for clerical marriage.

Protest against the new measure came swiftly and strongly. A petition by the Jōdo cleric Fukuda Gyōkai (1809–1888) that strongly denounced the government's efforts to end state enforcement of clerical regulations was signed by the chief abbots (Kanchō) of every Buddhist denomination except the Jōdo Shinshū and was submitted to the government just months after the new law was promulgated. The petition complained that the decriminalization of clerical marriage would lead to enormous confusion of the lay-clerical distinction in Buddhism and, by weakening the clergy, would result in further moral chaos for the Japanese nation. When government officials adamantly refused to reconsider the decriminalization measure, the leadership of the Buddhist clergy continued to meet with government officials and to submit a series of petitions calling for revocation of the new law. In addition, the leaders of almost every Buddhist denomination issued internal directives aimed at the clergy calling for continued adherence to the Buddhist precepts, despite the decriminalization.

The steady resistance of the Buddhist clerical leadership and a gradual moderation of the government's policy toward religious organizations led to a softening of the position with regard to clerical marriage. In 1878 the Naimushō (Ministry of Home Affairs), which now had jurisdiction over Buddhist affairs, issued a terse addendum to the 1872 *nikujiki saitai* law. The modification of the decriminalization measure stated, "Edict 133 [*nikujiki saitai* law], which states that the clergy are free to eat meat and marry, only serves to abolish the state law that had prohibited such activities. In no way does the law have anything to do with sectarian regulations." With that ruling the Naimushō officials turned over all responsibility for the maintenance of clerical discipline to the leadership of each Buddhist denomination, thus differentiating state laws from private religious and moral concerns.

The reaction of the clerical leadership to the modification of the government's position regarding clerical marriage was unified. Although clerical marriage was popular with most lower-ranking members of the Buddhist clergy, over the next several months the leadership of most denominations, including Sōtō, Nichiren, Jōdo, and Shingon, issued new sect laws and directives condemning or even banning clerical marriage. It was in the context of increased independence for the clerical leaders to regulate the behavior of the Buddhist clergy that *Dan sōryo saitai ron* was published in 1879.

Little is known about the identity of the author of *Dan sōryo saitai ron*, Uan Dōnin, but there is a strong possibility that the name Uan Dōnin was a pen name for the Sōtō cleric Nishiari Bokusan (a.k.a. Nishiari Kin'ei, 1821–1910). A prominent scholar of Dōgen's *Shōbōgenzō*, Nishiari served as the abbot of several Sōtō temples before becoming the chief abbot of the Sōtō denomination in 1902. Nishiari is known to have used the very similar pseudonym Uan Rōnin in some of his writings. Nishiari also was a vocal opponent of clerical marriage and expressed his views on the matter frequently. In 1875 he submitted two letters to the Sōtō leadership calling for them to observe traditional monastic strictures against the eating of meat, marriage, abandoning the tonsure, and wearing nonclerical garb. In his letters Nishiari warned his fellow clerics that they must be careful in both words and actions and that, despite changes in state law, they must continue to follow the Buddhist precepts.

Dan sōryo saitai ron is a prime example of the anticlerical marriage tracts that were published by private individuals and officially by the administrations of the various Buddhist denominations during the 1870s and 1880s. Written in question-answer dialogue format, the document presents the main justifications made by proponents of clerical marriage and the author's criticism of those positions. In this brief diatribe, the author refutes the main Confucian, Nativist, and government attacks on the Buddhist practices of *shukke* (home-leaving) and celibacy. Reiterating arguments frequently used by such Buddhist apologists as the Chinese layman Sun Ch'o (ca. 300–380), the Chinese Chan cleric Ch'i-sung (1007–1072, posthumously Ming-chiao Ta-shih; J., Myōkō Daishi), and the Japanese Ōbaku cleric Chōon Dōkai (1628–1695), Uan Dōnin challenges the common Buddhist dispensationalist argument that because in the Last Age of the Teaching (*mappō*) true practice is impossible, it is permissible for the Buddhist clergy to abandon the precept that proscribes sexual relations. Echoing the traditional Buddhist refutation of charges of unfiliality, the author asserts that "home-leaving" is the highest form of filial piety because, unlike laypeople, who are primarily concerned with the welfare of their immediate family in this life, Buddhist clerics work for the ultimate salvation of all beings.

In addition to responding to Confucian attacks on Buddhist celibacy, Uan Dōnin also attempts to neutralize Shintoist and Nativist critiques of monastic practice. To accomplish that end, the author ties the Buddhist abhorrence of sexual relations and marriage to the ultimate purity of the cosmos that is described in the foundational Shintō creation myths of the *Record of Ancient Matters* (*Kojiki*) and the *Chronicles of Japan* (*Nihon shoki*). Just as ritual purity and celibacy is demanded by the *kami* because of the original purity of the cosmos, Uan argues, so do the Buddhas demand the celibacy of those who enter the Buddhist order.

One of the primary rationales put forward to justify the state's liberalization of laws governing clerical behavior was that state-enforced celibacy was an unnatural and outmoded practice that rendered the Buddhist clergy useless in the efforts to build a "rich country and a strong army." Unlike such proponents of Buddhist modernization as Ōtori Sessō or Ugawa Shōchō, who were concerned with the pragmatic utilization of clerical manpower to strengthen the state, Uan Dōnin claimed that the true value of the clergy depends on their ability to insure the fortunes of the nation by serving the kami and the Buddhas, not on their utility as potential draftees and state proselytizers. The author even problematizes the very notions of progress and enlightenment as they were defined in the early Meiji period. Questioning the dominant emphasis on material progress as the hallmark of civilization, Uan Dōnin concludes that true "civilization and enlightenment" is impossible without the presence of pure, celibate clerics.

This is a translation of Uan Dōnin, "Dan sōryo saitai ron," in Meiji Bukkyō Shisō Shiryō Shūseihen Iinkai, ed., Meiji Bukkyō shisō shiryō shūsei, vol. 6 (Kyoto: Dōbōsha Shuppan, 1982): 171–175.

Further Reading

Winston Davis, "Buddhism and the Modernization of Japan," History of Religions 28, 4 (1989): 304–339; Richard Jaffe, "Neither Monk nor Layman: The Debate over Clerical Marriage in Japanese Buddhism, 1868–1937," Ph.D. dissertation, Yale University, 1995; Richard Jaffe, "The Buddhist Cleric as Japanese Subject: Buddhism and the Household Registration System," in New Directions in the Study of Meiji Japan, ed. Helen Hardacre and Adam L. Kern (Leiden: E. J. Brill, 1997): 670–702; Kawahashi Noriko, "Jizoku (Priest's Wives) in Sōtō Zen Buddhism: An Ambiguous Category," Japanese Journal of Religious Studies 22, 1–2 (1995): 161–183; James Edward Ketelaar, Of Heretics and Martyrs in Meiji Japan (Princeton: Princeton University Press, 1990); Uchino Kumiko, "The Status Elevation Process of Sōtō Sect Nuns in Modern Japan," Japanese Journal of Religious Studies 10, 1–2 (1983): 177–194.

A Treatise Refuting Clerical Marriage

The marriage of priests is a sign of the extinction of the dharma. The increase of licentiousness is an omen of the end of a nation. Therefore, I often admonish people about this. Although occasionally there are those who believe this, those who uphold [the prohibition against marriage] are quite rare. On occasion in response to this lament it is asked:

Question: In Heaven and Earth there are yin and yang. Accordingly, humans are male and female, husband and wife. Why do the Buddhists proscribe that which follows natural law? Those who disobey the law of nature will become obsolete, but those who accord with the law of nature prosper. Is that not why the celibate schools grow weaker daily and the schools that allow marriage grow more prosperous monthly?

Answer: You understand superficial worldly principles, but you do not understand the profound principles of heaven and earth. Excessive sexual desire harms the body, wrecks the family, and destroys the nation. Licentiousness originally arises from covetousness. When covetousness arises, inevitably greed, hate, delusion, and all the defilements also arise. When due to the three poisons and the defilements karmic causes are produced, retribution will inevitably follow.

Question: If people believe all the Buddha's teaching and, fearing karmic cause and effect, do not marry, then what will become of posterity? Mencius said, "Having no successor is the greatest act of unfilial behavior" [*Meng-tzu*, IV.A.26]. How do you resolve this problem?

Answer: The prohibition against marriage is aimed solely at "home-leavers." It is not an exhortation for all sentient beings to leave home. In Buddhism there are four groups of disciples and precepts appropriate for each of the seven assemblies: monks, nuns, male novices, female novices who receive the six precepts, female novices, laymen, and laywomen. You should understand this fact.

Mencius's words are specific for one situation; how can you take them to be unchanging for all time? This is clear because when Mencius explained the five types of unfilial behavior, he did not include not having an heir as part of the list [*Meng-tzu*, IV.B.30]. It also is said that Mencius wished to explain how Shun did not inform his parents of his marriage because Shun feared his parents would stop his marriage, thus preventing him from having an heir.

Even if it that was not the reason for Mencius making the statement about having an heir, his words still must be viewed as conditional, because having a child is dependent upon causes and conditions. It is not subject to human control. Even if one's family is prosperous and noble and one has both a wife and a concubine, one may not have even one child. By contrast, a poor husband and wife, barely able to eke out a living, may have many children even if they do not want them. How can we judge filial and unfilial behavior on the basis of that which is determined by causes and conditions?

Furthermore, Mencius had no children. The cause for this was Mencius's wife, who did not conduct herself with propriety, so he wished to be rid of her. Mencius's mother took pity on Mencius's wife; therefore his getting rid of his wife would have been unfilial. If he were to love his wife, [a woman who did not act with propriety,] that would compound the impropriety. Therefore he could neither get rid of his wife nor could he love her. Thus what can we tell from the fact that Mencius was without children? Mencius revered propriety; he did not lament that he was without an heir. If people flourish in numbers but are lacking in propriety, then they are animals, not humans. Mencius was successor to Confucius. This is an example of how he valued propriety and lightly regarded the matter of having descendants.

Furthermore, Confucius said, "If one hears of the Way in the morning, it is all right to die in the evening." That is how much Confucius valued propriety. He did not say, "If one has a child in the morning, it is all right to die in the evening." If one has descendants but does not follow the Way and lacks propriety, how could having descendants allow one to be at peace?

Such expressions as "not having children is unfilial," or "it is the natural law of yin and yang,"and so forth, are excuses used by hedonists. In fact, insuring posterity is rarely the aim of licentious behavior. Married men who visit prostitutes contract syphilis and transmit the disease to their wife and children. Does one visit prostitutes in order to have children or because of the principle of yin and yang? Sometimes one who is overwhelmed by sexual desire will even desert his wife who has borne his children. Or a wife and concubine will become jealous of each other, resulting in murder by poisoning or a knifing. Or a double love suicide occurs. Can we say that these occurrences are due to the heavenly principle or that these actions arise out of filial concern for having descendants?

If not having an heir makes one unfilial, then why is only the man unfilial? The same should hold true for the woman as well as the man. If that is so, then if a woman is childless with one husband, she should remarry. One hears that it is admirable if "a virtuous woman does not take a second husband." One does not hear that following the injunction "a virtuous woman should take a second husband in order to have descendants" is the basis for praise. You should think carefully about these things.

Question: Why do "home-leavers" abandon their parents and travel far away, thus not providing filial care for their father and mother?

Answer: The Buddha stated, "All sentient beings are my children." Thus the people of the world should all be considered our siblings. If one's siblings have difficulty, how can one not help them? For example, suppose one's sister marries into another family. If there is a fire or flood, even if one's parents are on their sickbed, one should do what is necessary to go to help her. Not only will one's father and mother not reprimand one for this, but their illnesses will be soothed by such action. If the flood or fire is said to be severe and one does not help because one's parents are ill, then parents' illness will only worsen. Is this not human nature?

In the defiled world the difficulties posed by the three poisons and the four devils [of evil passions, the five human constituents, death, and attachment] are even graver than those from flood or fire. The difficulties arising from a fire or flood are temporary and do not affect negatively one's future rebirths, but the three poisons and the four devils will eternally affect this and future lives. If that is not frightening then what is? If one is always diligent and leaves one's home and parents in order to devote oneself to the amelioration of difficulties caused by the three poisons and the four devils, ultimately there will be no time to worry about not having descendants. Therefore although people who engage in such activities are called "home-leavers," in fact they are "debt-repayers."

If a loyal retainer sacrifices his life for the sake of his lord, how can we say that he has been unfilial? If that is deemed a transgression and is construed as unfilial, then it will not do to laud [the imperial loyalist] Kusunoki Masashige or the retainers of Akō [the forty-seven rōnin warriors]. Home-leaving is undertaken for the sake of the Way. The Way saves sentient beings from their delusions and thereby enables them to escape future eternal suffering. Is that not Great Mind? Do you suppose that one who has manifested Great Mind has time to worry about having descendants?

Did not Confucius say, "Serving one's father and mother is taken to be the beginning of filial piety; achieving fame is the ultimate filial piety"? With respect to the filiality of home-leaving, although it is not undertaken for the sake of fame, those individuals whose pure name and world-saving skill are transmitted to all future generations are the most filial people of all. One cannot argue that the petty filiality of those who merely raised children pales by comparison. For more about the superiority of the filial piety of the home-leaver, you should carefully study the *Treatise on Filial Piety* [*Hsiao lun*] by Myōkyō Daishi [Ch'i-sung]. I will not go into detail here.

Question: If this is the case, then do all of the home-leavers today possess Great Mind of this sort?

Answer: We cannot guarantee that all put forth the Great Mind in this manner even in the past. Would this not be even more difficult to guarantee today? Have you not read that when Confucius expounded about humanity (*jen*), he was unable to make all benevolent? Or that when Lao-tzu expounded on spontaneity (*tzu jan*), he was unable to make everyone act with spontaneity? When Jesus expounded on faith and love, how could he make all people faithful and loving? Is it not even more so the case with the Buddha's exposition of putting forth the mind of the bodhisattva who strives to enlighten others before himself and the boundless great nirvana that extends through the three times and escapes the Triple World? If, due to the fact that one cannot make all people realize benevolence, nature, faith, and love, or the mind of the bodhisattva, one says those paths should be destroyed, then since ancient times no teaching should have been founded and no path should have been expounded in this ignorant world. If the sage's leaving the world ultimately is without benefit, we can only say that they are leading astray those in the world. How could it do to revere them? So long as the path that is difficult to enact and difficult to practice exists, no matter how unpopular it is there will be some in the world who follow it. Even if it is the Last Age of the Teaching, it is impossible that there is no one.

One who follows the Paths is called a person in possession of the Way. A person who possesses the Way tours the four directions and diligently preaches the Way, just as King Yu helped subdue the flood. It is impossible to predict how many people will be turned away from evil and toward the good by even one such person. It goes without saying that those who preach the Way aid the government.

Question: If people are made to uphold all the Buddhist precepts, won't this mean the extinction of humanity?

Answer: You should not worry too much about this. Even if one thousand Buddhas were to appear in the world and preach the Buddhist precepts, is it possible that they would make all sentient beings adhere to all the precepts, thereby causing the extinction of humanity? If due to the precepts the extinction of humanity were to result, then would not this filthy land become a Pure Land, and a race of humans who do not engage in impure relations between men and women be born?

Question: Why is it that those who serve the Buddha emphasize celibacy?

Answer: Why do you think that only those who serve the Buddha emphasize celibacy? Those who serve the kami are supposed to devote themselves to celibacy as well. At the very beginning, Heaven and Earth were truly pure essences. Thus the age of the kami began from one single kami. Even when there were male and female kami it is said there were no sexual relations. It is clear that the interaction of yin and yang resulted in the pollution of Heaven and Earth as well as the birth of the myriad things and human beings. Surely this is why the character *jin* (deity; *kami*) has the Japanese reading *kabi* (mysterious power).

Because human beings were born from the impurity of sexual relations, they only understand the impurity of sexual relations; they do not understand the pure essence [of all things]. They consider impurity to be the fundamental nature of Heaven and Earth and do not know that sexual relations are impure. They resemble insects who, because they are born in stagnant water, think that the original essence of water is stagnancy. The insects have not the slightest inkling of the essential purity of water.

The heavenly kami (*amatsu kami*) appeared at the beginning of Heaven and Earth so their love of purity is a necessity. Has not the Buddha taught that in the heavenly realms, the gods experience pleasure by different means–through intercourse, an embrace, the touch of hands, a smile, or a look? As one ascends, lust correspondingly weakens. Seeing the polluted acts of humankind, how could the heavenly kami not despise them? How much more so this must be true for a Buddha who has transcended the Triple World!

When those who serve the kami are pure, the kami are delighted; when those who serve the Buddhas are pure the Buddhas are delighted. We know this is so because when the kami and the Buddhas are delighted, they obey our prayers and always respond to our appeals. Since ancient times pure priests have moved the virtuous spirits and kami of Heaven and Earth; we know this by the extraordinary fashion in which their prayers were realized. Therefore those who have respect and faith for the Buddhas and the kami should love pure priests. The kami and the Buddhas take pleasure in an abundance of pure priests. When the kami and the Buddhas rejoice, then their protection grows stronger. Thus we can say when pure priests are numerous, those who protect the nation are numerous.

The fate of the Tokugawa family is a recent example of this. At the beginning of the Tokugawa reign the clergy's rules were upheld, in the middle the rules gradually slackened, and by the end the rules were in great disorder. This gave rise to the "abolish the Buddhas" movement of Lord Mito. Is it not the case that the vigor and weakness of the pure priests corresponded with the prosperity and decline of the Tokugawa family?

If you love your nation you should support the celibate schools, and you should pray that those who uphold the precepts will increase daily. You should not favor those who break the precepts.

Question: It is said that the decline of Roman Catholicism is due to their clinging to the outmoded custom of celibacy in service to God. Today, Buddhism in Japan is also like this. Is it not the case that the schools that allow marriage increase in strength daily, while the celibate schools decline daily?

Answer: The reasons for this are subtle and hidden and are difficult to explain. It is very difficult to say whether the prosperity of the schools that allow marriage is true prosperity or whether the weakness of the celibate schools is true weakness.

The decline of Tibet is most certainly the source of the decline of Lamaism. Although I don't know yet the source of Tibet's weakness, could it not be due to the oppressiveness of extravagant luxury and the topsy-turviness of too much "civilization"?

I am old-fashioned and there are things I do not understand about "civilization and enlightenment" (*bunmei kaika*). Should what is happening in Japan today be seen as progress or decline? The most striking things about the so-called "progress of civilization" are such external manifestations as machinery, tiled roofs, Western clothes, Western letters, and Western language. However, when we examine the disposition of those who are adolescents or younger, we find that those with flippant, servile, and resentful voices are numerous, but those with a sense of integrity are extremely few.

Precept violation by the clergy, the business enterprises of the nobles (*kazoku*), and ex-samurai (*shizoku*) pulling rickshaws are not considered contemptuous. A woman is not embarrassed about being a consort or a geisha, and it is considered foolish to be a "virtuous woman and a good wife" (*teijo seppu*). Deceit is a natural occurrence. It is difficult to loan and borrow money without collateral, even among fathers and sons or brothers. If this trend continues for a few more years, what will become of the nation, let alone the Buddha Dharma? When compared to the generations in which celibate priests were valued and virtuous women were admired, is the current state of affairs beautiful or ugly, progress or decline? Ultimately my grieving over the decline of the Buddha Dharma results in my grieving for the nation. With deep regret I forget about food and sleep and I, in isolation, can only let out a futile, heavy sigh. Some people remain silent and have withdrawn, but I have something more that attracts my eye. How splendid! I have had a dream. To explain the dream will require another work, so I lay down my writing brush for now.

Meiji 12/3/5 [1879]

LAY PRECEPTS

7

Eison and the Shingon Vinaya Sect

Paul B. Watt

Although the Kamakura period (1185–1333) is associated with the appearance of several new Buddhist sects—the Zen, Pure Land, and Nichiren sects among them—it is also an era that saw renewed activity in some of the older elements of the Japanese Buddhist tradition. Eison (1201–1290), or Kōshō Bosatsu as he was posthumously known, is a representative of that earlier tradition, coming out of the Shingon sect. He is remembered chiefly for having founded the Shingon Risshū, or Shingon Vinaya, sect, which combined Shingon teachings with a special emphasis on the vinaya or monastic discipline.

Eison was born in Yamato Province, the son of a scholar-monk of Kōfukuji in Nara. His mother died when he was eight, and because his father found it difficult to care for several children, Eison was sent off to the Shingon temple of Daigoji in Kyoto for his early education. After formally entering the clergy in his late teens, Eison focused his studies on Shingon, or Esoteric, Buddhist texts and rituals. When he was twenty-four, he traveled to Mount Kōya to pay his respects at the grave of Kūkai (774–835), the founder of the Shingon sect, and while there he received further training. For the next several years, Eison studied at various temples in the Nara-Kyoto area.

Eison's special interest in monastic discipline and the precepts does not seem to have emerged until his mid-thirties. While one may suspect that his dissatisfaction with the lack of attention paid to the precepts within the contemporary Buddhist community had been growing for some time, it was not until his thirty-fourth year (1234) that his reading of the *Sutra of the Great Luminous One* (*Dainichikyō*), the commentary on it by the T'ang dynasty monk I-hsing (683–727), as well as certain writings by Kūkai made him fully aware of the importance of the precepts. Particularly influential in this regard was the section from Kūkai's *Final Instructions* (*Yuikai*) in which he commands his followers to observe all Buddhist precepts. Kūkai's words, which Eison cites in his autobiography, read in part: "Never violate either Exoteric or Esoteric Buddhist precepts; firmly observe them and maintain yourselves in purity. . . . Unless one observes all these precepts, one's eye of wisdom will be dark. Knowing this, protect them as you would protect your life. Indeed, forsake your life rather than violate them."

In the same year that Eison was reading these materials, he learned that Son'en Shōnin of Tōdaiji, the Great Eastern Temple in Nara, was seeking six monks who would dedicate themselves to a life of discipline and religious practice at Saidaiji, a temple that had originally been established in the eighth century as the western counterpart to Tōdaiji. Eison quickly made known his desire to join the group and, in the first month of 1235, moved into the temple. This was apparently his first contact with the temple that would later become the center of his Shingon Vinaya movement. During 1235 Eison heard lectures by the monk Kainyo as well as Kainyo's disciple Ensei on a commentary on the vinaya by the famous T'ang dynasty master Tao-hsüan (596–667). He also visited Kainyo's disciple Kakujō at Kōfukuji and learned from him the procedure known as the *jisei jukai*, according to which, in the absence of qualified vinaya masters, one could administer the precepts for monks to oneself by taking a vow before an image of the Buddha. Following this procedure, Eison, Kakujō, Ensei, and another monk by the name of Yūgon took the precepts before the image of the Buddha at Tōdaiji in 1236.

Eison did not commence a sustained effort to establish Saidaiji as a center for the propagation of the precepts until 1238. For a short time just prior to that year, he was forced to leave the temple, apparently because of a dispute over the temple's control. During this period Eison took up residence in the Nara temple Kairyūōji, where he quickly wore out his welcome by criticizing aspects of monastic life there. From the time that he returned to Saidaiji in 1238 until he left for a brief stay in Kamakura in 1262, Eison concentrated on the propagation of the precepts among both the clergy and the laity and the establishment of Saidaiji as the center of his movement. Soon after his return, he built a five-story pagoda at Saidaiji and had a relic of the Buddha installed in it. This was the first of many indications of the special reverence Eison and his followers paid to Śākyamuni, the historical Buddha, who was also popular among others who worked to revive the precepts. In the tenth month of 1238, the first bimonthly religious retreat, or *fusatsu*, was held with Eison's close friend Kakujō as the leader of the assembly, and two years later, in 1240, the first rainy season retreat, or *ango*, was observed with eight senior monks and three novices in attendance.

Initially the Shingon Vinaya movement appears to have grown only gradually. Over the next two decades, Eison frequently traveled to temples in the Kyoto-Osaka area, lecturing on and bestowing the precepts. The types of precepts Eison bestowed depended, of course, on his audience. Most often it was the bodhisattva precepts (*bosatsukai*) of the *Sutra of Brahma's Net*, but he also administered the five and eight precepts to lay Buddhists and the complete precepts (*gusokukai*) to monks and nuns.

From the 1240s on, Eison often combined acts of charity with his efforts to spread the precepts. His disciple Ninshō (1217–1303) is actually better known for such social welfare activities, and it is generally recognized that Eison's move in this direction was due to Ninshō's encouragement. As a young man, Ninshō had developed a deep faith in Mañjuśrī, the bodhisattva of wisdom, whose cult called upon the believer to undertake acts of compassion. However, in both Eison's and Ninshō's case, the concern they felt for the needy was also related to the great respect they had for two earlier saints of the Japanese Buddhist tradition. One was Shōtoku Taishi (574–622), the prince famous for, among other things, his founding of Shitennōji, which included on its grounds a dispensary (Seyakuin), a hospital (Ryōbōin), and an asylum for the aged and homeless (Hiden'in). The other was Gyōgi Bosatsu (670–749), who himself had combined the propagation of the Dharma, or Buddhist teachings, with bridge and road construction, the digging of wells, and the founding of hostels and who, in the popular imagination, was regarded as a reincarnation of Mañjuśrī. Sites connected to both Prince Shōtoku and Gyōgi figure prominently in Eison's and Ninshō's biographies. Further, Eison established groups known as "Taishikō," dedicated to the veneration of Prince (Taishi) Shōtoku.

Eison's and Ninshō's acts of charity were directed chiefly at a group in Japanese society known as the *hinin* (literally, "nonpersons"), which included the chronically poor, lepers, and criminals. In 1242, for example, Eison visited the Nara prisons, saw to it that the prisoners were bathed, distributed food, and bestowed the precepts on them. In 1244, on the thirteenth anniversary of the death of Ninshō's mother, Eison conducted a memorial service for her and distributed food to more than one thousand hinin. Other activities in which they engaged were inspired by the precept that prohibited killing. Eison often sought to have lands set aside as places where all taking of life was forbidden or specific days designated when the members of a village or community would refrain from killing.

At the same time that Eison was pursuing such projects as these, he was also at work rebuilding Saidaiji. Mention has already been made of the 1238 construction of a pagoda to house a relic of the Buddha. In 1247 and 1249, respectively, a new monks' quarters and the Butsuden, or Buddha Hall, were completed. Also in 1249, Eison had installed in the Buddha Hall an image of Śākyamuni modeled on the famous standing image of Kyoto's Seiryōji, which the monk Chōnen had brought from China. This statue continues to serve as the main image of Saidaiji today.

While Eison's movement had slowly but steadily been winning followers during the 1240s and 1250s, records of donations made to the temple suggest that, in the 1260s, it entered an era of more rapid expansion. Two closely related factors can be seen in the background of this growth: greater contact between the Saidaiji order and the shogun's government or bakufu in Kamakura from the 1260s on, and greater attention on the part of Eison and his disciples to the Shingon element within their teachings.

In cultivating relationships with the bakufu, Ninshō appears to have again taken the lead, as he had done earlier in the area of social welfare activities. Ninshō had visited the Kantō area in the 1240s and moved there in 1252, staying at Mimuraji, a temple whose chief patron was Hatta Tomoie, the constable (*shugo*) of the province of Hitachi. By 1259, however, Ninshō had come to the attention of the bakufu. In that year, the former deputy regent (renshō), Hōjō Shigetoki, invited him to come to Kamakura to conduct services at Gokurakuji for the ailing former regent (shikken), Hōjō Tokiyori. But it was more than personal illness that had turned these men to religion. The late 1250s in the Kantō area was an especially chaotic time. A number of earthquakes and floods struck in 1257 and 1258; they were followed by a plague in 1259. By 1261 the situation had degenerated to the point that the bakufu issued new regulations that prohibited the selling of human beings and the discarding of the sick, orphans, and the bodies of dead persons and animals along the roadside. Further complicating the situation was the presence in Kantō of advocates of salvation by faith in Amida, who discounted the importance of observing the precepts, and the occasional diatribes launched by the Tendai visionary, Nichiren.

Having heard of Eison through Ninshō, the bakufu invited the Vinaya master to come to Kamakura in the hope that he would not only be able to cure Tokiyori's illness, but also help restore discipline to a society that seemed on the verge of collapse. Eison declined the bakufu's first invitation, and even after he had agreed to go to Kamakura, he refused to reside at Shōmyōji, the temple that had been prepared for him, choosing instead the far less lavish Shinseiyōji, also known as the Shakadō or Śākyamuni Hall. However, over the six months that Eison spent in Kamakura—lecturing on the precepts and bestowing them on people both high and low, while continuing his efforts to care for the poor—he did in fact win many influential supporters for the Shingon Vinaya sect, both within the Hōjō family and among its housemen or gokenin. With his visit to Kamakura, therefore, Eison's movement took its place fully on the national stage. It would retain that position throughout Eison's and Ninshō's lifetimes.

The greater visibility of Shingon elements in the movement can best be illustrated by reference to Eison's decision in 1264 to propagate the mantra of light (kōmyō shingon) and to his activities at the time of the Mongol invasion attempts of 1274 and 1281. Myōe Shōnin (1173–1232) is perhaps most commonly associated with the popularization of the mantra of light, but this mantra also came to hold an important place in the religious life of the Shingon Vinaya sect. Beginning in the ninth month of 1264, Eison had all monks and nuns related to Saidaiji gather at the temple annually to recite the mantra for seven days and nights without interruption. The benefits that were said to accrue from this mantra's recitation were not only the cessation of all afflictions and the eventual attainment of enlightenment, but, on another level, wealth and longevity and, at the end of one's present life, rebirth in the Western paradise. On the one hand, the institution of this annual ceremony served to strengthen the internal cohesion of the order; on the other, the dissemination of the mantra of light also widened Saidaiji's popular appeal.

The prominence of Shingon in Eison's teaching was also brought to the fore by the events surrounding the attempts by the Mongols to invade Japan. The first Mongol demand for tribute came in 1268 and launched the Japanese into a frenzy of military and religious activity aimed at turning back any possible attack. Eison himself seems to have been concerned about the Mongol threat, for although he seldom refers to secular events in his writings, he mentions the arrival of a letter from the Mongols in this year and states that he traveled to various religious sites, including Shitennōji, to perform Shingon ceremonies for the protection of the country. After another Mongol messenger arrived in 1271, Eison visited Ise Shrine, the chief shrine of the imperial family, in 1272 and 1273 to perform religious services. After the failure of the Mongol invasion of 1274, Eison visited Ise again in 1275, presenting to the shrine on that occasion a copy of the *Larger Perfection of Wisdom Sutra*. Similar events surround the second Mongol invasion attempt in 1281: in 1280 Eison presented a copy of the entire canon to Ise Shrine, and in 1281, at the Iwashimizu Hachimangū, he recited for seven days and nights the *sonshō darani*, which offers salvation from calamities, the removal of bad karma, and the extension of life.

During the 1270s and 1280s Eison continued to propagate the precepts and perform acts of charity (including, for example, the repair of the bridge at Uji south of Kyoto), but toward the end of his life his popularity rested as much, if not more, on his role as a Shingon master as on his role as a teacher of the precepts.

The following passages have been selected from "A Collection of Instructions and Admonitions Heard from Kōshō Bosatsu" (*Kōshō Bosatsu gokyōkai chōmonshū*). This short record of Eison's teachings was compiled when the master was in his eighties. Just who recorded these sayings is uncertain, although it would appear likely that his disciple Kyōe was responsible.

The translation is based on the text in Kamata Shigeo and Tanaka Hisao, eds., *Kamakura kyū Bukkyō* in Nihon shisō taikei 15 (Tokyo: Iwanami Shoten, 1971): 189–226.

Further Reading

Daigan and Alicia Matsunaga, *Foundations of Japanese Buddhism*, vol. 2 (Los Angeles: Buddhist Books International, 1976): 264–284; Inoue Mitsusada, "Eizon, Ninshō and the Saidaiji Order," *Acta Asiatica: Bulletin of the Institute of Eastern Culture* 20 (March 1971); Robert E. Morrell, *Early Kamakura Buddhism: A Minority Report* (Berkeley: Asian Humanities Press, 1987); Robert E. Morrell, *Sand and Pebbles (Shasekishū): The Tales of Mujū Ichien, a Voice for Pluralism in Kamakura Buddhism* (Albany: State University of New York Press, 1985).

A Collection of Instructions and Admonitions Heard from Kōshō Bosatsu

IN SCHOLARSHIP, SEEK THE ESSENTIALS

On one occasion the Master gave the [following] instruction: Scholarship is undertaken for the purpose of correcting the mind. People of the present generation only read with attention to details, and there are none who attempt to correct the mind. However, to understand first the meaning of the sacred teachings and to know always whether or not one's mind conforms to them, this is scholarship. To hold up one's mind to the mirror of the sacred teachings, to desist at those points where it is contrary to the teachings, and to make ever greater endeavors at those points where it naturally conforms, and thus to advance in the Way, this is what is called scholarship. You should always read the text closely. But first, each of you should quickly correct your mind. What use is it to engage in scholarship that does not correct the mind? No matter how well one learns the sacred teachings, a person who is without the mind that seeks enlightenment is without the invisible aid [of the Buddha's and bodhisattvas]. You should simply set aside all other things, raise up the mind that seeks enlightenment, and on that basis carry out your practice. Unceasing practice is that upon which you should rely, and you should regard correcting the mind as the starting point of practice.

MATTERS TO GUARD AGAINST IN PRACTICE

The true practitioner is one who corrects the mind that is attached to self and to things. A person who desires to receive the precepts must quickly bring to an end this [sort of mind]. One should receive the precepts solely in order to raise up the Dharma. If people desire to receive the precepts for their own benefit, in no way are [the precepts they receive] those of a bodhisattva. People who become resentful and angry upon hearing others speak ill of them, even in the slightest way, or who unreasonably rejoice at and are fond of those who only casually speak well of them—no matter how hidden these reactions may be—such people are not people of the Way. They do not have the mind of a bodhisattva. Even if someone should strike or kill you, you should only bear the pain and not have a mind [full of] hatred for that person. You should be like a mother who, when she is struck by her small child, is amused at this [behavior]. The mind of a bodhisattva is also like this. Should a cruel and foolish person inveigh against you, you should regard him or her with pity.

ON THE PARADOXICAL RELATIONSHIP BETWEEN LEARNING AND PRACTICE

Adopt the teachings of the Great Vehicle [Mahāyāna] and the practice of the Small Vehicle [Hīnayāna]. Adopt the language of the bodhisattva [who is commited to altruistic acts] and the mind of the śrāvaka [who is dedicated to the monastic life].

MATTERS TO BE MINDFUL OF IN PRACTICE

In reply to a certain person, [the Master] said: There are many things of which one should be mindful in practice. Simply not to fear the numerous pains of many eons [of transmigration] and singlemindedly to seek to become a Buddha for the salvation of all sentient beings is called "the mind that seeks enlightenment above." Firmly to be of a mind that regards both friends and enemies with equal compassion is called "the mind that transforms sentient beings below." And to raise up these two minds, not in the least moving from them, and in various circumstances to endeavor by all means to cease from deluded thoughts is called the practice of the Buddha Way. Even if you desire the Western Region, know that you should simply contemplate deeply the compassionate vow of Amitabha, keep in mind the secondary and primary rewards of the Pure Land, and, from this life onward, cease from even the slightest deluded thought. Although there are the various [techniques] of the sixteen meditations [listed in the *Sutra of Meditation on Amida Buddha*], know that they are simply means for ceasing deluded thoughts and quieting the mind's nature. To regard enemies as enemies and to distinguish them from friends is the root of deluded thinking. Know that this is something you should understand well.

ON FORGETTING THE SELF

In a sermon given when he was bestowing the precepts, [the Master] said: The mind that clings to the self in each and every instance conceals the Buddha-nature.

THE MEANING OF EXOTERIC AND ESOTERIC TEACHINGS ARE ONE AND THE SAME

In a talk given at the Muryōjuin of Kokawadera, [the Master] said: The sacred teachings of Hossō, Sanron, Tendai and Kegon, the Exoteric and Esoteric, the provisional and true, if properly understood, have just one meaning. In the end, it is discarding the self and, solely for the sake of others, setting aside personal gain. Even if later I spoke about it at leisure, it would not go beyond this.

MAKE SAVING ALL LIVING BEINGS THE ROOT OF YOUR PRACTICE

On holding firmly to the vow to benefit living beings. In a sermon given when bestowing the precepts, [the Master] said: Those before the eighth stage [of transmigration as beings in hell, hungry ghosts, animals, demons, humans, heavenly beings, *śrāvaka*, and *pratyeka* (solitary) buddhas] still have not cut off the obstacles [that prevent them from] benefiting living beings. It is upon reaching the ninth stage [of the bodhisattva] that they are cut off. How much more it should be the case that an ordinary person who has just aroused the thought of enlightenment should have many obstacles to their benefiting living beings. No matter what, one should simply work hard. The three collections of pure precepts [for observing the Buddha's rules, undertaking all acts of goodness, and benefiting all beings] have as their foundation the twofold mind that seeks enlightenment above and transforms sentient beings below. In short, it is simply the mind that seeks to benefit living beings. If you hold firmly to this mind and strictly observe the precept that encompasses all rules of conduct, then spontaneously there will be the benefit [that comes from observing the precepts] that encompass all acts of goodness and all beneficial acts.

OBSERVING THE PRECEPTS IS THE SUPREME CAUSE OF BUDDHAHOOD

What people of the world say—that following the five precepts leads to rebirth as a human being and that following the ten leads to rebirth in a heavenly realm—is nonsense. In particular the new school has made it clear that this is not the case. Whether it be the bodhisattva precepts, the five, eight, or ten precepts, or the complete precepts [for monks and nuns], all are causes of Buddhahood. . . .

ON MY TAKING UP THIS PRACTICE

At the time that I first entered the Buddha Dharma, I made a prayerful request to the gods, asking them which of the sects—Hossō, Sanron, Tendai, or Kegon—I should study. In a dream I was told to study Shingon. Therefore, although it was not my intention, acknowledging the dream I set aside the request regarding the four sects and studied Shingon, along with the Kusha [sect], until I was more than thirty. As I was doing so, [I realized that] many of those who study the teachings of Shingon fall into evil paths. When I examined their evaluation of the teachings, [I came to see that] this was because they were not grounded in the Vinaya. This conclusion fit perfectly with the meaning of the passage from the *Yu-ch'ieh-shih-ti-lun* (*Yugashijiron*) cited in the present collection. In the *Sutra of the Final Teachings* (*Yuikyōgyō*), it says, "If there were not the pure precepts, all of the various acts of goodness and virtue would not arise." The Great Vehicle takes benefiting others as its foundation. If there were no rules of conduct, there would also not be any acts of goodness or any acts benefiting others. Therefore, it is because I focus my intentions on benefiting others that I correctly follow the rules of conduct. Since there are ten benefits for each rule, the 84,000 virtues of the monks are always circulating and increasing. Further, by following the teachings of the precepts, one may discern principle and quickly win the shallow wisdom that enables one to meditate on principle. Since underlying each rule one may discern the Dharmakāya [body of truth], I took as my path the study of the various teachings of the Great Vehicle, and as much as possible I concentrated on their teachings regarding principle. As for my practice at that time, since all of the precepts are the bodhisattva's practice, in no way did I run counter to them. Although the teachings may differ, the intentions of the Buddha may all be traced back to the one principle. But people thoughtlessly express their opinions on the basis of their personal interpretations, some saying good and evil are the same, and others, one after another, expressing views not in conformity with principle. At ease, they pass the months and years—what principle might they discern? As for those who express various opinions and go against the practice that I have established, some [go off to] live alone, others take up their own practice—what can their practice be? When in Kantō at Saimyōji I had an encounter [with Hōjō Tokiyori], he said: "In those who receive the precepts of purity too, there is the discernment of principle." Since he practiced Zen and always sought to attest to the [true] mind, is not what he said indeed so?

8

Kokan Shiren's *Zen Precept Procedures*

William M. Bodiford

Zen Precept Procedures (*Zenkai ki*) was written by the Japanese Rinzai Zen monk Kokan Shiren (1278–1346) in 1325. Shiren was one of the outstanding leaders of the highly cultured Five Mountains (*gozan*) Zen monastic community in Kyoto. Today he is perhaps best known as the author of the *Buddhist Omnibus of the Genkō Era* (*Genkō Shakusho*, 30 fascicles, 1321), the first comprehensive history and ethnography of Buddhism written in Japan. Although Shiren's *Omnibus* describes all aspects of Japanese Buddhism, the founders of its various leading temples, its education system, its major public ceremonies, its outstanding icons, the regional gods (*kami*) that promote the religion, and so forth, the bulk of the text concentrates on biographies of Zen monks. In fact, its primary goal is to link Zen firmly to mainstream Buddhist traditions in Japan. It begins, for example, by describing how Bodhidharma, the legendary first patriarch of Zen, came to Japan and traded Japanese *waka* songs with Prince Shōtoku (547–622), Japan's foremost cultural hero and the founding patron of Japanese Buddhism. Its accounts of famous monks associated with rival styles of Buddhism rarely fail to emphasize the importance of Zen meditation in their spiritual development.

Shiren's *Zen Precept Procedures* also can be seen as an attempt to link Zen to mainstream Japanese Buddhism. It links Zen to the dominant Japanese interpretation of precepts. Based on old Japanese legends, Shiren identifies the exclusive Mahāyāna precept ordinations that were established by Saichō (767–822), the founder of Japanese Tendai, with the unique Zen lineage that Bodhidharma supposedly brought to China in the sixth century. This identification has no historical basis, but it has profound religious implications. This identification has, in fact, radically altered the religious characteristics of Japanese Zen.

The Japanese Tendai conceptions of exclusively Mahāyāna precepts and exclusively Mahāyāna precept ordinations differ radically from the traditional Buddhist precepts observed by Zen monks in China. Japanese Tendai monks labeled the 250 vinaya (*ritsu*) precepts observed by all Chinese monks, including Chinese

Zen monks, as "Hīnayāna" (Shōjō), literally, "inferior Buddhism." But it is important to note that Japanese Tendai monks did not regard their own bodhisattva precepts merely as a contrasting set of Mahāyāna (Daijō, i.e., "superior Buddhism") precepts. Instead the bodhisattva precepts were (and are) conceived of as a singular Buddha precept that transcends all distinctions between Hīnayāna and Mahāyāna, secular life and monastic life, or good and evil. This singular Buddha precept is the Buddha Mind, the mind of awakening, the vessel of salvation (jōkai itchi). The religious power of the precepts is such that proper ritual ordination alone will deliver man, woman, child, or beast from all suffering. In other words, the heart of the ordination is the symbolic confirmation of salvation; it need not represent a change of social status or a decision to join the clergy.

Shiren's Zen Precept Procedures identifies this special Tendai interpretation of the bodhisattva precepts with the Zen transmission of an exclusive patriarchal lineage, which supposedly conferred a unique legitimacy on Zen masters. He argues that the true Mahāyāna precepts that embody awakening are conveyed only within this unique Zen lineage: "Outside of Zen there are no precepts, and outside the precepts there is no Zen." What is important, therefore, is to have faith in the Zen lineage and faith in the ritual efficacy of the ordination procedure. Faith is the starting point. This ritual alone conferred the status of Buddha and patriarch on the participants. To confirm this spiritual transformation, the precept ordination ceremony concludes with the presentation of Zen blood-lineage charts (kechimyaku) to the participants. These lineage charts list the names of all of the Zen patriarchs, beginning with Śākyamuni Buddha and ending with the name of the lay person who was ordained. A red line connects all the names together, signifying that the lay person now has a direct link to the Buddha.

Shiren's Zen Precept Procedures also is known by the more descriptive title, Procedures for Bodhisattva Precept Ordinations in the Zen School (Zenmon ju bosatsukai ki). It consists of Shiren's preface plus the following ten sections: (1) Opening Sermon, (2) Exclusions, (3) Arousing Spiritual Aspirations, (4) Repentance, (5) Invoking the Presence of the Buddhas and Bodhisattvas, (6) Three Refuges, (7) Three Pure Precepts, (8) Ten Major precepts, (9) Minor Precepts, and (10) Transfer of Merit (ekō). Many elements in the precept ordination rituals practiced in Japanese Zen, both Rinzai and Sōtō, from the fourteenth century down to the present day conform to Shiren's procedures. Only the preface and sections 1, 2, and 4 are translated below. These sections emphasize the precepts as salvation, the unique Zen lineage, and the importance of repentance rituals. Although the text says that each ordinand must perform "repentance for three years," in actual practice usually much shorter terms were allowed. Often the entire precept ceremony would conclude within three days.

The translation is based on Zenmon ju bosatsukai ki in Zengaku taikei, vol. 7 (Tokyo: Ikkatsusha, 1913).

Further Reading

William M. Bodiford, *Sōtō Zen in Medieval Japan*, Studies in East Asian Buddhism, no. 8 (Honolulu: University of Hawaii Press, 1993); Paul Groner, *Saichō: The Establishment of the Japanese Tendai School*, Berkeley Buddhist Studies Series (Seoul: Po Chin Chai, 1984).

Zen Precept Procedures

PREFACE

In ancient times Bodhidharma brought the Buddha Mind Seal from southern India to China: pointing directly, a single transmission, fierce and rough. Thus were the bodhisattva precepts granted to the second patriarch and so on to the five houses and seven lineages of Zen. The granting and receiving of the precepts have continued without break. I have seen the precept charts of all other schools of Buddhism. None of their names are affiliated to this lineage. Only our Zen precepts have been handed down from the Buddha Śākyamuni to this day, interlinked without missing a single generation. Therefore, of all precepts, Zen precepts are best.

From the time I was first ordained with these precepts I have wanted to standardize the procedures and condense its elaborate text but lacked the time to do so. Now I have divided the ordination procedures into ten sections and explained the proper ceremony for each.

When an ordination is to be performed, always the chapel (*dōjō*) must be washed and swept. Each ritual furnishing, the incense stands, seating mats for masters and disciples, and so forth must be set out with care as specified in the procedures. First teach those who will receive the precepts to arouse pure faith. The *Brahma's Net Sutra* (*Bonmōkyō*) states: "You will become a Buddha. I have already become a Buddha." If one always believes in this way, then one is fully ordained with the precepts. The *Flower Garland Sutra* (*Kegonkyō*) states: "Faith is the origin of the Way. It is the mother of all virtues." Cultivate and develop all wholesome roots. Oh, you must not consider anything else!

Preface written autumn of 1325 by Kokan Shiren

PART 1: OPENING SERMON

The profound message of all awakened heroes of the past, present, and future consists of the Three Learnings. Meditation and wisdom are middle and last, but precepts come first. Precepts are visible in every action. They are the foundation of the six perfections. How could one's attainment of supreme perfect awakening not derive from them?

There are many varieties of precepts: the 5 and the 8 precepts for lay peo-

ple, the 250 of the vinaya, the 10 major and the 48 minor bodhisattva precepts. Of these, the 5 and the 8 precepts insure rebirth as humans or gods.
The 250 lead to realization of the Hīnayāna goal. Only the 10 major and 48
minor lead to accomplishment of the Supreme Way [i.e., Mahāyāna awak-
ening]. Ordination with Śrāvaka [i.e., Hīnayāna] precepts can be nullified. But
ordination with the bodhisattva precepts can never be revoked. Even if one
violates the precepts after ordination, one is still the Buddha's child. But one
who refrains from both ordination and violation is a non-Buddhist. Thus a
sutra states: "Just as the scent of champak blossoms, even when withered,
smells stronger than that of all other flowers, even precept-violating monks
are superior to non-Buddhists." Moreover, the *Brahma's Net Sutra* states: "Living beings who receive ordination with the precepts enter into the ranks of
the Buddhas, attaining the same great enlightenment. Truly they are the Buddha's children."

These Vajra Precepts (*kongō kai*) were transmitted from the Lotus throne
across the Lotus petals for 1,001 years by Śākyamuni Buddha, by forty-seven
Zen patriarchs in India to the West, and by twenty-three Zen patriarchs in
China to the East. The Chinese Zen patriarchs, beginning with the seventh,
were Nan-yüeh, Ma-tsu, Pai-chang, Huang-po, Lin-chi, Hsing-hua, Nan-yüan,
Feng-hsüeh, Shou-shan, Fen-yang, Tz'u-ming, Huang-lung, Hui-t'ang, Ling-
yüan, Wu-shih, Hsin-wen, Hsüeh-an, and Hsü-an (J. Nagaku, Baso, Hyakujō,
Ōbaku, Rinzai, Kōke, Nan'in, Fuketsu, Shuzan, Fun'yo, Jimei, Ōryō, Meidō,
Reigen, Mushi, Shinmon, Setsuan, and Koan). Only our Eisai made the pil-
grimage to Sung China to meet Hsü-an, to be ordained with the Buddha Mind
Seal. Hsü-an handed over his staff, whisk, as well as the bodhisattva precepts,
which constitute the Zen school's Single Great Affair (*ichi daiji*).

Certainly these great precepts do not resemble any of the other varieties.
They convey the Mind Seal of master Bodhidharma. Therefore, one who is
about to be ordained should arouse pure faith. In the old text of the *Zen Precept Procedures* the opening sermon stated: Good. Good. All children of the
Buddha now arouse the supreme faith of the bodhisattva. Seek to receive ordination with the supreme treasure, the precepts. Earnestly contemplate this.
All living beings consist of Buddha-nature. Since the beginningless past they
have always dwelled in purity: bright without dimness; understanding in constant knowledge. This fundamental state is thusness. It also is known as *tath-
āgata-garbha* [i.e., the spiritual womb of the Buddhas]. Yet merely because of
false thoughts it becomes obscured, and without one being aware of it one
sinks into attachments and engenders karma, thereby incurring the suffering
of birth and death (*saṃsāra*). The great awakened one, the Buddha, rues this.
He teaches that our true spiritual nature is pure, just like that of all Buddhas.
The scripture states: "At that time the Tathāgata surveyed all living creatures
throughout the universe and made this declaration: 'How marvelous. All living
beings possess the wisdom and virtuous characteristics of the tathāgatas. They
are no different from the Buddhas.' "

How sad! Since eons past we have never before encountered the true religion. We have turned our backs on the truth and sought the false. We have wandered through the six courses of rebirth, receiving all kinds of bodily forms. Thousands of births! Millions of deaths! Lacking our own wisdom eye, we have associated with evil companions. In our permissiveness we have committed infinite sins. Sometimes as an animal, sometimes as a human, we have transmigrated without end. Now, having encountered the ultimate teaching, believe that you are originally Buddha. Act in accordance with Buddha action. Match your mind to Buddha mind. Cut off your base habits. Return to the root. Go back to the source.

Children of the Buddha! Now you must want to discard the false and regain the true. You must want to receive the Buddhist precepts. The *Sutra of the Final Teachings* (*Yuikyōgyō*) states: "Precepts are the foundation that leads to liberation. As a result of precepts one is able to attain all meditative trances and develop the wisdom that eliminates suffering." The *Precept Sutra* says that all sentient beings should embrace the Buddha's precepts: "Living beings who receive ordination with the precepts enter into the ranks of the Buddhas, attaining the same great enlightenment. Truly they are the Buddha's children." Likewise, the *Sutra of Satyaka Niganthaputra* (*Sassha Nikenjikyō*) states: "If one does not observe the precepts, then one could not even achieve the body of a wild fox with scabies. How then could such a one expect to achieve the adornments of the Dharma Body of a Buddha?" The *Sutra on the Adornments of the Bodhisattva* (*Yōrakkyō*) states: "There is not a single bodhisattva who attained the Supreme Way, reaching the stage of equality of all things like an empty sky, who did not do so by means of the precepts." It also states: "If among all the living beings of the past, present, and future there is anyone who refuses the bodhisattva precepts, then that person should not be called a living being, should not be called a human. That person is no different from a beast. That person is eternally deprived of the Three Treasures. That person is not a man, is not a woman, is not a human. That person should be called a beast, known for false views, known for a heretical way." For these reasons all the Buddhas and all Zen patriarchs of every generation have been adorned with the pure precepts and have endeavored to propagate them widely throughout the universe. Master Nāgārjuna (Ryūju, ca. 2d–3d c.) said: "Just as someone without legs cannot run, someone without wings cannot fly, or someone without a raft cannot cross over to the other shore, likewise someone without the pure precepts cannot attain the marvelous goal of Buddhahood. If someone discards these precepts, even if he lives a religious life, retires to the mountains, and practices austerity, eating only fruit and medicine, still that person is no different from a beast."

Oh my! The Lord Śākyamuni has entered nirvāṇa. The ages of the True Teaching and Imitation Teaching have passed. We were born during the Decline of the Teaching (*mappō*), the evil age of five hardships. The spiritual faculties of living beings have grown weak. No one sees the true wisdom. Oh, we are witnesses to the disappearance of the virtuous and sagely, the destruction of the True Teaching. False teachers cover the land preaching false doctrines, practicing false ways, advocating false views, transmitting false explanations. They stir up the dimwitted, leading them to demons and ghosts. In their audiences, even people of noble spiritual faculties cannot distinguish the false from the true. Before they can escape, they are following the false teachers into false doctrines, slandering the True Teaching. It is just like one blind herdsman leading a flock of blind cattle into a fiery pit. Truly they are to be profoundly pitied.

It is for that reason that since long ago all the Zen patriarchs have simply presented the True Teaching, directly pointing to the human heart. Everytime they encountered a new student, the first thing they did was to ensure that he took vows and received the precept ordination. This is knowing the appropriate time. It is matching the teaching to the spiritual faculties of the audience. It is illuminating the meaning transmitted from Buddha to Buddha. It has the power to rescue us from the Decline of the Teaching, from the illness of following the false. Therefore, it is said that in studying Zen and inquiring of the Way, precepts come first. They are the foundation of all religious practices and the source of the six perfections. How else can one eliminate evil and stop error?

How can one become a Buddha and patriarch? Master Bodhidharma said, "One whose behavior and understanding correspond is called a patriarch." [That is, one's behavior and understanding must embody the precepts.] Yet there are many varieties of precepts. Of these, the 5 and the 8 precepts ensure rebirth as humans or gods. The 250 lead to realization of the Hīnayāna goal. Only the 10 major and 48 minor bodhisattva precepts lead to accomplishment of the Supreme Way. Ordination with Śrāvaka precepts can be nullified. But ordination with the bodhisattva precepts can never be revoked. How can this be? The 5 and 8 and other Hīnayāna precepts depend on physical ordinations. The bodhisattva precepts, however, are based on mind alone. If mind had a limit, then the bodhisattva precepts would have a limit. But because mind is without limit, the precepts are without limit.

The *Sutra on Contemplation of Mental Basis* (*Shinji kangyō*) states: "If a person arouses the mind of *bodhi* (*bodai*), he/she can attain the goal of completing the Supreme Way. By strictly adhering to these highest pure precepts one attains the body of a Dharma King, a Buddha, with its freedom in all activities, its supernatural powers that pervade the ten directions, its ability to embrace all types of living beings. Everyone who observes the bodhisattva precepts attains benefits and virtues freely. It is like the ability of a Wheel-Rolling King (*cakravartin*) to go anyplace his heart desires." The power of these precepts is such that even if one were to violate the grave prohibitions and thereby end up in hell, the precepts would cause one to be the king of all beings in that evil place. By this same principle, any sentient being who receives ordination with these pure bodhisattva precepts and observes them religiously without violations will always attain rebirth as a king in the human realm who protects the True Teaching of the Tathāgata (i.e., a perfected Buddha). But whoever does not receive ordination with the precepts will not even be able to achieve rebirth in the body of a fox. How could such an evil person ever become a king, the highest ranked, most pleasurable position in the human realm?

The *Sutra on the Adornments of the Bodhisattva* states: "If even one person in all the lands of the universe is converted and receives ordination with the bodhisattva precepts, the merit generated thereby would exceed that produced by erecting 84,000 Buddha stūpas." Just imagine the amount of merit generated by ordinations of two people, or three people, or a hundred, or a thousand. The benefits obtained thereby would be infinite. A husband or wife could receive an ordination and then ordain all the other members of the family. Even if one violates the precepts after ordination, one is still the Buddha's child. But one who refrains from both ordination and violation is a non-Buddhist. Thus a sutra states: "Just as the scent of champak blossoms, even when withered, smells stronger than that of all other flowers, even precept-violating monks are superior to non-Buddhists." Once ordained the efficacy of the precepts can never be lost, even in future lives. Even if one is reborn in hell or as a hungry ghost, ultimately the precepts are not revoked. If in a future life one is again ordained with the bodhisattva precepts, it is not called a new ordination. It just allows one's mind of enlightenment to push aside one's evil mind. Ordination with one precept produces a one-part bodhisattva. Ordination with two precepts creates a two-part bodhisattva, and so forth. Upon ordination with all ten major precepts, one becomes a fully-endowed bodhisattva. Thus, the precept text states: "You will become a Buddha. I have already become a Buddha." If one always believes in this way, then one is fully ordained with the precepts.

These Vajra Treasure Precepts (*kongō hōkai*) are the fundamental basis of all Buddhas, the basis of all bodhisattvas. They are the seeds of Buddha-nature. Know that these precepts were not preached for the first time by the Buddha of this age. These have been the original precepts of all Buddhas since long before. Buddhas after Buddhas have chanted these. Thus Vairocana (Rushana) Buddha seated on his lotus throne chanted these Treasure Precepts and bestowed them on the thousand million Śākyamuni Buddhas. The thousand million Śākyamuni Buddhas each sat under the tree of enlightenment, chanting these precepts fortnightly. Thereupon all the bodhisattvas chanted these precepts. All sentient beings consent to being ordained with these precepts. From the Buddhas and bodhisattvas above down to the most evil low-class beings below, the sagely and the common, Mahāyānists and Hīnayānists, all are included in the great net of these precepts. They are the profound, unobstructed, universal Buddhist teaching. Therefore, the forty-seven Zen patriarchs of the West in India and the twenty-three Zen patriarchs of the East in China each personally handed down these precepts. In China and in Japan all the Zen patriarchs are linked together through this unbroken continuum.

One who is about to be ordained should arouse pure faith and uphold this tradition. Faith is the origin of the Way. It is the mother of all virtues. Reflect on this well.

The great bodhisattva precepts handed down in the Zen school are the great precepts of the formless basis of mind. Master Bodhidharma bestowed the Buddha Mind Seal and the ordination ritual. Thus outside the Zen school there are no precepts, and outside the precepts there is no Zen.

All Buddhas and Zen patriarchs must rely first and foremost on the precept ordination to benefit living creatures. Therefore when Śākyamuni Buddha attained the supreme awakening under the tree of enlightenment, the first thing he did was to chant these precepts. When Bodhidharma came from the West he used these precepts to transmit the Mind Seal. Since then these precepts have been handed down from proper heir to proper heir, without missing a single generation. In this way they have been transmitted to me.

Today, in response to the pleas of the four groups of monks, nuns, laymen, and laywomen, I am about to perform the ordination ceremony. I embody neither understanding nor proper behavior. Embarrassed and ashamed, three times I refused, but in the end I could not avoid giving in to your requests. I will bestow on you the Zen precepts and blood-lineage chart (*kechimyaku*).

To be ordained with the great precepts of the Zen school is to obtain the True Teaching and precepts of the Buddhas and patriarchs. It is to arouse the precepts of the formless basis of mind, to open the Eye Perceiving the True Teaching (*shōbōgen*), to universally benefit gods and men. How could there be any doubt? How could you fail to arouse pure faith?

PART 2: EXAMINATION FOR EXCLUSIONS

Every good son who requests ordination with the bodhisattva precepts must be examined for the seven exclusionary sins. If even one of these sins has been committed, then the precepts cannot be conveyed. Naturally, one who has committed two or three exclusionary sins is completely unfit to receive the precept transmission. Only someone who is not guilty of any of the seven exclusions can receive the precept ordination. These seven exclusionary sins are: (1) injuring a Buddha, (2) killing one's father, (3) killing one's mother, (4) killing a senior monk, (5) killing a master of a Buddhist community, (6) violating a *saṅgha* (i.e., creating a schism), and (7) killing an *arhat* (an awakened one). Anyone guilty of these acts cannot receive the great precepts. Therefore, you will be questioned. The *Precept Sutra* says that the ordination master must not admit anyone who has committed the seven exclusionary sins in this present life. Now I will examine each of you. Answer truthfully. If you do not answer truthfully, you will only harm yourself and others. There will be no bounty.

Have you caused a Buddha's body to bleed? The ordinand answers, No. Have you killed your father?

Have you killed your mother?
Have you killed a senior monk?
Have you killed a master of a Buddhist community?
Have you violated a properly constituted saṅgha?
Have you killed an arhat?

The above questions are asked and answered three times.

Announce: The master permits those without the seven exclusions to receive the ordination. (The bell and gong are sounded three times. Everyone bows three times.)

PART 4: REPENTANCE

Instruct the ordinands to practice the repentance ritual. Since beginningless eons ago our bodies, speech, and thoughts have produced every type of evil karma. Now all of us must repent. It is like dyeing a cloth. If one first washes away the dirt and then dyes the cloth, its color will be clear and beautiful. Likewise the karmic stains of living beings must be washed clean by the water of repentance if the dye of the precepts is to soak past our defilements to refresh and transform our moral nature.

The Buddha entered nirvāṇa two thousand years ago. The True Teaching has drastically declined. The winds of false doctrines blow vigorously. Unfortunate living beings born into this age have difficulty arousing pure faith even if they happen to hear the truth. It is because their delusions and moral obstructions are so deep rooted. Unless one arouses a truly sincere mind, the karmic burden of one's sins will have no reason to disappear. If the burden of sins is not eliminated, the precepts cannot take hold. For this reason you cannot receive an ordination immediately. Everyone must proceed according to the correct ritual form. First practice the rites of repentance for three years. Then you can receive the precept ordination. You must experience profound penitence and shame by public repentance.

There are two types of repentance: abstract (ri) and concrete (ji). Concerning abstract repentance, the *Sutra on Contemplation of the Bodhisattva Universal Excellence* (i.e., Contemplation of Samantabhadra; *Fugen kangyō*) states:

> This ocean of all karmic obstructions
> Arises from our false thoughts.
> Let one who wishes to repent of them,
> Sitting in proper meditation posture,
> Contemplate the true aspect of reality.
> The burden of karmic sins, like frost,
> Evaporates in the sunlight of wisdom.

Concrete repentance consists of three grades. In the highest grade one throws one's body down on the ground, like a mountain crumbling, with blood oozing from every pore. In the middle grade, one publicly confesses one's crimes with tears of sadness flowing down. In the lowest grade, one acknowledges all faults as a Buddhist master recites a list. This grade relies on the great compassion of the Buddhas and bodhisattvas. But unless living beings become like newborn babies, they will not arouse sincere aspirations, and there will be no basis for a miraculous spiritual response (by the Buddhas and bodhisattvas). It is either like cleaning one's house before inviting a king to visit or like the reflection of the sun not appearing in muddy water. Now I will recite the text of the repentance on your behalf. You must reflect on your beginningless karmic obstructions. This repentance will cause them to be eliminated.

The Repentance Text says:

I, disciple *so-and-so*, reverently beseech all Buddhas, the revered ones throughout the cosmos filling the infinite empty sky, all revered ones free from attachments to elements, all revered ones among the communities of monks.

I, disciple *so-and-so*, throughout infinite lifetimes since the beginningless past until today, afflicted and confused by infinite unwholesome qualities such as lust, hostility, and ignorance, have committed every type of sin. I have violated Buddha stūpas, destroyed Buddhist temples, burned Buddhist scriptures, melted Buddha images, stolen the property of the Buddhist community, slandered the two vehicles, Hīnayāna and Mahāyāna, and spoken of faults in the holy teaching. I have obstructed, inhibited, obscured, and concealed all types of Buddhist practitioners: those who were ordained, those who were not ordained, those who observed the precepts, and those who violated the precepts. I have beaten, abused, and scolded them. I have gossiped about their faults and transgressions. I have imprisoned them. I have stolen their robes and forced them to return to lay society. I have whipped them and ordered them about. I have punished harmony and snuffed out life forces. I have killed my fathers and my mothers. I have caused Buddha bodies to bleed. I have killed *arhat* and violated *saṅgha*. Indulging in grave false views, I have murdered, stolen, and raped. My verbal karma has not been good. I have lied, told fantastic stories, criticized, and used deceitful language. My mental karma has not been good. With false views based on lust and hostility I have defiled my fathers and my mothers. I have defiled monks and nuns, as well as temple grounds. I have violated fasts, broken precepts, drunk alcohol, and eaten meat. I have abused the Three Buddhist treasures (the Buddha, His teachings, and His followers), as well as all creatures, both sentient and insentient, without giving any benefits in return. I have taught others based on views I created in accordance with the ways of the world. In these ways I have committed infinite, limitless sins. I cannot even count them all.

Today with sincerity I do earnestly and publicly repent. From the time

I finish this repentance ritual and forever after I do renounce my deluded, karma creating mind of continuous discriminations. I wholeheartedly request the three treasures to have compassion on me and certify my repentance. Please cause your disciple's burden of sins to disappear.

Let us recite the repentance verse from the *Chapter on the Vows of the Bodhisattva Universal Excellence* (*Fugen bosatsu gyōganbon*). Virtuous ones of the past all have recited this verse to repent. Each of you should chant aloud as I repeat the verse. (The verse is chanted three times. Everyone bows three times.)

> Formerly I committed every kind of evil deed.
> These evils all arose from beginningless lust, hostility, and ignorance.
> These evils produced by my body, by my voice, and by my mind,
> Of each and all of these I do now repent.

Ritual Practices

GODS

9

Records of the Customs and Land of Izumo

Michiko Y. Aoki

The tenth moon of the lunar calendar is called *kannazuki* in Japanese. There is more than one connotation for the word, but the interpretation favored by ordinary people is "the month without the gods," *kami-nashi-zuki*, which is contracted to *kannazuki*, because of the folktales that tell how the myriad deities of the Japanese pantheon leave their usual abodes and congregate in Izumo every year during the tenth month. This is the view, of course, of those who are not from Izumo, but for the people of Izumo, the tenth month is *kami-ari-zuki*, "the month filled with the gods." The gathering of these myriad deities is believed to have continued since time immemorial.

While the validity of this etymology awaits linguistic scrutiny, the land of Izumo has been known as the place in which sacral kingship prevailed long after most parts of the Japanese islands had come under the control of the Yamato clan. The Great God of Izumo is believed to dwell at the Great Shrine of Izumo, or Izumo Taisha, which is situated in the northwestern part of the main island of Honshū. It is one of the most important religious edifices of Japan, to which millions of the faithful pay a visit every year, especially during the tenth month. Officially recognized as one of the principal Shinto sects, the religious order based there is known by the name Izumo Taisha-kyō.

The headquarters of the Izumo Taisha-kyō are located in the city of Izumo, that is, the area that includes the township previously known as Kizuki. The name Kizuki has been known to the Japanese since the *Kojiki* and *Nihon shoki*, the earliest Japanese chronicles compiled in 712 and 720, respectively. According to the accounts in these documents, during the mythological Age of the Gods there was a long period of negotiation between an influential group in Izumo and the powerful clan in Yamato. The head of this quasi-mythological group in Izumo had enjoyed strong religious and political influence over his people until the powerful Yamato forces reached his sphere of influence. When finally the Izumo leaders agreed to reconcile themselves with the Yamato clan, the latter promised to build a mansion for the Great God of Izumo in the town of Kizuki. The present Izumo

Taisha is believed to be a replica of this legendary great mansion, which was said to be much grander in both height and structure than the one that stands today. In the Yamato-oriented mythology, this Izumo god is known as either Ohona-muchi or Ōkuninushi. In the Izumo tradition, he is known not only as Ohona-muchi, but also Omizunu, or the Lord of Great Water, the Lord of the Great Land, or Great Kizuki God.

Of many beliefs attached to the effectiveness of the Great God of Izumo today, one of the most popular aspects is his being a guardian of harmony and security, such as of a good marriage and the safe delivery of a newborn. Those who are affianced and the newly wed throng to Izumo Taisha for blessings. For those who are single and want to find suitable spouses, the Great God is believed to be an effective agent of matchmaking. Those who are in business also pray reverently for their success and profits. The Great God of Izumo and the deities who gather under him are the effective guardians of all these faithfuls. As the names of the month indicate (both *kami-nashi-zuki* and *kami-ari-zuki*), folk beliefs in Japan maintain that myriad deities congregate in Izumo to ensure harmony, happiness, and prosperity of the nation during the tenth moon.

From the *Institutes of the Engi Era* (*Engi shiki*), compiled in 927, we know that the high priest of the Great Izumo Shrine was given the privilege of conveying a congratulatory message to the reigning emperor, and that his congratulatory message, or *kamuyogoto*, was none other than the recitation of what great contributions the Great God of Izumo made to bring about peace between Old Izumo and Yamato. The *Izumo fudoki* identifies the exact location of the spring in which the high priest performed ablution before proceeding to the Yamato court for that purpose. It is told in relation with the story of Ajisuki Takahiko (Prince of the Shining Plough), the child of the Great God of Izumo, who had a speech defect. The Great God of Izumo wished so much to correct his son's impediment that he sought the help of the higher deities in prayer. His prayer was answered in his dream, in which he saw his son speak. Waking from the dream, the father let his son guide the way; they soon found a spring from which abundant water was flowing. Izumo residents say that the spring water has never stopped flowing ever since. It has therefore become one of the important places of worship in the land of Izumo. Surviving in the original form more than a millennium since its compilation in 733, the *Izumo fudoki* commands serious attention from researchers of religion now that it is considered one of the sacred scriptures of the Izumo Taisha-kyō.

The translation is adapted from Michiko Y. Aoki, *Izumo Fudoki: Translation with an Introduction* (Tokyo: Sophia University, 1971).

Further Reading

Masaharu Anesaki, *History of Japanese Religion with Special Reference to the Social and Moral Life of the Nation* (London: K. Trench, Trubner, 1930); Michiko Y. Aoki, *Records of Wind and Earth: A Translation of *Fudoki with Introduction and Commentaries* (Ann Arbor: Association for Asian Studies, 1997); Michiko Y. Aoki, *Ancient Myths and Early History of Japan* (New York: Exposition Press, 1974); Michiko Y. Aoki, *Izumo Fudoki: Translation with an Introduction* (Tokyo: Sophia University, 1971); William George Aston, tr., *Nihongi: Chronicles of Japan from the Earliest Times to A.D. 697* (Rutland, Vermont: Charles E. Tuttle, 1972); Felicia G. Bock, *Engi-shiki: Procedures of the Engi Era* (Tokyo: Sophia University, 1970); Joseph M. Kitagawa, *Myths and Symbols: Studies in Honor of Mircea Eliade* (Chicago: University of Chicago Press, 1969); Tsunetsugu Muraoka, *Studies in Shinto Thought,* tr. Delmer Brown and James T. Araki (Tokyo: Japanese Committee for UNESCO, 1964); Donald L. Philippi, tr., *Kojiki: Translated with an Introduction and Notes* (Tokyo: University of Tokyo Press, 1967); Joan R. Piggott, "Sacral Kingship and Confederacy in Early Izumo," *Monumenta Nipponica* 44 (1989): 45–74; Post Wheeler, *The Sacred Scriptures of the Japanese* (New York: Schuman, 1952).

Records of the Customs and Land of Izumo

Izumo was named after the words of the God Yatsukamizu Omizunu. The august Omizunu, who performed the land-pulling (*kunibiki*) spoke majestically: "Cloud Rising Izumo is a narrow strip of young land. When the creator gods established the land of Izumo they made it small. Therefore, it has to be enlarged by the addition of more land, which is to be fastened to the original land of Izumo."

"As I looked at the cape of white Shiragi in search for spare land," he said, "I could see Shiragi had an overabundance." Thereupon he took a wide spade shaped like a maiden's chest (*Otome no munasuki*), thrust it into the land as though plunging it into the gill of a large fish, and broke off a piece. Then he looped a three-ply rope around the land and pulled it. He pulled the rope slowly as if reeling in a fish line. As it came near, it looked like a huge riverboat pulled by his mighty strength. "Come land, come hither!" said the god. Thus he added the portion of land called the cape of Kizuki, which protrudes forth from the inlet of Kozu. The mooring post to fasten this land mass firmly was Mount Sahime. This mountain separates Izumo Province from Ihami Province. The rope used in the land-pulling was the long beach of Sono. . . .

Township of Mori. Mori is situated 13.1 miles southeast of the district office. The Great God Ohonamuchi, when he walked along Mount Nagaye on his return from his campaign to pacify Yakuchi in the land of Koshi, said, "The land that I have opened up and governed shall hereafter be entrusted to the Imperial Grandson for his peaceful administration. As to the land of Izumo, however, it alone shall be kept as my territory in which I will dwell forever. I will protect it like a precious jewel. The green hills and mountains shall surround Izumo, and I shall protect it. Therefore, the place is called Mori, meaning 'to defend.'"

Divine Cape of Kaga. There is a cave on this cape. Its height is about 100 feet; its circumference is 2,761 feet. It has three entrances: one in the east, one in the west, and another in the north. This is the place where the Great God Sada was born. When he was about to be delivered, the bow and arrow of his father became invisible. At this the mother Kisakahi, a daughter of the Spirit of Fertility, said in prayer, "May the gods make the bow and arrow reappear if my child is the son of my husband, who is the God of Bravery."

Thereupon a bow and arrow of horns appeared in the water. The mother took them up and showed them to the newborn child. "These are not the vanished bow and arrow," said she. Then she threw them into the water. Then a golden bow and arrow materialized in the water. The mother waited, then picked them up, saying, "What a dark cave it is!" She shot a golden arrow through the cave walls. (Immediately a ray of sunlight shone in the cave.)

The cape is the seat of the shrine of the Goddess Kisakahi. Whenever people today row around the cave, they shout loudly so that the echoes will subdue the spirit of the cave. If people proceed without making noise, the spirit of the gods will invariably appear and cause a gale to turn over their boat. . . .

Township of Misaha. It is located 8.3 miles southwest of the district office. Ajisuki Takahiko, a son of the Lord of the Great Land, was born dumb. Unable to talk, he kept crying day and night even after his beard grew long. His father took the prince on board a ship and navigated around the island to console him. Nevertheless, Ajisuki did not stop wailing. The Lord of the Great Land sought the will of the superior gods in his dream: "Tell me why my son cries so much, I pray." On the night he prayed, the Lord of the Great Land saw his son speaking in his dream. Awakening immediately, he spoke to his son. And the son uttered the word "misaha." "What place do you call by this name, my son?" asked the Lord of the Great Land. Whereupon Ajisuki set off from his father, crossed a river of pebbles, and walked up a slope. When he reached the upper part of the hill, Ajisuki stopped and said, "This is the place, my lord."

There was a spring at that place. Ajisuki bathed and purified his body with the spring water. This is why the *kuni no miyatsuko* began using the water of this spring to perform the custom of ablution before going to the court to present *kamuyogoto*. Because of Ajisuki, today a woman with child will not eat the rice grown in this village. If she were to eat the rice, her child would be born unable to speak.

─ 10 ─

Miraculous Tales of the Hasedera Kannon

Yoshiko K. Dykstra

Since the introduction of Buddhism into Japan, one may safely say that many embraced this religion for acquiring mundane benefits as well as spiritual salvation. As with statues and paintings depicting buddhas and bodhisattvas such as Shaka (Śākyamuni), Amida, Yakushi, Miroku, and the Four Heavenly Kings (Shitennō), those of Kannon (Skt: AvalokitŚevara), the bodhisattva of great compassion, were also believed to have been endowed with special powers and consequently became objects of popular devotion. The name Kannon literally means "to heed the sounds of the prayers of the world"; in Japan, the compassionate Kannon is conceptualized as being profoundly aware of the ubiquity of pain in life and consequently acts to free all sentient beings from their sufferings. For many centuries the most frequently recited and copied Buddhist text in Japan has been the *Lotus Sutra*, a scripture that contains a chapter exclusively related to devotion to Kannon. Believers have trusted in the ability of this text to bestow wealth, health, good fortune, and longevity to devotees. Largely due to the connection between the *Lotus* text and Kannon, over the course of time this bodhisattva has acquired great popularity among all classes of people in Japan.

Stories about the benefits and favors obtained through devotion to Kannon are abundant in the literature of the Heian (794–1185), Kamakura (1192–1336), and Muromachi (1338–1568) periods. Visits to the Kannon temples of Kiyomizu, Ishiyama, and Hase are frequently mentioned in literary works such as the *Tale of Genji* and the *Pillow Book* of Sei Shōnagon. The thirty-one chapters of the *Tales of Times Now Past* (*Konjaku monogatarishū*, ca. 1107), the largest tale (*setsuwa*) collection of Japanese literature, contain forty stories about Kannon, all describing the miraculous intervention of this merciful bodhisattva.

One of the most popular Kannon stories tells of a man, Warashibe Chōja ("Straw Rich Man"), who made his fortune through the help of Kannon, beginning with a single straw as his sole capital. This particular tale appears in various *setsuwa* collections and is set in different localities. Many people, of various occupations, must have heard and repeated the tale as they traveled through the different regions of Japan. Certainly the itinerant priests and preachers who spread the Buddhist teachings would have made a great contribution to the transmission of the story, and the propagating of such religious teachings seems to have played a significant role in the development of oral literature in medieval Japan.

During the Nara (710–784) and Heian periods, Buddhism was strongly patronized by the government and aristocracy and served to support the dominant political structure rather than provide any salvatory benefit for ordinary householders. As the center of sociopolitical power shifted in the Kamakura period, however, and began to be shared by the warrior class as well as the aristocracy, the influence of this state-related and court-related Buddhism was dispersed as opportunities arose for popular or "democratic" forms of Buddhism such as the Pure Land, Nichiren, and Zen schools. In addition to solemn ceremonies and profound lectures, there were simple sermons that catered to the masses, who were of course distanced from the court and the monasteries.

Professional preachers such as Chōken (ca. 1125–1205), the founder of the Agui school, appeared and stimulated these developments by engaging exclusively in the promulgation of religious teaching. These preachers preferred to tell simple stories and parables rather than to impart complicated ideas and profound concepts to their illiterate audiences. In their preaching, they often drew upon the propagation of religious teachings (shōdō) literature of the period, such as the *Hundred Daianji Temple Homilies* (*Daianji hyakuza hōdan*, 1110) and the *Collection of Things Heard* (*Uchigikushū*, 1134). Stories in these works were often adapted from Buddhist and Chinese sources, with suitable modifications made in keeping with the tastes of the Japanese audience. The sentences were usually sufficiently short for the narrator to deliver them effectively in one breath, and their focus was generally concentrated on plot and dialogue rather than on a tedious description of scenes and characters. To make the accounts more realistic and persuasive, however, the principal characters and scenes were usually identified in more detail. Although these homiletically oriented stories are generally written in a literary style that utilizes a combination of Chinese *kanji* characters and Japanese *kana* syllables, oral expressions and the typical colloquialisms of the time would have produced a strong effect on the common audience. The preachers were well aware that narratives and parables could be enhanced and thereby made more effective if told in everyday language accompanied by gestures, facial expressions, and appropriate pitch and tone, as the one described in the *Tales of Times Now Past*: "raising his voice, opening his fan, and stretching his arms."

Among numerous Japanese Buddhist works, the *Miraculous Tales of the Hasedera Kannon* (*Hasedera Kannon genki*, also known as *Hasedera reigenki*, c. 1210) deserves special attention since well-preserved copies of this collection are still extant. The Hasedera Temple, founded in the seventh century and rebuilt in 1650, is one of the "Thirty-three Places" sacred to Kannon in his "home province" around Kyoto. The temple is situated on the eastern and western flanks of the hills above the town of Hase in Nara Prefecture. The sixty-foot-long main hall stands half upon a cliff and half upon a lofty wooden platform built out from a rock; it commands an impressive view of the entire valley below.

According to a legend found in the *Tales of Times Now Past*, a large piece of wood once drifted to the Takashima district of Ōmi Province during a flood and wrought evil effects upon the local villagers. A man of Katsuragi in Yamato Province dragged the log to the Toma district with the intention of carving a statue of Kannon, but he died before finishing the work. Later, a strange disease swept the area and the local people, believing the log to be the cause of their misfortune, discarded it near the Hase River. When Priest Tokudo heard about this incident, he himself vowed to make a statue of Kannon from the miraculous piece of wood, and with the support of Emperor Shōmu, he finally completed the task. Priest Gyōgi (668–749) performed an inauguration ceremony for the Eleven-faced Kannon in 733. The statue stood two *jō* and six *shaku* (7.9 meters) high and, like the Kannon statues at Kiyomizu and Ishiyama, became immensely popular and the object of pious veneration.

The two volumes of the *Miraculous Tales of the Hasedera Kannon* contain a total of fifty-two stories about the miraculous powers of Kannon. Each of the nineteen stories of the first volume is concerned with one of his teachings, and the thirty-three stories in the second volume recount the same number of manifestations of Kannon, who changes form at will for the benefit of sentient beings.

In addition to their division into two volumes, the Hasedera Kannon stories can also be classified into two literary categories. The first includes stories related to the origin (*engi*), construction, statues (the Eleven-faced Kannon in particular), ceremonies, and periodic efforts taken in the rebuilding of the Hasedera. The temple has undergone periodic reconstruction on account of several fires in its long history, and mysterious, strange, and ominous events and signs were recorded to have occurred before each fire.

The second literary category includes stories that describe the various benefits gained by devotees. These stories may themselves be divided into the following five subgroups: (1) curing illness, (2) victory in battle and escape from dangers, (3) bestowal of health and success on poor people, (4) granting the desired birth of a child, and (5) obtaining salvation for oneself or one's parents.

These stories describe how in this mundane world Kannon grants the wishes of worshippers for blessings of health, wealth, and success. One of the most surprising tales of this kind recounts how Kannon even encouraged a poor woman to steal a robe belonging to someone else, and how this act effactually brings the story to a happy conclusion. From a strictly moralistic viewpoint, it is difficult to understand how Kannon, a bodhisattva who is inclined to respect laws prohibiting theft, could condone such an action. To audiences in medieval Japan, however, stealing may have been regarded as permissible in cases of hardship, especially when it had the sanction of Kannon, the most merciful and understanding bodhisattva, who with great compassion was deemed to grant any wish of his faithful worshippers. In addition, to the preachers of the Law (Dharma), Kannon's encouragement of stealing in such circumstances was merely another "skillful means" (*hōben*) of leading ignorant sentient beings to true enlightenment. A popular saying, "Even lying is a skillful means" (*uso mo hōben*), no doubt had its origin in this lenient, if not absolutely permissive, attitude. In light of this flexible moral viewpoint, it is possible to understand and better appreciate both this and other stories in the *Miraculous Tales of the Hasedera Kannon*.

The translation is based on various extant versions of *Hasedera Kannon genki*, including the Hasedera Tenshō text (1587 copy) edited by Nagai Yoshinori and owned at present by Hasedera Temple.

Further Reading

Yoshiko Kurata Dykstra, tr., *Miraculous Tales of the Lotus Sutra from Ancient Japan* (Osaka: Kansai Gaidai University, 1983); Yoshiko Kurata Dykstra, tr., "Tales of the Compassionate Kannon: The *Hasedera Kannon genki*," *Monumenta Nipponica* 31 (1976): 113–143; Yoshiko Kurata Dykstra, tr., *The Konjaku Tales: Japanese Section (1)* (Osaka: Kansai Gaidai University, 1997); Hori Ichiro, *Folk Religion in Japan*, ed. Joseph M. Kitagawa and Alan L. Miller (Chicago: University of Chicago Press, 1968); Marian Ury, tr., *Tales of Times Now Past: Sixty-two Stories from a Medieval Japanese Collection* (Berkeley and Los Angeles: University of Califomia Press, 1979).

Miraculous Tales of the Hasedera Kannon

HOW PRIEST KŌYA OBTAINED A SCROLL-ROD FOR THE *GREAT WISDOM SUTRA* THANKS TO THE REVELATION IN HIS DREAM [II:17]

During the reign of Emperor Murakami [r. 946–967], Priest Kōya wished to copy the *Great Wisdom Sutra* in gold on a paper scroll with a crystal rod. Obtaining a crystal rod, however, was difficult. Kōya sequestered himself in the Hasedera Temple and concentrated on praying to Kannon.

During the night of the twenty-first day of his confinement, Kōya dreamed of a golden boy appearing from the screen before the altar. The boy said to Kōya, "You should return today. Take shelter tonight. Your wish will be realized." The boy then disappeared behind the screen.

Kōya happily started on his return trip and took shelter that night at the Katsubeji Temple. The priest of the temple asked Kōya the purpose of his prayer. After his explanation, the priest said, "Long ago, someone in this temple made a vow to copy the *Great Wisdom Sutra* in gold. He obtained a crystal rod for the paper but passed away without fulfilling his vow. Before he died, he buried the rod in a stone casket with another vow that he would someday be reborn as a human being and complete his vow. Here I see the one who made the vow fulfilling his vow!"

Kōya and the priest dug up the stone casket and Kōya finally obtained the crystal rod. The rejoicing Kōya resumed his journey home.

When the dedication service for the *Great Wisdom Sutra* was held in the

Rokuharamitsuji Temple on the twenty-second day of the eighth month of Ōwa 3 [963], the Bodhisattva Monju [Mañjuśrī] was said to have been among the invited priests. The service was truly congratulatory and auspicious.

HOW A PRIEST WHO COULD NEVER REMEMBER TWO CHARACTERS OF THE [LOTUS] SUTRA FINALLY LEARNED THEM AND MET THE PARENTS OF HIS PRESENT AND FORMER LIVES [II:18]

During the reign of Emperor Murakami [r. 946–967], Priest Esō lived in the Daianji Temple. Since entering Buddhahood, he had relied solely on the Lotus Sutra and had memorized all the characters in the sutra except the two denoting "pure heart" in the fourteenth line of the "Verses for Priests" in the chapter on "Skillful Means" [chapter 2]. He had tried very hard to memorize these two characters for years. He remembered them when he saw them in the text but forgot them as soon as he left the text.

Lamenting his past sins, which had made him unable to remember these characters, Esō went to the Hasedera Temple sometime in the Kōho era [964–968] and sequestered himself in the temple to pray to Kannon.

Seven days passed. One night, Esō dreamed that an old man appeared from the screen before the altar and offered to help him learn the two characters by skillful means.

The old man began to explain, "In your previous existence, you were a man of the Kamo-no-Higashi district of Harima Province. Your parents are still living there. While you were alive, you recited the sutra by reading the copy before the fire. Sparks from the fire charred two characters of the sutra. You died before rewriting the characters. On account of this misdeed, you cannot learn the characters even in this existence. You should go there, pay your respects to the sutra, and supply the two characters as you repent of the sins from your previous life." In his dream, Esō repented of his sins and vowed to supply the characters.

After he awoke, he could remember the characters and never forgot them. Wishing to verify his dream, Esō soon went to the Higashi district. Since night was falling when Esō arrived at the house of his parents of his previous life, he decided to postpone his inquiry till the following morning. Meanwhile he began to recite the sutra, which he had always kept with him.

Hearing his reciting voice, his parents came to see him and said in tears, "Both your voice and appearance are no different from our deceased son's." Esō now described his dream to them. His parents immediately brought out the copy of the sutra. Esō examined it and verified that the two characters were charred and missing.

Overwhelmed by the skillful means of the Great Holy One [i.e., Kannon], Esō immediately supplied the characters and upheld the sutra for a long time.

Now that he had four parents, he was loyal to all of them and continued to practice the way of the sutra throughout his life.

Wonderful was the mercy of Kannon, who helped Esō to see his previous karma and meet the parents of his present and previous lives.

HOW A POOR MAN IN THE HASEDERA TEMPLE BECAME WEALTHY BY DONATING HIS STRAW COAT AND HOW HE THEN OFFERED A SERVICE FOR HIS PARENTS [14]

During the Kanpyō era [889–898] of the ex-Emperor Uda [r. 887–897], a man named Motomori lived in Yasuda village of the Uda district of Yamato Province. At the age of nineteen he lost his parents. Since he was extremely poor, he had no means to offer a service to console his parents' souls.

After the mourning period of forty-nine days, Motomori, with a strong wish for his parents' repose, began to make monthly visits to the Hasedera Temple. Thus a few years passed. Although he had nothing to offer, he never neglected his monthly visit to the temple.

Eventually his clothing wore out, and finally he had nothing to cover himself except an old straw coat. Yet, in rain or shine, he visited the temple in his tattered straw coat. One day, Motomori wished to know the efficacy of Kannon and concentrated on his prayer with the utmost sincerity. During the last night of his hundred-day prayer, he dreamed of a boy appearing from the screen before the altar who said to him, "A small offering brings no great return!"

"How could the Great Merciful One expect me to offer anything?" asked Motomori.

"There is no result without cause. If you offer little, accordingly your blessing will be as small as your life will be short," replied the boy.

After waking up, Motomori still wondered about the intention of the Great Merciful One but offered his sole possession, the broken straw coat before the altar, and left the temple.

At home, Motomori found nothing to eat except the vines of wild yams growing around his house. As he dug up one of the yams, he accidentally found a copper container filled with gold dust. He was most appreciative of Kannon's mercy.

Now Motomori became the richest man in the province and was popularly called the Straw-Coated Rich Man. In the thirteenth year after his parents' death, Motomori built a pagoda and offered a great Buddhist service for his deceased parents. Nearly a thousand priests with Priest Chigan as their leader were invited for the service. On that occasion, two heavenly persons appeared over the service hall, identified themselves as Motomori's parents, and shortly afterward disappeared in the clouds.

The present-day Yasuda Pagoda was originally built by Motomori. Although the original [structure] had been destroyed by fire and thunder, it was repeatedly rebuilt. It was truly noble that one consoled his parents' souls and enriched himself.

HOW NATSUNO OF KIYOHARA, MINISTER OF THE RIGHT OF FUTAOKA, WAS
QUICKLY CURED FROM LEPROSY [II:6]

During the reign of Emperor Kammu [r. 781–806], there was a man called
Natsuno of Kiyohara, minister of the right of Futaoka. Before he became a
minister, at the age of twenty, he contracted leprosy and suffered terribly from
the scabs on his face. Neither doctors nor divine efficacies proved to be effective
for his disease.

Thinking that the Hasedera Kannon would help those who were abandoned
by Buddhas and gods, Natsuno visited the temple and sat before the statue
fervently praying, "Oh, merciful Kannon, take my life away if my wish is not
realized!"

Thus, Natsuno fulfilled his seven-day prayers on the eighteenth [day] of the
ninth month of the twentieth year of Enryaku [801]. That night, about the
hour of the Tiger, he dreamed that a boy, appearing from the inner part of the
altar, said to him, "Although your disease is due to your karmic cause and
difficult to cure, the Great Holy One ordered me to come to help you." The
boy with his long tongue began to lick all the scabs spread over the entire body
of Natsuno. The surprised Natsuno awoke and found that his face was clean
and he was completely cured. Thereafter, he singlemindedly pledged to worship the [Hasedera] Kannon.

Later, Natsuno became a minister with the Second Rank, and finally, at the
age of fifty-six, on the twenty-ninth of the tenth month of Showa 4, he passed
away with a firm faith. Near the time of his departure, Natsuno sent a messen
ger to the temple to deliver his farewell to Kannon. With his correct view and
faith, he took his last breath when purple clouds draped the sky in the fragrant
air. He had wished for the encounter with Kannon in his new life. Certainly,
he must have been thereafter born in the Pure Land.

$$—11—$$

Japanese Puppetry: From Ritual Performance to Stage Entertainment

Jane Marie Law

In the United States and Europe, many world theater enthusiasts are familiar with what is often referred to as "Japan's classical puppet theater," Bunraku puppetry. This group of puppeteers, chanters, and shamisen (a stringed instrument used to accompany ballad recitation in Japanese performing arts) accompanists are centered in Osaka, where the National Puppet Theater is located. Now, they also perform at certain times of the year in the National Theater in Tokyo. The troupe certainly earns its praise as the "crown jewel" of Japan's puppetry traditions, yet the Bunraku theater is by no means the most representative of Japan's puppetry traditions. In part, Bunraku puppets have received such a high degree of international acclaim and display such aesthetic grace and subtlety because historically they literally stand on the shoulders (or in the *taka-geta*, tall wooden shoes used by puppeteers, as the case may be) of the widespread ritual and folk puppetry traditions that preceded this tradition. In this chapter, we will not be looking at this famous example of Japanese puppetry, but at the folk varieties that have dotted the Japanese countryside since the late Heian period.

These folk puppetry traditions in Japan may not on the surface appear to be as polished as the famous Bunraku puppets, but the power of these performances to evoke strong emotional and even religious feelings in people is impressive. One of Japan's leading authorities on ritual puppetry, the late Nagata Kōkichi, put it this way: "These puppets are like wild animals. If you restrict them to a stage, it is like putting them in a cage. They lose their innate raw and wild nature." Unlike Bunraku puppets, which are presented only in indoor theaters, most of the folk puppetry troupes have a long history of presenting their pieces in shrines, on roadsides, in entryways to homes, on fishing docks and boats, and even in rice fields as they are being planed or harvested. This quality of intimacy with the everyday lives of people tells us a great deal about the meanings these puppetry performances have had throughout Japanese history. Unlike the glamorous Bunraku examples, folk puppets are truly "puppets of the road."

The earliest text describing the activities of proper puppeteers is the *Chronicle of the (Wandering) Puppeteers* (*Kugutsu ki,* or *Kairaishi [no] ki*), written by Ōe no Masafusa (1041–1111), who was fascinated by the traveling artists who used puppetry to perform magic. The constellation of his description of the sexual allure of the women, the nocturnal worship activities, and the magical "transformations" of matter using puppetry strongly suggests a shamanic strain of Japanese ritual practice in the late Heian period. By far the most common type of itinerant ritual puppeteer in medieval Japan (and up through the early modern period) was the Ebisu-mawashi, or the manipulator of Ebisu. Ebisu is a maritime deity primarily devoted to safeguarding fishing, but also worshipped as a protector of commerce. Popularly depicted as a happy fisherman holding his freshly caught sea bream, he is also included as one of the seven gods of luck (*shichifukujin*). The *Dance of Ebisu* (*Ebisu-mai*) is a puppetry performance that invokes the presence of Ebisu and his capacity for bestowing good luck. Wandering puppeteers served an important purpose in spreading and maintaining Ebisu worship in outlying fishing villages where they presented performances telling of Ebisu's powers.

Ebisu was also identified as the Leech Child, the deformed offspring of Izanagi and Izanami. In *The Legend of Dōkumbō* (*Dōkumbō denki,* 1638), which also tells of the origins of the puppetry tradition on the island of Awaji, the abandoned Leech Child is said to have been found drifting on the ocean by a fisherman named Hyakudayū, who built a shrine for him in Nishinomiya. There a priest named Dōkumbō mediated for the Leech Child and received his messages, but after the priest died no one looked after the deity, who then caused bad weather and fishing disasters. Hyakudayū received an imperial command to make a puppet in the likeness of Dōkumbō, and the manipulation of the puppet in the shrine placated and calmed the Leech Child. The legend ends with a warning that the art of puppetry is for the appeasement of deities and should not be taken lightly.

Another overtly religious use of puppetry can be seen in the practice of *hotoke-mawashi*, in which itinerant Buddhist priests (often unordained or unauthorized by major Buddhist sects) used puppets to present miracle tales about the Buddha or the compassionate activities of bodhisattvas. By the early Edo period the demand for puppet performances allowed this art form to flourish and to develop the blending of three arts—dramatic recitation, musical accompaniment, and puppet manipulation—into one. Written and performed primarily for the entertainment of human audiences rather than the ritual appeasement of deities, the dramatic plays of this genre nevertheless draw upon the long traditions of Buddhist miracle tales (chapter 10).

Still popular today both in the provincial folk theaters and on the Bunraku stage, *An Account of the Miracle of the Tsubosaka Kannon* (*Tsubosaka Kannon no reigenki*) is a good example. The play was written by a woman from Awaji, Kako Chikajo. Her husband, Kako Nihei (1813–1898), was a *shamisen* player who performed under the stage name Toyozawa Danpei. He wrote the musical score for the piece. It was first performed in 1879 and became an extremely popular play after it was chanted at the Hikorokuza Theater in Osaka by Sanze Takemoto Osumidayū in 1887. It is considered to be both a representative work of Meiji puppetry and a fine example of Awaji puppetry. Further, it is faithful to the miracle story genre on a number of counts: first, there is a simple, easily discerned, remembered, embroidered, and retold plot that even a small child can understand. Second, the level of emotion in the play is extremely high, with a great deal of shedding of tears, heated dialogue, and celebration of the pathetic and helpless. Third, the play is heavily moralistic, and goodness is readily recognizable. It provides a basic ethical lesson: good wives are devoted to their husband, even unto death. Simple faith can be rewarded with miracles, and one can even escape the pronouncement of death through faith in Kannon. Fourth, the play presents didactic Buddhist interpretations of events. Fifth, the play teaches that the sufferings of this world are not without their causes in past lives and rewards in this or the next.

The play consists of only two short scenes and thus is often performed as a tragic interlude between two longer, more complex period pieces at an all-day puppetry performance. Since the simple play is highly cathartic and ends on a happy note, when placed between two historical tragedies it serves as a sort of breather for the audience. The play is usually performed with two simple sets. The first scene takes place in the teahouse where pilgrims on the Saikoku pilgrimage can rest on their ascent up Tsubosaka to worship before the Kannon there. In the second scene, to the right we see the small room in Sawaichi's home, and to the right, high up on a rocky slope, Tsubosaka Temple, a bell in its tower. In this scene, only three puppets are manipulated: Sawaichi, whose eyes are closed until the final part of the play; his wife Osato; and the elaborately costumed bodhisattva, Kannon. Each puppet is manipulated by three puppeteers. Since in each scene there are never more than a few puppets and in the final scene Kannon appears alone, the play can be staged with as few as six or nine puppeteers, one chanter and one *shamisen* player.

The translation is based on the performance score used in the Awaji Ningyō Jōruri Kan. Translations of *Kugutsu ki*, *Ebisu-mai*, and *Dōkumbō denki* can be found in Jane Marie Law, *Puppets of Nostalgia: The Life, Death, and Rebirth of the Japanese Awaji Ningyō Tradition* (Princeton: Princeton University Press, 1997): 97, 193–195, and 158–159, respectively.

Further Reading

C. J. Dunn, *The Early Japanese Puppet Drama* (London: Luzac and Co., 1966); Donald Keene, *Bunraku: The Art of the Japanese Puppet Theater* (Tokyo: Kodansha International, 1965); Jane Marie Law, *Puppets of Nostalgia: The Life, Death, and Rebirth of the Japanese* Awaji Ningyō *Tradition* (Princeton: Princeton University Press, 1997); Jane Marie Law, "Of Plagues and Puppets: On the Significance of the Name Hyakudayū in Japanese Religions," *Transactions of the Asiatic Society of Japan*, 4th series, 8 (Spring 1994): 108–132; Jane Marie Law, "The Puppet as Body Substitute: *Ningyō* in the Japanese *Shiki Sanbasō* Performance," in *Religious Reflections on the Human Body*, ed. J. M. Law (Bloomington: Indiana University Press, 1994); Jane Marie Law, "Religious Authority and Ritual Puppetry: The Case of *Dōkumbō Denki*," *Monumenta Nipponica* 47, 1 (Spring 1992); 77–97; Margaareta Niculescu, ed., *The Puppet*

Theater of the Modern World, tr. Ewald Osers and Elisabeth Strick (London: George G. Harrap and Co., 1967); A. C. Scott, The Puppet Theater of Japan (Rutland, Vermont: Charles E. Tuttle, 1963).

An Account of the Miracle of the Tsubosaka Kannon

SCENE ONE

The Pine Field of Tosa-machi (Tosa-machi Matsubara no Dan)

CHORUS: On a loom, she unwinds the spindle, weaving the water splash (*kasuri*) pattern. Although her body is adorned with tattered cloth, in her heart she weaves a brocade. This woman's conduct reflects chastity, and even the talk of the passersby reveals this. There is no fault in her, even on the day-to-day level.

There are eight paths down to Tosa-machi, and pine trees line the walk. In the distance below, we see a resting place, with sliding paper doors, where bitter tea is served. Smoke rises from the rest house, and the straw sandals of the people who come and go are hanging from the tea shop. The wife of the shop calls out to those who pass on this festival day for Kannon, as they stop for a rest on their pilgrimage.

TEA SHOP WIFE: Hey pilgrim! This is the perfect time for flower viewing! Stop and rest here a while.

CHORUS: She ladles out the water, and the floral fragrance that rises is as fine as that served in the eating houses of Yoshino. Each person takes a cup of fragrant tea, and the chatter begins to waft around as the guests settle down to rest.

PILGRIM: Oh, Gonza's wife! You sure are working hard today! Today is the eighteenth, and since this is the day for people to go and worship, the price of the tea will surely go up.

TEA SHOP WIFE: Thanks to the extreme spiritual power of Kannon, I am able to go on living in this life. Ah, it is a gracious blessing.

CHORUS: Across the spring fields comes a woman, fresh as the young grass, her skin the color of the first aster flower someone has just plucked, her hand-woven kimono carefully tied. One of the pilgrims calls out to her:

PILGRIM: Hey there! Sawaichi's wife! Where are you going? Come over here a moment and rest a bit with your friends!

OSATO: Oh! My, my! Since the weather is warm today, you can go and worship Kannon, but we have to work every day weaving cloth. We work and work but somehow can't make ends meet and are so poor!

CHORUS: When she says this, the pilgrims all break into a laugh.

PILGRIM: This Sawaichi is such a lucky fellow! Not only is his wife beautiful, but she cherishes him above all else, takes care of him, and does all the work to earn a living! I wish he could see her face just once!

ANOTHER PILGRIM: His wife is like the cherry blossoms in the valley pounded into sweet rice cakes: What a shame that Sawaichi only knows them by taste! What a shame!

CHORUS: As they praise her, Osato brushes off their compliments and laughs through her tears.

OSATO: It is not as you say. He was engaged to be my precious husband while he could still see, and this makes me very happy. But still, it would be my wish that he could see again.

CHORUS: She lets fall this one drop of her chaste sincerity, and they are all deeply moved.

PILGRIM: On top of all this, she's pure hearted too! Her beauty extends all the way to her heart! Listen, my dear! The Tsubosaka Kannon is not far away. You should go there and pray for him, and if you have enough faith, your mysterious reward will be right before your eyes. Go! Pray to Kannon!

OSATO: Thank you, but with all the work I have to do, I haven't any free time. I'll try to go this spring when the days are longer.

PILGRIM: Yes, do so! Do so! Well, let's go home down the seventh path.

ANOTHER PILGRIM: Yes, by all means let's go home! I'll go home and tell my wife about the lovely Osato, so *she* should cherish *her* man like that.

ANOTHER PILGRIM: Just let my wife hear this! Let my wife hear this! But at any rate, even with a husband who can see, she makes me feel like I am blind. All she does is spend, spend, spend, down to the last coins in my pocket!

CHORUS: Saying this, each of them scatters to the left and right. Osato, laughing, bids them farewell and heads toward her home.

SCENE TWO

From Sawaichi's Home to the Mountain (Sawaichi Uchi yori Yama no Dan)

CHORUS: Is a dream this floating world, or is the floating world a dream? In this town called Dream, the more we live, the more footweary we become. In the province of Yamato, in the area of Tsubosaka, in a town called Tosa, lives a poor blind man named Sawaichi. Honest by birth, he practices the *koto* and the *shamisen*. His life is thinner than the strings of his *shamisen*, fainter than a wisp of smoke. His wife Osato is sincere of heart and helps her husband by taking in mending and laundry and doing it by the piece. Her pounding as she starches the clothes beats out the rhythm of their indistinct existence.

The sound of birds, and even the sound of bells, soak into our body, recalling the tears that fell and flowed into the Imose River.

OSATO: What's this? What's this? Sawaichi! You've gotten your *shamisen* out and are playing away at it!

SAWAICHI: Oh! Osato! You think it's a sign that I am in a good mood to see me playing my *shamisen*?

OSATO: Yes, I do.

SAWAICHI: Well, I'm not in that kind of mood. I'm so blue. I'm so blue, I could just die. I am just feeling so very low. Hey! Osato! I have something I want to say to you. Come here for a minute. I say come right over here for a minute. There is something I have been wanting to talk to you about, so come here! Come here! There is nothing else, but . . . there is something I've been meaning to ask you about for a long time now, but . . . now is just the right time. Time flies like an arrow, the days and months go by so fast! Well, it has been three years since you and I have been together. You've been betrothed to me since childhood. We should know what is in each other's heart. Then why do you hide something from me? Tell me plainly! Confess!

CHORUS: The ends of his words trail off. Osato doesn't quite understand and questioningly asks:

OSATO: What is this, Sawaichi? What is it you are saying to me? In the three years that I have been your wife, really, truly, there hasn't been the slightest thing I have hidden from you. If there is something on your mind, then tell me what it is! Isn't that what husbands and wives are supposed to do?

SAWAICHI: Well, if you say so, then I will tell you.

OSATO: Tell me what it is!

SAWAICHI: Oh, shall I tell you? It is this, Osato: It has been a full three years that we have been married. Every evening, from a little bit after the seventh bell, there has not been a single time that you have been home. It's obvious that I am completely blind. Because of a terrible smallpox, my face has been ravaged. It is not unreasonable that you wouldn't find me attractive, but if there is another man you are thinking of, and if you had just come out and told me about it in the first place, then I wouldn't be this angry. You and I are cousins. Even when I hear people's sincere compliments, saying, "Oh, Osato is so beautiful, Osato is so beautiful," I am resigned and resolve never to get jealous. Come on! Please tell me!

CHORUS: Although he speaks bravely, he swallows back his tears, and his blind heart is breaking. Hearing this, Osato, unaware at this time of either herself or the world, throws herself at her husband's feet.

OSATO: What? You selfish man, Sawaichi! What kind of a detestable person do you think I am, that I can just discard you and take up with another man! Do you think I am that kind of a woman? I will hear none of this! None of this! Since the time I was separated from my parents I was under the care of my uncle and was raised with you as my brother three years older than I. I always admired how you, Sawaichi, always seemed on top of things, although you not only were blinded by smallpox after you were born but also had to endure poverty and suffering. Through fire and water, we are wedded together until our next life. Thinking only of this, every day for the last three years, when I hear the seventh bell at Tsubosaka, I slip out alone, trudge up the mountain path, and pray to Kannon restore your sight. What kind of reward is this we receive? There is no effect for my sincere supplication to her. I was just now resenting Kannon, since she doesn't hear my prayers, and without even knowing my heart, now in one sentence you start in with this business about another man. . . . Oh, it makes me so angry!

CHORUS: Saying this, a tear of sincerity rises in her eyes, its color pure. Sawaichi hears for the first time of the faithfulness of his wife. Now, he utters his apology in a tearful voice.

SAWAICHI: Oh, my wife. Please forgive me. I apologize. I apologize. I didn't know about this. It is just like this cripple to be such a fool. Please forgive me.

CHORUS: That is all he says, and, pressing his palms together, he sheds tears of apology. His entire sleeve is soaked with tears.

SAWAICHI: Ah, my wedded wife! What apology can I give you? Since it is clear I have doubted you, I wish I could just die! I just wish I could die! The more you say, the more ashamed I become. Despite your profound faith, my sight will not be restored.

OSATO: Now, now. What are you saying? With all the gloomy trials and hardships of these years and months! On rainy nights, on snowy nights, and foggy nights, I went barefooted to worship at the Kannon temple, and all for your sake!

SAWAICHI: Ah, with a vow such as that, you kept your determination. While it is very kind, and while I am very happy, what bad treatment the passing of the years and months have given you, the chaste woman who is so good to me. You speak of Kannon. I know I may bring the curse of heaven upon myself, but these eyes refuse to open and be healed.

OSATO: Don't say such things! What happens to you happens to me. Rather than doing all this complaining, be encouraged. Let's go together and make our request of Kannon. Come, let's go together and make our request.

CHORUS: Thinking of her husband like this, it is moving how dedicated her heart's intention is. In a flood of tears, Sawaichi says:

SAWAICHI: Ah, you are too good a wife for me. Your whole heart has been dedicated to only this. If flowers will bloom on a withered tree, perhaps my unseeing eyes are like a withered tree. Ah, how I wish those flowers would bloom! Even though I say this, I am so full of fault. The future, my wife . . . take my hand.

CHORUS: As he says this, his wife gladly races to change her clothes and hands him his thin cane. Her thin heart is full of her not so thin deep vow, as they trudge in the direction of the Tsubosaka Temple. It has been told of the Kannon of Tsubosaka that in the fiftieth generation of emperors, when Emperor Kammu was in Nara, he got a very bad eye ailment. The priest who resided there, named Dōki Shōnin, recited prayers for 107 days, and instantly the emperor's eyes were healed. Now, this site is the sixth station on the Saikoku pilgrimage route and is well known among people as a holy place.

Just as Sawaichi and his wife come near the temple at the marker on the road, from down the hill is heard the sound of pilgrims singing devotional songs to Kannon.

OSATO: Sawaichi, listen. Although a devoted heart is very important, the more depressed you are, the sicker you will become. At a time like this, it will cheer you up to sing some songs you know by heart. Why don't you sing something aloud and not be so serious?

SAWAICHI: Yes, that is really true. As you say, worrying over things is bad for my eyes. If that is the case, I will think of this as practice. But, is anybody watching us?

CHORUS: He begins to sing, as if playing the *shamisen* in accompaniment.

SAWAICHI: Is gloom compassion? Or is compassion gloom? As the dew disappears, my body. . . . Oops, I tripped! Oh, I forget the next part of that song.

CHORUS: The song becomes like the transitory grass on the road, and they climb up to the worship hall of the temple.

OSATO: Sawaichi. We've arrived at the hall of Kannon.

SAWAICHI: Oh, is this Kannon-sama? Oh, how fortunate, how fortunate. Namu Amida Butsu. Namu Amida Butsu. Namu Amida Butsu. Namu Amida Butsu.

OSATO: Here! Come over here! Tonight, on this very night, why don't we leisurely sing a devotional song all night long?

CHORUS: And the husband and wife's voices are pure as they chant together into the night.

SAWAICHI AND OSATO: Tsubosaka, Kannon, who builds mountains, and fills lakes with water. . . . The sands of the garden become the Pure Land. . . .

SAWAICHI: Oh! Osato! I thought this was impossible, but anyway, I followed your word and have come this far, but my sight is not being restored.

OSATO: Oh, you! You're being like that again! Here we go again! It was to this very Kannon on Tsubosaka, that Emperor Kammu in the Nara capital, when he was suffering from an eye disease, prayed. Immediately his eyes were opened. That is the reason I have encouraged you, because really there is no difference between the emperor and us who are like bugs. Having faith means being patient with a calm and concentrated heart throughout many steps of prayerful supplications. With such faith, anything is possible with Kannon's compassion. But instead of wasting time talking like this, why don't we continue chanting?

CHORUS: Saying this and gathering up their strength,

SAWAICHI: I guess you are right. From tonight, I am going to fast here for three days. You go home ahead of me and do your work. These three days will seal my fate as to whether my eyes will heal or not heal.

OSATO: I am so glad you said that. If that is the case, I will go on home and get things prepared. But Sawaichi, listen. This is a steep mountain road, and if you go to the right, there is a valley of unfathomable depths. So don't go anywhere.

SAWAICHI: Where would I go? For three days it will be just me and Kannon here.

CHORUS: He laughs. And while laughing, the wife leaves her heart behind in her footsteps, dew gathers and is scattered, and she flutters off, not knowing what kind of parting this is. Sawaichi remains behind alone, and, unable to endure his downhearted feelings, he lays himself down and cries.

SAWAICHI: I am happy, my wife. More than just nursing me these years and months, you have not begrudged the poverty and suffering. Moreover, not once did your love grow weary, and to me who cannot see, you have had patient endurance. Even so, without your knowing, I have had all kinds of doubts about you. Forgive me. Forgive me. Having just now parted, in what world should we meet again? I am such a pitiful person.

CHORUS: He throws himself on the ground and laments his failure. After awhile, he raises his face.

SAWAICHI: I won't let myself lament. Even though for three years my wife faithfully devoted herself to her prayers, there is no benefit in my living any longer. As it is said, if two people are miserable, let them go separate ways so that at least one of them can make a fortune. So my death can be my reward for you. While you are alive, marry into whatever good house you are able. As I heard from you just a little while ago, if when climbing the hill I go to the right, there is a valley of unfathomable depths. This will be my final resting place. If I become part of the earth of this sacred place, perhaps in the next life I may be saved. Luckily, night has fallen. While there is no one around, I'll do it. I'll do it.

CHORUS: Saying this, he stands and pulls himself together.

SAWAICHI: I hurry to my final moment.

CHORUS: He gropes his way along, tapping his cane forcefully side to side, and finally climbs up to the edge of the cliff. He hears the thundering sound of the waters below in the valley and, considering this to be a welcome from Amida, he thrusts his cane into the ground and propels himself forward,

SAWAICHI: Namu Amida Butsu.

CHORUS: and throws himself to his tragic death. Not knowing what has happened, his wife returns up the path, breathing heavily, her mind preoccupied with worries about her husband. Although she knows this path well, she slips and falls and finally makes her way to the top of the slope.

OSATO: I can't see him anywhere! Sawaichi! Sawaichi! Sawaichi!

CHORUS: She would ask someone if they have seen him, but she hears no voice and sees not even the shadow of a person. She staggers back and forth.

OSATO: Sawaichi!

CHORUS: Running here and there, from the light of the moon she can see something through the trees. She comes close and recognizes his cane, stuck into the ground. She lets out a cry of grief. Startled, she looks down into the valley, and in the shining moon she recognizes the dead form of her husband.

OSATO: What shall I do now! How sad!

CHORUS: Crazy with grief, she writhes back and forth. Even if she wished to fly down to him in the valley, she has no wings. She calls out to him, but to no avail. No one answers her but her own echo.

OSATO: I won't hear of this! I won't hear of this! I just won't hear of this! For all the hardships of these years and months, unbegrudgingly I bore all the difficulties. With a single heart I petitioned to Kannon that your eyes would soon be healed, that you would be saved. I have been praying ceaselessly for this, and on this very day, I am the one who is left behind. What shall I do? What shall I do? Come to think of it, that song you sang somehow bothered me. It stuck in my heart and made me worry. But now I realize that at that time you were already resolved to die. I didn't know! I didn't know! If I had known it would come to this, I would not have pushed you to come here with me. Forgive me. If I think about it, is there anyone more hopeless than I? To be separated for eternity from my husband to whom I am wedded in two worlds. . . . Ah, how miserable! Is this grief the result of sins from a previous life? How sorrowful! From the blind darkness of this world, he has gone on to the dark travels of death. Who will take his hand and keep him from getting lost in that world?

CHORUS: As she pleads into the silence, her tears of grief increase the water in the valley of Tsubosaka. Finally, she lifts her tearful face.

OSATO: I won't regret. I won't lament. Everything has been decided from a previous life. I will join my husband in death. Amida, show us the way as we leave this world.

CHORUS: As she voices this plea to Amida, she falls into the valley, her last gesture chaste. How piteous!

　　The time is early February. Near dawn, through an opening in the clouds, a beam of light shines forth. Surrounded by beautiful music, Kannon appears in the temporary form of a gracious and lovely woman. In a delicate voice, the bodhisattva speaks.

KANNON: Behold, Sawaichi! Due to events in a previous life, you became blind However, because of your pressing fate, and due to the chaste heart of your wife and the merit of her daily prayers, I will extend your lives. Since I have bequeathed this to you, go on the pilgrimage of the thirty-three sites, and in faith, show gratitude for the Buddha's compassion. Sawaichi! Sawaichi! Osato! Osato!

CHORUS: As she proclaims this in a divine voice, she disappears without a trace, and the early morning bells reverberate in four directions. The morning dawns, and as the light breaks in the dark valley, the two forms, not knowing if they are in a dream, slowly rise up.

OSATO: Ah! It's you, Sawaichi! It's you! Your eyes are open!

SAWAICHI: OH! It's really true! I can see! I can see! I can see! This is all due to Kannon-sama! Thank you very much! Thank you! Thank you! Thank you! And, you? Who are you?

OSATO: Who do you think I am? I am your wife!

SAWAICHI: You are my wife? This is the first time I have seen you. Oh how happy I am! How happy I am! This is indeed something very mysterious. I am sure I fell into the valley, and I thought I was dead. While I didn't know what was happening, Kannon appeared, and she explained everything that has happened to me from my previous life.

OSATO: Yes, and I followed in your footsteps, and there is no doubt that I, too, fell into the valley. But, there is not a single wound on my body, and on top of that, you can see! Are we dreaming?

SAWAICHI: If that is the case, then there is no doubt that it was Kannon who directly called me back to life, saying, "Sawaichiiiiii! Sawaichiiiiiii!!" Ha ha ha! I am so grateful!

CHORUS: It is indeed Kannon who saves the lives of this intimate husband and wife. Graciously rewarding them by opening Sawaichi's blind eyes, it is as if his youth has returned to him. Today is a happy day, for he sets aside his cane, and as the dawn breaks, he gives thanks to the gods and buddhas. It is Kannon who shows him these myriad things, it is the weight of Kannon's vow that builds mountains, and fills lakes with water. Even the sands become the Pure Land, and this revelation is the blessed Dharma.

— 12 —

The Shintō Wedding Ceremony:

A Modern *Norito*

Cherish Pratt

Some things are universal: every culture seems to have instituted some way of sanctifying the union of a man and woman. The ritual drama is not only for the sake of the couple; it is also for the sake of establishing ties between families and, through those ties, renewing the society that such rituals reflect and define. Intimate things are procedurally reconciled with social imperatives.

In Japan such ritual acts have developed out of ancient traditions. The Japanese wedding ceremony is informed by both continuity and change. Enactments of seemingly timeless formulaic rites have endured, allowing the newly formed Japanese couple to partake of the power of a shared mythic past; they participate in the legends and history that distinguish them as a society. At the same time, influences of Chinese culture—Buddhism, Confucianism, and Taoism—have been ritually incorporated and homogenized in order to exalt the ritual. The use of the verb "to listen," for example, in reference to the absorption of the aroma of incense, has strong Buddhist connotations. It is elements such as these that grace the service and the participants.

The wedding liturgy or *norito* that follows is an invocation of *kami*, the imperial gods, and is an ancient gesture to consecrate the marriage vows that the modern bride and groom make in the solemn presence of their family, go-betweens, shrine officials, and, figuratively at least, those primordial deities who created Japan and first performed this very ritual.

The potency of norito is legendary: it has been said that the Sun Goddess, Amaterasu, who had concealed herself in a cave, was lured from her hiding place by the power of the very kind of incantations that are preserved in the modern wedding liturgy. One of the earliest collections of norito, found in the ninth-century *Institutes of the Engi Era* (*Engi shiki*), documents the fundamental elements of Shintō ritual, outlines liturgical procedures, and insinuates indigenous notions of divine law. The *Institutes* instituted religious norms as it affirmed the divine mandate of the Imperial Sovereign.

Nori (from the verb *noru*, "to announce or tell") meant, among other things, "enjoinder or command," and as such it came to be the indigenous word for "law." The marriage ritual or norito that follows articulates and affirms this divine intent, the will, word, and work of the kami. Adoption of Chinese characters, phonetically read in both Japanese and Chinese, lent prestige to the texts and the rituals that performed those texts. In the modern norito, the phonetic reading was often indicated by the size of the character: small ideograms indicated a Chinese reading, while larger ones were the cue that it was to be read following the Japanese. Additional Chinese elements, mythological and philosophical, as well as those linguistic, were assimilated and formally incorporated into the norito without disrupting their authority as Japanese Shintō texts.

At various shrines throughout Japan, resident priests composed norito for the particular deity to whom their shrine was dedicated. Each priest followed the general principles for norito as outlined in the *Institutes*. The norito of each shrine reflected a fluidity of form, at once adhering to conventional ideals and patterns, and at the same time addressing the specific resident deities of each shrine district and, if applicable, the particular circumstances of the people for whom prayers were being offered.

These norito were literary, incorporating such poetic tropes as the use of pillow words (*makurakotoba*) and pivot words (*kakekotoba*), playful rhetorical figures that lent a telescopic and polysemous dimension, as well as an aesthetic mystique to each particular text, as intricate ideas and complex emotions were encapsulated in a minimum of uttered syllables.

For many years there was no uniform marriage ritual in Japan. There was but a relatively defined ritual etiquette that differed from individual to individual as determined by district, class, personal proclivities, or preferences. Standardization of the wedding ceremony did not occur until after May 10, 1900, the date on which Crown Prince Yoshihito wed Princess Sado. This imperial Shintō ceremony divulged the degrees to which traditional elements found in Shintō ritual and norito were coupled with political motives of the state. A desire or need to authenticate imperial sovereignty set the ceremonial mood of the performance that became the model for the modern wedding norito.

When individual shrines received requests for similar ceremonies, priests responded with liturgical compositions that conformed to standards of ritual practice in general (in their use of norito, *harai* or purification offerings, and a sacred feast); and yet, at the same time, each was unique in the ways in which it incorporated elements that conformed to the local practice and etiquette for marriage that had predated it.

The text that follows, typical of what is frequently used in wedding ceremonies today, is the script for a dramatic and formal rite of passage in which Japanese men and women find themselves transformed and united in terms of both a new life and a persistent past. Universal needs for the sanctification of intimacy are manifested in a particular social context and enacted by individuals who, through the ritual, are allowed to participate in something larger than themselves.

The translation is of a norito composed in the 1980s by the head priest at the Hawaii Daijingū Shrine, which stands in the lineage of Ise Shinto.

Further Reading

Felicia G. Bock, tr., *Engi-shiki: Procedures of the Engi Era* (Tokyo: Sophia University, 1970); U. A. Casal, *The Five Sacred Festivals of Ancient Japan: Their Symbolism and Historical Development* (Tokyo: Sophia University, 1967); Walter Edwards, *Modern Japan Through Its Weddings* (Stanford: Stanford University Press, 1989); Ofra Goldstein-Gidoni, *Packaged Japaneseness: Weddings, Business, and Brides* (Honolulu: University of Hawaii Press, 1997); Joy Hendry, *Marriage in Changing Japan: Community and Society* (London: Croom Helm, 1981); Donald L. Philippi, *Norito: A New Translation of the Ancient Japanese Ritual Prayers* (Tokyo: Institute for Japanese Culture and Classics, Kokugakuin University, 1959), reprinted by Princeton University Press, 1991; A. W. Sadler, "The Grammar of a Rite in Shinto," *Asian Folklore Studies* 35 (1976): 17–27.

The Shintō Wedding Text: A Modern Norito

We humbly speak before the Majestic and Sovereign Deity,
   who is awe inspiring and most highly revered.
We imitate the work of the deities who performed this in days of old.

Under the auspices of the go-between [*insert name*],
   who by grasping the middle of the majestic spear
   bids the bride [*insert woman's name*] and groom [*insert man's name*]
   make a wedding vow.

This day has been designated for ritual.
Due to its auspicious character we celebrate the wedding ceremony
   today.

It is because the law of marriage is majestically carried out in front of
   the great deities
   that the proper deportment of ritual must follow.
We make offerings of Sacred Food and Sacred Sake;
A variety of tastes are here arranged and set before you.
Eat with delight, listen to the aroma of the offerings, enjoy, and so
   accept.

The exchange of sake, three times drunk, shared, and poured for each
   other.
We do that because we are extending our congratulations to each
   other.
The vow does not exhaust itself; the cup is never dry.

The Vows we articulate are intricately inlaid into our lives in this
   world and the next.

Growing old together, until our hair is long and white, we have been
  caused to be tied.
So does our bond exist in the universe,
  just as the sun and moon exist in the heavens
  just as the mountains and rivers exist on earth.
Side by side, shoulder to shoulder, putting our home, the *ie*, in order,
  making it settled.

Maintain the family gate as a dignified one.
The connection to the ancestors is to be continued and not neglected.
The family name should flourish, be highly respected and widely
  known.

Our grandchildren and grandchildren should continue forever,
  just as the fifty red oak trees,
  just as the eight mulberry bushes prosper and propagate.

Thus we humbly and most respectfully speak.

SPIRITS

— 13 —

Tama Belief and Practice in Ancient Japan

Gary L. Ebersole

Recalling, Binding, and Pacifying Spirits of the Dead

Beliefs and practices surrounding the *tama*, the animating spirit that gives life to the physical body, constitute a central symbolic and ritual complex in early Japan. This is particularly apparent in the *Ten Thousand Leaves* (*Man'yōshū*, hereafter *MYS*), the anthology of Japanese poetry that is often cited as the earliest extant work of Japanese literature. It will be recalled that the *Ten Thousand Leaves* contains the lines "I cannot make out the sleeves / she waves in farewell" (*imo ga mode saya nimo miezu*, *MYS* 2:135). Although it is not clear from the translation, this is an obvious reference to the performance of a spirit-beckoning (lit., "spirit shaking," *tama-furi*) ritual. The intention behind the action of the poet's wife is to guarantee his safe return. The belief in the efficacy of this action is related in a general way to the familiar Western custom, now largely attenuated into metaphorical usage, of keeping a candle burning in the window while someone is away. In both cases, the belief is that the action will help the absent person find his or her way home again safely.

There are a large number of references to spirit-beckoning rituals in the extant poetry from early Japan, as well as in prose passages from the three texts. Again in the *Ten Thousand Leaves* (*MYS* 2:132; Levy 1981:99), Kakinomoto Hitomaro (d. ca. 708–715) says in one of the set of poems on parting from his wife:

Iwami no ya	O does my wife
Takatsuno-yama no	see the sleeves I wave
ki no ma yori	from between the trees
waga furu sode	on Takatsuno Mountain
imo mitsuramu ka	in Iwami?

Here again the ritual action of spirit-beckoning is visible. The following are the last lines of *Ten Thousand Leaves* (*MYS* 2:27; Levy 1981: 134–135), a ritual funeral lament by Hitomaro on, according to the headnote, the death of his wife. A messenger had just brought news of her passing.

iwamu sube	I did not know what to say,
namu sube shira ni	what to do,
oto nomi o	but simply could not listen
kikite ari eneba	and so, perhaps to solace
waga kouru	a single thousandth
chie no hito e mo	of my thousandfold longing,
nagasamuru	I stood at the Karu market
kokoro mo ariya	to where often she had gone
wagimoko ga	and listened,
tomazu idemishi	but could not hear
Karu no ichi ni	the voices of the birds
waga tachikikeba	that cry on Unebi Mountain
tamatasuki	where the maidens
Unebi no yama ni	wear strands of jewels,
naku tori no	and of the ones who passed me
koe mo kiezu	on that road,
tamahoko no	straight as a jade spear,
michi yuku hito mo	not one resembled her.
hitori dani	I could do nothing
niteshi yukaneba	but call my wife's name
sube o nami	and wave my sleeves.
imo ga na yobite	
sode so furitsuru	

Various elements of early Japanese belief and practice are found here. Note the frequent use of homonyms of *tama* here—*tamatasuki* and *tamahoko*—in addition to *tamazusa* earlier. The reference to the crying of birds alludes to the belief that the departing spirit of the dead often assumed the form of a bird. In waving his sleeves, Hitomaro was performing a spirit-beckoning rite to call back his wife's spirit. Unless one understands this, Hitomaro's action of waving his sleeves is meaningless. The early Japanese did not consider death to be a permanent or irreversible state, at least for a short period after an individual had expired. Since death was believed to be a result of the spirit having left the body, various spirit-beckoning-related rituals were performed in an effort to attract the animating spirit back into the body. In this light, even in the twentieth century we can appreciate Hitomaro's action as a desperate attempt to deny the reality of the death of a loved one. Though the specific ritual expression is historically and culturally bound, the informing emotional response to death is recognizably more universal.

The mobility of the spirit was a source of anxiety for the early Japanese, as we have seen. In addition to rituals to recall a departed spirit, they had rituals to bind it (*tama musubu*) and others to restrict or impose boundaries on its movement. The latter practice is alluded to in two elegies (*banka*) found in *Ten Thousand Leaves* (MYS 2:151, 154; Levy 1981: 108, 109), from the time of the temporary enshrinement of the corpse of the Emperor Tenji (r. 661–671):

(151)

kakaramu no	If I had known
kokoro shiriseba	it would come to this,
ōmi-fune	I would have tied signs of interdiction
hateshi tomari ni	around the harbor
shimeyu wa mashi o	where the imperial craft did berth.

(154)

Sasanami no	For whom does the guardian
oyamamori wa	of Sasanami's imperial mountains
taga tame ka	post his signs of interdiction,
yama ni shimeyuu	now that you, my Lord,
kimi mo aranaku ni	are no longer?

Here, following the death of Tenji, the imperial consorts retrospectively lament the fact that when he had fallen ill they had not had rituals performed that might have kept his life spirit from leaving his body and passing into the mountains, the realm of the dead.

If the conditions of death were not deemed proper, the spirit leaving the body could be in a state of aggravation that required pacification. The recitation of poems to pacify certain spirits, a major type of ritual poetry in early Japan, is found in different forms throughout the Japanese religious tradition. Although most of the poems collected in the *Ten Thousand Leaves* concern the imperial family or courtiers, there are others that deal with anonymous figures. Here is a good example of this type of poem (*MYS* 2:22; Levy 1981: 141–143):

Sanuki no Samine no shima ni, ishi no naka ni mimakareru hito o mite, Kakinomoto Asomi no Hitomaro no tsukuru uta isshu narabe ni tanka	**Poem by Kakinomoto Hitomaro upon Seeing a Dead Man Lying among the Rocks on the Island of Samine in Sanuki, with Tanka**
tamamo yoshi	The land of Sanuki,
Sanuki no kuni wa	fine in sleek seaweed:
kuni kara ka	is it for the beauty of the land
miredomo akanu	that we do not tire
kamu kara ka	to gaze upon it?
kokoda tōtoki	Is it for its divinity
ametsuchi	that we deem it most noble?
hi tsuki to tomo ni	Eternally flourishing,
tariyukamu	with the heavens
kami no mi omo to	and the earth,
tsugite kuru	with the sun
Naka no minato yu	and the moon,
funa ukete	the very face of a god—
waga kogi kureba	so it has come down
toki tsu kaze	through the ages.
kumo i ni fuku ni	
oki mireba	Casting off
toi nami tachi	from Naka harbor,

he mireba	we came rowing.
shiranami sawaku	Then tide winds
isana tori	blew through the clouds;
umi o kashikomi	on the offing
yuku funa no	we saw the rustled waves,
kajihiki orite	on the strand
ochikochi no	we saw the roaring crests.
shima wa ōke do	Fearing the whale-hunted seas,
mei kuwashi	our ship plunged through—
Samine no shima no	we bent those oars!
ariso mo ni	Many were the islands
iorite mireba	near and far,
nami no to no	but we beached on Samine—
shigeki hamabe o	beautiful its name—
shikitae no	and built a shelter
makura ni nashite	on the rugged shore.
ara doko ni	
koro fusu kimi ga	Looking around,
ie shiraba	we saw you
yukite mo tsugemu	lying there
tsuma shiraba	on a jagged bed of stones,
ki mo towamashi o	the beach
tamahoko no	for your finely woven pillow,
michi dani shirazu	by the breakers' roar.
oboboshiku	If I knew your home,
machi ka kōramu	I would go and tell them.
washiki tsumara wa	If your wife knew,
	she would come and seek you out.
	But she does not even know the road
	straight as a jade spear.
	Does she not wait for you,
	worrying and longing,
	your beloved wife?
hanka nishu	[Two envoys]
tsuma mo araba	If your wife were here,
tsumite tagemashi	she would gather and feed you
Sami no yamano no	the starwort that grows
e no uwagi	on the Sami hillsides,
tōgi ni kerazu ya	but is its season not past?
okitsu nami	Making a finely woven pillow
kiyoru ariso o	of the rocky shore
shikitae no	where waves from the offing
makura to makite	draw near,
naseru kimi kamo	you, who sleep there!

The poet opens by praising the geographical place in terms reminiscent of the *kunimi* poems discussed earlier. This praise is not accidental, for the poem participates in the same symbolic and ritual complex. The headnote provides the purported occasion of the poem's genesis, yet the long first section does not introduce any human figures. Rather, it is devoted exclusively to praise of the land, which it declares beautiful and divine (*miredomo akanu kamu kara ka*, etc.). The identity of the drowning victim is unclear, as even Hitomaro does not know his name or hometown. Why, then, does Hitomaro use the long form (*chōka*) for this banka? Most scholars agree that such poems must have been part of a ritual performed for the pacification of the spirit of the accident victim, whose fate had denied him the normal funeral rites. Itō Haku, for example, sees this chōka and the envoys as a product of Hitomaro's participation in the traditional belief and ritual complex surrounding travel and of his service in the imperial court. Here Hitomaro seeks to pacify both the spirit of the land, through stylized praise, and the spirit of the dead, through recalling the love of the dead man's wife and suggesting that if only she knew where the corpse was, she would dutifully lament at his grave site.

The poem, however, is even more complex, for if the chōka is read carefully, one can see that Hitomaro also identifies himself with the drowning victim; he, too, is on a dangerous journey over the same seas that claimed this man's life. The effect of this rhetorical identification is once again to focus, although in a deflected or oblique manner, on the danger Hitomaro and his companions face in undertaking a journey ordered by a member of the imperial family. Ostensibly a poem on an anonymous drowning victim, Hitomaro takes the opportunity to turn it into another variety of a "boastful complaint" as he rehearses the horrors of the storm that forced his ship to beach on Samine. The poem, then, is quite complex in intention and in address, for it is directed in part to the kami of the place, praising the site's beauty and offering thanks for the party having found refuge there; in part to the spirit of the drowning victim; and in part to the assembled traveling companions of Hitomaro and ultimately to his patron in the imperial family. This fact suggests that Hitomaro was himself enmeshed in the rationality informing court society. In the middle section of the chōka he is not so much performing a ritual of pacification of the spirit of the dead man as he is rhetorically positioning himself within the ranks of court functionaries. This internal linkage of the poet's own situation with that of the drowning victim was not lost on the compilers of the *Ten Thousand Leaves*, for the very next poem in the anthology, 2:223, is reputed to be Hitomaro's lament on his own impending death far from his wife and home.

Kakinomoto Asomi no Hitomaro, Iwami no kuni ni arite mimakaramu to suru toki, mizukara itamite tsukuru uta isshu	**Poem by Kakinomoto Hitomaro in His Own Sorrow as He Was about to Die in the Land of Iwami**
Kamo yama no iwa neshi makeru ware o kamo	Not knowing I am sleeping with the rocks on Mount Kamo for a pillow,

shira ni to imo ga   is my wife waiting,
machi tsutsu aramu   waiting for me?

Ten Thousand Leaves 3:426–437 are all similar in theme, concerning both men and women whose corpses had been discovered, and all are categorized as banka. According to the headnotes, the corpses of the women in 428 and 429–430 were apparently cremated, indicating that this Buddhist practice was not unknown in Japan in Hitomaro's lifetime.

Two Types of Imperial Funeral Laments

The discernible differences in rhetorical content and effect in *banka* are a function of the respective positions of the deceased in the line of succession. For those who occupied critical positions in the court hierarchy, banka tend to be much more political and mythological, in an effort to legitimate the succession and the newly reconstituted court hierarchy. On the other hand, for individuals who were neither serious contenders in the succession nor pivotal figures in its determination, banka tend to rehearse the sense of loss felt by a surviving spouse. Such banka are much closer to the type of laments performed for individuals outside the imperial family.

Poem 2:199–202 is an example of the banka concerned with the imperial succession, whereas 2:196–198 (Levy 1981: 124–126, adapted) is an example of the second type of imperial banka. The latter reads:

Asuka no himemiko Kinoe no araki no miya no toki, Kakinomoto Asomi no Hito maro no tsukuru uta isshu narabe ni tanka	**Poem by Kakinomoto Hitomaro during the Period of the Temporary Enshrinement Palace of Princess Asuka, with Tanka**
tobu tori no	Crossing a bridge of stone
Asuka no kawa no	(one source says "stepping stones")
kamitsu se ni	over the upper shallows
iwahashi watashi	of the Asuka River,
(hitotsu ni iu, iwanami)	where the birds fly,
shimotsu se ni	crossing a plank bridge
uchihashi watasu	over the lower shallows.
iwahashi ni	Even when the *tamamo* [water plants]
(hitotsu ni iu, iwa nami ni)	trailing from
oinabikeru	the bridge of stone
tamamo mo zo	(one source says "stepping stones")
tayureba ouru	breaks, it grows;
uchihashi ni	even when the river weeds
oi o oreru	spreading
kawamo mo zo	beneath the plank bridge
karureba hayuru	withers, it sprouts again.
nani shi kamo	Why, then,

wago ōkimi no	do you, our Princess,
tataseba	forget
tamamo no mokoro	the morning palace
koyaseba	of our splendid Lord
kawatamo no gotoku	who, when you rose,
nabikaishi	yielded to you
yoroshiki kimi ga	like the *tamamo*,
asamiya o	who, when you lay down,
wasuretamau ya	stretched out
yuiniya o	like the river weeds?
somukitamau ya	And turn away from
utsusomi to	the evening palace?
omoishi toki	I recall the time
harube wa	you were in this world,
hana orikazashi	how in spring
aki tateba	you broke off and decorated
momijiba kazashi	yourself with blossoms,
shikitae no	and when autumn came
sode tazusawari	decorated yourself
kagami nasu	with colored leaves,
miredomo akazu	how your hempen sleeves
mochitsuki no	crossed.
iya mezurashimi	Like a mirror
omōshishi	you never tired of gazing
kimi to tokidoki	on the Lord,
idemashite	who you thought
asobitamaishi	as precious as
mi ke mukau	the full moon.
Kinoe no miya o	Sometimes with the Lord
toko miya to	you would go out
sadametamaite	on formal excursions
ajisawau	to the palace at Kinoe,
megoto mo taenu	where the sacred food trays
shikare kamo	face each other.
(hitotsu ni iu, soko oshimo)	But now that you have established
aya ni kanashimi	that palace for all eternity,
nuetori no	gone are the eyes that met him,
katakoi tsuma	your words he heard.
(hitotsu ni iu, shitsutsu)	Is that why our Lord,
asatori no	(one source says "in deep regret")
(hitotsu ni iu, asakiri no)	choked with sorrow,
kayowasu kimi ga	moaning his unrequited love
natsukusa no	like the tiger thrush,
omoishinaete	goes back and forth,
yūtsutsu no	like the morning birds,
kayuki kakuyuki	(one source says "the morning mist")
ōbune no	to attend you?
tayutau mireba	When we see him

nagasamuru	wilting like the summer grass,
kokoro mo aranu	staggering
soko yue ni	like an evening star,
semu sube shireya	reeling
oto nomi mo	like a great ship,
na nomi mo taezu	with a heart that cannot be consoled,
ametsuchi no	we know not what to do.
iya tōnagaku	Thus, at least let us remember
shinoiyukamu	if only the sound,
mi-na ni kakaseru	if only the name,
Asuka-gawa	forever far and long
yorozuyo made ni	as heaven and earth.
hashikiyashi	Let us remember
wago ōkimi no	for ten thousand years
katami ka koko o	the Asuka River
	that bears her precious name—
	this the *katami* of our beloved Princess!

tanka nishu	Two Tanka

Asuka gawa	If they had piled branches
shigaramiwatashi	across the Asuka River
seka maseba	to stop its course,
nagaruru mizu mo	even the streaming waters
nodo ni ka aramashi	would have become quiet.
(hitotsu ni iu, mizu no	(one source says "would have
yodo ni ka aramashi)	become a pool")

Asuka-gawa	Asuka River!
ashita dani	Even tomorrow alone
(hitotsu ni iu, sae) mimu	(one source says "if only")
to omoeyamo (hitotsu ni iu, omoe kamo)	I want to see you!
wago ōkimi no	(one source says "hope to")
mi-na wasuresenu	I cannot forget
(hitotsu ni iu, mi-na	the precious name of my Princess.
Wasuraenu)	(one source says "I will not
	forget the precious name")

This lament was probably presented by Hitomaro as a surrogate for the husband of Princess Asuka. Princess Asuka, a daughter of the Emperor Tenji and Tachibana no Iratsume, died on 4/4/700. The lament comes out of the period of temporary interment of the corpse in the *mogari no miya*. The number of variants mentioned in the interlinear notes suggest that this lament may have been performed numerous times, either at this temporary enshrinement palace or, quite possibly, for others who had died at other times. If the early Japanese practice was similar to other cultures where oral laments are performed, a number of reciters or singers probably offered the same basic lament.

The chōka opens by recounting the journey to the site of the princess's *katami*, a site that is especially associated with the deceased and where it was believed to be especially easy to make contact with the spirit of the deceased. Misaki Hisashi has pointed out that the term *uchihashi*, here rendered as "a plank bridge," is found in five other *Man'yōshū* verses (4:528, 7:1193, 1:256 and 262, and 17:399), four of which refer to the meeting of lovers. Thus, the basic theme of the banka, the love of the bereaved prince and the deceased Princess Asuka, is heightened by even the nouns used. The poet then draws a pointed contrast between two types of water plants that seem to die yet return to life and the death of Princess Asuka. Then in accusatory form the deceased is reprimanded: "Why, then, / do you, our Princess / forget / the morning palace / of our splendid Lord?" The tone may strike the modern reader as irreverent, but oral laments often include this type of recrimination (Alexiou 1974: 46, 106–107).

A prose endnote appended to 2:202, an envoy to a banka for Prince Takechi, clearly indicates that the early Japanese themselves recognized this emotional aspect of the grieving process in the performance of oral laments. The widowed princess presents offerings at the shrine for her husband but also voices her bitterness at his death. The endnote says: "The *Forest of Classified Verse* [*Ruiju karin*] says the above poem is 'by Princess Hinokuma in her resentment against the Nakisawa Shrine.'" The speaker, here said to be Hitomaro, is a surrogate for the bereaved. Thus, we must not be misled into assuming that the first-person "I" in such verses refers to the poet and indicates his personal emotional responses; rather, such an "I" often indicates the surviving spouse and at times even the deceased.

The chōka then goes on to recall the past and the joyous times the princess and her husband had. Aoki Takako has argued that banka on a deceased spouse often recall an idyllic past. Although not mythical per se, it is described in such a way that the "ravages of time" do not appear. The idyllic love of the prince and princess, which would seem to have lasted forever, is recalled in order to bring out in stark contrast the emotional desolation the princess's death has caused. The tone is still accusatory in that in dying, Princess Asuka is said to have turned her back on her faithful and loving husband. The responsibility for the suffering he is experiencing, as well as the sense of disorientation everyone in the court feels, is laid squarely at the princess's feet. But then the lament shifts to note the fact that the Asuka River shares the princess's name and flows by the palace at Kinoe where the couple used to travel together. Thus, this place has become her *katami*. In addition to expressing regret, the envoys (termed *tanka*, although they function here and are normally referred to as *hanka*) seem to allude to ritual efforts to pacify the spirit of the deceased (*tama shizume*) and to call it back. If only the prince had done something differently, perhaps time, like the flow of the river, could have been stopped and the princess's *tama*, like the once surging water, could have become calm and settled. Note, though, that the poem as a whole focuses not only on the deceased but also on the living. Part of the professional poet's duty in such cases seems to have been to declare formally the undying love of the surviving spouse for the deceased.

Nowhere in the entire poem, though, is there ever any mention of other contemporary historical events. The focus is entirely on the imperial couple and their love. The imperial succession and the survivor's relative status in the court hierarchy find no mention. In this, 2:196–198 is similar to another banka, 2:194–195, performed by Hitomaro for Princess Hatsusebe and Prince Osakabe. This poem is in sharp contrast, however, to 2:199–202, a banka for Prince Takechi, a son of the Emperor Temmu. It is the longest sequence in the *Man'yōshū* and has been stirringly rendered by Levy (Levy 1981: 127–131; 1984: 137–146). It is not necessary to cite the entire sequence here. Instead, I will merely draw out a few of the elements that distinguish this type of "political" public banka from what we have just seen.

Prince Takechi was a son of Temmu and led his father's troops in the Jinshin War in 672 in which Temmu (then Prince Ōama) gained the throne. He was married to a daughter of the Emperor Tenji, Princess Minabe. Following the death of the Emperor Temmu in 686, the Crown Prince Kusakabe was to have succeeded to the throne, but he died on 4/13/689 and Temmu's widowed empress acceded as the Empress Jitō. There is some evidence to suggest that at this point Takechi became the heir apparent. An entry in the *Chronicles* for 7/5/69 says, "The Imperial Prince Takechi was made Prime Minister" (Aston 1956: 2:398) This entry indicates that Takechi would have been in control of much of the daily administration of the government. He died, however, on 7/1/696 at the age of forty-two or forty-three. The *Chronicles* entry recording his death is, like that for Kusakabe's death, very brief: "His Highness the Later Imperial Prince died" (Aston 1956: 2:420). The reference to Takechi as *nochi no miko no mikoto*, the Later Imperial Prince, suggests that he succeeded Kusakabe as the heir apparent. Whatever the case may have been, it is clear that he was a major figure in the court and that his death would have had a great impact on the future succession. As it turned out, his demise made much easier the abdication of Jitō in favor of her grandson, Prince Karu (the Emperor Mommu), almost a year later.

With this brief background, it is easier to understand why the public performative banka at Takechi's temporary enshrinement palace would center on the imperial succession. The poem 2:199 (Levy 1981:127) evokes recent history in mythological terms. First, the death of the Emperor Temmu is recorded in mythic terms:

Asuka no	Our Lord,
Makami no hara ni	who, while we trembled,
hisakata no	fixed the far and heavenly
amatsu mi kado o	halls of his shrine
kashikoku mo	on the fields of Makami in Asuka
sadametamaite	and, godlike, has secluded himself
kamusabu to	in the rocks there.
iwagakurirnasu	

Dying is itself transformed into the intentional act of a divinity (*kamusabu to iwagakarimasu*)—an act that parallels Amaterasu's secluding herself in the "heavenly rock grotto." The chōka then says that the emperor "went down / as from heaven / to the provinces," again recalling the descent of the grandson of Amaterasu, Ninigi no mikoto, from the High Heavens to the earth. Then, like Amaterasu, the banka says he "gave the task to his son, he being an imperial prince [miko nagara] to pacify the raging rebels, / and subdue the land" (Levy 1981: 127–128). This section is followed by a long passage in which the swirl and terror of battle are conjured up (Levy 1981:128–129). Once again, though, the historical events are remembered and recounted in mythic terms: the victory of Temmu's troops is described as a result of divine assistance.

yuku tori no	As they struggled
arasou hashi ni	like zooming birds,
Watarai no	the divine wind
itsuki no miya yu	from the Shrine of our offerings
kamukaze ni	at Ise in Watarai
matowashi	blew confusion upon them,
amakumo o	hiding the very light of day
hi no me mo misezu	as clouds blanketed the heavens
tokoyami ni	in eternal darkness
ōitamaite	

This rhetorical device gives the reign of the Emperor Temmu and that of his descendants legitimacy through appeal to the intervention of the kami in human history. The chōka then alters its focus and moves to Prince Takechi. It mentions that Takechi was positioned to succeed and establish his own rule when he passed away. It also describes an interesting ritual mourning practice in the court:

Haniyasu no	On the fields
mi kado no hara ni	before the Haniyasu Palace Gate
akane sasu	we crawl and stumble like the deer
hi no kotogoto	as long as the sun
shishi ji mono	still streams its crimson,
ihaifushitsutsu	and when pitch-black night descends
nubatama no	we crawl around like quail,
yube ni nareba	turning to look up at the great hall [ōtono].
ōtono o	
furisakemitsutsu	
uzura nasu	
ihaimotōri	

The focus of the chōka is now on the desolation and disorientation the prince's death has occasioned. This focus is similar to what we saw in the banka for Princess Asuka, and indeed it will be found in almost all such laments. Then the emphasis and focus shift to the site of the mogari no miya. Once again the frustrated expectations of the living are rehearsed, and the deceased is assured that he will never be forgotten by the living. In sharp contrast to the lament for Princess Asuka, there is no mention of the love his wives and consorts had for Takechi. Instead, his career is rhetorically situated in a larger mythistory.

To appreciate this lament, we must imagine the poem recited in the presence of a large assembly of members of the court who occupied critical positions in the hierarchy, as Takechi did. The public banka on the occasion of Takechi's temporary enshrinement were used to legitimate Temmu's violent assumption of power in the Jinshin War by rhetorically transforming the events surrounding it into a mythistory. In this way, in their public performative roles, poets like Hitomaro helped to give legitimacy to Temmu's successors as well.

Several different forms of ritual poetry from the imperial court have been introduced here. Oral performative poetry was an important expression of the ceremonial nature of the court, a daily spectacle of sight and sound. It was also a resource that could be used in performance by different individuals for different purposes; it served still others when some *uta* were committed to writing and recontextualized. Most important, this poetry gained its coherence and meaning in a dynamic world of political ceremony and intrigue, designed to create and demonstrate power and prestige. Rather than merely reflecting a timeless or static collective ideal, it served as a means of articulating responses to incongruities experienced by the community and of pressing individual and factional claims.

Further Reading

Margaret Alexiou, *The Ritual Lament in Greek Tradition* (London: Cambridge University Press, 1974); W. G. Aston, Nihongi: *Chronicles of Japan from the Earliest Times to* A.D. 697 (London: George Allen & Unwin, 1956 [tr. 1896]); Robert H. Brower and Earl Miner, *Japanese Court Poetry* (Stanford: Stanford University Press, 1961); Edwin A. Cranston, "The Ramifying Vein: An Impression of Leaves—A Review of Levy's Translation of the *Man'yōshū*," *Journal of Japanese Studies* 9 (Winter 1983): 120; Gary L. Ebersole, "The Buddhist Ritual Use of Linked Poetry in Medieval Japan," *The Eastern Buddhist* n.s. 16, 2 (Autumn 1983); Gary L. Ebersole, *Ritual Poetry and the Politics of Death in Early Japan* (Princeton: Princeton University Press, 1989), esp. pp. 54–78, on which this article is based; Mircea Eliade, *Images and Symbols: Studies in Religious Symbolism* (New York: Sheed and Ward, 1969), esp. "The 'God Who Binds' and the Symbolism of Knots," pp. 92–124; Norbert Elias, *The Court Society*, tr. Edmund Jephcott (Oxford: Basil Blackwell, 1983); J. H. Kamstra, *Encounter or Syncretism: The Initial Growth of Japanese Buddhism* (Leiden: E. J. Brill, 1967); Ian Hideo Levy, tr., *The Ten Thousand Leaves*, vol. 1 (Princeton: Princeton University Press, 1981); Ian Hideo Levy, *Hitomaro and the Birth of Japanese Lyricism* (Princeton: Princeton University Press, 1984); Donald L. Philippi, *This Wine of Peace, This Wine of Laughter* (New York: Mushinsho Books, Grossman Publishers, 1968).

14

Japan's First Shingon Ceremony

David L. Gardiner

The title of this selection could be misleading since there are various meanings of the word *shingon*. Since it literally means "true word(s)" and is a common translation for the Sanskrit *mantra*, a "shingon ceremony" could refer to any of a wide variety of Buddhist rituals that took place in Japan from the eighth century on that employed the recitation of the potent formulae known also as *dharani*. Or, since it also designates the name of the Buddhist school founded by Kūkai (774–835) around 816 some ten years after he returned from a two-year stay in China, the title could denote the first official ceremony conducted under the auspices of this representative organization of Esoteric Buddhism in Japan. In actuality, the title draws our attention to something in between these two possible interpretations: to the first recorded ceremony performed by Kūkai after his return from China prior to his efforts to establish a recognized school. Kūkai has become such a celebrated cultural hero in Japan that it may be hard for some to imagine that there was ever a time when he was not famous, but in fact he was not a very visible public figure until several years after he came back in 806, from studying Esoteric Buddhism in the T'ang capital of Ch'ang-an. He left China in the eighth month of 806, and it is thought that he arrived on the southern island of Kyushu by the tenth month. The present text, *Votive Text on the Occasion of a Memorial Ceremony for the Departed Mother of Lieutenant Governor Tanaka of Dazaifu (Ten no shōni ga sembi no kisai o makuru ga tame no gammon)*, was written in Kyushu in the second month of the following year and is the earliest record we have of Kūkai's activities after his travels abroad. Although traditional accounts have him leaving Kyushu within a year to reside in the capital area near Nara and Kyoto, there are indications that he may have resided in Kyushu for as long as three years before moving to the capital. In either case, his movements in these initial years are not well documented, so the present text offers an important opportunity to glimpse the early activities of the man whose later efforts were to have a profound and lasting impact on Japanese religion and culture.

The text is known in Japanese as a *gammon*, or a "votive document" that records

the performance of a religious rite and the circumstances in which it was performed. We know that Kūkai wrote more than forty such documents and that
both Japanese and Chinese precedents influenced their form and content. The
majority of his gammon were, like the present one, drafted on the occasion of a
memorial ceremony in honor of a deceased relative of someone whom Kūkai
knew. Moreover, most of these ceremonies were also, like this one, performed on
behalf of a government official for the sake of his former mother. Indeed, a large
number of Kūkai's extant gammon record ceremonies memorializing matriarchs
of the powerful Fujiwara family. The Fujiwara clan's role in aristocratic court
circles so dominated Japanese politics in the late ninth through eleventh centuries
that this period is often referred to as the Fujiwara era. Their dominance was
primarily acquired by the practice of marrying Fujiwara maidens to crown princes,
thus assuring that subsequent sons of the sovereign (and thus subsequent sovereigns) would be of Fujiwara blood and connections. This aspect of marriage-
politics is not directly reflected in Kūkai's numerous gammon, but the important
role of the mothers who resulted from such marriages is highlighted by the pre-
ponderance of memorial ceremonies in their behalf found in his writings.

The genre of Kūkai's gammon also reveals what must be considered a vital
dimension of the propagation of the new religious forms he brought back from
China. It is difficult to think about the dissemination of a religious teaching in
the purely abstract terms of doctrine, but when the concrete aspects of a memorial
rite come into focus, with paintings of deities, the hand-copying of scripture, the
recitation of sacred formulae, and the promise for the deceased of salvation in the
afterlife by encountering the beneficient power of the Buddha Dainichi ("Great
Sun," according to Shingon doctrine, the cosmic Buddha from which originate
all other Buddhas and bodhisattvas), it becomes easier to see how concepts related
to the symbols and functions of religious rites gained currency. One fundamental
way in which the Shingon school took root in the culture of Heian Japan was
through the appeal, on a sensory side, of its elaborate and beautiful liturgies, and
on a more intellectual side, of its comprehensive and compelling worldview. These
liturgies embraced not only memorial services but a variety of ceremonies for
which the power and blessing of the Buddha was invoked, such as initiatory rites,
rites to forestall or ameliorate the conditions of a natural or human disaster, rites
to assure the well-being of the Sovereign and peace throughout his realm and so
on. The liturgies employed colorful robes, sonorous chanting coupled with rhyth-
mic bell ringing, paintings and statues of mysterious deities (many of which were
new to Japan), and other alluring accoutrements of the Esoteric Buddhist cult.
And while the glamour of the elaborate paraphernalia and human movements,
on the one hand, and the coherent depiction of the virtues of a cosmic Buddha
and other deities who respond to such rites, on the other, ought both to be
considered parts of the quintessentially aesthetic attraction that Shingon Buddhism offered, it is particularly on the side of the materiel cult that we can discern
an important contribution made by the aristocratic sponsors of such ceremonies.
The production of paintings, copying of scriptures, and other components of the

rituals required patrons to fund them. It is thus hardly surprising that a religious specialist like Kūkai would have turned to persons of high rank and office in order to promote Shingon practices. It was a reciprocally beneficial relationship, however, and constituted an important type of "economy of exchange" within Heian court society. Indeed, the Esoteric (or Tantric) Buddhist tradition seems to have flourished throughout Asia primarily in close contact with the royal class.

The text translated here records a memorial for the mother of the lieutenant governor in Dazaifu, which was the central government's headquarters in western Japan. The content of this gammon is quite consistent with similar documents Kūkai wrote over the next thirty years. As do most of these texts, this one begins by praising the Buddha as being the most efficacious vehicle for repaying the great debt owed to one's parents. The reasoning behind this is that the Buddha has the power to liberate the spirit of the deceased, and what greater act of filiality could there be than the gift of salvation? As exhibited also in other Buddhist traditions, there operates here a belief in the special opportunities for enlightenment available to "spirits" after they have left the body. Unlike some traditions, however, there seems to be no particular time limit attributed to the spirit's existence, evidenced by the fact that the ceremony took place a year after the death. It is commonly recognized that very few Japanese accepted the "orthodox" Indian Buddhist concept of rebirth (for example, that for a human rebirth the intermediate state would be only forty-nine days) so that their views of the afterlife tended to be syncretic and reflected indigenous conceptions.

Following the praise of the Buddha is a eulogy to the deceased. Here Kūkai describes her virtues with flowery allusions to classical Chinese literature. This portrayal is coupled with a lamentation on the truth of impermanence and expressions of the grief felt by all who knew her. He then turns to an account of the rites performed, where he begins by noting the deity images that were reproduced in painting for the occasion and the scriptures that were copied. Although no mention is made, it should be understood that the act of reproducing sacred images and texts generates merit that in turn is to be dedicated to the spirit of the deceased. The particular combination of deities painted for this memorial (the Thousand-armed and -eyed Kannon and the Sixteen Great Bodhisattvas from the Diamond Realm mandala) does not appear in any of Kūkai's other extant gammon, but the two texts reproduced, the *Lotus Sutra* and the *Heart Sutra* (two of the most popular scriptures throughout all of Japanese history), not surprisingly were also copied for other memorial ceremonies.

Next follows a very brief description of the rites, which states only that the area was cleaned, special seats were arranged for the monks, flowers were placed, and prayers were made. The prayers are mostly for the benefit of the awakening of the deceased mother's spirit but extend also to the well-being of the bereaved. Beyond this, however, the prayers continue to radiate outward to include the sovereign, his ministers, and all beings of heaven and earth. The transfer of some of the merit of the rites to the royal court may strike some as sychophantic, and indeed it would be a mistake to think that Kūkai was unaware of the benefits that might (and eventually did) accrue to him from gaining favor from the throne. But this dedication is also consistent with a belief that the virtue of the sovereign is a power that covers the people in the nation like a beneficial rain. Thus in praying that the members of the court act righteously, Kūkai was in effect praying for the welfare of the entire realm. Furthermore, by dedicating the merit obtained from this ceremony to Lieutenant Governor Tanaka's mother, the sovereign court, and all beings, Kūkai was following a traditional pattern of expressing gratitude to the "four benefactors (*shi on*)—our parents, the sovereign, all sentient beings, and the Buddha (the last was expressed at the beginning)—a practice with a scriptural precedent and of which Kūkai was particularly fond.

Finally, it seems worthwhile to comment on an aspect of Buddhism during the Heian period that is reflected in this document. It is sometimes said that Buddhist teachings did not really penetrate deeply into the minds of Japanese people until the Kamakura period (1185–1333), when new forms of more "popular" Buddhism, such as Pure Land, Nichiren, and Zen, began to flourish. There can be no doubt that the reformation that took place during the Kamakura period brought forth simpler, more direct forms of Buddhist practice that were accessible to a much wider population than ever before. The dominant paradigm for the Heian period was Esoteric practice, which for the most part entailed complex rites for which few people could spare the requisite time, expense, and devotion. For various reasons it is fitting to claim that Heian Buddhism was primarily an upper-class affair. But this fact need not lead to the conclusion that Buddhist teachings were therefore only superficially understood and had no significant impact on the development of Japanese culture or of individual lives. Even if early on this world-view was limited, as were many of the rituals, to the aristocracy, the kinds of power intrinsic to this class of persons ensured that they were the bearers of cultural forms, symbol systems, and beliefs that unfolded over time into wider domains. The sort of worldview presented in this gammon—of the magnificent compassionate powers of a transcendent Buddha to which all beings living and dead have vital access through the performance of carefully regulated solemn ceremonies—was by all accounts an exceedingly influential one that eventually touched the lives of far more than just the handful of families in the court aristocracy. This text, and the many others like it, demonstrate one very concrete way in which a certain Buddhist model of the world began to take root in Japan.

The translation is based on the text published in Watanabe Shōkō and Miyasaka Yūshō, eds., *Sangō shiiki, Shūryōshū*, in Nihon koten bungaku taikei 71 (Tokyo: Iwanami Shoten, 1975): 332–335.

Further Reading

David L. Gardiner, "Kūkai and the Beginnings of Shingon Buddhism in Japan," Ph.D. dissertation, Stanford University, 1995; David L. Gardiner, "Mandala, Mandala on the Wall: Variations of Usage in the Shingon School," *Journal of the International Association of Buddhist Studies* 19, 2 (1996): 245–279; Yoshito Hakeda, tr., *Kūkai: Major Works* (New York: Columbia University Press, 1972); Taikō Yamasaki, *Shingon: Japanese Esoteric Buddhism* (Boston and London: Shambhala, 1988).

Votive Text on the Occasion of a Memorial Ceremony for the Departed Mother of Lieutenant Governor Tanaka of Dazaifu

With reverence, I consider that the debt we owe to our two parents for nourishing our bodies is great. In order to repay with our gratitude this debt as large as a mountain and as deep as the sea, on whom can we rely except the Buddha? There is no place where the Buddha's power does not extend. When depending on and looking up to Him, His attitude is like that of a parent toward its child: without consideration of like and dislike. Once we have established a relationship with His supernatural power, there is no limit to the reach of His compassionate vows. In both the bestowing of happiness and the removal of suffering, there is never any suspension of His activity. The vastness of His virtuous power is truly beyond our capacity to describe or even to conceive.

In humility, I recall that the former mother of Mr. Tanaka was a most virtuous wife, as can be seen in the progeny issued from her, which are as numerous as the creeping vines in a melon patch and as elegant as a grove of peaches. As an exemplar of motherhood, her renown was comparable to the fragrance of an orchid garden. It is our sincere wish that her descendants regard her for generations to come with the utmost in filial piety. It is hard to believe that she, who was as precious as an orchid or a pearl from the kingdom of Ch'u, could disappear as quickly as the morning dew. Oh, how we ache from our mournful cries. Our excessive grief is surely a recompense from nonvirtuous deeds performed in the past. The bereaved all feel as if they have swallowed fire or drunken poison and have been unmindful of the passage of time. But the months move as swiftly as an arrow; suddenly we are faced with the first-year memorial. Her virtue was rich and deep, and our longing to repay it knows no bounds.

Thus it is that on the eleventh day of the second month of the second year of Daidō [807], we most reverently made paintings of thirteen sacred deities: the Thousand-armed, Thousand-eyed Bodhisattva of Great Compassion [Kannon (Sanskrit: Avalokiteśvara)] as well as of the Four Great Bodhisattvas of Gathering and the Eight Great Bodhisattvas of Offering [attendants of the Buddha Dainichi in the Diamond Realm mandala]. In addition, we presented handscribed copies of the the *Lotus Sutra* in eight scrolls and of the *Heart Sutra* in two scrolls. Furthermore, in order to offer worship to the various deities, we swept clean the garden and sprinkled water about, set up a few seats for the performance of religious rites, and modestly arranged some fragrant flowers. We humbly prayed that the ocean of virtuous power of the Buddhas wash over her spirit so as to purify it; that the mist of delusion be lifted so that she may see the great sun [Dainichi]; and that she come to possess the mirrorlike wisdom that will illuminate the true nature of all things. May the marvels of the Dharma and its boundless workings also bring blessings to the relatives who remain, bestowing them with long life and good health.

When a vassal or a child is righteous, he always pays respect where it is due. We dedicate the superior merit derived from these rites in offering to the court of the sagely sovereign. May the golden wheel of the king who rules by the power of Dharma turn continuously, and the ten virtuous courses of action be augmented and renewed. May the crown prince, other princes, the state ministers and administrators unite together in wholehearted devotion to faithful service, and may happiness and plenty be secured for all. May the five kinds of heavenly beings and all living things of the ten directions together be gratified in the feast of Dharma that is of a single taste, and may they all move freely about within the palace of ultimate reality.

—15—

Shingon Services for the Dead

Richard Karl Payne

Most basically, Japanese thought divides the dead into two major categories: the proximate and remote dead. The proximate dead are the recently deceased. They are treated individually and carry with them all of the mingled, ambiguous feelings of love and fear. The remote dead are distinguished from the proximate dead by the fact that they are treated collectively. The remote dead are in turn divided into two categories, ancestors and *muenbotoke*. While ancestors provide protection and security, *muenbotoke* are ambivalently threatening and pitiful. *Muenbotoke* are "Buddhas" (*hotoke*, a euphemism for the dead) lacking (*mu*) a relation (*en*), that is, those dead who do not receive the proper ritual transformation, either because they have no living relations or because they die far from home. The difference between ancestors and *muenbotoke* is the relation between some living person and the deceased: ancestors are those who, having had such a relation while they were a soul in transition, were able successfully, positively to fade from the memory of the living group as a unique individual and join the anonymous collectivity of the ancestors. There is not one ancestor for a family, but rather many whose separate identities are lost as each one merges with the rest. *Muenbotoke*, lacking the support of relatives during the period of transition, fail to become part of any living family's (*ie*) anonymous collectivity of ancestors. They have failed to attain the status of ancestors because they have not been cared for while they were in their transitional status as proximate dead. From this perspective they are to be pitied rather than feared, although given the ambiguity of their identity as outsiders, even during the annual "Festival of the Dead" (*urabon, obon*), they are not invited into the house but fed outside.

Ritual actions facilitate the passage from recently deceased to ancestor. This transition can be divided into three phases—proximate, distant, and remote—with the addition of an intermediate stage between the beginning and end. The change from proximate to distant occurs on the forty-ninth day, while transition from distant to remote (i.e., status as a full ancestor) occurs on the thiry-third year. (Some ethnographic reports indicate that this process stretches out for fifty years.) Treatment of the memorial tablet (*ihai*) is what reveals these categories. At death two memorial tablets are made, one being left at the gravesite, the other staying in the home, where it is placed below the family altar, often together with a photograph. On the forty-ninth day, at the transition from proximate to distant, the memorial tablet is raised to the family altar and receives special treatment only on memorial days. At the time of the last memorial service (*tomurai age*), when the transition from distant deceased to remote ancestor takes place, the memorial tablet should be taken to the temple, though this seems to rarely happen. The anonymity of the ancestors is indicated by the fact that at this time the individual memorial tablet should be displaced by a tablet listing all of the generations of ancestors of a particular house (*ie no senzodaidai ihai*). This three-part division of the dead might be illustrated by distinctions found in the Japanese language between the three pronouns *kore*, *sore*, and *are*. *Kore* is used to refer to the location near to the speaker, while *sore* is used to refer to the location near to the hearer but at a distance from the speaker, and *are* is used for any location away from both the speaker and the hearer.

There are thirteen memorial days on which rites are performed for the sake of the deceased. These days have their associated buddhas or bodhisattvas, a grouping that dates from the Muromachi era (1338–1573). The mantra for these Thirteen Buddhas (*jūsan butsu*) are often recited as a group in contemporary Shingon service. The sequence of the Thirteen Buddhas is as follows:

first seventh day: (Skt.) Acala/(J.) Fudō
second seventh day: Śākyamuni/Shaka
third seventh day: Mañjuśrī/Monju
fourth seventh day: Samantabhadra/Fugen
fifth seventh day: Kṣitigarbha/Jizō
sixth seventh day: Maitreya/Miroku
seventh seventh day: Bhaisajyaguru/Yakushi
hundredth day: Avalokiteśvara/Kannon
first anniversary: Mahasthamaprapta/Seishi
third anniversary: Amitābha/Amida
seventh anniversary: Akṣobhya/Ashuku
thirteenth anniversary: Mahāvairocana/Dainichi
thirty-third anniversary: Ākāśagarbha/Kokūzō

At the end of this process, the deceased becomes an ancestor, no longer remembered as an individual. The basic division between proximate and remote dead is reflected in the rituals of the Shingon tradition. At the time of death the "Ritual of the Clear Light Mantra" (*Kōmyō shingon bō*) is performed for the salvation of the deceased. However, at Obon, the festival held at midsummer when both ancestors and *muenbotoke* are considered to return to this world, the "Ritual for Feeding the Hungry Ghosts" (*Segaki hō*) is performed for all of the dead. According to Buddhist cosmology coming from India, hungry ghosts (J. *segaki*, Skt. *preta*) are one of the six kinds of possible rebirths in the realm of material desire (J.

yokkai, Skt. *kamaloka*). They suffer from hunger and thirst that can never be satisfied. They are portrayed as having enormous stomachs and very tiny necks. Whatever they put into their mouths bursts into flames, and they are therefore also called "flaming mouths."

The Ritual for Feeding Hungry Ghosts seems to have been created in T'ang dynasty China. The Obon festival as we know it today in Japan results from the integration of the Indian Buddhist practice of making gifts to monks at the end of the rainy season retreat (Avalambana, Ullambana), the Hindu festival of Divali, indigenous Chinese practices associating offerings to the dead with the harvest season, and indigenous Japanese practices, for example, dances performed only at this time of year, the Bon Odori.

The political purpose for creating the Hungry Ghosts ritual was to present Buddhism as not running counter to the Confucian virtue of filial piety. One of the main sources for the Obon in China was the legend of Maudgalyāyana (Ch. Mu-lien, J. Mokuren), who makes offerings to monks at the end of the rainy season so as to free his mother from her status as a hungry ghost. All versions of the Mulien/Mokuren myth assume the unity of the ideals of Buddhism and the Chinese ideal of filial piety.

It may be that Amoghavajra (705–774), one of the patriarchs of Esoteric Buddhism in China, propagated the *segaki* ritual, for it was during Amoghavajra's time that the indigenous Chinese agricultural festival for the dead celebrated in the middle of the seventh lunar month was intermingled with two Buddhist ceremonies originating in India. One of these was offering food to the Buddha and sangha for the benefit of seven generations of one's ancestors, while the other was an offering of food to the hungry ghosts. Note that the distinction between these two Indian Buddhist rites matches the distinction between ancestors and *muenbotoke* described above.

An examination of *An Abbreviated Ritual for Feeding the Hungry Ghosts* (*Segaki ryaku sahō*), which is currently in use in the Shingon tradition, reveals that there is no identification between the practitioner and some chief deity. This is particularly surprising since ritual identification, that is, the practitioner's visualization of him/herself as identical with the deity evoked (*kaji*), is the defining characteristic of Esoteric Buddhist rituals. Three of Amoghavajra's Hungry Ghost texts are specifically ritual in character (T 1315, 1318, and 1320), and in none of these is ritual identification performed.

Indeed, the structure of the *Ritual for Feeding Hungry Ghosts* differs from the standard Shingon ritual format, which is based on the metaphor of feasting deities. Instead, the *Ritual for Feeding Hungry Ghosts* is structured around visualizing the feeding of the hungry ghosts and invoking the names of five Tathāgatas, who are referred to in Japanese as Kakohōshyō Nyorai, Precious Conqueror; Myōshikishin Nyorai, Beautifully Shaped Body; Kanrohō Nyorai, Nectar/Ambrosia King; Kōbakushin Nyorai, Wide and Vast Body; and Rifui Nyorai, Giver of Fearlessness.

While it is often said that Buddhism was transmitted to Japan from China, the rituals for the dead indicate that the statement needs two qualifications. First, there is a great deal of continuity between the Indic forms of Esoteric Buddhist practice and the Japanese forms. Second, given this continuity it is also important to realize that the Esoteric Buddhist tradition in Japan created new rituals. In fact, there are periods of great creativity. It would appear that the most important periods of ritual creativity were the T'ang period in China and the Kamakura era in Japan. Although the newly created rituals were based on existing paradigms and existing contents, it still indicates that the ritual tradition has not been as rigidly conservative as lineages of ritual practice are sometimes thought to be. Like any other performing art form, ritual practice must continue to change and grow to stay alive.

These rituals also tell us about changing conceptions of the dead in Japan. For instance, the now popular concept of *en* (cause or connection, that is, the opposite of *muen*) important for the Japanese ancestral cult, has its origins in Indian Buddhist discussions of causality. Buddhism contributes not only *hotoke* as a euphemism for the deceased, but also the concept of *en* as the means by which the recently deceased become ancestors, rather than wandering, hungry ghosts. It would seem then that one of the motivations for the spread of Esoteric Buddhism in Japan was concern for the status of the dead. The desirable outcome is for the recently deceased individual to be transformed into a member of the anonymous mass of ancestors. Buddhism has contributed to Japanese ways of thinking about the dead and has developed rituals appropriate to that transformation. This ritual and its history show both the continuity of Esoteric Buddhist ritual practice from India to Japan and the way in which ritual practices are created by a living lineage.

The translation is based on Nakagawa Zenkyō, ed., *Shingon-shū jōyō shokyō yōshu, Shōwa shintei* (Kōyasan: Kōyasan Shuppansha, 1980): 337–348.

Further Reading

Emily M. Ahern, *The Cult of the Dead in a Chinese Village* (Stanford: Stanford University Press, 1973); Gary L. Ebersole, *Ritual Poetry and the Politics of Death in Early Japan* (Princeton: Princeton University Press, 1989); William H. Newell, ed., *Ancestors* (The Hague and Paris: Mouton Publishers, 1976), esp. Maeda Takashi, "Ancestor Worship in Japan: Facts and History," pp. 139–161; Herman P. Ooms, "A Structural Analysis of Japanese Ancestral Rites and Beliefs," pp. 61–90; and Takeda Choshu, "'Family Religion' in Japan: Ie and Its Religious Faith," pp. 119–128; Charles Orzech, "Saving the Burning-Mouth Hungry Ghost," in *Religions of China in Practice*, ed. Donald S. Lopez, Jr. (Princeton: Princeton University Press, 1996): 278–283; Robert J. Smith, *Ancestor Worship in Contemporary Japan* (Stanford: Stanford University Press, 1974); Stephen Teiser, *The Ghost Festival in Medieval China* (Princeton: Princeton University Press, 1988).

An Abbreviated Ritual for Feeding the Hungry Ghosts

One should face in an easterly direction, and must avoid (standing) beneath a peach, willow, or pomegranate tree.

First, the rite for protecting the body. (Perform) quietly, please.
Next, the Three Refuges:

Homage to the Buddhas in the ten directions.
Homage to the Dharma in the ten directions.
Homage to the Sangha in the ten directions.
Homage to the Greatly Compassionate Bodhisattva Avalokiteśvara.

Next, the *gatha* for giving food:

This sacred dharani empowers and purifies food and drink; give these to each of the departed spirits, as multitudinous as the sands of the Ganges.

Fulfilling my vow, abandoning attachment to my body, [I pray that] they may speedily escape the hell-realms, start on the good path, and take refuge in the Three Jewels, thereby generating the aspiration for enlightenment [*bodhicitta*] and in the end realizing the highest awakening and merit without limit. Til the end of time may all sentient beings be equally filled with food.

Next, the mudra that gathers together all of the hungry ghosts [*preta*]:

Extend the five fingers of the right hand, twist the thumb and middle fingers together, beckon with the index finger, [and recite]:

Naubo bo ho rikya ritari tatagyataya, three times.
[Homage to the Tathāgata who resides everywhere on earth, fulfilling his (religious) mission for the salvation of all beings.]

Imagine all the *preta* in the entire *dharmadhatu* gathering together here.

Next, the mudra that bursts open the gate of the earth prison and causes the constricted throats to open:

With the prior mudra, do not beckon with the index finger, snap the thumb and middle two fingers together with each *dharani*.

On bo ho teiri. Kyari tari tatagyataya, three times.
[Same meaning as above.]

Next, the mudra that empowers food and drink:

With the prior mudra, rub the thumb with the tip of the middle finger three times. Then snap the thumb and index fingers once for each recitation:

Naumaku saraba tatagyata barokitei. On sanbara sanbara un, three times.
[Homage to all the Tathāgatas who look down upon the world, merciful ones, *om*, gather here.]

Imagine each of the *preta* receiving seven [times] seven Magadha bushels (*koku*) of food. After consuming it all, [they find themselves] already reborn in one of the eight pure lands. [They] perform devotions, and their evil karma is eradicated and their life span increased.

Next, the mudra of the ambrosia-flavored Dharma. [Form] mudra of fearlessness [, and recite:]:

> *Naumaku soro haya tatagyataya. Tanyata on soro soro hara soro
> hara soro sowaka,* three times.
> [Homage to the Tathagata of the superior form, please come out,
> come out and show us, *svaha*]

Imagine the food and drink, as well as the water, transforming, becoming
milk and ambrosia, and that the many *preta* receive it equally.

Next, visualization of the water *cakra*. Mudra of offering all *preta* food and
drink:

> Open the fingers of the right hand like the lid to a food dish, [and recite:]
>
> *Nomaku samanda bodanan ban,* three times.
> [Homage to all the buddhas, *vam*]

Imagine that milky water of ambrosia pours forth endlessly from the gate of
the water syllable (*vam*); and that all *preta* are satisfied without the slightest
scarcity.

Next, disburse the food.
Next, sincere praise of the names of the Five Tathāgatas.

> Ring the bell three times. [Because a bell may scare the hungry ghosts,
> wooden clappers are used instead.]
> Homage to Kankohōshyō Nyorai: remove petty karmic attachments and per-
> fect merit and wisdom.
> Homage to Myōshikishin Nyorai: destroy [these] hideous forms and perfect
> the marks [of a Buddha].
> Homage to Kanrohō Nyorai: fill the heart of the Dharmakaya with order
> [, so all may] receive pleasure.
> Homage to Kōbakushin Nyorai: open [their] throats so as to receive large
> [quantities] of food and drink.
> Homage to Rifui Nyorai: abolish fear, and prevent any likelihood [of rebirth
> as] a hungry ghost.

Next, [the mantra of] producing *bodhicitta* [the aspiration for enlightenment].
(Ring the bell.)

> *On boji shitta bodahada yami,* three times.
> [*Om,* produce the mind of awakening.]

Next, [the mantra of] the *Samaya* precepts. (Ring the bell.)

> *On sanmaya satoban,* three times.
> [*Om,* you, the pledge]

Next, Clear Light (*kōmyō*) mantra. [Form the] mudra of the five colored lights
[, and recite]:

> *On abokya beiroshano maka bodara mani handoma jimbara hara bari*
> *taya un*, three times.

(Next, [recite the] *Heart Sutra*.)
  (Next, prayers)
  The vow to give this food produces merit here.
  Now distribute the offering everywhere [to] all *preta* [and] sentient beings
    in the *dharmadhatu* [so that] both will be born in a pure land and swiftly
    become Buddhas.

Next, leave-taking.

> *On bazara bokisya boku*, three times.
> [*Om* perpetual liberation *muh*]

Next, transfer of merit.

> [I] vow that all of this merit,
> being given over entirely
> to self and others, causes
> all living beings to enter the path of the Awakened Ones.

—16—

Genshin's Deathbed Nembutsu Ritual
in Pure Land Buddhism

James C. Dobbins

Buddhism is sometimes depicted as a religion of reason rather than of myth. In it individuals take control of their fate and attain enlightenment and liberation through their own mental and moral efforts. This depiction of Buddhism, though valid in many ways, does not do justice to Buddhism's mythic dimension, pervasive especially in Mahāyāna, nor to the blurring of inward and outward forces that lead to enlightenment. Pure Land Buddhism, one of the Mahāyāna schools, is a study in contrasts to this depiction. It sees sacred story, or myth, not as an obstacle to religious advancement but as the only viable path. Part of that story is that the powers leading to liberation originate not with the individual but with an all-pervasive and resplendent Buddha known as Amida.

Pure Land Buddhism had its beginnings in India, but it emerged as a widespread movement in China and Japan. It is predicated on the idea that among the countless Buddhas that populate the universe, all of whom are expressions of the single reality of nirvana, there is one, Amida, who offers a particularly felicitous and compelling path to enlightenment. In a series of vows, Amida made clear that he would create a Buddha sphere, or a Pure Land, in which nirvana is assured to all born there. He is constantly at work trying to bring living beings to birth in Pure Land. His inexhaustible light extending in all directions is a symbol of his constant presence and reflects his ubiquitous embrace of all sentient beings. The key to attaining birth in Pure Land is not the rigorous practices often associated with Buddhism—e.g., breaking all attachments and achieving insight into the true nature of reality—but rather the special practices and devotions of the Pure Land scriptures: aspiration to be born in Pure Land, meditative visions of Amida's radiance and Pure Land's splendors, offering up good works in dedication to the Buddha and Pure Land, and chanting single-mindedly and with reflection Amida's name, known as the *nembutsu*, in the form *Namu Amida Butsu*, "I take refuge in the Buddha Amida." Generally speaking, meditative visions were seen as the more efficacious practice but, based on passages in the Pure Land scriptures, even ten reflections on Amida or ten successive chants of the nembutsu were deemed sufficient for birth in Pure Land. In fact, because the nembutsu is a pure religious practice created by Amida, it is considered potent enough to eradicated the karmic effects of profound wrongdoings. Through these practices one could be born in Pure Land at death and would attain enlightenment expeditiously, if not instantaneously.

There is a tendency to view Amida and Pure Land in the worst sense, as mythic creations abandoning the rarified truths of Mahāyāna Buddhism—e.g., the idea of emptiness, or that nirvana is none other than *saṃsāra*, or that ultimate reality is inherent in every circumstance and experience. The Pure Land path, by contrast, comes across as a dualistic worldview, a flight from this flawed world to a perfect world after death. To appreciate Pure Land, it is crucial to realize that its mythic visions were never considered at odds with Mahāyāna truth of nondualism. Functionally, Amida and Pure Land may be treated as independent realities, but the school always acknowledged them to be inherently empty, or undifferentiated from the very minds of living beings. The importance of Pure Land Buddhism is not that it posits a new dualistic vision to supplant Mahāyāna nondualism, but that it assumes that Mahāyāna higher truths are inaccessible to human beings in their present state. Pure Land therefore offers a path to those truths through form, specifically mythic form. If one can use the ideal images of Amida and Pure Land to develop an intensity of mind and clarity of vision, then one is set irrevocably on the path to highest realization, nirvana, albeit in the next life. Pure Land is intended, therefore, not to contradict Mahāyāna's ultimate truths but to actualize them.

The following text is from the *Collection on Essentials for Birth in Pure Land* (*Ōjōyōshū*) by the eminent Tendai priest Genshin (942–1017). It describes the deathbed ritual for Pure Land adherents, including practice of the nembutsu, visions of Amida and Pure Land, and a sequence of reflections conductive to birth in Pure Land. Death was always seen in Buddhism as a crucial event, for one's last moment of consciousness could condition one's next birth. The Pure Land school inherited this concern and sought to focus the dying person's thoughts on Amida and Pure Land. According to the scriptures, Amida and a retinue of saintly figures would appear before the dying believer and usher the person into Pure Land at death. This belief became the basis for the deathbed ritual that Genshin and his fellow Pure Land enthusiasts popularized among Buddhists of eleventh-century Japan. In trying to define the procedures for this ritual, Genshin drew passages from a variety of Buddhist texts. He organized them into a description of the ideal conditions for the ritual and appended ten reflections that attendants of the dying believer should encourage in the person during the deathbed watch. Of the ten, he considered the seventh, eighth, and ninth most important: visions of Amida's physical characteristics, his all-embracing light, and his appearance at the believer's deathbed. The tenth reflection is reserved for the moment of death. This ritual was followed widely in Japan during premodern times.

The translation is an excerpt fronm chapter 6 of the *Ōjōyōshū* in *Genshin* in Nihon shisō taikei 6, ed. Ishida Mizumaro (Tokyo: Iwanami Shoten, 1970): 206–214.

Further Reading

Allan A. Andrews, *The Teachings Essential for Rebirth: A Study of Genshin's* Ōjōyōshū (Tokyo: Sophia University Press, 1973); Robert E. Morrell, *Early Kamakura Buddhism: A Minority Report* (Berkeley: Asian Humanities Press, 1987); August Karl Reischauer, "Genshin's Ojoyoshu: Collected Essays on Birth into Paradise," *Transactions of the Asiatic Society of Japan*, second series, 7 (1930): 16–97.

Genshin's *Nembutsu for Special Occasions*

With regard to the deathbed ritual, I will first explain the practice and then explain the reflections encouraged during it.

First, concerning the practice, [the following] is a quotation from *Accounts of the Middle Kingdom* (*Chung-kuo ch'eng-ch'uan*) [as cited] in the "Caring for the Sick and Dying" section of *Notes on the Four-Part Vinaya* (*Ssŭ-fēn lü ch'ao*):

> In the northwest corner of the Jetavana retreat where the setting sun [can be seen], there is constructed the Impermanence Hall. If people are ill, they are placed within it. The reason they are moved to this separate location is that people subject to craving will have no dispassion of mind and will give rise to all types of attachments if they gaze on their robe, begging bowl, and other implements in their own building. The name given to this hall is Impermanence. There are many who have come here, but only one or two who have returned from it. In this immediate setting one seeks [Pure Land] and reflects on the Dharma single-mindedly. Within that hall a standing image [of the Buddha] is installed. It is covered in gold leaf, and it is turned facing the western direction. The right hand of that image is raised, and the left hand is grasping a single, five-colored pennant, the tail of which hangs down to the ground. The sick person should be placed behind the image, holding the tail of the pennant in the left hand. As [the sick person] follows the Buddha, thoughts of going to the Buddha's pure realm should be generated. Those caring for the sick should light incense, sprinkle flowers, and adorn the sick person. Moreover, if there is any excrement or vomit, it should be removed right away.

Or, it also states:

> Have the image of the Buddha facing east, and place the sick person in front of it.

(I would add: If there is no separate place [to move to], simply have the sick person face the west, light incense, sprinkle flowers, and give various forms of encouragement. Or, you should have the person look at a fully adorned image of the Buddha.)

The Master Shan-tao said:

Whether believers are ill or not, when their life is about to end, they should compose their mind and body using exclusively the *nembutsu* meditation method described above. They should turn their countenance toward the west, concentrate their mind, and contemplate Amida Buddha. They should coordinate mind and voice with each other, and there should be constant chanting [of the nembutsu]. They should generate the thought of being born in Pure Land without fail and of [Amida's] saintly host coming with a lotus throne on which to usher them into Pure Land. If the sick see this scene before them, they should turn to those caring for them and describe it to them. Those looking after them should record it just as described once they have heard the complete description. If the sick are unable to speak, then those caring for them should by all means ask the sick what scenes they are seeing. If they describe images of wrongdoing, then those by their side should say the nembutsu for them and assist them by performing repentance with them. By doing so, all wrongdoing will be eradicated without fail. If wrongdoing is successfully eradicated, then the saintly host with the lotus throne will appear before them in accord with their thoughts. That also should be recorded as before.

If the believers' relatives or six next-of-kin wish to visit the sick, do not admit any person who has consumed liquor, meat, or the five pungent foods. If such people do come in, by all means do not allow them to approach the side of the sick. Otherwise, they might lose the correct [train of] thought, and baleful spirits might confuse them. The sick might die in a state of madness and fall into one of the three unfortunate rebirths. Our wish is that believers will tend toward self-restraint by themselves, that they will uphold the Buddhist teachings, and that at the same time they will generate a karmic bond leading to a vision of the Buddha.

To generate thoughts of birth in Pure Land or of being ushered into Pure Land is well grounded in principle. The *Treatise of Great Wisdom and Liberation* (*Ta lun*) expounds on the mysterious workings of mind in the following way:

When the apprehension of the image of ground is dominant, one can walk on water as though it were ground. When the apprehension of the image of water is dominant, one can enter into ground as though it were water. When the apprehension of the image of fire is dominant, one's body can give off smoke, fire, and so forth.

One should realize that, whatever might be sought, when one apprehends its image, one is able to assist the thing along and to actualize it. This does not occur only at the point of death. It is similar in ordinary circumstances also.

Master Tao-ch'o said:

To have ten uninterrupted reflections in succession would not seem difficult. But most unenlightened individuals have a mind as untamed as a horse and a consciousness as impetuous as a monkey. It races among the six types of sensory objects wondering what would ever make it rest. Properly speaking, you should generate faith, and from the beginning engrave it on your heart; you should train yourself repeatedly so it becomes second nature; and you should fortify yourself in the root of good works. The great king [Bimbisāra] said the following: "If a person accumulates good practices, then at death there will be no evil thoughts. When a tree tips over and falls, it always seems to follow the direction in which it is bent." Whenever the winds of death and dissolution come in a single instant, then a hundred pains will gather in the body. If you have not trained prior to this time, how can you assume that the nembutsu will come to mind then? Each person should thus make a pact in advance with three to five people of like conviction. Whenever the time of death approaches [for any of them], they should offer each other mutual encouragement. They should chant the name of Amida for the dying person, they should long for that person to be born in Pure Land, and they should continue chanting to induce the ten moments of reflection [in the person's mind].

The ten reflections mentioned here have been interpreted in many different ways, but by and large they have been defined as single-minded reflection and chanting of *Namu Amida Butsu* [the nembutsu] ten times. This definition is in accord with passages in the sutras. . . .

Next, [I will describe] the reflections encouraged during the deathbed [ritual]. Good friends and fellow believers who have these religious concerns—in order to follow the Buddhist teachings and to benefit sentient beings, as well as to cultivate the good and [beneficial] karmic bonds—should visit the person's sickbed from the first moment that illness arises and should graciously offer encouragement. But the content of that encouragement should accord with the thoughts of the sick person. If I were addressing myself, I would tentatively frame these words:

> You, as a follower of the Buddha, have spent years overcoming worldly ambitions and performing just [the nembutsu,] the practice leading to the Western Paradise. What you have been anticipating above all else from the very beginning are these ten moments of *nembutsu* reflection at death. Now as you lie in your sickbed, it is impossible not to be afraid. But you should simply close your eyes, hold your hands together in reverence, and single-mindedly vow in expectation. You should not visualize any form except the features of the Buddha. You should not hear any sounds except the Buddha's words of Dharma. You should not speak of anything except the true teachings of the Buddha. You should not think of anything except birth in Pure Land. In this way when your life at last comes to an end, you will find yourself seated on a jeweled lotus throne, following behind Amida Buddha,

surrounded by his saintly host, and passing by billions of worlds. Thus you should not establish a karmic bond with any other land. You should go directly to the seven-jeweled pond of [Pure Land's] realm of paradise. Once there, you will open your eyes, hold your hands together in reverence, behold the blessed appearance of Amida, hear his profound words of Dharma, smell the fragrant virtues of all the Buddhas, taste the joy of Dharma and the delight of meditation, prostrate yourself before the oceanlike assembly of saints, and actualize Fugen Bodhisattva's vows of practice.

Now we come to the ten items [of reflection]. You should listen to them and reflect on them single-mindedly. Reflect on them one at a time, and do not allow doubt to arise in your mind.

1. You should understand how Mahāyāna's knowledge of the real arises and the origins of *saṃsāra*. A verse from the *Great Perfect Enlightenment Sutra* (*Ta yüan-chiao ching*) says the following:

Ignorance, dreamlike and beginningless in all sentient beings, arises out of the perfectly enlightened mind of all the Tathāgatas.

You should realize that *saṃsāra* is none other than nirvana, that mental afflictions are none other than enlightenment, that they are all melded together perfectly without obstruction, and that they are neither dual nor separate from each other. But you entered the world of *saṃsāra* from your first moment of illusory thought. From that time, you have been blinded by the sickness of ignorance and have long forgotten the path of original enlightenment. All Dharmas from the very beginning constantly bear the mark of quiescence in themselves. Like a dream, they have no set nature, but they are transformed [into what they are not] by the mind. Thus, as a follower of the Buddha, you should reflect on the three treasures [Buddha, Dharma, and Sangha]. You should overturn what is false and return to what is true. The Buddha is the physician, the Dharma is the medicine, and the Sangha is the person caring for the sick. There is no equal to the Buddha, the Dharma, and the Sangha for eliminating the sickness of ignorance, for opening the eye of right views, for revealing the path of original enlightenment, and for guiding one to Pure Land. Hence, as a follower of the Buddha, you should first bring to mind the great physician, and reflect single-mindedly on the Buddha. . . . *Namu Amida Butsu†* (ten times or more). Next, you should bring to mind the marvelous medicine and reflect single-mindedly on the Dharma. . . . Next you should bring to mind the guardians surrounding you and reflect single-mindedly on the Sangha. . . .

(If it seems appropriate, chant along in unison [with the sick person]. Or, keep cadence with a bell to enhance proper *nembutsu* practice. . . .)

2. Dharma-nature is all-pervasive, but it does not stand apart for our relative existence. Amida Buddha has said: "All dharmas are empty and devoid of individual identity. To comprehend this, seek the Buddha's Pure Land exclusively, and you will attain [birth in] that land without fail." In order to be born in Pure Land, the first step is weariness of this world. The present *sahā* world is affected by evil acts and is the source of all types of sufferings. You transmigrate without end through birth, old age, sickness, and death, and there is not one torment of these three realms that is desirable. If you do not grow weary of this world in the present, then in what lifetime will you be able to escape transmigration? But Amida Buddha is imbued with a wondrous power. If you chant his name single-mindedly, then amid the succession of nembutsu reflections the karmic effects of grave wrongdoings that would bind you for eight billion eons in *saṃsāra* will be eradicated. Thus, you should now reflect on the Buddha single-mindedly, and you will be released from this realm of suffering. You should generate the thought: "My aspiration is for Amida Buddha to come to my aid. *Namu Amida Butsu†*."

(When you see that the faith derived from these ten nembutsu has expended its energy, you should then encourage [the sick person] in the next item. . . .)

3. You should long for Pure Land. The Western Paradise is the Mahāyāna realm rooted in good works and is a place without suffering or affliction. When you have once been granted a lotus throne, you will forever escape *saṃsāra*. Your eyes will behold the saintly appearance of Amida; your ears will hear the sublime and revered teachings; and there will be no joy or happiness lacking whatsoever. If you chant and reflect on Amida Buddha ten times when dying, it is certain you will be born in that land of bliss. You, as a follower of the Buddha, [have been fortunate enough to] receive a human body in this [lifetime] and also to encounter the Buddhist teachings. [Such an event is as rare] as a one-eyed turtle [swimming to the surface and poking its head] through a hole in a floating log. If you do not attain birth in Pure Land at this time, you will again fall into the three unfortunate rebirths with their eight types of miseries. It will be even more difficult to hear the Dharma. How much more so will it be to attain birth in Pure Land? Thus, you should single-mindedly chant and reflect on the Buddha's [name]. You should generate the thought: "My aspiration is for the Buddha to guide me and bring me to birth in paradise without fail today. *Namu Amida Butsu*."

4. Because you desire to be born in that land, you should pursue practices leading to it. Among the Buddha's principal vows is the following:

> Were I to attain Buddhahood, and yet if sentient beings of the ten directions were not to achieve their reward even though they heard my name, concentrated their thoughts on my land, cultivated the basis of manifold virtuous acts, sincerely offered up [those acts] in dedication, and desired to be born in my land, then I would not accept true enlightenment.

As a follower of the Buddha, you have earnestly performed practices leading to the western [Pure Land] throughout your life. Although the practices performed are many in number, your goal has been only one, paradise. You should now draw together once more whatever good works of the three times [past, present, and future] that are rooted in you, and offer them all up in dedication to the paradise. You should generate the thought: "My aspiration is that, based on the power of all the good works rooted in and possessed by me, may I be born in paradise without fail today. *Namu Amida Butsu.*"

5. Among the principal vows, there is also the following:

> Were I to attain Buddhahood, and yet if I were not to appear surrounded by my great host before sentient beings of the ten directions at the time of their death, even though they gave rise to the aspiration for enlightenment, performed manifold virtuous acts, and sincerely established a vow desiring to be born in my land, then I would not accept true enlightenment.

You, as a follower of the Buddha, have always given rise to the aspiration for enlightenment. You have also offered up in dedication to paradise the manifold good works rooted in you. You should now give rise once more to the aspiration for enlightenment and reflect on the Buddha. You should generate the thought: "My aspiration is to be born in paradise without fail today, so that I might bring benefit and happiness to all sentient beings. *Namu Amida Butsu.*"

6. You know already that, as a follower of the Buddha, you have equipped yourself from the beginning with the [nembutsu] practice that leads to birth in Pure Land. Now as you reflect exclusively on the Tathāgata Amida, you should apply yourself to that practice all the more. The virtues of the Buddha are limitless and immeasurable and can never be described completely. Each of the other Buddhas residing in the ten directions, as countless as the sand of the Ganges, constantly praises the virtues of this Buddha. They could spend countless eons praising them in this way and still not exhaust them all. You, as a follower of the Buddha, should take refuge in that Buddha's virtues single-mindedly. You should reflect: "May I, in this moment of reflection now, take refuge in all the manifold virtues of the Tathāgata Amida. *Namu Amida Butsu.*"

7. As a follower of the Buddha, you should reflect on the physical appearance of Amida Buddha and allow that single image to reside in your mind. It is said that the physical body of the Buddha is gold like the riverbed in the Jambu forest. He is towering in his stateliness, like the golden mountain king, and his body is adorned with immeasurable features. Among them, the white tuft of hair (Skt. *ūrṇā*) between his eyebrows curls gracefully to the right, [as majestic] as five Sumeru mountains. Seven billion fifty-six million rays of light blaze out from it, as brilliant as thousands or millions of suns and moons. This is the result of his manifold untainted virtues, flowing from his great meditation, wisdom, and compassion. If you reflect on this feature for even an instant, then the karmic effects of grave wrongdoings that would bind you for nine billion six hundred million eons in *saṃsāra*—or for trillions or for as many as the Ganges' sand or as particles of dust—will be eradicated. Thus, you should now concentrate on this feature [of the Buddha], and you will eradicate the karmic effects of wrongdoings. You should generate the thought: "My aspiration is for the light from that feature, the [Buddha's] white tuft of hair, to eradicate all my wrongdoing. *Namu Amida Butsu.*"

8. The variegated light from this feature, the white tuft of hair, constantly shines on sentient beings of the nembutsu in the worlds of the ten directions. It embraces them and never forsakes them. You should know that the light of great compassion shines upon you unfailingly. A verse from the *Flower Garland* (Hua-yen) [*Sutra*] says the following:

> Emitting the light refers to seeing the Buddha. The light causes those who are dying to awaken to enlightenment. In the nembutsu meditation they will definitely see the Buddha. At the point of death they will be born in the presence of the Buddha.

Thus, you should now generate the thought: "My aspiration is for Amida Buddha to emit his pure light, shining upon my mind afar, causing my mind to awaken to enlightenment, overturning my three attachments—to objects, to self, and to rebirth—allowing me to complete the nembutsu meditation and attain birth in the paradise. *Namu Amida Butsu.*"

9. The Tathāgata Amida, in addition to emitting his light from afar, constantly comes himself with [the Bodhisattvas] Kannon and Seishi to guard over believers. How indeed the father and the mother are earnestly heavy of heart over their sick child! [The Buddha] moves the [unshakable] mountain of Dharma-nature and plunges into our ocean of *saṃsāra*. You should know that at this moment the Buddha is emitting his light, he is coming with all his saintly host, and he is guiding you and guarding you. Even though confusions and obstructions intervene making it difficult for you to see [the Buddha], you must not doubt his great compassionate vow. It is certain that he will enter this room. Thus, as a follower of the Buddha, you should generate the thought: "My aspiration is for the Buddha to emit his great light and to come without fail to usher me into birth in the paradise. *Namu Amida Butsu.*"

(You should constantly offer encouragement [to the sick] using items seven, eight, and nine above. Use the other items on an occasional basis.)

When the strength of the sick is about to dissipate at last, you should say: "The Buddha has arrived along with Kannon, Seishi, and his immeasurable saintly host. They are offering you the jeweled lotus throne, and they are guiding you, the follower of the Buddha [, to Pure Land]."

10. When the end has truly come, you should say: "Follower of the Buddha, do you realize it? This is your last thought. This single reflection at death outweighs [all] the karmic acts of a hundred years. If this instant should pass you by, rebirth [in *saṃsāra*] will be unavoidable. Now is precisely the time. Perform the nembutsu reflection single-mindedly, and it is certain you will be born on the seven-jeweled lotus throne amid the pond of eight virtues in the sublime Pure Land of the Western Paradise. You should generate the thought: "The principal vow of the Tathāgata is not off the mark even by a hair. My aspiration is for the Buddha to guide me [to Pure Land] without fail. *Namu Amida Butsu.*" Or, you should use the somewhat abbreviated form of reflection: "My aspiration is for the Buddha to guide me unfailingly. *Namu Amida Butsu.*"

Thus, you should monitor the condition of the sick and adopt whatever accords [best] with it. Make the item [above] the very last reflection, and do not allow [the person] to have an abundance [of thoughts]. Use great care in the words you instruct [the person to say]. Do not allow [other] objects of perception to arise in [the mind of] the sick.

17

Women and Japanese Buddhism:
Tales of Birth in the Pure Land

William E. Deal

By the middle of the Heian period (794–1185), aristocratic Buddhism centered increasingly on a desire for birth in the Pure Land, or the Western paradise of Amida Buddha. Birth in the Pure Land was to be achieved by a combination of the recitation of the name of Amida Buddha (*nembutsu*) and the five practices of upholding, reading, chanting, preaching, and copying the *Lotus Sutra*. It was believed that the merit accrued by such ritual acts gained one entrance into the Pure Land, a view expressed time and again in Heian period texts.

These ideas arose from the Tendai school's association of *Lotus Sutra* practices with birth in the Pure Land (*ōjō*). Founded in the early Heian period, Tendai was an interpretation of the Chinese T'ien-t'ai school. From its inception, Japanese Tendai included a rather eclectic array of practices, incorporating Pure Land, Esoteric, and other Buddhist ideas into its Buddhological views. Thus, Japanese Tendai monks meditated, recited the name of Amida Buddha, performed Esoteric rituals, and took vows to uphold the monastic precepts. The Enryakuji temple on Mount Hiei, the Tendai headquarters, became an important center for Buddhist thought and practice in the Heian period.

This eclecticism was not something confined to the monasteries but was also embraced by Heian aristocrats. Nowhere was this more apparent than at the Hōjōji, the great Heian aristocrat Fujiwara no Michinaga's temple complex. The Hōjōji was a monument to both the depth of Michinaga's faith and the disparate practices that marked Heian period religiosity. For instance, the different halls that comprised the Hōjōji included the Shakadō (Śākyamuni Hall), the Midō (Amida Hall), the Godaidō (Hall of the Five Great Mystic Kings), the Yakushidō (Healing Buddha Hall), and the Sammaidō (Contemplation Hall), represent teachings from a broad cross-section of East Asian Buddhist traditions.

In the mid-Heian period the promotion of Pure Land aspirations within the structure of Tendai thought came especially from the monk Genshin (Eshin, 942–

1017), whose famous *Ōjōyōshū* (The Teachings Essential for Birth in the Pure Land) vividly depicts the vicissitudes of hell and the pleasures of the Pure Land of Supreme Bliss (*gokuraku jōdo*). Genshin believed that recitation of the name of Amida Buddha, done with a faithful attitude, was enough to gain one birth in the Pure Land. Unlike the later Kamakura Pure Land schools, however, Genshin did not think that nembutsu practice was the only means to salvation. Genshin's Buddhology was situated within the context of the eschatological belief that Japan was about to enter into the age of the degenerate Dharma (*mappō*), a period in which it would be extremely difficult to gain salvation through one's own efforts alone. In such a time, one needed to rely on the vow of Amida Buddha to save all who would faithfully recite his name. The *Ōjōyōshū* is frequently referred to in subsequent Heian period texts.

Genshin's treatise on the Pure Land required a well-educated readership able to grasp the many quotes from Buddhist texts. There was another genre of Buddhist literature, however, that taught Pure Land faith through short didactic tales that told the spiritual biographies of those who had gained birth in the Western paradise. Biographies of people born into the Pure Land of Amida Buddha are known generically as "biographies of those born into the Pure Land" (*ōjōden*). The earliest collection of such stories, *A Record of Japanese Born into the Pure Land* (*Nihon ōjō gokuraku ki*), was compiled by the scholar Yoshishige no Yasutane (934?–997) around the year 985. He had been involved in starting the Kangaku-e, or Assembly for the Encouragement of Learning, in 964. Its membership included both Tendai monks and scholars of Chinese studies who came together for the purpose of studying the *Lotus Sutra*, writing devotional poetry, and reciting the nembutsu. Yasutane and his colleagues are typical of the mid-Heian period practice of combining the *Lotus Sutra* with Pure Land rituals in hopes of gaining birth in the Pure Land.

One of the distinctive aspects of this literature is the inclusion of stories about pious women, often from aristocratic or bureaucratic families, who were able to attain birth in the Pure Land. The issue of whether women could attain enlightenment was a topic of debate within Buddhism. The *Lotus Sutra*, clearly prized in the Heian period, states that women are capable of gaining salvation. In the "Devadatta" chapter (chapter 12) of the *Lotus Sutra*, the story is told of the eight-year-old daughter of the Dragon King, who is said to have gained enlightenment upon hearing the *Lotus Sutra* preached. There are bodhisattvas who do not believe this is possible. The dragon girl appears before the assembled bodhisattvas, one of whom questions her, saying:

> You say that in no long time you shall attain the unexcelled Way. This is hard to believe. What is the reason? A woman's body is filthy, it is not a Dharma-receptacle. How can you attain unexcelled bodhi [wisdom]? The Path of the Buddha is remote and cavernous. Throughout incalculable kalpas [ages], by tormenting oneself and accumulating good conduct, also by thoroughly cultivating perfections, only by these means can one then be successful. Also, a woman's body even then has five obstacles.

It cannot become first a Brahmā god king, second the god Śakra, third King Māra, fourth a sage-king turning the Wheel, fifth a Buddha-body. How can the body of a woman speedily achieve Buddhahood? (Hurvitz 1976: 200–201)

The dragon girl, in response to the doubts expressed about her ability to gain enlightenment, instantaneously turns into a man and achieves Buddhahood. Important to understanding Heian views of women and salvation is the *Lotus Sutra's* articulation of the concept of the five obstacles (*goshō*), that is, the five kinds of births that are denied woman because their bodies are too impure to gain Buddhahood directly. There is strong evidence that the five obstacles were well-known in the Heian period, and that women were aware of the Devadatta chapter and the story of the dragon girl. Tale 40 of the *Biographies of Japanese Born into the Pure Land, Continued* (*Zoku honchō ōjō den*) makes explicit reference to the five obstacles and suggests, as does the *Lotus Sutra,* the possibility that these need not be an insurmountable hindrance to birth in the Pure Land.

Further support for women's salvation is provided in chapter 23 of the *Lotus Sutra,* "Former Affairs of the Bodhisattva Medicine King," which makes explicit the possibility of birth in the Pure Land for women who uphold the *Lotus Sutra.*

> If a woman, hearing this chapter of the Former Affairs of the Bodhisattva Medicine King, can accept and keep it, she shall put an end to her female body, and shall never again receive one. If after the extinction of the Thus Come One, within the last five hundred years, there is then a woman who, hearing this scriptural canon, practices it as preached, at the end of this life she shall straightway go the world-sphere Comfortable (Sukhāvatī) [the Pure Land], to the dwelling place of the Buddha Amitāyus [Amida], where he is surrounded by a multitude of great bodhisattvas, there to be reborn on a jeweled throne among lotus blossoms, never again to be tormented by greed, never again to be tormented by anger or folly, never again to be tormented by pride, envy, or other defilements. (Hurvitz 1976: 300)

It is notable that in tales of birth in the Pure Land men are often depicted as engaging in a combination of *Lotus Sutra* rituals and nembutsu practice. Women, however, are usually portrayed as only reciting the nembutsu. Thus, the religious lives of Heian men and women, though directed toward the same goal, were distinguished by conceptions of spiritual differences based on gender. Men apparently held the attitude that women were only capable of the "easy" practice of the nembutsu, whereas men, able to read and understand the profundity of the *Lotus Sutra,* could engage in both kinds of rituals. The tales about women translated below mention only nembutsu practice. Of the forty-two tales that comprise *A Record of Japanese Born into the Pure Land* (*Nihon ōjō gokuraku ki*), nine are about women and do not mention the *Lotus Sutra.* The eight tales that explicitly mention *Lotus Sutra* practice and birth in the Pure Land are about men. Further gender distinctions are evident in the fact that women are not often identified by name, but rather in terms of their relationship to men, such as husbands, fathers, and brothers.

Tales of birth into the Pure Land are typically formulaic. For instance, in the stories about women translated below, the women are often depicted as having been pious from an early age. Frequently they have not married, or have otherwise exhibited a disinterest in the mundane affairs of daily life. Rather, they are depicted as having directed their energies toward Buddhist practice. Descriptions of their often gentle and compassionate natures provide further evidence of their spiritual insight. Finally, these tales, even when they do not state explicitly that someone was born into the Pure Land, describe the auspicious signs that are proof that Amida has come to welcome one into the Western paradise, such as heavenly music, purple clouds, and the beatific countenance of the newly deceased.

The stories of women born into the Pure Land translated here are from two collections of tales, *A Record of Japanese Born into the Pure Land* (*Nihon ōjō gokuraku ki*), compiled by Yoshishige no Yasutane around the year 985, and *Biographies of Japanese Born into the Pure Land, Continued* (*Zoku honchō ōjō den*), compiled by Ōe Masafusa (1041–1111) in 1101.

Translations are based on Inoue Mitsusada and Ōsone Shōsuke, eds., *Ōjōden-Hokke genki*, Nihon shisō taikei 7 (Tokyo: Iwanami Shoten, 1982). Bureaucratic ranks, lists of names of otherwise unknown people, alternative readings for names, and other such material have sometimes been omitted from the translations in the interest of readability. Quotations from the *Lotus Sutra* are taken from Leon Hurvitz, tr. *Scripture of the Lotus Blossom of the Fine Dharma* (New York: Columbia University Press, 1976).

Further Reading

Allan A. Andrews, *The Teachings Essential for Rebirth: A Study of Genshin's* Ōjōyōshū (Tokyo: Sophia University, 1973); William E. Deal, "The Lotus Sutra and the Rhetoric of Legitimization in Eleventh-Century Japanese Buddhism," *Japanese Journal of Religious Studies* 20, 4 (December 1993): 261–295; Yoshiko Kurata Dykstra, tr., *Miraculous Tales of the Lotus Sutra from Ancient Japan: The* Dainihonkoku hokekyōkenki *of the Priest Chingen* (Osaka: Intercultural Research Institute, Kansai University of Foreign Studies, 1983); Hori Ichirō, *Folk Religion in Japan: Continuity and Change*, ed. Joseph M. Kitagawa and Alan A. Miller (Chicago: University of Chicago Press, 1968); Leon Hurvitz, tr., *Scripture of the Lotus Blossom of the Fine Dharma* (New York: Columbia University Press, 1976); Edward Kamens, tr., *The Three Jewels: A Study and Translation of Minamoto Tamenori's* Sanbōe, Michigan Monograph Series in Japanese Studies 2 (Ann Arbor: Center for Japanese Studies, University of Michigan, 1988).

A Record of Japanese Born into the Pure Land

TALE 30

There was a nun who was the granddaughter of the Emperor Kōkō. She married at a young age and gave birth to three children. One after the other these three children died. Shortly thereafter, her husband also passed away. Widowed, she profoundly felt the impermanence of this world and so took the tonsure and became a nun. She ate only once a day. Several years passed and the nun suddenly developed a pain in her hips and was unable to move very easily. A doctor told her that she suffered from fatigue and that if she did not eat meat, her condition would not improve. However, the nun valued neither her body nor her life. More than ever, she recited the name of Amida Buddha. Her pain subsided of its own accord.

The nun was by nature gentle and deeply compassionate. Mosquitoes and flies would feed on her body, but she would not even try to swat them away. When she was more than fifty years old, she suddenly suffered a slight pain. Music reverberated in the sky, causing the neighbors to marvel. The nun said, "Amida, you have already come to welcome me into the Pure Land. I now desire to depart this world." So saying, the nun breathed her last.

TALE 31

There was a nun who was the older sister of Great Bishop Kanchū. Long a widow, toward the end of her life she entered the Buddhist path. Kanchū welcomed her to live in the vicinity of his temple and took care of her daily needs. As the nun approached the end of her life, she did nothing but recite the name of Amida Buddha. She said to Kanchū, "The day after tomorrow I will go to paradise (the Pure Land). In the interim, I wish to practice the meditation known as the Continuous Nembutsu." Kanchū had the monks of his temple practice nembutsu meditation for three days and nights. The nun again spoke to Kanchū, her words mingling with her tears: "Right in front of me there is a jeweled cart that has flown here from the west. However, Amida and the bodhisattvas think this place is impure and have gone back." Kanchū twice had music played and the sutras chanted. The next day the nun said, "The holy assembly has again come. It is now time for me to be born into the Pure Land." She sat leaning against a small table and, reciting the nembutsu, died.

TALE 32

There was a nun from the village of Kamutsuhira in the Iidaka district of Ise Province. She renounced the world late in life and fervently recited the name of Amida Buddha. For many years she had thought of peeling off the skin on her hand and reverently drawing a picture of the Pure Land paradise on it. Although her wish was sincere, she had been unable to peel off the skin herself. At that time, a monk came along, peeled off the skin on her hand, and immediately disappeared. The nun reverently drew an image of the Pure Land on it. Not once did she let it out of her possession. When she died there was music in the heavens. The Dharma teacher Shinrai of Ishiyama-dera was her descendant. It is said that one of Shinrai's younger sisters was also born into paradise. Three people from the same family achieved birth in the Pure Land.

TALE 37

A woman disciple, the wife of Tomo no Hikozane, governor of Ōmi Province, constantly recited Amida's name from the time she was a child. She married in her thirties, but, because she was Hikozane's niece, they did not share the same bed. On the last day of her life, she sat in front of the Womb Realm mandala. She said to Hikozane, "For a long time I have made the female servant do disgusting work. I will surely receive retribution for this sin. In order to expiate this sin, I want to give the female servant a house." Hikozane at once consented to her request. She spoke again: "There is a small thing preventing my birth into paradise. When I calmly consider it, I recall that some years ago someone sent me several carp. Among these, two were still alive so I released them at once into a well. Because the well is small, these carp have undoubtedly longed for the rivers and lakes. Is this not what is preventing my birth in the Pure Land?" Accordingly, she had the carp taken out of the well and released into the river. As this woman was about to breathe her last, the fragrance of lotus blossoms filled the room and a cloud wafted in through the bamboo screen. Without pain in her body, she faced the west and died.

TALE 38

A woman disciple was the daughter of Ono no Takaki, governor of Yamashiro Province, and the mistress of Sukeyo, major controller of the right. From the time she was very young, her heart was with the Buddha's Dharma. She addressed her older brother Enkyō, a priest, saying, "I desire knowledge of the path to enlightenment. I pray that you will grant me this understanding." Enkyō excerpted important passages from the *Sutra of Meditation on Amida Buddha* (*Kanmuryōjukyō, T* 365) and various sutra commentaries and gave them to her. She studied them day and night, reverently, without ever losing interest. At twilight on the fifteenth of each month she prostrated herself on the ground, and, facing the west, she prayed, chanting, "Praise to the Western Pure Land." Her father and mother admonished her, saying, "Young people are not normally like this. We fear that you will trouble your spirit and destroy your body." When she was twenty-five years old, she gave birth, for the first time, to a girl. About a month later, she suddenly suffered pains. In the end, after spending ten days lying in distress, she died. That evening, music filled the skies, and the neighboring villagers were filled with sacred joy.

TALE 39

A woman disciple of the Fujiwara family was by nature gentle and deeply compassionate. She always yearned for birth in paradise, ceaselessly reciting the nembutsu. Late in her life she remarked to others, "I can hear music far off in the distance. This is surely an auspicious sign that I will be born into the Pure Land." The following year she again said, "The music is gradually getting closer." The following year she remarked again, "The music gets closer with each passing year. It has come very close now—I can hear it from above my bedroom. Now surely the time has come for me to be born into the Pure Land." No sooner had she spoken these words than she passed, without pain, from this world.

TALE 40

There was a woman of the Okinaga family from Sakata district in Ōmi Province. Every year she picked the lotus flowers growing in the Tsukuma inlet and gave them as an offering to Amida Buddha. She fervently hoped for birth into paradise. In this way, many years passed. When she died, a purple cloud enveloped her body.

TALE 41

There was an old woman from Iidaka district in Ise Province. The first fifteen days of each month she fervently engaged in Buddhist practices, while she attended to her worldly affairs for the last fifteen days. As part of her Buddhist practices she always bought incense and reverently offered it at the Buddhist temples in Iidaka district. Every spring and autumn she picked flowers and included them in her offerings. She also gathered up such things as salt, rice, fruit, and vegetables and gave them as alms to the monks. She regularly did things like this. The woman passed many years with the desire to be born into paradise.

She became sick for several days and her children helped her sit up so that she could eat. Her clothes, which she had worn for a long time, had naturally become dishevelled. She clutched the stalk of a lotus flower in her left hand. The petal was about twenty-four centimeters wide and did not resemble any flower from this world. It had a beautiful bright color, and from it emanated a lovely fragrance. Her nurses asked her where the flower came from, and she replied, "The beings who will welcome me into the Pure Land previously gave me this flower." Immediately she died. Those who witnessed this were filled with joy.

TALE 42

There was a woman in Kaga Province whose husband was wealthy. After he died, she had no desire to remarry, and she lived as a widow for several years.

A lotus flower grew in a small pond near her house. She always prayed, saying, "When this flower opens into full bloom, I will surely be born into the Western paradise. Then, with this flower, I will make an offering to Amida Buddha." Whenever there were blossoms, she would take them from her pond, divide them up, and give them as offerings to the temples in her district. One time, after the widow grew old, she became ill when the lotus bloomed. She rejoiced, saying, "My flower has bloomed and I've gotten sick. I will surely be born into paradise." At once she invited her family and neighbors together, providing food and drink for each person. She remarked, "Today I will leave this world." So saying, she died. That evening, the lotus flower in her pond bowed to the west.

Biographies of Japanese Born into the Pure Land, Continued

TALE 38

The wife of the Imperial Advisor Fujiwara no Kanetsune was the daughter of the Assistant Middle Counsellor Fujiwara no Takaie. She was the mother of such notables as the governors of Mutsu and Iyo provinces. She was extremely virtuous and by nature gentle. The people in her house never saw her show excessive emotion. Throughout her life she devoted herself to the recitation of the nembutsu. Her aspiration for the Way matured and she had no attachment to life in this world. As she was dying, an extraordinary fragrance filled her room. She said, "I can see the full moon shining down on me." With great joy, she breathed her last. The clothes of her son and female servant were permeated with the extraordinary fragrance, which remained for several months.

TALE 39

The daughter of Minamoto no Yoritoshi, the former governer of Mutsu Province, yearned for nothing but Amida's paradise all her life. She was by nature gentle and never got angry. She fervently thought of birth in the Pure Land and never married. She dared not engage in anything but Buddhist practices. She died reciting the nembutsu, and a brilliantly colored cloud filled the room.

TALE 40

The nun Ganshō was the younger sister of the monk Genshin. From an early age, she sought to follow the way of the Buddha. She never married. Although she had received a woman's body with its five obstacles to enlightenment, she exhibited clarity and wisdom in her contemplation of the two truths, the absolute truth, and the conventional truth lived by those caught in the samsaric cycle. Her learning and aspiration for enlightenment surpassed that of her older brother. People called her the Pure Land nun. Her nembutsu practice increased with each passing day, and her aspiration for enlightenment deepened with the years. When she died, her wonderful countenance was indescribable. She truly resides on a blue lotus in paradise.

TALE 41

The nun Emmyō was the granddaughter of Kamo no Yasunori. Her mother, called the Kamo woman, excelled at writing poetry. Emmyō was called Gen no kimi before she renounced the world. Her first sexual experiences occurred while she was in service to Fujiwara no Norimichi. Later, aspiring to enlightenment, she took the tonsure and entered the way of the Buddha. She wandered through town and country reciting nothing but the words "Buddha-nature is eternal." She preached to others, encouraging them to lead a Buddhist life. She lived for over eighty years. At the time of her death, many auspicious signs spontaneously occurred, and there is no doubt that she gained birth in the Pure Land.

TALE 42

Onshi was the wife of Minamoto no Tadatōshi and the granddaughter of Minamoto Oshu, governor of Musashi Province. From an early age, she was full of compassion and displayed neither joy nor anger. She accompanied her husband to his government post at Dazaifu. In the first month of the third year of the Kōwa era (1101), she gave birth. For some forty days thereafter there was a fog in the air that would not clear. Finally, it passed. Dwelling peacefully in the right thought of Amida Buddha, she was never lax in the practice of the nembutsu. She personally remarked, "This room has a marvelous fragrance. It greatly resembles that of a plum blossom."

—18—

Epic and Religious Propaganda
from the Ippen School of Pure Land Buddhism

Sybil Thornton

In the ninth month of the year corresponding to 1400, the train of the provincial governor Ogasawara Nagahide (d. 1424) was attacked by an alliance of local magnates at a place near Kawanakajima in Shinano. The rearguard under the command of Nagahide's cousin Banzai Nagakuni was cut off and besieged in an abandoned fort at Ōtō. After twenty days without supplies, Nagakuni and some three hundred men decided to commit suicide or die fighting. Nagahide made it back to Kyoto and a life as an expert on court ceremonial and etiquette. The shogunate sent another as governor.

This incident is memorialized in the military epic (*gunki monogatari*), *The Tale [of the Battle] of Ōtō* (*Ōtō monogatari*). As a narrative whose subject is a battle or war in which a great family has been destroyed, the epic is usually a compilation of many accounts culled from many sources, including religious stories about those defeated and killed, the victors shocked by the horror of battle into leaving the world, and the servants, lovers, wives, and mothers who entered religious life to pray for the souls of the dead. Such religious material tends to be concentrated in the third and last section, which describes the aftermath of the battle. The translation selections below from the *Ōtō* are typical of the genre.

The religious material of *The Tale of Ōtō* was produced by propagandists of the closely related but independent communities of the Ippen school of Pure Land Buddhism at Mount Kōya (Wakayama Prefecture) and Zenkōji (Nagano City, Nagano Prefecture). Although there were many confraternities, orders, and communities looking to Ippen Shōnin (1239–1289) as founder, they were not placed under the common jurisdiction of the Ippen school order known as the Jishū (Ji sect, formerly Yugyō-ha or Itinerant school) until the Tokugawa period. There were also communities of nembutsu practioners founded by others and belonging to other schools of Pure Land Buddhism. All the religious of these communities were known as *jishū* (the time sect) because of their practice of chanting the nembutsu six hours of the day. Although all these *jishū* were nembutsu practioners, the Ippen school *jishū* in particular represented a conflation of several traditions: the *hijiri* (holy man) movement through the practices of itinerancy and amulet distribution; the Seizan school of Pure Land Buddhism in the doctrine of the mutual dependence of Amida and practioner for achieving Buddhahood and rebirth in Amida's Pure Land paradise; and the mysticism of the Tendai school in the practice of walking meditation through itinerancy and the dancing (*odori*) nembutsu.

The stories are typical of those used to advertise the ministries performed by the monks and nuns of the Ippen school communities: mortuary and memorial services for those killed in battle, informing survivors and supervising their tonsures, providing a refuge for warriors and relatives suffering posttraumatic stress syndrome, and their mission of touring the country to bring religious awakening and salvation to ordinary people. The stories advocate the principal practice of these communities, chanting the name of Amida Buddha (nembutsu), and point out its benefits to those facing death in battle, as a memorial service, and as a way of life for those attempting to deal with deep, personal suffering. The temple Zenkōji, enshrining a statue of Amida Buddha believed to be the Buddha on Earth, was the center of a great independent Amidist cult that once had about one hundred branch temples. Although it was officially partly Tendai and partly Pure Land, a community of Ippen school Pure Land Buddhist religious served within the temple doors. These were the Tsumado *jishū* who are featured in the text.

Zenkōji was also a center for female Pure Land believers, who were denied access to the exclusively male enclave of Mount Kōya. This is also reflected in the *Ōtō*. A principal protagonist of the text, Hachirō's mother, is said to have joined a Pure Land community there. One assumes it was the Ippen school community, since the community is called the *jishū* and the preceptor at her tonsure was a Tsumado *jishū*. Ippen school temples, I might note, were unique in that they housed both male and female religious.

The story of the courtesans Tamagiku and Kaju follows a pattern of stories connected with Zenkōji of women taking the tonsure. First, they come in a pair, like Tora and Shoshō in the *Tale of the Soga*. Second, Kaju's name is similar to those of heroines of other tales connected with Zenkōji: Shoshō (originally Shoju) of the *Tale of the Soga* and Senju of the *Heike monogatari* (not to mention Anju of the *Sanshō dayū*, the product of a separate tradition). The "-ju" ending in the women's name is said to correspond to the "-a" or "-ami" suffix in men's names found in groups of semireligious entertainers of the Pure Land, or nembutsu, sects. It is now generally accepted that these stories were preserved and transmitted by women who functioned principally as religious specialists of one sort or another, as mediums or fund raisers.

The relationship between Zenkōji and Mount Kōya is indicated in the text by the story of the messenger monk sent to Hachirō's mother. Mount Kōya, although officially a Shingon complex, was dominated by its community of retreatants almost exclusively of the Ippen school, who were forced to convert or leave by the Tokugawa shogunate in 1615. The vast majority were engaged in fund raising (*kanjin*); they also collected bits of bone for burial at Mount Kōya, which, because it was considered the Western Pure Land paradise, guaranteed rebirth in paradise.

The *Ōtō* refers indirectly to the Mount Kōya tradition of the retreat of warriors—from both the winning and the losing sides of battles—to that temple complex. Such warriors congregated in hermitages at Renge Valley (like Kumagai Naozane and Sasaki Takatsune), and the temples Kayadō, the Kongō sammai-in, and the Shinbessho. It has been suggested that there was a custom of getting together and confessing reasons for taking the tonsure, and that these confessions may well have been circulated around Mount Kōya as stories of religious awakening and spread throughout the country by the temple's fundraisers. Repeating the story as confession (*zange*) for oneself or for another was considered, it is proposed, a way of eradicating sin (*metsuzai*). This is analagous to the concept that reading the story of the origins of a god or holy site (*engi*) is equal in merit to going on pilgrimage or to worshipping in person.

Mount Kōya was a center for ascetic Pure Land practitioners, a refuge for world-weary warriors, and a transmitting station for the mass media of the day, oral religious narratives. So much of this activity centered on the Kayadō chapel that the Pure Land ascetics came to be known as Kayadō ascetics. The mention in the *Ōtō* of the Kayadō as the place where the enemy warrior Munetsugu undertook three years of austerities indicates the site of the production and transmission of his story.

More importantly, the Kayadō is famous for the religious awakening story "Karukaya," which reflects the relationship between Mount Kōya and Zenkōji and is also carried by the Pure Land temples Ōjōji and Saikōji, neither far from the Zenkōji. This relationship between two large Pure Land communities, specifically Ippen school Pure Land communities, is also seen in the religious awakening story of the preceptor of the mother of Tokiwa Hachirō. Although already serving as a Tsumado *jishū* at Zenkōji, he flees to Mount Kōya to escape further exposure to human suffering.

Jūnenji, not a ten-minute walk from Zenkōji, belongs now to the Pure Land sect. There is no documentation of an Ippen school community at Jūnenji at this time. However, Jūnenji was known to have had a special relationship with Kobodera Shōkaku'in. And, according to the *Ōtō*, Munetsugu went from the Kobodera Kannon to Mount Kōya. That would indicate, again, an Ippen school connection.

We can reasonably attribute the provenances of these religious-awakening stories to independent communities of Ippen school Pure Land Buddhist practitioners based at Mount Kōya and Zenkōji. But what purpose do these propaganda traditions serve in this epic?

The stories, except for the single description of a self-immolation in battle after chanting the invocation of Amida Buddha's name (nembutsu), are all stories that explain how and why an individual experiences religious awakening (*hosshin*). One achieves religious awakening through suffering. A woman who has lost a husband and two sons becomes a nun. Two courtesans who have lost their lover enter religious life. A religious sent to inform the first woman is so affected by her grief that he abandons his ministry for a life of asceticism. And the warrior traumatized by the atrocities he has seen abandons rank and family for the same. The author himself indicates the purpose of telling these stories in his rhetorical cry, "Those who have heard what men have seen and have not achieved religious awakening at this time, [just] what time are they waiting for?" The purpose of a religious awakening story is to spark religious awakening in others. The warrior lay priest Munetsugu becomes a traveling ascetic and preacher, a bringer of en-lightenment to ordinary people. "It is the Buddha's work to lead men to enlight-enment by showing the reality of suffering, which is the reality of living beings in the world of desire" (Nakamura 1973: 160). The importance of these stories is that they are links of a chain reaction of religious awakening that extends to anyone who even hears the story; the importance of the battle at Ōtō is that it triggered this chain reaction.

Munetsugu's own real religious awakening comes when, witnessing the maim-ing and mutilation of the wounded and dead at Ōtō, he realizes that this "is nothing more than the Six Realms (rokudō)." In the Tendai doctrine of the Six Realms, which is the basis of the Pure Land movement, there are six stages of existence in this world, and in all of them, from heaven to hell, there is as much suffering in one as in the other. In this degenerate age (mappō), an individual can, like the Empress Kenreimon'in in the Tale of the Heike, experience all the realms in a single lifetime. The only complete and absolute release from the law of cause and effect that causes the soul to be born again and again into this world of suffering is the vow of Amida Buddha to rescue all sentient beings who believe in him and call on his name.

If this world is the Six Realms, then the battlefield is specifically the place of the antigods (shurajo) and the existence of fighting men is that of the antigods (shuradō). The identification of the battlefield with the antigods (shura) is much more explicit in some texts, such as the Tale of the Heike, and implicit in others, such as the Tale of the Soga. Actually, the author of the Ōtō identifies the battlefield with the realms of hungry ghosts and animals, the lowest of the Six save hell, with a description of the men eating the raw meat of their horses as the blood runs from their mouths and the expression, "realm of hungry ghosts and animals (gaki-chikushō-dō)."

Identifying Ōtō with the Six Realms identifies historical time and space with Buddhist time and space. History is placed in the perspective of Tendai/Pure Land doctrine. For the protagonists of the aftermath section, the battlefield at Ōtō, the scene of so much suffering, is where the realization about the true nature of the world—of existence in the Six Realms—is made clear. Those who experience religious awakening by seeing or hearing about it bear witness to it in their stories. All five aftermath protagonists are (or are made to be) personal witnesses to faith. Their function in the narrative is religious, to illustrate suffering as the only reality in this world. Their status as chief protagonists of the narrative, indeed as tragic heroes, is based more strictly on their identity as the catalysts to religious awakening in others, as religious propagandists. But their credibility is enhanced by the fact that they are at one and the same time witnesses to a historical event. For, through them, the battle at Ōtō is identified with and indeed proves the tenets of Pure Land Buddhism.

The translation is from *Ōtō monogatari* in *Zoku gunshoruijū* 21/2, ed. Hanawa Hokiichi (Tokyo: Zoku Gunshoruijū Kanseikai, 1933).

Further Reading

Nakamura Kyōko, tr. and ed., *Miraculous Stories from the Japanese Buddhist Tradition: The Nihon Ryōiki of the Monk Kyōkai*, Harvard Yenching Institute Monograph Series 20 (Cambridge: Harvard University Press, 1973); William H. and Helen Craig McCullough, tr., *A Tale of Flowering Fortunes*, 2 vols. (Stanford: Stanford University Press, 1980); Helen Craig McCullough, tr., *The Tale of the Heike* (Stanford: Stanford University Press, 1988).

Selections from the Tale of [the Battle] of Ōtō

In all this, especially tragic was the end of the lay priest Tokiwa. Father and two sons, on the point of suicide, joined hands and faced west. In loud voices they earnestly chanted the nembutsu, the promise and the prayer [of Amida] to receive them and not to abandon them. And each, with repeated blows, committed suicide. . . .

Now, the next day, the eighteenth day of the tenth month, in the hour of the tiger (3:00–5:00 A.M.), the forces of the vanguard attacked. They raced each other around and around the fort, took the heads of the dead, and dispatched the dying with a blade through the throat. They stopped those fleeing and cut off their arms and legs. They pursued the dying to the scattered places they had crawled to and took their heads. Their actions were indescribable. Now, the lay priest Kōsaka Munetsugu, [styled] second in command of the horse of the left, shut his eyes for a time. What he thought in his very heart was that this was nothing more than the Six Realms. There was before his eyes only the fate of those who take up arms. It was in all his own fate. The cause lay solely in greed. All took pride in honor and wealth and failed to reflect on this transient life, which disappears so easily. All this because they sought one hundred years of glory and pleasure. As he pondered this deeply, he thought them fools beset by attachments and passions. The agonies of the road to hell were surely like this. Now their desperate situation would make a mountain of gold worthless to them, would make them willingly reject an emperor's throne. How strange it was that people who thought they tired of the transience of this corrupt world could tire of it, that people who thought they wanted to abandon the world could abandon it. It was the way of an evil destiny, that of arms. Thinking this, he wheeled about and gave an order.

Now, the Tsumado *jishū* of Zenkōji and similarly the holy men (*hijiri*) of Jūnenji heard that the men at Ōtō had committed suicide. They hurried there and inspected the miserable state of the battlefield. It was a sight too awful to look upon. Men who only recently had appeared so fine and grand all lay dead upon the moor. The corpses of men lay strewn together with the carcasses of horses. [A carpet of] blood-stained creepers, fluttering in the wind like the red leaves of [Mount] Kōya, resembled red brocade spread out in the sun. Monks and priests who were relatives collected the remains and embraced the dead bodies. They grieved and wept without limit. Such a thing has never been heard of in the past nor seen in our own time. Men of old fled the world seeking asylum in the moon of Mount Kōya (Nanzan) and hid themselves in the clouds of bamboo groves. After hearing what people have seen, those who do not awaken to religion at this time, [just] what time are they waiting for? Those *jishū* gathered up one by one the corpses lying scattered here and there. Some they burnt and others they buried. They set up stupas and on each they bestowed nembutsu. Everywhere they raised the hope that Amida would come to lead them to paradise. More and more they acted with the mercy of Buddha. They went as far as to collect [the last] writings from the dead as souvenirs which were sent to the widows and orphans.

Now, two courtesans named Tamagiku and Kaju of the Sakurakōji [district], having of late realized a dream of love with Banzai no Jirō, could not forget their feeling for him. Setting out, they sought out his body at Ōtō; lamenting and weeping profusely, they appealed to a *jishū* who kindly interred his body. They returned to Zenkōji and put on poor clothes dyed black. They earnestly prayed for his rebirth as a buddha. That they did all this was most laudable. They composed this single poem: "I never thought that living so short a time in this fleeting world, I would have to lament so long a journey in a dream."

Now, one who met with great sorrow was the wife of the lay priest Tokiwa. As for the poems that her son Hachirō had written at Ōtō, they were sent from Zenkōji through a Tsumado *jishū*. This *jishū* soon arrived at Igara village. When he saw the house where Tokiwa had lived, [he saw] it had become dilapidated surprisingly quickly. The garden was buried in tree leaves, and there was no trace of a single person who might have walked there. The mournful orchids on the broken bamboo dripped so much dew they seemed to weep. An old cypress in the garden moaned in the wind. He saw that it was the house where a lonely person must be living, and [then] he heard the sound of the plucking of a *koto*, which only added to his sadness. It seemed to him like the sound of a caged crane crying fearfully in the middle of the night after its young. Hearing this, he thought how piteous love between parent and child was. This *jishū* approached the front gate and called for admittance. Presently there came out an old man with hair as white as frost hanging down his back. Then, when he told him why he had come, the old man in confusion went into the house and thus informed Hachirō's mother. The lady, hearing this, felt she was in a dream and, coming out, asked the *jishū* what had happened. Her grief was as he thought it would be. He spoke not at all, only wept, choked with tears, and taking out the deceased's souvenirs, the poems written in the field and the lock of hair from his temple, gave them to her. The lady clutched them and, pressing them to her face, she fell prostrate. Words cannot express her agony, her pining, and her lamenting. After a little while, the *jishū* gently told her about the battle and how her husband and sons had met their end. A great stir filled the house, faces were knit in pain; nothing could compare with their grief. As the lady's pain remained unassuaged, the *jishū* was made her preceptor and her head was shaved. How sad indeed that she should clad herself in a hermit's robe. This *jishū* thought that now he saw how the world really was. One might leave the world once, but it might not turn out as one wished. Day and night, morning and evening, one comes into contact with daily events. Because of this there is no way one can avoid the things that break the heart. How sad, indeed, it was that he had not already abandoned the world. "Yet, will I find a place where I will not see or hear sad things, if I go deep into the Yoshino mountains?" While composing this poem, without returning to Zenkōji, he went straightaway to Mount Kōya and entrusted himself to Amida's vow to draw him near. Cutting himself off from the world, he walked the path he hoped would take him to the cloud on which Amida would come to take him to paradise . . .

Now. Hachirō's mother arrived at Ōtō and looked for a trace of her dead. She found a mound of newly bleached bones and a stupa. When she enquired, they said it was the marker of the Tokiwa grave. She approached, her heart quieted, and chanted the invocation of Amida Buddha's name. The intimacy of a long time, words of endearment during a night's light sleep, words of complaint. But there is not even an echo in the valley. She has no husband, nor does she see her children. Only the grass far and wide and the cold, cold dew. Her condition is such that she pours out her pain, tottering on her feet. Her sadness is that of a heart burdened with memories. Thus grieving, she leaves all this. By herself, she went to Zenkōji and, prostrating herself, worshipped [the enshrined image,] the living body of Amida. Then she became a *jishū*. She did not neglect the six hours of prayer through the day and night. Blessed indeed is the example she set, meeting the situation properly, asking for memorial services to pray for the afterlife of her husband and two sons and their birth as buddhas.

Now, as for the lay priest Kōsaka Munetsugu, [styled] second in command of the horse of the left, the deaths of the men at Ōtō weighed heavily on his mind. He saw it was daylight, but he did not return home. From camp he went to the Kannon of Kobodera. On the twenty-first day after their deaths he prayed throughout the night, asking for a heart of faith and firmness. He relied on the vow of great mercy and compassion; would there be no sign? Then he received various dreams, and Munetsugu's wish was fulfilled. Giving his entire inheritance to his son, the [styled] vice-minister of justice, he left his family and went up to Mount Kōya. For three years he underwent austerities at the Kay-adō, and, becoming an ascetic Pure Land practitioner, he traveled the various provinces in pursuit of truth and acted charitably on behalf of the common people. And yet, so they say, how thankful we are for the original causes [however dreadful] having such rewarding consequences. How awesome! How true! How pitiable!

— 19 —

Buddhism and Abortion: "The Way to
Memorialize One's Mizuko"

William R. LaFleur

Mizuko, literally a "child of the waters," is the term used in modern Japan to refer to an aborted fetus or a stillborn. In today's Japan, Buddhist institutions feel uneasy about condoning abortion but are also reluctant to condemn it outright. Abortion has been legal in Japan since 1948 and there is no great interest in changing the law. Many Buddhist temples provide a ritual called a *kuyō* through which both "parents" of a *mizuko* can pray for its well-being in the "beyond," that is, in the "realm of the gods and Buddhas." The bodhisattva Jizō is prayed to as the powerful and compassionate figure who guides deceased children through the realm of the dead. Some observers hold that this ritual does much to relieve the so-called postabortion syndrome. In the public press as well as in some Buddhist periodicals, however, some temples have been criticized for being crassly commercialized in the provision of these rituals. Shiun-zan Jizō-ji (Purple Cloud Mountain Jizō Temple), a relatively new establishment on the outskirts of Chichibu, itself an object of such criticism at times, provides promotional brochures, one of which is translated below.

This translation of a brochure published by Shiun-zan Jizō-in first appeared as an appendix in William R. LaFleur, *Liquid Life: Abortion and Buddhism in Japan* (Princeton: Princeton University Press, 1992): 221–223.

Further Reading

Samuel Coleman, *Family Planning in Japanese Society: Traditional Birth Control in Modern Urban Culture* (Princeton: Princeton University Press, 1983); Hoshino Eiki and Takeda Chōshū, "Indebtedness and Comfort: The Undercurrents of *Mizuko Kuyō* in Contemporary Japan," *Japanese Journal of Religious Studies* 14, 4 (December 1987): 305–320; William R. LaFleur, *Liquid Life: Abortion and Buddhism in Japan* (Princeton: Princeton University Press, 1992).

The Way to Memorialize One's *Mizuko*

1. The *mizuko* resulting from a terminated pregnancy is a child existing in the realm of darkness. The principal things that have to be done for its sake are the making of a full apology and the making of amends to such a child.

In contrast to the child in darkness because of an ordinary miscarriage or by natural death after being born, the child here discussed is in its present location because its parents took active steps to prevent it from being born alive in our world. If the parents merely carry out ordinary memorial rites but fail to make a full apology to their child, their *mizuko* will never be able to accept their act.

Think for a moment how even birds and beasts, when about to be killed, show a good deal of anger and distress. Then how much more must be the shock and hurt felt by a fetus when its parent or parents have decided to abort it? And on top of that it does not even yet have a voice with which to make complaint about what is happening.

It often happens that the living children of persons who have repeatedly had abortions will in the middle of the night cry out "Father, help!" or "Help me, Mommy!" because of nightmares. Uncontrollable weeping or cries of "I'm scared! I'm scared!" on the part of children are really caused by dreams through which their aborted siblings deep in the realm of darkness give expression to their own distress and anger. Persons who are not satisfied with this explanation would do well to have a look at two publications of the Purple Cloud Villa; these are entitled *Mizuko Jizō-ji's Collection of the Experiences of Departed Souls* and *The Medical Dictionary of Life*.

2. The next thing to do in remembering the *mizuko* is to set up an image of Jizō on the Buddhist altar in one's own home. That will serve as a substitute for a memorial tablet for the *mizuko*. Such a Jizō can do double service. On one hand it can represent the soul of the *mizuko* for parents doing rites of apology to it. Simultaneously, however, the Jizō is the one to whom can be made an appeal in prayer to guide the fetus through the realm of departed souls. Such Jizō images for home use can be obtained from the Purple Cloud Villa but can also be purchased at any shop specializing in Buddhist art and implements. As long as one performs this worship with a pure heart, it is bound to have a positive effect.

Some prices follow. Jizō images made of metal are either 3,000 yen for silver ones or 4,000 yen for gold. Add 1,100 yen to the price of either of these if home delivery is desired. These are prices as of September 1984.

3. Inasmuch as the Jizō image on the Buddhist altar also does double duty as a memorial tablet for a terminated fetus, it is allowable—after asking permission of the Jizō—to give it a place on the altar lower than the memorial tablets for one's parents and ancestors. Also it does not matter greatly whether it is to the right or the left on the altar.

4. The next thing of importance is to set up a stone Jizō image either in the cemetery of the Mizuko Jizō Temple or at one's own family temple. Such will serve as substitute for a gravestone for the aborted child and will constitute an eternal, ongoing ritual of apology and remembrance. Such action will undoubtably have a good effect—a fact shown in things published in our monthly periodical *The Purple Cloud.* The expenses involved in setting up a stone Jizō Buddha at our place are fully detailed in our publication *Concerning the 10,000 Jizōs.* If requested, we will be pleased to send it.

5. The following pertains to the number of images needed if a person is the parent of more than one *mizuko.* One of each on the home altar and in the cemetery will suffice if all the *mizuko*s were produced by a single couple—whether married or not. If, however, the father of a later *mizuko* was different from that of an earlier one—and, of course, also had a different family registry—separate Jizō images will be required. An exception to this could be made if a woman were to discuss this candidly with her second husband and get his permission. Then it would be just as in the case of a woman bringing along into her second marriage the children begotten in an earlier one. In such a case, if she requests that the deceased ancestors understand the situation, it is allowable for all her *mizuko*s to be collectively remembered with a single image.

6. When at your home altar you are giving a daily portion of rice and water offering to your deceased ancestors, be sure to include the *mizuko* too—and let them know of their inclusion. Also pray for the well-being of your *mizuko* in the other world. Do this by standing before the Buddhas there and reciting either the *Heart Sutra* or the *Psalm to Jizō* used at the Jizō cemetery in Chichibu. In addition to that, if as an ongoing remembrance of your *mizuko* you write out in longhand a copy of the *Heart Sutra* once a day, you will at some point along the way receive the assurance that your child has most certainly reached Buddhahood. Until you receive such an assurance, you should continue to perform these rites of apology and remembrance.

7. To make amends for the fact that you never had to pay anything for the upbringing and education of a *mizuko,* you should give to the Buddha every day an offering of 100 yen for each of your *mizuko.* However, if you have had as many as ten terminated pregnancies, there may be hardship in laying out 1,000 yen every day; in such cases it is permissable to give only 300 or 500 yen—or even to give more or less depending on one's income. This is an expression of apology to the child for not having given it a love-filled upbringing. Therefore, you should put your love into these acts of remembrance, not being stingy with your time and resources. Once you get into the habit of thinking how much easier it would be simply to make a 10,000-yen contribution once a month, you are missing the whole point. It is far better to put a daily offering on the altar every day and then on a special, designated day pay a visit to the Jizō Temple at Chichibu and make a contribution to the temple. Alternatively, you could do it while making the eighty-eight-temple pilgrimage

on the island of Shikoku or the pilgrimage to the one hundred Kannon sites
in western Japan. [See Reader, chapter 37.]

8. When a person has awakened to the value and importance of remembering *mizuko*, one gains a much deeper faith and makes efforts to live as a
bodhisattva, setting one's mind to performing at least one act of goodness each
day. Also vowing to go on pilgrimage to Shikoku or the Kannon sites is an
excellent way to be total and thorough-going in one's act of apologizing to and
remembering the *mizuko*. It is important to be of a mind to do more than
enough; to be of the opinion that one has already done plenty is just the kind
of attitude that evokes a bad effect.

9. Children who are miscarried, born dead, or die shortly after being born
differ, of course, from those whose lives are cut short by being terminated by
their parents. Nevertheless, they too are *mizuko* and, when one gives consideration to his or her responsibility for the fact that these too did not enter life
successfully, it would seem good to provide them too with *mizuko* rites, just
as one would in the case of aborted fetuses.

10. Households whose members think about the seriousness of karmic laws
related to abortion are also households that can take advantage of such occasions in order to deepen the faith of those within them. By continuing to
perform adequate rites of apology and memorial, such persons later are blessed
with the birth of fine, healthy children. Or, as an extension of good fortune,
there are many instances of people really thriving. Some persons find that their
own severe heart diseases are cured or that the rebelliousness of children or
neuroses go away. When on top of all that there is increased prosperity in the
family business, there is good cause for lots of happiness.

Why not find out more about this by simply paying a visit to the Jizō Temple
in Chichibu?

RITUALS OF REALIZATION

—20—

The Contemplation of Suchness

Jacqueline I. Stone

The Contemplation of Suchness (Shinnyo kan) is attributed to the great scholar and teacher of the Tendai school of Buddhism, the prelate Genshin (942–1017). However, it actually dates from around the twelfth century. Tendai writings of medieval times were often compiled by unidentified authors who attributed them to earlier Tendai masters. By the early medieval period, a few Buddhist thinkers had begun to write in vernacular Japanese rather than the literary Chinese that formed the accepted scholarly medium for works on Buddhist doctrine. The Contemplation of Suchness is an example of this new development. It may have been written for an educated lay person, rather than a monastic reader, and reflects a number of significant developments within early medieval Japanese Buddhist thought.

One important intellectual trend to develop within Tendai Buddhism of the medieval period is known as original enlightenment thought (hongaku shisō). This doctrine denies that enlightenment is achieved as the result of a long process of religious cultivation; rather, it holds that all beings are, from the outset, enlightened by their very nature, that is, "originally." From this perspective, Buddhist practice is to be approached, not as a means to "attain" a future result, but to realize that oneself is Buddha already. The present writing describes this in terms of knowing, or believing, that "oneself is precisely suchness." "Suchness" or "thusness" (Skt., tathatā; J., shinnyo) is a Buddhist term for the true nature of reality, or what an enlightened person is said to realize. Like many such terms, it is intended to designate without describing, for the Buddha wisdom can be neither described nor grasped conceptually but only indicated as being "such."

In this text, the idea of original enlightenment is explained in terms of traditional Tendai (C. T'ien-t'ai) forms of doctrinal classification and meditative practice, as well as the Tendai school's particular reverence for the Lotus Sutra. The historical Buddha, Śākyamuni, was said to have preached for fifty years. According to the Tendai systematization of doctrine, for the first forty-two years the Buddha taught provisional teachings that were accommodated to his listeners' understanding, while in the final eight years of his life he taught the true teaching, the Lotus

Sutra, said to be the direct expression of his own enlightenment. *The Contemplation of Suchness* assimilates this distinction between true and provisional teachings to two different views of enlightenment. The provisional teachings preached before the *Lotus Sutra*, it says, teach that one can attain Buddhahood only after many kalpas (aeons) of austere practices, while the *Lotus Sutra* uniquely reveals that all beings are enlightened inherently.

In terms of meditative practice, the "contemplation of suchness" discussed in this text is equated with the "contemplation of the Middle Way" or the "threefold contemplation in a single thought" set forth in the *Great Calming and Contemplation* (*Mo-ho chih-kuan*), the influential treatise recording the teachings on meditation of Chih-i (538–597), founder of the T'ien-t'ai school, the Chinese precursor of Japanese Tendai. T'ien-t'ai meditation aims at perceiving all things from the threefold perspective of emptiness, provisional existence, and the Middle, known as the threefold truth. By contemplating all phenomena as empty—that is, as dependent upon conditions and without permanence or underlying essence— one is freed from delusive attachments. This is said to correspond to the practice and insight of persons of the two vehicles (the Hīnayāna teachings) and bodhisattvas of elementary Mahāyāna. However, merely to be freed from attachment is not enough. Therefore, while knowing all things to be empty, one also contemplates them as provisionally existing. In this way, one is able to understand them correctly as conditioned aspects of conventional reality, without imputing to them false notions of essence, and so act wisely and compassionately in the world. This is said to correspond to the insight and practice of bodhisattvas of the higher Mahāyāna teachings. Lastly, by contemplating all things as both empty and provisionally existing, one maintains both views simultaneously, the two perspectives holding one another in perfect balance and preventing one-sided adherence to either. This is said to correspond to the practice and insight of Buddhas. In explaining the threefold truth, one must unavoidably explain its three aspects sequentially, and novice practitioners were also taught to contemplate the three truths of emptiness, provisional existence, and the Middle as a progressive sequence. However, this sequential meditation was regarded as a lesser form of the threefold contemplation. Its ultimate form is to cognize all three truths simultaneously, "in a single thought."

Within the traditional T'ien-t'ai/Tendai structure of meditative discipline, the threefold contemplation, or the contemplation of the Middle Way, required formal meditative practice, usually performed in a monastic context and often carried out in seclusion for a specified number of days, weeks, or months. The "contemplation of suchness" discussed in this writing, however, is not a formally structured meditation but rather the cultivation, in the midst of daily activities, of a particular mental attitude—namely, of seeing oneself and all others as identical to suchness. As the text says,

> Clergy or laity, male or female—all should contemplate in this way. When you provide for your wife, children, and retainers, or even feed oxen, horses, and the

others of the six kinds of domestic animals, because the myriad things are all suchness, if you think that these others are precisely suchness, you have in effect made offerings to all Buddhas and bodhisattvas of the ten directions and to all living beings, without a single exception.

Because suchness is the real aspect of all things, to think of both oneself and others in this way is to open a perspective from which individuals are not separate, unrelated, or conflicting existences but nondual—each identical with the totality of all that is and encompassing all others within itself. In other words, it is to see all beings manifesting original enlightenment just as they are.

Some evidence suggests that the "contemplation of suchness" described in this text may actually have been conducted as a form of lay practice during the early Kamakura period (1185–1333). A late twelfth- or early thirteenth-century anthology of tales called *A Collection of Treasures* (*Hōbutsu shū*), attributed to Taira Yasuyori (fl. 1190–1200), refers to the above passage from *The Contemplation of Suchness* and says:

When you eat, visualize [this act] as making offerings to the thirty-seven honored ones [i.e., the Buddhas and bodhisattvas depicted on the Diamond-Realm mandala of Esoteric Buddhism], and when you feed others, form the thought that you are, upwardly, making offerings to the Buddhas of the ten directions and three periods of time, and downwardly, giving alms to hell-dwellers, hungry ghosts and those in the animal realm. And you should likewise form this thought when you feed your servants and retainers, or give food to horses and cattle, birds and beasts. For lay people, men and women engaged in public and private affairs, what practice could possibly be superior? [*DNBZ* 147:426]

By cultivating the attitude that "all things are precisely suchness," the simplest acts of daily life in effect become Buddhist practice.

The Contemplation of Suchness links notions of original enlightenment to several other trends that characterized much of Japanese Buddhism in the medieval period. One is a growing emphasis on simple practices, which developed within both older, established schools of Buddhism—Tendai, Shingon, and the Nara schools—and the new Buddhist movements of the Kamakura period. Practices such as the repeated chanting of the nembutsu, the Buddha Amida's name (*Namu-Amida-butsu*), or of the *daimoku*, the title of the *Lotus Sutra* (*Namu-myōhō-renge-kyō*), gained popularity during this time. Such practices were of course accessible to a great range of persons, including lay people unable to undertake demanding religious disciplines or to read difficult Buddhist texts. Beyond the issue of accessibility, however, the emphasis on simple practices was connected with the idea that the world had entered a period known as the Final Dharma age (*mappō*), regarded as a time of decline when traditional Buddhist disciplines would be beyond the capacity of most persons. The "contemplation of suchness" described here, which can be undertaken by anyone even in the midst of daily activities, appears to have been one of the simple practices regarded as particularly suited to those people born in the Final Dharma age.

While the simple practices were on the one hand touted as appropriate to people of limited capacity unable to undertake traditional Buddhist disciplines, they were at the same time extolled as being superior to those disciplines, in that they were said to encompass all merit in a single religious act and thus offer direct access to the Buddha's enlightenment without lifetimes of austere practice. For example, Hōnen (1133–1212), founder of the Japanese Jōdo or Pure Land sect, praised the nembutsu as encompassing the Three Bodies, Ten Powers, and Four Fearlessnesses—in short, all the virtues of the Buddha Amida. Nichiren (1222–1282), who preached a doctrine of exclusive devotion to the *Lotus Sutra*, similarly taught that the *daimoku* contains the merit of all the virtuous practices carried out by Śākyamuni Buddha in his quest, over countless lifetimes, for supreme enlightenment; by chanting the *daimoku* of the *Lotus Sutra*, Nichiren said, one can immediately access the Buddha's merits. Here, at a slightly earlier date, we find similar claims made for the "contemplation of suchness," which is said to encompass all merit within itself.

Related to the notion of simple practices was the idea that sincere devotion to the particular religious act in question was more important to one's salvation than the cultivation of moral conduct. In the present writing, even those who "violate the precepts without shame" are nonetheless said to be able to realize enlightenment and achieve birth in the Pure Land by diligently contemplating suchness. Such passages link this text to broader medieval concerns about the possibility of the salvation of evil persons. For many, the Final Dharma age was a time when proper observance of the Buddhist precepts was thought to be impossible. These concerns also reflected the rise to power of the warrior class, people whose hereditary profession required them to violate the traditional Buddhist precept against killing.

When Saichō (767–822), who established Tendai Buddhism in Japan, studied in China, he received instruction not only in the T'ien-t'ai *Lotus* teachings but also in Esoteric Buddhism, Ch'an (Zen), and the bodhisattva precepts. Building upon this foundation, his successors sought to develop a comprehensive religious system that would encompass all practices within the "one vehicle" of the *Lotus Sutra*. This all-encompassing approach would become characteristic of Japanese Tendai, and strands of Buddhist thought other than the original Tendai/Lotus teachings are accordingly evident in *The Contemplation of Suchness*. The most obvious of these is Pure Land Buddhism, centering on contemplation of and devotion to the Buddha Amida (Skt. Amitābha), said to live in a pure land called Utmost Bliss (Sukhāvatī, Gokuraku) in the western quarter of the universe. Birth after death in Amida's Pure Land, the goal of many Pure Land practitioners, was seen as liberation from the sufferings of the round of rebirth and equated with the stage of nonretrogression on the path of achieving Buddhahood. Pure Land practices in premodern Japan were extremely widespread, transcending sectarian divisions, and assumed a number of forms. These ranged from various Pure Land meditations that developed within the Tendai school; to the chanting of Amida's name, interpreted as both contemplation and devotion; to popular uses of the nembutsu, for example, as a deathbed practice, to transfer merit to the deceased, and to placate unhappy spirits. The medieval period also witnessed the rise of independent Pure Land traditions, such as the Jōdo (Pure Land) sect of Hōnen, the Jōdo Shin (True Pure Land) sect of Shinran (1173–1262), and the Ji sect of Ippen (1239–1289). *The Contemplation of Suchness* reflects the Pure Land tradition that developed within Tendai Buddhism. Genshin, to whom it is attributed, was a key figure in the development of this tradition and the author of an extremely popular work on Pure Land faith and practice, the *Essentials of Birth in the Pure Land* (*Ōjōyōshū*). It will be noted that *The Contemplation of Suchness* on one hand speaks of birth after death in Amida's pure land as a real event and yet, on the other, urges the necessity of realizing that oneself and the Buddha are nondual in essence. This dual perspective is not altogether uncommon in the Tendai Pure Land writings of this period, which may describe the pure land as both a real place in the western part of the universe and immanent in this world, and Amida, as both a transcendent Buddha and identical to one's own mind. For example, *Questions and Answers on the Nembutsu as Self-Cultivation* (*Jigyō nembutsu mondō*), another medieval Tendai text retrospectively attributed to Genshin, says: "Even though one knows Amida to be one's own mind, one forms a relationship with Amida Buddha of the west and in this way manifests the Amida who is one's own mind" [*DNBZ* 31: 212].

Although less prominent than the Pure Land references, elements of the Esoteric strand within Tendai Buddhism also occur in this text. The Buddha revered in the Esoteric teachings is Dainichi (Skt. Mahāvairocana), the cosmic Buddha said to pervade and be embodied by the entire universe: all forms are his body, all sounds are his voice, and all thoughts are his mind, although the unenlightened do not realize this. In Esoteric practice, the practitioner is said to realize the identity of one's own body, speech, and mind with those of Dainichi through performance of the "three mysteries": the forming of ritual gestures (*mūdras*) with the hands and body, the chanting of mantras or secret ritual formulas with the mouth, and the mental contemplation of mandalas or iconographic representations of the cosmos as the expression of Dainichi. Portions of *The Contemplation of Suchness* not included here suggest that contemplating suchness is identical to the adept realizing one's identity with Dainichi in the act of Esoteric practice.

The Contemplation of Suchness makes clear that, although all beings are said to be enlightened inherently, this does not amount to a denial of the need for Buddhist practice: Original enlightenment, according to this text, must be manifested by cultivating the attitude that oneself and all others are inseparable from the Buddha. Its concluding passage admonishes the reader to "think that we are precisely suchness, night and day, whether walking, standing, sitting, or lying down, without forgetting." Moreover, while all creatures, even insects, are deemed to be enlightened innately, there is an implicit privileging of the human state, in that only humans can realize their identity with suchness and so free themselves from the suffering of transmigration. It is also recognized that, due to individual differences in human capacity, not everyone will be able to achieve and sustain this insight with equal speed. Some will require "a day, two days, a month, two months, a year, or even a lifetime," though the implication is that everyone can do so within this present existence.

The translated excerpts are from *Shinnyo kan*, in Tada Kōryū et al., eds., *Tendai hongaku ron*, in Nihon shisō taikei 9 (Tokyo: Iwanami Shoten, 1973): 120–149.

Further Reading

Allan A. Andrews, *The Teachings Essential for Rebirth: A Study of Genshin's Ōjōyōshū* (Tokyo: Sophia University, 1973); Neal Donner and Daniel B. Stevenson, *The Great Calming and Contemplation: A Study and Annotated Translation of the First Chapter of Chih-i's Mo-ho chih-kuan* (Kuroda Institute/ University of Hawaii Press, 1993); Paul Groner, "Shortening the Path: Early Tendai Interpretations of the Realization of Buddhahood with This Very Body (*Sokushin Jōbutsu*)," in *Paths to Liberation: The Mārga and Its Transformations in Buddhist Thought*, ed. Robert E. Buswell, Jr., and Robert M. Gimello (Kuroda Institute/University of Hawaii Press, 1992): 439–473; Paul Groner, "The Lotus Sutra and Saichō's Interpretation of the Realization of Buddhahood with This Very Body," in *The Lotus Sutra in Japanese Culture*, ed. George J. Tanabe, Jr., and Willa Jane Tanabe (University of Hawaii Press, 1989): 53–74; Ruben L. F. Habito, *Originary Enlightenment: Tendai Hongaku Doctrine and Japanese Buddhism* (Tokyo: International Institute for Buddhist Studies, 1996); Leon Hurvitz, tr., *Scripture of the Lotus Blossom of the Fine Dharma* (New York: Columbia University Press, 1976); A. K. Reischauer, tr., "Genshin's Ōjōyōshū: Collected Essays on Birth into Paradise," *Transactions of the Asiatic Society of Japan*, second series, vol. 7 (1930): 16–97; Daniel B. Stevenson, "The Four Kinds of Samādhi in Early T'ien-t'ai Buddhism," in *Traditions of Meditation in Chinese Buddhism*, ed. Peter N. Gregory (Kuroda Institute/University of Hawaii Press, 1986): 45–97.

The Contemplation of Suchness

Volume 1 of the *[Great] Calming and Contemplation* states: "Of every form and fragrance, there is none that is not the Middle Way. So it is with the realm of the self, as well as the realms of the Buddha and of the beings" [*Mo-ho chih-kuan*, J. *Maka shikan*, T 46:1c]. The "realm of the self" is the practitioner's own mind. The "Buddha realm" indicates the Buddhas of the ten directions. "The beings" means all sentient beings. "Every form and fragrance" means all classes of insentient beings, including grasses and trees, tiles and pebbles, mountains and rivers, the great earth, the vast sea, and empty space. Of all these myriad existents, there is none that is not the Middle Way. The different terms for [this identity] are many. It is called suchness, the real aspect, the universe [Skt. *dharma-dhātu*, J. *hōkai*] the Dharma body, the Dharma nature, the Thus Come One, and the cardinal meaning. Among these many designations, I will for present purposes employ "suchness" and thus clarify the meaning of the contemplation of the Middle Way that is explained in many places in the sutras and treatises.

If you wish to attain Buddhahood quickly or be born without fail in [the pure land] of Utmost Bliss, you must think: "My own mind is precisely the principle of suchness." If you think that suchness, which pervades the universe, is your own essence, you are at once the universe; do not think that there is anything apart from this. When one is awakened, the Buddhas in the worlds of the ten directions of the universe and also all bodhisattvas each dwell within oneself. To seek a separate Buddha apart from oneself is [the action of] a time when one does not know that oneself is precisely suchness. When one knows that suchness and oneself are the same thing, then, of Shaka (Śākyamuni), [A]mida (Amitābha), Yakushi (Bhaiṣajya-guru) and the other Buddhas of the ten directions, as well as Fugen (Samantabhadra), Monju (Mañjuśrī), Kannon (Avalokiteśvara), Miroku (Maitreya), and the other bodhisattvas, there is none that is separate from oneself. Moreover, the Lotus Sutra and the others of eighty thousand repositories of teachings and the twelve kinds of scriptures, as well as the myriad practices of all Buddhas and bodhisattvas undertaken as the cause for their enlightenment, the myriad virtues they achieved as a result, and the boundless merit they gained through self-cultivation and through teaching others—of all this, what is there that is not within oneself?

When one forms this thought, because all things are the functions of the mind, all practices are encompassed within one mind, and in a single moment of thought, one comprehends all things: This is called "sitting in the place of practice" (zadōjō). It is called "achieving right awakening" (jōshōgaku). Because one [thus] realizes Buddhahood without abandoning this [present body], it is also called realizing Buddhahood with this very body. This is like the case of the eight-year-old dragon girl who, on hearing the principle of the Lotus Sutra that all things are a single suchness, immediately aroused the aspiration for enlightenment and, in the space of a moment, achieved right awakening [Hurvitz, 199–201]. Moreover, for one who contemplates suchness and aspires to be born [in the pure land] of Utmost Bliss, there is no doubt that one shall surely be born there in accordance with one's wish. The reason is: Attaining Buddhahood is extremely difficult, because one becomes a Buddha by self-cultivation and by teaching others and thus accumulating unfathomable merit, enough to fill the universe. But achieving birth in [the land of] Perfect Bliss is very easy. Even those who commit evil deeds, if, at life's end, they wholeheartedly chant Namu Amida-butsu ten times, are certain to be born there.

Thus, when one contemplates suchness, one can quickly realize even Buddhahood, which is difficult to attain. How much more is one certain beyond doubt to achieve birth in [the pure land of] Utmost Bliss, which is easy! This being the case, those who wish by all means to be born in the Pure Land should simply contemplate suchness. A hundred people out of a hundred are certain to be born there, surely and without doubt. But if one does not believe [that oneself is suchness], that person slanders all Buddhas of the ten directions in the past, present, and future periods of time. This is because the Buddhas of the ten directions, as well as the Lotus Sutra, all take suchness as their essence. One who has slandered the Buddhas of the ten directions or the Lotus Sutra falls into the Hell without Respite (*muken jigoku, avīci*) and will not [readily] emerge. The "Parable" chapter expounds the karmic retribution for the sin of slandering the *Lotus Sutra*, saying: "Such a person, at life's end, shall enter the Avīci hell, where he shall fulfill one kalpa. When the kalpa is exhausted, he shall be reborn there, transmigrating in this way for kalpas without number" [*Miao-fa lien-hua ching*, T 9:15b–c].

How awesome! Whether we fall into the Hell without Respite or are born in the land of Utmost Bliss depends solely on our [attitude of] mind in this life-time. We ourselves are precisely suchness. One who does not believe this will surely fall into hell. But one who believes it deeply without doubting will be born in the Pure Land. Whether we are born in [the land of] Perfect Bliss or fall into hell depends on whether or not we believe in [our identity with] suchness. How pointless that by not believing that one can be born in [the land of] Perfect Bliss by the power of the contemplation of suchness, one falls into the Hell without Respite and suffers for countless kalpas, when, simply by believing deeply, one may be born in [the pure land] of Perfect Bliss and experience happiness that shall not be exhausted in kalpas without number! Therefore we must each firmly believe in the contemplation of suchness. In lifetime after lifetime and age after age, what greater joy could there be than to learn in this life of this way by which one may so easily become a Buddha and be born in [the pure land of] Utmost Bliss? Even if one should break the precepts without shame, one should simply—without the slightest negligence, even while lying down with one's sash unloosed, even for a moment—think, "I am suchness." How extremely easy and reliable [a mode of practice]!

Bodhisattvas of the provisional teachings, who did not know this contemplation of suchness, for countless kalpas broke their bones and discarded bodily life; without even a moment's neglect, they engaged in difficult and painful practices (*nangyō kugyō*), undertaking them because they valued the path of attaining Buddhahood. And in the case of our great teacher, the Thus Come One Śākyamuni, there is no place even the size of a mustard seed where, throughout countless kalpas in the past, he did not throw away his life [for the beings' sake]. Precisely by cultivating such difficult and painful practices, he was able to become a Buddha. But in our case, we have learned of the way of realizing Buddhahood and achieving birth in [the pure land] of Utmost Bliss in a very short time, without cultivating such difficult and painful practices for countless kalpas and without practicing the six perfections [the *pāramitās* of giving, keeping the precepts, forbearance, assiduousness, meditation, and wisdom], simply by a single thought with which we think, "I am suchness." In all the world, [encountering this teaching] is the thing most rare and to be appreciated.

During the time when we did not know that our own mind is precisely the principle of suchness, we thought that the Buddha and ourselves differed greatly and were widely separated. We thought so because we are ordinary worldlings who have not yet extirpated delusions, while the Buddha, throughout countless kalpas, carried out difficult and painful practices, both for his own self-cultivation and to teach others, and is fully endowed with unfathomable merits. Of the Buddha's six perfections and myriad practices, what merit do we possess? Not even in this lifetime have we broken our bones and thrown away our lives [for enlightenment's sake], let alone for countless kalpas! Rather, since it has been our habit since the beginningless past, we value only worldly fame and profit, aspiring to this estate or that temple or shrine; hastening in pursuit of the world's pleasures and prosperity, we have not sustained our aspiration for birth in [the land of] Utmost Bliss, or for Buddhahood and enlightened wisdom (bodhi), which are the important things. Having spent this life in vain, in our next life we are certain to sink into the depths of the three evil paths [of the hells, hungry ghosts, and animals]—so we have thought, but this was merely the deluded mind at a time when we did not yet know the contemplation of suchness.

From today on, knowing that your own mind is itself suchness, evil karma and defilements will not be hindrances; fame and profit will instead become nourishment for the fruition of Buddha[hood] and enlightened wisdom. Even if you should violate the precepts without shame or be negligent and idle [in religious observances], so long as you always contemplate suchness and never forget to do so, you should never think that evil karma or defilements will obstruct your birth in [the pure land of] Utmost Bliss.

Someone asks: I do not understand this about all beings being Buddhas originally. If all beings were Buddhas originally, people would not resolve to become Buddhas through difficult and painful practices. Nor would there be the divisions among the six paths [of transmigration], that is, hell dwellers, hungry ghosts, animals, asuras, humans, and heavenly beings. Thus the Buddha himself taught that the beings of the six paths always exist. In the *Lotus Sutra* itself, it states, "[I, with the eye of a Buddha,] see the beings on the six courses, reduced to poverty's extreme, having neither merit nor wisdom" [Hurvitz, 42]. Moreover, phenomena do not exceed what they actually appear to be. In reality there are humans and horses, cows, dogs and crows, to say nothing of ants and mole crickets. How can one say that all [such] beings are originally Buddhas? And, as people in the world are accustomed to thinking, "Buddha" is one endowed with the thirty-two major and eighty minor marks of physical excellence, an unrestricted being whose supernatural powers and wisdom surpass those of all others. That is precisely why he is worthy of respect. How can such creatures as ants and mole crickets, dogs and crows, be deemed respectworthy and revered as Buddhas?

Now in reply it may be said: Oneself and others are from the outset a single reality that is the principle of suchness, without the distinctions of hell-dwellers, animals [, etc.]. Nevertheless, once ignorance has arisen, within the principle that is without discrimination, we give rise to various discriminations. Thinking of suchness or the universe merely in terms of our individual self, we draw the distinctions of self and other, this and that, arousing the passions of the five aggregates [the physical and mental constituents of existence: forms, perceptions, conceptions, mental volitions, and consciousness] and six dusts [the objects of the senses of sight, sound, smell, taste, touch, and thought]. [Toward objects that accord with our wishes, we arouse the defilement that is greed;] toward objects that do not accord with our wishes, we arouse the defilement that is anger; and toward objects that we neither like nor dislike, we arouse the defilement that is folly. On the basis of the three poisons—greed, anger, and folly—we arouse the eighty-four thousand defilements. At the prompting of these various defilements, we perform a variety of actions. As a result of good actions, we experience the recompense of [birth in] the three good realms of heavenly beings, humans, and asuras. And as a result of evil actions, we invite the retribution of [birth] in the three evil realms of the hells, hungry ghosts, and animals.

In this way, [living] beings and [their insentient] environments of the six paths emerge. While transmigrating through these six realms, we arbitrarily regard as self what is not really the self. Therefore, toward those who go against us, we arouse anger and we abuse and strike or even kill them; thus we cannot put an end to the round of birth and death. Or toward those who accord with us, we arouse a possessive love, forming mutual bonds of obligation and affection thoughout lifetime after lifetime and age after age. In this case as well, there is no stopping of transmigration. In other words, transmigrating through the realm of birth and death is simply the result of not knowing that suchness is oneself, and thus of arbitrarily drawing distinctions between self and other, this and that. When one thinks, "Suchness is my own essence," then there is nothing that is not oneself. How could oneself and others not be the same? And if [one realized that] self and others are not different, who would give rise to defilements and evil actions and continue the round of rebirth?

Thus, if while walking, standing, sitting, or lying down, or while performing any kind of action, you think, "I am suchness," then that is realizing Buddhahood. What could be an obstruction [to such contemplation]? You should know that suchness is to be contemplated with respect to all things. Clergy or laity, male or female—all should contemplate in this way. When you provide for your wife, children, and retainers, or even feed oxen, horses, and the others of the six kinds of domestic animals [that is, horses, oxen, sheep, dogs, pigs, and chickens], because the myriad things are all suchness, if you think that these others are precisely suchness, you have in effect made offerings to all Buddhas and bodhisattvas of the ten directions and three periods of time, as well as to all living beings, without a single exception. This is because nothing is outside the single principle of suchness. Because the myriad creatures such as ants and mole crickets are all suchness, even giving food to a single ant is praised as [encompassing] the merit of making offerings to all Buddhas of the ten directions.

Not only is this true of offerings made to others. Because we ourselves are also suchness [with each thought-moment being mutually identified with and inseparable from all phenomena], one's own person includes all Buddhas and bodhisattvas of the ten directions and three time periods and is endowed with the hundred realms, thousand suchnesses, and three thousand realms, lacking none. Thus, when you yourself eat, if you carry out this contemplation, the merit of the perfection of giving at once fills the universe, and because one practice is equivalent to all practices, the single practice of the perfection of giving contains the other perfections. And because cause and effect are non-dual, all practices, which represent the causal stage, are simultaneously the myriad virtues of the stage of realization. Thus you are a bodhisattva of the highest stage, a Thus Come One of perfect enlightenment.

And not only are living beings suchness. Insentient beings such as grasses and trees are also suchness. Therefore, when one offers a single flower or lights one stick of incense to a single Buddha—because, "of every form and fragrance, there is none that is not the Middle Way"—that single flower or single stick of incense is precisely suchness and therefore pervades the universe. And because the single Buddha [to whom it is offered] is precisely suchness, that one Buddha is all Buddhas, and the countless Buddhas of the ten directions without exception all at once receive that offering. . . . When one contemplates suchness with even a small offering, such as a single flower or stick of incense, one's merit shall be thus great. How much more so, if one chants the Buddha's name even once, or reads or copies a single phrase or verse of the sutra! [In so doing], the merit gained by thinking that each character is the principle of suchness [is so vast that it] cannot be explained in full.

In this way, because all living beings, both self and others, are suchness, they are precisely Buddhas. Because grasses and trees, tiles and pebbles, mountains and rivers, the great earth, the vast sea, and the empty sky are all suchness, there is none that is not Buddha. Looking up at the sky, the sky is Buddha. Looking down at the earth, the earth is Buddha. Turning toward the eastern quarter, the east is Buddha. And the same is true with the south, west, north, the four intermediate directions, up and down.

—21—

The Purification Formula of the Nakatomi

Mark Teeuwen and Hendrik van der Veere

There is little about *Reading and Explanation of the Purification Formula of the Nakatomi* (*Nakatomi Harae Kunge*) that can be said with certainty. Neither the date of composition nor the author(s) of this text is known. The oldest manuscript, on which this translation is based, is preserved at Kanazawa Bunko and dates from the early fourteenth century.

Tradition ascribes the text to Kūkai (774–835), but this is obviously apocryphal. A colophon found in the first printed edition, published in 1691, mentions that the text was first copied in 1191 but gives no details concerning the identity of the copyist or the provenance of the original. Recent research (e.g., by Okada Shōji) has produced a number of indications, both bibliographical and based on the contents of the text, that suggest that the text does indeed date from the late twelfth century. Its author, however, remains unidentified, and all we can say about him (or, perhaps, them) is that he must have been a Buddhist ritual specialist with considerable knowledge of Esoteric doctrine.

The text can be divided into three parts. Part 1 is a theoretical introduction that recommends the Nakatomi Purification Formula to the reader as an excellent ritual tool and summarizes the main doctrinal themes that feature in part 2. Part 2 discusses selected phrases from the formula and gives information about their mythological, doctrinal, and ritual backgrounds. Interestingly, the text refers to the *Chronicles of Japan* (*Nihon shoki*, 720) for mythological data, and to Esoteric Buddhist scriptures and practices when discussing doctrine and ritual. Finally, part 3 contains scriptural evidence from various sources. Large sections of part 3, however, have little bearing on the main subject of the text (the formula) and can be readily identified as later additions, appended in the thirteenth century.

Ritual Background

As indicated by its title, the text deals with a ritual formula called the Nakatomi Purification Formula. This is a slightly adapted version of the Formula of Great Purification (*Ōharae no kotoba*), which was recited by a priest from the Nakatomi clan on the occasion of the semiannual court ceremony of Great Purification. This formula is recorded in book 8 of the *Procedures of the Engi Period* (*Engi shiki*, 927). The adapted version of this formula, which forms the subject of our text, was developed at the court itself as early as the ninth century, for private use.

In the tenth century, recitation of the Nakatomi Purification Formula became part of the rituals of so-called Yin Yang Masters (*onmyōji*), experts in rituals of largely Chinese origin who specialized in the performance of private purification. First mention of this practice is made in the diary of Murasaki no Shikibu (entry 1008, 9th month, 10th day), where an *onmyōji* recites the formula at the bedside of a court lady in labor. Only slightly later, the formula was incorporated in Buddhist ritual. It must have been in the setting of such a ritual that the formula attracted the attention of our author. This is made all the more probable by the following passage from the latter part of part 1:

> When one makes reverence and recites this [formula] seven times, one will not be defiled by the mud of the passions that accompany the state of ignorance. When one worships at a stream and touches it seven times, one can cleanse the waves of the water and purify the source of one's mind.

This passage seems to refer to an Esoteric Buddhist ritual called *rokuji ka-rinpō*, which appears in the documents of the eleventh century. This ritual took seven days to complete and culminated in a *goma* session conducted on a large boat on the last day. As this boat passed through seven rapids, the Esoteric ritual of *rokujikyō-hō* (based on the seed-syllables of the six Kannon who save sentient beings in each of the six realms of transmigration) was repeated seven times. The pollution of the sponsor of the ritual was transferred to three kinds of effigies, which were subsequently burned on the *goma* fire stage, and some of the ashes were swallowed by the sponsor. While it is in essence Buddhist, many elements from this compound ritual can be traced back to the rituals of the Yin Yang Masters; the reciting of the Nakatomi Purification Formula is one of these.

The passage translated above mentions the number "seven" and talks about a "stream"; moreover, elsewhere in part one, the text discusses ritual objects such as "three kinds of effigies." All of this suggests that *Reading and Explanation of the Purification Formula of the Nakatomi* was written with the aim of providing a doctrinal explanation for the working of the Formula as it was used in Buddhist rituals, notably *rokuji karinpō*. This places our text in the genre of *hishaku* or "Esoteric expositions," doctrinal texts that elucidate the value of Esoteric, but also (apparently) Exoteric or even non-Buddhist, practices or concepts for the Esoteric practitioner. Examples of earlier works in this tradition are the Esoteric explanations of the nembutsu by Saisen (1026–1115) and Jitsuhan (1089–1144), and of the syllables of Amida's name by Kakuban (1095–1144).

Relevance of the Text

Our text not only had a place in the older tradition of Esoteric expositions but at the same time marked the beginning of two new traditions or genres, both of which rose to prominence in the ensuing centuries. As a Buddhist treatise about a Shintō ritual formula, *Reading and Explanation of the Purification Formula of the Nakatomi* is generally regarded as the oldest known text of Ryōbu Shintō, a school of Shintō thought that explored new ways of combining Buddhist and Shintō notions into one integrated teaching. Moreover, the text is the first of a large body of commentaries on the Nakatomi Purification Formula.

Ryōbu Shintō was not an independent sect, but a school of thought and ritual that had adherents among Buddhist monks as well as Shintō priests. Its name, which was invented only much later, by Yoshida Kanetomo (1435–1511), means "the Shintō doctrine that is based on the Two *Mandara*" and refers to the Ryōbu Shintō thesis that the two Ise shrines (the Inner and the Outer Shrine) are emanations of the *Taizō* and *Kongōkai Mandara*. In Shingon thought, these *mandara* are seen as two possible depictions of Dainichi, the "cosmic Buddha" who is conceived of as the ultimate reality of the universe. The *Taizō* or "Womb" *Mandara* is described as a depiction of Dainichi's "presence" (*ri*)—Dainichi's compassion through which the universe is brought into existence. The *Kongōkai* or "Diamond Realm" *Mandara* depicts "wisdom" (*chi*), or the insight into Dainichi's presence, and thus into the unity of all existence in Dainichi, which the practitioner must strive to obtain.

According to Esoteric Buddhist doctrine, the entire universe partakes of Dainichi. Accordingly, a human, being no exception, is endowed with an "inherent enlightenment" (*hongaku*) that is innate in all beings. Thus a human has an "original bond" (*hongan*) with Dainichi, which allows the person to attain instantaneous enlightenment in this life. When the practitioner attains the insight that the presence of Dainichi's compassion (*ri*) and wisdom (*chi*) are one and the same, both being modes of description of Dainichi, he or she will be able to attain union with Dainichi, and "inherent enlightenment" will be realized.

Ryōbu Shintō's most important contribution to religious thought was the introduction of the concept of "inherent enlightenment" into Shintō. This led to a radical reinterpretation of the concept of ritual purity that is central to Shintō thought and ritual. Consistent with the Esoteric Buddhist view that the impure partakes of Dainichi as does the pure, our text explains that "the duality of pure and impure does not arise in reality" and recommends meditation as a means of purifying our minds from the ignorance that leads us to make this unreal distinction. The formula is treated as a series of steps through the meditation process, resulting in union with Dainichi and immediate enlightenment. Thus, the text sees purification as a mental process that aims at helping the practitioner realize "inherent enlightenment." This was a radical departure from the traditional conception of purification, in which the aim of this ritual had been to exorcise evil external influences.

The Text's Connection with Ise

A further tradition for which this text was of tremendous importance is Watarai or Ise Shintō, the Shintō of the Ise shrines, or more specifically of the Outer Shrine of Ise and its priests, the Watarai.

The text contains several passages, especially in parts 2 and 3, that point to Ise as their source. In part 2, names of deities and shrines are mentioned that belong to the Ise tradition, suggesting that the original author, who was a Buddhist, consulted an Ise priest on Shintō matters. Part 3 includes quotations from the so-called Secret Books of the Watarai, which date from the mid-thirteenth century.

The Ise priests were more than willing to cooperate with the Buddhist author of the text because they had a keen interest in the Nakatomi Purification Formula. Recitation of this formula was not a traditional practice at Ise but had been adopted by Ise priests in the late twelfth century. In the Heian period, the economy of the Ise shrines had been based almost exclusively on funding from the imperial court. However, as the Heian period gave way to the Kamakura period and the imperial court lost much of its power, court support decreased rapidly, and the priests of Ise were forced to seek new sources of income from private benefactors. This led them to adopt the practice of performing private purification, and of reciting the Nakatomi Purification Formula, from the Yin Yang Masters

The Ise priests employed various means to make this new practice their own. They argued that the gods who, according to the formula, remove the impurity from the Japanese islands are in fact spirits of the gods of the Inner and the Outer Shrine. This theory figures in part 2 of our text, and one might imagine that the Ise priests were more than happy to see their claim recognized by Buddhist monks. Moreover, Ise priests used *Reading and Explanation of the Purification Formula of the Nakatomi* to construe their own secret tradition of recitation of the Formula. They made some small changes to the formula text, resulting in an "Ise-style" Nakatomi Purification Formula. The first results of this process can be seen in *Commentary on the Nakatomi Purification Formula* (*Nakatomi harae chūshō*), which was compiled in or shortly before 1215. Interestingly, some of these changes can be shown to have been inspired by the explanations of phrases from the formula in part 2 of *Reading and Explanation of the Purification Formula of the Nakatomi*.

The interest of the Ise priests in this text is also apparent from the numerous interpolations and additions they made to it, especially in part 3. Most of these can be readily identified because they are quotations from the Secret Books of the

Watarai, and because they are concerned with the sanctity of the Ise shrines and their position in the religious world—a subject altogether absent from part 1. It should be noted that no manuscript survives of the "original" text—the text as it was before it was rewritten by the Ise priests. Even the oldest extant manuscript goes back to a copy from Ise.

In part 1 there is one passage that we have identified as a Watarai interpolation. The phrase "In olden times, when Heaven and Earth first separated and the Divine Treasure of the Sun appeared" was added at the beginning of a sentence that describes how Dainichi brought the universe into existence. This phrase was taken from the *Record of Yamato-hime no Mikoto* (*Yamato-hime no Mikoto seiki*), one of the Secret Books of the Watarai. It is inconsistent not only with Esoteric Buddhist doctrine in general, but also with the following sentence, which states that the "Great God" (which is unambiguously identified as Amaterasu only by the above interpolation) served as a defendant of Buddhism only *after* Dainichi had produced the universe.

The idea that purification is a means of realizing one's "inherent enlightenment" (*hongaku*) remained central to Shintō thought and practice until the seventeenth century, when Neo-Confucian interpretations of Shintō myth and ritual supplanted Buddhist ones. At Ise, this idea was reflected in a secret "oral tradition" of Ise style recitation of the Nakatomi Purification Formula, laid down in a *Collection of Purification Rites* (*Shoharae shū*, fifteenth century). This text prescribes that at a crucial point in the Formula, priests must, under their breath, add a verse from the *Diamond Peak Sutra* (Kongōchōgyō):

> You pure ones, remember this: All dharmas are like reflecting images. They are pure and without a speck of defilement. This is beyond words. They are all produced from karmic causes.

This verse was quoted by Kūkai in his (posthumous) *Collected Works of Prose and Poetry* (Shōryōshū), and, from there, by our unknown author in part 2 of *Reading and Explanation of the Purification Formula of the Nakatomi*, where he comments: "When you contemplate on this [verse], you will see the wondrous presence [of Dainichi's compassion] (*myōri*) that is beyond comprehension and explanation."

Thus this verse, which points out that impurity does not exist in reality, and that from the viewpoint of the absolute, all dharmas are pure, was incorporated in the execution of purification by Ise priests. They adopted the verse as an expression of the Esoteric meaning of purification and thereby transformed purification into a quest for union with Dainichi's "wondrous presence," or, in other words, instantaneous enlightenment.

This excerpt is a translation of part 1 only; an annotated full translation, with a detailed introduction and analysis has been published under the title *Nakatomi*

Harae Kunge: Purification and Enlightenment in Late-Heian Japan, Buddhist Studies 1/1998 (München: iudicium verlag, 1998).

Further Reading

Basic Terms of Shinto, rev. ed. (Tokyo: Kokugakuin Daigaku, 1985); F. G. Bock, tr., *Engi-Shiki,* 2 vols. (Tokyo: Sophia University, 1970 and 1972); Allan G. Grapard, "The Shinto of Yoshida Kanetomo," *Monumenta Nipponica* 47, 1 (Spring 1992): 27–58; James Legge, tr., *The Chinese Classics*, vol. 1: *Confucian Analects, The Great Learning, and The Doctrine of the Mean* (Oxford: Clarendon Press, 1893, reprinted by Southern Materials Center, Taipei, 1983); Nelly Nauman, *Die Einheimische Religion Japans*, vol. 2 (Leiden: E. J. Brill, 1994); Donald L. Philippi, tr., *Norito, a New Translation of the Ancient Japanese Ritual Prayers* (Tokyo: Kokugakuin University, 1959; new edition by Princeton: Princeton University Press, 1990); Jacqueline Stone, "Medieval Tendai Hongaku Thought and the New Kamakura Buddhism: A Reconsideration," *Japanese Journal of Religious Studies* 22, 1–2 (Spring 1995): 17–48; Mark Teeuwen, "Attaining Union with the Gods; The Secret Books of Watarai Shintō," *Monumenta Nipponica* 48, 2 (Summer 1993): 225–245.

Reading and Explanation of the Purification Formula of the Nakatomi

Although the origin of the manifestation [in our human world] of the Buddha's light [in the form of the kami] is described in the National Histories and House Records, there are still matters that are left unsaid, and people are unable to recognize its true meaning. Here, I shall briefly indicate the essential road that leads to the mind from which all things spring, on the basis of the Esoteric teaching of [Dainichi,] the Lord of Enlightenment.

It is generally understood that the Nakatomi Purification Formula, also known as *Ama-tsu-Hosata* or *Hafurita no Nonto-Kotoba* [or, traditionally, *Ama-tsu-Norito no Futo-Noritogoto*, "the Heavenly Norito, the Great Norito"], is a Divine Message of Izanagi no Mikoto, [who first recited it after his visit to Izanami in the Nether World,] and was recited by Ame no Koyane no Mikoto [, the divine ancestor of the Nakatomi, when Susanowo performed purification after Amaterasu had left the Rock Cave of Heaven]. [However, the words of this formula are more than that:] they are the beneficent truth that one's own mind is pure, and they are Sanskrit words of Daijizaiten [, Maheśvara, who is an emanation of Dainichi and is also associated with Izanagi]; they are helpful means of all the buddhas of the past, the present, and the future, and a field of bliss for all sentient beings; they contain the extensive and great wisdom that springs from the mind, and the great teaching that in essence all is pure; [this formula] is a *darani* that dispels fear, and a divine spell of repentance for one's transgressions. In truth, it begets the most superior and greatest beneficence and boundless salvation; it is the Way of the teaching for the worldly and the supraworldly and a hidden technique that removes suffering and bestows bliss. [He who recites this formula] will live eternally in harmony with Heaven and Earth, and be blessed eternally in harmony with the Sun and the Moon.

In olden times, when Heaven and Earth first separated and the Divine Treasure of the Sun appeared, Dainichi—who is the Dharma Realm, and the Dharma Body, and the Ultimate Mind—in order to save sentient beings who are without opportunities [to meet a buddha and hear the teaching] and who are suffering from bad karma, entered the Lotus Meditation by means of his wisdom to apply all conceivable manner of helpful means; he created the great bond of purity, he made apparent his compassion springing from his love and pity, and he manifested himself in a temporary transformation [as Śākyamuni]; he left his footsteps in Jambudvīpa, demanded the seal of power from King Māra, [ruler of the World of Desire,] and wielded the divine power that subjugates [evil]; he sent Śākyamuni's teaching and disciples in all directions and spread his compassion and blessings everywhere. And ever since this time, the Great God [Amaterasu] has acted as a divine warrior who, although on the surface performing ceremonies that are different from the Buddhist teachings, in essence protects the Buddhist Law. Although within and without [the Buddhist teachings] the words are different, [kami and buddhas] are identical as means of salvation. Kami are the spirits of the various buddhas; the Buddha constitutes the essence of the various kami. Therefore it is written in a sūtra: "The Buddha dwells in nonduality and always manifests himself in the form of kami."

Thus we know that through the permeating power of [the Buddha, mediated by] the kami, [this formula] leads erring sentient beings to the Buddhist Way by means of the power of the bond that leads to salvation. This [formula] is one of good and adequate helpful means, it contains the real wisdom of the great compassion, it constitutes the original bond according to which there is no duality of mind and matter, and according to which all benefit from the equality [of human and Dainichi]. Thus it makes manifest the workings of the kami in this world and activates their majestic power, and delivers [humans] from a lifetime of suffering and provides them with a hundred years of bliss. Humans will escape from the five fundamental conditions of passions and delusions and leave the cage of the three worlds; they will see the wondrous presence of Suchness and experience the domain of the flower-dais that is adorned with mysteries [mitsugon kedai, Dainichi's universe in which the identity of wisdom and compassion is realized].

This Purification Formula is the ultimate great divine spell. The manner in which it fulfills all wishes can be compared to the blowing of a swift wind. The manner in which it completely realizes what is sought after can be compared to [the realization of] Jizaiten [that is, Maheśvara, but here probably meaning "the deity that is omnipresent"]. Therefore it is the Original Way of the equality of the ten worlds [of the six realms of hell of hungry spirits, animals, asura, humans, and heavenly beings; and the four worlds of "listeners," pratyekabud-

dhas, bodhisattvas, and buddhas]; it is a dharma-gate offered by the various Honored Ones out of their great compassion; it is one aspect of the permeating power that stems from Uncreated Nature (*hōni*); and it is a secret technique of all Devas and of the Three Treasures of Buddhism. For the wise, it is a teaching of meditation [through which one can attain union with] the various Honored Ones; for the foolish, it is a good incentive to become a *pratyekabuddha* or a disciple.

Harae (purification) is called *yaraimasu* (to exile) in the first volume [of the *Chronicles of Japan*] on the Age of the Gods [in which Susanowo no Mikoto was exiled as part of his purification]. The correct reading is *harahe*. When we scrutinize its true meaning, we find that it destroys the four [categories of] demons who are our enemies with the help of the supernatural power of wisdom. In a work on this formula called *Hongi*, it is said:

> The enemies of the past, the present, and the future recede from the border and will not approach. The evil thoughts of the countless people cross the border and will perish in the distance. The three disasters and seven calamities disappear as snow sprinkled with hot water; the hundred poisons and nine unnatural deaths vanish as fire drenched with water; the countless evils and hindrances disappear as hair burnt in the fire. Thus the evil demons flee ten thousand miles, and the seven hardships do not approach and will not occur. The fortress [constructed in Taoist rituals of exorcism] invites the Five Emperors [who lead Heavenly Armies from the north, east, south, west, and the center], and countless good fortunes approach and will arise. He who performs this purification once will be freed of hindrances for a hundred days; he who performs it a hundred times will be freed of a thousand days of divine wrath.

The form of the *ōnusa* [tree branch used in purification rites] is a representation (*samaya*) of the purity of one's original nature and a symbol of the *samādhi* of [Dainichi's] Universal Presence [*fugen*, the omnipresent nature of Dainichi's concentration]. [The celebrant,] wearing a robe of endurance and holding a *shaku* of uprightness [, the wooden object held in the right hand as part of the formal wear of Shintō priests and court nobles], sweeps away the three poisons and the seven calamities and liberates [the sponsor] of the five impurities and the eight sufferings. The ritual robe is an armor of endurance. When one holds the *shaku* while resisting evil thoughts, it will become a sword of wisdom that deters all enemies. Its form is straight; its working is perfect.

Harae-tsu-mono [, offerings made to expiate past errors or impurities,] and *agamono* [, which include effigies thrown into a river after one's impurities or misfortunes have been transferred onto them,] such as rice, cloth, effigies of gold, silver, and iron, bows and arrows, and long and short swords, are all implements that the divine warriors use to dispell evil demons. The various buddhas graciously receive these [offerings] and activate their power to use helpful means; when [the celebrant] shoots off the arrows of wisdom from the bow of concentration [associated with the left hand] and brandishes the sword of wisdom [associated with the right hand], he sends the *cakravartin* Taishak-uten and Bonten to the east and the west and dispels the Devas, demons, those outside Buddhism, and so forth, to the south and the north. The sun and the moon, the five stars, the twelve gods, and the twenty-eight constellations dim their light and mingle with the dust [of our world] in order to benefit sentient beings. [The celebrant] makes a vow and joins his hands. As for the offerings of cloth, and so forth: because for humans the benevolence of Heaven and Earth is the most august in life after life, and the power of buddhas and the kami is the most delightful in birth after birth, we offer these things in return for their benevolence.

To perform *harae* is to purify oneself of all transgressions and divine wrath by means of a mystic ritual formula; this is the same as to return to the won-drous state in which everything is originally unborn, represented by the syllable A, and to realize the real wisdom of the subtle brightness of one's own nature. The duality of pure and impure does not arise in reality. And so, the condi-tioned is in fact attachment, and the unconditioned is in fact the entity that is pure. This, [the unconditioned,] is the essence of our minds. If one practices meditation, one's mind will gradually become pure. Because of this, when one makes reverence and recites this [formula] seven times, one will not be defiled by the mud of the passions that accompany the state of ignorance. When one worships at a stream and touches it seven times, one can cleanse the waves of the water and purify the source of one's mind. Thus one will escape from the net of the ten passions and not be caught in the three existences [*san'u*, the realms of desire, form, and nonform that together constitute the world of trans-migration]. This is called "purification." It is a secret technique to extinguish transgressions, to produce good, and to attain instantaneous enlightenment.

I hear the following: When one worships the gods of heaven and earth, [the gods] attend benevolently to one's concerns if one is pure and clean. Because of [their purity,] the gods abhor impurity (heavenly spirits are called *shin*, earthly spirits are called *gi*, and human spirits are called *ki*; therefore one speaks of heavenly *shin*, earthly *gi*, and human *ki*). The Imperial Words [of Emperor Shōmu (r. 724–749)] of the Sacred dynasty say: "In driving away misfortune and courting good fortune, we depend upon the other world. In revering the gods and worshipping the buddhas, first of all we must make sure to be pure." A sūtra says: "When your mind is pure, the buddhas will dwell in it." To be pure is to activate the wisdom that one's own mind is pure; it is the original nature of quiescence and bliss. Impurity is the karmic cause of cycles of birth and death, and the karmic result of the burning hell of eternal suffering. There-fore the defilements of birth and death are the gravest of all. The Buddha has taught:

> The admonitions of the manifestations are in accord with the precepts of the various buddhas; he who follows the admonitions of the kami is [at the same

time] abiding by the precepts of the various buddhas. Some will observe the months of fasting and the various days of celebration, and others will undertake pilgrimages; rich and poor either present flowers and incense to the Three Treasures of Buddhism, or offer herbs to the *kami*. Those who perform these acts thus create a cause that will lead them into the Inner Teaching [of Buddhism]. Creating a cause for [rebirth in] a Pure Land, they will cross the sea of birth and death and reach the shore of enlightenment. If sentient beings have no goodness, I will give them goodness; if they have no enlightenment, I will turn toward them with enlightenment, with which I will illuminate their inner realization (*naishō*).

Thus we know with certainty that humans possess the wisdom of the buddhas of past, present, and future and can attain perfect salvation in the present and the future. This is beyond words, this is beyond words.

The teaching says:

To the east, beyond the eighty myriad worlds, countless as the grains of sand in the river Ganges, lies the Buddha Land. It is called the Original Land of Dainichi [*Dainichi hongoku* or *Dai-Nippon-goku*, "Great Japan"]. A kami dwells in this land, named Ōhirume no Muchi [, which is another name for Amaterasu]. Know this: all sentient beings who are born in this land receive the majestic and divine power of the buddhas, and here they dwell in bliss together with the various buddhas. This is what the Buddha teaches us; these are not my own words.

— 22 —

Dōgen's *Lancet of Seated Meditation*

Carl Bielefeldt

In modern times the early Zen master Dōgen (1200–1253) has become known as one of the greatest philosophical minds of premodern Japan and is widely celebrated for his distinctive theories of being, time, and the Buddha nature. Among Dōgen's descendants in the Sōtō school of Zen, however, he is most revered for what we might loosely call his "soteriological" teachings—i.e., his views on spiritual practice and its goal. Here he is known especially for his doctrine that Buddhist practice and its goal of Buddhahood are one (a doctrine often called by the school "the unity of practice and verification" [shushō ittō]), and for his advocacy of a style of meditation (typically referred to as "just sitting" [shikan taza]) in which the practitioner is advised to abandon all strategies of mental control and pretense of spiritual advancement and to abide simply in the mysterious state known as "body and mind sloughed off" (shinjin datsuraku).

There is no doubt that Dōgen was one of the most original and articulate interpreters of Zen practice in the history of the school, and that his extensive corpus of writings is replete with material on the central practice—from which the school got its very name—of seated meditation (zazen). In addition to several manuals on the theoretical principles and practical techniques of zazen, he left a number of important essays on the practice that are included in his famous collection, *The Treasury of the Eye of the True Dharma* (*Shōbō genzō*). Among the most interesting of these is the text translated here: the *Zazen shin*, or "Lancet of Seated Meditation," originally composed in 1242 at Dōgen's Kōshōji monastery near Kyoto and subsequently presented to his monks in the winter of 1243, shortly after its author had retired from Kōshōji to the remote province of Echizen.

Like most of the representative texts of the *Treasury*, the *Lancet* takes the form of a series of comments on selected passages from the Chinese Ch'an literature—especially the famous stories of the masters that often served as *kōan*, or "public cases" for commentary and study in Sung period Ch'an. The Sōtō contemplative style of "just sitting" is often said to do away with the use of such cases in meditation (in contrast to the style of the Rinzai school, which typically encourages a practice focused on the *kōan*); but, as is clear from the *Zazen shin* and many other texts of the *Shōbō genzō*, Dōgen's own Zen was deeply indebted to the historical record of the Ch'an masters' stories and intimately bound to their study and interpretation. Indeed, much of the power of Dōgen's writing derives from his almost uncanny ability to draw out rich and surprising meanings from these stories—an ability that is well exemplified in our text here.

The "Lancet of Seated Meditation" is divided into four sections. The first is devoted to the *kōan* known as "thinking of not thinking," a saying of the early eighth-century master Yüeh-shan Wei-yen (Yakusan Igen, 745–828). Although the discussion of it here is very brief, this *kōan* is central to the Sōtō understanding of Dōgen's meditation; for it appears as a description of (or perhaps prescription for) the practice in his *Universal Promotion of the Principles of Seated Meditation* (*Fukan zazen gi*), a manual recognized by the school as the chief source for its style of *zazen*. As might be expected, therefore, a great deal of effort has gone into the interpretation of the key epistemological terms in this saying: "thinking," "not thinking," and something described as "nonthinking." Dōgen himself is not much help here; indeed, his attention in this passage seems to be focused as much on the image of the master "sitting fixedly" in meditation as it is on his state of mind. This is an important clue, I think, to the entire text and to Dōgen's approach to meditation teaching more broadly: that the spiritual significance of meditation lies as much in the wholehearted participation in the historic practice of *zazen* as in any particular psychological technique.

The first section of the *Lancet* closes with a criticism of those who misunderstand *zazen* as either a method of mental calm or a preliminary exercise unnecessary for those who realize that everything they do is naturally Zen. Dōgen then offers his own interpretation of the practice, in a passage that is one of the most important statements of his understanding of *zazen*. The passage is quite difficult, and readers will disagree on its meaning; but since it is important and difficult, let me hazard here a possible paraphrase.

Zazen is the orthodox practice of Buddhism. At the same time, this practice, properly understood, is not merely a utilitarian device for producing a perfected state of enlightenment (what Dōgen calls here "making a Buddha") but the expression of a more fundamental perfection inherent in all beings ("the practice of a Buddha"). When we understand it in this way, the practice of *zazen* itself becomes the actualization of ultimate truth ("the realization of the *kōan*"), and the practitioner, just as he is, becomes the incarnation of perfect enlightenment ("the embodied Buddha"). This higher understanding, free from the "baskets and cages" of our ordinary understanding, reveals the seated practitioner as a "seated Buddha" and, in this sense, "makes a Buddha." In this revelation, we recognize what was always true "from the very beginning": that our enlightenment extends to all our states (even those in which we become "Māra The Evil One") and indeed to "the ditches and moats" of the world around us.

In his second section, Dōgen turns to the famous story known as "Nan-yüeh Polishes a Tile." In this story, Nan-yüeh Huai-jang (Nangaku Ejō, 677–744) likens his disciple Ma-tsu's (Baso Dōitsu, 709–788) attempt to "make a Buddha" by sitting in meditation to someone's trying to make a mirror by polishing a tile, or trying to drive an ox cart by whipping the cart instead of the ox. Buddhahood, says Nan-yüeh, has no fixed form, and to fix on the form of the "seated Buddha" is to "kill the Buddha." On the face of it, the story would seem to be a criticism— often in fact seen in the sayings of the masters—of the view that *zazen* practice is central to Zen soteriology. But Dōgen's commentary goes through the story to bring out in each line of the dialogue his own vision of the higher understanding of the practice—a vision in which Buddhahood becomes the act of polishing a tile, beating the cart is the way to move it along the path of the Buddha, and killing the Buddha is what it means to be a Buddha.

The brief third section of the text praises *zazen* as the very essence of the tradition of the Ch'an patriarchate in India and China and laments the failure of most Ch'an monks to appreciate it. Returning to his earlier attack on the contemporary Chinese treatment of meditation (a theme that becomes quite prominent in his writings from this period), Dōgen dismisses the understanding of the Sung Ch'an abbots and the meditation literature appearing in the Sung historical records of the school. Only one such abbot is an authentic representative of the patriarchate; only one meditation text is a true expression of Buddhist enlightenment. With this, Dōgen introduces the poem from which his own work takes its name: the "Lancet of Seated Meditation (*Tso-ch'an chen*) by Hung-chih Cheng-chüeh (Wanshi Shōgaku, 1091–1157), the most famous master in the recent history of Dōgen's Ts'ao-tung lineage and former head of the T'ien-t'ung monastery where Dōgen had studied in China.

The final section of the text, then, is taken up with Dōgen's commentary on Hung-chih's poem. Here, we see our author in high Zen literary form as he plays through the terms in each line and adorns his play with obscure allusions to the classical sayings of the masters. Then, in the end, with a formal announcement of the solemnity of the occasion, Dōgen offers his own, upgraded version of the poem.

My translation is based on the edition of the *Zazen shin* published in Ōkubo Dōshū, ed., *Dōgen zenji zenshū*, vol. 1 (Tokyo: Chikuma Shobō, 1969): 90–101. I have tried not to litter the translation with notes on its technical terminology and references to its many literary sources; but, given the difficulty of the text, I have added a few emendations (in square brackets) and occasional notes suggesting a possible interpretation of particularly murky passages. Readers seeking more detailed annotation can consult the appendix to my *Dōgen's Manuals of Zen Meditation* (Berkeley: University of California Press, 1988).

Further Reading

Carl Bielefeldt, *Dōgen's Manuals of Zen Meditation* (Berkeley: University of California Press, 1988); Carl Bielefeldt, "Recarving the Dragon: History and Dogma in the Study of Dōgen," in *Dōgen Studies*, ed. William R. LaFleur (Honolulu: University of Hawaii Press): 21–53; William M. Bodiford, *Sōtō Zen in Medieval Japan* (Honolulu: University of Hawaii Press, 1993); Bernard Faure, *The Rhetoric of Immediacy: A Cultural Critique of Chan/Zen Buddhism* (Princeton: Princeton University Press, 1991).

Lancet of Seated Meditation

at Kannon Dōri Kōshō Hōrinji

Once, when the Great Master Hung-tao of Yüeh-shan was sitting in meditation, a monk asked him, "What are you thinking of, sitting there so fixedly?"
The master answered, "I'm thinking of not thinking."
The monk asked, "How do you think of not thinking?"
The Master answered, "Nonthinking."

Verifying that such are the words of the Great Master, we should study and participate in the correct transmission of fixed sitting. This is the investigation of fixed sitting transmitted in the way of the Buddha. Although he is not alone in "thinking fixedly," Yüeh-shan's words are singular: he is "thinking of not thinking." These words express what is the very "skin, flesh, bones, and marrow" of "thinking" and the very skin, flesh, bones, and marrow of "not thinking."

"The monk asked, 'How do you think of not thinking?'" Indeed, though the notion of "not thinking" may be old, here it is the question, "how do you think" of it? Could there be no "thinking" in sitting "fixedly"? In sitting "fixedly," how could we fail to penetrate this? If we are not the sort of fool that "despises what is near," we ought to have the strength—and the "thinking"—to question sitting "fixedly."

"The master answered, 'Nonthinking.'" Although the employment of "nonthinking" is "crystal clear," when we "think of not thinking," we always use "nonthinking." There is someone in "nonthinking," and this someone maintains us. Although it is we who are sitting "fixedly," our sitting is not merely "thinking": it presents itself as sitting "fixedly." Although sitting "fixedly" is sitting "fixedly," how could it "think" of sitting "fixedly"? Therefore, sitting "fixedly" is not the "measure of the Buddha," not the measure of awakening, not the measure of comprehension.[1]

The single transmission of this sitting "fixedly" by Yüeh-shan represents the thirty-sixth generation directly from the Buddha Śākyamuni: if we trace back from Yüeh-shan thirty-six generations, we come to the Buddha Śākyamuni. And in what was thus correctly transmitted from the Buddha there was already [Yüeh-shan's] "thinking of not thinking."

Recently, however, some stupid illiterates say, "Once the breast is without concerns, the concentrated effort at seated meditation is a state of peace and calm." This view does not compare with that of the Hīnayāna scholastics; it is inferior even to the lowest Buddhist vehicles of men and gods. How could one who holds such a view be called a person who studies the teaching of the Buddha? At present there are many such practitioners in the Great Sung. How sad that the path of the Patriarchs has become overgrown.

Then there is another type that holds that to pursue the way through seated meditation is a function essential for the "beginner's mind and the latter-day student," but it is not necessarily an observance of the Buddhas and Patriarchs.

As the saying goes, "Walking is Zen, sitting is Zen; whether in speech or silence, motion or rest, the substance is at ease."[2] Therefore, they say, do not adhere solely to the present concentrated effort of seated meditation. This view is common among those calling themselves a branch of the Lin-chi lineage. It is because of a deficiency in the transmission of the orthodox lineage of the teaching of the Buddha that they say this. What is the "beginner's mind"? Where is there no "beginner's mind"? Where do we leave the "beginner's mind"?

Be it known that, for studying the way, the established means of investigation is pursuit of the way in seated meditation. The essential point that marks this investigation is the understanding that there is a practice of a Buddha that does not seek to "make a Buddha." Since the practice of a Buddha is not to make a Buddha, it is the "realization of the kōan." The embodied Buddha does not make a Buddha; when "the baskets and cages are broken," a seated Buddha does not interfere with making a Buddha. At just such a time—from one thousand, from ten thousand ages past, from the very beginning—we have the power, as they say, "to enter into Buddha and enter into Māra." Walking forward or back, "its measure fills the ditches and moats."[3]

When the Ch'an master Ta-chi of Chiang-hsi was studying with the Ch'an master Ta-hui of Nan-yüeh, after intimately receiving the mind seal, he always sat in meditation. Once Nan-yüeh went to Ta-chi and said, "Worthy one, what are you figuring to do, sitting there in meditation?"

We should give concentrated effort to the investigation of this question. Does it mean that there must be some "figuring" above and beyond "seated meditation"? Is there no path to be "figured" outside of "seated meditation"? Should there be no "figuring" at all? Or does it ask what kind of "figuring" occurs at the very time we are practicing "seated meditation"? We should make concentrated effort to understand this in detail. Rather than "love the carved dragon," we should go on to love the real dragon. We should learn that both the carved and the real dragons have the ability to produce clouds and rain. Do not "value what is far away," and do not despise it; become completely familiar with it. Do not "despise what is near at hand," and do not value it; become completely familiar with it. Do not "take the eyes lightly," and do not give them weight. Do not "give weight to the ears," and do not take them lightly. Make your eyes and ears clear and sharp.[4]

Chiang-hsi said, "I'm figuring to make a Buddha."

We should clarify and penetrate the meaning of these words. What does it mean to speak of "making a Buddha"? Does it mean to be "made a Buddha" by the Buddha? Does it mean to "make a Buddha" of the Buddha? Does it mean that "one or two faces" of the Buddha emerge? Is it that "figuring to make a Buddha" is "sloughing off [body and mind]," and that what is meant here is a "figuring to make a Buddha" as the act of sloughing off? Or does "figuring to make a Buddha" mean that, while there are ten thousand ways to "make a Buddha," they become "entangled" in this "figuring"?

It should be recognized that Ta-chi's words mean that "seated meditation" is always "figuring to make a Buddha," is always the "figuring" of "making a Buddha." This "figuring" must be prior to "making a Buddha"; it must be subsequent to "making a Buddha"; and it must be at the very moment of "making a Buddha." Now what I ask is this: How many ways of "making a Buddha" does this one "figuring" entangle? These entanglements themselves "intertwine" with entanglements. At this point, entanglements, as individual instances of the entirety of "making a Buddha," are all direct statements of that entirety and are all instances of "figuring." We should not seek to avoid this one "figuring": when we avoid the one "figuring," we "destroy our body and lose our life." Yet when we destroy our body and lose our life, this is also the entanglement of the one "figuring."[5]

At this point, Nan-yüeh took up a tile and began to rub it on a stone. At length, Ta-chi asked, "Master, what are you doing?"

Who could fail to see that he was "polishing a tile"? Who could see that he was "polishing a tile"? Still, "polishing a tile" has been questioned in this way: "What are you doing?" This "what are you doing?" is itself always "polishing a tile." This land and the other world may differ, but the essential message of "polishing a tile" never ceases. Not only should we avoid deciding that what we see is what we see, we should be firmly convinced that there is an essential message to be studied in all the ten thousand activities. We should know that, just as we may see the Buddha without knowing or understanding him, so we may see rivers and yet not know rivers, may see mountains and yet not know mountains. The precipitate assumption that the phenomena before one's eyes offer no further passage for understanding is not Buddhist study.

Nan-yüeh said, "I'm polishing this to make a mirror."

We should be clear about the meaning of these words. There is definitely a principle in "polishing a tile to make a mirror": there is the "*kōan* of realization"; this is no mere empty contrivance. A "tile" may be a "tile" and a "mirror" a "mirror," but when we exert ourselves in investigating the principle of "polishing," we shall find there are many examples [of "polishing a tile to make a mirror"]. The "old mirror" and the "bright mirror" [often spoken of in Ch'an as metaphors for the inherent Buddha mind]—these are "mirrors" made through "polishing a tile." If we do not realize that these "mirrors" come from "polishing a tile," then the Buddhas and Patriarchs have nothing to say; they do not open their mouths, and we do not perceive them exhaling.

Ta-chi said, "How can you produce a mirror by polishing a tile?"

Indeed, though the one who is "polishing a tile" be "a man of iron," who borrows no power from another, "polishing a tile" is not "producing a mirror." Even if it is "producing a mirror," it must be quick about it.

Nan-yüeh replied, "How can you make a Buddha by sitting in meditation?"

This is clearly understood: there is a principle that "seated meditation" does not await "making a Buddha"; there is nothing obscure about the essential message that "making a Buddha" is not connected with "seated meditation."

Ta-chi asked, "Then, what is right?"

These words resemble a simple question about this practical matter of "what" to do, but they are also asking about that final "rightness." You should realize that the relationship between "what" and "right" here is like, for example, the occasion when one friend meets another: the fact that he is my friend means that I am his friend. Similarly, the meanings here of "what" and "right" emerge simultaneously.[6]

Nan-yüeh replied, "When someone is driving a cart, if the cart doesn't go, should he beat the cart or beat the ox?"

Now, when we say "the cart doesn't go," what do we mean by the cart's "going" or "not going"? For example, is the cart's "going" analogous to water's flowing, or is it analogous to water's not flowing? There is a sense in which we can say that flowing is water's "not going," and that water's "going" is not its flowing. Therefore, when we investigate the words, "the cart doesn't go," we should approach them both in terms of "not going" and in terms of not "not going"; for it is a question of time. The words "if the cart doesn't go" do not mean simply that it does not go.

"Should he beat the cart or beat the ox?" Does this mean that there is a "beating of the cart" as well as a "beating of the ox"? Are "beating the cart" and "beating the ox" the same or not? In the mundane world, there is no method of "beating the cart"; but, though ordinary men have no such method, we know that on the path of the Buddha there is a method of "beating the cart," and this is the very eye of Buddhist study. Even though we study that there is a method of "beating the cart," we should give concentrated effort to understanding in detail that this is not the same as "beating the ox." And even though the method of "beating the ox" is common in the world, we should go on to study the "beating of the ox" on the path of the Buddha. Is this "ox-beating" the water buffalo? Or "ox-beating" the iron bull or the clay ox? Is this beating with a whip, with the entire world, the entire mind? Is this to beat with the marrow? Should we beat with the fist? The fist should beat the fist, and the ox beat the ox.[7]

Ta-chi did not reply.

We should not miss the import of this. In it, there is, as they say, "throwing out a tile to take in a jade"; there is "turning the head and reversing the face." By no means should we do violence to his silence here.[8]

Nan-yüeh went on, "Are you studying seated meditation or are you studying seated Buddha?"

Investigating these words, we should distinguish the essential activity of the Patriarchal ancestors. Even without knowing the full reality of "studying seated meditation," we do know here that it is "studying seated Buddha." Who but a scion of true descent could say that "studying seated meditation" is "studying seated Buddha"? We should know indeed that the "seated meditation" of the beginner's mind is the first "seated meditation," and the first "seated meditation" is the first "seated Buddha." In speaking of this "seated meditation," Nan-yüeh said,

"If you're studying seated meditation, meditation is not sitting still."

The point of what he says here is that "seated meditation" is "seated meditation" and is not "sitting still." From the time the fact that it is not "sitting still" has been singly transmitted to us, our unlimited "sitting still" is our own self. Why should we inquire about close or distant familial lines? How could we discuss delusion and awakening? Who would seek wisdom and eradication of the spiritual "afflictions"? Then Nan-yüeh said,

"If you're studying seated Buddha, Buddha is no fixed mark."

Such is the way to say what is to be said. The reason the "seated Buddha" is one or two Buddhas is that he adorns himself with "no fixed mark." When Nan-yueh says here that "Buddha is no fixed mark," he is describing the mark of the Buddha. Since he is a Buddha of "no fixed mark," the "seated Buddha" is difficult to avoid. Therefore, since it is adorned with this mark of "Budddha is no fixed mark," "if you're studying seated meditation," you are a "seated Buddha." "In a nonabiding dharma," who would "grasp or reject" anything as not the Buddha? Who would "grasp or reject" it as the Buddha. It is because "seated meditation" has sloughed off all "grasping and rejecting" that it is a "seated Buddha."[9] Nan-yüeh continues,

"If you're studying seated Buddha, this is killing Buddha."

This means that, when we further investigate "seated Buddha," we find that it has the virtue of "killing Buddha." At the very moment that we are a "seated Buddha," we are "killing Buddha." Indeed, when we pursue it, we find that the [thirty- two] marks and [eighty] signs and the radiance of "killing Buddha" are always a "seated Buddha." Although the word "kill" here is identical with that used by ordinary people, its meaning is not the same. Moreover, we must investigate in what form it is that a "seated Buddha" is "killing Buddha." Taking up the fact that it is itself a virtue of the Buddha to "kill Buddha," we should study whether we are killers or not.[10]

"If you grasp the mark of sitting, you're not reaching its principle."

To "grasp the mark of sitting" here means to "reject the mark of sitting" and to touch "the mark of sitting." The principle behind this is that, in being a "seated Buddha," we cannot fail to "grasp the mark of sitting." Since we cannot fail to "grasp" it, though our "grasping the mark of sitting" is crystal clear, we are "not reaching its principle." This kind of concentrated effort is called "sloughing off body and mind."

Those who have never sat do not talk like this: such talk belongs to the time of sitting and the one who sits, to the "seated Buddha" and the study of the "seated Buddha." The sitting that occurs when the ordinary human sits is not the sitting of the "seated Buddha." Although a man's sitting naturally resembles a "seated Buddha," or a Buddha's sitting, the case is like that of a human's "making a Buddha," or the human who makes a Buddha: though there are humans who make Buddhas, not all humans make Buddhas, and Buddhas are not all humans. Since all the Buddhas are not simply all humans, a human is by no means a Buddha, and a Buddha is by no means a human. The same is true of a "seated Buddha."

Here, then, in Nan-yüeh and Chiang-hsi we have a superior master and strong disciple: Chiang-hsi is the one who verifies "making a Buddha" as a "seated Buddha"; Nan-yüeh is the one who points out the "seated Buddha" for "making a Buddha." There was this kind of concentrated effort in the congregation of Nan-yüeh and words like the above in the congregation of Yüeh-shan.

Know this, that it is the seated Buddha that Buddha after Buddha and Patriarch after Patriarch have taken as their essential activity. Those who are Buddhas and Patriarchs have employed this essential activity, while those who are not have never even dreamt of it. To say that the teaching of the Buddha has been transmitted from the Western Heavens [i.e., India] to the Eastern Earth [i.e., China] implies the transmission of the seated Buddha, for it is the essential function of that teaching. And where the teaching of the Buddha is not transmitted, neither is seated meditation. What has been inherited by successor after successor in this transmission is just this message of seated meditation; one who does not participate in the unique transmission of this message is not a Buddha or a Patriarch. When one is not clear about this one teaching, one is not clear about the ten thousand teachings or about the ten thousand practices. And without being clear about each of these teachings, one cannot be said to have a clear eye. One has not attained the way; how could one represent the present or past in the lineage of the Buddhas and Patriarchs? By this, then, we should be firmly convinced that the Buddhas and Patriarchs always transmit seated meditation.

To be illumined by the radiance of the Buddhas and Patriarchs means to concentrate one's efforts in the investigation of this seated meditation. Some fools, misunderstanding the radiance of the Buddha, think it must be like the radiance of the sun or moon or the light from a pearl or fire. But the light of the sun and moon is nothing but a mark of action within the realm of trans-migration in the six destinies; it is not to be compared with the radiance of the Buddha. The radiance of the Buddha means receiving and hearing a single phrase, maintaining and protecting a single teaching, participating in the single transmission of seated meditation. So long as one is not illumined by the ra-diance of the Buddha, one is not maintaining, nor has one accepted, the Bud-dha's teaching.

This being the case, throughout history there have been few who understood seated meditation as seated meditation. And at present, in the [Ch'an] moun-tains of the Southern Sung, many of those who are heads of the principal monasteries do not understand, and do not study, seated meditation. There may be some who have clearly understood it, but not many. Of course, the monasteries have fixed periods for seated meditation; the monks, from the abbot down, take seated meditation as their basic task; and, in leading their students, the teachers encourage the practice. Nevertheless, there are few ab-bots who understand it.

For this reason, although from ancient times to the present there have been one or two old worthies who have written texts entitled *Inscriptions on Seated Meditation*, *Principles of Seated Meditation*, or *Lancets of Seated Meditation*, among them there is nothing worth taking from any of the *Inscriptions on Seated Meditation*, and the *Principles of Seated Meditation* are ignorant of its observances. They were written by men who do not understand, do not par-ticipate in, its unique transmission. Such are the *Lancet of Seated Meditation* (*Tso-ch'an chen*) in the *Ching-te ch'uan teng lu* (Record of the Transmission of the Lamp from the Ching-te Era) and the *Inscription on Seated Meditation* (*Tso-ch'an ming*) in the *Chia-t'ai p'u teng lu* (Universal Lamp Record from the Chia-t'ai Era). What a pity that, though the authors of such texts spend their lives passing among the "groves" [or Ch'an monasteries] of the ten directions, they do not have the concentrated effort of a single sitting—that sitting is not their own, and concentrated effort never encounters them. This is not because seated meditation rejects their bodies and minds but because they do not as-pire to the true concentrated effort and are precipitately given over to their delusion.

What they have collected in such texts is nothing but models for "reverting to the source and returning to the origin," vain programs for "suspending con-siderations and congealing in tranquility." Such views of meditation do not approach the stages of transmundane contemplation known as "observation, exercise, infusion, and cultivation," or the understandings of bodhisattvas ad-vanced to the "ten stages and equivalent enlightenment"; how, then, could they be the single transmission of the seated meditation of the Buddhas and Patri-archs? The Sung chroniclers were mistaken to record such texts, and later students should cast them aside and not read them.

Among the *Lancets of Seated Mediation*, the only one that is an expression of the Buddhas and Patriarchs is that by the Reverend Cheng-chüeh, the Ch'an Master Hung-chih of the Ching-te Monastery at T'ien-t'ung, renowned Mount

T'ai-po, in the district of Ching-yüan in the Great Sung. This one is a true *Lancet of Seated Meditation*. This one says it right. It alone radiates throughout the surface and interior of the realm of the teachings. It is the statement of a Buddha and Patriarch among the Buddhas and Patriarchs of past and present. Prior Buddhas and later Bddhas have been lanced by this *Lancet*; present Patriarchs and past Patriarchs appear from this *Lancet*. Here is that *Lancet of Seated Meditation*.

LANCET OF SEATED MEDITATION

by Cheng-chüeh
by imperial designation the Ch'an Master Spacious Wisdom

Essential function of all the Buddhas,
Functioning essence of all the Patriarchs—
It knows without touching things;
It illumines without facing objects.
Knowing without touching things,
Its knowing is inherently subtle;
Illumining without facing objects,
Its illumining is inherently mysterious.
Its knowing inherently subtle,
It is ever without discriminatory thought;
Its illumining inherently mysterious,
It is ever without a hair's breadth of sign.
Ever without discriminatory thought,
Its knowing is rare without peer;
Ever without a hair's breadth of sign,
Its illumining comprehends without grasping.
The water is clear right through to the bottom;
A fish goes lazily along.
The sky is vast without horizon;
A bird flies far far away.

The "lancet" in this *Lancet of Seated Meditation* means [such classical Ch'an sayings as] "the manifestation of the great function," "the comportment beyond sight and sound"; it is "the juncture before your parents were born." It means "you had better not slander the Buddhas and Patriarchs"; "you do not avoid destroying your body and losing your life"; it is "a head of three feet and neck of two inches."

"Essential function of all the Buddhas." The Buddhas always take the "Buddhas" as their "essential function"—this is the "essential function" that is realized here; this is "seated meditation."

"Functioning essence of all the Patriarchs." The saying, "My master had no such saying"—this principle is what is meant here by "the Patriarchs." It is in this that the teaching and the robe [of the First Patriarch, Bodhidharma] are transmitted. The faces that are reversed when we "turn the head and reverse the face" are what is meant here by the "essential function of all the Buddhas"; the heads that turn when we "reverse the face and turn the head" are the "functioning essence of all the Patriarchs."

"It knows without touching things." "Knowing" here, of course, does not mean perception; for perception is of little measure. It does not mean understanding; for understanding is artificially constructed. Therefore, this "knowing" is "not touching things," and "not touching things" is "knowing." Such "knowing" should not be measured as universal knowledge; it should not be categorized as self-knowledge. This "not touching things" means the saying "When they come in the light, I hit them in the light; when they come in the dark, I hit them in the dark." It means "sitting and breaking the skin born of mother."

"It illumines without facing objects." This "illumining" does not mean the "illumining" of luminosity or spiritual illumination; it means simply "without facing objects." In this meaning, the "illumining" does not change into the "object," for the "object" itself is "illumining." "Without facing" means the saying "it is never hidden throughout the world"; "it does not emerge when you break the world." It is "subtle"; it is "mysterious"; it is as they say "interacting without interacting."

"Its knowing inherently subtle, it is ever without discriminatory thought." "Thought" is itself "knowing," without dependence on another's power. "Its knowing" is its form, and its form is the mountains and rivers. These mountains and rivers are "subtle," and this "subtlety" is "mysterious." When we put it to use, it is what they call "brisk and lively" as the leaping carp. [The carp is said to become a dragon as it climbs the Yellow River beyond the Yü Gate, but] when we make a dragon, it does not matter whether we are inside or out of the Yü Gate. To put this single "knowing" to the slightest use is to take up the mountains and rivers of the entire world and "know" them with all one's power. Without our intimate "knowing" of the mountains and rivers, we do not have a single knowing or a half understanding. We should not lament the late arrival of "disciminatory" thinking: the Buddhas of previous "discrimination" have already been realized. "Ever without" here means "previously"; "previously" means "already realized." Therefore, "ever without discrimination" means as they say "you do not meet a single person."[11]

"Its illumining inherently mysterious, it is ever without a hair's breadth of sign." "A hair's breadth" here means the entire world; yet it is "inherently mysterious," inherently "illumining." Therefore, it is as if it is never brought out. The eyes are not to be doubted, nor the ears to be trusted. Such sayings as "you should clarify the essential meaning apart from the sense"; "do not look to words to grasp the rule"—this is what is meant by "illumining." Therefore, it is said to be "without peer"; therefore, it is "without grasping." This has been preserved as what the text calls "rare" and maintained as "comprehending," but I have my doubts about it.

"The water is clear right through to the bottom; a fish swims lazily along." "The water is clear." The "water" that has to do with the sky does not get "right through to the bottom" of what is meant here by "clear water"; still less is that which forms clear, deep pools in the "vessel world" of our environment the "water" intended by the expression "the water is clear." That which has no shore as its boundary—this is what is meant by "clear water" penetrated "right through to the bottom." If a "fish" goes through this "water," it is not that it does not "go"; yet, however many tens of thousands the degree of its progress, its "going" is immeasurable, inexhaustible. There is no shoreline by which it is gauged; there is no sky to which it ascends, nor bottom to which it sinks. And therefore there is no one who can take its measure. If we try to discuss its measure, all we can say is that it is only "clear water" penetrated "right through to the bottom." The virtue of seated meditation is like the "fish going": who can calculate its degree in thousands or tens of thousands? The degree of the "going" that penetrates "right through to the bottom" is like that on what is called the "path of the bird," along which the body as a whole does not "go."

"The sky is vast without horizon; a bird flies far far away." The expression "the sky is vast" here has nothing to do with the heavens: the "sky" that has to do with the heavens is not the "vast sky"; still less is that space extending everywhere here and there the "vast sky." Neither hidden nor manifest, without surface or interior—this is what is meant by the "vast sky." When the "bird" flies this sky, it is the single truth of "flying" the "sky." This conduct of "flying" the "sky" is not to be measured: "flying" the "sky" is the entire world, for it is the entire world "flying" the "sky." Although we do not know how far this "flying" goes, to express what is beyond our calculations, we call it "far far away." This is equivalent to the saying "you should go off without a string beneath your feet." When the "sky" flies off, the "bird" flies off; when the "bird" flies off, the "sky" flies off. In an expression of the investigation of this flying off, it is said, "It is just here." This is the lancet of sitting fixedly: through how many tens of thousands of degrees does it express this "it is just here"?[12]

Such, then, is the Ch'an Master Hung-chih's *Lancet of Seated Meditation*. Among the old worthies throughout all the generations, there has never been another *Lancet of Seated Meditation* like this one. If the "stinking skin bags" throughout all quarters were to attempt to express a *Lancet of Seated Meditation* like this one, they could not do so though they exhaust the efforts of a lifetime or two. This is the only *Lancet* in any quarter; there is no other to be found. When he ascended the hall to lecture, my former master [Ju-ching] often said, "Hung-chih is an old Buddha." He never said this about any other person. When one has the eye to know a man, he will know as well the voice of the Buddhas and Patriarchs. In truth, we know that there are Buddhas and Patriarchs in the tradition of Tung-shan.

Now, some eighty years and more since the days of the Ch'an Master Hung-chih, reading his *Lancet of Seated Meditation*, I compose my own. The date is the eighteenth day of the third month in the cyclical year Mizunoe-tora, the third year of Ninji [1242]; if we calculate back from this year to the eighth day of the tenth month in the twenty-seventh year of [the Southern Sung era of] Shao-hsing [1157, when Hung-chih died], there are just eighty-five years. The *Lancet of Seated Meditation* I now compose is as follows.

LANCET OF SEATED MEDITATION

Essential function of all the Buddhas,
Functioning essence of all the Patriarchs—
It is present without thinking;
It is completed without interacting.
Present without thinking,
Its presence is inherently intimate;
Completed without interacting,
Its completion is inherently verified.
Its presence inherently intimate,
It is ever without stain or defilement;
Its completion inherently verified,
It is ever without the upright or inclined.
Intimacy ever without stain or defilement,
Its intimacy sloughs off without discarding;
Verification ever without upright or inclined,
Its verification makes effort without figuring.
The water is clear right through the earth;
A fish goes along like a fish.
The sky is vast straight into the heavens,
A bird flies just like a bird.

It is not that the *Lancet of Seated Meditation* by the Ch'an Master Hung-chih has not yet said it right, but it can also be said like this. Above all, descendants of the Buddhas and Patriarchs should study seated meditation as "the one great concern." This is the orthodox seal of the single transmission.

Notes

1. This is one of the more obscure "arguments" in the text. I understand the passage to say something like the following. Although nonthinking is an enlightened activity, free from all obstructions to knowledge (as in the Zen expression, "all eight sides are crystal clear"), it is a distinct act of cognition, with its own agent (the enlightened "someone" who is present in all our cognitive states). But the activity of nonthinking in meditation is not merely a matter of cognitive states: it is the identification with the act of "sitting fixedly" itself. When one is thus fully identified with the act, it

is beyond what can be thought of or measured, even through the notions of Buddhahood or awakening.

2. From the *Cheng tao ko* (Song of Verification of the Way) attributed to Hui-neng's disciple, Yung-chia Hsüan-chüeh (Yōka Genkaku, 665–713).

3. For a paraphrase of this difficult passage, see my introduction, above.

4. From the old Chinese sayings, "To give weight to the ears and take the eyes lightly is the constant failing of the common man," and "The ordinary man values what is distant and despises what is near." The "carved dragon" here alludes to the Chinese story of the man who loved the image of the dragon but was terrified of the real thing.

5. From the famous problem, posed by the ninth-century figure Hsiang-yen Chih-hsien (Kyōgen Chikan, d. 898), of the man hanging by his teeth over a thousand-foot cliff who is asked the meaning of Bodhidharma's advent: "If he opens his mouth to answer, he will destroy his body and lose his life." One way of paraphrasing what seems to be the point of this tangled passage is this: the effort to practice and achieve the goal of Buddhism "entangles" us in Buddhism; yet complete entanglement in Buddhism—both in its discourse and in its cult—is itself the goal of Buddhism; hence, the practice of "figuring" is completely "entangled" in the goal of "making a Buddha." Dōgen is clearly enjoying himself here with the multivalent notion of "entanglements": as the constricting language within which we ordinarily "figure," as the liberating language of the Zen *kōan*, and as the interdependence of the two in Zen study.

6. Ma-tsu's question here might be more naturally put, "Then, what should I do?" But (as in his earlier treatment of "how do you think" and "not thinking") Dōgen seems to be reading the question as a declarative sentence and suggesting that the interrogative term "what" is itself what is ultimately "right," or that, like the relationship between the effort of "figuring" and the goal of "making a Buddha," the two are interdependent.

7. The various bovines here are allusions to a number of well-known sayings in the Ch'an literature, in which they typically symbolize the basic nature of the mind or the fundamental issue of the religion. Huai-jang's metaphor of the cart and ox is itself an allusion to a scriptural passage (attacking an ascetic practice), where the terms indicate body and mind, respectively.

8. To "throw out a tile and take in a jade" is a polite way to ask another for capping verse for your poem; here it no doubt refers to the give and take of Ch'an repartee. "Turning the head and reversing the face" suggests the notions both of a spiritual reversal and of the inseparability of awakening and delusion—or, as probably in this case, of master and disciple.

9. Dōgen is here alluding to a sentence from Nan-yüeh's answer to Ma-tsu that he does not bother to quote: "In a nonabiding Dharma, there should be no grasping or rejecting." The discussion of the "mark" of the Buddha here derives from the Mahāyāna doctrine that the true mark of a Buddha is not his thirty-two major and eighty minor physical marks of spiritual excellence but precisely his transcendence of all "marks," or phenomenal characteristics.

10. Dōgen is no doubt alluding here to one of the most famous sayings of Ch'an, attributed to the T'ang dynasty master Lin-chi (Rinzai Gigen, d. 866): "If you meet the Buddha, kill the Buddha; if you meet a Patriarch, kill the Patriarch."

11. I interpret this rather obscure passage to mean something like the following. The "subtle knowing" of the Buddhas clearly discriminates every phenomenon. We should not think that this (higher) "discriminatory thinking" is something for which we must wait; it is "already realized" in each mind's inherent power of discrimination ("the Buddhas of previous discrimination"). Cheng-chüeh's "ever without discriminatory thought" here refers to this inherent power, which is "realized" even in ordinary perception. The spiritual practice of one who understands this is as free as what the T'ang dynasty master Tung-shan called "the way of the birds," on which one is said not to "meet anyone."

12. Dōgen is here alluding to a conversation between the T'ang dynasty masters Po-chang and Ma-tsu over a passing flock of wild geese. When Ma-tsu asked where the birds were going, Po-chang said they had flown away. Ma-tsu twisted Po-chang's nose and said, "You say they've flown away, but from the beginning they're just here."

— 23 —

Chidō's *Dreams of Buddhism*

William M. Bodiford

Dreams of Buddhism (*Buppō yume monogatari*) was written by a Japanese Buddhist monk known as Chidō sometime during the latter half of the thirteenth century. Little is known about Chidō other than his name and the contents of several short treatises attributed to him. He seems to have enjoyed renown as a master of Shingon Esoteric practices. Only one of his works, *Ten Causes of Favorable Dreams* (*Kōmu jūin*), was dated, and this only with the vague notation: "During the Kōan Era" (i.e., 1278–1287). Other works attributed to him include *Proper Mental Attitude during Illness* (*Byōchū yōjinshō*), *The Uncreated* (*Fushōshō*), and *Procedures for Performing the Mantra of Radiant Light* (*Kōmyō shingon shiki*).

The usual Japanese titles for this text are *Buppō yume monogatari* (Tale of the Buddhist Doctrine of Dreams) or *Yume chishiki monogatari* (Tale of the Dream Teacher). The English title is intended to suggest the ambiguous role of dreams in Chidō's treatise. The text attempts to reveal both what Buddhism teaches about dreams and what dreams can teach us about the true nature of reality, or how Buddhists view reality. The text assumes that the reader already accepts the Buddhist critique of our commonsense world of individual existence as being dreamlike and lacking ultimate validity. It further assumes that the reader already seeks the goal of liberation from such false reality. Its real emphasis, therefore, is not dreaming itself, but the experience of waking up afterward. Chidō insists that our familiar habit of awaking each day should convince us of the possibility of experiencing a similar process of religious awakening. His ultimate goal is to convince us to believe in the efficacy of Buddhist practice. If we are able on our own to awake from sleep-induced dreams, he argues, we must be equally capable of pursuing Buddhist awakening. Thus, Chidō stands in opposition to Pure Land Buddhist leaders who taught that people no longer possessed the ability to attain awakening through individual effort.

The format of *Dreams of Buddhism* is quite simple. It presents a dialogue between a host and a guest on a quiet night in a humble hermitage. As in other Japanese didactic treatises, the guest serves only as a convenient prompt for the host's lengthy instructions. Speaking through the host, Chidō attempts to explain how people can attain liberation from the endless cycle of birth and death, or transmigration, that all sentient beings endure. Chidō's solution consists of merely eliminating the false belief in individual existence that serves to sustain our illusion of transmigration. We should view existence as we already view dreams and should awake from our mistaken belief in existence just as we wake from our dreams each day. In explaining this remedy, Chidō discusses the proper mental attitude toward life and death, ignorance as the source of mistaken beliefs, the equivalence of Buddha and living beings, the principle of moral consequences (i.e., karmic etribution), and meditation on the syllable A (A-ji kan). He concludes by arguing against Pure Land doctrines that would deny people's aptitude for Esoteric Shingon Buddhist practices during the present degenerate age of Buddhist decline (mappō). Section headings have been inserted in the text to identify these themes.

The text also mentions several well-known individuals, the Indian prince Ajātaśatru (Pali, Ajātasattu; J., Ajase), the Chinese Taoist sages Lieh-tzu (Resshi) and Chuang-tzu (Sōshi, 4th c. B.C.E.), and the Korean Buddhist master Wŏnhyo (Gangyō, 617–686), as well as one obscure Japanese monk, Rishō-bō of Sennyū Temple. Ajātaśatru is infamous as the evil prince who murdered his father, Bimbisāra the king of Magadha, to usurp the throne. Ajātaśatru's subsequent remorse and concern with the workings of karmic retribution are discussed in a number of Buddhist texts, most notably the Sutra of the Great Cessation (Daihatsu nehangyō, T 374) and the Limitless Life Buddha Sutra (Muryōjukyō, T 360). The writings attributed to the Taoist sages Lieh-tzu and Chuang-tzu both emphasize the illusionary nature of our commonsense categories of reality. Their discussions of the transformations of dreams into reality and reality into dreams are well known to all students of Chinese literature and thought. Wŏnhyo is famous both for his prodigious commentaries on Buddhist scriptures (he wrote more than one hundred treatises) and his sometimes bizarre behavior. In Japan, he was regarded as an important patriarch of the Kegon school, the doctrines of which constitute the metaphysical foundation for the Shingon Esoteric practices advocated by Chidō. Wŏnhyo's awakening in a cemetery midway during his aborted journey to China is reported in Biographies of Eminent Monks of the Sung Dynasty (Sung Kao-seng chuan, T 2061).

The translation is of the text found in Miyasaka Yūshō, ed., Kana hōgoshū, in Nihon koten bungaku taikei 83 (Tokyo: Iwanami Shoten, 1964).

Further Reading

Robert E. Morrell, tr., Early Kamakura Buddhism: A Minority Report (Berkeley: Asian Humanities Press, 1987); Robert E. Morrell, tr., Sand and Pebbles (Shasekishū): The Tales of Mujū Ichien, a Voice for Pluralism in Kamakura Buddhism (Albany: SUNY Press, 1985); George J. Tanabe, Jr., Myōe the Dreamkeeper:

Fantasy and Knowledge in Early Kamakura Buddhism (Cambridge: Harvard University Press, 1993); Taikō Yamasaki, *Shingon: Japanese Esoteric Buddhism*, tr. Richard and Cynthia Peterson (Boston: Shambhala, 1988).

Dreams of Buddhism

BIRTH AND DEATH

One calm night a guest asked for lodging at a monk's rustic hermitage. In the course of discussing affairs ancient and modern, the guest said, "I have encountered the difficult-to-encounter teachings of the Buddha. Although I have not completely lacked a sincere fear of birth and death (*saṃsāra, shōji*), I've been habitually involved in worldly filth. Because I wasted my days hither and thither, only now have I noticed that my limited life span has grown short. I have crossed distant mountains and rivers to come and inquire of you concerning just one issue. What attitude can I adopt so as to attain liberation from birth and death during this life?"

The host replied, "You say that you have spent many years nominally in Buddhist training, yet you have never before given consideration to the single great affair of birth and death? Just regard the dreams you see night after night as your teacher. Then at least you will not deepen your attachments to the world. When people lie down and dream, the things they see do not actually exist. Yet under the conditions of sleep they see all kinds of affairs: different places, living creatures, oneself, and others. Because one's own self is involved, if things go contrary one becomes angry. If things go well one rejoices. It is no different from one's waking reality.

"Lieh-tzu dreamed for sixty years. Chuang-tzu dreamed that he spent one hundred years as a butterfly. In just one night they saw many months and years come and go. Just imagine how many karmic acts they performed during that time! How many thoughts of good and evil! While dreaming one never thinks that one's imaginary experience is false. Yet if one considers it after awakening, it is obvious that not one of the imaginary objects seen while lying down in bed actually existed. Each living being's entire experience of transmigration through birth and death is no different from such dreams. Therefore, again and again the Buddha preached in response to various types of ignorance that we should regard the six courses and four modes of rebirth as dreams."

IGNORANCE

"'Ignorance' means not knowing that one's own mind is Buddha. Within a single mental instant of this delusion, one leaves the palace of Dharma Nature [i.e., reality as it actually is,] and wanders among the impoverished villages of false thoughts [i.e., our commonsense world of existence]. One might think that the experience of transmigration is real. But if upon encountering the Buddha's teaching that life and death is a dream, one listens with faith, then suddenly one leaves the mistaken beliefs of dreams and awakens on the bed of inherent enlightenment. The fact that one has not yet awakened from dreams is simply because one thinks of them as actually existing. The Buddha appeared in the world to make us become aware of our long night of dreams.

"For those of shallow aptitude, Buddhists first explain the principle of the emptiness of self. This approach is known as the Lesser Vehicle (Hīnayāna, Shōjō). Thoughts of self-existence are what habitually cause infinite sins to arise. If one understands that the self is empty, then the power generated by this understanding transports one out of the three realms of desire, form, and no-form to a land outside of our world system. This approach, however, has the defect of emphasizing the existence of the elements of experience (dharma, hō). Therefore, for those of deeper aptitude, Buddhists explain the emptiness of both self and these elements. This approach is known as the Great Vehicle (Mahāyāna, Daijō). The emptiness of dharmas teaches that everything seen in dreams, every type of element, are all emptiness: because everything arises from mind, none has reality. Therefore, the knowledge that every type of dharma consists completely of dreams is the doctrine of the Great Vehicle.

"For these reasons, over the course of years in this humble hermitage, during night after night of dreams, I have seen all kinds of things. Sometimes I became upset. Sometimes I became happy. Sometimes I entered the marvelous realm of the immortal sages and became friends with Buddhas and bodhisattvas. Sometimes I tormented myself with the afflictions of demons and poisonous serpents. While viewing these events one thinks they exist. But after awakening they leave no trace. From this experience one should realize that birth and death fundamentally are nonexistent.

"Due to various kinds of causes and conditions, within one's tiny brain one can see ten thousand miles of mountains and rivers. Within the span of a short nap one can experience the passing of many months and years. One should realize, based on this same principle, that a single instant of thought can pervade the Dharma Realm, the entire cosmos. The elements that one sees do not come into existence from the future when one dreams. They do not go out of existence into the past when one awakes. Even while one sees them they do not abide, do not persist in the present anywhere. Based on this experience, one can understand the meaning of the saying that the three periods of past, present, and future cannot be grasped. This being so, any sentient being who awakens to this realization can be called a Buddha or a Patriarch.

"The reason I believe there is no teacher better than dreams is that the process of sleeping in bed, resting my head on the pillow of inherent enlightenment, allows me to see how the production of delusions causes birth and death within dreams. My awaking at dawn reveals the similar process of realizing the wisdom of spiritual awakening in all its clarity. Thus living in clear realization of the fundamental nonbeing of birth and death, I know that the sense objects experienced while awake are not different from those experienced in dreams. Joys and sorrows are both forgotten, and my mind is ready to encounter the infinite teachings of the Buddha.

"So long as you do not know that your self exists only as a dream, then no matter how much good karma you cultivate, the best benefit you can attain is rebirth in a human or heavenly realm. You will not realize the salvation of liberation from the cycle of birth and death. But if you know that your self exists only as a dream and that all sights, sounds, sensations, and thoughts exist only as a dream, then even a simple act of good karma, such as reciting one line of scripture or chanting the Buddha's name once, is a powerful enough act to produce Buddhahood.

"You must thoroughly investigate this thing known as our mind of thought (*ichinen no shin*). When the interaction of sense organs and sense objects produces an instant of awareness, it does not come from somewhere in the future. When the awareness stops, it does not go to someplace in the past. If one investigates where this mind abides in the present, it is not inside the body nor outside the body. It cannot be found between the inside and the outside. Yet it is not something nonexistent. Because it is this mind that projects the visions of dreams and waking reality, both consist of elements that are fundamentally nonexistent."

THE EQUIVALENCE OF BUDDHA AND LIVING BEINGS

"You must thoroughly investigate what are called 'Buddha' and 'sentient beings.' The scripture says: 'Because of false thoughts, therefore sinking in birth and death; because of knowing reality, therefore realizing *bodhi* [i.e., wisdom].' This means that Buddhas and sentient beings, because both are pure in their fundamental nature, lack the slightest bit of difference. Yet if false thoughts arise, one becomes a sentient being drowning in birth and death. If one knows reality as it is, then one becomes a Buddha who realizes *bodhi*.

"What does the scripture mean by 'false thoughts'? Merely a confused mind. It is like pointing to the east and thinking it is the west. There is a story told about a man, Rishō-bō of Sennyū Temple. Once as Rishō-bō absentmindedly returned to his temple from Kyoto, he walked across the Fifth Avenue Bridge all the while thinking only that he was traveling west. Then he thought to himself: 'If I am returning from the capital to my temple, then I must be facing east. Why am I thinking that I'm going west?' Although it felt odd, he could not get rid of this thought until he had finished crossing the bridge.

"Your false thoughts of birth and death resemble Rishō-bō's confusion. Sentient beings will, because of a single thought of confused discrimination, cling to no-self as a self and construct dreams of birth and death. Just like when Rishō-bō later thought to himself, 'Since I must be facing east, why do I think that I am facing west?' the realization that our mind plays tricks on us resembles encountering Buddhism, awakening to the mental origin of reality, and knowing the principle of no-self. His knowing how to distinguish east and west, but not changing his mind while crossing the bridge, resembles the persistence of false thoughts—due to habitual karmic tendencies formed during many previous lives—even though one trusts in the teachings of the Buddha. His regaining his senses after crossing the bridge resembles putting an end to false thoughts by believing in and practicing the teachings of the Buddha.

"Rishō-bō realized his mistake in thinking that east is west. Thus he did not stop on the bridge but continued on his way home. If he had been taken in by the false opinion of thinking that east is west, then he would have stopped in midjourney and would not have continued on his way home. Because we know that our false mind is fundamentally empty, we should not be stopped by it. Therefore, [Vasubandhu's] *Treatise on Arousing the Bodhi Mind* (*Hotsu bodaishin gyōron, T* 1659) states: 'If the false mind should arise, recognize it and do not follow it.'

"Once a person known as Wŏnhyo journeyed from the Korean kingdom of Silla to the T'ang empire of China in search of the Buddhist Teaching. Encountering rain, he took shelter in a cave. Feeling thirsty, he drank water from a pool in the cavern. The taste of the water resembled sweet nectar. He drank and drank. At dawn he saw a corpse lying in the water. Remembering the water he had drunk, he vomited it up. At that moment he awakened to the fact that all elements of existence (*dharma*) in themselves are neither pure nor impure, but merely coincide to the artifice of the One Mind. Thinking, 'Now there is no further Teaching to seek,' he returned to Silla.

"Not knowing that body and mind are empty with respect to purity and impurity, one performs infinite karmic acts for the sake of the body and thereby randomly engenders suffering. Suppose, for example, there was a crazy person who took a corpse, set it on the side of the road, and decorated it in various ways. Suppose he built a house for it and traveled about getting food and clothing for it. Suppose he became happy when a passerby admired the corpse and became angry when one criticized it. Just for this one corpse he suffered mental and physical exertion. Anyone who saw this would probably say, 'Well, he's crazy!' But our manner of transmigration through birth and death differs not in the slightest. We receive bleached bones from our fathers and obtain red flesh from our mothers. None of this is our own. Yet, what we do every day for ourselves is all just for our corpses, is it not?

"Chinese poets described man's worldly striving as:

> Working late until the stars appear overhead;
> starting early so as to brush off the morning frost:
> Such is one who seeks fame and covets profit.

> Polishing jeweled floors, decorating with embroidered banners, sewing
>   fancy clothes:
> Such is one who is concerned only with outlandish beauty.

"If one considers these activities thoroughly, it is clear that we are just slaves to our corpses. Our mental and physical toil infects not just this life, but also engenders pleasures and pains for eons to come. How could our craziness be less than that of the crazy person above? Thus, because we cling to no-self as a self and cling to the false and nonexistent as truly real, we have become ordinary unawakened beings (bonpu) caught in birth and death. Therefore, realizing that mind and body absolutely lack any self-sustaining permanent essence and believing that they are just like phantoms and dreams is the event to which the scripture quotation above refers when it says: 'because of knowing reality, therefore realizing wisdom (bodhi).'"

THE PRINCIPLE OF MORAL CONSEQUENCES

The guest asked, "You say good and evil in reality do not exist. If that is so, then couldn't one perform evil without incurring karmic sins, and couldn't one cultivate good without obtaining karmic benefits?"

The host replied, "If you understand in such a manner, then you would be denying the law of cause and effect, a horrific false view. In fact, it is because of the lack of permanent essence that the performance of evil leads to baleful retributions and that the cultivation of good engenders pleasant benefits. You should understand that the principle of things lacking any fixed nature implies that the karmic connections between good and evil causes and effects are not random.

"Suppose, for example, that in a dream you see someone killed and see a king investigate and judge the crime. While dreaming, the principle of cause and effect cannot be disrupted. Thinking upon this after awaking, however, it is clear that the murderer, the murder victim, the performance of the crime, and the king actually did not exist. Therefore, if one truly believes that both good and evil are dreams, one will transcend cause and effect and realize highest awakening. Because at that time both karmic sin and karmic benefit are totally nonexistent, it is possible even for one who performed the five heinous crimes to attain Buddhahood.

"But as long as one has not attained Buddhahood, the law of cause and effect is completely inviolable. While one is at the level of ordinary unawakened beings, how could the burden of karmic sin not exist? Nonetheless, if one believes that one's sinful heart from its very bottom is fundamentally nonexistent, then there is no doubt that the burden of karmic sin will disappear. Therefore, one should contemplate evil acts before doing them, asking oneself, 'Since these are dreams, how can I do them?' and thereby carefully control body and mind. Because the evil acts that one is about to commit exist only within dreams, they too completely lack any ultimate reality. Even if one seeks throughout the ten directions and three periods for the mind that commits sins, in the end it cannot be grasped. One should reflect well, thinking: 'Since this mind that commits sins actually does not exist, how can it engender any karmic retribution?' This form of mental reflection is known as repentance of the uncreated (*mushō no sange*).

"King Ajātaśatru murdered his father. When he visited the Buddha to repent of his sins, the Buddha told him that all elements of existence are completely without fixed forms. What is that thing called 'father'? What is that thing called 'son'? The Buddha explained that the idea of father and son result at random from temporary relations between a pair of the five groups ('heaps,' *skandha*, of dharma elements) that constitute sentient beings. By means of the power of this wisdom, in no time at all, Ajātaśatru's karmic sins dissolved into the state of fundamental nonbeing. This process is known as the elimination of sins (*metsuzai*).

"Your attempt to rationalize your desire to commit sins by saying, 'Since they are just dreams, how could I suffer consequences?' is a big mistake. You must analyze this distinction well. Just always focus your attention on the situations in which such thoughts arise. Suppose, for example, just when an unexpected thought of dislike toward a person has arisen, you maintain that train of thought in your mind and carefully analyze this occasion of resentment. In the end, you would realize that estrangement characterizes what is called the un-awakened being trapped in the currents of life and death. If just when an evil thought is about to arise one asks: 'From where does this thought arise? Who is its subject? Who is its object?' then that train of thought, which initially was hateful, suddenly would disappear without a trace. Suppose, for example, at night one mistakes a post for a demon and runs away in fear. If one asks what kind of demon could be there and goes back to look more carefully, then one would see that the demon fundamentally is a post. All thoughts of fear would vanish. Whenever an instant of false thought is about to arise, carefully return to that instant of arising and ask what is the basis of that instant of thought. Because the fundamental nature of mind is emptiness, ultimately one reaches that state of fundamental nonbeing.

"This attainment is liberation from birth and death. While the mind of an instant of thought has no basis from which to arise, the thought that things actually exist maintains a continuous train of thought that results ultimately in the sea of life and death. Yet if one traces back this thought and analyzes what kind of thing it is, then one realizes that fundamentally it is nothing. Therefore, after reflecting back for awhile, one knows that one is uncreated. Thus, the process of birth and death—heretofore maintained by previous life-times of thought—is eliminated."

MEDITATION ON THE SYLLABLE "A" (A-JI KAN)

"The Buddha placed all of the Great Vehicle's doctrines of the uncreated into the one syllable 'A.' Thus, if one unpacks the syllable 'A' it becomes many different doctrines, and if one compresses these, they become the single syllable

'A.' *The Great Sun Sutra* (*Dainichikyō,* T 848) states: 'The syllable "A" is itself uncreated, ungraspable, fundamental emptiness. It universally encompasses all Buddhist teachings. By means of mutual empowerment through this emptiness, one is able to embrace all Buddhist teachings and thereby attain Buddhahood.'

"This syllable 'A' consists of color, shape, sound, and meaning. Sometimes one can practice by focusing one's mind on its color and shape. Sometimes one can practice by vocalizing its sound. When one wishes quietude, one can practice by continuous contemplation of its meaning. Because it offers several forms of practice, one's mastery of the highest principle occurs in no time.

"The Pure Land practice of chanting *Namu Amida Butsu,* by contrast, involves many words and is prone to distraction. Because the breath that comes out when one simply opens one's mouth always is the sound 'A' even when one is distracted, no other practice is as easy as this one. Because all the doctrines preached in the hundreds and thousands of scriptures and treatises in their entirety are encompassed by this one syllable, reciting this one syllable produces the same amount of merit as reading the entire Buddhist canon. Moreover, the doctrines I mentioned above [i.e., no-self, uncreated, and elimination of sins], in their entirety constitute the meaning of this syllable. Therefore, even the merit produced by reciting without any knowledge is no trivial amount. The amount of merit produced by adding to one's recitation of this syllable even one instant of belief in the principle of the uncreated, therefore, could not be explained completely even after infinite eons.

"Thus, at the very last when facing the end in death, one should merely open one's mouth, place one's attention on the 'A' breath, and experience the end. At that moment, because all affairs also come to an end, no matter what one ponders over, it is beyond one's ability to imagine something better. If one tries to contemplate the meaning of 'A' too intently, it will become a hindrance. Merely ending one's life on the single 'A' syllable without any intense contemplation is attainment of self-realization beyond thought [i.e., perfect awakening without delusion or mental effort]."

APTITUDE FOR BUDDHIST PRACTICE

The guest asked, "The principles of no-self and noncreation probably are, as you say, the foundation of Buddhism. Yet when I reflect on my own mind, there is not even half a moment when I forget about clinging to a self. Never have I been attentive enough to notice the instant when feelings of happiness or joy come over me. Thus, doctrines and practices like these that you've described must be for wise, flawless people only. Some people [e.g., Pure Land leaders] say that during this evil and declining age ordinary unawakened men should not consider such matters. When I evaluate this in my own mind, I think truly there must be reason in their position. Right?"

The host replied, "Because people's aptitudes for Buddhist practice diverge, the Buddha preached the Dharma of a single taste in various ways. One must not necessarily use one version to block all other ways of practice. Because this doctrine of no-self and noncreation is profound, one who lacks affinities from previous lives will not believe it for an instant. But someone who has established many such affinities will, without being able to say why, feel the value of this doctrine upon hearing it. If one arouses even a single instant of faith, then the power of that faith will eliminate the heaviest sins from the beginningless past. One should see that this will plant the seed of Buddhahood in the Storehouse Consciousness (*ālaya vijñāna*).

"Thus, the class of beings who have aptitude for the Great Vehicle does not even exclude those who violate the precepts and freely perform evil. Merely one instant of faith and understanding qualifies one for inclusion. The reason for this is that even before one thinks that 'the permanent self must be something that really exists,' the Great Vehicle already extends to whatever good or evil karmic nature exists within one's heart. Once one believes that birth and death [i.e., *saṃsāra*] and Nirvana are the same as yesterday's dreams, then the power of this faith transports one beyond the distinctions of good and evil. Therefore it matters not in the least if there has been a good or evil determination prior to one's unawakened cognition [i.e., the power of an unawakened person's faith is not limited by his or her moral nature, which has been determined by prior karmic acts]. In this regard, it is because the beginningless cycle of false thoughts and karmic influences has made such a deep impact that people believe only in themselves and distrust the words of the Buddha that promise salvation through the syllable 'A' and think thoughts such as: 'Since I am evil, how could I have the proper aptitude for Buddhism?'

"Examine your lowly self! You are a person within a dream, wherein both good and evil are fundamentally empty. Because everything is fundamentally empty, you are not the slightest bit different from the Buddha. What basis is there for thinking that your aptitude has been fixed at an inferior grade?

"None of the doctrines or practices mentioned above state that one must discard all evil thoughts. Rather they merely encourage one to have faith in the fundamental nonexistence of whatever good or evil thoughts arise. Buddhist tradition has provided the three practices of morality, meditation, and wisdom so that we will attain inner and outer purity, that is, mental insight and physical decorum. Yet even if I were to beg people to practice these, in this latter age they have become too weak to do so. Even if one is unable to manage any kind of multiple practices, I believe that faith in the doctrines of the Great Vehicle for just one instant of thought right now will plant the proper seed of Buddhahood.

"Confused thoughts are characteristic of ordinary unawakened people. Therefore, as long as one is an ordinary person it is impossible for false thoughts not to arise. From this, it is clear that not a single ordinary person who lacks aptitude for the Great Vehicle exists. It is precisely for ordinary unawakened people who lack any foundation in the Buddhist Way that one explains knowledge of the Tathāgata's secret treasure of esoteric contemplation of the syllable 'A.'

"I observe that people of this world, in terms of their attitude toward Buddhism, would rather think only of relying on the merit produced by acts such as chanting Amida Buddha's name (*nembutsu*) or chanting scripture to attain transport to Pure Land in their next life. Hardly anyone exists who expends even a single instant of trust in the Buddhist doctrine. Here is what I know. The Buddhist doctrine is difficult to encounter and difficult to believe. Knowing that it is difficult to believe, upon believing it one obtains inconceivable benefits. The saying that the chanting of one line of verse from the Buddhist scripture will destroy infinite eons worth of sins, being the words of the Buddha, could not possibly be a lie. Yet if these sins were really existing things, then their disappearance would take some amount of time. Because these sins are fundamentally empty, upon chanting the name of the Buddha who awakened to this truth, even without understanding anything, they are eliminated. By adding even an instant of faith in this truth to one's chanting, just think how much more merit would be produced! One should reverently arouse one's mind of faith. My speaking like this also is nothing more than words in a dream. . . ."

As these words were spoken the guest disappeared as if erased. Then the host also disappeared. There was just the humble hermitage and the sound of the wind in the pine trees.

Chidō, who harms the nation, wrote this.

$$— 24 —$$

A Japanese Shugendō Apocryphal Text

Paul Swanson

Shugendō, the "Way of Cultivating Spiritual Powers" through ascetic practices in the mountains, is a syncretistic Japanese religious tradition that has been remarkably influential through much of Japanese history. Although it claims the semi-legendary figure of En-no-Gyōja (En the Ascetic) as founder, it took form as an organized religion only in the Heian period (9th–12th c.) when ancient religious practices came under the influence of foreign religions. Contributing to the formation of Shugendō were the pre-Buddhist folk religious practices of Japan, such as shamanism and *kannabi shinkō* (the belief that agricultural deities and the spirits of the dead reside in the mountains); aspects of Tantric Buddhism, including the use of spells, and magic rituals; Buddhist ethics and cosmology; and elements of yin-yang and Taoist magic. Its followers are popularly known as *yamabushi*, "those who lie in the mountain," or *shugenja*, "those who accumulate spiritual power or experience" through ascetic austerities in the mountains, such as fasting, seclusion in caves, solitary meditation, group pilgrimage, chanting of spells and sutras, and sitting or standing under waterfalls. Shugendō has been a strong and influential presence for much of Japanese history. Its influence has been felt in many cultural areas, such as literature, folk festivals, dance, theater, and rituals.

En-no-Gyōja (c. 7th century C.E., also known by his personal name En-no-Ozunu or En-no-Kimi) is the prototypical ascetic of Shugendō. The text translated below is said to have been transmitted to him by Mañjuśrī (Monju), the bodhisattva of wisdom. Legends concerning his life and wondrous works abound in all mountainous areas of Japan, though historically he operated mainly in the Katsuragi-Yoshino and Kumano areas (including the Ōmine mountains) south of Nara. The *Continued Chronicles of Japan* (*Shoku Nihongi*, coverage 697–791) includes the following entry for the 5th month of 699:

> 24th day. En-no-Kimi-Ozunu was banished to the peninsula of Izu [in Yamato]. Originally Ozunu had lived on Katsuragiyama and had been reputed as an adept in magic. Karakuni no Muraji, Hirotari . . . took him as his teacher. Later, jealous of his

art, he slandered him in saying that he led people astray by weird arts and therefore he was banished to a far-away place.

It was said among the population that he often commanded spirits to draw water or to gather firewood for him. If they did not obey his orders, he bound them with magic.

Many legends relate the supranormal powers and deeds of En-no-Gyōja, especially his defeat and control of evil spirits to allow (or "open") a mountain to be used for spiritual practices.

Records show that Buddhist monks and other wandering ascetics have entered the mountains for religious purposes in various parts of Japan from an early time, certainly before the Nara period (710–784). In the Heian period and later, these monks were gradually organized into two major groups: the Honzan-ha, affiliated with the Tendai school of Buddhism, and the Tōzan-ha, affiliated with the Shingon school. Shugendō was proscribed by the Japanese government in 1872 in an attempt to universalize the government's Shintō ideology, and the *yamabushi* were forced to declare themselves either Buddhist monks or Shintō priests. As a result, much of traditional Shugendō organization, ritual, and practices was lost. After World War II and the proclamation of the freedom of religion, however, independent Shugendō individuals and groups began to recover their tradition, and some traditional pilgrimages, rituals, and other practices have been resurrected. The influence of Shugendō on the origin of many of the new religious movements in Japan, for example, is increasingly recognized.

The Shugendō text translated below is considered apocryphal. The study of "apocryphal" Buddhist texts (*gikyō*) is increasingly recognized as an important part of understanding East Asian Buddhism. The use of such a term, of course, implies a standard for designating certain texts as part of the Buddhist canon. The situation is much more complicated than, for example, the Christian or Islamic tradition, where canonical scripture was defined and limited relatively early. Strictly speaking, the Buddhist canon is limited to the words of Śākyamuni, the historical Buddha. Under this narrow definition, however, few if any Buddhist texts could be safely considered "nonapocryphal." The followers of Mahāyāna Buddhism in particular have a rather liberal view of scripture, accepting the idea that teachings "inspired" under trance or in accord with Buddhist principles are fully acceptable as "teachings of the Buddha." In the words of the *Treatise on the Great Perfection of Wisdom* (*Ta chih tu lun*, T 1509, 25.66b2–4), "All good and beautiful words are part of the Buddha-dharma." We thus find a very tolerant attitude among many Buddhists concerning the writing and acceptance of new scriptures.

China saw a proliferation of such "home-grown" Buddhist texts. For many of the more "orthodox-minded" Buddhists, however, only texts originating in India were accepted as canonical, and such home-grown texts were classified apocryphal. A scholastic discipline developed among the Chinese Buddhists for cataloguing the canon, and part of the task of the cataloguer was to identify the origin and translator of each text; those identified as either having an "anonymous" translator or being "doubtful," "spurious," or "suspicious" were classically referred to as apocryphal texts. The great number and variety of these apocryphal writings in China are such that they defy satisfactory classification. A quick look at the traditional catalogues shows that anywhere from a fifth to a third of the Buddhist texts in China were apocryphal (i.e., composed in China), and recent work by Buddhist scholars indicate that many of the most influential works in Chinese Buddhism may be of this type. For many scholars it is the "home-brewed" nature of the apocryphal texts that makes them interesting, for "it is apocryphal texts, rather than exegeses of translated Indian scriptures, that often exhibit what is most distinctly Chinese about Chinese Buddhism" (Buswell 1990: 14).

In contrast to China, there are very few Buddhist apocryphal texts that can be identified as originating in Japan. This makes the *Sutra on the Unlimited Life of the Threefold Body* (*Bussetsu sanjin juryōmuhen kyō*), the text analyzed and translated below, particularly unusual and interesting. It is significant that the text is part of the Shugendō tradition, for Shugendō is a distinctive development of Buddhism in the Japanese context. A study of this text reveals much about features of Buddhism peculiar to Japan, and particularly about Shugendō ways of thinking.

The *Sutra on the Unlimited Life of the Threefold Body* is a short text of about seven hundred Chinese characters. The title includes the claim that it is "taught by the Buddha" (*bussetsu*), but it is attributed to the "inspired vision" (*kantoku*) of En-no-Gyōja. Legend has it that the contents were revealed by Mañjuśrī while En-no-Gyōja was practicing esoteric contemplation on Mount Ōmine, one of the most important mountains for Shugendō practice, and that En-no-Gyōja transmitted the teachings/text to his disciples Gikaku and Gigen. It comes down to us today as part of a collection of Shugendō texts, the *Shugen jōyōshū* (Collection of Shugen [Texts and Liturgies] Used Daily), edited and compiled by a certain Kankō. Kankō was helped by Gyōchi (1778–1841), a *shugenja* best known for his Shugendō writings such as *A Robe of Leaves* (*Konohagoromo*). The *Shugen jōyōshū* was published in 1825 and used by the Tōzan-ha branch of Shugendō as their basic liturgical sourcebook. The *Sutra on the Unlimited Life of the Threefold Body* was chanted as part of the daily morning service, along with the *Heart Sutra* (*Hannya shingyō, T* 251) and some more standard Esoteric texts, spells, and hymns of praise to the Buddhas.

The sutra opens with a manifestation of Mañjuśrī as he is depicted in the Womb Realm Maṇḍala (one of the most important symbolic representations of Buddhist cosmology and aid to meditation in Esoteric Buddhism): with a five-knotted crown, dark "blue" hair to his shoulders, body shining like gold, holding a blue lotus and a five-pronged *vajra* (Esoteric Buddhist ritual implement symbolizing the power of wisdom) in his left hand, and holding a sutra-box "backpack" in his right. This backpack (*oizuru*) is of particular interest: used by *yamabushi* to carry their gear, including scriptures, during their sojourns, it is one of the traditional accoutrements of the *yamabushi* and is given important symbolic meaning, such as the mother's womb from which the ascetic is reborn. The term *oizuru* originally referred to the leaves on which Sanskrit scriptures were written; these leaves were preserved by placing them between blocks of wood, and these stacks resembled boxes. Eventually in the Shugendō tradition the term came to refer to the boxlike backpack.

Mañjuśrī, having made his appearance, poses a series of questions to the Buddha on the source of the Buddha's teachings and, by extension, the source of his authority. In short, where and from whom did the Buddha—or the Tathāgata (Nyorai, the "Thus Come"), one of the titles of the Buddha—hear the Dharma? The answers lead to progressively profound levels of revelation. The Buddha himself, after attaining and passing through the forty-one stages of enlightenment, heard the Dharma directly from Mahāvairocana, the "Great Sun" Buddha who is considered the basic, eternal, universal Buddha in Esoteric Buddhism. Mahāvairocana, in turn, received the Dharma from "the beginningless and endless original Buddha who is of one mind and one thought." Here we go beyond even Mahāvairocana to an "original" Buddha who underlies all reality. But there is one more step. This original Buddha heard the Dharma from "the beginningless and endless original Buddha of no mind and no thought." This is as deep as we go. The sutra assures us that there is "no Buddha above and beyond" this Buddha. This Buddha is beyond conceptual understanding, comprises the basis of all reality, and is the fundamental nature of all, that in whom we live and move and have our being.

As if further authority were required, the Tathāgata named King of Imposing Sound (Bhīṣmagarjitasvara-rāja; J., Ion-ō butsu) makes an appearance to praise Mañjuśrī for his good work. This Tathāgata appears in the *Lotus Sutra* as the Buddha before whom there is no Buddha. Thus he symbolizes the "original" Buddha, the Buddha of the most distant past, the fundamental source.

Finally, Mañjuśrī and the assembly of eighty-four thousand people all join the Buddha in his enlightenment through the supranormal power of the Buddha. The sutra is summarized in a verse in which we are reassured that we can realize the same mind of enlightenment as that of the Buddha through entering the concentrated trance of meditation (*samādhi, sanmai, jō*). The enlightenment of the Buddha is available to us directly, revealed in and through the nature of reality itself. For the *shugenja*, this must have provided reassurance and expectation that one can experience direct insight and enlightenment by practicing austerities in the mountains, and by following his Shugendō rituals and religious practice.

Who wrote this sutra, and why? There is no way of knowing, and in a sense it does not matter, for it teaches that a direct experience of and insight into the truth is available to all of us. By implication, it is the content of the text, and not the identity of the author, that is more important. It is safe to assume, however, that it was most likely composed by an anonymous *shugenja* to share his own vision and spiritual experience. In any case, we have eight or nine layers of transmitted revelation teaching that we can go directly to the source and learn the truth from the "original" Buddha, the nature of reality. The message is transmitted to us through the compilation of the *Shugen jōyōshū*, passed down by En-no-Gyōja's disciples, based on the visionary inspiration of En-no-Gyōja himself, an inspiration given by Mañjuśrī, based on questions asked to and answered by the Buddha, who learned it by hearing the preaching of the Dharma by the Great Sun Buddha, who heard and learned the Dharma from the "original Buddha of one mind and one thought," who in turn heard it from the "original Buddha of no mind and no thought," who is beyond conceptual understanding. Here the circle is complete, for through religious practice and experience one can tap the source directly. The authority of the historical Buddha, and even all the historical texts and traditions, are bypassed in favor of an enlightenment realized directly through meditative concentration and, presumably, other Shugendō practices. The implication is that authority and meaning rest in spiritual experience that one can have through austerities in the mountains, not on some abstract teaching attributed to the historical Buddha Śākyamuni in India.

Some final textual comments: "threefold body" refers to the Mahāyāna Buddhist theory that the Buddha has (at least) three "bodies": (1) the Dharma Body (*dharmakāya, hosshin*), the body of the Law, the fundamental way things are regardless of whether or not a historical Buddha appears in this world to teach us about it; (2) the Reward or Enjoyment Body (*sabhogakāya, hōjin*), the body of the Buddha in which he enjoys the fruits or reward of his enlightenment; and (3) the Transformation Body (*nirmāṇakāya, ōjin*), the body in which the Buddha appears historically in this world as a result of his good deeds in past lives and for the benefit of unenlightened beings. In this text it would appear that these are all various forms of the one fundamental and original Buddha, so I have translated the term as "threefold body."

Also, one version of this text belonging to the Hōkaku-ji, a Tōzan-ha temple, claims it to be a translation by the famous Kumārajīva (344–413). Nevertheless, a number of features in this text suggest that it was in fact composed in Japan: the appearance of the *oizuru* (backpack, sutra-box), the depiction of Mañjuśrī as he appears in the Womb Realm Mandala, the use of the theory of forty-one bodhisattva stages, the reference to the Tathāgata of the *Lotus Sutra*, and the general thrust of the sutra toward the inherent (or "original") enlightenment ethos (*hongaku shisō*), the idea that all beings are Buddhas just as they are. This final point—the buddhahood of all things—was pervasive in Japanese Buddhism and also an integral part of Shugendō.

The translation is based on the text published in Nihon Daizōkyō Hensankai, ed., *Shugendō shōso* 1 (Tokyo: Meicho Shuppan): 1–2.

Further Reading

Irit Averbuch, *The Gods Come Dancing: A Study of the Japanese Ritual Dance of Yamabushi Kagura*, Cornell East Asia Series 79 (Ithaca: Cornell University East Asia Program, 1995); Carmen Blacker, *The Catalpa Bow: A Study of Shamanistic Practices in Japan* (London: George Allen & Unwin, 1975); Robert E. Buswell, Jr., ed., *Chinese Buddhist Apocrypha* (Honolulu: University of Hawaii Press, 1990); H. Byron

Earhart, *A Religious Study of the Mount Haguro Sect of Shugendō*, Monumenta Nipponica Monographs 39 (Tokyo: Sophia University, 1970); Miyake Hitoshi, "The Influence of Shugendō on the 'New Religions,'" in *Japanese Buddhism: Its Tradition, New Religions and Interaction with Christianity*, ed. Minoru Kiyota et al. (Tokyo and Los Angeles: Buddhist Books International, 1987): 71–82; Paul L. Swanson, "Shugendō and the Yoshino-Kumano Pilgrimage: An Example of Mountain Pilgrimage," *Monumenta Nipponica* 38 (Spring 1981): 55–79; Paul L. Swanson, "Tapping the Source Directly: A Japanese Shugendō Apochryphal Text," *Japanese Religions* 13 (July 1993): 95–112; Royall Tyler and Paul L. Swanson, eds., *Shugendō and Mountain Religion in Japan*, special issue of *Japanese Journal of Religious Studies* 16, 2–3 (1989).

The Sutra on the Unlimited Life of the Threefold Body as Taught by the Buddha

At one time the bodhisattva [of wisdom] Mañjuśrī was seated on a jewelled lotus, having a five-knotted crown on his head, his dark blue hair hanging down to his shoulders, his bodily form that of shining gold, his left [hand of] concentration holding a blue lotus with a five-pronged vajra above it, his right [hand of] wisdom grasping a sutra-box [backpack], and his body shining like an autumn rainbow.

Peacefully dwelling in [the state of concentration called] the "moon-ring," he spoke to the Buddha, saying, "World-Honored-One. We all have, from the distant past, listened to the Tathāgata's preaching of the Dharma [sermons]. From which Buddha did the Tathāgata hear this preaching of the Dharma-sounds?"

The Buddha spoke to Mañjuśrī, saying, "I received the preaching of Mahā-vairocana (Great Sun Buddha) after passing through the forty-one levels to enter the great inner chamber."

The bodhisattva Mañjuśrī again spoke to the Buddha, saying, "Who is within the inner chamber of the forty-one levels?"

The World-Honored-One again said, "After passing through the ten stages of abodes, the ten stages of practices, the ten stages of merit-transferrence, ten bodhisattva stages (*bhūmi*), the stage of becoming comparable to enlightenment, and entering the inner chamber, I received the preaching of the Dharma by Mahāvairocana, who is at the stage of wonderful enlightenment."

The bodhisattva Mañjuśrī again spoke to the Buddha, saying, "From what Buddha did Mahāvairocana on the stage of wonderful enlightenment receive this preaching of the Dharma?"

The World-Honored-One replied, "Mahāvairocana on the stage of wonderful enlightenment received the preaching of the Dharma from the beginningless and endless original Buddha who is of one mind and one thought."

The bodhisattva Mañjuśrī again spoke to the Buddha, saying, "From what Buddha did 'the beginningless and endless original Buddha who is of one mind and one thought' receive the preaching of the Dharma?"

The World-Honored-One again said, "'The beginningless and endless original Buddha who is of one mind and one thought' received the preaching of the Dharma from the original Buddha of no mind and no thought."

Mañjuśrī again spoke to the Buddha, saying, "From what Buddha did the 'original Buddha of no mind and no thought' receive the preaching of the Dharma?"

The World-Honored-One again said, "There is no Buddha above and beyond the 'original Buddha of no mind and no thought.' There is no Buddha before and no Buddha after 'no mind and no thought.' The original Buddha is in essence beyond conceptual understanding. From the beginning he/it does not go nor come, does not have the nature of the threefold body, does not have the nature of the ten destinies [from hell to Buddhahood]."

Mañjuśrī again spoke to the Buddha, saying, "If above and beyond the original Buddha of no mind and no thought there is no nature of the threefold body and the ten destinies, from what basis do the threefold body and ten destinies arise?"

The World-Honored-One again said, "The original Buddha of no mind and no thought is by nature beyond conceptual understanding. Both the conceptually understood natures of the threefold body and sentient beings in the ten destinies, and the nature of that which is without a nature, arise from the nature that is beyond conceptual understanding."

Mañjuśrī again spoke to the Buddha, saying, "If this is so, then is there no Buddha who teaches at the beginning?"

The World-Honored-One again said, "There is nothing that teaches or receives above and beyond the original Buddha of no mind and no thought. Moreover, this is a single Buddha, and there are not two Buddhas. You all should shut your eyes and contemplate the original Buddha that is without beginning and without end."

Mañjuśrī spoke to the Buddha, saying, "That which the World-Honored-One preaches is exceedingly profound. It is true yet beyond our power to comprehend. It is good; it is good. I gladly preach this sutra."

At that time the Tathāgata named King of Imposing Sound [Bhīṣmagarjitasvara-rāja] spoke to Mañjuśrī, the prince of the Dharma, saying, "Well done, prince of the Dharma. You have questioned the Tathāgata in such a way that it is cause for a great event. Now, listen carefully; listen carefully. Reflect well on these things."

The Buddha, after preaching this sutra, sat in the lotus position and entered the concentration [samādhi] that is wonderful and supreme. At that time Mañjuśrī, prince of the Dharma, and everyone in the assembly of eighty-four thousand monks, all entered this samādhi through the supranormal power of the Buddha.

The following events were seen. The Buddha, from within his state of concentration, emitted a great circle of light from his own face, illuminating with insight Mañjuśrī and the eighty-four thousand monks. A sword of wisdom [appeared] from the top of Mañjuśrī's head, and from his side ["liver"] emerged a golden-haired lion. The Tathāgata's ray of light extended everywhere, and the color of his body was like that of gold.

Mañjuśrī spoke to the Buddha, saying, "World-Honored-One. We have attained unprecedented [insight]. Our hearts greatly rejoice."

The Tathāgata again preached in a verse, saying,

> The supreme path of all Buddhas
> Has the marks of perfect light and eternal abiding.
> Those who enter meditative concentration together with [the Buddha]
> In the same way realize the mind of enlightenment [*bodhicitta*].

When the Buddha finished preaching these verses, the great monks in the assembly at once stood up, bowed, and went on their way.

The Sutra on the Unlimited Life of the Threefold Body
as Taught by the Buddha

FAITH

—25—

On Attaining the Settled Mind: The Condition
of the Nembutsu Practitioner

Dennis Hirota

On Attaining the Settled Mind (*Anjin ketsujō shō*) is an influential tract of the Pure Land Buddhist tradition, treasured since the fourteenth century for its incisive exposition of the interrelationships between the person of the nembutsu and Amida Buddha. The "settled mind" refers to the entrusting of oneself to Amida's Primal Vow, and attainment of this condition signifies that one's liberation from painful samsaric existence in ignorance and self-attachment has become certain.

The author and date of composition are unknown. The tract employs a number of concepts and expressions characteristic of the Seizan branch of the Jōdo school, developed by Hōnen's disciple Shōkū (1177–1247), and the dominant opinion among contemporary scholars is that it is a writing of the Seizan tradition. Historically, however, it has been the Shin tradition of Shinran (1173–1263) that has studied, annotated, and transmitted the work. Kakunyo (1270–1351), the third head of Shinran's Honganji lineage, and his son Zonkaku were familiar with it, and Rennyo, the eighth head of the tradition, in whose time the Honganji Temple developed into a major social and political force, called it a "gold mine" for its presentation of the nature of true entrusting. The tract appears to have exerted a powerful influence on Rennyo's thought and expression. Further, it was even a Shin scholar-priest, Ekū (1644–1721), who first argued for Seizan provenance. *On Attaining the Settled Mind,* then, is an important document in the development of Japanese Pure Land thought and practice from the later medieval period on, and, in view of the sharp sectarian distinctions solidified in the Edo period, it is significant as a Seizan work adopted into the Shin tradition. The background for the tract may be viewed through a brief comparison of the teachings of Shōkū and Shinran.

Shōkū was one of Hōnen's chief disciples. He entered the Yoshimizu following at the age of fourteen and remained a disciple for twenty-three years, until Hōnen's exile. Distinguished both for his grasp of the master's teaching and for his scholarly capabilities, he was, at age twenty-two, among the handful of disciples who aided Hōnen in the composition of *Passages on the Nembutsu Selected in the Primal Vow (Senjaku hongan nembutsu shū)*. This was in 1198, several years before Shinran resolved to descend Mount Hiei. Moreover, in his later career he faithfully followed Hōnen in holding the *Sutra of Meditation on Amida Buddha (Kammuryō jukyō, T* 365) and Shan-tao's works at the center of his teaching. Indeed, in developing a highly systematic doctrine based on these writings, he sought to give firm grounding to Hōnen's nembutsu teaching. Shōkū stands together with Shinran on several major issues. Above all, they both emphasize the centrality of a conception of "faith" underlying utterance of the nembutsu rather than practice of repeated recitation, and because of this, they both were critical of the view that attainment of birth in the Pure Land was also possible through performing various good practices other than the nembutsu.

In viewing the teachings of Shinran and Shōkū together, there emerges the following generalized structure of religious transformation based on the fundamental Mahāyāna concept that, because authentic wisdom transcends the dichotomy of self and other, aspiration for enlightenment necessarily involves the desire to bring all beings to awakening:

1. Underlying human salvation is the dynamic activity of true reality as wisdom-compassion that fulfills itself in its working to make itself known to us.

2. In our ignorance, we resist this activity and cling instead to our own, inevitably egocentric, judgments and designs. Moved by greed, envy, and fear, we devote our energies to worldly or "religious" ends for the sake of self-gratification. As a result, we are bound to false, imagined selves and lives of compulsive repetition of pain.

3. Salvation lies in genuine entrusting of ourselves to that which is true and real, the Vow of Amida. This is an awakening that cannot be brought about through any exertion of will or effort by the ignorant self, but rather itself represents the abandonment of self-will.

4. To entrust ourselves is to undergo an instantaneous transformation in which we become one with the dynamic activity of the true and real; in this way, we are freed from bondage to samsaric life.

5. Because of this transformation, there is a fundamental change in our ongoing lives in the present. While we are still possessed of passions, at the same time our lives are characterized by the unobstructedness of the compassionate activity that grasps us.

This general understanding of the human situation and the nature of salvation underlies *On Attaining the Settled Mind*. In addition, the tract displays some of the areas of difference between Shōkū's path and Shinran's. It is frequently compared with *Tannishō*, the record of Shinran's words, both works seen as early vernacular writings in the indigenous Pure Land tradition that retain their power for contemporary readers. In content, they are also contrasted. It may be said that Pure Land thought includes both (1) a polarity of beings, who are evil and powerless to bring about their own emancipation, and Amida Buddha, the embodiment of wisdom-compassion, and (2) the nonduality of beings and Amida in the Buddha's compassionate working. *Tannishō* focuses on the self-reflection of persons of nembutsu, whose religious awareness entails an awakening to the nature of their existence as pervaded in its depths by uneradicable blind passions rooted in self-attachment. In Shōkū's thought, entrusting is understood rather in terms of realization of Amida Buddha's compassion and the Buddha's fulfillment in the infinite past of birth in the Pure Land for all beings. Thus, *On Attaining the Settled Mind* emphasizes this latter aspect. This is particularly apparent in the usage of Shōkū's term, the "oneness of *ki* (practicer) and Dharma (Buddha) (*kihō ittai*)," which occurs twenty times throughout the work. Scholars have distinguished various implications of the phrase depending on context in the tract, but here we may simply note that it develops two general dimensions of the oneness: that based on the nature of the Vow as inherently including the religious fulfillment of beings (oneness of Amida's attainment of perfect enlightenment and beings' attainment of birth in the Pure Land), and that based on the actual working of the Vow in beings (oneness of beings and Amida Buddha in Namu-amida-butsu). The first sense of oneness is closely related to the realization that one need accomplish no practice because one's birth in the Pure Land has already been won by the Buddha, while the second sense of oneness expresses the presence of Amida's activity in every act of one's ongoing existence.

The translation is based on *Anjin ketsujō shō* in *T* 83, no. 2679: 921–929.

Further Reading

Dennis Hirota, tr., "On Attaining the Settled Mind: *Anjin ketsujō shō,*" *The Eastern Buddhist* 23, 2 (Autumn 1990): 106–121, and 24, 1 (Spring 1991): 81–96; Dennis Hirota, "Shinran's View of Language: A Buddhist Hermeneutics of Faith," *The Eastern Buddhist* 26, 1 (Spring 1993): 50–93, and 26, 2 (Autumn 1993): 91–130; Dennis Hirota, *No Abode: The Record of Ippen* (Kyoto: Ryūkoku University, 1986), rev. ed. (Honolulu: University of Hawaii Press, 1997); Dennis Hirota (head translator), Hisao Inagaki, Michio Tokunaga, and Ryushin Uryuzu, *The Collected Works of Shinran* (Kyoto: Jōdo Shinshū Hongwanji-ha, 1997); Minor L. and Ann T. Rogers, *Rennyo: The Second Founder of Shin Buddhism* (Berkeley: Asian Humanities Press, 1991); Yoshifumi Ueda and Dennis Hirota, *Shinran: An Introduction to His Thought* (Kyoto: Hongwanji International Center, 1989).

On Attaining the Settled Mind

FULFILLED ASPIRATION: AMIDA'S PRIMAL VOW

To actualize [with your own existence] the living core of the Pure Land way, you must first of all understand the dynamic that informs the Primal Vow.

Forty-eight universal Vows have been established [by Amida], but their fundamental intent is expressed in the Eighteenth. The other forty-seven are for the purpose of bringing beings to entrust themselves to this Vow. [The Chinese Pure Land master Shan-tao] paraphrases the [Eighteenth] Vow in his *Hymns of Birth (Ōjō raisan,* T 47:447c):

If, on my becoming Buddha, sentient beings throughout the cosmos say my Name, be it only ten times, and yet fail to be born [in my land], then may I not attain perfect enlightenment.

In other words, if the sentient beings of the cosmos attain birth—the necessary awakening of profound aspiration and performance of practice (*gangyō*) having been accomplished—I also will become Buddha; if they do not attain birth, I shall not attain perfect enlightenment.[1]

The Buddha's realization of perfect enlightenment, then, must depend on whether or not we are born in the Pure Land. This being so, it is difficult to understand [Amida's] having achieved enlightenment before the sentient beings of the cosmos have in fact been born into the Pure Land. Nevertheless, Amida Buddha has already arranged the birth of beings there by wholly fulfilling, in our place, the resolute vow or aspiration and the practice [that are essential in the Buddhist path]. When, for every sentient being throughout the cosmos, the awakening of aspiration and performance of practice were thoroughly realized and birth in the Pure Land thereby accomplished, Amida attained the perfect enlightenment embodied in Namu-amida-butsu as the oneness of practicer and Dharma. The birth of foolish beings, then, is inseparable from the Buddha's realization of perfect enlightenment. When the birth of all sentient beings throughout the cosmos was consummated, the Buddha attained enlightenment; thus, the Buddha's realization of enlightenment and the fulfillment of our birth in the Pure Land were simultaneous.

Although our birth has been effected on the part of the Buddha, we sentient beings differ in coming to grasp this truth; hence, there are those who have already been born in the Pure Land, those who are now being born, and those who will be born in the future. The times of past, present, or future may vary according to the individual practicers; nevertheless, beyond the moment (*ichinen*) of perfect enlightenment in which Amida achieved the attainment of birth in our place, there is nothing else necessary, nothing at all that we contribute.

To give an analogy, when the sun emerges, the darkness in all directions vanishes instantly, and when the moon appears, the waters throughout the Dharma-realm simultaneously reflect its image. The moon, in ascending, casts its reflection on all streams; the sun, in rising, unfailingly sweeps away the dark. You need only know, then, whether the sun has risen, and should not worry about whether or not the darkness has been dispelled. You should discern whether the Buddha has attained perfect enlightenment, and not be anxious about whether or not foolish beings will attain birth. . . .

Birth has been accomplished on the part of the Buddha, without any pain or effort whatsoever on our part; nevertheless, tormented by blind passions, we have long been transmigrating in samsara and do not accept in trust the

Buddha's wisdom, wondrous beyond conceivability. Because [our birth has already been effected by the Buddha], the thought-moment in which a sentient being of the past, present, or future takes refuge [in Amida] returns to the one thought-moment of [Amida's fulfillment of] perfect enlightenment, and the mind settled on saying the Name that arises in the living beings of the cosmos also returns to the one thought-moment of [Amida's fulfillment of] perfect enlightenment. Not a single utterance or thought [of aspiration or trust] remains with the practicer [as his or her own good act].

The Name in itself wholly embodies [Amida's] perfect enlightenment, for it is the practice of the universal Vow in which Name and Buddha-reality are nondual (myō-tai funi). Because it embodies this perfect enlightenment, it embodies the birth in the Pure Land of the sentient beings throughout the cosmos. Because it embodies our birth, it holds fully and unfailingly the aspiration and practice necessary for us. . . .

The nembutsu utterance of a person in the lowest grade of the lowest level—the utterance at the point of death by one incapable of focusing thoughts on the Buddha—is taught to be possessed of aspiration and practice; know, concerning this, that the person's own aspiration and practice is not at all involved. For it is the aspiration and practice [accomplished] by Bodhisattva Dharmākara over a span of five kalpas [of reflection on his Vows] and billions of years [of practice] that fulfills the aspiration and practice of foolish beings. Apprehending the truth that Amida Buddha perfected the aspiration and practice for foolish beings is called realizing the "three minds," or the "threefold trust," or the "mind of trust." To express verbally the profound reason for which Amida fulfilled foolish beings' aspiration and practice in the Name is "Namu-amida-butsu." Hence, apprehension of it does not remain with the practicer but returns to the actuality of the Buddha's Vow. Neither does the Name remain with the practicer; when one says it, it immediately goes back to the universal Vow. Thus, the Dharma-gate of the Pure Land [way] lies in nothing but authentically grasping the Eighteenth Vow. . . .

To grasp the Eighteenth Vow is to grasp the Name. To grasp the Name is to realize that at the very moment Amida Buddha accomplished beforehand the birth of foolish beings—fulfilling the necessary aspiration and practice in their place—he made the birth of sentient beings throughout the cosmos the substance of his enlightenment. Hence, whenever we who practice the nembutsu hear the Name, we should realize, "Already my birth has been accomplished! For it is the fulfilled Name embodying the perfect enlightenment of Dharmākara Bodhisattva, who vowed not to attain it unless the birth of the sentient beings of the cosmos were achieved."

Whenever we pay homage before the image of Amida Buddha, we should realize, "Already my birth has been accomplished! For this is the form embodying the perfect enlightenment realized by Dharmākara Bodhisattva, who vowed not to attain it unless the birth of the sentient beings throughout the cosmos were fulfilled."

And whenever we hear the name "Land of Perfect Bliss," we should realize, "The Buddha has prepared the place where I will be born—the Land of Ultimate Bliss fulfilled by Dharmākara Bodhisattva, who vowed not to attain perfect enlightenment unless sentient beings are born there!" For such practicers as ourselves, who know only committing evil and who lack both the roots of good taught in the Buddha-Dharma and those valued in mundane life, virtues countless as the sands of the Ganges have been fulfilled on the part of Buddha; hence, that land is called "Perfect Bliss," being immeasurable bliss for the sake of such foolish and wrong-viewed sentient beings as ourselves.

It would be a sad thing for people for to assume that they will attain birth only if they have accumulated utterances of the Name, believing—even though they say the Name trusting the Primal Vow—that it represents the Buddha's virtue existing apart [from their own birth]. When faith has arisen in us that our birth having been firmly settled is manifested by "Namu-amida-butsu," then we see that the substance of [Amida's] Buddhahood is itself none other than the practice bringing about our birth. Thus, where there is a single voicing, birth is firmly settled.

Whenever we hear the Name "Amida Buddha," we should immediately recognize it as our attainment of birth and grasp that our birth is none other than the Buddha's perfect enlightenment. . . .

Even though people hear the Name or pay homage to [Amida's] image, they may, on hearing it, fail to realize that it is the manifestation [revealing] that Dharmākara's Vow to attain Buddhahood only if he bears us across [to nirvana] has not been in vain, and that he has attained perfect enlightenment; this is to hear without hearing, to see without seeing.

The *Sutra of the Enlightenment of Nondiscrimination* states: "On hearing [Śākyamuni Buddha] teach the Dharma-gate of the Pure Land, [beings] dance with joy and the hair of their bodies stands on end." This is not vaguely to rejoice. We may endeavor in some practice to bring about our emancipation, but in doing so we find that we are wanting in genuine aspiration for enlightenment and without wisdom. Since we are existences lacking the eyes of wisdom and the legs of practice, we can only sink in the burning pit of the three evil courses; nevertheless, aspiration and practice have been fulfilled on the part of Buddha, and when we are struck with gladness that the Buddha has attained the perfect enlightenment in which practicer and Dharma are one, then our joy is so great that in its abundance we leap and dance. The *Larger Pure Land Sutra* expresses this: "During that time [after the three treasures have disappeared], people who hear [the Name] and realize one thought-moment [of joy will all attain birth]," and "Those who, hearing the Name, rejoice in it and praise it, [will all attain birth]." To cease disregarding the Name, viewing it as something applying only to others, and [to hear] it as itself our own birth already fulfilled, and to see [Amida's] form as [the embodiment of] our having attained birth, is called "hearing the Name" or "seeing the Buddha's form." To apprehend this truth is called knowing and entrusting oneself to (*shinchi*) the Primal Vow.

NEMBUTSU-SAMADHI

Those who seek settlement of the mind of trust in the practice of nembutsu-samadhi should understand that their bodies are Namu-amida-butsu, their minds are Namu-amida-butsu.

The human body arises through a mergence of the four elements—earth, water, fire, and air—and in the Hīnayāna tradition it is said to be composed of minute particles. But though it be crushed again into such particles, not a single one will fail to be suffused with the virtue of the fulfilled Buddha. Thus, the physical body that actualizes the oneness of practicer and Dharma is itself Namu-amida-butsu.

The mind is wholly formed of blind passions and attendant blind passions; from moment to moment it arises and perishes. Though it be divided a thousand times, not a single instant will fail to be pervaded by Amida's aspiration and practice. Hence, manifesting the oneness of practicer and Dharma, the mind also is itself Namu-amida-butsu.

Sentient beings, who are forever foundering [in samsaric existence], fill Amida's heart of great compassion; therefore, practicer and Dharma are one and are themselves Namu-amida-butsu. The virtues of the Buddha, who is the body of the Dharma-realm, fill our ignorant and inverted minds to their depths; again, therefore, practicer and Dharma are one and are Namu-amida-butsu.

The two kinds of fruition constituting the Pure Land—Buddha-body and the land itself—are also thus. There is nothing in the fulfillment of the land—down to even a single leaf of a jewel-tree—that is not for the sake of us, who are utterly evil; hence, practicer and Dharma are one and are Namu-amida-butsu. The fulfillment of Amida's Buddha-body—from the white hair between the eyebrows to the thousand-spoked wheels on the soles of the feet—consists of forms manifesting the complete realization of the aspiration and practice of sentient beings, who are constantly sinking [in samsaric existence]; hence, again, practicer and Dharma are one and are Namu-amida-butsu.

Our bodies and our hearts and minds—our activity in its three modes and our deportment in its four states—are all thoroughly pervaded by the virtues of the fulfilled Buddha. Hence, the practicer—"Namu"—and Amida Buddha are never separated for even an instant; every point in time is Namu-amida-butsu. Since there is not a moment when exhaled breath and inhaled breath are separated from the Buddha's virtues, all is the embodiment of Namu-amida-butsu. . . .

THE PERSON OF NEMBUTSU

Nembutsu-samadhi refers to the entrusting of oneself to Amida in the awareness that the aspiration (Vow) and practice embodying the great compassion of the fulfilled Buddha has, from the very beginning, entered the minds and thoughts of ignorant sentient beings, so that without our knowing, from the

side of Buddha, the perfect enlightenment of Namu-amida-butsu in which practicer and Dharma are one has been attained. Because aspiration and practice
have both been accomplished on the part of Buddha, our hands in worship,
our lips in utterance, and our minds in trust are all Other-power.

For this reason, in the eighth exercise [of the *Sutra of Meditation on Amida
Buddha*] it is taught, concerning nembutsu-samadhi that embodies the oneness
of practicer and Dharma: "The Buddha-tathāgata Amida is the body of the
Dharma-realm, entering the minds of all sentient beings." In commentary,
[Shan-tao] states: "'Dharma-realm' refers to the field of enlightening activity,
the world of sentient beings." Note that it is all the sentient beings of the
Dharma-realm—not "sentient beings who perform meditative good" or "sentient beings who awaken aspiration for enlightenment"—who are the objects
of enlightening activity. This is what Shan-tao means when he says, "'Dharma-
realm' refers to the field of enlightening activity, the world of sentient beings."
Further, he states that precisely because the Buddha's mind transfuses [beings],
the Buddha's body also transfuses them. The virtues of Amida's body and mind
penetrate and fill the bodies of the sentient beings of the Dharma-realm and
the depths of their minds; hence the words, "entering the minds of all sentient
beings." The person who accepts this in trust is called a sentient being of the
nembutsu.

Further, Shan-tao explains concerning the contemplation of the true Buddha-body: "The three modes of activity of sentient beings of the nembutsu and
the three modes of activity of Amida Tathāgata are mutually inseparable."[2] The
Buddha's perfect enlightenment consists of the birth of sentient beings, and the
birth of sentient beings consists of the Buddha's perfect enlightenment; hence,
the three modes of activity of sentient beings and those of Amida are wholly
one. Those who hear with genuine understanding that there is no birth of
sentient beings apart from the Buddha's enlightenment, and that both aspiration and practice have been fulfilled on the part of Buddha, are the sentient
beings of the nembutsu. Their entrusting of themselves to the Vow, when given
verbal expression, is Namu-amida-butsu. . . .

In China there was a venerable master named Fu who achieved a remarkable
realization of the Mahāyāna and who was also versed in non-Buddhist scriptures. Among his sayings is the following: "Together with Buddha I rise morning after morning; clasping Buddha I lie down night after night." Although
"Buddha" here refers to Buddha that is ultimate reality or suchness, as taught
in the general Dharma-gate of the Path of Sages, there is nothing at all to
prevent us from considering it from the perspective of Amida's practice and
realization. If we come to be illumined and protected by the light of Amida's
mind, which grasps beings, we are like Master Fu. Morning after morning we
rise bearing the virtues of the fulfilled Buddha, and night after night we lie
down together with Amida's Buddha-wisdom.

The Buddhas unrelated to us being remote, what can we do to receive their
virtues? And although the true reality of suchness or Dharma-nature is near,

unenlightened beings like ourselves are powerless to attain it. While having long possessed in our very existence the aspiration and practice of Other-power, which do not require any capabilities or awakening on our part, we have meaninglessly remained fettered by the attachments of self-power, so that we return in vain to our old village of samsaric life. This is truly lament-able!

NEMBUTSU AS UNCREATED

People commonly think that the nembutsu is a matter of mentally contem-plating the features of the Pure Land and Amida Buddha or vocally saying the Name, and that when we are not contemplating or reciting, there is no nem-butsu. If it were such, we could hardly speak of the uncreated and eternal nembutsu. If it appeared when we said it and vanished when we did not, the nembutsu would truly be ephemeral and constantly changing. . . . In the Ma-hāyāna tradition, the eternal, unchanging reality of suchness or Dharma-nature is spoken of as uncreated. Thus, in the preface to his *Commentary on the Sutra of Meditation on Amida Buddha*, Shan-tao states, "Dharma-body is eternal, like empty space," expressing the Pure Land's benefit of transcendence of time. The statement that the Land of Bliss is the uncreated and eternal realm means, therefore, that it neither vanishes nor emerges through the acts of foolish be-ings. Nembutsu-samadhi is precisely thus. It does not emerge for the first time when a sentient beings thinks on [Amida] or disappear because it has been forgotten. . . .

When we disregard the Buddha's perfect enlightenment as something rele-vant in general but not our very own, and seek to attain birth by somehow awakening aspiration for enlightenment and diligently performing practice, we manifest a deplorable self-attachment. Since Amida's perfect enlightenment is itself the reality that brings about sentient beings' birth, the Buddha-reality itself embodies our aspiration for birth and our practice. This practice does not depend on whether or not sentient beings are mindful. Thus, no practice for birth is discussed other than the perfect enlightenment of Buddhahood. . . .

Although we say the Name, worship, and think on the Buddha, these are not practices of the self; they are simply the practicing of Amida Buddha's practice. This means that when we, with the mind taking refuge, allow our-selves to be carried by the Primal Vow and our bodily, verbal, and mental acts all ride upon the reality of Amida's Buddhahood, then the body is no longer an existence separated from Buddha, the mind is no longer a mind separated from Buddha. Saying the Name aloud, we verbally express our deep gratitude for the perfect enlightenment in which practicer and Dharma are one, and paying homage [with our bodies], we venerate the joy that we experience at the compassionate virtue of Other-power, a joy that floods our existence. Hence, although we worship, and although we say the Name, these acts do not arise from the efforts of the practicer; they are simply the enacting of that which has been fulfilled in Amida Buddha's accomplishment of the practice of foolish beings.

SELF-POWER AND OTHER-POWER

Suppose the sun to be Avalokiteśvara Bodhisattva. Newborn children may receive Avalokiteśvara's light with their eyes, but while in infancy they do not realize it. As they grow slightly cognizant, they assume that the light is their own power, the light of their eyes. But someone who knows the significance of the sun explains, "If it were the light of your own eyes, you would be able to see even at night. Quickly turn your trust instead to the primal light of the sun!" For those who turn to the light of the sun in the heavens, the light of their own eyes immediately becomes the light of Avalokiteśvara (Kannon).

Such is the meaning of taking refuge (kimyō). Our life when we are unaware is still the life of Amida; nevertheless, in infancy we are ignorant of this. When we have become slightly aware and exert our powers, we think our life is our own. Then, listening to a good friend who teaches us to turn to the primal life of Amida, we take refuge in the Buddha of Immeasurable Life, and thereby come to apprehend in trust that our life is none other than Immeasurable Life. In this way, to take refuge is explained as "attaining right mindedness." Those who have once taken refuge in the Vow and attained right mindedness may fall into an indeterminate state of mind, for their karmic bonds are heavy, but will nevertheless be born in the Pure Land. . . .

The *Buddha-Contemplation Samadhi Sutra* (*Kanbutsuzammaikyō*, T 643) states:

> There was a wealthy man who had one daughter. In his final disposition of his property, he gave her purest gold of the Jambu River. She wrapped it in a filthy cloth and buried it in mud. The king of the realm sent retainers to seize the gold. Though they tread in the mud, they did not realize it was hidden there and left empty-handed. Afterward, the daughter retrieved the gold and used it in trade, so that it increased to even greater worth than before.

This is a parable. The "king of the realm" stands for our own mind-king, the "treasure" for good acts, and the "retainers" for the six thieves—our senses and consciousness. To be bereft of all means of support, our good acts seized by the six thieves, is an analogy for lacking any condition for emancipation. Retreiving the gold from the mud and its worth working freely represents the mind of entrusting becoming definitely settled through nembutsu-samadhi, so that we swiftly attain birth in the Land of Happiness. Wrapping the gold in filthy rags and placing it in the mud presents an analogy indicating that the true practicer in accord with the Vow is none other than the foolish being of the five defilements, the woman of defilement and evil.

Once flame has been set to firewood, it cannot be separated out from it. The firewood represents our hearts and minds; the flame, Amida's light grasping and never abandoning us. Since we are illumined and protected by the light of the Buddha's mind, there is no Buddha-mind apart from our own minds, and no hearts and minds of our own apart from the Buddha's mind. It is this that is named "Namu-amida-butsu."

Notes

1. There are two fundamental elements in the Buddhist path: aspiration for enlightenment formulated in vows (gan) to give resolve and direction to practice, and the religious cultivation and good works (gyō) performed through many lifetimes in order to bring that aspiration to fruition. The Pure Land practicer must also conform with these fundamental requirements of awakening of aspiration for enlightenment and performance of practices. In Anjin ketsujō shō, however, the scheme of aspiration (Vow)-practice functions as a forceful device for teaching the unity of Amida's compassion and human aspirations, for concretely it refers to Amida's Vow and the aeons of practice performed as Dharmākara, which are transferred to living beings.

2. The contemplation of the true body of Amida (shinshinkan), the ninth exercise of the Sutra of Meditation on Amida Buddha, focuses on the Buddha's transcendent features and the light they emit: "Each ray of Amida's light shines everywhere upon the worlds of the cosmos, grasping and never abandoning sentient beings of the nembutsu" (T 12:343b). In his commentary on the light grasping and never abandoning people of the nembutsu, Shan-tao describes three relationships that exist between the practicer and Amida Buddha. The first is the "intimate" or "close" relationship: if a person always utters the Name, worships Amida, and thinks on him, the Buddha hears, sees, and recognizes the person; thus their three modes of activity are inseparable. "Three modes of activity" (sangō) refers to all actions categorized as bodily, verbal, and mental; in the case of the practicer, concretely it refers to worship, saying the nembutsu, and thinking on the Buddha. The quotation in Anjin ketsujō shō is a paraphrase based on Commentary on the Sutra of Meditation on Amida Buddha, "On Meditative Practice" ("Jōzengi," Kangyōsho, T 37:268a). This aspect of oneness pervading the practicer's acts in ordinary life is not developed in Shinran's thought but is emphasized by Shōkū, who, after Hōnen's death, studied Tendai esoteric teachings and adopted esoteric terms and concepts to express it. This strain of Japanese Pure Land thought finds its fullest development in Ippen (1239–1289).

—26—

Plain Words on the Pure Land Way

Dennis Hirota

The following selection consists of sayings and anecdotes transmitted by wandering monks or "holy men" (*hijiri*), who began to appear in large numbers from the eleventh century, and who played an important role in spreading Buddhist teachings and practices beyond temple walls and in areas outside the urban centers. Some of these men had abandoned their positions within the major temples, dissatisfied with their practice or disillusioned by the worldliness that pervaded the ecclesiastic institutions; others had never been formally ordained to begin with, having shaved their heads, donned monk's robes, and pursued their activities without government authorization.

Many such wandering monks withdrew to secluded temples or huts where they meditated, chanted sutras, and performed austerities, sometimes adopting Shintō and native folk religious practices to cultivate spiritual powers. Often, however, they went down to the cities or traveled the countryside, guiding lay people by giving sermons and leading worship and chant. Those who followed a mendicant life lived by begging, stopping before houses to recite passages from sutras or incantations for warding off misfortune. At times they performed rites for the dead or to cure illness, and some collected contributions for temples they had formed affiliations with, to be used for construction or for an image or bell.

Kūya (or Kōya; Kōshō, 903–972) was the first such monk successfully to spread the practice of the nembutsu—the recitation of the Name of Amida Buddha, "Namu-amida-butsu"—as a means of attaining birth in Amida's Pure Land after death. It is said that he chanted it in the Kyoto marketplace while rhymically beating a gong, and that his joy in the nembutsu emerged in dance. Prior to him, nembutsu recitation had been regarded chiefly as an incantation for pacifying spirits of the dead and was shunned by the common people as inauspicious. It was also used as an adjunct to meditation practices, particularly within the Tendai sect, and in the later Heian period came to be widely used in Shingon as well.

In the latter part of the twelfth century, Hōnen (1133–1212) established the doctrinal foundation for the "sole-practice" (*senju*) Pure Land path, teaching that all those who simply said the nembutsu would attain birth in the Pure Land. According to Hōnen, this practice was superior to others because it was determined by Amida, who, in vowing to save all sentient beings, selected for them a practice that all people could perform. Any more demanding act, though it might seem inherently more efficacious in religious cultivation, would be inaccessible to some—if not to all—during the period of the Latter Days of the Dharma (*mappō*), which was calculated as beginning in 1052 C.E. Thus, those with genuine trust in the Buddha's all-embracing compassion would devote themselves to the nembutsu alone as the specific act in accord with the Buddha's Vow. This Pure Land teaching came to be spread widely through the activities of monks like those represented in the following sayings, despite periodic persecutions instigated by the established temples and concerned civil authorities.

Plain Words on the Pure Land Way (*Ichigon hōdan*, literally "one-word talks fragrant [with Dharma]") includes over 150 statements in the form of personal instruction, anecdote, and dialogue. Many of the passages are anonymous, like the compilation as a whole, but the names of over forty monks are also recorded. Some of the named were revered monks of the distant or recent past, but others survive in no other records. The depiction of religious practice in Plain Words is striking for several reasons. First, the work exhibits a broad sense of tradition, rooting the Pure Land movement in the ancient legacy of wandering holy men and mountain ascetics by embracing within its past such figures as Gyōgi Bosatsu (668–749), a Buddhist leader of the Nara period who is regarded as the forerunner of the wandering *hijiri* and Tendai's Saichō and Shingon's Kūkai, the founders of the Heian period Buddhism. These men advanced the indigenization of Buddhist practice by going beyond the limited, largely ritual functions assigned to monks and nuns in the temples established by the state. Such emphasis on the adaptation of the path to personal life was often related to syncretic tendencies. This is reflected in *Plain Words*, which places native sources rather than the texts and schools from the Asian continent at its foundations, invoking in its opening section a revelation received by the monk Genshin (Eshin, 942–1017) at the Great Shrine at Ise, from early times the most sacred place of Shintō worship in the country. Genshin was the author of the influential Pure Land work *Essentials of Birth* (*Ōjōyōshū*, 985); hence, this passage implies that the central message of that scholarly treatise is in fact available to all, having been delivered in Japan by the Sun Goddess herself, often regarded since the Nara period as a manifestation of the Great Sun Buddha (Dainichi Nyorai).

Further, *Plain Words* defines this tradition of practice for personal emancipation in terms of an ideal of complete and unadorned sincerity. It thus conveys with immediacy the day-to-day resolve of the wandering monks of the Kamakura period. Through talk of backpacks, meals of bean paste, and death on the road, we sense the tough-minded practicality that they valued, and references to archery and horsemanship reflect the warrior background of many of them. It is said that two broad streams of Pure Land thought are brought together in *Plain Words*, that of Hōnen's teaching of "just saying Amida's Name" in ordinary life and that of a nembutsu practice influenced by indigenous and Esoteric traditions and performed by reclusive and itinerant monks based on Mount Kōya. Shunjō, Myōhen, and Kyōbutsu represent this latter strain. From the perspective of the work itself, however, the various streams are grasped together as a single tradition of wholehearted aspiration, free of mundane—and priestly—attachments. This breadth of vision, in which the loftiest models are those who have been able to strip away all self-attachment by abandoning learning and monastic precepts, reflects the religious energy of a time before the fine doctrinal distinctions of the different Pure Land schools solidified.

Finally, *Plain Words* follows upon the creative religious developments of the first part of the Kamakura period, and out of its historical awareness, it includes passages that lament the degeneration of reclusive practice. Life as a wanderer had represented for many unauthorized, "self-ordained" monks a means by which to evade taxation and conscription labor or to circumvent the responsibilities and social restrictions of one's class. Saigyō, for example, is thought to have taken up the life of a wandering monk partly to gain the freedom to nurture his talents as a poet. At the same time, wandering monks shared the road with the itinerant actors and acrobats who performed at temples and shrines, and it was tempting for some to cross the fine line that divided preaching from storytelling and poetry, sutra-chanting from musical recitation, rite from dance. *Plain Words*, in its criticism of monks who are overly concerned with "tales of war"—originally adopted as the stuff of sermons on decline and impermanence—or of self-satisfied hermits "intoning verses in their still and tasteful retreats," foreshadows the emergence of professional artists and entertainers who would invoke for their own purposes the traditions of the wandering monks, not only the numerous "lute priests" who chanted the *Tales of the Heike*, but also such figures as Noh performers, linked-verse poets, and the "recluses" (*tonseisha*) who advised the shoguns on matters of taste.

The translation follows the earliest extant text, published in 1648 with a note stating that it is based on a manuscript dated 1463. It is included in Miyasaka Yūshō, ed., *Kana hōgo shū*, in Nihon koten bungaku taikei 83 (Tokyo: Iwanami Shoten, 1964).

Further Reading

Dennis Hirota, tr., *"Ichigon Hōdan, Two Parts,"* The Eastern Buddhist 9, 2 (October 1976): 88–106; and 10, 1 (May 1977): 92–110; Dennis Hirota, *No Abode: The Record of Ippen* (Kyoto: Ryūkoku University, 1986), rev. ed. (Honolulu: University of Hawaii Press, 1997); Dennis Hirota, *Plain Words on the Pure Land Way: Sayings of the Wandering Monks of Medieval Japan* (Kyoto: Ryūkoku University, 1989); Dennis Hirota, *Wind in the Pines: Classic Writings of the Way of Tea as a Buddhist Path* (Fremont: Asian Humanities Press, 1995); Hori Ichiro, *Japanese Religion* (Tokyo: Kodansha, 1972); Hori Ichiro, "On the Concept of Hijiri (Holy-Man)," *Numen* 5, 2–3 (1958): 128–160; 199–232; Hori Ichiro, *Folk Religion in Japan: Continuity and Change*, ed. Joseph M. Kitagawa and Alan L. Miller (Chicago: University of Chicago, 1968).

Plain Words on the Pure Land Way

It is told: Genshin made a pilgrimage to the Great Shrine at Ise to spend seven days in secluded prayer. During the final night, in dream, the portals of the holy shrine suddenly opened and a gentlewoman stepped forth in an aura of sanctity. She declared:

> The Goddess of the Great Shrine has returned to the capital, the primal enlightenment. I am caretaker in the absence. Instructions were left, saying: "If sentient beings of the last age should seek the essential path of liberation, advise them to say the Name of Amida Buddha." [1]

It is told: The venerable Shunjō was in the closing night of a vowed week-long seclusion at the inner sanctuary of Mount Kōya. When it had drawn into the deep of night and all had grown still, from within the chapel of the Founder's Samadhi [where Kūkai is entombed], there emerged a single, distinct voicing of the nembutsu. Those who heard it were overcome with both sorrow and joy, and their sleeves were wet with tears. [2]

On his way back from a pilgrimage to Zenkōji Temple, Bishop Myōhen of Mount Kōya had an interview with Hōnen. Myōhen asked, "How can I break the bonds of samsaric existence with this lifetime?"

Hōnen replied, "Just say the nembutsu."

"That's surely the answer," Myōhen said. "But what should I do about the delusional thoughts and feelings that fill my mind?"

"Even though deluded thoughts arise, you will attain birth though the power of the Primal Vow."

Satisfied with this answer, Myōhen left.

Afterward Hōnen murmured to himself, "Trying to attain the Pure Land by suppressing delusional thoughts is like casting away the eyes and nose you're born with in order to say the Name." [4]

Dharma-seal Myōzen said: Simply dedicate yourself to saying the nembutsu. This may seem but a pouring of water to stone, but utter it, and there will be benefit. [5]

It was said: Most likely you never awaken any genuine compassion, but you must harbor no hatred for anyone. [8]

Zen-amidabutsu of Kurodani told this story: A *hijiri* went to [the priest] Gedatsu and asked permission to live and study with him.

Gedatsu replied, "Good monk, I perceive that aspiration for enlightenment is awake within you. Engaging in study is altogether useless; swiftly return whence you came. Those here lack desire for the world beyond, and I put them to study only because it's better than aimlessly doing nothing at all."

Thus he drove him away. [12]

Myōzen said: A *hijiri* knows it's good being good for nothing. [17]

Acts you must ponder whether to do or not are, as a rule, better left undone. [22]

For the person who actually wants to attain the world beyond, nothing is more pointless than withdrawal from ordinary life. [23]

Hōnen said: If, because it is taught that birth is attained with but one or ten utterances, you say the nembutsu heedlessly, then faith is hindering practice.

If, because it is taught that you should say the Name "moment by moment without interruption," you believe one or ten utterances to be indecisive, then practice is hindering faith.

As your faith, accept that birth is attained with a single utterance; as your practice, endeavor in the nembutsu throughout life. [26]

Without fretting about whether your passions are superficial or deep-seated, without weighing the magnitude of your karmic evil, just say Namu-amida-butsu with your lips and through your voicing bring about the settlement of birth. [30]

Shōkō said: If people who have been steadily and deeply mindful of birth into the Pure Land find that their practice is regressing, they should consider well: the time of death is approaching. [34]

Kyōbutsu-bō said: Recluses these days, once they have cut off the topknots they wore in mundane life, become superb scholars and preachers. Going up to Mount Kōya, they turn into illustrious Shingon masters and eminent explicators of the commentaries . . . and acquire a serviceable hand at the standard Sanskrit and Chinese characters. But it's extremely rare to see one whose abhorrence of samsaric existence runs deep, or who is wholly immersed in practice for attaining the world beyond. When they first cut their topknots, they seemed resolved never to be thus possessed of ambition, but they have aroused thoughts driven by fierce self-attachment and concern for reputation.

Up to the time that I abandoned the world, all of us were taught that since renunciation meant giving up all we possessed, seeking more was inexcusable. We therefore embraced a determination never to engage in any activity, secular or religious, which—though it might mean mastering the arts and skills of this life—would turn into a lingering attachment to samsara and in the end become a hindrance to birth. . . . Hence, though I was long at Ōhara and Mount Kōya, I learned not even one chant melody nor a single Sanskrit letter. [40]

To feel attached to your implement box or wicker pack is to lose sight of why you use it in the first place. Earnestly resolve in your heart: this life is one night's lodging, this world but dream and illusion, so let it be as it may.

As a means to taking your existence lightly and aspiring for the world beyond, you should become keenly aware that being alive is a matter of this day only, of the present moment alone. Realize this, and what is now scarcely endurable will be easily borne; your endeavor for the world beyond will be dauntless. If you imagine even casually that your life will be long, things of this world will swell in importance and all those concerns unrelated to the aspiration for enlightenment will arise.

For more than thirty years I have taken this truth of impermanence as my support, and to this day I make no error. I have looked as far to the future as the possibility of death by the year's end, but never contemplated life extending into the next year. I am now in old age. In all matters I think only of today. Ultimately, the key to liberation lies in setting your mind on impermanence.

People of ancient times, on casting off worldly life, lived with purity and simplicity of heart. Nowadays reclusion is but poorly understood, and through it people are instead corrupted in spirit.

Although the person aspiring for the world beyond chops wood and draws water, it should be the chopping wood and drawing water of one who is thinking of birth.

Those who seek the world beyond abide in the thought that they are out on a journey. Though you travel to the limits of cloud or sea, as long as you have physical existence, you cannot do without the bare essentials of food, clothing, and shelter. Nevertheless, whether you are attached to them or not makes all the difference. When you are constantly aware that you have but one night's lodging, not a permanent dwelling, nothing can obstruct your saying of the nembutsu.

That learning is worthless to the outcast monk is a matter of degree. The person with the capacity for it should occasionally skim Genshin's *Essentials for Birth* in an elementary way, taking a look at the concrete descriptions of the transience of samsaric existence and the bliss of the Pure Land. . . . But you should never labor after a thorough mastery or lucid understanding of every word and phrase just because study is recommended. In reading the text, it is enough to be able to grasp the gist without too much effort and to survey generally the most important passages. Once you have mastered this proven method, you will never deviate from the teaching, the fundamental intent of which lies in encouraging us to attain the world beyond. This is its living core.

Although you study only to this degree, if you sense your self-attachment or concern for reputation growing, you should resolutely desist. To turn medicine into poison is complete folly. On the other hand, if through your grasp of even a single sentence or phrase you find yourself more earnest in saying the nembutsu or your aspiration for birth strengthened, or you experience a fresh sense of urgency welling up within, you should indeed read the sacred words from time to time.

The person whose natural abilities are meager, however, should wholeheartedly say the Name without even this level of learning. If you endeavor in practice with genuineness of heart and mind, you will never stray from the basic intent of the teaching. The mind of faith—the mind aspiring for enlightenment—will arise of itself if you practice. [42]

The old warriors of the eastern provinces used to say that if they stayed long in the capital, they'd lose their nerve. This reveals, likewise, the wisdom of those who aspire to the world beyond. Bodily repose and lucidity of mind come only after you have eradicated even the slightest concern for fame and profit. Many of those who dwell in solitude cling to their way of life, believing that their minds are pure because they pass their time wholly in intoning verses in their still and tastful retreats: they are deceiving themselves. [44]

Myōhen often said: Personally, I regret the day I began to dwell in this mountain monastery. I imagined that, after withdrawing from worldly life, I would be heating bean-paste over a fire of twigs and brushwood for my meals, but quite the contrary, I have become known as a "man of the Way" and live in splendid circumstances: this is altogether at odds with my original intention. And unaware of my inmost feelings, people see my secluded life here and think it worthy of admiration.

This he would say with a wry expression. [47]

Gyōsen said: Heaven and earth answer no practical purpose yet embrace all things. Thus is the person of the Way. In becoming one of no consequence whatsoever lies the supreme consequence. [49]

Wholly aspiring to the Buddha Way is not an involved task. Allow yourself time, putting the Way before all else and setting your mind to no other business: this is the primary step. [50]

Shinkai crouched but never sat. Asked about this, he replied: "Where in the three realms and the six paths can I settle back with an easy mind?" [53]

Kenshō-bō of Shōin said: When you come to a landing just as the ferry is pulling away, there is only one thing to be done: just grab hold and get aboard.

If the crossing you seek traverses the river of passions surging through this life, then once you have encountered Amida's Name there is nothing else to be done: just say the Name, reverently entrusting yourself to it. None of us really realize how much we suffer because of our own calculating wisdom. [54]

None of us genuinely perceive that it's saying Namu-amida-butsu that is crucial, without deliberating whether we are wholehearted in it or not. [55]

Extraordinarily rare are those who, casting aside the desires and ambitions that torment the spirit, seek to devote themselves wholly to saying the Name with their hearts and minds unadorned, just as they are. No one has truly wakened the aspiration just to say the nembutsu single-heartedly, becoming one who does not even distinguish between black and white.

Do we realize what power is embodied in the mystery of Amida Buddha's Primal Vow? We are all busy fashioning our places in the world, neither reflecting on the evil of our existence nor turning a thought to the power of the Buddha and the Dharma. Thus our evil karma runs on unchecked. This is a miserable attitude. [58]

When the late Jakugan-bō was confined to his sickbed, Kyōsen-bō gave this advice: People who practice mounted archery learn a full-dress etiquette and ceremony that accompanies shooting. When it comes down to the actual day of contest, however, they are so filled with eagerness to shoot that once they have sprung forth on their horses, they forget everything but the desire to get their arrows to the target.

Likewise, you have been engrossed with one thing and another concerning the world beyond and have studied ceaselessly, but already you lie sick. Now you must embrace the aspiration to attain birth, saying the nembutsu with no other thought. [62]

Kyōbutsu said: Words of the Dharma for the person aspiring to the world beyond will not exceed a single page. [64]

Kyōbutsu once told Shinbutsu-bō: When people in secular life like blacksmiths and carpenters train apprentices in the ways of their trade, they do not necessarily teach in complete detail. Nevertheless, if the novice becomes competent at the essentials, they say that the way has been transmitted.

Similarly, even if you have nothing to show for these two or three years you've spent with me except that, as one who has broken away from the world, you do not lose sight of impermanence, then my original purpose will have been fulfilled. [66]

Shunjō said: Those mindful of the world beyond recognize that they should own nothing, not so much as a crock for salted bran. [67]

It was said: Seeking the world beyond is no different from carrying out your life on the paths of this world. This day is already at dusk. How easy it is to be slack in your labor. The year too drifts to a close; a lifetime is elapsing without any sense of urgency. At night, lie down and lament this meaningless procession of hours, and at dawn awaken and resolve to endeavor in your practice to the day's end.

When slovenly and negligent, set your mind on the transience of samsaric existence. When wayward thoughts take hold in your heart, raise your voice and utter the nembutsu. When confronted by demons and imps, arouse your compassion and try to help them; do not feel you must overcome them.

Poverty is the seed of awakening that day by day advances us along the Buddha-path. Possessions are the chains of birth-and-death, and night after night they move us to further evil. [69]

Someone asked Kyōjitsu-bō, "I say the Name knowing utterance to be the key to attaining birth, but my thoughts wander off to the moors and mountains of this world and I say it merely from my lips. What should I do?"

He answered, "When you set out with the idea of coming here, surely you did not think 'I'm going there,' 'I'm going there' with every step. You made your way here with your mind full of unrelated thoughts. Nevertheless, you did not cease walking and you have arrived.

"In this way, once you have wakened the aspiration for birth into the Land of Bliss, if you continue saying the Name of Amida to the end of your life, then even though your mind strays while doing so you will unfailingly attain birth." [75]

It is told: At a shrine of Mount Hiei, a young court lady disguised herself as a priestess. In the middle of the night, after everyone had retired, she beat out clear raps on a drum before the inner shrine of Jūzenji, singing with perfect lucidity of heart: "Let it be as it may. Please, please. . . ."

After persistent questioning, she explained, "When the transience of samsaric existence fills my mind, I say: 'Let the things of this world be as they may. Please bring me to the world beyond!'" [78]

It was said: I have seen a *hijiri* heartened to learn that provisions had run out. For that leanness when the smoke of the cooking hearth dies away holds what it truly means to be a hermit. [81]

Ji-amidabutsu of Shimotsumura said: Do not stand conspicuous in people's eyes, like crimson leaves dotting the far hillside or a single tree in a field: the best *hijiri* are bamboo in a brake. [83]

Hōnen said: Wakening aspiration for enlightenment is best accomplished by stealth. [84]

Ganshō said: Long ago I met Myōhen and, upon being initiated in the eighteen elements of esoteric practice, requested instruction in the samadhi of the Sanskrit characters in a lunar ring. Whereupon the master admonished me: "Do not cherish the thought of becoming learned or wise. Even Śākyamuni, when performing practices for his Buddhahood, was neither scholar nor sage. He was an aspirant for enlightenment who sacrificed himself to learn the second half of a gatha and cast away his life to feed his body to a tigress. Of what use, then, are abstruse teachings? It is the aspiration for enlightenment that is paramount."

Although permission to receive instruction in the ring-samadhi was then granted, I felt drawn to abstain from learning it. [85]

It was said: As you pursue your vagrant life of alms-begging and practice, carefully weigh the advantages and disadvantages of various locations as sites for your end. Determine beforehand a place where you will be able to exert your efforts for the world beyond with a tranquil heart, leaving behind all self-attachment and concern for reputation, and where you will be able to fulfill your final moments. People lacking aspiration are devoid of such foresight. [88]

Hongan of Hōdō-in said: For the venerable monks of old, the great issue throughout their lives was whether or not they possessed the aspiration for enlightenment. Those of later times fell to discussing texts. Now they speak of nothing but their tales of war. [93]

Myōhen said: Having renounced worldly life and become a hermit means that you have resolved, at bottom, to meet death at the road's edge or in a field. Bear this in mind, and you will never for a moment envy others, however disheartening your experience. But even in this, you must rely on the Buddha's power. [94]

The learned Kyōshin, who settled in Kako, built no fence to the west: toward the Land of Bliss the gate lay open. Nor, befittingly, did he enshrine an image of worship; he kept no sacred books. In appearance not a monk nor yet worldly, he faced the west always, saying the nembutsu, and was like one to whom all else was forgotten. [98]

Hōnen said: To speak deeply about the meaning of the nembutsu is, on the contrary, a sign of shallowness. Even though your reasoning does not go deep, if only your aspiration is deep, you are certain to attain birth. [99]

The way to say the nembutsu lies in having no "way." If you just say it earnestly, without taking account of your conduct or the good and evil of your heart, you will attain birth. [100]

Ji-amidabutsu of Shimotsumura said: Gyōgi taught, "Always be a companion to others and not yourself at center." In acting as a support to others lies true equanimity of heart. [102]

Kyōbutsu said: I had to rebuke some fellow practicers: You're like those who add baggage to the *hijiri*'s pack in order to strengthen their footing. [106]

While performing practice in Shikoku, Shinkai wrote on the wall of a farmhouse: Say the nembutsu without becoming a "person of the nembutsu" and you will attain birth.

Hongaku-bō of Chinzei asked Myōhen, "It is said that uttering the Name when you are distracted does not constitute good; you must first still the mind and then recite it. How should I go about this?"

Myōhen answered, "That statement applies to the most adept. Inferior practicers like myself are wholly incapable of ridding the heart and mind of distractions. Hence, without concern about whether we are agitated or not, we simply take a rosary with a sturdy strand and turn the beads, saying the Name. To wait expectantly for the moment the mind is concentrated would mean never being able to say the nembutsu." [111]

Shōkō said: The late Master Hōnen said, "When you say the nembutsu for the sake of attaining birth, the great significance of this act fills your heart and, thus encouraged, you wish to utter it always. With this, know that you are already possessed of the three essential attitudes." [117]

After his attainment of birth in the Pure Land, Hōnen appeared to Jūshin-bō of Miidera in a dream and answered his question: Though you ask, Amida Buddha is completely without appearances. One can only say the Name. [122]

Hōnen said: If you abide in an attitude of self-power, even saying the Name but a single time will be an expression of self-attachment. If you entrust yourself to Other-power, utterance after utterance, nembutsu after nembutsu, will be the manifestation of Other-power. [127]

Nen'a said: How lamentable it is that those who believe in causality are weak in their faith in Other-power, and those who believe in the Primal Vow do not acknowledge the law of causality. If you entrust yourself wholly to Amida's Vow and further believe in causation, you will be in accord with the Buddha's intent and will attain birth. [129]

It was said: If you truly desire to attain birth, just say the nembutsu, without becoming solicitous about others or involving yourself in sundry matters. You can hope to aid other sentient beings when you return to this defiled world from the Pure Land. [132]

Kyōjitsu said: Learn well the taste of the nembutsu! [133]

It was said: Reclusion has nothing to do with harboring a deep aversion for humankind. And to fear people without cause also reflects a warped outlook. Rather, at the heart of abandoning the world lies a profound rejection of the craving for esteem and wealth.

Since all practicers in their foolishness find it difficult to manage alone, you would probably do well to associate with one or two others who do not arouse strong yearnings for fame and possessions. If the number increases, however, there are bound to be problems. [140].

— 27 —

Shinran's Faith as Immediate Fulfillment
in Pure Land Buddhism

James C. Dobbins

Pure Land Buddhism underwent diversification and development in Japan, particularly during the twelfth and thirteenth centuries. Independent Pure Land schools emerged, giving an institutional base to the ideas of Japan's most illustrious Pure Land teachers: Hōnen (1133–1212), Shinran (1173–1263), and Ippen (1239–1289). Among them, Shinran's teachings are frequently cited as a provocative and compelling interpretation of Pure Land thought, and as the starting point for the largest Pure Land school in Japan, the Jōdo Shinshū, or true Pure Land school. Shinran went beyond the premises laid down by Genshin (942–1017), seeking to shift the focus of religious fulfillment from the next life to this one. The key to understanding Shinran is his concept of faith (*shinjin*), mentioned in Amida's eighteenth vow in the Pure Land scriptures. For Shinran, faith is not the believer's individual act of volition, a conscious decision in favor of Amida and Pure Land; instead, it is a state wherein humanly contrived choices cease and one reposes effortlessly in Amida's embrace. Amida's mind and purpose become one's own mind and purpose. In fact, faith is none other than Amida's mind transmuted in the person. What this means is that the crucial moment when one is embraced by Amida never to be forsaken is not death but rather the first instant of faith. Hence, there is no reason for the person of faith to look to death as the great transformation, nor to plan meticulously for the deathbed nembutsu ritual. That transformation occurs in this life. Faith is thus immediate confirmation here and now.

Shinran used a variety of ideas to elucidate the special nature of faith. He indicated, for instance, that there is no self-effort (*jiriki*) in faith, only Other-power (*tariki*). That is, faith is a transformation effected solely by Amida, not by the effort of the believer. One's own efforts not only fall short of faith but can actually obscure it. Shinran acknowledged that many people seek birth in Pure Land through a variety of practices—e.g., meditative visions of Amida, performing good works, intensive chanting of the nembutsu. But fulfillment via that path is contingent on the capacity of the individual. Because the process can be so long and arduous, most people will never complete it. Amida Buddha realized these difficulties when he made his vow assuring sentient beings of birth in Pure Land. The important thing, therefore, is not for people, upon each failing, to rededicate themselves all the more to self-effort, but to rely on Other-power. Everything necessary has already been accomplished by Amida. When this realization dawns upon people and when they confront forthrightly their own inability to win birth in Pure Land, they move from a mindset of contrivance (hakarai) to faith. In contrivance, one constantly seeks to calculate and define the exact terms of one's birth in Pure Land and to fulfill them through one's own efforts. Faith is none other than an end of contrivance and of defining one's own terms.

Many other Buddhist thinkers, like Shinran, consider this world to be the locus of Buddhism's affirming experience. But Shinran's great innovation was to place this experience in the context of people's encounter with their own wrongdoing and corruptibility. Faith does not mean perfection in the sense of overcoming all wrongdoings and evil inclinations. Evil inevitably persists. Indeed, people of faith succumb to it in certain circumstances, when karmic tendencies are too intense to suppress. But evil does not nullify faith. Faith endures amid the vicissitudes of human action, good or bad. The encounter with evil, in fact, may be the best occasion for faith to arise in a person, for in confronting it one comes to acknowledge the limited capacity of humans to perfect themselves through self-effort. It is precisely this realization that leads one to Other-power and faith. Shinran's candid discussion of evil was not without its dangers. Some of his followers mistakenly assumed that faith frees one to commit whatever wrongdoing one pleases. Shinran responded vigorously against such interpretations. Faith may flourish in a world fraught with evil, but it does not give one license to commit capricious wrongdoings. To think so is another instance of contrivance on one's part, at odds with faith.

Shinran's idealization of faith was grounded completely in the traditional themes and symbols of Pure Land Buddhism, though they took on slightly different significances when refracted through Shinran's ideas. Invoking Amida's name, the nembutsu, is very much a part of the life of faith but is not viewed in the traditional sense as a person's religious practice or act of good. Rather, the nembutsu is Amida's act, emerging out of his principal vow, the eighteenth vow, to bring all sentient beings to Pure Land. When a person of faith says the name, it is a tangible sign of Amida at work in the person. For people seeking birth in Pure Land as a reward for their practices and good works, birth there can never be certain until death. But for the person of faith, birth is certain from the first moment faith arises. In fact, some interpreters of Shinran regard this moment as one form of birth in Pure Land, inextricably linked to birth in Pure Land at death when the person of faith attains immediate enlightenment. Enlightenment at death, however, is already assured in this life to the person of faith, just as it is to the next Buddha, Maitreya. Hence, the sense of fulfillment begins in this life rather than at death.

The following passages are drawn primarily from Shinran's letters to his followers. Also included is an excerpt from *Notes Lamenting Deviations* (*Tannishō*), the most famous collection of sayings attributed to Shinran, and one from *Teaching, Practice, Faith, and Enlightenment* (*Kyōgyōshinshō*), his most extensive doctrinal treatise. Shinran was steeped in Buddhist learning, and consequently doctrinal terminology and obscure allusions to scripture surface even in his personal letters. But the density of his writing should not detract from the power of his message: that the weight of human failings, while persisting, cannot undermine or invalidate the liberating experience of faith. The extent to which Shinran acknowledged his own failings is reflected in his pen name, Gutoku, meaning Head-Shaven Fool. He saw himself as a fool in priest's guise, buffeted by waves of his own wrongdoing, but sustained by the power of Amida's vow.

The translations are from *Shinran-shū Nichiren-shū*, in Nihon koten bungaku taikei 82, ed. Nabata Ōjun et al. (Tokyo: Iwanami Shoten, 1964): *Mattōshō* 1:115–117; *Mattōshō* 2:117–121; *Tannishō* 3:194–195; *Mattōshō* 17:138–139; *Mattōshō* 24:151; and also from *Kyōgyōshinshō*, in *Shinran*, in Nihon shisō taikei 11, ed. Hoshino Gempō, Ishida Mitsuyuki, and Ienaga Saburō (Tokyo: Iwanami Shoten, 1971): 108.

Further Reading

Alfred Bloom, *Shinran's Gospel of Pure Grace* (Tucson: University of Arizona Press, 1956); James C. Dobbins, *Jōdo Shinshū: Shin Buddhism in Medieval Japan* (Bloomington: Indiana University Press, 1989); Ueda Yoshifumi and Dennis Hirota, *Shinran: An Introduction to His Thought* (Kyoto: Honganji International Center, 1989); Taitetsu Unno, tr., *Tannishō: A Shin Buddhist Classic* (Honolulu: Buddhist Study Center Press, 1984); Ueda Yoshifumi, ed., *Letters of Shinran: A Translation of* Mattōshō (Kyoto: Hongwanji International Center, 1978.)

Selections on Shinran's Faith

SHINRAN'S LETTERS (*MATTŌSHŌ* 1)

The [expectation of] being ushered into Pure Land [by Amida] belongs to those who seek birth in Pure Land through religious practices. Their practices are grounded in self-effort. Death is also [seen as the crucial moment] to those who seek birth through religious practices. They still have not attained true faith. Also, there are references to evil people who, having committed the ten wrongdoings and the five heinous offenses, encounter a good teacher for the first time [on their deathbed] and are urged [to say the nembutsu]. But believers of true faith, because they are embraced [by Amida] never to be forsaken, reside already at the stage whereby they are truly assured [of enlightenment]. For that reason, they have no need to look toward death or to depend on being ushered into Pure Land. When faith is established in them, birth in Pure Land is likewise established. They do not have to look toward the [deathbed] ceremony of being ushered into Pure Land.

True nembutsu reflection refers to the establishment of faith based on Amida's principal vow. People proceed without fail to unsurpassed nirvana because they have attained faith. Faith means single-mindedness. Single-mindedness means the indestructible mind. The indestructible mind means the mind aspiring for complete enlightenment. This is in fact the Other-power [of Amida at work], which supersedes all other-power.

Concerning true nembutsu reflection, there are two [other] types. One is that of believers in a meditative state of mind; the second is that of believers in a nonmeditative state. These two true nembutsu reflections, though included in Other-power, are actually reflections based on the believer's self-effort. Whatever good derives from such meditative and nonmeditative practices lies in the sphere of those who seek birth in Pure Land through religious practices. This good, though included in Other-power, is actually good based on the believer's self-effort. Believers who rely on their self-effort will not be born even on Pure Land's fringes, or in embryonic form, or in the realm of idleness, without [having to] wait for [Amida] to usher them into Pure Land [at death]. For that reason [Amida's] nineteenth vow [,which is aimed at them,] states: I vow to appear at the death of, and to usher into Pure Land, those people who perform good deeds, who offer their merit up in dedication to Pure Land, and who aspire to be born there. Thus, waiting [expectantly] for death and attaining birth by being ushered into Pure Land apply to believers in the meditative or the nonmeditative state of mind.

As for the principal vow singled out by Amida, neither formal reflection nor formless reflection [are relevant]. Formal reflection refers to thought involving colors and forms. Formless reflection refers to not having forms lodged in the mind and not thinking of colors in the mind, so that not even the word reflection [is appropriate]. Both of these are teachings from the [rigorous religious] path of sages. This path of sages includes Mahāyāna's advanced teachings from the Busshin (Buddha Mind), Shingon (True Word), Hokke (Lotus Flower), Kegon (Flower Garland), and Sanron (Three Treatises) schools. The Busshin school is commonly known in the world as the Zen (Meditation) school. These are teachings through which people who have already attained Buddhahood seek to advance our state of mind. Also included are the adapted teachings, the Hīnayāna teachings from the Hossō (Dharma Character), Jōjitsu (Realization of the Actual), and Kusha (Kośa) schools. All of these belong to the path of sages. The term "adapted" refers to the fact that Buddhas and Bodhisattvas, having already attained Buddhahood, appear provisionally in various guises in order to advance them.

In the Pure Land school also there are the ideas of formal reflection and formless reflection. Formal reflection means good practices of the nonmeditative type; formless reflection means good practices of the meditative type. Formless reflection in the Pure Land [teachings] is not like formless reflection in the path of sages. Also, within formless reflection in the path of sages there is a type of formal reflection too. Ask [others about this] in greater detail.

Within the Pure Land school, there is the true and the provisional. The true is based on the principal vow singled out by Amida. The provisional is based on the two types of good practices, meditative and nonmeditative. The principal vow singled out by Amida is the true essence of Pure Land. The two types of good practice, meditative and nonmeditative, are the provisional gate of expedient means. The true essence of Pure Land is Mahāyāna's most advanced [teaching]. Within the provisional gate of expedient means, there are both Mahāyāna and Hīnayāna, adapted and genuine, teachings. There have been 110 good teachers of Śākyamuni Tathāgata. They appear in the *Flower Garland Sutra* (*Hua-yen ching*).

Namu Amida Butsu.

1251, 9th month, 20th day

Gutoku Shinran,
79 years of age

SHINRAN'S LETTERS (*MATTŌSHŌ* 2)

In response to questions from *nembutsu* adherents at Kashima.

Among the ideas found in the true teachings on Pure Land, there are [the concepts of] Other-power and self-effort, [as applied] to a person's capacity for birth in Pure Land. These ideas appeared previously in the sayings of the Indian treatise masters and the Pure Land patriarchs. Self-effort, though it depends on the circumstances of each believer, means to chant and reflect on the names of Buddhas other than [Amida], to perform practices rooted in good other than [the nembutsu], to rely on oneself, to rectify the mind of physical, verbal, and mental disturbances by means of one's own contrivances of mind, and thereby to distinguish oneself so that one can assume one will be born in Pure Land. Other-power means to have faith in the principal vow, the eighteenth, whereby one is is born in Pure Land through the nembutsu, which was singled out and adopted by Amida Tathāgata from among his vows. Because this is the vow of the Tathāgata, one of the sayings of Master [Hōnen] was that, in Other-power, to be free of definition is the [best] definition. Definition here indicates contrivance. The contrivance of the believer is self-effort; it is [the person's act of] defining. Other-power is [simply] having faith in the principal vow whereby birth in Pure Land is undoubtedly established. Thus, it is completely free of any definition [on the part of the person]. Consequently, one need not wonder as a result of one's evil whether the Tathāgata would usher one into Pure Land [at death].

Unenlightened beings have from the beginning been overwhelmed with evil inclinations, so it is natural for them to think of themselves as evil persons. It is not appropriate for them to consider themselves upright in mind and thus deserving of birth in Pure Land. One cannot be born in the true Land through the contrivances of self-effort. What I have been told is that, with a faith based on the individual self-effort of the believer, one can only be born in the realm of idleness, or on the fringes of Pure Land, or in embryonic form, or in Pure Land's castle of doubt.

Through the fulfillment of his eighteenth vow, Amida Tathāgata attained [his status as the Buddha]. He assumed a form that was the ultimate in its miraculous benefit [to sentient beings]. The Bodhisattva Vasubandhu described [this Buddha] as the Tathāgata of Unobstructed Light Suffusing the Ten Directions. Hence, you should know that [light] does not disdain good or evil people; it does not prefer [or reject] a mind of evil inclinations; it is never at a distance; and so undoubtedly there is birth in Pure Land. Thus, Master [Genshin] of the Eshin temple said in his *Collection on Essentials for Birth in Pure Land* (*Ōjōyōshū*), in the place describing the nature of faith in the nembutsu of the principal vow: "There is no preferred [circumstance]—walking, standing, sitting, or lying; nor is there any disadvantageous time, place, or condition." He makes it clear that the person who has attained true faith is enveloped in [Amida's] embracing light. Therefore, Śākyamuni Tathāgata taught that, because one is born in the Pure Land of tranquility while still overwhelmed with ignorance and evil inclinations, one undoubtedly attains the fruit of unsurpassed Buddhahood. But it is unlikely that we, [born in] this evil world of five corruptions, will receive in faith the words of this one Buddha, Śākyamuni; hence, as Master Shan-tao has indicated in his commentaries, Buddhas in the ten directions as numerous as sand also bear witness [to this truth]. This shows that Śākyamuni, Amida, and the Buddhas of the ten directions are all of like mind and are never far from sentient beings of the principal vow's nembutsu, accompanying them as shadows do their objects.

Hence, Śākyamuni Tathāgata joyously declares the person of faith to be his beloved companion. The person of faith is also said to be the true disciple of the Buddha. This person is the one who dwells in true nembutsu reflection. Since the person is embraced never to be forsaken, we say that the person has attained the indestructible mind. The person is also described as the highest of the high, the exquisite person, the magnificent person, the all-surpassing person, and the extraordinary person. You should know that this person is established at the stage of those truly assured [of enlightenment]. Thus, the person is said to be the equal of Maitreya Buddha. You should know that because the person has attained true faith, the true Land is where the person is born. You should also know that attaining this faith is something bestowed [on people] through the expedient efforts of Śākyamuni, Amida, and the Buddhas of the ten directions. Consequently, you should not denigrate the teachings of any of the Buddhas, nor denigrate people who perform other practices

rooted in the good. You should neither revile nor denigrate those who revile and denigrate people performing the nembutsu. Rather, you should have
compassion and bear feelings of pity for them. That is what Master [Hōnen]
said.

Respectfully . . .

1255, 10th month, 3d day

Gutoku Shinran
written at 83 years of age

NOTES LAMENTING DEVIATIONS (*TANNISHŌ* 3)

Even the good person attains birth in Pure Land. How much more so the evil
person! But ordinarily people in the world say: "Even the evil person is born
in Pure Land. How much more so the good person!" At first glance this statement seems reasonable, but it runs counter to the idea of Other-power
[grounded] in the principal vow. The reason is that people who perform good
works through self-effort are not in [accord with] Amida's principal vow, for
they lack any sense of relying fully on Other-power. But when they overturn
their self-effort mindset and rely on Other-power, they attain birth in the true
Land. We who are overwhelmed by evil inclinations are unable to escape *saṃsāra* by any practices [of our own]. Out of compassion [for us, Amida] has
established his vow. The primary intent of it is for the evil person to attain
Buddhahood. Thus, the evil person's reliance on Other-power constitutes above
all else the true cause of birth in Pure Land. Hence, "Even the good person is
born in Pure Land. How much more so the evil person!"

TEACHING, PRACTICE, FAITH, AND ENLIGHTENMENT (*KYŌGYŌSHINSHŌ*)

Truly I know how lamentable it is! I, Gutoku Shinran, languish in a vast ocean
of attachments and desires. I wander vainly after mountains of fame and benefit. I take no joy that I am included among those assured [of enlightenment].
I do not delight that I am approaching the realization that is true realization.
How shameful and painful it should be!

SHINRAN'S LETTERS (*MATTŌSHŌ* 17)

Without knowing the teachings of the scriptures or the true underpinnings of
Pure Land's message, you are telling those among you who are senselessly
[inclined toward] remorseless indulgence that evil can be done just as they
please. By no means should this be said. Did you not see how I finally had to
distance myself from the person named Zenjōbō of the northern counties? If

people can do whatever they please [simply because] they are unenlightened beings, should they steal, or kill others, or whatever? If those who are originally inclined to steal should aspire for the paradise and say the nembutsu, there might well be some change in their original, misguided sentiments. But on no account should you say to others who have no such symptoms that evil is not a hindrance. Crazed by evil inclinations, people may commit things that they should not do, say things that they should not say, and think things that they should not think, even without realizing it. But if a person, thinking that there is no obstruction [to birth in Pure Land], is duplicitous with others and does things that should not be done and says things that should not be said, then it is not a matter of being crazed by evil inclinations. The person is intentionally doing what should not be done. Hence, on no account should this occur.

If you speak out against the wrongs of the people of Kashima and Namekata and bring under control the particularly misguided [situation] of the people of that region, then it will be an indication of what I am expressing on my part. It is [altogether] shameful for people to say that one should act giving free rein to one's heart in every way. To abandon the evils of this world and to refrain from doing shameful things [reflects] weariness of the world and the saying of the nembutsu. But when people who have said the nembutsu for years do or say evil things to others, this is no indication of weariness of this world. Hence, among Shan-tao's teachings, specifically among those on sincerity, he taught that you should take care to distance yourself from people who love evil. When [did he ever say] you should act giving free rein to the evils of your heart? On no account should you offer such advice, in your general state of ignorance about the scriptures and the Tathāgata's words.

Respectfully,

Also, since birth in Pure Land depends on the Tathāgata's vow in every way and not on the contrivances of unenlightened beings, it lies in Other-power. For you to continue your contrivances to the bitter end is improper.

Respectfully,

10th month, 24th day

Shinran

SHINRAN'S LETTERS (MATTŌSHŌ 24)

In the *Treasure Name Sutra* (*Pao-hao ching*) it states that Amida's principal vow is not a practice nor a good act; it is simply that which undergirds [the nembutsu], the Buddha's name. The name is [Amida's] good act and [Amida's] practice. The word practice here is a term that concerns performing good. The principal vow is to be understood as the Buddha's primordial promise; but it is not a good act nor a practice [per se]. [Amida's] name, which is [grounded] in the principal vow, is the primary agent causing people to be born in Pure Land. This cause of birth in Pure Land is therefore their father. [Amida's] light of great compassion is the supporting condition of those born in Pure Land. This supporting condition of those born is therefore their mother.

Institutional Practices

COURT AND EMPEROR

— 28 —

The Confucian Monarchy of Nara Japan

Charles Holcombe

The *Continued Chronicles of Japan* (*Shoku Nihongi*) follows immediately after the more famous *Chronicles of Japan* (*Nihon shoki*, 720) as the second of six official, Chinese-style, histories of ancient Japan. The text was completed in 797 and provides in forty *maki* (thin volumes) a year-by-year—sometimes even day-by-day—account of important events at the court (which was located in Nara during most of this time) from 697 to 791. Except for a number of especially august imperial proclamations (*semmyō*), which were transcribed phonetically in the Japanese language, the text is written entirely in a rather austere classical Chinese. Despite, or because of, the *Continued Chronicles'* dry, annalistic flavor, however, it is regarded by some modern scholars as being a relatively reliable source for the study of Nara Japan.

The selection translated here, covering the first few months of 757, is intended to highlight typically Confucian court concerns, especially the ideal of rule by imperial grace and ethical example, and the emphasis on filial piety (*kō*) as the fundamental moral principle linking state to family. The court's obvious fascination with omens is also a reflection of early Chinese Confucian practice, although one that had already come under imperial criticism in China itself. Noteworthy, too, is the apparently smooth integration of Confucianism, Buddhism, and Shintō portrayed in this passage. The issue of Korean immigration and assimilation is also addressed with the granting of Japanese surnames to those who so desired and qualified for them. It is estimated that by 761 C.E. about two thousand immigrants had changed their names according to this provision.

This translation is based on the superb new annotated *Shoku Nihongi* (compiled originally by Sugano no Mamichi and Fujiwara no Tsugutada et al. in 797 C.E.) in *Shin Nihon koten bungaku taikei*, vol. 3 (Tokyo: Iwanami Shoten, 1992): 20.174–185.

Further Reading

James Legge, tr., *The Sacred Books of China*, pt.1: *The Texts of Confucianism*, in *The Sacred Books of the East*, vol. 3, ed. F. Max Müller (1879; New Delhi: Motilal Banarsidass, 1966), esp. pp. 447–488 (*The Classic of Filial Piety*); Sakamoto Tarō, *The Six National Histories of Japan*, trans. John S. Brownlee (Tokyo: University of Tokyo Press, 1991); Aat Vervoorn, *Men of the Cliffs and Caves: The Development of the Chinese Eremitic Tradition to the End of the Han Dynasty* (Hong Kong: Chinese University Press, 1990).

Continued Chronicles of Japan

In the first month of spring of the initial year of the Tempyō-hōji (Precious Ideograph of Heavenly Peace) reign period (757), on the New Year of Keng-hsü according to the Chinese cyclical calendar, court was dismissed for reasons of imperial mourning [for Retired Emperor Shōmu, who had died the previous year]. By imperial command, eight hundred persons were ordained as monks.

The fifth day. It was commanded that since [in compliance with an earlier edict] the *Net of Brahma Sutra* (*Bonmōkyō, T* 1484) is to be expounded in every province from the fifteenth day of the next fourth month until the second day of the fifth month [to commemorate the first death anniversary of the late emperor], this year's "Quiet Dwelling" [Summer Seminar, which normally be-gan on the fifteenth day of the fourth month] shall begin immediately afterward on the third day of the fifth month. It was also decreed:

> Recently, commoners have been employed as district heads [*gunryō*] and colonels [*gunki*]. For this reason, people become accustomed to seeking of-fice from their homes and are unaware that their salaries come from serving the ruler. The loyalty that is a transference from filial piety [which also extends to the emperor] therefore gradually declines, and the Tao of en-couraging others becomes truly difficult. From now on, we should order the bureau director of the Ministry of Ceremonial not to allow any unranked persons to be considered for appointment. Colonels should be selected by the Ministry of War from those among the Six Guards whose capacities have been distinguished, employing those who are talented, courageous, and strong. Other kinds of fellows are not to be permitted indiscriminate appeal. All other matters remain as in the statutes and codes.

The sixth day. The former Senior First Rank Minister of the Left Tachibana Moroe (684–757) died. Ki Iimaro, of the Junior Fourth Rank, upper grade, and Ishikawa Toyohito, of the Junior Fifth Rank, lower grade, were dispatched to superintend the funeral. The obligatory funerary objects were officially pro-vided. The Minister [Tachibana] was the grandson of Prince Kurikuma of the

Posthumous Junior Second Rank, and the son of Prince Mino of the Junior Fourth Rank, lower grade.

The ninth day. The Fujiwara surname was bestowed upon Prince Iwatsu, of the Junior Fifth Rank, lower grade, and he became the son of Major Counselor [Fujiwara] Nakamaro of the Junior Second Rank [who was then ascendant at court, and a longstanding rival of the recently deceased Tachibana Moroe].

The twentieth day of the third month. In the ceiling of the Imperial Residence, the four ideographs "Great Peace Under Heaven" materialized spontaneously.

The twenty-second day. The imperial princes and all of the ministers were summoned and commanded to witness these auspicious ideographs.

The twenty-seventh day. [To avoid taboos on the names Fujiwara and Kimi (Lord),] it was proclaimed that from now on the surname Fujiwarabe would be changed to Kuzuwarabe, and Kimikobe to Kimikobe [written with different ideographs].

The twenty-ninth day. Crown Prince Funato was in imperial mourning, but his mind was set on debauchery. Although he was given imperial instruction, he never repented. Therefore, all of the ministers were summoned, shown the late emperor's last will, and then consulted as to the matter of whether to depose him or not. Everyone from the minister of the right on down memorialized together: "We dare not disobey the final imperial command." On this day, the crown prince was deposed, and he was returned to his brothers as an ordinary prince.

Summer, the fourth day of the fourth month. The empress summoned all of her ministers, asking: "Which prince should we establish as imperial heir"? The Minister of the Right Fujiwara Toyonari (704–765) and the Minister of Central Affairs Fujiwara Nagate (714–771) said: "Prince Funato's elder brother Prince Shioyaki could be established." The High Steward of Settsu Fumiya Chino and the Great Controller of the Left Ōtomo Komaro said: "Prince Ikeda could be established." Major Counselor Fujiwara Nakamaro said: "No one knows his ministers like their lord. No one knows his sons like their father. We will merely serve whoever it is Heaven's inclination to select." It was decreed: Within the imperial house, the two princes [sons of the late prince] of the Imperial Guards Niitabe are most senior. Therefore, having formerly established Prince Funato only to have him disobey the imperial teachings and give in to his debauched intentions, we may now select from among the sons of the Prince of the Imperial Guards. But Prince Fune is unreformed in the women's apartments. Prince Ikeda's filial conduct is deficient. Prince Shioyaki was upbraided by the late Emperor [Shōmu] for lacking propriety. Only Prince Ōi, although he is not yet mature, has never been known for doing wrong. We wish to establish this prince. What do all the ministers think about this?

Thereupon, from the minister of the right on down, they all memorialized, "Whatever is the Imperial Command will be complied with." Before this, Major

Counselor [Fujiwara] Nakamaro invited Prince Ōi to live in his residence at Tamura. Today he dispatched his son Inner Imperial Guard Fujiwara Satsuo with twenty of the Central Guards to meet Prince Ōi and establish him as crown prince. It was decreed:

> The state takes its lord as master. The lord takes his heir apparent as his assurance. Therefore, the late emperor in his last will established Prince Funato as crown prince. But before the imperial mourning was over, and while the grass on the imperial tomb was not yet dry, the prince had illicit intercourse with a young attendant, without respect for the late emperor. In the ritual of mourning, he did not grieve suitably. This confidential matter was moreover entirely disclosed to the people. Despite repeated imperial instructions, he is still without feelings of remorse. He is fond of using women's language, and rather often disobedient. He suddenly departs his official residence in the Spring Palace, and at night he returns home alone. It is said that if a minister is clumsy and simple as a person, he is not fit to undertake weighty responsibilities. Therefore We secretly planned to depose this prince and establish Prince Ōi. We personally beseeched the Three Treasures of Buddhism and prayed to the [Shintō] deities, hoping for a sign that Our rule was either good or bad. Then, on the twentieth day of the third month, in the screen on the ceiling of Our residence, the ideographs "Great Peace Under Heaven" appeared clearly and brightly. This, then, is help from Heaven above, and a sign from the deities. Looking far back into high antiquity, and examining past events in succession, this is something that has never been recorded in books and was unheard of in former ages. Then We knew that the [Three] Treasures of the Buddha, the Dharma, and the Priesthood have prescribed great peace for the nation, and the various deities of Heaven and Earth foretell permanence for Our ancestral altars. Bearing this token of good fortune, we are truly delighted. Even a compassionate father finds it hard to sympathize with his unfilial son; the sage ruler still identifies ministers who are lacking in propriety. We should follow Heaven's instructions and return him [Prince Funato] to his original position.

It is also thanks to the utterly loyal and proper assistance of the aristocracy that we owe this noble omen. How could it have been sent in response to Our single person? We should receive Heaven's bequest together with the princes, nobles, gentlemen, and commoners, and in response to Heaven wash away our old flaws and universally receive the new blessings. We can proclaim a general amnesty throughout the empire. All crimes are forgiven, from capital offenses on down, committed before dawn on the fourth day of the fourth month of 757, whether they are minor or serious, discovered or undiscovered, atoned or un-atoned, or resulted in imprisonment or exile. Only those who commit the [unpardonable] Eight Atrocities [such as treason or depravity], intentionally kill people, privately mint coins, violently rob, or secretly steal are excluded from this provision.

The common people of the empire are registered for light compulsory labor in the year they become youths [at age seventeen, according to the East Asian mode of reckoning], and in the year when they are capped [at age twenty-one] they become eligible for full labor service. Sympathizing with their labor, We are distressed at heart. Formerly, the late Emperor [Shōmu] also had this inclination, but he did not act on it. From now on, we should take eighteen as the age of youth for males, and twenty-two and up as the age for fully adult males.

The ancients, in governing the people and pacifying the country, had to use the principle of filial piety. As a source of all action, nothing takes priority over this. We should command each family in the empire to possess and diligently memorize a copy of the [Confucian] Classic of Filial Piety, and redouble their instruction. Among the common people, if there is someone who surpasses other persons in filial conduct and is looked up to in the village, we should order the senior officials in their native places to recommend them all by name. If there are those who are unfilial, disrespectful, unfriendly, or disobedient, they should be banished to Momunofu District of Michinoku Province [Mutsu] or the Okachi District of Dewa Province [on the far Northern front, in confrontation with the supposedly "savage" Emishi] to purify their practices, and to defend the frontier. If there are others who sleep loftily in retirement at Ying River and hide their traces under Mount Chi [as the admirable hermit Hsü Yu did after supposedly refusing an offer of the throne in mythical Chinese antiquity], who are fit to be [paragons like the legendary] Ch'ao or Hsü for Our age, they should be visited with propriety and released from legal requirements to nourish their spirits.

As for the priests and nuns of the Office of Monastic Affairs, and in the vicinity of the capital, from the [minor clerical office of] Fukui on up, We bestow goods in proportion to their status. The servants on inner attendance, the attendants conferred with swords, and all of the men and women responsible for preparing the various materials for the imperial fast commemorating the anniversary of Emperor [Shōmu's] death [5/2], who have labored from morning until night without neglect, each absolute in their sincerity, We should command to be promoted two ranks, and bestow silk on them. Officials who have been remiss will also be reduced one rank. The remaining inner and outer officials, from the master of ceremonies on up, and aged persons above eighty throughout the empire, the Central Guards, the Military Guards, the Palace Gate Guards, commanders, miscellaneous artisans, and soldiers on duty and commoners on government service who have continuously served more than thirty years will be promoted one rank. Only those of senior sixth rank, upper grade, and above, and those who are not serving, are excluded from this provision. To those civil and military officials on official duty in the capital, of the senior sixth rank, upper grade, and above, and those shrines celebrating the monthly fast, we confer goods in proportion to their rank. Widowers, widows, orphans, and childless persons throughout the empire, those who are seriously ill or disabled, and those who are unable to sustain themselves will be given a measure of relief. For those persons [who are descendants of immigrants] from Koguryō, Paekche, and Silla [the three Korean states that were united under Sillan rule in 668] who have long desired to be transformed by the presence of a sage [i.e., civilized by contact with imperial Confucian virtue], and who have attached themselves to our customs, hoping to be bestowed with a surname, they are all to be permitted one. Recording their household registers without ideographs for their surnames and families is untenable in principle and ought to be corrected. Also, the workmen at Tōdaiji, the laborers who built the imperial tomb, and the soldiers of the left and right sections of the capital, the four home provinces, Iga, Owari, Chikatsuafumi [Ōmi], Taniwa, Taniwa no michi no shiri [Tango], Tajima, Harima, Mimasaka, Kibi no michi no kuchi [Bizen], and Kii provinces, the defenders, garrisons, imperial guards, supervisors of cooks, commoners on government service, the households attached to the advocate at the Ministry of War, and the head of the household that provided conveyance [at Emperor Shōmu's funeral] are all exempt from this year's rice-field tax.

The numerous officials proceeded to the audience chamber and submitted a memorial congratulating the empress on the appearance of the auspicious ideographs.

The second day of the fifth month, the anniversary of the late emperor's death. Over fifteen hundred monks were invited to Tōdaiji to hold a fast.

The fourth day . . .

29

The Founding of the Monastery Gangōji
and a List of Its Treasures

Miwa Stevenson

Gangōji or the "Monastery of the Original Flourishing" is perhaps best known for being the home monastery of the Sanron or "Three Treatises" tradition, one of the most prominent of the six Buddhist schools of the Nara period. However, the Gangōji of the Sanron school that we find situated in the vicinity of Kōfukuji monastery and the Kasuga Shrine in downtown Nara today is a later incarnation of the original Gangōji that is the subject of our treatise here, the *Circumstances Leading to the Founding of the Monastery Complex of Gangōji and a List of Its Accumulated Treasures* (*Gangōji garan engi narabi ruki shizaichō*). The Gangōji described in the *Circumstances* refers to a monastery that was located in Asuka to the southeast of Nara, known also as Hōkōji (Monastery of the Flourishing of the Law) or Asukadera (Asuka Monastery). According to the *Chronicles of Japan, Continued* (*Shoku Nihongi,* 791 C.E.), construction of the Gangōji in Nara was begun in 716. The following year, the clerical staff and functions of the original Gangōji or Hōkōji in Asuka were relocated to the new complex at Nara, ultimately eclipsing the former in importance as the imperial court and its growing bureaucracy, itself newly settled at Nara, got into full swing.

But while the Asuka-based Gangōji (or Hōkōji) may have fallen by the wayside as an active center of Buddhist learning and influence, in the historical hindsight of the Nara imperial court and its Buddhist ecclesiastica the importance of the ancient Gangōji grew to mythic proportions. According to legend, the Gangōji (or Hōkōji) in Asuka was the first Buddhist monastery ever established in Japan, founded through the struggle and spiritual foresight of the two great cultural heroes, Empress Suiko (Empress Daidaiō) and Shōtoku Taishi (Prince Umayado Toyotomimi). Buddhism, as the Japanese chronicles tell us, was introduced to Japan from the Korean peninsula during the sixth century, bringing with it a rapid assimilation of continental Chinese culture that radically unsettled and transformed the ancient indigenous traditions of Japan. A century and a half later, these changes culminated in the consolidation of the Nara imperial bureaucracy and state-sponsored Buddhist priesthood, a system that would continue to dominate Japanese life throughout the medieval period. In their efforts to come to grips with these momentous developments, the court and ecclesiastical chroniclers of the Nara period found in figures such as Shōtoku and Suiko the basis for articulating a new historical mythology. The text of the *Circumstances Leading to the Founding of Gangōji* represents one among several eighth century attempts to put the events of past and present into focus.

According to its postscript, the *Circumstances Leading to the Founding of Gangōji* was compiled in the nineteenth year of the Tempyō period (747) in compliance with an order issued by the Government Bureau of Buddhist Clerical Management in the previous year. There are extant two other treatises and treasure lists of similar provenance—one for the influential state monastery of Daianji, the other for Shōtoku's famous monastery of Hōryūji—both of which bear nearly identical postscripts and dates of compilation. Of the three, however, the Gangōji treatise is by far the most detailed when it comes to historical narrative. As one of the few early accounts of Buddhism's triumphant, yet troubled, introduction to Japan—the other major source being the court-sponsored *Chronicles of Japan* (*Nihon shoki,* submitted in 720)—the *Circumstances Leading to the Founding of Gangōji* provides us with invaluable insights into religious events of early Japan, as well as the diverse ways in which recollections of those events were manipulated and interpreted.

The term *engi*, which is rendered in the title of the *Gangōji engi* as "circumstances of founding or origin," has an explicit technical meaning in the Buddhist tradition as the Chinese translation of the Sanskrit term *pratītyasamutpāda* (J. *engi*), meaning "conditioned or dependent origination." While the use of this expression within the genre of monastery chronicles is closer in sense to the term "history" or "origins," its fundamental Buddhist significance cannot be overlooked. For, in effect, what the *Gangōji engi* or *Circumstances Leading to the Founding of Gangōji* purports to describe are the subtle spiritual influences—the mysterious nexus of karmic "causes and conditions"—that, historically speaking, precipitated the founding of the ancient Gangōji and the "original arising and flourishing of the Buddhist Law (Dharma)" (*gangō* or *hōkō*) in Japan for which it is named. Thus, it is history as a pulse of sacred influences that extend far deeper and wider through space and time than the phenomenal human hand that appears to wield them— the miraculous, almost inconceivable, dawning of the light of true religion and civilization in a land that was originally ignorant and unaccepting of it.

The *Circumstances* was one of the first of this sort of "miraculous origin" chronicles in Japan. And, just as the history of Buddhism there did not stand still with the founding of Gangōji, *engi* chronicles continued to be produced for any number of later major monasteries and holy sites, becoming a fairly standard Buddhist literary genre in medieval Japan. *Ruki shizaichō* or "lists of accumulated treasures," akin to the one attached to the Gangōji record, likewise were produced continuously from the eighth century on. The term *ruki* probably means something more like "transmitted," referring not just to monastery wealth, but to holy treasures that were bestowed on a monastery and transmitted as hereditary belongings of that monastery. Many of these accrue cult significance, such as the cast bronze statues and bowls for performing the ceremony of "bathing the infant Buddha" detailed in the Gangōji chronicle. According to certain scholars, treasury inventories of this sort were taken and submitted to the government on a regular basis during the Nara period, probably to keep the court and its official priesthood apprised of any objects of holy power that might be employed in the spiritual service to the state.

Much of the action in the *Circumstances* devolves around the struggles between two factions at the ancient Asuka court: a group of continent-gazing "progressives" with strong connections to expatriate communities from the kingdoms of Paekche, Koguryŏ, and Silla on the Korean peninsula, and more "conservative" factions centered on indigenous Japanese aristocratic clans. The former is epitomized by the Grand Minister Iname and his grandson, the Grand Minister Umako (contemporary of Empress Suiko, supporter of Shōtoku), who was a scion of the Soga clan; the latter, by the "miscellaneous ministers" of the Mononobe, Nakatomi, and various other aristocratic clans, most of whose ancestries were deeply bound to the emergent imperial house by established indigenous traditions of vassalage and mythological descent. The Nakatomi and Mononobe, we are informed by the *Record of Ancient Matters* (712) and the *Chronicles of Japan* (720), served as court priests and ritual specialists for the indigenous proto-Shintō royal religion, a role that, for religious as well as political reasons, would put them at odds with the new tradition of Buddhism.

The frequent reference to manifestations of the "displeasure" of the native kami in the form of natural disasters and epidemics—or, at least, the rhetoric to that effect—illustrates just how profoundly the "religious" and "political" spheres were intertwined in the early Japanese (and northeast Asian) experience of the world. What we might call "historical" events pulsate not only to matters of economic wealth and political power but also to age-old Shintō norms of ritual purity and pollution and the a priori truths of sacred clan hierarchy and solidarity, with religious value and perception shaping human action as seminally as material culture. The clash over Buddhism that transpires between the Soga and clans such as the Nakatomi and Mononobe is, thus, a contest between two different ways of seeing and organizing the world, the reverberations of which extend through all reaches of Japanese society and culture.

The extent of this expansion of cultural horizons in early Japan finds one of its most effective illustrations in the term hō (C., fa), the term that is used, simultaneously, to refer to both the cosmic Buddhist Dharma or "Law" and the comprehensive system of state "law" and imperial bureaucracy imported to Japan from Korea and the Chinese continent. Viewed in light of these extended nuances, it is important to ask ourselves just what expressions such as "submitting to the Buddhist Law" and "[monk] Master of the Law," or "Monastery of the Flourishing of the Law" (hōkōji) and "Monastery of the Original Flourishing [of the Buddhist

Law]" (Gangōji), might mean within the changing socioreligious discourse of early Japan. Just what is this divine "Law" and what is the significance of its sudden historical appearance?

Indeed, this sort of resonance between the manifest social order and the Buddhist concept of a universal law (hō) of moral cause and effect underscores just how deeply the Japanese reception of continental culture threatened to transform indigenous views of humankind and the world. The Circumstances presents its historical events with a certain teleological inevitability—the certainty of eighth-century Nara hindsight; but in its religious language and in its tales of confrontation and indecision we can still detect the wrenching tensions of the period.

One of the points for which the Gangōji engi has long been renowned is its claim that Buddhism was officially introduced by Emperor Kimmei in the seventh year of his reign (Senior Year of Earth with Horse, corresponding to 538 C.E.), a date that conflicts with that of 552 C.E. provided in the imperial Chronicles. While there has been much speculation among scholars as to the possible reasons for this discrepancy, it appears that during the Nara period the date offered in the Circumstances was widely accepted as authoritative by the Nara clergy.

The heroes of the tale are Prince Toyotomimi (Shōtoku Taishi) and Princess Daidaiō (Empress Suiko), a scion of the imperial line who was also tied by maternal descent to the current Grand Ministers Iname and Umako of the Soga clan. The Circumstances goes to extraordinary lengths to place Suiko herself at the epicenter of the entire saga surrounding the introduction and acceptance of Buddhism at the imperial court. Not only is she conspicuously present when the Paekche emissary first presents Kimmei with the Buddhist Law in 538, but she remains its faithful advocate through decades of trial, finally winning the support of the aristocracy on her "hundredth birthday" nearly a century later in 613. The significance of Suiko as the first imperial devotee of the Buddhist religion, her involvement in the founding of the monastery, or the fact that its first native ordinands were women (i.e., the three nuns) would not have been lost on an early Japanese audience, for women held positions of extraordinary religious influence in ancient Japan as miko or "shamanesses" who were called to serve as oracles and priestly mediums to the indigenous gods and spirits (kami).

Along related lines, one must look carefully at the circumstances surrounding the formal establishment of the Buddhist church in Japan. According to the Buddhist monastic codes (the Vinaya), a specific quorum of duly ordained clergy (usually ten full monks) is required in order to give ordination to new members of the priesthood. The ordination of nuns is carried out in the presence of both a quorum of ten nuns and a quorum of ten monks, with supervision of the ceremony placed firmly in the hands of the latter. Thereafter, nuns are required to convene twice a month (on the days of the uposatha fast) in the presence of monks in order to review and confess infractions of the precepts.

Clearly the adopting of Buddhist restraints such as fasting, chastity, and other precepts with purificatory overtones resonated closely with indigenous traditions of ritual restraint applied in routine service to the kami, those involving women's oracular and hieratic role as *miko* being a perfect example. At the same time, the formalities of the religious profession introduced by the Buddhist Vinaya profoundly reinscribed the traditional lineaments of authority with which these hieratic functions were traditionally connected, especially by routinizing the subordinate status of women through the institution of the order of nuns.

Clearly there is an interesting tension in the fact that the monumental changes described in the *Circumstances*—the rather turbulent introduction of Buddhism— come chiefly through the figure of Suiko, a woman whose role carries strong overtones of the courtly *miko*. Questions that we might want to ask in light of the *Circumstances* are how politicoreligious power might have been relocated under this new cosmic canopy of the Buddhist Law, and where this intersects the concept of the new imperial state. Here one might bear in mind the ancient Japanese idea of *matsuri-goto* or the inseparability of ritual and statutory functions on the part of the imperial court, as well as the polysemic sense of "law" (*hō*) as both Buddhist Dharma or cosmic order and the governmental system of bureaucratic offices and civil law (*ritsuryō*). To what extent, for example, does routinization of religious role through the institution of the state Buddhist Sangha and monastic code devolve as a counterpart to the use of continental models of imperial bureaucracy as a means to hierarchically subordinate regional clans and traditional forms of religious and socioeconomic polity to the imperial line?

Finally, it is important to step back and look at the *Circumstances* not just as a repository of historical data, but as a rhetorical document designed—in this case by the high Buddhist clergy of the Nara court—to impart a particular historical perception and identity to its contemporary audience. Here one might fruitfully compare the narrative strategies of the *Circumstances* with that of the *Nihon shoki*, bearing in mind that this kind of totalizing historiographical practice was itself newly emergent during the Asuka and Nara periods. What kind of history, for example, is being related in these works, and to what end? What sort of special attributes, cultural cues, or narratological devices are brought into play in these respective historical narratives? How do they differ from or play off one another? To what extent are they complementary or competitive, and how?

As a case in point, Suiko and Shōtoku are both descendants of the imperial house, with complex ties to various eminent clans of ancient standing (notably the Soga). Is their historical role—and that of other major *dramatis personae*— formulated differently in the *Circumstances* and the *Chronicles*? Note, for example, that in the *Circumstances* biological descent and quasi-mythical connections to the imperial line are by no means the sole determinant of their identity. What is the text implying when it suggests that the three nuns sponsored by Suiko were possibly incarnations of the bodhisattva Avalokitesvara (Kannon), or that Suiko herself was a "manifestation of a likeness of the Great Sage (the Lord Buddha)" as prophesied in the Buddhist scriptures? Or when later Buddhist documents identify Shōtoku as a manifestation of the Chinese T'ien-t'ai (J. Tendai) patriarch Nanyue Huisi (515–577)? What does it mean to juxtapose these multidimensional identities and such classic Buddhist ritual *topoi* as installation of sacred images and establishment of the Sangha with the overarching historical event of the emergence of the imperial court?

Set within the historical context of the symbiotic coemergence of the Japanese imperial court and the Japanese Buddhist Sangha during the Nara period, the *Circumstances* can be read as a document that explicitly sought to utilize contemporaneous forms of historical myth and narrative to construct a meaningful paradigm for the relationship between Sangha and court. So doing, it both anticipated and informed the narrative stratagems and rhetoric that later Buddhists such as Saichō, Kūkai, and even Nichiren would use to establish the central place of Buddhism in Japanese social and cultural life.

The translation is based on critical editions of the text published by Iwaki Takatoshi, ed., *Zōho Gangōji hennen shiryō*, vol. 1 (Tokyo: Yoshikawa Kōbunkan, 1975); Sakurai Tokutarō, ed., *Jisha engi* in *Nihon shisō taikei*, vol. 20 (Tokyo: Iwanami Shoten, 1975); and Tanaka Takashi, ed., "Gangōji garan engi narabi ruki shizaichō," *Nanto Bukkyō* 4 (1957). All three of these editions are based on a Daigōji manuscript dated 1207.

Further Reading

W. G. Aston, tr., *Nihongi: Chronicles of Japan from the Earliest Times to A.D. 697* (London: George Allen & Unwin, 1956); Isamu Kanaji, "Three Stages in Shōtoku Taishi's Acceptance of Buddhism," *Acta Asiatica* 47 (1985): 31–47; J. Edward Kidder, *Early Buddhist Japan* (New York: Praeger, 1972); Daigan and Alicia Matsunaga, *Foundations of Japanese Buddhism*, vol. 1 (Los Angeles: Buddhist Books International, 1974); Donald L. Philippi, tr., *Kojiki* (Princeton: Princeton University Press, 1968); J. B. Snellen, tr., "Shoku Nihongi: Chronicles of Japan, Continued, A.D. 697–791 (Books I-VI)," *Transactions of the Asiatic Society of Japan*, second series, 11 (1934), 14 (1937); Enchō Tamura, "Japan and the Eastward Permeation of Buddhism," *Acta Asiatica* 47 (1985): 1–30; M. W. de Visser, *Ancient Buddhism in Japan: Sutras and Ceremonies in Use in the Seventh and Eighth Centuries A.D. and Their History in Later Times*, 2 vols. (Leiden: E.J. Brill, 1935).

The Founding of the Monastery Complex of Gangōji

On the ninth day of the first month in the cyclical Junior Year of Water with Cock (*mizunoto tori*, 613 C.E.), when Toyomike Kashikiya Hime (Empress Suiko, r. 592–628), who ruled the realm from the palace at Sakurai Toyura, was one hundred years old, Prince Umayado no Toyotomimi (Shōtoku Taishi, 574–622), by imperial command, made a record of the origins of Gangōji as well as the vow of the Empress Toyomike and the vows of the various ministers.

The Buddhist Law (Dharma) was first transmitted to the land of Great Yamato in the twelfth month of the Senior Year of Earth with Horse (*tsuchinoe uma*, 538). It was the seventh year of the reign of Emperor Amekuni Oshiharuki Hironiwa (Emperor Kimmei), who ruled the realm from the palace at Shikishima, assisted by the Grand Minister Soga Iname no Sukune. King Sŏngmyŏng of Paekche (r. 523–554) sent an image of Prince Siddhārtha, together with a vessel and set of implements for [performing the ceremony of] bathing the Buddha and a single case containing a scroll explaining the emergence of the Buddha in the world. It said, "As the Buddha's Law is supreme among all the laws of the world, your country should also put it into practice."

Upon receiving this charge the Emperor [Kimmei] notified the ministers, saying, "Is it permissible to use this object sent to us from a foreign land? Consider the matter carefully and let me know." At that time the rest of the ministers spoke saying, "In our land we worship and serve together the 108 divinities of the heavenly legions (amatsu-kami) and the legions of our native land (kunitsu-kami). It is not permissible to pay homage to divinities of a foreign land for fear that we may offend the divinities of our own land." The Grand Minister Soga Iname no Sukune alone spoke up, saying, "It may be fitting for our country to prize something that other countries treat as precious."

Thereupon the Emperor asked the Grand Minister, "Where shall we install this object so that we may worship?" The Grand Minister replied, "The house that has been set aside as the rear palace for the Princess Daidaiō (the future Empress Suiko, r. 592–628) might be a suitable place." Thereupon the Emperor summoned the Princess Daidaiō and said, "We wish to make use of your rear palace at Mukuhara as the palace for the deity from the foreign land." Princess Daidaiō said, "In accordance with your august intentions I shall remove myself from the palace."

This is how the image of the Buddha first came to be installed in the hall and worshipped. After that a handful of people from Paekche, Koguryŏ, and China privately carried on worship of the divinity on a very small scale there. Over the next year there were many instances when the native divinities showed their anger. The other ministers spoke out, saying, "It is the violation of worshipping the foreign deity that causes the hearts of the deities to be so often aroused to anger." The Grand Minister Iname countered, "The reason for these events is the offense of not paying worship to the deity of the foreign land." The various other officials said, "As the children of the divinities, how could we not listen to their words and thereby bring disturbance to our land!" Having listened to these deliberations, the Emperor said to the Grand Minister [Soga Iname], "Since the offense of worshipping the foreign deity is held to be the cause behind the frequent disasters and high incidence of fatal illnesses in our land, we cannot very well allow it to continue." The Minister, having reflected for a long time, said, "Although outwardly I will follow the other officials, in my heart I will not abandon the divinity of the foreign land." The Emperor [Kimmei] said, "I also feel that way."

Some thirty years later when the Grand Minister Iname lay critically ill, he addressed the Prince Ike no Be (the future Emperor Yōmei, r. 585–587) and the Princess Daidaiō (future Empress Suiko) standing before him as follows:

"On the basis of my council to embrace the Buddha's Law, his Highness the Emperor [Kimmei] agreed to institute it. But various other officials continued to harbor plans to exterminate and abandon the religion, so that the rear palace at Mukuhara, originally offered by imperial decree as the palace of the Buddhist divinity, came to be destroyed. Nevertheless, His Highness, the Emperor, and I were of one heart. O Prince and Princess! You also should be of the same heart and never abandon the Buddhist Law.

At that time the Princess held the position of consort to Prince Hinamishi (the heir apparent, future Emperor Bidatsu, r. 572–585). Prince Ike no Be was designated as successor to Prince Osata (Hinamishi, future Emperor Bidatsu). This situation will be explained later. But after the Grand Minister Iname died in the Junior Year of Earth with Ox (*tsuchinoto ushi*, 569), the other officials schemed together, and in the Senior Year of Metal with Cock (*kanoe tora* 570) they [set out to] burn the hall where the Buddha was enshrined and to throw the Buddha image and scriptures into the Naniwa River. On that occasion the Prince [Ike no Be] and Princess [Daidaiō] said, "This palace was never intended to be the [final] divine palace for the Buddha; it was merely adopted as a temporary site to install the deity. It is, in fact, the rear palace of Daidaiō." Thus, they did not have it burned. Regrettably, the image of the Prince Siddhārtha was taken away. Having been hidden beforehand, the vessel for bathing the Buddha was not removed. Those that are now kept in Gangōji are these.

Later, in the Junior Year of Metal with Rabbit (*kanoto u*, 571), the wrath of the divinities increased. Many people in the realm died of illness, and there was a great drought when it did not rain for a long time. Then, once again, a great deluge fell from heaven [causing floods]. Finally, the grand palace burned down when a divine fire broke out.

The Emperor [Kimmei], alarmed by these unexpected events, fell ill, his condition becoming quite critical. At that point he summoned the Prince Ike no Be and the Princess Daidaiō and said, "This Buddha divinity is a fearsome being. Bear in mind and do not forget the parting words of your grandfather [Soga Iname no Sukune]: The Buddha deity should not be slighted or abandoned. Princess Daidaiō, you should offer your palace at Mukuhara completely to the Buddha, without any second thought. You must not retain any part of it as your personal property. In its stead you will receive the Miminashi no Miyakihita as your rear palace."

Thus the Prince [Ike no Be] and Princess [Daidaiō], touching the crown of their heads [to the floor in obeisance], received the decree that he bestowed on them. That same year of Junior Year of Metal with Rabbit (*kanoto u*, 571) the Emperor [Kimmei] passed away.

In the Junior Year of Metal with Ox (*kanoto ushi*, 582), eleven years after the Emperor [Kimmei] departed, the Empress Daidaiō addressed His Majesty, the Emperor Bidatsu (r. 572–585), saying, "Formerly, during the Junior Year of Earth with Ox (*tsuchinoto ushi*, 569), our great grandfather the Grand Minister [Soga Iname] bequeathed us his last words, charging that the Buddhist

Law must not be neglected or abandoned. We did as he charged. However, in the Senior Year of Metal with Cock (*kanoe tora*, 570), due to the prohibition of the Buddhist Law it came to a stop. Then once again, in the Junior Year of Metal with Rabbit (*kanoto u*, 571) we received the last words of our father, the late Emperor [Kimmei]. He summoned the Prince Ike no Be and myself and told us that the Buddhist Law should not be neglected or abandoned, and that furthermore, I, Daidaiō, must offer the rear palace at Mukuhara to the Buddha divinity without any further thought of retaining it as my personal property. Thus, we have received final injunctions to this effect on two separate occasions. However, due to the ordinance prohibiting the Buddhist Law, we have stood immobile for the past ten-odd years."

Thereupon, the Emperor Osata (Bidatsu) announced to her, "Even now the ministers are not disposed toward [the Buddha divinity], so if you wish to carry this out perhaps it may be done in secret."

Having thereby received the imperial command, in the Senior Year of Water with Cock (*mizunoe tora*, 582), the Empress Daidaiō and the Prince Ike no Be (future Emperor Yōmei), like-minded in their intentions, transferred the Palace of Mukuhara to Sakurai. In the following year of Junior Year of Water with Rabbit (*mizonoto u*, 583) they began to construct the chapel at Sakurai and concealed the vessel for bathing the Buddha there. Having suffered the disasters that were ravaging the realm, later during the same Junior Year of Water with Rabbit (*mizonoto u*, 583), the son of the Grand Minister Iname, Umako no Sukune, sought the advice of a shaman-diviner. The latter told him: "This is the will of the divinity that was worshipped during the time of your father." The Grand Minister thereupon became quite fearful and made a vow to propagate the Buddhist Law. He sought for persons who might leave home [as a Buddhist mendicant], but no one responded.

At the time in the province of Harima there was an old monk from Ko[gu]ryŏ named Hyepyŏn who had given up the priestly robes and returned to lay life, as well as an old nun named Pŏpmyŏng. Three girls—Shimame, the seventeen-year-old daughter of Tatto, the head of the saddle-makers; Tokome, a daughter of Ayahito Hōshi; and Ishime, daughter of Nishigori no Tsuho—together had attached themselves to Pŏpmyŏng and were currently receiving instruction in the Buddhist Law. They all said, "We wish to leave home [as nuns] and be taught the Buddhist Law." The Grand Minister was overjoyed and arranged for them to be ordained. (The Buddhist name of Shimame was Zenshin; that of Tokome was Zenzō, and that of Ishime was Ezen.)

Overjoyed at this turn of events, the two [royal siblings], Daidaiō and Ike no Be no Mikoto, invited them to settle in the Sakurai chapel. Later on, Kōga no Ōmi arrived from Paekche bearing a stone image of the Bodhisattva Maitreya. The three nuns installed it in the entrance to the mansion, made offerings, and performed obeisance to it. The Kuratsukuri no Obito, at the time of the Onjiki, obtained a *shari* relic and presented it to the Grand Minister. On the fifteenth day of the second month in the Junior Year of Wood with Snake (*kinoto mi*, 585), the Grand Minister held a great ceremonial gathering to celebrate the erecting of the central pillar of the *stūpa* reliquary at Toyorasaki. At the time of this gathering the Emperor Osata (Bidatsu) wished to eradicate the Buddhist Law. So on the very same day of fifteenth of the second month he cut down the *stūpa*-pillar and once more reprimanded the Grand Minister and those persons who followed the Buddhist Law. The images of the Buddha and their chapel palaces were crushed and burned to the ground. The Emperor dispatched the Saiki no Mimuro, Kono Miyatsuko, to summon the three nuns. As they departed they looked at the Grand Minister, tears streaming down their faces. When the three nuns reached the *nagaya* in Tsubakiichi they were defrocked of their Buddhist robes, and the Buddhist Law was eradicated. As for the Sanctuary of Sakurai, the Empress Daidaiō issued an edict that it was not to be harmed. Claiming, "It is my rear palace," she prevented it from being burned.

The instant that the Buddhist Law was extinguished an epidemic of pox broke out in the realm. Many people died of the epidemic. People who suffered from the illness all said things like, "I burn," "I feel like I'm being chopped apart," or, "I feel like I'm being cut into pieces." During this period the three nuns did not go out and continued to guard [their self-discipline] firmly, even though they had returned to lay status. Then the Grand Minister also contracted the disease. Because of this he addressed His Majesty, the Emperor Osata (Bidatsu), saying, "I wish that we might once again worship the Three Jewels [of Buddhism]." But the Emperor only gave permission to the Grand Minister to do this. The Grand Minister again invited the three nuns to his house, where he worshipped the Three Jewels.

The Emperor Osata passed away during that same Junior Year of Wood with Snake (*kinoto mi*, 585). Prince Ike no Be (Emperor Yōmei, r. 585–587) succeeded him to the throne. Prince Umayado (Shōtoku Taishi) said to him, "Since the persecution of the Buddhist Law has caused our calamities to increase, perhaps it is advisable to install the three nuns in the Sakurai Chapel so that offerings may be presented to the Three Jewels." The Emperor gave his permission and had them take up residence in the Sakurai Chapel and make offerings.

At that time, the three nuns said to the attending officials, "We have heard it said that persons who leave home must take the monastic precepts as their spiritual foundation. As there are no masters of the Buddhist monastic codes (*vinaya*) [in Japan], we would like to travel to Paekche to receive the precepts." However, before long, in the Junior Year of Fire with Ram (*hinoto hitsuji*, 586), guest retainers arrived from Paekche. The officials inquired of them, "These three nuns wish to go to Paekche to receive the precepts. What should we do about this?" The retainer said, "According to the established procedure by which a nun receives the precepts, one first invites ten nuns to administer [the monastic vows] in a nunnery. After the basic precepts have been received, she then goes to a monastery and asks ten monks to confirm it. Combined with the previous ten nuns, precepts are received in the presence of a total of twenty clerics. Since you only have a nunnery in this country and there are no monasteries nor any assembly of monks, for the nuns to be in full accordance with the [Buddhist] Law you must establish a monastery and invite monks and nuns to come from Paekche. Then you can arrange for them to receive the precepts."

At that time the Emperor Ike no Be (Yōmei) issued an order to Daidaiō and the Prince Umayado (Shōtoku Taishi): "Settle on a site where a monastery may be built for the monks [Dharma-masters]." At the time the Paekche retainer said, "In my country the monasteries and nunneries are constructed in locations where [they are in close enough proximity to one another that] the sounds of each other's monastery bells can be heard, and where there is no difficult terrain to hinder their going out and returning before noon when they perform such difficult services as the fortnightly [recitations of the precepts]." Prince Umayado Toyotomimi (Shōtoku Taishi) and the Grand Minister Umako together looked around and settled upon a site on which to raise a monastery.

In the Junior Year of Fire with Ram (*hinoto hitsuji*, 586) the emissary from Paekche returned to his country. Upon that occasion the Emperor Ike no Be (Yōmei) said, "We wish in the future to propagate the Buddhist Law. Therefore, we wish to obtain monks conversant in the Law, as well as craftsmen to build a monastery. As I am ill, it would be good if you could send them to us quickly." However, the Emperor passed away before any official envoys [from Paekche] arrived.

Subsequently, in the Senior Year of Earth with Monkey (*tsuchinoe saru*, 588), during the reign of Emperor Kurahashi (Sushun, r. 587–592), [Paekche] sent six monks [who were masters of the Law] and four craftsmen, including the Vinaya Master Lyóngcho, his disciple Hyechong, the Master of the Law Lyóng'ui, his disciple Hyehun, Master of the Law To'óm, and his disciple Lyóngki, as well as the four craftsmen, Ünsol, Sujin, and others. They also presented a miniature model of a golden hall [to the Emperor], which is none other than [the model] kept at present at the [Gangōji] monastery. On that occasion, the Prince Toyotomimi (Shōtoku Taishi) said to Princess Daidaiō (Suiko), "In the past the request was made for [monks who were] masters of the Law, as well as craftsmen, to be sent from Paekche. Now we have received them. How shall we handle this matter?" The Princess Daidaiō said, "We shall explain these prior events to the reigning Emperor [Sushun]."

Thus Prince Toyotomimi recounted the events of the past in detail for the Emperor [Sushun]. The Emperor said, "Deal with it as was originally planned under the late Emperor [Yōmei]."

The three nuns said to an official, "Only six monks came [from Paekche]. It does not make up the full twenty that are required [for our ordination]. Hence, we wish to go to Paekche to receive the precepts." The minister asked the [Paekche] monks, "These three nuns wish to journey to Paekche to receive the precepts. How do we go about doing this?" The reply that the monks gave was no different from that of the previous retainers. But the nuns pleaded that they strongly desired to go [to Paekche], so the minister gave his permission. Altogether five nuns, including the two disciples Shinzen and Zenmyō, were sent. They set out in the Senior Year of Earth with Monkey (*tsuchinoe saru*, 588).

At that time the Prince Toyotomimi (Shōtoku) addressed the Empress Daidaiō (Suiko), "The ministers have already given their permission to propagate the Buddhist Law. How shall we go about doing it?" The Empress Daidaiō said to both Prince Toyotomimi and the Grand Minister Umako, "At present we plan to build two monasteries with the help of the craftsmen from Paekche. However, as a nunnery already exists from previous times, for now have them work on the monastery for the monk masters of the Law." Thus the two highnesses, Prince Toyotomimi and the Grand Minister Umako, jointly established a temporary compound and quarters for the monks on the site where they were to build the future monastery for the masters of the Law. They had the six [Paekche] masters of the Law take up residence there. This was the Senior Year of Earth with Monkey (*tsuchinoe saru*, 588).

In the Senior Year of Metal with Dog (*kanoe inu*, 590) the nuns returned from Paekche. They said to the Grand Minister, "We went away in the Senior Year of Earth with Monkey (*tsuchinoe saru*, 588) to receive the precepts. In the third month of the Junior Year of Earth with Cock (*tsuchinoto tori*, 589) we received full ordination, and now, in the Senior Year of Metal with Dog (*kanoe inu*, 590), we have returned." They took up residence in the original Sakuraidera.

At that time the nuns said, "Please build a hall as soon as possible in which we can worship the Buddha. Furthermore, please build a monastery for the monks as soon as possible so that we may perform the fortnightly *karmavācanā* [confessional ceremony]." As such, a temporary hall was set up within the precincts of Sakuraidera. In the Senior Year of Water with Tiger (*mizunoe tora*, 592), when the Empress Daidaiō (Suiko) was ruling the realm from the palace at Toyura, the Empress summoned the Prince Toyotomimi and said, "You and I must never neglect or abandon this Sakurai monastery. The Buddhist Law had its beginnings at this monastery. Furthermore, it was at this monastery that we received the august last words of the Emperors [Kimmei and Yōmei]. During our lifetime this monastery was once nearly laid to waste. Your royal highness, in utmost sincerity, should offer this monastery in order to create blessings for the sake of the Emperor [Kimmei] who ruled the world from the palace at Shikishima. Since I intend to make this palace at Toyura into a monastery, you should move into this palace and quickly convert it [into a monastery]. I do not know whether you, my Prince, will be able to accomplish this speedily, but please also build a palace for me at Owarida. Also, construct the monastery for the monk masters of the Law, so that the nuns may perform the *karmavācanā* confessional."

Thus, in the Junior Year of Water with Cock (*mizunoto tori*, 613), having moved into the palace precincts, [Shōtoku Taishi] set about building a rudimentary golden hall and the hall for worshipping the Buddha, and the palace at Toyura thereby became a monastery. Furthermore, on the first day of the month of spring in the Junior Year of Water with Cock (*mizunoto tori*, 613), during the reign of Empress Daidaiō (Suiko), a celebration was held. It was the hundredth birthday of the Empress. On that same day we have heard that the Prince Toyotomimi said, "At present we have no way of actually calculating our day of birth, but on the occasion of this hundredth-year celebration we make testimony to the establishment of the Buddhist Law for householders and mendicants. It represents the establishment of the arising (*kenkō*), and the establishment of penetrating understanding (*kentsū*) [of Buddhism] in the world. As I ponder this, how can such an event not be the pinnacle of virtue?

"At the time when the Buddhist Law first came [to Japan, the Empress] prevented the rear palace from being destroyed and moved out of Sakurai so that it might be made into a chapel for Buddhist practice. At that time three girls left home as nuns. Rejoicing at this event, the Empress had them take up residence at the chapel, thereby sowing the seed of the Buddhist Law. For this reason [the chapel] was named Gangōji, 'Monastery of the Original Arising and Flourishing [of the Law].' As for the three nuns, it is said in a sūtra, 'For those who shall gain salvation through the form of a monk, [the Bodhisattva Kannon] manifests and preaches the Dharma in the form of a monk.' Indeed, it has happened just as the text describes.

"Now furthermore, Gangōji was built in the age when the Buddhist Law first appeared and began to spread throughout the world. On the basis of the original name it may be known as Kenkōji, 'Monastery of the Establishment of the Arising.' As for the monastery for the monk masters of the Law, monk after monk came from Ko[gu]ryó and Paekche to expound the Buddhist Law. Thus a monastery was built and called Kentsūji, 'Monastery of the Establishment of Penetrating Understanding.' In the age of our august Empress [Suiko], all came to understand the Law of the Buddha. Having witnessed the establishment of both its initial presence (origin) and comprehension [at this time], we can surmise that the Great Sage (the Buddha) must have manifested his likeness [here in Japan]. A sūtra says, 'In the rear palace of the King he magically appeared in the form of a woman in order to preach the Law.' Indeed, it happened just as it is written. Because this manifestation [of the Buddhist Law] can only occur in sympathetic response with the spiritual circumstances and capacity of our native land, we know that we are in accord with the intent of the Buddha's sacred teaching. I propose to name her 'Empress Who Caused the Law to Arise and Flourish (*hōkō*).' By these three epithets she shall be known in the world for eternity. And in this fashion she will tally with her subjects." Having spoken these words, [Shōtoku Taishi] thereupon made a vow, saying, "I respectfully vow to receive the charge of the Three Jewels. Together with Her Highness the Empress [Suiko], I will strive to bring tranquillity and happiness to all within heaven and earth and the four seas, and cause the True Law to prosper so that its sagely transforming influence will never be exhausted."

At that point the Empress rose from her seat, joined her palms, looked up to heaven, and, shedding the most heartfelt tears, repented, saying:

My current parents and six relations followed persons who held ignorant and depraved views. Thus they caused the [paraphernalia] of the Three Jewels to be annihilated, burned, and cast into the river. Items that they had previously given in offering they took back and destroyed. To atone for this, I now have turned the rear palace at Toyura into a nunnery and have endowed it with hills, forests, gardens, cultivated fields, lakes, households, and slaves. Furthermore, I have reverently built a monastery for the monk masters of the Law and endowed it with fields, gardens, households, and slaves. In addition I will piously fashion two [Buddha] images for these monasteries, each six feet in height. I myself have also strived to cultivate all manner of wholsome [karmic] roots. Through these meritorious deeds I pray that I may expiate the sins of burning and rejecting away the Buddhist Law and the sins of retracting offerings that were committed by our parents, relatives, and their entourages. May they meet Maitreya face to face, hear the True Law, realize the truth of the unoriginated nature of all things, and speedily attain the perfect enlightenment of Buddhahood.

In the presence of all the Buddhas of the ten directions and the four divine guardian kings, I pledge and pray with utmost sincerity that the two monasteries and the two six-foot images fashioned for them will never again be destroyed, cast into the river, or burned, and that the objects kept in these two monasteries will never again be taken back, destroyed, violated, or become the objects of deception. If I myself, my successors, my descendants, or any other person treats these two monasteries and the two six-foot images irreverently—demolishing them, casting them in the river, or setting them aflame—if they seek to repossess offerings that they have made previously to these two images, or if they even deceitfully harbor such a thought, they are sure to be visited by all sorts of great calamity and great shame.

Those who esteem and hold faith in the Lord [Buddha], make offerings to him, worship him, repair and generously care for [his image and sanctuaries], they shall receive the support of the Three Jewels. These persons will be tranquil and at ease, and their lives will be long. They will receive all sorts of blessings. The myriad affairs will proceed as they wish, and their family lines will not be cut off for ten thousand generations. I have already come to know this for certain.

Whoever slanders or defames the Lord [Buddha] or snatches away what he has previously offered in alms will each suffer appropriate misfortune. Having given much thought to this, I urge you to take great care! Take great care! The Three Jewels must not be treated lightly, and the objects that pertain to the Three Jewels must not be violated.

We should practice [the religion] according to our ability and discharge this responsibility well. May we instruct our descendants and the descendants of our descendants to accept this charge of the [Buddhist] Law and strive to lead beings in both the present and the future to gain supreme tranquillity and bliss. May we embrace this Dharma without ever losing faith, so that for ages to come it never knows an end. May we, together with all beings endowed with consciousness and form, share equally in this merit and thereby speedily achieve perfect enlightenment.

When the Empress had finished her vow, the earth trembled, thunder roared, and a great rain suddenly fell, washing every corner of the realm clean. The Prince Toyotomimi and the various ministers having all listened to the Empress's vow, Prince Toyotomimi then said to the various ministers, "Please take heed. If the Empress practices the True Law we too should follow her. If Her Highness entertains false views, we should correct her and try to direct her to the right path. Witnessing the vow that the Empress has professed, [I can say that] it is a true and correct vow. All the people of the realm should follow her example."

Thereupon the various ministers, led by Nakatomi Muraji and Monobe Muraji, said with one heart, "From now on we will never again destroy, burn, cast in the river, or slight the Law of the Three Jewels. Nor will we seize or violate offerings made to the Three Jewels. From now on, with the Three Jewels resting at our left shoulder and our native divinities (kami) resting at our right shoulder, we will worship them together, treasure them, and make offerings to them. If anyone dares to break this pledge or make it in deceit, may he or she suffer great calamity and shame just as the Empress has pledged. We reverently pray that, through the merit of this excellent vow, Her Highness the Empress and all [beings] beneath heaven, the sun, and the moon may dwell in tranquillity and happiness. May our descendants accept this charge and realize benefits identical to our own, even though they live in a different age."

The Prince Toyotomimi, having listened to this, reported the entire matter to the Empress. The Empress in praise said, "That is all very well. I am also pleased." Thereupon, summoning the Prince Toyotomimi (Shōtoku Taishi), she told him, "Learn the details of this affair and make a complete record of how Buddhism arose during my reign, and how [the two monasteries of] Gangōji and Kentsūji came to be built, as well as my making of the vow." Furthermore she told him, "Do not allow any pollution to occur at the sites where the stūpa-pillar was erected or the site where the two six-foot images were fashioned. Do not allow these areas to be polluted by human dwellings. Anyone who violates or deceitfully [tries to circumvent] this measure will suffer great calamity and shame, as in my previous vow."

The aforementioned stūpa-pillar stands at the site of the Eastern Buddha Gate of the Jeweled Gallery. The spot where the two six-foot images were made is thought to be located north of Monomi no Oka. To the east of this site there is a large hall, eleven feet [in height], where the six-foot images of bronze were cast. To the west there is an octagonal hall, which is the place where the decorations were made.

On the first day of the first month of the Junior Year of Water with Cock (*mizunoto tori*, 613), the anniversary of the day when Toyo Mike Kashikiya Hime (Empress Suiko), ruler of the realm from the palace at Sakurai Toyura, became one hundred years old—that very day when the auspicious affair was openly celebrated—Prince Umayado Toyotomimi, the imperial Prince [Shōtoku], son of the Emperor Tachibana no Toyohi (Yōmei), who ruled the realm from the palace at Ike no Be no Manitsuki, made a record of these events and presented it [to the throne], in obedience to the Empress' command.

The Empress Daidaiō (Suiko) issued an edict stating, "In private I shall be called by the name Novice Zenki. The [two six-foot images] and the myriad objects conferred on the two foregoing monasteries must be carefully guarded from evil men. Also, this written record must not be given out, copied, or revealed to any such person. If the text of this record is destroyed or errors are introduced, one should be aware that the two monasteries will eventually be destroyed. You three masters of the Law, Master Kanjun, Master Myōrō, and Master Ikan, must preserve it carefully."

On the fifth day of the first month of the Junior Year of Metal with Boar (*kanoto i*, 651), during the reign of Emperor Naniwa (Kōtoku), the inscription for the dew basin of the *stūpa* was presented. It reads:

> During the reign of the Emperor of the land of Yamato, Ame Kuni Oshiharuki Hironiwa (Kimmei), who ruled the realm from the palace at Shikishima with Soga no Iname serving as Grand Minister, King Sóngmyóng of Paekche submitted a message, saying, "Of all the laws of the world, that of the Buddha is the most exalted." The Emperor and the Grand Minister having heard this proclaimed, "How excellent! We will welcome the Buddhist Law and establish it in our land of Wa." However, the [good] karma behind this fortunate recompense of the Emperor and the Grand Minister became depleted.
>
> Then a daughter of the Emperor who ruled the world from the palaces at Sakurai and Toyura, who had the name Toyomike Kashikiyahime no Mikoto (Suiko), and her nephew, the prince named Umayado Toyotomimi (Shōtoku Taishi), led by the Grand Minister Soga, named Umako, together with the various other ministers praised and said, "How awesome! How wonderful! How excellent! It was our father the Emperor and our father the Grand Minister who established the Buddhist Law." Having aroused the intention to seek enlightenment, they vowed before the Buddhas of the ten directions to transform and deliver living beings and to bring the great peace to the nation. In reverence they built the *stūpa* [and monastery]. They dedicated the power of this merit to the seven generations of ancestors of the Emperor, the Grand Minister, and the various other ministers, and broadly extended it to all sentient beings everywhere throughout the six destinies who belong to the four classes of birth, as well as to the pure realms of the ten directions. They dedicated it universally, that through this vow all might realize the fruit of Buddhahood. So that their descendants from generation to generation

would not forget [this vow] and the Law not be cut off, they named the monastery Kentsūji, "Monastery of the Establishing of Penetrating Understanding."

In the Senior Year of Earth with Monkey (*tsuchinoe saru*, 588) for the first time they requested monk Masters of the Law and Buddhist images from the sovereign of Paekche, named Sóng [Mmyóng]. Thus they were sent Vinaya Master Lyóngcho, Master of the Law Hyechong, the basin inlayer Shōtokuji Maejun, the monastery architects Daramida and Monkekoshi, the tile craftsmen Manamonnu, Yōkimon, Horyōki, and Shakuma Taimi. Those who were involved in the construction were the Ōatai Yamato no Aya, whose name was Makokōki, and the Atai Ototokashi. The scribes included the scholar Byatsuka and the scholar Yōko. The work was completed in the eleventh month of the Senior Year of Fire with Dragon (*hinoe tatsu*, 596).

On that occasion, those responsible for doing the metal work included the chief of the Onimi guild (*be*), whose name was Shinshō, the chief of the Asatsuma guild, named Karani, and the chief of the Kawachi guild, named Toki. The task was accomplished through the assistance of various people, with the chiefs of these four guilds acting as overseers.

—30—

Hagiography and History: The Image
of Prince Shōtoku

William E. Deal

Perhaps no figure in Japanese history has had more written about him, when so little is actually known, than Shōtoku Taishi (Prince Shōtoku; 574–622). Shōtoku Taishi became crown prince during the reign of his aunt, Empress Suiko (r. 592–628), overseeing the affairs of state from 593 until his death in 622. He is noted for his wise rule and his profound understanding of and devout engagement with Buddhism. These details of Shōtoku's life can be gleaned from the several extant biographies of Prince Shōtoku, including the two accounts translated here. Surprisingly, though, these biographies provide few details about Shōtoku the person, such as his personality, considering his importance throughout Japanese history. A study of the texts dealing with the life of Shōtoku situates the reader at the intersection of history and hagiography. These texts purport to tell us the historical facts about the life of Prince Shōtoku, but they also reveal how he has been idealized as the father of the Japanese nation and the founder of Japanese Buddhism.

The two biographies of Prince Shōtoku translated here are the sections on Shōtoku taken from the *Nihon shoki* (or *Nihongi*; Chronicles of Japan, 720 C.E.) and a text called the *Jōgū Shōtoku hōō teisetsu* (The Imperial Record of Shōtoku, Dharma King of the Upper Palace). The *Imperial Record* is the oldest biography of Shōtoku Taishi that is not part of some other text and was composed mostly during the eighth century; its author is unknown. A concluding section, which recounts the five generations after Emperor Kinmei, was likely composed during the tenth century. The *Chronicles*, the first of the Six National Histories, was compiled by members of the court and aristocracy at imperial command some one hundred years after the death of the prince. These two biographical texts are particularly important because they have served as the foundation for most subsequent interpretations—ancient and modern—of Shōtoku's life and times, although they focus on different aspects of his life and are organized in different ways.

The sections on Shōtoku Taishi in the *Chronicles* are but a small part of this very long text, which recounts the history of Japan from the age of the gods to the abdication of Empress Jitō in 697 C.E. The *Chronicles* places Shōtoku within the larger context of the political and religious struggles occurring in early Japanese history. The text is organized chronologically, lending credibility to the veracity of its historical claims. But the *Chronicles* accounts of Prince Shōtoku are not simply historiographical; there is strong textual evidence that this version of the life of Shōtoku Taishi is a compendium of historical, literary, legendary, religious, and other materials placed within this chronological framework. Because the *Chronicles* was written at imperial command, in part to legitimate claims of the imperial family's right to rule, the narrative of the life of Shōtoku Taishi represents an "authorized biography." This portrayal of Shōtoku meshes the image of Shōtoku as statesman with that of Shōtoku as devout Buddhist.

The *Imperial Record* was composed in the eighth century, though, like the *Chronicles*, some of the accounts concerning Shōtoku Taishi were likely derived from earlier sources. The *Imperial Record* also reveals the importance of Shōtoku as both ruler and Buddhist. Arguably, unlike the *Chronicles* account, the *Imperial Record* is primarily a Buddhist biography because it emphasizes Shōtoku's Buddhist activities, such as temple building and sūtra study. Shōtoku is but one important moment in the *Chronicles*' expansive treatment of Japan's entire history up to 697 C.E. By contrast, the *Imperial Record* features Shōtoku Taishi as its main protagonist, conveying Shōtoku's prodigious capabilities as both Buddhist and ruler. Ultimately, because both texts were written at least one hundred years after Shōtoku's death, we must be careful not to confuse claims about historical fact with the valorization of the Prince's political and religious accomplishments. What, if anything, can we discover about the "true" Shōtoku from the *Chronicles* and the *Imperial Record*? Even if we can never recover the historically factual Shōtoku Taishi, we can learn something about what his image has meant in different historical periods, and how this image was utilized to promote religious practices and political agendas.

The composite image of Shōtoku Taishi that we hold today was crafted over many centuries and embellished and elaborated on in the many "tellings" of Shōtoku's life over the centuries. In the Nara and Heian periods alone, numerous narratives existed that chronicled the life of Prince Shōtoku in addition to the two texts translated here. These narratives, along with modern interpretations of their meaning and significance, reflect mostly idealized representations of Shōtoku. The prince is shown to be a great and compassionate statesman and nation-builder, and a wise and holy Buddhist in two of the most common constructions of his image. Such representations of Shōtoku can be discerned in varying degrees in the two biographies translated here, as well as in many modern interpretations.

The view of Shōtoku as statesman emphasizes Shōtoku's statecraft, particularly his authorship of the Seventeen-Article Constitution (*Jūshichijō kempō*, 604), his creation of the twelve-cap court rank system, and his embrace of Confucian values as a cornerstone for the administration of government. The image of Shōtoku as statesman is derived in part from the view that he was a great scholar who studied the Confucian and Taoist classics extensively in addition to the subtleties and profundities of Buddhist doctrine.

In the *Chronicles* and the *Imperial Record* biographies, Shōtoku the statesman and Shōtoku the Buddhist are interrelated images because Buddhism and the state had become inextricably linked in early Japan. During Shōtoku's lifetime and after, Buddhism was utilized, at least in part, to legitimate and secure the power and authority of the imperial family. Aristocratic families, like the powerful Soga, also embraced and promoted Buddhism around this time. The rising popularity of Buddhism among some of the aristocracy necessitated imperial control over this powerful ideology, which was itself becoming a central part of the imperial family's claim to the throne. The imperial embrace of Buddhism was epitomized by Shōtoku's prodigious faith, which secured the importance of this religious tradition in Japan.

In Shōtoku's time, Japan was beginning to emerge as a nation under imperial rule. As the accounts below indicate, Shōtoku was given administrative control over the government, and thus he played an important role in articulating the rhetoric of the imperial family's claim to dominance over Japan. The imperial family wielded the religious power believed to reside in Buddhist texts, images, and rituals as another way of justifying their ruling authority. One of the most conspicuous examples of the connection between Buddhism and ruling power occurs in the depiction of the political struggle between the Soga and Mononobe. The Mononobe were associated with the worship of the indigenous kami, while the Soga family supported Buddhism. Shōtoku's pivotal role in the military defeat of the Mononobe involved his vow to build a temple for the worship of the Four Heavenly Kings—Buddhist protective deities. The temple was promised in exchange for the kings' divine assistance in securing a Soga victory over Moriya's Mononobe troops, and hence, Soga influence at court. The Soga victory occurred, we are told, because of the efficacy of Shōtoku's Buddhist rituals. The imperial family, aided by the Soga family, was thus able to claim legitimacy as Japan's sovereigns because the Buddhist deities favored them with victory in battle. This intimate connection between Buddhism and politics is a central component of the rhetoric of the *Chronicles* and the *Imperial Record*. In passages like those summarized above, Buddhist rituals often have both spiritual and political implications, and Shōtoku is depicted as a master of both the political and religious realms.

The *Chronicles* and *Imperial Record* also focus on the sincerity of Prince Shōtoku's personal Buddhist faith and the depth of his understanding of the Buddha's teachings. This wise and pious image of Shōtoku has been further promoted by some modern interpreters. He is described, for instance, as the first Japanese truly to understand the profundity of the Buddhist message because he was said to have read Buddhist sutras for their meaning rather than simply chanting them for their salvific efficacy, as was often done in his day. It is sometimes suggested by modern scholars that Shōtoku Taishi was a lone beacon of knowledge and insight in the dim cultural backwater of sixth- and early seventh-century Japan.

Shōtoku's sutra commentaries, mentioned in the texts translated here, are considered evidence of his Buddhist erudition. A careful examination of these commentaries, however, reveals that they are mostly glosses or paraphrases of Chinese commentaries studied by Shōtoku under the tutelage of Korean Buddhist monks. While Shōtoku may have been a great and sincere Buddhist genius with a profound understanding of Buddhism, no specific evidence survives to substantiate this view. The influence of Chinese and Korean Buddhism on Shōtoku's faith is one of the most revealing details to be gleaned from his commentaries, a fact often glossed over in evaluations of Shōtoku's Buddhist expertise. Aside from the depth of his understanding of the Dharma, the *Chronicles* and *Imperial Record* passages also indicate that Shōtoku and his coterie were concerned with the magico-religious efficacy of Buddhist rituals. They commissioned the construction of temples and Buddhist images and ordered sutras expounded in hopes of curing illnesses and effecting favorable rebirths for the newly deceased.

Although there are many similarities between the accounts in the *Chronicles* and the *Imperial Record*, they do not always agree on the details of Shōtoku's life, or they present details missing from the other. These discrepancies reflect the variety of oral and textual sources for these two biographies and attest to the different religious and political agendas of their authors.

The *Chronicles* is important for understanding the official attitude of the state toward Buddhism, and the extent to which Shōtoku Taishi is understood to have effected that relationship and promoted Buddhism to undergird nationhood. Because the *Chronicles* was written at imperial command to legitimate claims to ruling authority, we can assume that the portrayal of Shōtoku Taishi was directed in part toward validating those claims. To the extent that the *Chronicles* made a case for Shōtoku's brilliance and holiness, the political goals of the imperial family were also justified. Perhaps Shōtoku was personally able to keep his Buddhist spirituality out of his politics, but the compilers of the *Chronicles* took special interest, for political reasons, in securely connecting Shōtoku's temporal power with the salvific power of Buddhism.

The *Chronicles* account is also important because it is the only place where the articles of the Seventeen-Article Constitution are actually listed. The *Imperial Record* only mentions that Shōtoku wrote the Constitution but provides no other details (it should be noted also that the date offered by the *Imperial Record* for the promulgation of the Constitution differs slightly from the date given by the *Chronicles*). The Seventeen-Article Constitution seeks to establish an ethical foundation for the bureaucratic governance of the emerging Japanese nation. It delineates a three-tiered social hierarchy: the lord or sovereign (in this case, the Japanese emperor), bureaucrats, and the people. The seventeen articles that comprise the Constitution delineate the proper actions and attitudes that ideally operate between and within these three statuses. When propriety is established among these three, it asserts, concord will flourish in the nation.

The Constitution is usually described as a mix of Confucian and Buddhist ideas, reflecting, from a Western perspective, the syncretic nature of Japanese religion.

One of the foundations for Shōtoku's ethical bureaucracy was the concept of harmony (wa). Many scholars suppose that this concept was derived from the Confucian notion of harmony, which carries with it the idea of acting in consonance with others according to one's social status. Those who would see a Buddhist inflection in the Constitution's notion of harmony claim it is derived from the Buddhist notion of benevolence. The Buddhist content of the Constitution— explicit reference to Buddhism is limited to the second article—is stressed by scholars who wish to draw a comparison between Shōtoku and the Indian king Aśoka, who established a Buddhist state in India in the third century B.C.E. Shōtoku Taishi's enterprise was on a decidedly lesser scale, however. Even when Shōtoku Taishi's authorship of this ethico-legal document is called into question, it is often said that it nevertheless reflects his thinking. How this is known is unclear, but it is part of the historical valorization of Shōtoku.

The Imperial Record presents details missing from the Chronicles account, just as the Chronicles has inclusions neglected in the Imperial Record. Descriptions of Buddhist rituals performed at the illness or death of members of the imperial family are of particular interest. The Imperial Record documents the interrelationship between Buddhist vows made to assure the curing of an illness or a good rebirth in the next life and the crafting of Buddhist images. These images were the currency with which the faithful hoped to purchase fulfillment of their desire for a cure or good rebirth. Similar circumstances surrounded the creation of images such as the Śākyamuni (the historical Buddha) and Yakushi Nyorai (the Healing Buddha) statues found in the main hall (kondō) of the Hōryūji Temple, and the Tenjukoku mandala embroidery, originally in the Hōryūji but now housed in the Chūgūji Nunnery.

According to the Imperial Record, the image of Yakushi was constructed after the death of Emperor Yōmei, Shōtoku's father, by Shōtoku and Empress Suiko in 607 C.E. This image may or may not exist today—the one in the Hōryūji is likely a late seventh-century reconstruction replacing the original thought to have been lost in the Hōryūji fire of 670 C.E. The Śākyamuni image was fashioned as a result of a vow made by Shōtoku's followers seeking his recovery from the illness that eventually took his life. Shōtoku died, but the image was finally completed a year after his death in order to ensure his rebirth in the Pure Land and immediate enlightenment. This bronze image, cast by the famous Buddhist sculptor Tori Busshi, is still found in the Hōryūji today.

The Imperial Record also records the reasons for the execution of the Tenjukoku mandala embroidery. When Shōtoku died, two embroidered tapestries were crafted by his consort and her attendants to depict his life in paradise, where he was believed to have been reborn. The Tenjukoku (Land of Celestial Immortality) mandala exists today in fragments at the Chūgūji Nunnery adjacent to the Hōryūji. It depicts a scene of paradise, probably either the paradise of Amida, the Buddha of the Western Paradise, or Miroku, the Buddha of the future. In its original form, the embroidery depicted one hundred tortoises with four Chinese characters written on the back of each one. Of this total of four hundred characters, only twenty-nine remain on the surviving fragments. The Imperial Record account is important because it preserves these four hundred characters in its description of the Tenjukoku mandala, which is apparently a transcription of the characters from the embroidery itself.

The *Chronicles* and the *Imperial Record* sometimes nuance the same historical events by describing them in differing degrees of detail, sometimes offering different dates as well. For instance, the *Imperial Record* (along with the *Gangōji garan engi narabini ruki shizai chō* [A History of the Gangōji Temple Complex and a List of Its Treasures]) gives a date of 538 C.E. for the introduction of Buddhism to Japan (see chapter 29 in this volume). This differs from the date of 552 C.E. stated in the *Chronicles*. It may be that an earlier date for the introduction of Buddhism to Japan was meant to lengthen the duration of the relationship between the imperial family and Buddhism, thus strengthening their claim of control over this religion. The description of the conflict between the Soga and the Mononobe is recounted in considerably more detail in the *Chronicles*, suggesting a greater concern with establishing the supremacy of the Soga over the Mononobe. The *Chronicles* account develops Soga no Umako's role in these events, whereas the *Imperial Record* account solely emphasizes Shōtoku's role. Shōtoku's death is also treated in different ways: the *Imperial Record* devotes considerably more attention to Shōtoku's illness and death.

Whether or not Shōtoku Taishi did and said everything that is attributed to him in the *Chronicles* and the *Imperial Record*, we can safely assume that his biographies represent an idealized Shōtoku and the ideal of the period in which the biographies were written. The portrayal of Shōtoku Taishi as a holy person, or *hijiri*, evidences the extent to which Shotoku was esteemed by the eighth century. It also reveals the hagiographic process through which Shōtoku's persona was constructed and he was set apart from others because of his holy nature and miraculous powers. The conception we hold today of Shōtoku Taishi represents an aggregate image that articulates the mystique of the person originally represented in the *Chronicles* and the *Imperial Record*.

Passages translated from the *Nihon shoki* are taken from *Nihon shoki*, vol. 2, Nihon koten bungaku taikei 68, ed. Sakamoto Tarō et al. (Tokyo: Iwanami Shoten, 1965). The *Jōgū Shōtoku hōō teisetsu* translation is taken from *Shōtoku Taishi shū*, Nihon shisō taikei 2, ed. Ienaga Saburō et al. (Tokyo: Iwanami Shoten, 1975). Bureaucratic ranks, lists of names of otherwise unknown people, alternative readings for names, and other editorial deletions have sometimes been made from the translations in the interest of readability. These translations use the Japanese pronunciation of Korean names and places.

Further Reading

W. G. Aston, tr., *Nihongi: Chronicles of Japan from the Earliest Times to A.D. 697* (London: George Allen & Unwin, 1956 [tr. 1896]); Hanayama Shinshō, "Prince Shōtoku and Japanese Buddhism," *Philosophical Studies of Japan* 4 (1963): 23–48; Kanaji Isamu, "Three Stages in Shōtoku Taishi's Acceptance of Buddhism," *Acta Asiatica* 47 (1985): 31–47; Robert E. Morrell, "Shōtoku Taishi," in *Great Thinkers of the Eastern World*, ed. Ian P. McGreal (New York: HarperCollins, 1995): 291–294; Nakamura Hajime, "The Ideal of a Universal State and its Philosophical Basis—Prince Shōtoku and His Successors" (Chapter 1), in *A History of the Development of Japanese Thought I* (Tokyo: Kokusai Bunka Shinkokai, 1967); Charles S. Terry, "Legend and Political Intrigue in Ancient Japan: Shōtoku Taishi," in *Great Historical Figures of Japan*, ed. Murakami Hyoe and Thomas J. Harper (Tokyo: Japan Culture Institute, 1978): 1–15; Tsunoda Ryusaku et al., eds., *Sources of Japanese Tradition I* (New York and London: Columbia University Press, 1958 and 1964): 48–51; Alex and Hideko Wayman, tr., *The Lion's Roar of Queen Śrīmālā* (New York: Columbia University Press, 1974).

Chronicles of Japan

586 C.E. SPRING, 1ST MONTH, 1ST DAY

Anahobe no Hashihito, the imperial princess, was made empress. She gave birth to four sons. The first was called Prince Umayado [Stable Door, i.e., Shōtoku Taishi]. (He was also called Toyomimito [Excellent Discernment and Wisdom] Shōtoku, Great Dharma King Toyotomimi [Excellent Wisdom and Discernment], and Dharma Master King.) Prince Shōtoku first resided at the Upper Palace and later moved to Ikaruga. During the reign of Empress Suiko, he resided at the Eastern Palace, serving as crown prince. He administered the government on behalf of the empress. These words appear in the Imperial History of Empress Suiko.

587 C.E. AUTUMN, 7TH MONTH

Soga no Umako counseled the imperial princes and government officials to plot the destruction of Mononobe no Moriya. Umako and the others, leading an army, advanced to attack Moriya. . . . Moriya himself led an army of family and servants. They built a fortress from bales of rice and engaged in battle. . . . Moriya's army fought furiously. . . . The army of the imperial princes and government officials was seized with fear, and three times they retreated. At this time, Prince Shōtoku . . . reflected on the course of the battle: "Will we not be defeated? Unless we make a vow, it will be difficult to achieve victory." So saying, he cut down a sacred *nuride* tree and quickly fashioned images of the Four Heavenly Kings, Buddhist guardian deities. He affixed the images to his hair and made a vow: "If we are allowed to defeat our enemy, I will build a temple and stūpa to the Four Heavenly Kings who protect the world." Soga no Umako also made a vow: "If we obtain the benefit of being saved and protected by the Four Heavenly Kings and the protector deity Daijinnō, I vow to build a temple and stūpa to them, and to propagate Buddhism." Having made these vows, they prepared their army and urged them into battle. A man named Tomi no Obito Ichii shot at Mononobe no Moriya from up in a tree, killing Moriya and his children. Consequently, Moriya's army was quickly routed. . . .

After this conflict had been suppressed, the Four Heavenly Kings Temple (Shitennōji) was constructed at Tsunokuni. Half of Mononobe no Moriya's servants were made to serve as the servants of this temple, and Moriya's estate was made into the private rice fields of the temple. Also, 490 acres of rice lands were presented to Tomi no Obito Ichii. Soga no Umako, in keeping with his vow, constructed the Hōkōji Temple in Asuka.

593 C.E. SUMMER, 4TH MONTH, 10TH DAY

Shōtoku Taishi was designated crown prince. He governed the affairs of state and was completely entrusted with its administration. Shōtoku was the second child of Emperor Yōmei. His mother, the empress, was named Anahobe no Hashihito. On the day Shōtoku was born, she went around the imperial palace inspecting each of the government offices. When she came to the Bureau of Horses she entered as far as the stable door. Suddenly, and without any pain, she gave birth. Shōtoku was able to speak at birth and possessed the wisdom of a holy person. When he reached adulthood, he could listen to the lawsuits of ten people at the same time and judge them without error. He was also able to know things that were going to happen before they occurred. He learned Buddhism from the Korean monk Eji and studied the Confucian Classics with the scholar Kakuka. He made an exhaustive study of both areas. The emperor loved his son and had him to take up residence in the south upper hall of the palace. Thus, he was praised as the Prince Born Before the Stable Door, Residing in the Upper Hall, Gifted with the Power of Great Discernment.

594 C.E. SPRING, 2D MONTH, 1ST DAY

Empress Suiko issued an imperial edict to Shōtoku Taishi and Soga no Umako instructing them to promote the Three Treasures (Buddhism). At that time, all of the lords and ministers, in order to repay their debt of gratitude to the empress and their parents, competed with each other to build Buddhist dwelling places. These were called "temples."

595 C.E. SUMMER, 5TH MONTH, 10TH DAY

The Korean monk Eji came to Japan and became Shōtoku's Dharma teacher. Another Korean monk, Esō, also arrived in Japan in the same year. These two monks propagated the Buddha's teachings and together became the upholders of the Three Treasures.

601 C.E. SPRING, 2D MONTH

Prince Shōtoku began construction of a palace at Ikaruga.

603 C.E. WINTER, 11TH MONTH, 1ST DAY

Prince Shōtoku addressed the officials, saying, "I possess a sacred Buddha image. Who will take this image and reverently worship it?" Hada no Miyakko Kawakatsu stepped forward and said, "I will worship it." He immediately received the Buddha image and built the temple Hachinooka-dera (Kōryūji) to enshrine it.

This month, Prince Shōtoku asked Empress Suiko for permission to make large shields and quivers, and also to paint images on banners [for use in rituals].

604 C.E. SUMMER, 4TH MONTH, 3D DAY

Shōtoku Taishi personally set down the Seventeen-Article Constitution for the first time.

Article 1

Value harmony and follow the principle of nonopposition. All people have factional interests and few are wise. Therefore, some do not follow their ruler and their father, while others are at odds with the neighboring village. However, when the superior is harmonious and the inferior is congenial, and when there is agreement in the discussion of different matters, then understanding will naturally occur and no matters will remain unfinished.

Article 2

Fervently revere the Three Treasures: the Buddha, the Dharma, and the Monastic Community (*sangha*). They are the final refuge of all living beings, and the supreme principle in the world. Is there anyone in any age who does not revere the Dharma? People who are extremely bad are rare. They, too, can be taught to follow Buddhism. If they do not take refuge in the Three Treasures, how will they correct their wickedness?

Article 3

When you receive imperial decrees, you must heed them. The ruler is like heaven; the government official is like earth. Heaven covers and earth supports. The four seasons move in an orderly fashion, and all things in the world develop accordingly. If earth desires to cover heaven, then only destruction will result. Therefore, when the ruler makes commands, the government official must carry them out. The superior acts; the inferior follows. Therefore, receive imperial decrees with the necessary humility. Without humility, things will naturally fail.

Article 4

All government officials should follow the principle of propriety. The principle of governing the people must be found in propriety. When there is no propriety above, there will be disorder below. When there is no propriety below, offenses will necessarily result. Therefore, if the government officials maintain propriety, there will be no confusion about the order of ranks. If the people maintain propriety, the state will govern itself naturally.

Article 5

Abstain from gluttony and abandon desire. Fairly judge legal matters. The legal matters of the people number as many as one thousand in a single day. Although there may be this many in a single day, how many more will there be over a number of years? These days, those who decide legal matters are in the habit of obtaining a profit, hearing lawsuits after receiving a bribe. Consequently, the lawsuits of the wealthy are like throwing stones in the water—they will be favorably received, while the lawsuits of the poor are like throwing water on stones—they will not be favorably received. Therefore, what are poor people to do? The duty of the government official is deficient here.

Article 6

Punish bad and encourage good—this is a good and ancient rule. Therefore, do not conceal the good in people, and when you see bad, correct it. People who flatter and deceive are sharp swords who undermine the state and destroy the people. Flatterers like to explain the errors of inferiors to superiors, and when they meet with inferiors, they emphasize the errors of the superiors. These kinds of people are neither loyal to their lord nor benevolent to the people. This is the source of great civil disorder.

Article 7

Every person has a responsibility. There must not be disorder in the conduct of government. When a wise person is appointed to office, voices of praise sound immediately. When a wicked person holds office, repeated disorder occurs in the world. In this world, few people are naturally wise—it is through careful deliberation that they become sages (*hijiri*). Regardless of the relative importance of any state matter, if the right person is appointed, peace will necessarily prevail. Whether it is a time of emergency or not, if you meet with a wise person, the world will naturally be well-ordered. Owing to this, the state will long endure and be free from danger. Therefore, the sage-kings of old sought good people for government offices; they did not seek government offices for favored people.

Article 8

All government officials should arrive at court early and leave late. There is no leisure time in the conduct of government business. Even working all day long does not exhaust the business to be done. Therefore, if government officials arrive late at the court, they will not be able to deal with emergencies. If they leave early, business will not be completed.

Article 9

Sincerity is the foundation of righteousness. All things possess sincerity. The essence of good and bad and of success and failure is found in sincerity. If government officials together are sincere, what cannot be accomplished? If they are not sincere, all matters will end in failure.

Article 10

Refrain from hatred and angry looks. Do not be irate when people disagree with you. All people have hearts, each with their own deep attachments. If you are right, then I am wrong; if I am right, then you are wrong. I am not necessarily a sage and you are not necessarily a fool. We are both only ordinary people. Who can decide for certain what is right and what is wrong? Both of us are alternately wise and foolish, like an endless circle. For this reason, although other people become angry, I, on the contrary, fear my own errors. Even if I alone fully comprehend, I will follow the others and act like them.

Article 11

Clearly discern merit and demerit, and apply the necessary reward or punishment. Recently, reward has not been applied to merit and punishment has not been applied to wrongdoing. Government officials in charge of these matters should fairly apply rewards and punishments.

Article 12

Provincial and local officials must not extort the people. There are not two sovereigns of the country and there are not two lords of the people. The emperor is the lord of the people. Appointed officials are retainers of the emperor. How can they extort the people while at the same time conducting the affairs of the government?

Article 13

Those appointed to various offices must endeavor to fulfill their duties. Whether because they are ill or because they are away on business, there will be times when they cannot attend to work. However, on days when they can work, they should be in accord with their colleagues and endeavor to catch up on the work they missed while absent. Do not refuse to do official business just because it has not been entrusted to you.

Article 14

Government officials must not be jealous. If you are envious of people, they will also be envious of you. The affliction of jealousy knows no limit. Therefore, we are displeased when others are wiser than us, and we are jealous when others surpass our ability. Thus, it is not until after five hundred years pass that we finally encounter a wise person, and even with the passage of one thousand years it is difficult to find a sage. If we can find neither a wise person nor a sage, how can we govern the country?

Article 15

The duty of the government official is to turn away from private benefit and to turn instead toward the public good. If people are concerned with private benefit they necessarily feel resentment. When there is resentment, disagreement necessarily arises. If there is disagreement, the public good is obstructed for the sake of private benefit. If resentment arises, it conflicts with the system of rules and destroys the law. Therefore, the first article stated that superior and inferior should be harmonious and congenial. The meaning of these two articles is similar.

Article 16

People should be forced to do public service work during suitable times of the year—this is a good and ancient rule. Therefore, it is good to employ the people in public service when there is free time during the winter months. From spring to autumn, when the people labor at agriculture and sericulture, they must not be made to do public service. What would we eat without agriculture? What would we wear without sericulture?

Article 17

Important matters should not be decided by one person alone. They must be discussed together with many people. Less important matters need not be discussed with others. In the discussion of important matters, there is concern that mistakes will be made. Therefore, discussion with many people leads to the proper course of action.

605 C.E. SUMMER, 4TH MONTH, 1ST DAY

Empress Suiko issued an imperial decree to Shōtoku Taishi and Soga no Umako and to the princes and ministers commanding them to vow together to begin crafting one copper and one sewn Buddha image. She also commanded Kura-tsukuri no Tori to supervise the making of these images. At this time, the Korean King Daikō heard that the empress of Japan was making Buddha images so he gave 300 *ryō* [1 *ryō* = 37.5 grams] of gold as tribute.

606 C.E. AUTUMN, 7TH MONTH

The empress requested Shōtoku Taishi to lecture on the *Queen Śrīmālā Sūtra* (Shōmangyō, Śrīmālādevīsi*mhanāda-sūtra, *T* 353). He expounded on it for three days. This year, Prince Shōtoku also lectured on the *Lotus Sūtra* (Hokekyō; Saddharma puṇḍarīka, *T* 262) at the Okamoto Palace. The empress, greatly rejoicing at this, presented Shōtoku with 100 *chō* [1 *chō* 2.45 acres] of rice fields in Harima Province. Accordingly, Shōtoku offered this land to the Ikaruga Temple (Hōryūji).

607 C.E. SPRING, 2D MONTH, 15TH DAY

Prince Shōtoku and Soga no Umako led the government ministers in worship of the deities of heaven and earth.

613 C.E. WINTER, 12TH MONTH, 1ST DAY

Prince Shōtoku traveled to Kataoka. At that time, a starving man was lying by the side of the road. Accordingly, the Crown Prince asked him his name, but the man did not respond. Shōtoku, observing this situation, provided the man with food and water and removed the coat he was wearing and covered the starving man with it. He said to him, "Lie there in peace." Shōtoku then sang this verse:

> On Mount Kataoka,
> the poor traveler,
> collapsed, starving for food.
> Were you raised without parents?
> Are you without a lord prospering like the bamboo?
> The poor traveler,
> collapsed, starving for food.

2D DAY

Prince Shōtoku dispatched a messenger to check on the starving man. The messenger returned, saying, "The starving man has already died." The crown prince was extremely saddened by this. Accordingly, he immediately had the starving man buried at the place by the side of the road. The grave was firmly sealed. Several days later, Shōtoku summoned his attendants and said to them, "The starving man who was lying by the side of the road the other day was no ordinary man. He must surely have been a holy person (*hijiri*)." Shōtoku dispatched a messenger to investigate. When he returned, the messenger said, "When I went to see the grave the earth covering it had not been moved, but when I opened the grave and looked inside the corpse was not there. Only your coat was there, folded and place on top of the coffin." At this, Shōtoku sent the messenger back to retrieve his coat. The crown prince then wore the coat again as before. People at this time thought these events most strange and remarked, "It is true that only a holy person (*hijiri*) knows a holy person (*hijiri*)." They were all the more awed by this situation.

620 C.E.

This year, Prince Shōtoku and Soga no Umako consulted together and recorded the *History of the Emperors*, the *History of the Nation*, and the *True Record* of the Omi, the Muraji, the Tomo no miyakko, the Kuni no miyakko [titles for government ranks], the 180 occupational families [*be*], and the people.

621 C.E. SPRING, 2D MONTH, 5TH DAY

Shōtoku Taishi died in the middle of the night at the Ikaruga Palace. At this time, the princes, ministers, people of the nation, and all the old people, who felt as if they had lost a beloved child, did not even taste the flavorful food in their mouths. Children, as if a dear parent had died, raised their voices in sorrowful anguish that could be heard in the streets. Farmers stopped ploughing and the women who pounded the rice stopped pounding. Everyone said, "The sun and the moon have lost their brilliance, and heaven and earth have fallen into ruin. Henceforth, on whom can we depend?"

This month, Shōtoku Taishi was buried in the Shinaga imperial mausoleum. At this time, the Korean monk Eji was greatly saddened upon hearing that Prince Shōtoku had died. He requested the Buddhist monks to hold a vegetarian meeting (*sai-e*) as a memorial to Shōtoku. Accordingly, on that day Eji expounded sūtras, vowing, "There is a holy person in Japan named Shōtoku Taishi. Heaven granted him a superior nature. Endowed with the immeasurable virtue of a holy person, he was born in the country of Japan. He propagated the way of the ancient wise and virtuous rulers and continued the great projects of the former emperors. He revered the Three Treasures and saved the people from their hardships. He was truly an august holy person (*hijiri*). Now the Crown Prince is dead. Although I am from a foreign country, it is difficult to sever the emotional bond between us. What is the use of living alone? I will, without fail, die next year on the fifth day of the second month [the one-year anniversary of Shōtoku's death]. I will join Prince Shōtoku in the Pure Land and together we will spread the Buddhist teachings to all sentient beings." Eji died on the day he vowed he would. The people of that time remarked to one another, "Prince Shōtoku is not the only holy person. Eji is also a holy person."

Imperial Record of Shōtoku, Dharma King of the Upper Palace

Emperor Yōmei married his half sister, Anahobe no hashihito no miko, and she became the empress. She gave birth to Shōtoku Taishi, Kume no Miko,

Uekuri no Miko, and Manda no Miko. Emperor Yōmei also married the daughter of Soga no Iname, Ishikina no Iratsume, who gave birth to Tame no Miko. The emperor also married the daughter of Katsuragi no Tagima no Kurabito-hiroko, Ihiko no Iratsume, who gave birth to Omaroko no Kimi and Sukateko no Miko (this princess worshipped the kami at the Ise Shrine during three imperial reigns). In all, Shōtoku Taishi's siblings numbered seven princes and princesses.

Shōtoku Taishi married the daughter of Kashiwade no Katabuko no Omi, named Hokikimi no Iratsume, who gave birth to Tsuishine no Miko, Hatsuse no Miko, Kuhata no Miko, Hatori no Miko, Sakikusa no Miko, and others— eight children in all. Shōtoku also married Tojiko no Iratsume, the daughter of Soga no Umako, who gave birth to Yamashiro no Ohine no Miko (this prince had a wise and noble heart, threw away his own life, and had compassion for the people—later generations mistakenly confused him with his father, Shōtoku Taishi), Takara no Miko, Hiki no Miko, and Kataoka no Oka—four children in all. Shōtoku also married Inabe no Tachibana no Miko, the daughter of Ohari no Miko, who gave birth to Shirakabe no Miko and Teshima no Miko. In all, Shōtoku Taishi had fourteen children.

Yamashiro no Ohine no Miko married his half-sister, Tsuishine no Miko, who gave birth to Naniwa no Maroko no Miko, Maroko no Miko, Yuge no Miko, Sasa no Miko, Mishima no Miko, Kōka no Miko, and Ohari no Miko.

Shōtoku Taishi's half brother, Prince Tame no Miko, after the death of their father Emperor Yōmei, married Shōtoku's mother, Anahobe no Hashihito no Miko, who gave birth to Princess Saho no Miko.

Emperor Kinmei (Shōtoku Taishi's grandfather) married Ishihime no Mikoto, the daughter of Emperor Senka, who gave birth to Emperor Bidatsu (Shōtoku Taishi's uncle). Emperor Kinmei also married Kitashihime no Mikoto, the daughter of Soga no Iname, who gave birth to Emperor Yōmei (Shōtoku Taishi's father) and his younger sister, Empress Suiko (Shōtoku Taishi's aunt). Emperor Kinmei also married Oane no Mikoto, Kitashihime no Mikoto's younger sister, who gave birth to Emperor Sushun (Shōtoku Taishi's uncle) and his older sister, Anahobe no Mashihito no Miko (Shōtoku Taishi's mother).

The five emperors and empresses mentioned above ruled successively without interruption. (Actually, Emperor Sushun was the fourth and Empress Suiko the fifth in order.)

During the reign of Empress Suiko, Shōtoku Taishi, along with Soga no Umako, assisted in the administration of government, promoted Buddhism, constructed temples such as the Gangōji and the Shitennōji, and instituted the twelve-cap ranking system, which consisted of the following ranks: Greater Virtue, Lesser Virtue, Greater Benevolence, Lesser Benevolence, Greater Propriety, Lesser Propriety, Greater Faith, Lesser Faith, Greater Righteousness, Lesser Righteousness, Greater Wisdom, and Lesser Wisdom.

When Anahobe no Hashihito, Emperor Yōmei's empress, went out to the stable door, she suddenly gave birth to Shōtoku Taishi. Prince Shōtoku was wise from a very young age. When he became an adult, he was able to listen to the statements of eight people simultaneously, and to differentiate their points. He heard one thing and understood many. Accordingly, he was called Prince Stable Door, Gifted with the Power of Great Discernment, Eight Ears.

Emperor Yōmei loved his son, Shōtoku Taishi, the crown prince, very much. Because the emperor had Shōtoku live in the south upper hall of the palace, he was called Prince Upper Palace.

Shōtoku Taishi took the Korean monk Eji as his Dharma teacher. Shōtoku was able to understand the principle that nirvana is immutable and unchanging, and that there are five kinds of buddha-nature. He also clearly discerned the meaning of the *Lotus Sūtra* teaching concerning the three vehicles and the two kinds of wisdom. He perceived the import of the *Vimalakirti Sūtra*'s teaching of the wondrous nirvana. Moreover, Shōtoku knew the Hīnayāna teachings known as the Sautrāntika and the Sarvāstivāda. He also knew the meaning of the three profound Chinese teachings and the five Chinese Classics. At the same time, he also studied astronomy and geography. He wrote seven volumes of commentary on the *Lotus Sūtra* and other sutras. These are called the "Upper Palace Commentaries."

Once, Shōtoku asked a question his teacher could not answer. That evening, Shōtoku dreamed that a gold-colored person appeared and taught him the meaning of what he did not understand. After he awoke, Shōtoku was able to explain the point. When he explained it to his teacher, he, too, was able to understand it. This kind of thing occurred several times.

Shōtoku Taishi built seven temples: Shitennōji, Hōryūji, Chūgūji, Tachibanadera, Hachiokadera (also known as Kōryūji), Ikejiridera, and Kazurakidera.

On the fifteenth day of the fourth month of the sixth year (598) of Empress Suiko's reign, the empress requested Shōtoku Taishi to lecture on the *Queen Śrīmālā Sūtra*. Shōtoku's appearance was like that of a monk. Many princes, princesses, government dignataries, and others heard this lecture, gained faith, and were greatly overjoyed. The lecture ended after three days.

The empress made an offering to Shōtoku Taishi of 15,000 *shiro* of land at Iiho no kohorisase, in Harima-kuni. The prince gave this land to the Hōryūji.

Shōtoku Taishi's teacher, the monk Eji, took Shōtoku's three sūtra commentaries and returned to Korea (Koma), where he had these texts disseminated. In the middle of the night on the twenty-second day of the second month of the thirtieth year (622) of Empress Suiko's reign, Shōtoku Taishi died. When Eji heard this, he had sūtra lectures conducted and made a vow, saying, "I met Shōtoku Taishi and he wished to receive an education. I, Eji, will die next year on the twenty-second day of the second month, and I will necessarily meet Shōtoku in the Pure Land." At last, just as Eji had said, the following year on the twenty-second day of the second month, he became ill and died.

When Emperor Yōmei became ill during the first year of his reign (586), he summoned Suiko and Shōtoku, and made this vow: "I desire to be cured of my disease. Therefore, I command you to build a temple and enshrine there an image of Yakushi." However, the emperor died at that time and the construction did not take place. In the fifteenth year of Empress Suiko's reign (607), the empress and Shōtoku carried out the construction following the emperor's command. The above is the inscription on the back of the halo of the Yakushi image enshrined in the Golden Hall (Kondō) of the Hōryūji. It is the initial reason for building this temple.

In the twelfth month of the first year of Hōkō gansei (621 C.E.), the empress dowager, Shōtoku Taishi's mother, Anahobe no Hashihito, died. On the twenty-second day of the first month of the following year (622 C.E.), Shōtoku Taishi became ill. Unfortunately, on account of this, the Kashiwade Empress, Shōtoku's wife, became exhausted and took ill. Both became bedridden. At this time, queens, princes, and various retainers—Dharma friends—with great sadness together made the following vow: "Because of our reverence for the Three Treasures, we will make an image of Śākyamuni with the body proportions of Shōtoku Taishi. Receiving the power of this vow, we hope that Shōtoku's illness will be cured, his life extended, and he will live peacefully in the world. Should it be that he dies because of karmic consequence, we hope that he is born into the Pure Land and quickly ascends to the realm of enlightenment."

On the twenty-first day of the second month, the Kashiwade Empress died. The following day, Shōtoku Taishi also died. In the middle of the third month of the thirty-first year of Suiko's reign (623), as had been vowed by the Dharma friends, an image of Śākyamuni with attendants and decorative implements was reverently completed. Sharing this bit of good fortune, these Dharma friends, who had faith in the way of the Buddha, reverently followed these three (the empress dowager, Shōtoku Taishi, and the Kashiwade Empress) even now peaceful in death. They promoted the Three Treasures, desiring finally to reach the other shore [enlightenment] together. Also, they hoped that the deluded sentient beings everywhere in the samsaric cycle would escape from their painful karmic connections and proceed to the world of enlightenment. The image of Śākyamuni was made by Shiba Kuratsukuri no Tori [Tori Busshi]. The above is similar to the account on the inscription on the back of the halo of the Śākyamuni image enshrined in the Golden Hall of the Hōryūji.

When Shōtoku Taishi died, his consort Tachibana no Ōiratsume, stricken with grief, respectfully addressed Empress Suiko: "I fear that I cannot stop my feelings. As was expected, Shōtoku Taishi and his mother have died. There is nothing to compare with my sadness. Our dear Prince Shōtoku said, 'The world is ephemeral, only the Buddha is real.' When we appreciate this teaching, Shōtoku Taishi will be born into Tenjukoku [paradise]. However, this country's appearance is difficult to visualize. I pray I will see Prince Shōtoku's condition of rebirth."

Empress Suiko heard this and sadly replied, "Prince Shōtoku's words are true." She issued an imperial order to the palace women and others to create two embroideries. The artists were Aya no Maken from Japan, and Kasei and Aya no Nukakori from Korea. The project supervisor was Kurahitobe no Hata no Kuma. Shōtoku Taishi's words are written on the back of a tortoise shell on the embroideries which is stored at the Hōryūji Temple.

When Shōtoku Taishi died, Kose no Mitsue no Machigimi composed three poems:

> If the Tomi stream in Ikaruga should cease to flow
>   our great prince's name would be forgotten.
> Flowers growing on Mount Tabasami where the gods eat;
>   People grieve for our great prince.
> The branches of the mountain trees hang down surrounding Ikaruga
>   like a fence,
>   We desire to tell our lord a wish that won't be realized.

Around the sixth or seventh month of the second year of the reign of Emperor Yōmei (587 C.E.), when Soga no Umako battled with Mononobe no Moriya, Umako's troops fled without victory. Consequently, Shōtoku Taishi constructed images of the Four Heavenly Kings in front of the troops and vowed, "If we can destroy Moriya, I will build a temple for the Four Heavenly Kings and reverently worship there." Thereupon, Umako's troops were victorious, killing Moriya. Because of this, the Temple of the Four Heavenly Kings was constructed at Naniwa. This occurred when Prince Shōtoku was fourteen years old.

During the reign of Emperor Kinmei, in the tenth month of the twelfth day of 538 C.E., King Myoo, of the Korean kingdom of Kudara, for the first time offered as tribute Buddhist images, sūtras, and monks. By imperial edict, Soga no Iname received these things and propagated Buddhism.

In 570 C.E., a fire destroyed a Buddha Hall. The Buddha Hall was thrown into the Naniwa canal.

In the thirteenth year of the reign of Empress Suiko (605 C.E.), Shōtoku Taishi planned with Soga no Umako to construct a Buddha Hall and propagated Buddhism. Thereupon, in conformity with the teaching of the five elements, Shōtoku Taishi established the twelve-cap court rank system. In the seventh month, he wrote the Seventeen-Article Constitution.

Shōtoku, Dharma King of the Upper Palace, also known as King Dharma Master, was born in 574 and died on the twenty-second day of the second month of 622. He was forty-nine years old. He served as Empress Suiko's crown prince. His mausoleum is located in Kōchi no shinaga no oka.

—— 31 ——

Nationalistic Shintō: A Child's Guide
to Yasukuni Shrine

Richard Gardner

The following text is excerpted from a pamphlet, intended for children, explaining the history of Yasukuni Shrine, one of the more controversial religious and political sites in Japan. The shrine was established in 1869 at its present location, the top of Kudan slope in Tokyo's Chiyoda-ku, at the request of Emperor Meiji. It served to enshrine and pacify the spirits of those who had died on both sides of the fighting in the Boshin War (1868–1869), which resulted in the overthrow of the shogunate and restoration of the emperor to power. The shrine came to be understood as the place for enshrining all of those who lost their lives in battle for the sake of the nation in both civil and foreign wars. From early on, Yasukuni had a close connection with the imperial family, came under military jurisdiction, and served as a center for nationalistic propaganda.

Following the Japanese defeat in the Second World War, State Shintō was banned by the occupation authorities and the new Japanese constitution included a provision formally separating church and state. Yasukuni Shrine thus became an independent religious organization. While many younger Japanese rarely if ever think of the shrine, it has remained, nevertheless, a site of contention and dispute. Traditionalists, conservatives, and the Association of Bereaved Families (Izokukai) have, since the mid-1950s, waged a campaign to reestablish the connection between Yasukuni Shrine and the state. Liberals, leftists, Christians, and others have fought to oppose any effort to reforge such a link. The shrine is also a point of contention throughout Asia. For many Asian countries, Yasukuni Shrine is a symbol of Japan's aggression during the war years. The last major "event" in the history of the shrine—Prime Minister Nakasone's official visit to the shrine in 1985—sparked a vehement protest by China and other nations in the region.

The controversy surrounding the shrine today is inevitably bound up with living memories of the period of Japan's militarism in the 1930s and 1940s.

Soldiers departing for the battlefield were told not to worry because they would be taken care of at Yasukuni Shrine. Heading into battle, soldiers would often say to one another, with either seriousness or irony, "See you at Yasukuni!" While some former warriors make their annual pilgrimage to the shrine fully embracing the shrine's views of history, others repudiate what the shrine officially stands for but see their visit as a means of fulfilling promises to or communing with the friends and comrades they lost in the war. Japanese religion provides many occasions for honoring and communing with the dead. The power of Yasukuni for some lies in its claim to provide the most appropriate, the most intimate space for communing with the dead.

Not all of the Japanese war dead are enshrined at Yasukuni. The criteria for enshrinement has shifted over the course of history. Most civilian Japanese war dead, such as the victims of the fire bombing of Tokyo in 1945, are not enshrined here. Within the shrine compound, there is, however, a very small, hidden-away shrine, usually unnoticed by visitors, that enshrines all the war dead of all countries not enshrined in the main shrine.

Much of the support for the shrine comes from those with living memories of family and friends who lost their lives in Second World War and are enshrined at Yasukuni. As the numbers of those with living memories of the dead pass on, it has become necessary for the shrine to attempt to awaken in the young a sense of the meaning and significance of the shrine.

The text translated here is *Yasukuni daihyakka: Watashitachi no Yasukuni Jinja* (Tokyo: Office of Yasukuni Shrine, 1992).

Further Reading

Haruko Taya and Theodore F. Cook, *Japan at War: An Oral History* (New York: The New Press, 1992); Wilhelmus H. M. Creemers, *Shrine Shintō after World War II* (Leiden: E. J. Brill, 1968); Helen Hardacre, *Shintō and the State, 1868–1988* (Princeton: Princeton University Press, 1989); Mark R. Mullins, Susumu Shimazono, and Paul L. Swanson, eds., *Religion and Society in Modern Japan* (Berkeley: Asian Humanities Press, 1993); David M. O'Brien with Yasuo Ohkoshi, *To Dream of Dreams: Religious Freedom and Constitutional Politics in Postwar Japan* (Honolulu: University of Hawaii Press, 1996).

A [Child's] Guide to Yasukuni Shrine: Our Yasukuni Shrine

Dear Fathers and Mothers:

The whole family can have an intimate visit with the gods by worshipping at the inner sanctuary of the Main Sanctuary. Please feel free to make an application at the reception office. We also look forward to welcoming your visit on days of celebration such as Coming of Age Day, the Children's Festival, and the First Visit of Newborns to the Shrine.

THE CHERRY TREES OF YASUKUNI

At the time of the construction of the Main Sanctuary of Yasukuni Shrine in Meiji 3 (1870), Someiyoshino cherry trees were planted within the shrine grounds. This was the beginning of the cherry trees of Yasukuni. The graceful, beautiful cherry trees of Kudan, which all the gods are very proud of, are a symbol of Yasukuni Shrine. At present there are about a thousand cherry trees—including Someiyoshino, mountain cherry, and others—within the shrine gardens. As spring approaches every year, the Meteorological Agency examines the Someiyoshino at Yasukuni in order to predict when the cherry trees will bloom in Tokyo.

THE WHITE PIGEONS OF YASUKUNI

There are about six hundred of Poppo the Pigeon's friends here. They are all pure white carrier pigeons [*hato*, which also means dove, the symbol of peace], a type born only once every ten thousand births. Twice every day Leopold Mozart's "Toy Symphony" wafts throughout the grounds to tell Poppo and his friends that it is time to dine.

POPPO THE WISE PIGEON'S "ANSWERS TO ANY AND ALL QUESTIONS ABOUT YASUKUNI"

POPPO: Good day everyone! I'm Poppo the White Pigeon. There are about six hundred of my friends living together peacefully here at Yasukuni. We've come to be great friends with everyone looking after and visiting the shrine and are always having fun playing about the shrine grounds. So if it is something to do with Yasukuni, we know every nook and cranny of the place. Let's talk a bit about the history and festivals of Yasukuni Shrine, which everyone is always asking about.

Q: Who built Yasukuni Shrine and when?

A: Yasukuni Shrine is a shrine with a long tradition and was built over 120 years ago in 1869. Throughout the time of national seclusion before the Meiji period, Japan did not have relations with the other countries of the world. But the people of foreign countries gradually took a critical attitude toward Japan and pressured Japan to open itself to the outside world.

Wondering "what in the world should we do," the whole country was in an uproar and public opinion was widely split between those wanting to open the country and those wanting to keep it closed. In this situation, the Tokugawa Bakufu, which had been entrusted with the governing of Japan for over three hundred years, lost the power to quell this disturbance and so returned the authority to govern to the emperor.

At this point was born the idea of everyone in Japan becoming of one heart and mind under the emperor in order to restore the beautiful traditions of Japan, create a splendid modern nation, and become good friends with all the people of the world.

Then in the midst of trying to achieve this great rebirth, the Boshin War—an unfortunate, internal dispute—occurred, and many people came forth to offer their lives for the country. In order to transmit to future ages the story of the people who died in the Meiji Restoration, which aimed at creating a new age, the Emperor Meiji built this shrine, then named Tokyo Shokonsha (Shrine for Summoning the Spirits), here at Kudan in Tokyo in the sixth month of 1869. In 1879 the name was changed to Yasukuni Shrine.

Q: What does "Yasukuni" mean?

A: The Honorable Shrine Name "Yasukuni Shrine" was bestowed on the shrine by Emperor Meiji. The "Yasukuni" in the name means "Let's make our country a place of tranquility and gentle peace, an always peaceful country" and reflects the great and noble feelings of the Emperor Meiji. All the gods who are worshipped at the Yasukuni Shrine gave their noble lives in order to protect Japan while praying for eternal peace, like the Emperor Meiji, from the depths of their heart.

Q: What gods are worshipped at Yasukuni Shrine?

A: I explained a bit about the Boshin War earlier. The over 3,500 pillars (when counting gods, we count not "one, two" but "one pillar, two pillars") who died at that time were the first gods worshipped here. Later, all of those who died devoting themselves to the country, from 1853 (the year the American Admiral Perry led four warships to Uragaoki in Kanagawa Prefecture and everyone was saying with shock, "Black ships have come!") to the end of the Bakufu fifteen years later, were also enshrined and worshipped here.

After that there were also numerous battles within the country—such as those of the Saga Disturbance and the Seinan War [both of which were revolts against the newly established Meiji government]—until the new Japan was firmly established. All those who died for their country in those battles are also worshipped here. Everyone's ancestors helped carry out the important mission of creating a marvelous Japan with the emperor at its center.

However, to protect the independence of Japan and the peace of Asia surrounding Japan, there were also—though it is a very sad thing—several wars with foreign countries. In the Meiji period there were the Sino-Japanese War and the Russian-Japanese War; in the Taishō period, the First World War; and in the Shōwa period, the Manchurian Incident, the China Incident, and then the Great Pacific War (the Second World War).

At the start of the Russian-Japanese War, Emperor Meiji expressed his deep sorrow by composing and reciting an August Poem: "Though all are linked like the waters of the four seas, why do storms arise in the world?" (Why does peace give way to the storms of war when all the countries of the world should be like brothers?)

War is truly a sorrowful thing. But it was necessary to fight to firmly protect the independence of Japan and to exist as a peaceful nation prospering together with the surrounding countries of Asia. All those who offered up their noble lives in such disturbances and wars are worshipped at Yasukuni Shrine as gods.

Q: Could you please teach us some more about the gods?

A: Do you all know how many gods there are at Yasukuni Shrine? The answer is over 2,467,000! There are this many gods in front of all of you who have come to worship here! Let me tell you a little about the gods.

Among the gods at Yasukuni Shrine, there are gods such as Hashimoto Sanai [1834–1859], Yoshida Shōin [1830–1859], Sakamoto Ryōma [1836–1867], and Takasugi Shinsaku [1839–1867], who you all know well from history books and television dramas and who worked hard for the country from the end of the Edo period to the beginning of the Meiji period [by opposing the shogunate and supporting the emperor]. Also worshipped here are the many soldiers who died in battle during the wars of the Meiji, Taishō, and Shōwa periods.

But there are not just soldiers here; there are also over fifty-seven thousand female gods here. There are also children like you, and even younger, who are worshipped here as gods.

Let me tell you a little about the Great Pacific War, which took place over fifty years ago. When the American Army attacked Okinawa, there were junior high school students who stood up and resisted with the soldiers. To defend Okinawa and their hometowns, over sixteen hundred boys of nine schools— Okinawa Shihan School, the Number One and Number Two Prefectural Junior High Schools, etc.—formed groups such as the Blood and Iron Imperial Brigade and fought just like soldiers. Also, over four hundred students of girls schools, such as Number One Prefectural Girl's High School, Number Two Prefectural Girls High School, and Shuri Girls High School, served as nurses on the battlefield or made their way through the battlefield carrying food and ammunition. Most of those boy and girl students fell in battle. Now they are enshrined in Yasukuni Shrine and are sleeping here peacefully.

There are also fifteen hundred who met their sad end when the *Tsushima Maru* transport ship, which was evacuating them from Okinawa to Kagoshima to escape the bombing, was hit by torpedoes from enemy submarines. Among them were seven hundred grade school children.

There are also many, just like your older brothers and older sisters, who died in bombing attacks when they gave up their studies because of the war and worked hard producing goods in factories.

The next story is something that happened on August 20, 1945. Though the war was already over, the Soviet Army suddenly attacked Karafuto (now Sakharin). The girl telephone operators of Maoka in Karafuto continued reporting the movements of the Soviet Army to the mainland as the enemy approached. Their last message before losing their lives was, "Farewell everybody, this is the end, sayonara." All of them are here.

Also among the gods here are many who fell leading the fight to put out the fires caused by enemy bombing attacks on Japan. Nurses attached to the army on the battlefield who bore the noble insignia of the Red Cross and were adored like a mother or older sister. The crews of military transport ships who one and all sank to the bottom of the sea while heading to the southern battlefront. Cameramen and newspaper reporters attached to the army who fell from enemy bullets while gathering stories on the battlefield. Many people like this are worshipped here with great devotion as noble, godly spirits who gave their lives for their homeland Japan.

There are also those here who took the responsibility for the war upon themselves and ended their own lives when the Great Pacific War ended. There are also 1,068 who had their lives cruelly taken after the war when they were falsely and one-sidedly branded as "war criminals" by the kangaroo court of the Allies who had fought Japan. At Yasukuni Shrine we call these the "Shōwa Martyrs" [including General Tōjō Hideki], and they are all worshipped as gods.

YASUKUNI SHRINE IS THE SHRINE WHERE ALL JAPANESE GO TO WORSHIP

So now you know what gods are worshipped at Yasukuni Shrine. The gods of Yasukuni Shrine gave their noble lives on the battlefield with the hope that Japan might continue forever in peace and independence and that the marvelous history and traditions of Japan bequeathed by our ancestors might continue on and on forever. That Japan is peaceful and prosperous is thanks to all of those who have become gods at Yasukuni Shrine. From now on you must treasure "Our Japan," which these people protected by giving their lives in times of war. So let's all come to worship at Yasukuni Shrine, offer up our feelings of thanks to the gods, and promise to become splendid people. Flying above the shrine grounds, all us pigeons will be looking forward to your coming to worship.

SECTARIAN FOUNDERS, WIZARDS,
AND HEROES

— 32 —

En the Ascetic

Linda Klepinger Keenan

At the end of the seventh century there lived in the mountains of central Japan a man named En no Ozunu, who came to be known as En no Gyōja. The word *gyōja* means "one who performs religious practices." It was used especially of holy men who devoted themselves to rigorous ascetic disciplines deep in the rugged mountains in pursuit of spiritual powers. "Ascetic" is perhaps the closest English equivalent.

Today most people associate the name of En the Ascetic with the Japanese mountain religious tradition called Shugendō, for eventually he did come to be revered as the spiritual ancestor of men who went into sacred mountain areas to chant incantations and perform ascetic practices. These practitioners of Shugendō are sometimes called *yamabushi*—literally, "those who lie down in the mountains."

In fact, however, En the Ascetic did not take his place as the patriarch of Shugendō until several centuries after his death, during a period when mountain ascetics were beginning to organize into groups and thus felt the need to identify a progenitor. In his own time, so far as we can learn, En did not gather about himself a group of disciples, establish any kind of religious sect, or hand down any specific body of teachings. And long before he was adopted as the official founder of Shugendō, many stories about him circulated among the people and appeared in the literature—in histories, tale collections, and poetry.

The earliest written account of En the Ascetic appears in an official imperial history, the *Chronicles of Japan Continued* (*Shoku Nihongi*). This document was completed in the year 797, nearly one hundred years after the twenty-fourth day of the fifth month of the third year of the Emperor Mommu (699 C.E.) when, it records, a man named E (En) no Ozunu was banished to a distant island:

> E no Kimi Ozunu was exiled to the island at Izu. Ozunu first lived on Mount Katsuragi and was known for his magic. The Outside Junior Fifth Rank Lower Grade Chieftain of Korea Hirotari apprenticed himself to him. Later he came to envy his Master's

powers and slandered him, saying that Ozunu was leading the people astray. As a result, Ozunu was exiled to a distant place. People say that Ozunu enslaved the gods and demons and forced them to draw his water and gather his firewood. If they did not follow his orders, he bound them with spells.

This brief notation raises many questions. What manner of man was this "E no Kimi Ozunu"? How did he "lead the people astray," and why did this result in his exile? Some answers are suggested by the political and religious situation in seventh- and eighth-century Japan. This period was characterized by the continuing effort of the ruling Yamato clan to centralize and rationalize the power of the state. They looked to T'ang China for a model of government organization and adopted Buddhism as a state-sponsored religion. Buddhism was so closely allied with the state, in fact, that the temples themselves were organized under a government bureau. Priests were examined and promoted by the government and held bureaucratic rank, while the state maintained strict control over their activities. No one was allowed to become a priest or wear priestly attire without official approval from the imperial court. Thus, no matter how earnestly one desired to practice the Buddhist path, it was quite difficult to enter the priesthood. As a result, many "lay priests" took their religious practices into the mountain forests, far from the centers of population. This trend made the government so apprehensive that it promulgated more and more regulations—against preaching the doctrine outside the temples, against fortune-telling and sorcery, and against healing with unorthodox practices. Only officially recognized monks and nuns were allowed to make retreats in the mountain forests, and then only under the close supervision of their superiors and on condition that they would not mix with the populace.

In the eyes of the officials, the primary function of Buddhism as the state-established religion was to protect the state, to buttress government authority. Religious practice outside the state structure was viewed as potentially inimical to its interests. Most threatening to officials was any charismatic figure who might attract to himself the loyalties of the common people. And since the religious needs of ordinary people were not addressed by official state Buddhism, they were indeed vulnerable to the influence of "holy men" who professed to have the power of performing miracles and of controlling the invisible forces of chaos and destruction that threatened their meager existence. The authorities feared with some justification that such a man might stir up the people, threatening the peace and order of society. And there is evidence that many such figures did practice in the mountains during this period despite strict government regulations. The vigilance of the Yamato government to detect and crush out any charismatic holy man provides a likely context for the *Chronicle*'s statement that the ascetic on Mount Katsuragi was "leading the people astray."

Still, the authorities must have been impressed with En early on, for one of their own officials apprenticed himself to the magician on Mount Katsuragi. Historical records indicate that this man, Hirotari, was a member of the Bureau of

Court Physicians. (Later, in the year 732, he is said to have become director of that bureau.) Hirotari was an exorcist or physician (*jugonshi*), whose role was to expel evil influences through the chanting of incantations. He must have been seeking new and effective techniques through his apprenticeship with En the Ascetic, but apparently he or his superiors concluded that this man and his practices were dangerous. So En the Ascetic was banished to a distant island. Perhaps, too, the authorities felt especially nervous to have him practicing his powerful magic on Mount Katsuragi so close to Fujiwara, the capital of the reigning Emperor Mommu.

What precisely were En the Ascetic's religious practices? The *Chronicles* refer succinctly to the "magic" he practiced on Mount Katsuragi, but they do not identify it as belonging to any particular tradition. Japanese scholars agree that it is impossible to determine the exact nature of his practices, but they surmise that he (and others like him in that age) engaged in some combination of native and imported magic—perhaps a mixture of indigenous Japanese shamanistic practices with early Esoteric Buddhist rituals and elements of religious Taoism. Whatever the nature of En the Ascetic's knowledge and techniques, however, they must have been in some sense new or unique, or he must have demonstrated particular efficacy in their use, to have drawn so much attention to himself.

Ascertaining En the Ascetic's precise religious lineage may be problematic, but clearly he must be discussed in the context of the mountains of Japan and religious practices in those mountains. The *Chronicles of Japan Continued* state that En the Ascetic practiced his "magic" on Mount Katsuragi, which lies on the western rim of the Yamato Plain, the political and cultural center of Japan for centuries. And this theme of religious practice on sacred mountains is the ground bass that runs through every variation of En the Ascetic's story over the centuries.

Japanese religious practice drew from many sources, accommodating both the imported religion of Buddhism and the native Shintō tradition, while accepting Chinese yin-yang beliefs and other aspects of religious Taoism. Yet perhaps far more important in the religious life of the Japanese people than any sectarian label or doctrine are certain constant themes, such as that of mountains and the many beliefs and practices associated with them. Scholar Kishimoto Hideo describes two very different, indeed precisely opposite, attitudes toward mountains in Japanese religious practice—one "symbolic," the other "behavioral." In the first, the mountain functions as a symbol in the mind of the people. They do not approach it, and the mountain may in fact be tabooed so that no ordinary person may set foot upon it. This view of the mountain may relate to the belief that agricultural deities come down to the fields during the growing season and then return to the mountain to dwell there on high until the following spring. Another reason for revering the mountain from a distance is the belief that certain mountains shelter the souls of the dead. This "symbolic" sense of the mountain as sacred, inhibitive, and to be worshipped from afar may reflect ancient, indigenous traditions.

By contrast, the "behavioral" attitude toward mountains regards them not as objects of worship but rather as training grounds for attaining religious ideals.

Here, people do not keep their distance from the mountains but climb the steepest peaks and brave the deepest and most threatening recesses to undertake arduous ascetic practices. From the earliest accounts, En the Ascetic is described as performing his practices on the mountain, so clearly he represents this more active attitude. This is consistent also with his later adoption as the patriarch of Shugendō, whose practitioners either traveled about to various sacred mountains to perform their practices or secluded themselves on one particular mountain, where they cultivated ascetic disciplines to attain "Dharma power" and the ability to subjugate evil demons.

As the legend evolved, the name of En the Ascetic became linked with one after another mountainous region in Japan. The earliest instance of this linkage is seen in the second written account of his story, found in a collection of tales entitled *Miraculous Stories of Karmic Retribution of Good and Evil in Japan* (*Nihonkoku genpō zen'aku nihon ryōiki,* commonly abbreviated as *Nihon ryōiki*). The monk Kyōkai (or Keikai) of Yakushiji Temple in Nara compiled this collection, completing his work in the year 823. He writes that En the Ascetic

> gathered the multitude of gods and demons and exhorted them, saying, "You are to build a bridge reaching all the way from Mount Katsuragi to Mount Kinpu in Yamato." The deities were distressed at this, and during the reign of the emperor at the Fujiwara Palace, the Great Deity Hitokotonushi of Mount Katsuragi became enraged and slandered him, saying: "E no Ubasoko [or Ubasoku, an unordained Buddhist ascetic,] is scheming to overthrow the emperor." . . . The Great Deity Hitokotonushi was bound in a spell cast by En the Ascetic and has not to this day been released from that spell.

Mount Kinpu, or Kinpusen, here refers to the entire mountainous region south of the Yamato Plain, including the modern Ōmine and Yoshino. This area had long been known both as a beautifully secluded spot and as the home of the deities who provide water for the fields of the Yamato Plain. Located close to the imperial capitals—which, until the Nara period (710–784), moved at the beginning of each new reign—these mountains had been the destination of imperial excursions since the third century. Some of the early emperors even built detached palaces there. The beauty of the area was idealized in poetry and sometimes even described as the abode of Taoist immortals. Eventually, Mount Kinpu came to be regarded as the Pure Land of the Bodhisattva Maitreya (Miroku Bosatsu).

Moreover, with the introduction of metal techniques in the eighth century, the area's natural resources began to be developed, and it was imagined—and subsequently rumored as true—that there was gold to be found in these mountains. This very likely was the source of the name Kinpu, meaning "golden peak." Thus it was that this mountainous area—known variously as Kinpusen, Yoshino, or Ōmine, famous for its lovely natural environment, rumored as a source of gold, important for its historic connections to the imperial house, and considered to be the realm of Taoist immortals and the site of Buddhist pure lands—came eventually to be regarded as sacred, as a destination for religious pilgrimages.

The awe in which these mountains were held was enhanced by various religious and social taboos enforced in the area. Women were prohibited from a very early period, and those men who desired to enter the mountains were required to conform to strict rules of abstinence and purification. The peaks of Kinpusen had a particular sanctity that was not to be violated. Even in later times, Shugendō practices undertaken in these mountains were perceived as having greater efficacy than those performed elsewhere.

The bridge episode in *Miraculous Stories* thus linked En the Ascetic, a mountain holy man celebrated for his magical powers, with Kinpusen, a mountainous area renowned for its sacred character. This is the first of many tales that connect the name of En the Ascetic to particular mountains and mountain temples throughout the country. From another perspective, En's confrontation with the gods over the bridge serves to illustrate the simple statement of the *Chronicles of Japan Continued* that the magician of Katsuragi had the power to enslave gods and demons, and to bind them in spells when they failed to follow his orders.

Most Heian period tales identify the deity who refuses to work on the bridge in the daylight for fear of being seen by human beings as Hitokotonushi, the local deity of Mount Katsuragi, who, despite being identified as male in earlier sources, is depicted as a female deity in Heian narratives of En the Ascetic. The Ascetic, in his wrath at this insubordination, casts Hitokotonushi into the bottom of a deep valley and binds her there under a spell. The deity then takes revenge by possessing someone in the imperial court and, through that medium, informing authorities that En the Ascetic is plotting treason. (Hitokotonushi here takes over Hirotari's role as the slanderer.) This precipitates the Ascetic's arrest and banishment to an island near Mount Fuji, far from the capital. Later storytellers during the Heian period adhere rather closely to a fairly standard narrative of the legend, depicting the confrontation about the bridge, the binding of Hitokotonushi under a spell in the valley, the Ascetic's exile in Izu, his pardon and release, and his experiences on the Asian continent after flying away from Japan.

Toward the close of the Heian period (ca. 1120), the collection *Tales of Times Now Past* (*Konjaku monogatari*) introduces a new element into its version of the story. Here, En the Ascetic—through the power of religious devotions performed on Mount Kinpu—is vouchsafed the vision of a new divine figure, the Bodhisattva Zaō, who becomes an important guardian deity for mountain ascetics. This wrathful figure, burning with rage, is deemed particularly appropriate for a protector of religious practitioners in the perilous mountain heights.

En the Ascetic's vision of the Bodhisattva Zaō in *Tales of Times Now Past* is a harbinger of developments of his legend during the Kamakura period (1185–1333). Kamakura versions of the tale do repeat Heian storytellers' motifs, but they also add new, predominantly religious themes that are designed to emphasize and legitimize En the Ascetic as the model for lay monks practicing austerities in the sacred mountains. Typical is the account in a mid-Kamakura (1257) Buddhist tale collection entitled *One Hundred Cases of Karmic Origins, Personally Gathered* (*Shishū hyaku innen shū*) by Jūshin, a Buddhist priest of the Pure Land sect. This narrative includes a very important statement revealing that, at least by the middle of the Kamakura period, mountain practitioners consciously modeled themselves on the image of this mountain holy man: "If one were to inquire into the origins of the lonely, perilous practices of the *yamabushi*, these all arose out of actions first taken by En the Ascetic."

The account of En the Ascetic in *One Hundred Cases of Karmic Origins* seems almost a miscellany of everything the author had ever heard about this man. Clearly the writer's priority, though, is to emphasize the Ascetic as a religious figure, a paradigm for practitioners of mountain austerities. The focus has shifted away from the magician of Katsuragi's confrontation with a local deity named Hitokotonushi. More important is the demonstration of En's credentials as a holy man—auspicious signs appearing from the time he was in his mother's womb, his faith from the age of seven in the Three Treasures of Buddhism (the Buddha, the teachings, and the community), his ascetic practices on the many different sacred mountains of Japan, and his legitimate place in the transmission of the teachings. The text claims that En was the first to "open" sacred mountains all over Japan for religious practices, in particular manifesting many wonders in Ōmine, "the most sacred peaks in Japan." In these mountains he left 120 hermitages, built a three-story stone edifice at Jinzen, encountered his own skeleton from his third lifetime, and set up one thousand stone monuments as an offering for his parents' enlightenment.

Perhaps most important from a Shugendō point of view is the account of how En the Ascetic received the Esoteric teachings from the great Buddhist patriarch Nāgārjuna during his retreat at the waterfall on Mount Mino'o. This episode acquired great significance in the tradition, for it established the Ascetic's legitimate place in the transmission of the teachings. Moreover, he is said to have appeared on various mountains as different manifestations of the Buddha—as the Bodhisattva Hōki on Mount Kongō, and elsewhere as the Peacock King.

In the author's eagerness to establish the religious credentials of En the Ascetic as prototype and patriarch of all ascetic practitioners in the sacred mountains of Japan, he even downplays the single (probably) historical fact—that imperial authorities had sent the man named En no Ozunu into exile on an island far to the east, off the Izu Peninsula. This event is mentioned almost as an afterthought, near the end of Jūshin's account in *One Hundred Cases of Karmic Origins, Personally Gathered*. Ironically, modern Japanese scholars seem to agree that the historical core of all that was told and written about En the Ascetic very likely boils down to these few bare facts: that in the late seventh century there was a man living on Mount Katsuragi in the Yamato area who was particularly adept at certain magical practices, and that he was for some reason sent into exile by imperial order in the year 699 C.E.

The translation is based on Jūshin, *En no Gyōja no koto* (En the Ascetic), in *Shishū hyaku innen shū*, in *Dainihon bukkyō zensho* 148 (Tokyo: Bussho Kankōkai, 1912): 136–140.

Further Reading

H. Byron Earhart, "Shugendō, the Traditions of En no Gyōja, and Mikkyō Influence," in Kōyasan Daigaku, ed., *Studies of Esoteric Buddhism and Tantrism* (Kōyasan: Kōyasan University, 1965): 297–317; Ichirō Hori, "On the Concept of *Hijiri* (Holy Man)," *Numen* 5 (1958): 128–160, 199–232; Linda Klepinger Keenan, "En no Gyōja: The Legend of a Holy Man in Twelve Centuries of Japanese Literature," including an English translation of the drama "En the Ascetic" by Tsubouchi Shōyō, Ph.D. dissertation, University of Wisconsin-Madison, 1989; Hideo Kishimoto, "The Role of Mountains in the Religious Life of the Japanese People," in *Proceedings of the Ninth International Congress for the History of Religions, 1958* (Tokyo: Maruzen, 1960): 545–549; Paul L. Swanson and Royall Tyler, eds., "Shugendō and Mountain Religion in Japan," special issue of *Japanese Journal of Religious Studies* 16, 2–3 (Summer 1989); Royall Tyler, ed. and tr., "The Wizard of the Mountains," in *Japanese Tales* (New York: Pantheon, 1987): 127–130.

One Hundred Cases of Karmic Origins, Personally Gathered: En the Ascetic

We respectfully relate that one hundred years or more after the Buddha's teaching crossed into our realm, from the end of the reign of Emperor Tenji and into the reigns of Empress Jitō and Emperor Mommu, there lived a remarkable ascetic. This was the Lay Priest En. His father was Takakamo no Makagemaro, his mother Shirataume Totokimaro of the same clan. He was born in Yabako Village in Upper Kazuraki (Katsuragi) district in the land of Yamato, where in later times was built Chihara Temple.

En was possessed of uncanny qualities from the time he was in his mother's womb. From the age of seven, he took refuge in the Three Treasures. As a young man of nineteen he repaired to Mino'o Falls in the land of Settsu, where he accumulated merit by assiduously performing ascetic practices—chanting mantras and sitting in meditation. He amassed power through his perseverance in these practices.

Before too many years passed, he effected the appearance of thirty-six Diamond princes [deities in the form of furious-looking boys] in billowing white clouds above the dragon cave. Thereafter, he devoted himself to the practice of the Buddhist teachings, renewing his wondrous powers again and again. Vowing to save and benefit sentient beings of the coming final age, he placed images of the Diamond princes in many locations: the so-called Fifteen Diamond Princes remain in Mino'o, the Eight Great Diamond Princes in Ōmine, and the Seven Diamond Princes in Kazuraki. However, for the peak called Not-Yet-Illumined, he pledged one Diamond prince for the future; in those days it had not yet taken form.

We respectfully relate that an amazing event occurred at Mino'o Falls. The Ascetic, borne up by his holy powers, entered from the head of the falls into the dragon cave in the cloud-wreathed rocky heights. After proceeding some distance into its innermost regions, he espied an exquisite scene, all golden and bejeweled, and bearing no resemblance to anything seen in this material world of Jambūdvīpa. Suddenly there was a Diamond gate. He knocked on the gate, and a voice answered from within.

The Ascetic responded, saying, "I am the Lay Priest En from Jambūdvīpa."

The voice within said, "Know you not? I am the Great King Tokuzen, and this is the Pure Land of Nāgārjuna."

Whereupon he opened the gate, and En went in and gazed about at this place. Neither thought nor speech could encompass it. By setting foot in that pure realm in his earthly frame, he was washed clean of defilement in body and mind alike. He met the Great Sage Nāgārjuna and was blessed with the means for salvation and equipped to follow the Buddha Path. Truly he was graced.

Further, En the Ascetic established the One Vehicle Enlightenment Temple on Golden Peak in Kumano (at the southern end of the Ōmine Mountains). He began going onto holy peaks here and there and was the first to set foot on the holy mountains of many districts. With clouds for his shelter and a stone for his pillow, he reclined upon a mat of moss. If one were to inquire into the origins of the lonely, perilous practices of the *yamabushi*, these all arose out of actions first taken by En the Ascetic. All things in the beginning are admirable, but by the end of the corrupt age they tend to become unimaginably degraded. However, the example that he passed on to his descendants has not deteriorated in the least. There has not been one person in this whole country since the time the prayers were recited who has donned a monk's garments and implored the merciful protection of heaven, who has not fervently desired to forge a karmic linkage with the One Vehicle Wisdom peaks of the two mandalas, the Womb-store and Diamond mandalas. There are a great variety of circumstances in which to practice the Path of the Buddha, but the circumstances of the *yamabushi* are truly noble and awesome. They prize the unexcelled Way without regard for their own lives. Verily, what practice is the equal of their forsaking their lives in the mountain forests for the Way of the Buddha? None! And in particular, the one whose will to seek immortality was most profound was En the Ascetic. And thus, for over thirty years he dwelled in a stone grotto on Mount Kazuraki, covering himself with a cloak of wisteria and sustaining his life on pine needles. At last, having acquired merit, he rode upon a cloud of five colors and came to the contemplative retreats of the immortals.

Mount Kazuraki is the same as Mount Kongō. Because the Ascetic established a sacred precinct on this high mountain for the sake of the life to come, this miraculous peak became in its entirety *The Sutra of the Lotus of the Wonderful Dharma*. Thus it is that Mount Kazuraki is called "The Peak of the One Vehicle.". . .

And the mountains of Ōmine comprise the peaks of the two mandalas, the Womb-store and Diamond mandalas. The mountains known as Kumano comprise the Mandala of the Womb-store Realm (which presents the Buddha mind as cause for awakening), where provisional manifestations of the Buddhas have left their traces in twelve locations. Mount Kinpu is the Diamond Mandala (which presents the result of awakening), and there in thirty-eight places they have softened their light (to appear to humanity). That peak was not originally in the country of Japan; it was actually a mountain in the land of the Buddha's birth and came flying through the air to our realm and alighted here. The deities who have manifested themselves there are likewise protector deities from the land of the Buddha's birth. The original form of the manifestation of Kumano Shōshō Gongen is Amida Buddha, who is the main Buddha of the Lotus Section of the Karma Assembly in the Diamond Mandala. Kongō Zaō is the Buddha Śākyamuni. Śākyamuni is also called Vairocana, who is the Great Sun of the Diamond Realm. Thus, the mountains of Ōmine are the most sacred peaks in Japan. . . . Further, in these mountains the Ascetic left behind hermitages in 120 places. Three hundred eighty immortals dwell therein.

At Jinzen [in Ōmine], there is a three-story stone edifice. The lowest level is the Amida Mandala; the middle level is the Mandala of the Womb-store Realm; while the top level is the Mandala of the Diamond Realm. On every level is a great dais. Carefully arranged upon the stone on each dais are ritual Diamond bell posts with strings of the five colors.

We respectfully relate that in the cave of the immortals there is an old skeleton. All of its joints are still intact and have not fallen apart. It lies on its back facing upward, grasping in its left hand a single-pronged Diamond pounder and holding in its right hand the sword of wisdom. It is more than nine feet long. It has a withered tree growing up through its eye. Upon seeing these things (the Diamond pounder and the sword), the Ascetic tried to take them. When he tried with force to budge them, they were as solid as a mountain and could not be removed.

He petitioned the gods and Buddhas, and his guardian deity granted this revelation in a dream: "These are your remains from a previous life. You have been traversing these mountain peaks for seven lifetimes already since you first received life. In your first three lives you left behind your skeletons. Your stature in the first life was over seven feet. In your second life it was over eight feet, and in the third life more than nine feet. This is your third skeleton. If you wish to ascertain the truth of this, intone the Mystic Formula of the Thousand-hand Kannon five times. And then if you pray the *Heart Sutra* three times, you should be able to take these things."

Both hands of the skeleton then opened immediately and, as he had been told in his dream, this also opened the three-story stone edifice that he had constructed during his first, second, and third lifetimes.

Further, this Ascetic had long practiced the teaching [and chanted the mantra] of the Peacock King, readily manifesting its mystical powers. Some say that the Ascetic perfected the "Mantra of Compassionate Salvation" at the age of seven and recited it one hundred thousand times every day.

It might be asked: When En the Ascetic was in the land, the mantra teachings had not yet even reached T'ang China, let alone Japan. How is it then that the ceremonies of the Ascetic and the rituals of Ōmine are essentially in accord with the mantra teachings? To reply: In contrast to those of lofty intentions, whether of high rank or low, En the Ascetic is celebrated as a sage for all eons. Thus how could he entirely forget his previous existences? How could he not practice teachings that are eternal through all time?

All in all, the Lay Priest En appeared on Mount Kinpu as the Great Sage Itokuten; on Mount Kongō as the Bodhisattva Hōki; and it is also said that in some places he took form as the Peacock King.

This was a remarkable ascetic—he ran floating across the ocean's surface as though treading upon dry land and soared among the mountain peaks like a bird in flight. Moreover, the Ascetic was not shallow in his resolve to repay the kindnesses of his mother and father. During his lifetime he built a temple to make an outward gift of his sincere respect and to repay the kindnesses of his father and mother. One hears also of the offering he made to Taima Temple. . . . During the reign of Emperor Temmu, . . . for the sake of his parents' enlightenment, En donated to Taima Temple several hundred acres of mountain forests and fields that he had inherited from his ancestors. In the Main Hall of his father's temple the Ascetic deposited within the sixteen-foot statue of Maitreya a small gilded bronze image of the Peacock King, who for many years had been his guardian deity.

The Outside Junior Fifth Rank Lower Grade Chieftain of Korea Hirotari initially revered the Ascetic but later came to envy him. The courtier slandered him, saying, "This fellow has the evil look of someone who is sure to agitate the realm. He is bound to be bad for the nation, for the ruler, and for the people."

Another time the Ascetic called to account the Great Deity Hitokotonushi of Kazuraki, for she had utterly failed to finish building the stone bridge of Kume. He bound her seven times around with silky floss from the sacred *sakaki* tree and left her at the bottom of a ravine. As a result, the deity took possession of someone in the imperial palace and in this way reported the matter to the ruler. This was during the reign of Emperor Mommu.

The great king dispatched emissaries to arrest En the Ascetic, but he flew up into the sky so they were not able to do so. Then they went to take his mother Shirataume into custody. The Ascetic appeared at the Wisteria Court and—his heart taken captive by his mother's sad plight—he begged them to arrest him in her place, thus exemplifying the bond of compassion between parent and child.

Nonetheless, in the fifth month of the third year of Emperor Mommu's reign, he was exiled to the island at Izu. In the daytime, in obedience to the sovereign, he dwelt on the island performing his religious practices. At night, he flew over to Mount Fuji in the land of Suruga to practice. After three years passed, in the fifth month of the first year of Taihō, they summoned him. Slowly he made his way toward the imperial court and then flew up into the air.

He wished to leave the country but regretted that he would not then be able to repay his parents' kindnesses in their homeland, so he erected one thousand stone monuments at Jinzen in Ōmine, dedicating these to them on Kūhachi Peak. . . . The records of the ancients report that after that, when the Ascetic was about to leave the country of Japan, his mother Shirataume was distressed at parting from her loved one. The Ascetic, too, was at a loss, loath to think of the separation of mother and son. Unable to forsake his mother, he had her ride in a bowl while he sat upon a woven grass mat, and they were transported ten thousand *ri* across the billowing waves to the kingdom of Silla (Korea).

At that time, the Buddhist teacher Dōshō of our realm had crossed over to T'ang China under imperial orders to seek the Buddhist teachings. He had gone to Silla at the invitation of the five hundred Silla "tigers" and was teaching the *Lotus Sutra* deep in the mountains there. At one session, a participant raised a question in the language of Japan. The Venerable Dōshō asked who he was. He answered, "I am the Lay Priest En from the country of Japan. I left my country because the hearts of the gods are unruly and the hearts of the inhabitants are defiled and confused. But even gods and immortals find it difficult to forsake the bond between parent and child, so my mother has accompanied me to these foreign regions. And since the remains of my loving father are still in Japan, I now travel back and forth to that country regularly. I came to hear you speak because you are a spiritual leader from my homeland."

When Dōshō came down from the speaker's platform to seek him out, the voice was audible but he did not see anyone. . . .

Another account says that the Ascetic prayed, and the figure of Śākyamuni appeared. "How in these latter days can he benefit the sentient beings of the defiled world in *this guise?*" the Ascetic wondered, and he prayed again. Then appeared the wrathful form of Zaō. The Ascetic offered him great reverence and accepted him in faith. He who long ago expounded the *Sutra of the Lotus of the Wonderful Dharma* on Vulture Peak now is revealed in the body of Zaō on Mount Kinpu. And his attendant protectors are Fudō and Bishamon. We respectfully relate that Zaō's embodiment is a stone image that is three feet high on Mount Kinpu; on Mount Kongō it is five feet high, in a stone box enshrined deep down in holy ground.

— 33 —

The Founding of Mount Kōya and Kūkai's
Eternal Meditation

George J. Tanabe, Jr.

Mount Kōya, the headquarters of the Shingon sect, is one of the most beautiful of the monastic complexes in Japan. Situated high in the mountains of Wakayama Prefecture south of Nara, Mount Kōya can be reached by train and cable car or by a long, winding road through exceptionally verdant mountains. The monastery consists of dozens of temples scattered in a heavily forested, flat-bottomed bowl several miles across. Ancient cryptomeria trees as straight and majestic as redwoods surround the ornate temples and give to the artifice of sacred architecture the natural sanctity of the mountain. Splendid in isolation from the distant valleys of farms and factories, Mount Kōya is nevertheless crawling with people.

The visitors, mostly pilgrims, come from all over Japan. In this time of modern "tourist Buddhism," most of the temples, in fact, function as inns providing food and lodging for the faithful. They come to sightsee, but they do so as people of faith, filled with unquestioning belief in the sacred virtues of the mountain and its monasteries. Specifically, they believe in the holiness and power of Kūkai (774–835), the founder of the Shingon sect, who is more popularly known as Daishi-sama, a contraction of his posthumous title Kōbō Daishi, the Great Master and Propagator of the Teaching. Whereas believers of other sects chant praises to certain buddhas or scriptures, the Shingon faithful chant the name of their savior, Kōbō Daishi. He is their god.

The apotheosis of Kūkai began shortly after his death when admiring disciples expressed their adoration by writing legends of the virtues and miraculous feats of their master. Unlike fairy tales, which are totally fictional about make-believe people and places, legends center around real personalities and locations. There is a certain veracity to legends, at least to the degree to which they deal with real facts. These facts, of course, are then surrounded with a great deal of fabrication. The stories, however, do more than merely entertain by exaggeration; they make serious arguments as well.

It is these legends that define a good part of what people understand to be the content of their religion. The sublime doctrines studied by scholars and monks seldom reach the popular understanding, and the ordinary believers, if asked about the teachings of their sect, will often reply with reference to legends rather than philosophies. The stream of the philosophical teachings does not always converge with the rivers of popular belief, but it would be a mistake to think that their divergence is due to their having different sources. It is not the case that the popular legends, so filled with miracle and magic, originate from the unsophisticated minds of peasants and farmers and then are only tolerated by educated scholar/priests who know better than to accept those amazing fictions as facts. The origins of the legends can be traced, and the trail leads back to the scholar/priests themselves. They concocted the legends and propagated them to the people, who were the recipients, not the originators. The propagation of these legends was immensely effective: the same stories are still being told and are still attracting the faithful in large numbers.

The temples and shops at Mount Kōya sell a huge number of comic books, banners, plaques, and other paraphernalia that depict three legends in particular. The first of these enduring stories speaks of how Kūkai was led to Mount Kōya by two dogs loaned to him by a hunter. The second legend tells of how Kūkai, led by the dogs, arrived at Mount Kōya only to find hanging from a pine tree (a scion of which still grows at the main compound) a three-pronged ritual implement he had thrown from China. The third is perhaps the most important and claims that Kūkai did not really die but is still alive in his mausoleum (Oku no In), sitting in eternal meditation. The stories of the dogs and the pine tree were first written by a scholar/monk in *A Record of the Practices and the Establishment of the Temple of the Diamond Peak* (*Kongōbuji konryū shugyō engi,* 968). This text, from which the following translation is made, tells of the founding of the Temple of the Diamond Peak, the main compound at Mount Kōya, and weaves all three legends along with a variety of other stories into a more or less coherent account.

The stories are entertaining, but all have serious points to make. While Kūkai was granted the land on Mount Kōya by an imperial decree, the exact boundaries were not fixed. By the eleventh century, when this text was written, the monastic complex had grown, and neighboring landlords complained of encroachments into their properties. The story of the hunter's dogs makes it clear that Kūkai did not wander into the place by accident, and, furthermore, the king of the mountain as well as the resident Shintō deities gave the property to Kūkai. The temple's claim to the lands it occupied was therefore legitimate, and even preordained, as the story of the ritual implement in the pine tree attempts to argue. The land, which only ostensibly belonged to a Shintō deity, was originally the "ancient place of an old buddha." In the hands of Buddhist monks, the land is now possessed by its rightful owners and is vitalized by the power and sanctity of Kūkai, who still reigns over Mount Kōya. The conclusion of the arguments is clear: Mount Kōya was chosen in a divinely special way to be Kūkai's monastery and continues to exude its power and virtue through the majesty of its trees, the loftiness of its mountains, the sanctity of its temples, the purifying practices of its priests, and the living presence of its saint.

The stories are engaging, and their arguments are persuasive to scores of people who take them seriously and go to Kōyasan to worship and make offerings. Take away the philosophy and Mount Kōya will still thrive, but remove its legends and the monastery will lose its call to the people.

The text for this translation of *Kongōbuji konryū shugyō engi* is from Hase Hōshū, ed., *Kōbō Daishi den zenshū* 1 (Tokyo: Pitaka, 1977): 53–55. Authorship of the text is traditionally atributed to the scholar/monk Ninkai (951–1046), but since the work is clearly dated for the year 968, when Ninkai was only seventeen years old, scholars doubt the authenticity of this attribution. Kongōbuji is the name of the main temple that still serves as the headquarters of the Shingon sect at Mount Kōya.

Further Reading

Yoshito S. Hakeda, *Kūkai: Major Works* (New York: Columbia University Press, 1972); Edward Kamens, tr., *The Three Jewels: A Study and Translation of Minamoto Tamenori's* Sanbōe (Ann Arbor: Center for Japanese Studies, University of Michigan, 1988); Robert E. Morrell, tr., *Sand and Pebbles: The Tales of Mujū Ichien, a Voice for Pluralism in Kamakura Buddhism* (Albany: State University of New York Press, 1985); Kyoko M. Nakamura, tr., *Miraculous Tales from the Japanese Buddhist Tradition*: The Nihon Ryōiki *of the Monk Kyōkai* (Cambridge: Harvard University Press, 1973); Marian Ury, tr., *Tales of Times Now Past: Sixty-two Stories from a Medieval Japanese Collection* (Berkeley: University of California Press, 1979).

A Record of the Practices and the Establishment of the Temple of the Diamond Peak

In midsummer of the year 816, Kūkai left the capital to travel beyond it. In Uchi County in the province of Yamato, he met a hunter, who was deep red in appearance and stood about eight feet in height. He wore a short-sleeved blue coat and had long bones and thick muscles. He carried a bow and arrows strapped to his body, and he was accompanied by dogs, one large and one small. He saw Kūkai pass by and asked some questions. Kūkai stopped and also inquired about certain details.

The hunter said, "I am a dog keeper from the southern mountains. I know of a mountain area of about ten thousand square measures, and in that area there is a marvelous flat plain. The place is full of mysterious signs. You should take up residence there; I will help you accomplish this. I will release my dogs and have them run ahead or you will get lost."

Kūkai thought silently about this and proceeded. They stopped for a rest when they came to a large river on the boundaries of Kii Province. Here they met a man who lived in the mountains. Upon being told the details of the place, he said, "South of here there is a flat, swampy plain. The mountains range on three sides and the entry way from the southwest is open. Myriad rivers flow to the east and terminate by converging into one. During the day there are strange clouds, and at night there are always mysterious lights." Upon further investigation, it turned out to be directly south of Ito-no-kōri in Kii Province.

The next day, he followed this mountain man, and they arrived at the swampy plain a short distance away. As he examined the place, he thought that this certainly was the spot where he should build a monastery.

The mountain man secretly said to Kūkai, "I am the king of this mountain, and I donate the land under my control to you in order to increase my power and blessings. I am accustomed to mountains and rivers and remain distant from the activities of men. Fortunately I have met a saint, much to my merit."

The next day they went to Ito-no-kōri and Kūkai thought, "When the Sacred King Who Turns the Wheel of the Buddhist Teaching (tenrinjōō; cakravartin) ascends the throne, he takes a river willow and offers it to the holy men. If, however, they do not grant him a single iron needle or a single blade of grass, then he is in error."

Therefore, in the middle of the sixth month, Kūkai submitted his request to the emperor for a place for meditation. He built one or two thatched huts. He had myriad things to do and did not have much time, but he managed to go up once a year. On one side of the path in the mountains there was a swamp of about ten square measures. It was the shrine of the mountain king, the Great August Deity Niu. Today it is called the palace of Amano.

The first time Kūkai ascended the mountain, he spent a night in the area of the shrine. He received an oracle saying, "I have been a follower of the way of the Shintō deities, and I have hoped for power and blessings for a long time. Now you have come to this place, much to my great fortune. In the past when I was a human being, the deity Kekunisuera-no-mikoto gave me about ten thousand square measures of land for houses. The boundaries are south to Nankai, north to Yamato River, east to Yamato Province, and west to the valley of Mount Ōjin. I wish to donate this to you for all eternity as an expression of my belief."

In addition, Kūkai was granted an official decree.

While they were clearing the trees in order to build a monastery, they found the three-pronged ritual implement that he had thrown from China hanging majestically from a tree. Kūkai was filled with joy. Then he realized that this was a place suitable for the Esoteric teaching, just as the mountain king, the owner of the land, had said.

At the spot where they were digging in the ground, they uncovered a jewelled sword from beneath the earth. An imperial decree ordered that it be examined, but there was a curse. Diviners did a reading of the curse and found out that the sword should be put into a copper tube and returned to its place. The interpretation of this was that the non-Buddhist protector, the Great August Deity, regretted its loss.

Kūkai said to all of his disciples, "I think I will be leaving this world sometime during the third month of next year. To the great worthy Shinnen (804–891), I bequeath the Temple of the Diamond Peak, the construction of which is still not complete. Since, however, the efforts of this great worthy alone will not suffice, the great worthy Jitsue (785–847) should help him.

"Initially I thought that I might be able to live in this world for a hundred years, propagating the Esoteric Buddhist teachings and attracting ordinary people. Meditation masters are particularly possessed about this, but my own vow is sufficient. You should know that I gave no regard for my own life as I crossed ten thousand waves of the ocean and traveled over a thousand miles to seek the Buddha's teaching. The teaching of the way I have transmitted to you will protect and uphold this place. It will bring peace to the country and nourish the people."

On the fifteenth day of the third month of the year 835, Kūkai said, "I expect to enter the state of eternal meditation in the early morning of the twenty-first day. From now on I will not resort to human food. You should not shed tears of sadness, and do not wear mourning clothes. While I am in eternal meditation, I will be in the heaven of the future Buddha Maitreya, the compassionate one, in whose presence I shall serve. After more than five billion six hundred million years have passed, the compassionate one will descend to earth. At that time I will surely accompany Maitreya, and I will be able to see my old places. Do not let this Diamond Peak fall into neglect. Outwardly it appears that this place is the property of the mountain king Niu, but I have requested this imperial deity to entrust it to me. What no one knows, however, is that this is the ancient place of an old buddha. All the deities of the Diamond and the Matrix mandalas were assembled and enshrined here. To look at a site on this mountain is to know the majesty of its appearance. To hear its sounds is to hear explanations of the compassionate wrath of the deities. My future worth will be a million. Although people will not know my face in person, those who see an elder from one of these temples or who spend some time on this mountain will surely be able to surmise my intentions. When I see that my teaching is not doing well, I will mingle with the black-robed monks to promote my teaching. This is not a matter of my own attachments but is simply to propagate the teachings and that is all."

In the early morning hours of the twenty-first day of the third month of the year 835, Kūkai sat in the lotus position, formed the ritual hand gesture of the Great Sun Buddha (Mahāvairocana), and peacefully entered the state of eternal meditation.

For ten consecutive days services were held four times a day during which his disciples chanted the name of Maitreya. His entry into meditation simply meant that he had closed his eyes and did not speak. In all other respects he was like a living person. He was sixty-two years old at the time. Since he was [still living] like an ordinary person, no funeral was performed and he was positioned in a dignified manner. According to ordinary custom, memorial services were carried out every week for seven weeks. When his disciples looked upon him, they saw that the color of his face had not faded, and that his hair and beard had grown long. Therefore they shaved him and took care of his clothing. They closed off the stone structure and people had to get permission to enter it. They asked a stone mason to build a tombstone on top of it to represent the five elements, and they placed a book of Sanskrit mantras in it. They also built a jewelled pagoda on top of the structure and enshrined some relics of the Buddha in it. These matters were all arranged by Abbot Shinnen.

Sometime around 852 during the reign of Emperor Montoku, Abbot Shinzei (800–860) petitioned the court to grant Kūkai the rank of high abbot. In 921, during the reign of Emperor Daigo, the court granted Kūkai the title Great Master and Propagator of the Teaching (Kōbō Daishi) in response to a request submitted by Abbot Kangen (853–915).

— 34 —

Legends, Miracles, and Faith in Kōbō Daishi and the Shikoku Pilgrimage

Ian Reader

Pilgrimages have, since at least the Heian era, been a major area of religious activity in Japan. Numerous pilgrimage routes, mostly associated with Buddhist temples, but some with important Shinto shrines, have flourished, including the pilgrimage to the Shinto shrines of Ise, which in peak years during the Tokugawa period attracted several million pilgrims; the Saikoku pilgrimage in western Japan in which the pilgrim visits thirty-three temples dedicated to the bodhisattva Kannon; and the Shikoku pilgrimage, a nine-hundred mile route around the island of Shikoku that takes the pilgrim to eighty-eight temples and is focused on the miracle-working popular Buddhist figure Kōbō Daishi. Besides these pilgrimages, many smaller, regional pilgrimage routes with thirty-three or eighty-eight sites and modeled on either the Saikoku or Shikoku pilgrimages have developed from the mid-Tokugawa period onward.

Pilgrimage is an activity that manifests virtually every aspect of Japanese religious behavior—from the intensely ascetic to the touristic—and the experiences, devotions, motivations, and activities of pilgrims have ranged across a broad spectrum. Pilgrims have set out on pilgrimages to seek cures for diseases, to expiate sins, to venerate deities, Buddhas, and other holy figures of worship, and to petition them and pray for benefits and rewards, both in this life and in terms of salvation after death. At the same time many pilgrims have been motivated by more touristic motives and by the need or desire to escape from their everyday environment, travel, let off steam, and experience new places.

Such themes also permeate contemporary pilgrimage, and many of the routes popular in earlier eras have continued to flourish in the modern day. There has been a growth, in the modern era, in the numbers of pilgrims traveling routes such as Shikoku, for the availability of mass transportation has opened up the possibilities of pilgrimages to far places to greater numbers than ever before. Nowadays, while some pilgrims in Shikoku still go by foot in the time-honored way, most make use of modern means of travel such as cars and buses.

Perhaps no pilgrimage is better known in Japan, and none has a more devout following in contemporary times, than the eighty-eight-stage pilgrimage around the island of Shikoku. The pilgrimage is focused on the holy Buddhist figure Kōbō Daishi, who in pilgrimage lore watches over and protects each pilgrim. Kōbō Daishi ("the great teacher who spread the law of Buddhism") is the posthumous title of Kūkai (774–835), the ninth-century Buddhist monk who founded the Shingon Buddhist sect in Japan and the holy center of Mount Kōya. Legends have transformed Kōbō Daishi into a popular, miracle-working, saintlike figure who has become one of the most widely venerated of all figures in Japan. The legends were originally spread by itinerant priests from Kōya who traveled the country building up faith in the Daishi, as he came to be known, and they have subsequently entered folklore and contributed to the development of a whole genre of Kōbō Daishi legends (*Kōbō densetsu*) as well as to a powerful popular devotional cult. In the legends, Kōbō Daishi travels the countryside in the guise of an itinerant priest or pilgrim, dispensing miracles, curing the sick, bestowing benefits on the good and virtuous, especially those who help him and display charity, and punishing the greedy and mean.

One of the predominant manifestations of faith in the Daishi (*Daishi shinkō*) is the Shikoku pilgrimage, which takes the pilgrim around the island where the historical Kūkai was born and did some of his religious training. Although popular lore has it that Kūkai founded the pilgrimage himself, there is no historical evidence to suggest this. The pilgrimage appears to have developed over a number of centuries, out of the travels of ascetics from Kōya, who went to Shikoku to seek out sites connected with the holy founder of their religious institution. Gradually, from the twelfth through the seventeenth centuries, Shikoku came to be a major focus of Daishi devotion, and by the mid-seventeenth century a pilgrimage route around the island, incorporating various local temples and mountain religious centers, with eighty-eight sites in all (a number for which no reliable reason has been ascertained) had come into existence. It is from this era that the first pilgrims' diaries, guidebooks, and collections of pilgrimage legends and miracle tales date, including Shinnen's *Account of the Merits of the Shikoku Pilgrimage* (*Shikoku henro kudokuki*), the first collection of pilgrimage miracle stories.

The pilgrimage involves the pilgrim in a close relationship with the saint; indeed, Kōbō Daishi is believed to travel spiritually with each and every pilgrim, and it is common for pilgrims to wear a white pilgrimage shroud with four Japanese ideograms written on it, with the meaning "two people, one practice" (*dōgyō ninin*), representing the notion that the pilgrim is not alone but traveling with the saint. Pilgrims also carry a staff that symbolizes, among other things, the body of the saint, and they recite prayers to him along the way as well as at the temples, each of which has a special hall of worship dedicated to him. The immanent presence of Kōbō Daishi is strongly emphasized by pilgrimage lore and by pilgrims' tales, many of which (in both the written and oral traditions) are still widely told today. Indeed new oral stories of miraculous intercession continue to appear in the present day, and to be reported among pilgrims and Daishi devotees.

Legends and miracle tales are important expressions of religious faith and meaning, relevant for, and inspirational to, ordinary people. In the case of pilgrimage, such legends and miracle stories have inspired people to become pilgrims and offered them the hope of benefits that might be received through pilgrimage. They have also provided moral messages elevating the religious status of the pilgrim in the eyes of the people whom the pilgrim encounters, and upon whom, in premodern times, the pilgrim was often dependent for food and lodging. Since the pilgrim was closely associated with Kōbō Daishi, he or she could be seen in many ways as representing the saint, and such stories, by praising the saint and admonishing people to be kind to the pilgrims who were travelling with, or might even be, him (as some of the stories translated below demonstrate), served to emphasize this point. In the Tokugawa era, when many pilgrims were impoverished, often diseased people or even fugitives from their home villages, and in which legal authorities were rarely kindly disposed toward pilgrims, tending to view them as a drain on the local economy, this association with sanctity played an important part in strengthening the self-esteem of pilgrims.

The earliest collection of miracle stories outlining the merits and benefits of pilgrimage was compiled by Yūben Shinnen and published in 1690. Although few clear details of his life exist, we know that Shinnen was an ascetic and a devotee of Kōbō Daishi, who had contacts at Mount Kōya and spent much of his time in Shikoku, performing the pilgrimage at least ten, and possibly as many as twenty, times. He also devoted great efforts to developing and promoting the pilgrimage, collecting donations and using them to erect a number of stone pilgrimage route markers to guide pilgrims along the way, and establishing a small wayside shrine in Tosa (present-day Kōchi Prefecture) at which pilgrims could lodge. He also produced the first guidebook to the pilgrimage, the *Guide to the Shikoku Pilgrimage Route* (*Shikoku henro michishirube*) in 1687. This brief guide was supplemented by a longer one, *An Account of the Pilgrimage Sites of Shikoku* (*Shikoku henro reijōki*) written, based on Shinnen's information, by the scholar-priest Jakuhon from Mount Kōya, and published in 1689. This guidebook became a standard source of information on the pilgrimages for much of the Tokugawa era, and several editions were published. In 1690 Shinnen, seeking to emphasize what he saw as the wondrous and salvific nature of the pilgrimage (a theme that was less prominent in Jakuhon's more academic account), produced his collection of miraculous stories, with an introduction and comments appended by Jakuhon.

The *Account of the Merits of the Shikoku Pilgrimage* is a seminal work in the development of popular pilgrimage in Japan, and in the development of Daishi worship, for it is the first textualized source in which are heard the voices of pilgrims in Shikoku and the stories that they transmitted to each other, which underline their hopes and the religious perspectives within which they operated. It also served to promote the pilgrimage, encouraging people to give alms to pilgrims, and promoted a message vital to the success of any pilgrimage: the notion that pilgrimage is an efficacious means of directly encountering the holy.

Since the appearance of Shinnen's collection, others have appeared, and many temples in Shikoku have developed their own collections of miracle tales. In the present age, too, similar stories of wondrous happenings and of the benefits of pilgrimage appear in numerous published pilgrims' journals and in various contemporary collections of pilgrimage tales. Prominent among these has been a volume produced in 1984 by the Shikoku Reijōkai (Association of Pilgrimage Temples in Shikoku), which reflects many of the themes first expounded in Shinnen's text and demonstrates that pilgrimages speak to a continuing need for dramatic salvific experiences, and that the presence of Kōbō Daishi continues to be central to the experiences of pilgrims. The value of Shinnen's text is that his was the first and most influential of all such texts during the Tokugawa era, and it set the tone in terms of motifs for subsequent, and even modern, texts.

Shinnen's text revolves around a number of basic themes that emphasize the virtues of doing the pilgrimage, and of aiding pilgrims. It contains twenty-seven brief tales of merit, miracle, and retribution, many of which reiterate similar forms of events and meanings; nine representative tales, which encapsulate the themes of the whole work, are translated here. Many of the tales are undated and can be seen as stories from the wider corpus of Kōbō Daishi legends found throughout Japan but here are placed in the setting of the Shikoku pilgrimage. Others place in a textual form legends that had widely circulated among Shikoku pilgrims for some while prior to Shinnen's activities: the tale of Emon Saburō (tale 24) was in existence in the latter part of the sixteenth century (according to graffiti evidence found in Shikoku) and had been mentioned in two mid-seventeenth-century pilgrimage journals kept by priests. Shinnen's text, however, was the first to bring it in written form to a wider audience. Some of the stories are dated as occurring in the 1680s, in the years immediately preceding the publication of the text, and many of them report not just dates, but places and names as well.

They tell stories of the miraculous benefits that come to pilgrims, of how resolving to do the pilgrimage led to rapid cures of diseases or the acquisition of good fortune, and how the pious who help pilgrims and offer them alms are rewarded with blessings. They also tell of the retributions that befall those who insult or refuse to help pilgrims. In the tales, as is common in many other of the miracle stories found in Japanese religious literature, karmic rewards and retributions for one's deeds are direct and immediate; illnesses are rapidly cured and sins immediately punished. However, as the Emon Saburō story shows, with proper repentance and religious practice, even a sinner may attain absolution through pilgrimage and faith. Repentance may even lead to further spiritual rewards, as in tale 17, when the fisherman, having realized the folly of his meanness and the transient nature of the goods he coveted, repents and achieves a complete spiritual awakening.

In all the tales one sees the overarching presence of Kōbō Daishi and of the identification between him and the pilgrim. It is Kōbō Daishi, as an anonymous pilgrim, who is insulted or given alms, and it is through his power that the sinner is punished and the benefactor rewarded. It is also he who watches over and protects all pilgrims, as in tale 8, where he appears and gives succor to a stricken pilgrim, thereby giving emphasis to the notion, emblazoned on the pilgrims' clothing, that he walks with and guards over every pilgrim.

One reason why people went on pilgrimages to Shikoku in the Tokugawa era was to seek cures from disease. This was an important theme in an age without adequately developed medical practices, where recourse to spiritual healing and prayer was often the only hope. Stories of Daishi's miraculous intercessions, such as tale 2, which tells of how a man with a speech defect acquires the ability of speech after embarking on the pilgrimage, spurred such faith and encouraged the sick to set forth on pilgrimage. Moreover, the notion that simply performing the pilgrimage was a meritorious enough action to attain rebirth in the pure land meant that those who did not find a cure through the grace of Kōbō Daishi, or who died on the way, could be assured that their pilgrimage was not in vain.

Many pilgrims in earlier times were sufferers of leprosy, exiled from their own villages because of this affliction, and were thus forced into a life of mendicancy. The Shikoku pilgrimage offered them spiritual solace as well as the chance to solicit alms to keep themselves alive. As tale 13 shows, even this most feared of diseases was not excluded from the possibility of miraculous cure should the sufferer exhibit the faith to become a pilgrim.

Besides promoting the salvific powers of Kōbō Daishi and the efficacy of the pilgrimage, Shinnen's intent was to cajole, by tales of reward and retribution, the people of Shikoku into giving help to pilgrims. Several of his stories illustrate these themes well and will be recognized by students of Japanese folklore as similar to other stories found throughout Japan, often in connection with Kōbō Daishi. Tale 4, of the woman who is rewarded for giving the water she had fetched for her child to a needy pilgrim, and tales 6 and 17, in which the person who is asked for alms refuses to give the pilgrim anything and is suitably punished, are examples of this. Those who help pilgrims in effect share the grace of the pilgrimage, as in tale 10, in which a priest repays the lodgings he receives by doing the pilgrimage on behalf of the parents of a sick girl, who rapidly gets better, and in tale 23, in which a devotee who is unable through illness to go on the pilgrimage does good deeds and gives shelter to pilgrims, as a result of which he is cured and is able to go on pilgrimage.

If such tales have a manipulative dimension, encouraging people to give alms to pilgrims, they also express a simple sense of morality in which selflessness and virtue are praised and the perils of miserliness and greed are highlighted. Thus the woman who has made great efforts to get water for her thirsty child displays great charity and selflessness in giving it to a pilgrim in need, and the place where she lives is forever rewarded with an abundant supply of water for her good deed. Other tales show how a local product—shellfish in tale 16 and peaches in tale 17—that was in great abundance became useless because of the mean-spiritedness of locals toward passing pilgrims. The moral is that covetousness and miserliness, especially from those who are well-off and thus able to help the less fortunate, are reprehensible sins that lead to the loss of what one cherishes. The practical angle of such stories, of course, is that they encourage people to give alms to pilgrims.

The most famous of all such stories in Shikoku is the aforementioned legend of Emon Saburō, which Shinnen repeats in a rather truncated form that suggests that it was widely enough known not to require fuller narration. Since Shinnen's version is abridged, the translation given here has been expanded to incorporate the broader story as it is known to Shikoku pilgrims. Basically, the story is set in the ninth century and involves a man depicted as the richest and meanest man in Iyo (present-day Ehime) Prefecture, Emon Saburō. He is visited by a begging priest, and not only does Emon refuse to give him alms, but he attacks the priest and breaks his begging bowl. He soon discovers that the priest must have been Kōbō Daishi, for his eight sons die in quick succession. In grief and repentance, Emon sets out to find the Daishi and seek his forgiveness. He travels many times around Shikoku (indeed, some legends attribute the founding of the pilgrimage to him, with the sites representing the places where he stopped overnight) until he finally falls, dying. At this point Kōbō Daishi appears before him to absolve him of his sins, a message that tells pilgrims that through the pilgrimage even the most heinous sin can be forgiven. At this point the story also becomes the foundation legend for one of the largest and most popular temples on the pilgrimage, Ishite (Stone Hand) Temple in Matsuyama. Emon asks Kōbō Daishi to allow him to be reborn to a good family in his home province, so that he can continue that family line and do good deeds; the saint grants his wish and writes the words "Emon Saburō reborn" on a stone, which Emon dies clutching. Shortly after, a baby is born to the family concerned. The baby clutches a stone that says "Emon Saburō reborn," and he goes on to restore the temple now known as Ishite Temple and to perform numerous good deeds.

That legend may be accompanied by material remains is illustrated by the existence in Shikoku of a burial mound near Matsuyama, which, according to local lore, contains the remains of Emon's eight sons and a grave said to be Emon's at the place where he is reputed to have fallen, while at Ishite Temple there is a casket, which according to temple lore contains the stone he was born clutching. This story, which has long been a favorite among Shikoku pilgrims, in many respects rounds off Shinnen's collection of tales; after it Shinnen appends three short moralizing tracts, which are in fact brief homilies about doing good and eschewing bad deeds toward pilgrims, and which thus reiterate the broader moral meanings contained in the text.

The text of the *Shikoku henro kudokuki* is found in Kondō Yoshihiro, ed., *Shikoku reijōki shū* (Tokyo: Benseisha, 1973), appendix: 1–18; a virtually identical version, to which reference was also made, is found in Iyoshi Dankai, ed., *Shikoku henroki shū* (Matsuyama: Ehimeken Kyōka Tosho, 1981): 209–232.

Further Reading

Carmen Blacker, "Religious Travellers of the Edo Period," *Modern Asian Studies* 18, 4 (1984): 593–608; Winston B. Davis, *Japanese Religion and Society* (Albany: SUNY Press, 1992): 45–80; James Foard, "The Boundaries of Compassion: Buddhism and National Tradition in Japanese Pilgrimage," *Journal* of Asian Studies 16, 2 (1981): 231–251; Helen Hardacre, "Maitreya in Modern Japan," in Maitreya, the Future Buddha, ed. Allan Sponberg and Helen Hardacre (Cambridge: Cambridge University Press, 1988): 270–284; Joseph Kitagawa, On Understanding Japanese Religion (Princeton: Princeton University Press, 1987): 127–136; Ian Reader, "Miniaturisation and Proliferation: A Study of Small-scale Pilgrimages in Japan," Studies in Central and East Asian Religions 1, 1 (1988): 50–66; Ian Reader, "Dead to the World: Pilgrims in Shikoku," in Pilgrimage in Popular Culture, ed. Ian Reader and Tony Walter (Basingstoke, UK: Macmillans, 1993): 107–136; Ian Reader, "Pilgrimage as Cult: The Shikoku Pilgrimage as a Window on Japanese Religion," in Religion in Japan: Arrows to Heaven and Earth, ed. P. F. Kornicki and I. J. McMullen (Cambridge: Cambridge University Press 1996): 267–286; Ian Reader and Paul L. Swanson, eds., "Pilgrimage in Japan," special issue of Japanese Journal of Religious Studies 24, 3–4, (Fall 1997) (articles on Japanese pilgrimage in historical, comparative, and theoretical perspectives with definitions of Japanese terms relating to pilgrimage); Paul L. Swanson, "Shugendō and the Yoshino-Kumano Pilgrimage: An Example of Mountain Pilgrimage," Monumenta Nipponica 36, 1 (1981): 55–79.

Account of the Merits of the Shikoku Pilgrimage

TALE 2

In the fief of Kōya in the province of Ki [modern-day Wakayama], there lived a man called Zensaburō who, since birth, had had great difficulty speaking, and who could only stammer and cry, and who could not pronounce one word clearly. This caused him great distress. One day he determined to pray for help to Kōbō Daishi, and he set out on the Shikoku pilgrimage. On the third day of his pilgrimage he started to be able to say things without any problem, and his speech became fluent, so that it appeared as if his tongue had been changed.

TALE 4

In Kaifu in Awa [modern-day Tokushima] Province, there is a river called the Hahagawa [Mother River]. In olden times this was just a parched and arid area that was hard to live in. A woman who lived there, distressed because her infant was thirsty, set out to a distant valley in search of water. Finding some there, she thankfully set off homeward in joy. On her way she met a pilgrim who, although knowing that the water was very important to her, asked her if she would give him a little. Although she had intended to use it to slake the thirst of her child, the woman thought that, since the pilgrimage priest was there before her, she should give it to him, and so she did. The pilgrimage priest felt great gratitude to her and thought that he would return her favor by giving back to her water in great quantity. So he performed an Esoteric rite five times, and in that place a pure, flowing river appeared. That river is the Hahagawa. It is said that the pilgrim was Kōbō Daishi, and that this event was a divine miracle.

TALE 8

From Fujii Temple to Ryōsan Temple [two of the pilgrimage sites] in Awa Province is a distance of seven or eight miles along a steep mountain track. There is no water along the way, and during the summertime one pilgrim on his own passed along this route and, after around five miles, became tired. Although his throat was parched, there was no water to be found, and he fell down. As he lay there he saw a solitary priest appear carrying the branch of a river willow tree; the priest performed a ritual invocation there, and immediately pure water gushed out nearby. The pilgrim was saved and revived by the water; realizing the priest was Kōbō Daishi, he gave thanks to and venerated him. He planted the willow branch in the ground there, and it grew into a tree. From its roots spring pure water, and this has [ever since] been of great benefit to people passing along the way. This spring is known either as Willow Spring or as River Willow Branch Water, and there is a stone marker at the spot.

TALE 10

In the province of Tosa [modern-day Kōchi Prefecture] at Nonegaura, in Aki district, there was a man called Amejiya Shichiyūemon, whose daughter at birth had, on the nape of her neck, a growth the size of a peach. As she grew, so too did the growth, and at times it gave her great pain. By the time she was five or six years old it was huge [literally, "the size of a pillow"], and she was suffering immensely. Her parents were plunged into grief and lamented this, and they attempted all manner of healing and also religious rituals, but to no avail. Thinking this growth must be the result of some retribution from the past, they felt there was no other solution than to make supplications to Kōbō Daishi. Accordingly they gave lodging to a fine priest who was doing the Shikoku pilgrimage and told him about their daughter's problem. He said that, when the child became fifteen years old, she should do the pilgrimage along with her parents, and that, until that time, they should make a vow to do the pilgrimage every year, by giving the pilgrim's paper offerings [osamefuda, slips of paper on which pilgrims write their names and vows, and which are left at each pilgrimage site as a sign of the pilgrim's visit] to him; they should trust him to leave the offerings at the temples and thus do the pilgrimage on their behalf, and they should pray to the Daishi. So saying, he left, but from that month onward, the illness gradually got better, and within that year, it was completely healed. There are no people who, hearing this story, have not become believers.

TALE 13

In the place called Itsumi in Izumi Province [modern-day Osaka area], there was a man suffering so seriously from leprosy that he was unable to keep company with other people. This caused him grave distress, and so he set out traveling for a year with a priest called Unkai and went on the Shikoku pilgrimage. After fourteen or fifteen days of pilgrimaging, a miraculous omen occurred, and from that time on his condition got better until, when he returned [to his home,] all the signs of leprosy had disappeared, and everyone marveled at the divine power of the Daishi.

TALE 16

At the foot of Kōnomine Temple in Tosa Province, at the place called Tōnohama, there lived a fisherman. In ancient times, a pilgrim passed by and saw him collecting large numbers of shellfish, and he asked the fisherman for one. The fisherman, replying that these shellfish were inedible, refused to give him anything, and the pilgrim, saying, "I see, I see," went on his way. However, at that moment, all the shellfish turned into stones and became totally inedible. The fisherman was amazed and realized that this pilgrim was Kōbō Daishi, and he immediately repented. He hurled the shells into the valley and at that time had a complete religious awakening. This valley is now called Stone Shell Valley, and there are many shells here. Go there and pick a shell up, and you will realize that this is not a fabricated story.

TALE 17

In the place called Ikumi Village in Aki region of Tosa Province, peaches had been a local delicacy since olden times. Their reputation had reached as far as other villages, and they were widely admired. In 1684 a pilgrim came by begging for alms and asked [the people there] for a peach. They told him they would not give him one. Saying "All right, all right," he passed on by. From the next year onward, in that village not a single peach grew, and the trees all withered and died. However much they lamented it, the peaches did not reappear. Realizing that that pilgrim must have been Kōbō Daishi, the villagers were struck with awe.

TALE 23

In the village of Shimomura in Uwajima in Iyo Province there was a man named Konya Shōhei. He had great faith in Kōbō Daishi but, because of ill health, was unable to do the pilgrimage. However, he did good deeds, and even though he was sick he did not let this prevent him from giving lodging and hospitality to pilgrims. One day, all of a sudden, he was cured and, realizing that this was due to the miraculous powers of the Daishi, he and his wife set out on the pilgrimage and gained great peace of mind from increasingly being amidst other pilgrims.

TALE 24 (The Tale of Emon Saburō)

The story of Emon Saburō comes from the Ukaana area of Iyo Province and is widely reported in Shikoku. Emon was a greedy and irreligious man. When a pilgrim came to his door and held up his begging bowl, Emon struck him with his staff and knocked the begging bowl flying, causing it to break into eight pieces. However, in the next eight days his eight sons died one by one, and thus he was stricken with grief and repentance [because he realized that the pilgrim he had insulted was Kōbō Daishi]. Thus he set out to do the pilgrimage [in search of the Daishi to seek forgiveness] and did it twenty-one times in reverse order [at this point, some versions of the story say he did it twenty times in the normal, i.e., clockwise, order and, failing to meet the Daishi, then went on his twenty-first circuit counterclockwise], before falling down, dying, at the foot of Shōsan Temple in Awa Province. As he did so, Daishi appeared before him and [absolving him of his sins] granted his request [to be reborn, in his old province, as the son of a good family in a position that would enable him to do good deeds], then wrote his name on a stone. Emon was reborn as the son of the village headman Kōno; at birth his hand was clenched, and [when it was opened] they found this same stone, with the words "Emon Saburō reborn" written on it, in his hand. He grew up, succeeded to the Kōno family line, and restored the Anraku Temple in Matsuyama, building numerous shrines there, enshrining the stone that had been clenched in his hand, and renaming the temple Ishite [Stone Hand] Temple. The Kōno family flourished for several centuries, and from this event a long story has evolved and become the foundation story [engi] of Ishite Temple.

— 35 —

A Personal Account of the Life of
the Venerable Genkū

Allan A. Andrews

The *Genkū Shōnin shinikki* (A Personal Account of the Life of the Venerable Genkū), a hagiography of Hōnen-bō Genkū (1133–1212), is an enigmatic work. First, its author and date are uncertain, but on the basis of internal evidence many think it was compiled by Shinkū (1145–1228), Hōnen's earliest disciple, or by one of Shinkū's disciples, between the years 1214 and 1227. Its title is unclear as well. "*Shinikki*" means literally "my daily account," implying that the work was composed as a sort of journal by a witness to the events described. However, the *Personal Account* is not an original composition, but a compilation of preexisting biographical materials on Hōnen edited and supplemented with additional material by the compiler. This is clear because certain sections still exist as separate works whose provenance is also obscure (sections 12, 16, 19, and 21); others contain passages with quite different styles resembling, for example, folk tales (sections 8 and13); and still others are more matter of fact and provide dates (sections 1, 2, 4, 5, 6, 15, 16, 18, and 19). The purpose of the compiler and his intended audience are also unclear and will have to be determined from the contents of the work itself. We will return to these issues below.

The central theme of the *Personal Account* is, however, quite clear. From the opening passage to the final conclusion, the constantly reiterated refrain is that Hōnen was a manifestation in this realm of bondage to birth-and-death (*samsāra, rinne*) of the bodhisattva Seishi (Mahāsthāmaprāpta), come to make available for all sentient beings salvation through birth (or "rebirth"; *ōjō*) into the Pure Land of Amida Buddha.

Pure Land (*ching-t'u, jōdo*) faith was introduced from India to China in the second century of the common era with the first of several translations into Chinese of the *Larger Pure Land Sutra* (*Sukhāvatīvyūha-sūtra*), of which the most influential was that ascribed to Sanghavarman in 252 C.E. This Mahāyāna Buddhist scripture describes the heroic spiritual works of the Buddha Amitābha (Omi-t'o, Amida), which generated a purified Buddha realm or "Pure Land" called Boundless Bliss (*Sukhāvatī, Gokuraku*) situated in the far western region of the universe into which this Buddha vowed to save by rebirth after death all beings who "reflect" (*nien-fo, nembutsu*) on him with deep faith. To "reflect" on the Buddha meant several kinds of meditative and devotional activities that might be pursued separately or simultaneously, including deep meditation on the Buddha's physical characteristics and spiritual essence, just thinking about and recalling the Buddha's compassion and wisdom, and also merely calling his name repeatedly with deep faith in him.

Between the fifth and the ninth centuries a movement of popular Pure Land piety emerged and grew in China based upon this sūtra and related scriptures and also upon two major beliefs that originated in India but were developed in China: (1) the notion that to "reflect" on Amitābha Buddha as specified in the Buddha's vows meant nothing more than to call on his name repeatedly with the invocation, "Homage to the Buddha Amitābha in whom I take refuge" (*nan-wu O-mi-t'o Fo, namu Amida Butsu*), and (2) the belief that the character and ability of human beings had so degenerated, and thus the Dharma, that is, the teachings of the historical Buddha Śākyamuni, had become so corrupted as to plunge China into an "age of the final Dharma" (*mo-fa, mappō*), a time when liberation from birth-and-death by means other than Pure Land rebirth was extremely difficult, if not impossible. Pure Land piety based upon these scriptures and ideas was most concisely formulated by the T'ang period monk Shan-tao (Zendō, 613–681), from whose time Pure Land devotionalism became a mass movement in China.

As we are told in the *Personal Account*, Hōnen was born in 1133 in western Japan. His father was a provincial law enforcement officer (*ōryōshi*) and thus belonged to the military class. In 1141 Hōnen suffered a personal tragedy when his father was killed in a skirmish with the superintendent (*azukari dokoro*) of the agricultural manor or estate on which they lived. Hōnen was then only eight years old (nine according to the traditional method of calculation; in all cases subtract one year from Hōnen's age as given in the *Personal Account*). This was surely one of the many small clashes then occurring nationwide in the growing struggle between the imperial government and the military clans for control of land and for political power, which was not resolved until the defeat of the Taira clan by the Minamoto at the battle of Dan-no-ura in 1185.

This civil strife provided the background to much of Hōnen's life. Probably to protect him from further attack, Hōnen was immediately placed in a temple, and in 1145 or 1147 he was sent to Mount Hiei, the headquarters of the ancient and powerful Tendai school of Japanese Buddhism, for further training and ordination. There he studied Buddhism broadly and deeply, but in 1150 when he was seventeen he withdrew from the busy center of Tendai ecclesiastical life at the top of Mount Hiei to the secluded monastic retreat of the venerable nembutsu teacher (*nembutsu shōnin*) Eikū (Jigembō, d. 1174?) on the western flanks of the mountain. Some of this information is contained in sections 1 to 6 of the *Personal Account*.

The *Personal Account* also relates (section 11) that Hōnen read the entire Buddhist canon, including the works of Shan-tao and a Japanese work called *Essentials of Pure Land Rebirth* (*Ōjōyōshū*), three times before he found convincing proof that the only salvation available for himself and his contemporaries in the final age of the Dharma—which began in 1052 C.E. according to most Japanese calculations—lay in calling on the name of Amida Buddha. The *Essentials* was composed by the Tendai scholar monk Genshin (942–1017). Like Shan-tao in China, Genshin also aspired to Pure Land rebirth and in 984, about 150 years before the birth of Hōnen, compiled for himself and his contemporaries the *Essentials*, a voluminous collection of scriptural passages, including some from Shan-tao's works, on the Pure Land of Amida Buddha, on Pure Land rebirth, and especially on how to practice reflection on the Buddha (nembutsu).

Genshin was of two minds on the practice of Buddha-reflection. On the one hand, his Tendai training taught him that deep meditation on the physical appearance and profound essence of Amida was authentic Buddha-reflection and an excellent practice because not only could it bring about Pure Land rebirth at death, but for those of pure conduct it could also result in the immediate realization of enlightenment and liberation from birth-and-death. This was the orthodox interpretation of Buddha-reflection in the Tendai school and the interpretation accepted by most Japanese until Hōnen's time. On the other hand, Genshin learned from the works of Shan-tao and other Chinese Pure Land masters that in the final age of the Dharma very few persons were capable of this kind of profound meditation and that for most people reflecting on the Buddha by calling on his name (with the invocation *namu Amida Butsu*) was the best practice. Genshin became convinced that—as taught by Shan-tao and others—under ideal circumstances even those burdened with the most evil karma, if they would repent upon their death-beds and call upon the compassion of the Buddha by invoking his name unceasingly with deep faith and longing, could be reborn into the Pure Land. Having been born into the Pure Land, like all others reborn there, they would sit at the feet of Amida Buddha, personally hear his teachings, and quickly achieve complete enlightenment. It was these views of Genshin, and especially the teachings of Shan-tao upon which they were largely based, that converted Hōnen to the exclusive way of Pure Land rebirth through calling on the name of Amida.

After his discovery of the single practice of calling on Amida's name (*senju nembutsu*) (*Personal Account*, 12) Hōnen had a dream in which Shan-tao urged him to go forth and spread this practice. Elsewhere Hōnen wrote that he considered Shan-tao to be none other than an incarnation of Amida Buddha. The *Personal Account* also claims that in 1175, shortly after this discovery of the power of the Buddha's name and his dream of Shan-tao, Hōnen established in Japan the Pure Land school (Jōdo shū; see sections 14 and 16). Most scholars identify this as the year of Hōnen's departure from monastic seclusion and from the Tendai school, and of his establishment of his own center for worship and teaching at Ōtani in the suburbs of the capital. There he soon attracted a large band of disciples and lay followers.

The official Buddhist schools of the day, especially the Tendai, strongly objected to Hōnen's teachings, in particular his claim of having established in Japan a Pure Land school, and his insistence that the only practice (*senju*) necessary for liberation from bondage to birth-and-death was calling on the name of Amida. In 1207 they finally gained the proscription of the sole practice of calling on the name and Hōnen's exile (see sections 14 and 18). However, it was too late to halt the spread of his Pure Land faith. Though Hōnen died in 1212, shortly after return from exile (*Personal Account*, 19), his teachings were rapidly disseminated throughout the country by his disciples and followers and eventually took the form of two major denominations of Japanese Buddhism, the Jōdo shū (Pure Land school) and the Jōdoshin shū (True Pure Land school).

Thus Hōnen's significance for the history of Japanese religion looms large. He was in the forefront of the gradual shift of Japanese Buddhism from a religion of the aristocratic and monastic elites to the faith of all Japanese. Increasingly after Hōnen, deep faith and simple practices became the prime requisites of salvation. In Hōnen's wake followed other teachers, some his disciples, some his emulators, who brought a variety of exclusive faiths and single practices to the country folk and the provincial warriors as well. Thus Hōnen and his followers participated in and stimulated far-reaching changes in Japanese religious life.

The *Personal Account of the Life of the Venerable Genkū* was intended as an instrument for proselytizing a varied audience of monks and laypersons, both conservative and renovative in their attitudes. As such, it reflects the tensions of the age swirling about Hōnen and his movement. First of all it is clear that the work represents a strong reaction to the harsh criticism and vilification that descended on Hōnen from just before his death. With its bold depiction of the miraculous and its unabashed adulation of Hōnen, the *Personal Account* attempts to demonstrate that far from being a heretic and an outcast, Hōnen was a great scholar and saintly bodhisattva. And while it is clearly in the style of the traditional Pure Land hagiographies (*ōjō den*), which had originated in China and been produced for centuries in Japan, the *Personal Account* does not, like most of those earlier works, merely present for the edification of the faithful an account of a pious life-style or miraculous rebirth. Rather, it attempts to mythologize Hōnen as a savior and central object of worship for converts to his fledgling Pure Land school.

Moreover, the compiler of the *Personal Account* tries to reconcile two contrary perspectives on Hōnen and his teachings that prevailed among Hōnen's own disciples—that of the disciples who remained within the Tendai school, among whom the compiler himself must be counted, and the view of those who left the Tendai and other older schools to establish Hōnen's Pure Land school. Thus, while the compiler records that Hōnen founded the Pure Land school, he fails to mention Hōnen's major work, his *Passages on the Selected Nembutsu of the Original Vow* (*Senchaku hongan nembutsu shū*, 1198; disseminated 1212), which defined that school and set out its teachings, probably because the Tendai school had condemned this work. And although the *Personal Account* clearly describes as momentous the discovery by Hōnen of the single practice of calling on the Buddha's name (i.e., invocational Buddha-reflection; see section 11), it also emphasizes that he continued to practice so-called Buddha-reflection *samādhi* (*nembutsu sammai*), a deep meditative state in which a visualized icon of Amida comes to life in the meditator's mind (see sections 14 and 16). This meditative practice was the kind of Buddha-reflection favored by the Tendai school, but a practice that in his *Passages on the Selected Nembutsu* Hōnen had rejected. Furthermore, the *Personal Account* describes Hōnen donning just before his death a Tendai clerical surplice (*kesa*; see section 19). These depictions of Hōnen, in spite of his founding of a Pure Land school, as a Tendai monk cultivating typical Tendai, or "path of the sages" (*shōdōmon*), practices reflects not only the conflicting views of Hōnen among his followers in the first several decades following his death (some of which may have originated with inconsistencies in Hōnen's own teachings and practices), but also the dynamic tensions between old and new forms of Buddhism that Hōnen's life and teachings had intensified.

In addition to these insights into Hōnen's movement and his times, the *Personal Account* gives us, or corroborates, many facts. While some of the events it describes, such as Hōnen's conferral of the Buddhist precepts (rules of conduct) upon Cloistered Imperial Consort Jōsei [Jōseimon-in, 1126–1189], his dream of Shan-tao and the Ōhara debate (sections 8, 9, 12, and 15), are of doubtful veracity, other facts and events, such as Hōnen's parentage, the dates of his entry into the priesthood and then into monastic seclusion (sections 1–6), the circumstances of his discovery of the single practice of calling on the name (section 11), his relationship with the Regent to the Throne Fujiwara Kujō Kanezane (1149–1207; Regent, 1186–1196; section 17) and his exile and death (sections 18 and 19), provide indispensible historical data. Thus the *Personal Account of the Life of the Venerable Genkū* presents us with a rich mix of myth and history, or perhaps of history mythologized, and moreover provides insights into the significance of Hōnen for both his followers and foes.

Finally, we should note that the *Personal Account* initiated a whole genre of Hōnen biographies amounting to fifteen or more by the close of the Kamakura period (1185–1333), culminating in the voluminous forty-eight-chapter illustrated biography by Shunjō (d. 1335) first published around 1320 (see Coates and Ishizuka 1925 for a translation).

The translation is based on the text in *Saihō shinan shō* (Compendium of Guidance to the Western Land), a collection of works by and about Hōnen transcribed by Shinran, in *T* 83:875c–877c. Section numbers have been supplied by the translator.

Further Reading

Allan A. Andrews, *The Teachings Essential for Rebirth: A Study of Genshin's Ōjōyōsū* (Tokyo: Sophia University Press, 1973); Harper Havelock Coates and Ryugaku Ishizuka, tr., *Honen the Buddhist Saint:*

His Life and Teachings Compiled by Imperial Order—Translation, Historical Introduction, Explanatory and Critical Notes (Kyoto: Society for the Publication of Sacred Books of the World, 1925); Julian F. Pas, *Visions of Sukhāvati: Shan-tao's Commentary on the Kuan Wu-Liang-Shou-Fo Ching* (Albany: State University of New York Press, 1995).

A Personal Account of the Life of the Venerable Genkū

1. GENKŪ'S BIRTH

The secular name [of Genkū, i.e., Hōnen] was Uruma. He was the son of Uruma no Tokikuni, an official of Mimasaka Province. His place of birth was the Inaoka estate in the southern region of the Kume district of the same province. In the second year of the Chōjō Era [1133] when the Venerable One [Genkū] first emerged from the womb of his mother, dual banners descended from the sky. This was a rare and miraculous sign of the rebirth of a manifestation [of a Buddha or bodhisattva]. It is said that those who saw this joined their palms in reverence and those who heard of it were amazed.

2. THE DEATH OF GENKŪ'S FATHER

In spring of the seventh year of the Hōen Era [1141], his kind father was mortally wounded in a night attack and died. The Venerable One, who was only a boy of nine, aimed his small arrow and shot the cruel enemy between the eyes. Because of this wound they knew who he was. It was the superintendent of the estate, the warrior Akashi Gennai. Because of this he [Akashi] fled and hid.

3. SENT TO BODAIJI TEMPLE

At that time the Venerable One became a disciple of Kangaku the Learned of Bodaiji Temple in the same province.

4. SENT TO MT. HIEI

In the second year of the Ten'yō Era [1145] he ascended Mount Hiei. In a letter to Meditation Master Jihōbō [Genkō, dates unknown] of West Pagoda, North Valley, Kangaku the Learned wrote, "I am sending you an image of the great and revered bodhisattva Monju [Mañjuśrī]. When he read the letter he thought that this must be a rare lad indeed that had been sent him. The Venerable One was then thirteen.

5. GENKŪ BEGINS HIS STUDIES

When he was seventeen he began to read the sixty volumes [of Chih-i, the Chinese founder] of the Tendai school.

6. ENTERS INTO SECLUSION

In the sixth year of the Kyūan Era [1150] when he was eighteen years old he asked permission of his master and entered into seclusion.

7. MIRACLES RELATED BY SHINKŪ

Once while he was engaged in the *Lotus [Sutra]* repentance practice, the bodhisattva Fugen [Samantabhadra] appeared before him and revered him, and while pursuing the *Garland Sutra* a small serpent appeared. The venerable Shinkū saw this and was astonished. That night Shinkū had a dream [in which the serpent appeared and said], "I [have observed that] when the Venerable One [Genkū] studies the scriptures at night, even though there is no lamp the room is as bright as day." Shinkū (also named Horembō, a fellow disciple [with Genkū] of the Venerable One [Eikū]) also saw this light. And once when Genkū was cultivating the Shingon teachings, upon entering the meditation hall he beheld the five mystic visions. His contemplative practices revealed these to him.

8. A SERPENT LISTENS TO GENKŪ DELIVER A SERMON ON THE PRECEPTS

Once while Genkū was delivering a seven-day sermon on the precepts at the residence of Cloistered Imperial Consort Jōsei [Jōseimon-in, 1126–1189], a small serpent came and listened. On the seventh day the serpent climbed upon a Chinese-style fence and died. Those who where there saw its head break open and a deity or a butterfly fly out. Perhaps because of listening to the sermon on the precepts it was able to overcome its karmic retribution (*mukui*) as a serpent and gain rebirth immediately in a paradise.

9. GENKŪ AND THE PRECEPTS

It was during the reign of the Emperor Takakura (r. 1168–1180; cloistered, 1180–1181) that these precepts were received [by Jōseimon-in from Genkū]. These were the same precepts that had been transmitted by Grand Master Nan-yüeh [Hui-ssu, 515–576] and were transmitted everywhere without a break in the tradition right down to [Genkū and] our own day.

10. GENKŪ'S MASTERY OF THE TEACHINGS OF THE OTHER SCHOOLS

Four learned masters of various schools under whom the Venerable One had studied became, on the contrary, his disciples. Truly, even when he studied a large work of many volumes, after reading it three times the text became clear and the meaning thoroughly understood. Nonetheless, even after more than twenty years of effort, there was one school [the Pure Land school] the great truths of which he could not grasp. Therefore he studied the teachings of the various schools and became enlightened to the inner principles of both the Exoteric and Esoteric teachings. In addition to the profound principles of the eight schools, those of the Buddha-mind or Daruma [Zen] school, etc., became clear to him as well.

Then the Venerable One went to visit a learned scholar of the Sanron school who resided at Daigoji Temple and discussed with him the essential ideas [of that school]. The scholar said nothing at all but rose from his seat, entered his own room, and came out with ten or more boxes of texts and said, "I have nothing more to teach you about my Dharma-gate, therefore I bestow these on you." Then he offered up successively without pause many beautiful hymns of praise. Moreover, when Genkū met Clerical Supervisor Zōshun [Zōshun Sōzu, 1104–1180] and discussed with him the Hossō school Dharma-gate, Zōshun said, "You are surely not a mere person but the manifestation of a Buddha or bodhisattva. Your wisdom is deep and broad and your countenance is bright. I vow to make offerings to you for the rest of my life." Therefore, every year he sent offerings and kind thoughts. Even though they had already mastered the fundamental principles, great scholars and elders [of the various schools] without exception revered him and were converted [to the Pure Land way].

11. GENKŪ DISCOVERS THE SINGLE PRACTICE OF CALLING ON THE NAME

Though he had examined once all of the holy scriptures, biographies, and catalogs that had been transmitted to our land, he was still troubled over the path to liberation and unable to find peace of body or mind. Beginning with T'an luan [Donran, c. 488–551], Tao-ch'o [Dōshaku, 562–645], Shan-tao [Zendō, 613–681], and Huai-kan [Ekan, d. 710], and continuing all the way to the *Essentials of Pure Land Rebirth* by the ancient worthy of Shuryōgon'in Temple [Genshin], he searched a second time for the inner truth, and yet even on this reading he found Pure Land rebirth to be difficult. Finally on the third reading he discovered that for confused common sentient beings there is nothing equal to the single practice of calling on the name [of Amida Buddha], and that this is in fact our sole reliance in this defiled world, that which will liberate and enlighten sentient beings in the final age [of the Dharma]. Indeed, he realized that this was especially his own path to liberation as well. However, even though he wanted to spread this practice for the benefit of the world and all its beings, it was difficult for him to judge the readiness of the age and to know the response he would receive.

12. GENKŪ'S DREAM OF SHAN-TAO

While pondering this he lied down for awhile and had a dream. A broad and huge purple cloud rose up and covered all Japan. Limitless light shone from the cloud, and from this light birds hued like a hundred gems flew out and filled the sky. Then he climbed a high mountain and suddenly beheld the living Shan-tao. From his hips down he was golden. From his hips up he was as usual human. The eminent priest [Shan-tao] said, "Even though you are [my] unworthy [successor], reflection on the Buddha will flourish everywhere under the heavens. I have come so that the exclusive practice of calling on the name may reach [all] living beings. I am Shan-tao." Therefore he [Genkū, decided to] spread this Dharma so that eventually over the years it would flourish and extend everywhere.

13. THE MASTER OF HIGO'S REBIRTH AS A SERPENT

The venerable [Genkū] said, "My teacher, the Master of Higo [Higo Ajari, Kōen, d. 1169], said, 'Human beings have deep and broad wisdom, but if we examine our situation carefully we will realize that we are not likely to escape from the round of birth-and-death in this lifetime. And if we are reborn again and again, we will surely forget the Buddha-Dharma because of our moral corruption. It is best, I think, to earn a long life so that we will be able to encounter the arrival of the compassionate [future] Buddha [Miroku, Maitreya] in this world. Therefore, I would like to be reborn as a great serpent. However, if I dwell in the great ocean there might be a calamity.' Thinking thusly, he made up his mind and, obtaining from the proprietor a writ of transfer for a pond called Sakura-ike on Kasahara estate in the region of Tōtomi, he made a vow to be reborn there and to dwell in that place. Later, when he was about to die, he asked for water and, pouring some into the palm of his hand, he died. Then when the wind was not blowing suddenly waves arose on the pond and all the mud was stirred up. Those who saw this took it for a sign and informed the proprietor [of the estate]. When the date and hour were investigated it was discovered that this was the time of the master's death. Therefore, because he was wise he realized the difficulty of gaining release from birth-and-death, and because he was strongly motivated to follow the Dharma he made this vow to encounter the [future] Buddha. However, because he did not yet know of the Pure Land Dharma-gate he made this evil vow. If at that time I had been asked about this [Pure Land] Dharma, regardless of whether or not he had faith in it, I would have taught it to him. In any case, within the Dharma-gate of the path of the sages, if one is strongly motivated to follow the Dharma, one will desire karmic circumstances for prolonging one's life; if one is not motivated to follow the Dharma, one will merely seek fame and profit. This is reliable proof that those who desire easily to avoid the round of birth-and-death by means of self-power cannot succeed."

14. GENKŪ FOUNDS THE PURE LAND SCHOOL

After studying the sūtras and commentaries for some years the Venerable One came to understand from the scriptural passages that the Buddha Shaka [Śākyamuni] extensively taught that erring, evil, common sentient beings bound in birth-and-death can be reborn in [the land] Boundless Bliss by means of the practice of calling Amida's name. At that time he cultivated Buddha-reflection *samādhi* [*nembutsu sammai*] and founded the Pure Land school. Then the eminent scholars of the southern capital [Nara] and the northern mountain [Mount Hiei] slandered and ridiculed him beyond all limits.

15. THE ŌHARA DEBATE

About the time of the second year of the Bunji Era [1186], Tendai Archbishop and Imperial Counselor, Seal of the Dharma Kenshin [1131–1192] came to despise this world [called] Endurance [*saha sekai*] and longed for the Land of Boundless Bliss. He retired to Ōhara Mountain [near Kyoto] and entered the Dharma-gate of Buddha-reflection. At that time his disciple, the Lord of Sagami, said, "The venerable Hōnen has established the principles of the Pure Land school. Perhaps we should invite him here and ask him about them." Kenshin responded, "Yes indeed, let us do that. However, we should not limit the inquirers to just us." So they decided to invite and assemble scholars from everywhere. After assembling at Ōhara's Ryūzenji Temple they invited the Venerable Hōnen. He came before them unaccompanied. Kenshin was overjoyed. Those who assembled were:

> Myōhen [1141–1224], the clerical supervisor of Mount Kōmyō—an elder of the Tōdaiji Temple, Sanron school
> The venerable Gedatsu [1153–1213] of Kasagi Temple—imperial chamberlain and senior lecturer, Jōkei, of the Hossō school
> Honjōbō of Ōhara Mountain—the moderator
> Shunjōbō [1121–1206], the venerable solicitor [*kanjin shōnin*] of Tōdaiji Temple (he changed his name to Namu-Amida)—Chōgen
> Nembutsubō [b. 1156] of Saga's Ōjōin Temple—a Tendai priest
> Myōjōbō of Ōhara's Raikōin Temple—Renkei, of the Tendai school
> Renkōbō of Mount Bodai, Nagao—of Tōdaiji Temple
> Chikai, Seal of the Dharma and chief clerical supervisor—Rinsenbō, of the Tendai school's East Pagoda, West Valley
> Shōshin, Seal of the Dharma and assistant chief clerical supervisor—Hōchibō, of the Tendai school's East Pagoda, East Valley

Altogether there were about three hundred listeners. At that time the Venerable One [Genkū] expounded with the utmost clarity the essential principles of the Pure Land school, the karmic merit of Buddha-reflection and the purport of Amida's original vow. At that time Honjōbō was the moderator, but he was converted and remained silent. Everyone who was assembled there shed tears of joy and completely surrendered themselves [to the Pure Land way], and from that time the Venerable One's school of Buddha-reflection (*nembutsu shū*) flourished. From the time long ago of the monk Dharma Treasure [Hōzō; Dharmākara] to the present age of Amida Buddha, for the first time the import of the original vow and the circumstances of [Pure Land] rebirth were unambiguously explained, and there was not one among the three hundred listeners who had any doubts concerning the scriptures on the path of the sages and on the Pure Land [way]. When the profound import was explained to them, [amazed] they began to stare into space and no one uttered a word. Those assembled declared, "He appears to be the venerable Genkū, but is he not actually a manifestation of Amida Buddha?" Therefore, to commemorate the debate they held at the same temple a service of unceasing Buddha-reflection [*fudan nembutsu*] for three days and nights. On the [last] morning when [they took] vows of dedication Kenshin urged everyone to add an "Amida-Butsu" name to the name they already had of characters from the *Lotus Sutra*. From that time the Venerable One of the great Buddha image [at Tōdaiji Temple, Chōgen] began to use the name "Namu-Amida-Butsu."

16. GENKŪ'S VISIONS OF THE PURE LAND

During the reign of Cloistered Emperor Takakura in the first year of the Angen Era [1175], when the Venerable One was forty-three years old, he first entered the Pure Land Dharma-gate and quietly began to contemplate the Pure Land. On the first night he beheld the jewelled trees, on the second night the ground of lapis lazuli, and on the last night the palaces [of the Pure Land]. Amida and his two accompanying bodhisattvas appeared continually. Also when he was engaged in a twenty-one-day service of unceasing Buddha-reflection at Ryōzenji Temple the chamber was illumined even though there was no lamp. On the fifth night the bodhisattva Seishi joined the circumambulation and stood in the same row. A certain person [Shinkū?] beheld this as if in a dream. The Venerable One said, "Has such a thing ever been seen before?" Yet the others were unable to see this.

17. MIRACLES WHILE VISITING KANEZANE

Lord Zenjō Tsukinowa Kanezane (his clerical name was Enshō) was extremely devoted [to Genkū]. Once when the Venerable One was leaving after a visit to Kanezane's mansion he strode upon lotus blossoms raised high above the ground. His halo was brilliant. Thus we know that he was a manifestation of Seishi.

18. GENKŪ IS PERSECUTED AND EXILED

Such good karmic causes as these, however, when we consider it, brought about a quite different karmic effect. The eminent scholars of the south [Nara] and the north [Mount Hiei] and the luminaries of the Exoteric and Esoteric teachings either slandered our school or said that we maligned the path of the sages [*shōdō*], and claiming this and that sought to fault us in every way. This was apt to alarm the throne, and even while [Genkū was] admonishing his followers, suddenly, without considering other things, an imperial censure was imposed and a sentence of exile was carried out. However, in no time at all [Genkū] was allowed to return to the capital. The assistant imperial counselor, Lord Fujiwara Mitsuchika [1176–1221], as the shōgun's commissioner, obtained an imperial pardon. The following year, the first year of the Kenryaku Era [1211], on the twentieth of the eleventh month, Genkū returned to the capital and took up residence at a villa located at Ōtani on Mount Higashiyama and there quietly awaited his welcoming escort into the Western Pure Land.

19. GENKŪ'S REBIRTH

On the third day of the first month of the third [actually the second] year of the same era, in ill health due to age and lost in thought, he awaited the dark end [of life]. But oh the joyfulness of that which he expected and sought for! And he began to call the Buddha's name loudly and ceaselessly.

On one occasion the Venerable One spoke to his disciples, saying, "I used to be one of the disciple-monks in India always performing austerities. Originally I was in the realm of Boundless Bliss and now I have come to the land of Japan to study the Tendai school." Again he urged Buddha-reflection. He had no pain or distress in body or mind, and suddenly his consciousness cleared.

On the eleventh at about eight in the morning he sat up straight, joined his palms, and began calling the Buddha's name ceaselessly. He said to his disciples, "All of you should loudly call the Buddha's name. The bodhisattvas Kannon [Avalokiteśvara] and Seishi with the holy assembly [of other bodhisattvas] appear before us just as described in the *Amida* [smaller *Sukhāvatīvyūha*] *Sutra*. Tears of joy flowed as if his heart would break with longing. A vision of the adornments of the realm of absolute formlessness [the Pure Land] filled his eyes, and the sound of the turning of the wheel of the wonderful Dharma filled his ears.

On the twentieth day of the same month a purple cloud spread high above, and in the midst of the cloud appeared something round, brilliant, and clear just like a painting of a Buddha image. Those who saw this—clergy and layman, noble and commoner, from near and far—shed tears of wonder, and those who heard of it were amazed. At about two in the afternoon on the same day he joined his palms and looked up from the east to the west five or six times. His disciples wondered and asked him, "Is the Buddha coming to welcome you [to the Pure Land]?" The Venerable One answered, "Yes indeed."

On the twenty-third and twenty-fourth the cloud remained, becoming larger and spreading wider. An old charcoal peddler on Mount Nishiyama [west of Kyōto] and woodcutters carrying kindling on their backs saw it. The great and the small, the young and the old, beheld it.

On the twenty-fifth just at twelve noon, his posture still faultless, the strength of his voice calling the Buddha's name finally began to weaken, and his eyes beholding the Buddha seemed to be sleeping. The purple cloud hovered overhead, people assembled from near and far, and an unusual fragrance filled the chamber. Those who saw and heard this gazed upward in faith. The last moments had finally come. Putting on the nine banded clerical surplice [kesa] of Grand Master Jikaku [Ennin, 794–864], he faced the west and intoned [a line from the Amitabha Contemplation Sutra (Kammuryōjubutsu kyō, T 365)]: "Each and every ray of Amida's light illumines all the worlds in the ten regions of the universe, embracing and never abandoning those who reflect upon the Buddha" [and he expired]. It was exactly twelve noon.

20. GENKŪ AND SHAKA

It was in the spring of the year that venerable Shaka preached and passed away, and that the venerable Genkū preached and passed away. For venerable Shaka it was on the fifth day of the middle third [the fifteenth] of the second month, and for the venerable Genkū it was on the fifth day of the last third [the twenty-fifth] of the first month. It was at the age of eighty that the venerable Shaka preached and passed away, and that the venerable Genkū preached and passed away. The venerable Shaka had reached four-score years, and the Venerable One had reached four-score years.

21. KŌIN'S DREAM OF GENKŪ

On the night after he had led a service Archbishop Kōin [Daisōjō; d. 1216], the Abbot of Onjōji Temple, had a dream [verifying Genkū's rebirth in the Pure Land]. In it he heard:

Benefiting from Genkū's teachings, Kōin is able to preach well, and the [karmic] effects [of his preaching] will be inexhaustible. At death received into the Pure Land, Genkū's original embodiment was the bodhisattva Seishi who returns again and again to this world to teach and save sentient beings.

Thus a manifestation of [the bodhisattva] Seishi is named the Great Master [Genkū], the Venerable One, and Seishi, praised as boundless light illumining all beings everywhere with the light of wisdom, is adored as the Venerable One, called first in wisdom, who enriches the seven routes [of Japan] with his adamantine virtue. Amida sent Seishi as the agent of his salvation; Shan-tao sent the Venerable One to prepare those beings whose karma is ripe.

22. CONCLUSION

Know with certainty that upon encountering the fame of the master [Genkū], sentient and nonsentient beings of all the innumerable worlds in the ten regions of the universe in the three periods [of past, present, and future] will first be awakened to the path of equal liberation within the five vehicles [of humans, deities, monks, solitary Buddhas, and bodhisattvas], and that even divine rulers and divine beings of the triple world [of desires, desireless forms, and form-lessness] dwelling in space, in the four degrees of concentration [in the world of desire] or in the eight degrees of concentration [constituted by the four in the world of desire and the four beyond desire and form] will all be spared most gratefully through the birth of the Venerable One from the misery of the five kinds of decay at the death of a divine being. [And thus] all the more are we sentient beings of this evil world in the age of the final Dharma able, each and every one of us, through the transmission of the teachings and establish-ment of the practice by the venerable Genkū, to realize by means of the single practice of calling upon the name of Amida Buddha our cherished wish of [Pure Land] rebirth. Therefore, it was to spread and urge these [teachings] that he came here into our world.

23. INVOCATION AND DEDICATION

Namu Shakamuni Butsu [buddha];
Namu Amida Butsu;
Namu Kannon Bosatsu [bodhisattva];
Namu Great Seishi Bosatsu;
Namu Wonderful [Pure Land] Three Part Scripture of the One Vehicle [to salvation].
May this [account] benefit equally all living beings throughout all worlds.

—36—

Priest Nisshin's Ordeals

Jacqueline I. Stone

The *Virtuous Deeds of Nisshin Shōnin* (*Nisshin Shōnin tokugyō ki*) is a hagiographical account of the life of Kuonjōin Nisshin (1407–1488), an evangelizer of the Nichiren or Lotus sect (Hokkeshū). The historical Nisshin was born or adopted into the Haniya family, a warrior clan in Kazusa Province in eastern Japan, and was tonsured as a young man in the Nakayama lineage of Nichiren Buddhism. In his early twenties, he journeyed to the imperial capital of Kyoto and began his career of disseminating faith in the *Lotus Sutra* by roadside preaching. Over the course of his life, he traveled throughout the country, based primarily in Kyoto and in Hizen in Kyushu, and founded more than thirty temples. Among these was the Honpōji in Kyoto. *Virtuous Deeds* was written by Honji-in Nisshō (1628–1689), the Honpōji's twentieth chief abbot. Its twenty sections deal with Nisshin's early mastery of doctrine; the mysterious portents of his proselytizing mission; his successes in preaching and converting; his confrontation with the shogun; his resulting imprisonment, torture, and eventual release; his founding of temples; and the manifestations following his death of his supernatural power to answer prayers. Nisshō wrote the *Virtuous Deeds* in literary Chinese; later, however, the Honpōji's twenty-seventh chief abbot, Jōon-in Nichidatsu, expanded and rewrote it in the Japanese syllabary for accessibility to a broader readership. This version was published in 1704. The following translation is of seven sections from Nichidatsu's edition of the text.

Nisshin's efforts to spread faith in the *Lotus Sutra* were modeled on those of Nichiren (1222–1282), the originator of the Hokke sect. Nichiren is regarded as one of the founders of the new Buddhist movements of the Kamakura period (1185–1333). Like others of these founders, Nichiren taught that only one, universally accessible form of Buddhism led to enlightenment in the Final Dharma age (*mappō*). For Nichiren, this single form was faith in the *Lotus Sutra*, expressed in the chanting of its *daimoku* or title, *Namu-myōhō-renge-kyō*. Nichiren, who began his religious life as a monk of Tendai Buddhism, adopted the premise of that school that the *Lotus Sutra* represents the Buddha's true teaching, and all other sutras, his provisional teachings. However, while the Tendai school tended to encompass other forms of Buddhism as "skillful means" leading to the one vehicle of the *Lotus*, Nichiren took a strongly exclusivistic approach. In the Final Dharma age, he claimed, teachings other than the *Lotus* were utterly ineffectual. To disbelieve the *Lotus Sutra*, or to hold some other teaching to be its equal, was in his eyes tantamount to "slander of the Dharma" and the cause for falling into the hells. He therefore adopted the practice of *shakubuku*, the "harsh method" of spreading the *Lotus* by actively rebuking attachment to other teachings. *Shakubuku* was for him an act of compassion necessary to awaken others from the sin of "slandering the Dharma" and enable them to form a karmic connection with the *Lotus Sutra* that would eventually assure their enlightenment. He therefore believed himself bound to declare the exclusive truth of the *Lotus*, even at the risk of his life.

In Nichiren's view, belief or disbelief in the *Lotus Sutra* was not merely an individual matter but had implications for society as a whole. Based on Tendai notions of the nonduality of the self and the objective world, he argued that a succession of disasters besetting Japan in his day—drought, famine, epidemics, and earthquakes—had come about because the people at large had abandoned the *Lotus Sutra* in favor of Pure Land, Zen, and other "erroneous" teachings. His *Treatise on Establishing the Right [Teaching] and Bringing Peace to the Country (Risshō ankoku ron)* urges that the ruler cease offering support to the priests of such teachings and uphold the *Lotus* alone in order to restore peace to the land. Nichiren submitted this treatise as a memorial to Hōjō Tokiyori, the most powerful figure in the Kamakura *Bakufu* or warrior government, in 1260. In it, he warned that two further disasters—internecine strife and attack from abroad—would occur if his advice were not heeded. An attempted rebellion in 1271 and the Mongol invasion attempts of 1274 and 1281 lent seeming credence to his predictions.

Nichiren's attacks on other forms of Buddhism aroused hostility among both leading clergy and government officials. He was exiled twice, attempts were made on his life, and his followers were occasionally imprisoned or had their lands confiscated. Nichiren saw the persecutions he met as opportunities to expiate his own past acts of slander against the Dharma that he believed he had committed in prior lives. Moreover, the *Lotus Sutra* speaks of trials that its practitioners shall encounter in the evil age after the Buddha's nirvaa. Probably a reflection of the difficulties encountered by the emerging Mahāyāna community that had compiled the sutra, these passages appeared to Nichiren as predictions being fulfilled in his own person. The harsh treatment he encountered thus served to confirm in his own eyes the righteousness of his actions. The idea that one meets persecution as a validation of one's faith recurs throughout the Nichiren tradition and has played an important though double-edged role in its history. At times, it has provided adherents with a moral basis for resisting secular authority, as well as the courage to endure brutal opposition. However, it has occasionally inspired some among them to court oppposition deliberately, thus becoming a self-fulfilling prophecy. The theme of willingness, even eagerness, to suffer for the sutra's sake emerges clearly in *Virtuous Deeds*, as does Nisshin's desire to follow in Nichiren's footsteps in this regard. Judging from his writings, Nisshin believed that being Nichiren's Dharma heir was not merely a matter of belonging to a Hokke lineage, but of acting as Nichiren had acted and experiencing the hardships he had experienced. Like Nichiren, he was also convinced that facing persecution on account of the *Lotus Sutra* would guarantee his eventual achievement of Buddhahood.

After Nichiren's death, the memory of his uncompromising stance and his readiness to give his life for his faith provided an inspiration that helped shape the early tradition. Virtually all monks (and also some nuns) among his following took Buddhist names having as their first character the *nichi* of Nichiren, indicating that they were heirs to his teaching and task of proselytizing. Leaders among the fledgling order also carried on his practice of *shakubuku* through preaching, debate, and memorializing officials. A distinctive activity of the emerging Hokke sect was "admonishing the state" (*kokka kangyō*), a practice modeled on Nichiren's submission of the *Risshō ankoku ron* as a memorial to Hōjō Tokiyori. Letters of admonition (*moshijō*) were submitted to the ruler—the emperor or, more often, the shogun, or his local officials. Such letters restated the message of the *Risshō ankoku ron*, urging the ruler to discard provisional teachings and uphold the *Lotus* alone for the peace and prosperity of the country. Sometimes a copy the *Risshō ankoku ron* itself was appended or, less frequently, a composition of similar purport by the writer of the letter, such as the admonitory treatise written by Nisshin in *Virtuous Deeds*. Going up to Kyoto to "admonish the state" was almost expected of any monk who was chief abbot of a Hokke lineage in eastern Japan. An early example was Jōgyōin Nichiyū (1298–1374) of the temple Hokekyōji of the Nakayama lineage in Shimōsa Province, who figures in *Virtuous Deeds* as Nisshin's forebear and spiritual protector. In 1334 he went to Kyoto to present a letter of admonition to the Emperor Godaigo. He was arrested and imprisoned for three days, counting it an honor to meet persecution, even briefly, for the sutra's sake. Six years later he made the journey again to admonish the first Ashikaga shogun, Takauji. By Nisshin's time, the tradition seems to have elaborated on Nichiyū's activities. In the *Transmission of the Lamp* (*Dentō shō*), his history of the various Nichiren lineages, Nisshin wrote that Nichiyū was nearly beheaded in the course of another remonstration attempt in 1356. Nisshin, who was also of the Nakayama lineage and who practiced as a young man at the Hokekyōji, must have been deeply impressed by Nichiyū's example. Nisshin himself is said to have remonstrated with nobles and warrior officials on eight occasions.

Following the initial efforts of Higo Ajari Nichizō (1269–1342), who first preached Nichiren's doctrine in Kyoto, the major Hokke lineages all began to establish temples in the imperial capital. By the mid-fifteenth century, it is estimated that nearly half the population of Kyoto belonged to the Hokke sect. While its major social base was among the rising urban mercantile population or *mach-*

ishū, converts were also made among aristocrats and powerful samurai. As the various Hokke lineages became well established, Nichiren's exclusivistic stance and the practice of confrontational *shakubuku* became harder to sustain. The history of the sect can in fact be seen in terms of ongoing tensions between conciliatory factions seeking to make practical accommodations with ruling authorities and other forms of religion to ensure the sect's welfare and prosperity, and those who insisted on a strongly exclusivistic position. Nisshin was among a number of monks, chiefly from new lineages that had split off from older ones, who believed that the Nichiren order was becoming excessively accommodating and losing the strict spirit of proselytizing by *shakubuku*, the refutation of other Buddhist teachings. As suggested in the *Virtuous Deeds*, Nisshin was an uncompromising purist. In 1433, a few years after his first journey to Kyoto in 1427 when he preached by the Returning Bridge, Nisshin was dispatched to Kyushu to oversee branch temples of the Nakayama Hokekyōji in Hizen Province. There, to his dismay, he found images enshrined of Buddhas and bodhisattvas unrelated to the *Lotus Sutra* or the Nichiren teachings. His repeated remonstrations and criticisms on that score, addressed to the leading local lay patron and to the Hokekyōji's chief abbot, eventually resulted in his expulsion from the lineage in 1437. Memorializing the shogun, as Nisshin did in 1439—while undeniably true to the founder Nichiren's example—was also viewed with alarm by the leaders of older Hokke lineages as a possible threat to their temples' security. While overtly an attempt to convert the ruler and benefit the country, by this time, "admonishing the state" also carried implicit criticism of more conciliatory elements within the Nichiren tradition. It is quite possible that Nisshin had as many enemies among the moderates within his own sect as he did outside it.

Nevertheless, it is undeniable that men like Nisshin won the Hokkeshū large numbers of converts and kept alive the normative Nichiren Buddhist ideal of exclusive devotion to the *Lotus*, acting as a check on accommodations made to social custom and secular authority. Nisshin himself appears to have been an enormously charismatic figure, as popular among the people as he was detested by government officials and prominent clerics. In 1460 the bakufu received complaints from temples of other sects in Hizen, where Nisshin was engaged in proselytizing under the protection of the local landholder Lord Chiba Taneshizu, and decided to impose sanctions on him. Lord Chiba was ordered to bring him back to Kyoto. Although the journey usually required only one month, it took them nine months to reach to the capital. Lord Chiba explained that they had been delayed by throngs of people crowding the roads and demanding to meet Nisshin and receive his teachings.

The *Virtuous Deeds* generally follows the known facts of Nisshin's career, while providing considerable embellishment. From Nisshin's own writings, we know that he did indeed memorialize Ashikaga Yoshinori in 1439, was told not to do so again, composed the *Risshō jikoku ron* in defiance of this order, and was arrested before completing the fair copy. The description of the low, cramped cell with the nails protruding point first from the ceiling is also taken from his own account.

The treatment he received while incarcerated was undoubtedly harsh; Nisshin writes that he was "tormented by water and fire." However, he does not go into detail. The specific, gruesome tortures so enthusiastically elaborated in *Virtuous Deeds*—including the celebrated incident of the pot—are almost certainly the products of a later imagination. As the text indicates, Nisshin was released in an amnesty following Yoshinori's assassination, but there is no indication that the Ashikaga clan converted en masse to faith in the *Lotus Sutra*.

Virtuous Deeds reflects several themes that recur in Nichiren's writings and in the later literature of the Nichiren tradition: propagation of the *Lotus Sutra* in the Final Dharma age is invariably accompanied by great trials; the *Lotus* has a higher claim on the believer's loyalty even than does the ruler; and giving up one's life for the sutra's sake is a supreme honor and will assure one's future enlightenment. At the same time, the image of Nisshin depicted in *Virtuous Deeds* also reflects a type of practitioner not confined to Nichiren Buddhism or indeed to Buddhism at all, but found elsewhere in Japanese religions. This is the figure of the ascetic who acquires magical or supernatural abilities through a regimen of harsh disciplines, and whom it is dangerous to cross because of his command of magical powers.

Virtuous Deeds does not address the doctrinal or philosophical side of Nichiren Buddhism; it is a work of popular hagiography. It may well have served to provide entertainment and promote support for the Honpōji, as well as to encourage piety. It is clear that it both reflected and advanced an emerging cult of devotion to Nisshin that flourished in Kyoto and the surrounding area during the Edo period (1600–1868). Nisshin's extraordinary strength of purpose as reflected in the legends told about him, especially his ability to withstand the most horrific tortures, was regarded by many as proof of immense spiritual power. Temples sprang up around sites connected with him. Picture scrolls depicting his ordeals, many of them based on the descriptions in *Virtuous Deeds*, were issued by these temples and were valued as talismanic. The "pot-wearing saint" was believed to answer prayers for healing, safe delivery, worldly success, freedom from misfortune, long life, and so forth. A wooden image of Nisshin enshrined at the Honjōji in Sakai attracts believers even today.

The translation is based on *Nisshin Shōnin tokugyō ki*, in Washio Junkei, ed., *Kokubun tōhō Bukkyō sōsho*, series 1, vol. 5 (Tokyo: Kokubun Tōhō Bukkyō Sōsho Kankōkai, 1925–1927): 541–590.

Futher Reading

Ruben L. F. Habito, "Lotus Buddhism and Its Liberational Thrust: A Re-reading of the *Lotus Sutra* by Way of Nichiren," *Ching Feng* 35, 2 (June 1992): 85–112; Alicia and Daigan Matsunaga, *Foundation of Japanese Buddhism, vol. 2: The Mass Movement* (Los Angeles and Tokyo: Buddhist Books International, 1976): 137–181; Laurel Rasplica Rodd, *Nichiren: Selected Writings* (Honolulu: University of Hawaii Press, 1980); Jacqueline Stone, "Rebuking the Enemies of the *Lotus*: Nichirenist Exclusivism in Historical Perspective," *Japanese Journal of Religious Studies* 21, 2–3 (June–September 1994): 231–259;

Burton Watson et al., tr., and Philip B.Yampolsky, ed., *Selected Writings of Nichiren* (New York: Columbia University Press, 1990).

The Virtuous Deeds of Nisshin Shōnin

MAKING A VOW AND RECEIVING A SIGN [3]

At one time in the year Ōei 33 (senior Fire, Horse) [1426], when Master Nisshin was twenty, he made a vow. "One's body is insignificant, but the Dharma is profound. To spread the Wonderful Dharma [of the *Lotus Sutra*] without begrudging bodily life—this is the teaching of the Thus Come One. The World Honored One also admonishes against witnessing enmity toward the Buddha-Dharma and failing to rebuke it. Our founder [Nichiren] received the Buddha's mandate to spread this sutra in the Final Dharma age. He upheld the golden words, 'We do not cherish bodily life,' and, even though he encountered many great trials, he endured them all, spreading the Wonderful Dharma, widely benefiting beings stained by the five impurities [of the kalpa, mental defilements, beings, views, and life-span] and repaying the great debt owed to all Buddhas. I am privileged to number among his later disciples. How should I not carry on his task of converting and guiding? Ready to discard bodily life, I will single-mindedly spread the *Lotus Sutra* and help fulfill the original intent of our founder." So he resolved. Then he further reflected: "To spread [the *Lotus Sutra*] in the Final Dharma age will surely entail many trials. [The Buddha] restrained even great bodhisattvas from undertaking it. Without the protection of the Three Treasures [the Buddha, the Dharma teaching, and the Sangha community] and of the founder, how could one successfully accomplish the great deed of disseminating [the sutra]? If I have a sign of their response, I will commit myself to its propagation."

At the end of that year, from autumn through winter, for a hundred days, he went each night during the hours of the Rat and the Ox [11:00 P.M. to 3:00 A.M.] to the graveyard of the Shōchūzan [the Hokekyōji]. Seating himself firmly before the many stone stūpas [marking the graves], he recited the *Jiga* verses [from the *Lotus Sutra*] each night a hundred times. In the place where the graves were was a line of trees that obscured the light of the sun and moon. The only inhabitants were foxes and badgers; it was far removed from any place that people frequented. The wind blew through the bare branches of the trees, and the scene of snow and frost in the depths of night was utterly frightful. Nevertheless, Master Nisshin's resolve was firm, and he did not miss a single night. Strangely, on the hundredth night, the stone stupas all recited the *Jiga* verses together with him. One had a particularly high and awe-inspiring voice that rang out clearly. Master Nisshin wanted to identify the stūpa, but because the sky so late at night was thoroughly dark, he could not make out whose grave it was. He embraced the stone stūpa and pulled it over; then he left. When day dawned, he hurried back. When he examined it, it proved to mark the grave of Nichiyū Shōnin, who had been chief abbot of the Hokkekyōji. Nisshin rejoiced greatly and shed tears of emotion. Bowing with his palms placed together, he thought with gratitude, "Nichiyū Shōnin was truly the founder of our sect reborn. Now he has displayed this mysterious sign that he will aid my efforts. My wish has been splendidly fulfilled, and I am resolved to preach the Wonderful Dharma widely." From then on, his faith was all the firmer, and he pledged himself to fulfill the great vow to disseminate and teach [the *Lotus Sutra*].

A SUPERNATURAL DREAM [5]

One night Nisshin dreamed that Nichiyū Shōnin came to where he was study-ing and announced, "You have resolved to spread this sutra. When one person launches such a vow, he himself rejoices, and others are delighted as well. Now I will confer upon you a sign that your propagation [of the *Lotus*] will be accomplished." Thereupon he conferred upon Nisshin his written seal. Nisshin awoke, filled with joy, and suddenly noticed the shape of that seal inpressed on the ashes in the incense burner before the altar. From that time until his death, Master Nisshin used that seal as his own. The sacred objects of worship, [the *daimoku* mandalas inscribed by him,] which have been handed down until this day, all bear this written seal. On another occasion, Master Nichiyū taught him the method of inscribing the characters "Dharma" (*hō*) and "lotus" (*ren*) of the *daimoku* as it appears on the mandala. This is recorded in Nisshin's *Transmissions Concerning the Mandala* (*Mandara sōjō shō*). The founder [Ni-chiren] conferred the *Prayer Sutra* [compendium of passages from the *Lotus Sutra* recited for protection] (Kitōkyō) upon Toki Nichijō Shōnin, and Nichijō transferred it to Nichiyū. Nichiyū's saying he would give Nisshin a sign means that he encompassed the *Prayer Sutra* within his seal and conferred it upon Master Nisshin. For that reason, Master Nisshin was neither killed nor harmed, even when tortured by fire or water, and at last he fulfilled his vow to spread the [*Lotus*] sutra. Therefore, those who are born after Master Nisshin's time should, with deep and single-minded resolve, believe in and revere the objects of worship inscribed by him as well as his virtuous deeds. It is as clear as the palm of one's hand that, by so doing, one can transmit the Wonderful Dharma with perfect wisdom and firm faith, widely benefiting others.

GOING UP TO THE CAPITAL AND SPREADING THE DHARMA [6]

His resolve to preach widely and transmit the Wonderful Dharma having be-come firmly established, and having beheld with his own eyes wondrous signs of the Buddhas and patriarchs, Master Nisshin lost no time in setting out for the capital. He was twenty-one at the time, and it was near the end of the first month of the year Ōei 34 (junior Fire, Snake) [1427]. On the eighth day of the second month of the same year, he first began to preach in the vicinity of

the Returning Bridge (Modori-bashi) on First Avenue in the capital. He chanted
the Wonderful Dharma [i.e., the *daimoku*] and firmly rebuked the error of
slandering the Dharma. Before his time, Bodhisattva Nichizō had [similarly]
spread the doctrines of the [Hokke] sect in the Einin era [1293–1298]. That
was the beginning of the spread of [faith in] the king of sutras in the capital.
At that time, the followers of other schools who slander the Dharma had profound attachments to the provisional teachings that could not immediately be
controlled, so [Nichizō's] admonitions about doctrine and observance were not
strict. Since then, with the passage of time, there were many people of the one
[Hokke] sect who, like those of other sects, visited the shrines of deities who
protect the provisional teachings [other than the *Lotus*], or who pasted heretical
amulets on the gates of their homes and looked up to them with reverence.
However, when they came to hear Nisshin's teachings, a great change occurred.

Because no one of the sect, monk or layperson, would give him a night's
lodging, Nisshin went day and night to the roadside near the Returning Bridge.
Using a stone as a seat and raising an umbrella, he chanted the *daimoku* as
loudly as he could and vigorously preached the errors of other sects. He declared that sutras other [than the *Lotus*] do not lead to Buddhahood, and he
clarified the sin of slandering the Dharma, which leads to the hells. He preached
that, through the power of the wondrous sutra of the one vehicle, there is not
a single person who shall not attain Buddhahood, expounding the scriptural
passages in detail and recommending the Wonderful Dharma that accords with
both the time and human capacity. However, people both high and low
frowned and grew angry, or clapped their hands and laughed. What is more,
men and women of other sects pelted him with rocks and tiles, while monks
and nuns who slandered the true teaching plotted single-mindedly to do him
harm. There was no one who treated him cordially or approached him. However, Nisshin truly expounded the doctrine, now rebuking [errors], now citing
sutras to demonstrate his point. His wisdom opened [the meaning of] the sutras
of the Buddha's lifetime and the treatises written about them, while his elo-
quence was like flowing water that knows no obstruction. At first people
shunned and despised him, but later they revered and esteemed him. Day after
day, they congregated to hear him preach. It so happened that two men from
Kajiori Village (also called Kajiwara) in Shimagami district of Settsu Province,
Uno Magozaemon and Nishimura Hikohyōe, came up to the capital and mingled with the crowd, where Nisshin sat preaching at the Returning Bridge and
heard him. Because of good karma from the past, they at once realized the truth
of his teaching. Both bent their heads and stepped beneath the umbrella to
receive his Dharma. [Later they helped Nisshin establish his first temple.] Not
only men and women of other sects bent their heads in faith and acceptance,
but persons of the Hokke sect also reformed the impurity of their slanders of
the Dharma. In this way, the spread of the *Lotus Sutra* [in the capital] was
begun by Master Nichizō, while the fact that people came to adhere strictly to
the admonitions of the sect was solely because of Nisshin's teaching. After that,

the sect prospered and the Wonderful Dharma spread all the more. That followers of the Nichiren sect today in both city and countryside strictly avoid slanderous acts is due largely to the virtuous achievement of Master Nisshin.

At that time, there was a stone near the Returning Bridge on which Master Nisshin seated himself to preach. From then on, it was called the "preaching stone." It is said that whoever sat on it by mistake, even briefly, or those who treated it disrespectfully, received some supernatural warning. In the past it was called the Seimei Stone [possibly in memory of the yin-yang master Abe no Seimei]. For some reason, in the year Genroku 15 (senior Water, Horse) [1702], on the sixteenth day of the eighth month, the stone was moved to the Honpōji. Since the Ōei era, it had weathered 280 years, remaining undisturbed. It had never been moved anywhere, and then finally it happened to be brought to Master Nisshin's chief place of practice. Surely this is most mysterious.

"TREATISE ON GOVERNING THE COUNTRY" [9]

In carrying out his original pledge to spread the Wonderful Dharma in the imperial capital, Nisshin admonished the shogun on multiple occasions. In the year Eikyō 11 (junior Earth, Ram) [1439], when he was thirty-three, he again admonished the Great Barbarian-Subduing General Minamoto no Yoshinori [the sixth Ashikaga shogun]. Lord Yoshinori grew enraged. Glaring, he said in a rough voice, "The reason you have still not been taught a lesson is that I have not yet given orders [to that effect]. If you come appeal to me again, I will make sure that you are punished." Master Nisshin heard him out [and replied], "I am a disciple of the Buddha, a vassal of the Dharma. How could I go against the Buddha's teaching out of fear of your commands? No matter what punishments you may inflict on me when I appeal to you again, I will be like the Venerable Āryasiṃha [, who was killed by King Danmira, an enemy of Buddhism,] or the Tripitaka Master Fa-tao [, who opposed Emperor Hui-tsung's attempts to suppress Buddhism]. Would it not rather be a great happiness to discard my wretched body in this [one] insignificant lifetime for the sake of the *Lotus Sutra* and thus ensure that the great Dharma will remain for ages to come?" So stating, he returned. After that, he composed the *Treatise on Establishing the True [Teaching] and Governing the Country* (*Risshō jikoku ron*) in one volume, modeling it on the founder [Nichiren]'s *Treatise on Establishing the True [Teaching] and Bringing Peace to the Country* (*Risshō ankoku ron*). He intended to submit it in remonstration on the occasion of thirty-third annual memorial service for Yoshinori's father, Rokuon-in Yorimitsu. In it he widely cited from the sūtras, making clear that faith in wrong teachers is the root cause of disorder in the realm. He set forth in detail the words and principles of the Wonderful Dharma and demonstrated that establishing the true teaching is the basis for governing the land. Its words were indisputable and its reasoning was clear. This writing is stored in the treasure repository of the Honpōji.

IMPRISONMENT AND TORTURE [10]

No sooner had Nisshin finished the *Risshō jikoku ron* than someone got word of it and slandered him in various ways to the shogun, saying, "Priest Nisshin pays no heed to my lord's prohibition but instead has composed a writing of appeal. This is how he violates your order." The shogun grew very angry on hearing this but did not immediately order punishment. [Instead,] he summoned eminent priests of the Zen and Nembutsu [sects]. The shogun Lord Yoshinori addressed them as follows: "Priest Nisshin has on several occasions appealed to me to take faith in the *Lotus Sutra*. I do not believe nor have I accepted his appeals, but last year he came to appeal to me again. At that time, I said that if he came to memorialize me any further, I would have heavy punishment inflicted on him. Nisshin replied, 'I am a disciple of the Buddha and a vassal of the Dharma. How could I go against the Buddha's teaching out of fear of your commands?' So saying, he returned. This is how he disregards my orders. Moreover, he has now composed a treatise intending to memorialize me again. This priest reveres the *Lotus Sutra* alone; he holds his person in disregard but values the Dharma. I have not yet determined the rights and wrongs of the other teachings. You priests must each ascertain [in debate with Nisshin] in my presence the relative profoundity of the various sutras and whether or not they lead to Buddhahood."

In their hearts, the majority of the Zen and Nembutsu priests feared to debate with Master Nisshin, so they replied to Lord Yoshinori: "Of all the various Exoteric and Esoteric schools based on the eighty thousand sacred teachings, there is none that does not represent the essential teaching of the Buddha. How could the *Lotus Sutra* alone be true? Moreover, when the Buddha was about to enter nirvana, he entrusted the Dharma to the ruler and his ministers. How could one propagate the Dharma if he goes against your command? Nisshin is completely ignorant of Buddhism. What point could there be in debating pros and cons with him? All he does is malign others. To fling away one's life in vain, reaping the world's derision, is to become a laughingstock. And even though he may speak boldly now, if he is punished as serious criminals are, he will at once abandon the *Lotus Sutra* and chant the sacred name of [A]mida. We ask that you deal with him in this manner." Slandering [Nisshin] in various ways, they made this recommendation. Lord Yoshinori did not know that, among the teachings of the Thus Come One, there are various expedients [and not all represent the ultimate truth]; nor did he know of men like Āryasiṃha or Fa-tao, who went against the ruler's command in order to teach the Dharma. He simply believed the errors and deceptions of the Zen and Nembutsu priests, who were ignorant and of limited ability, and he grew more and more enraged.

On the sixth day of the second month of the twelfth year of the Eikyō era (senior Metal, Monkey) [1440], Nisshin was seized and roughly thrown into prison. He was thirty-four at the time. His prison cell measured four feet, five inches high, and its width accommodated only four mats. Nails, seven or eight inches in length, hung pointing down from the ceiling. At this time there were eight people together in this cell. There had been thirty-six originally, but the jailor, feeling pity, had removed twenty-eight of them to a broader, six-sided cell. The remaining eight could neither sit nor stand readily, nor could they urinate and defecate as they wished.

[On one occasion,] Master Nisshin was taken out into the prison yard in the fierce heat of the summer sun. Firewood was piled up, and he was made to cross through the flames. Forced to confront the fire, he was admonished, "If you think the pain will be hard to bear, then quickly say [the name of A]mida." Master Nisshin replied, "The heat is truly difficult to bear. However, when one commits the sin of slandering the Dharma, he will fall into the Hell without Respite and be scorched in the flames of [the Hell of] Great Heat. Nothing can compare to the heat of those fires. How could I, because I shunned a brief spell of suffering from this heat, plant the seeds for long ages of torment?" And he chanted the *daimoku* in a loud voice. Again, at night in the freezing cold of winter, he was led out into the yard where the frost lay thick. There he was stripped naked, tied to a plum tree, and flogged throughout the night. "This is what the suffering of cold is like. Why don't you rely on Amida?" Master Nisshin replied, "There is no way to describe how hard the cold is to endure. However, one who receives the Dharma of an evil teacher falls into the eight cold hells and is pierced by the ice of [the Hell of] the Great Crimson Lotus. No comparison can describe how many times the suffering of cold [in that hell] exceeds my present torments. How could I, because I shunned a brief spell of cold in this world, plant the seeds for long kalpas of suffering?" He did not flinch but chanted the *daimoku* in a loud voice. When day dawned, Lord Yoshinori came to see the sight. Nisshin was chilled from the night's cold, and when he appeared to shiver slightly, Yoshinori said, "Whom does the practitioner of the *Lotus Sutra* fear, to tremble in this way?" Master Nisshin replied, "If you had been treated like this, you would have soon frozen and perished. In my case, thanks to the power of the *Lotus Sutra*, I am still alive."

On another occasion, he was locked in a bathhouse that was heated [with firewood] for three hours. At first his voice could be heard loudly chanting the *daimoku*, but then it gradually subsided until no sound could be heard. People said that he must have died. But when they opened the door, Master Nisshin was there looking just as he had before, chanting the Wonderful Dharma in a soft voice. Or [at another time], he was tied to a ladder, and water was scooped up in a ladle and poured into his mouth. He himself was able to count up to thirty-six ladles-full; after that, he did not know how many [he was forced to swallow]. Though he was tormented in this way, he did not relax or weaken [in his resolve] even in the slightest. [On occasion,] bamboo skewers were applied to his testicles, or [the blades of] hoes, heated red-hot, were placed in his armpits. But although he was tortured in countless ways, he gave no sign of being troubled or pained. At one time, a bamboo saw sharp as a metal blade had been hung near his prison cell. When Nisshin asked its purpose, the jailor replied, "It is a saw to remove your reverence's head." Nisshin then took the saw and bashed it against the earthen floor of his cell. The jailor grew angry and said, "Even if you break that saw, it will be to no purpose. There are other saws, to put an end to your life." To this, Master Nisshin declared, "I do not shun suffering in the slightest, nor do I begrudge my life. But if you cut off my head with a sharp, swordlike blade such as this, it will be altogether too easy. Because my life will be discarded solely in order that I may offer my body to the *Lotus Sutra* and widely benefit others, I would wish the suffering to be longer and more intense. That is why I am trying to dull this sharp blade." Truly, because of such deep resolve, he was able to endure these many tortures, and his life was not harmed. His bearing was as composed as ever. Filled inwardly with the virtues of wisdom and meditation, he outwardly displayed forbearance and compassion. Were it not for the protection of the Buddhas and kami, who could do as he did?

CROWNED WITH A POT [11]

Though subjected to numerous tortures, Master Nisshin did not waver in the least. Out of resentment of his firm resolve, on one occasion, a pot was heated until it glowed like flames and then placed over his head. This too he endured well, and he gave no sign of extreme pain. From that time on, people in the world all called him "the pot-wearing saint." It was because of this torture that he came to be revered by this name. On another occasion, Lord Yoshinori commanded that his tongue be cut out. The person who received the order had pity on him, and, in his sympathy, sliced off only a bit of the tip. After that, Master Nisshin lisped like a child. The top of his head scarred where the pot had rested, so he was unable to shave it as he wished and had to trim his hair with scissors as it grew out. Thus his head looked like that of a small boy [with a cropped haircut]. It remained so, even when he grew old. Master Nisshin would joke, "The saying, 'In old age, one becomes a child again,' must refer to me." Thus, taken out [of his cell], he was tormented in various ways, and returning to it, he underwent numerous sufferings. The term of his imprisonment exceeded a year, lasting 503 days. Who else could have endured as well as Master Nisshin did, unless he were the founder [Nichiren] reborn? In the Honpōji, there is an object of worship dated the first year of the Kakitsu era (1441) that he inscribed while in prison. Day and night in his cell he chanted the Wonderful Dharma and refuted [the doctrines] of false teachers. His voice carried beyond the prison. Among those who heard him, there were some who slandered him, and some who took faith and converted. And when he was tortured, there were many who quickly realized that he was no ordinary person and revered him.

YOSHINORI'S PUNISHMENT [12]

On the thirteenth day of the third month of the first year of the Kakitsu era (junior Metal, Rooster) [1441], the shogun Lord Yoshinori sent a messenger to demand of Nisshin in his prison cell: "One who torments a practitioner of the *Lotus Sutra* will surely receive punishment in this life—so it is written in the sutra itself. I have tormented you harshly for more than a year now, but there is no sign of anything untoward. Can the sutra be false? Or if not, it is clear that you are surely no true practitioner of the *Lotus*." Master Nisshin replied, "How could the sutra be false? And I am a true practitioner of the *Lotus*. Before three years have passed, my lord will surely incur punishment." The shogun sent a further message: "What you say is foolish. If after three years were I to meet some misfortune, how could one say it was specifically on account of tormenting you?" Master Nisshin replied, "If you think three years would be too late, then before a hundred days are out, you will quickly incur heavy punishment." Hearing this, the shogun laughed with derision. He was extremely angry. Declaring that he would never lose his life, he passed the days in various counsels. Then, on the twenty-fourth day of the sixth month, ninety-nine days after the messenger had been sent [to Nisshin], the lay priest Aka-matsu Mitsusuke Shōgu murdered the shogun Yoshinori in his mansion. (This is related in the *Summary of Reigns* [*Ōdai ichiran*] and other sources.) Thus Nisshin's words that Yoshinori would incur punishment within a hundred days were fulfilled. In the past, the regent in Kamakura, the governor of Sagami [Hōjō Tokimune], exiled the founder [Nichiren] to the island of Sado, and within a hundred days fighting broke out in his domain. On investigating the past case of the founder and comparing with it the more recent case of Master Nisshin, thoughtful persons, considering Yoshinori's immediate punishment, will revere Nisshin's virtuous deeds and take faith in him. Throughout the capital, men and women all said, "Because Yoshinori inflicted various tortures on a noble priest, he met with this misfortune." Word spread from the streets to every house. On this account, the shogun's clan pardoned a great number of criminals as a memorial offering for Lord Yoshinori. Their intent was solely that Nisshin be pardoned and released, and to nullify Yoshinori's offenses. But Master Nisshin refused to leave the prison. He had borne grave sufferings and upheld the *Lotus Sutra* without begrudging his life, solely in order to lead others to embrace the Wonderful Dharma. The shogun had not discerned this and brought disaster on himself. Master Nisshin announced, "If those close to the shogun, down to the last man, do not now receive this Wonderful Dharma that I uphold, I will never leave prison." Yoshinori's family and retainers were unable to oppose him, and the shogun's entire clan became devotees of the *Lotus*. Thereupon Master Nisshin left prison. He was thirty-five at the time. During his days of incarceration, he had tirelessly preached the Dharma. Those who had muttered that it was only the noise of an arrogant priest were many, while those who had taken faith were few. From that point on, however, both high and low, men and women, were awestruck by the power of Master Nisshin's virtue and believed and revered him. Master Nisshin himself practiced *shaku-buku* all the more with respect to other sects and widely declared the Hokke doctrine. Those who heard him directly at once embraced the Dharma, while those to whom the word was passed also converted as they heard it. There were very few who slandered him and none who tried to do him harm. That same year, Yoshinori's heir, Lord Yoshikatsu, at eight years of age, was invested as shogun by the emperor. However, on the twenty-first day of the seventh month in the third year of the Kakitsu era (junior Water, Boar) [1443], the Great Barbarian-Subduing General Minamoto no Yoshikatsu fell from his horse and died an early death. This was due to the sin of his father in tormenting a practitioner of the *Lotus*. Nisshin's predictions of "three years" and "a hundred days" came true as exactly as matching tallies. How fearful! Was he not a sage who knew beforehand what was yet to happen?

—— 37 ——

Makuya: Prayer, Receiving the Holy Spirit,
and Bible Study

H. Byron Earhart and Etsuko Mita

Makuya, literally "tabernacle," is the abbreviated name for a Japanese new religion, known also as Kirisuto no Makuya, "Tabernacle of Christ," or by its full name Genshi Fukuin Undō: Kirisuto no Makuya (The Original Gospel Movement: Tabernacle of Christ). Because members of the movement refer to it as Makuya, we will follow this precedent.

Makuya was founded by Teshima Ikurō (1910–1973), whose life was shaped both by his Japanese heritage and by his acceptance of Christianity. He became a Christian in his teens, was baptized and later joined the Nihon Kirisuto Kyōkai (The Christ Church of Japan), was active in the Non-Church movement (Mukyō-kai, or Non-Church Christianity), and later formed his own Bible study group. Teshima was heavily influenced by the pattern of Mukyōkai laid down by its founder Uchimura Kanzō (1861–1930), who stressed independence from official church structures, instead relying on individuals' personal experience of God linked to independent Bible study, and attending formal lectures on the Bible. These lectures, held in public halls rather than churches, were formal, academic analyses of the Bible intended to help individuals in their own study of the Bible and direct experience of God. In other words, this "Non-Church" view of Christianity saw the structures of the church as hindering rather than helping the individual in meeting God, and Uchimura wanted to go around ecclesiastical structures to return to the early or original Christianity.

The translation from *Our Master Teshima Ikurō* (*Wagashi Teshima Ikurō*) provides two excerpts describing crucial experiences for Teshima: first, when he decided to enter the Christian ministry, and second, several years later, when he developed a new and more effective style of preaching. Teshima's 1948 decision to devote himself to religion was partly the result of his being forced to hide in the mountains from the American Occupation forces—he had led a demonstration against an Occupation directive about a local school and was ordered arrested. While in the mountains he prayed and meditated, experiencing directly the power of God. Later, when he began his ministry, Teshima followed the Mukyōkai pattern of rigorous Bible study and formal lectures on the Bible, but at first he was not very successful. Later, during a 1950 Bible study meeting, frustrated by his inability to persuade listeners, he began crying and praying emotionally—which moved the people. From that time he changed his style to a more "pentecostal" character—emotional sermons emphasizing not just conversion to Christianity but receiving the Holy Spirit, often in the context of miracles and healing. This approach enabled him to attract a large following; although Makuya may be seen, historically, as developing out of Mukyōkai (Non-Church Christianity), it has grown much larger than Mukyōkai, with a headquarters in Tokyo, eighty-two branches, and many followers. Since there is no strict membership system and reliable figures are difficult to obtain, it is not possible to say how many members there are, although some estimates give figures in the 50,000 to 60,000 range. Teshima is known by Makuya followers as *sensei* (teacher), in the sense of "Master." Makuya is best known outside Japan for its close ties with Israel: Makuya views the emergence of the state of Israel as a fulfillment of biblical prophecies. Makuya followers who become teachers may study Hebrew, students live in Israeli kibbutzim, and adults go on pilgrimage to Israel.

Japanese new religions primarily are *Japanese* in character, being composed of elements of Buddhism, Shintō, and Confucianism. Although there is some influence of Christianity in Japanese new religions, Christianity has not been a major source of new religious movements in Japan. (In Korea, by contrast, Christianity is a major watershed of new religious movements, such as the Unification Church, followers of which are known by its detractors as "Moonies.")

Makuya is interesting to students of Japanese religion for a number of reasons. For one thing, although hundreds of Christian missionary groups from many Western countries have been active in Japan for more than a century, they have been rather unsuccessful, with Christians (church members) accounting for less than 1 percent of the Japanese population. Both Mukyōkai and Makuya represent Japanese attempts to develop an indigenous form of Christianity in Japan—Mukyōkai on a more intellectual level, and Makuya on a more popular level. For another thing, although most Japanese new religions appear to be reconfigurations of Shintō, Buddhism, and Confucianism, Makuya presents one convincing example (along with several other Christian movements) of how a movement can be both Christian and a Japanese new religion. Makuya also shows us how the actual practice of a religion—not just its official teachings and institutional structure—are crucial to its acceptance and growth.

One of the best ways to understand Makuya, and indeed other new religions as well, is to listen to what these religions and their members have to say about their founding figures and the revelations or inspiration they experienced. The materials at hand present a dramatic "inside" view of the experiences that led Master Teshima to become a founder, and the experiences of three people who became his followers. These stories are not dispassionate, "objective" accounts verified with historical evidence; they are passionate, subjective idealizations emerging from personal experiences. If we want to understand how and why individuals become founders, and how and why people join new religions, we will learn much from these accounts. Although these stories are not the raw experiences of the individual founder or member—they are in fact the reconstructed experiences as idealized memories— nevertheless they give us one of the best pictures of how a new religion views its founder and its founding event, and how members understand their lives within the new religion in relation to the founder.

The first translation is taken from *Wagashi Teshima Ikurō*, an official account published by Makuya of the life of Teshima Ikurō, the founder of Makuya. This 369-page work carefully traces the background of Teshima's family and early life. His family devoutly practiced Shintō, and he was taught the spirit of Bushidō (the way of the warrior) from the time he was a small child. When he was twelve he went with his older sister to a Baptist church and experienced conversion while listening to hymns at an outdoor meeting. This led him to his study of Christianity, and he was baptized at age sixteen.

He started his career as a teacher at Kumamoto Higher Commercial School. Around this time he began to participate in the study meetings of Mukyōkai and married Teruyo, the daughter of a minister of Nihon Kirisuto Kyōkai, The Christ Church of Japan. When he was twenty-nine he quit his teaching position and went to China and Korea, where he started his own businesses. After World War II he went back to his hometown and was successful in managing a number of businesses. During this time he conducted Bible study with his employees and also published magazines based on his religious belief. The missionary work that he was conducting during his free time changed dramatically in 1948, when he was thirty-eight. In the first translation we pick up the story of *Wagashi Teshima Ikurō* where it describes the crucial event that led to his calling into a full-time ministry.

The second translation consists of episodes related by three of his followers in *Under Kumamoto Skies (Kumamoto no sora no shita ni)* which was published in 1991, eighteen years after Teshima's death. The title refers to the prefecture of Kumamoto on Kyushu, the southernmost of the four main Japanese islands, where Teshima lived for most of his life and had his crucial religious experiences. These episodes from his life were compiled and published so that people who did not have a chance to meet Teshima could know more about him—not just his formal life and public teachings, but his everyday activities and personal experiences. In these two volumes more than 150 followers tell their stories about how they came to know and be taught by Teshima. The editor of these stories writes in the afterword that Teshima did not have a uniform plan for all his followers—he saw into the character of each person's soul and guided each one accordingly. As the three selected stories show, his followers' love for him comes from the fact that through his guidance they all came into contact with the life of Christ.

The translations are based on Yoshimura Kiichirō, *Wagashi Teshima Ikurō* (Tokyo: Kirisuto Seishojuku, 1990), and *Kumamoto no sora no shita ni*, 2 vols. (Tokyo: Kirisuto Seishojuku, 1991).

Further Reading

Carlo Caldarola, *Christianity: The Japanese Way* (Leiden: E. J. Brill, 1979); Carlo Caldorola, "The Makuya Movement in Japan," *Japanese Religions* 7, 4 (December 1972): 18–34; H. Byron Earhart, "Gedatsu-kai: One Life History and Its Significance for Interpreting Japanese New Religions," *Japanese Journal of Religious Studies* 7, 2–3 (June–September 1980): 227–257; Mark R. Mullins, "Christianity as a New Religion: Charisma, Minor Founders, and Indigenous Movements," in *Religion and Society in Modern Japan*, ed. Mark R. Mullins et al. (Berkeley: Asian Humanities Press, 1993); Teshima Ikurō, *The Original Gospel Faith*, 3d ed. (Tokyo: Makuya Bible Seminary, 1982); Uchimura Kanzō, *How I Became a Christian: Out of My Diary* (Tokyo: Keiseisha, 1895).

OUR MASTER TESHIMA IKURŌ

THE LORD'S VOICE

The Master Teshima, fearing arrest by the military police of the American Occupation Forces, fled to the Jigoku Heights deep within the Minami Aso Mountains, where Mount Okamado rises up. This is on the back side of Mount Aso, an area people hardly visit at all.

The mountain called Okamado is not known well even to the local people, so only a few people could tell where it was. Mount Okamado presents its steep, rocky surface when viewed from the summit of Mount Eboshi, located to the north of Mount Okamado. The origin of the name Okamado comes from its appearance, which looks like an oven (*kamado*). When the Master retreated to the mountain, it was a wilderness never visited by humans. Miscanthus and pampas grass were growing there as tall as most adults. There was no path of any kind. It is a frightening place with fissures that look like cracks of the Earth scattered here and there, and not a drop of water is to be found no matter how far you go. There were people who got lost in this wilderness and, not finding the way out, eventually died due to fear and fatigue—and not only in winter.

The Master wandered around this valley of the shadow of death nearly a month. In the morning while it was still dark the Master would sneak out of Hotel Seifusō because of his fear of the police, hiding himself in the deep grass on the far side of a nearby mountain during the day and sneaking back to the hotel after dark each night. Fortunately, he was never caught in the rain, but his spirit was completely broken, spending each day in fear of arrest. He was so fearful of capture by his oppressors that he had to turn to God. "Oh, God, please help me. Just save me from being sent to Okinawa for heavy labor," he kept praying.

He began praying, and two or three days, and then a week, passed. One day when he was praying on top of Jigokudani, where plumes of sulphur smoke were rising, suddenly everything around him was radiant.

He wondered if the air was shimmering or if the sun had started to shine;

his body trembled and he could not stand. His praying was not complicated. He just repeated over and over, "God, please help me. Help." The Master was flat on the ground.

At that time he heard deep within him a message, like an arrow hitting home, "And though the Lord give you the bread of adversity and the water of affliction, yet your Teacher will not hide himself any more, but your eyes shall see your Teacher. And your ears shall hear a word behind you, saying, 'This is the way, walk in it,' when you turn to the right or when you turn to the left." The Lord inspired him with a biblical passage from Isaiah 30 [Isaiah 30:20–21, cited here from the Revised Standard Version].

"Lord, if you really stand by me and guide me, I will be content no matter how poor I am. If you just say 'Go,' I will go anywhere for mission work." When he came to himself the sun was about to set, painting the grass around him a bright red. He could never forget the scenery at that time, beautiful beyond description. The Master went down Mount Aso with fear and trembling. However, as Christ had promised, he was under the wonderful protection of God. When he went down the mountain to see, the military police had been ordered to another area.

It was early May 1948.

A FOUR-LEAF CLOVER

After returning home from Mount Aso and having a symbolic spiritual dream, the Master set out on his first mission work. When he fled into the mountains of Aso and prayed in the wilderness, he heard the holy voice of God and was given a divine call and descended the mountain, but when he began his mission work, he found no believers at all. Even though he vowed before God, "I will give up everything and devote myself to mission work," he was totally at a loss as to how he should go about his mission work.

One day about that time his son, a second grader, picked a handful of four-leaf clovers and brought them home.

"Father, look how many four-leaf clovers there were. Surely we're headed for good luck, right?"

"There's no place that has so many four-leaf clovers!" his father replied.

"No, father. There are places where they can be found."

Early in the morning on the day after this conversation, in a dream the Master heard a spirit say, "Get up early tomorrow and find a four-leaf clover before the sun rises. Start your mission work at the place where you first find a four-leaf clover."

The Master thought, "All right, should I go to Tokyo? Or should I go to Kyoto? If I go to a big city there are many people and my mission work will probably be successful." He thought about the time after St. Ignatius Loyola had met the resplendent Christ in a cave near Manresa [Spain]: he went to look for students at the Sorbonne and found St. Francis Xavier.

At that point he recalled the melody and words of a school song—"Good, I'll go to the Fifth High School. That campus is probably full of clover. That's where I will start my mission work."

On the wide campus the green clover was shining wet with the morning dew. But he couldn't find any four-leaf clovers. Even worse, his attention was drawn to a large group of pitifully emaciated students.

"I was wrong to come here. There's no time to lose. I should talk to adults. Sick people are the best ones to talk to about religion. Yes, I'll go to the university hospital."

Dragging his tired legs, he pushed his bicycle up to Kumamoto Castle and walked around Fujisakidai where the patient wards and classrooms of the hospital were built next to each other. However, he couldn't find any four-leaf clovers here, either. The sun had already risen high. He was upset with himself for daydreaming, and he went home heaping scorn on himself for believing in revelation or inspiration.

"Oh, it's no good. There wasn't any four-leaf clover. And the sun has already risen high," he mumbled to himself. He went out the back door of his house and squatted down. When he looked right in front of him, he couldn't believe it at all, but there was a four-leaf clover. There was just one, mixed in with some small weeds by the side of the dirt road. Opening his eyes wide, he was surprised: "It really is a four-leaf clover! In a place like this." He had to gasp for breath.

But after he picked it up he was disappointed. It was dirty, faded clover not worth looking at. However, he said to himself, "Wait, the dream I had this morning was truly a spiritual dream. The four-leaf clover is a symbol of faith, hope, love, and charity. But the one I just found is not like that kind of four-leaf clover. It is weak and yellowish, and after being trampled terribly by people it is starting to wither. The sun is at its highest point. And soon, will my destiny be the same as the setting sun?"

"But, it's a four-leaf clover, a four-leaf clover!"

While saying this, he picked up again the clover he had thrown away.

For the Master, he had to feel that this was some kind of symbol of his own destiny. He called his students Minami, Kojima, Yoshimura, and Torikai, "Now, let's begin our Bible study again!" To himself, the Master proclaimed, "My destiny begins at this address, 88 Karashima."

Through coaxing he gathered a number of young students, and after a year's interval he reopened Bible meetings at his home. This was June 1948.

As the name of the address Karashima ("Suffering Island") indicates, it was a place of a series of misfortunes for the Master.

However, once he set out, he could not turn back. Exactly as he learned in the divine calling at Aso, although the Master tasted the bread of adversity and the water of affliction, Christ never hid from him. When he turned to the right or when he turned to the left, Christ was behind him and kept saying in his ear, "This is the way, walk in it."

In the excerpt translated above, Teshima had the transforming experience in the mountains that persuaded him to give up business and begin a full-time ministry. In the passage of the book not translated here, Teshima's ministry from 1948 to 1950 is described—including missionary work and visiting a leprosy sanatorium every Sunday to preach the gospel. However, he was haunted by the question of what the real Christianity is, and whether there wasn't a serious fault in Japanese Christianity at the time.

Although he himself had come into contact with the life of Jesus and was filled with joy, he did not know the best way to convey the life of Jesus to the people. While pondering this he met Tsukamoto Toraji, a Mukyōkai teacher, who said, "Sometimes I think my thirty years of missionary work—lectures on the Bible—were wrong. The result was creating intellectual Christians who just think with their brains." And he advised Teshima, "Don't follow our way of missionary work. You should find your own way." We pick up the story from *Wagashi Teshima Ikurō* as Teshima is striving to conduct his ministry and reach people with his message.

THE SPIRIT OF THE LORD FALLS ON US IN RESPONSE TO MASTER TESHIMA'S PRAYER

In the summer of 1950, within Makuya there was an intense awakening of the Spirit of the Lord. On June 25 of the same year, suddenly hostilities broke out on the Korean Peninsula. The United Nations Emergency Security Council, with the Soviet Union absent, decided to send UN forces to the war front and appointed MacArthur supreme commander in chief. Japan set up the Police Reserve Force and reinstated previously purged officers of the Japanese Armed Forces. At the same time a red purge was begun among the workers of companies. Just when the protracted World War II had finally ended, the Japanese feared that once again they would become involved in the turmoil of war. Especially those of us in Kyushu could not hide our fear about when the sparks of war from the neighboring Korean shores might fall on us.

The Master Teshima earnestly encouraged us, who were weak in faith, to arm ourselves with the Spirit of the Lord. There was a tense air among the members at Kumamoto gatherings. We were told that we were not Christians unless we accepted the Spirit of the Lord. We wondered what the Spirit of the Lord was and thought about how we could receive it. Our eagerness to know the Spirit of the Lord started to intensify.

We opened a Bible study session at the Jigoku Heights in August 1950. The thirty of us, the Kumamoto Bible Study Group, together with new members, arrived at the Yamaguchi Inn, Tarutama, on a dilapidated, charcoal-burning bus. The inn was packed with farmers enjoying the hot baths, taking a break after the harvest. The smell of sulfur stung my nostrils. The Tarutama Falls poured down the slope of rough rocks overlapping one another. It was surrounded with verdant growth. We were distracted by such beautiful scenery, and the Master warned us, "We came up the mountain not simply for sightseeing but for the sole purpose of seeking Heaven. Heaven is where we love each other. We are here to learn how much we can love each other. We want to live with love, forgetting everything else, for a mere three days. We are here to practice our love."

I presided over this first session. Master Teshima picked "First Corinthians" and gave six lectures. Master Teshima was perplexed about how to proceed. No matter how well he chose his words and ideas, they would not reach the people's hearts because beautiful words, lovely to hear, might satisfy the people's intelligence but not provide anything for their hungry spirits. Master Teshima did not know what to do and agonized over this. He planned for his lectures thoroughly, but the night before the session he changed his mind: he abandoned his former lecture style—a soft, wordy, and thoughtful manner. No matter how sharp the members' opposition, no matter how many people dropped out, he decided that he should inject the life of Christ—unadulterated—into their hearts. He preached that belief in the Lord is our life and led us to pray seriously. He also said, "We should not lose our Japanese spirit." However, our hearts were not spiritually prepared, so we just enjoyed ourselves by eating a big breakfast and bathing in the hot springs in the morning. And although it was inexcusable, during his desperate lectures, we dozed, absent-minded, hearing the Master's voice like a pleasant breeze blowing through the mountains. We were beyond his control, even though we only numbered thirty. From time to time Master Teshima's angry voice roared.

THE SPIRIT OF THE LORD WORKED AFTER MASTER TESHIMA'S ENERGY WAS EXHAUSTED

Beginning with 5:30 early morning prayers, he continued rigorously with his Bible lectures and testimonies. We had to help each other with cooking, cleaning, and gathering firewood during the camp. On the third day we were all about to fall down. Some of the weak-willed members complained of stomachaches and headaches. However, Master Teshima kept on lecturing to us, not paying attention to our complaints. He said, "The Kingdom of God does not rely on words, but on power. The words of the cross are foolishness to those who perish. However, without receiving the blood of the cross, the spiritual world will not open to you. If you cannot bear the physical strain of a mere three days, what do you think 'faith' is? Won't the power of the divine spirit confront you? Your heads are stubborn, your reasoning is argumentative, and your flesh is greedy for three meals a day—they must be smashed! They must be emasculated! If you do not eliminate your own heart and mind, how will you ever understand the voiceless voice of the cross calling out from the world of death! My beloved friends! I will speak clearly to your spirits. You whose ears are not circumcised, it is useless no matter how much I talk to your eardrums."

Master Teshima was so serious, and he was almost pathetically spurring us on. His last lecture finally ended on the third day. His energy exhausted, with head hanging down, he collapsed on the desk. Soon we heard a prayer escape like a groan. It was a small, low voice that seemed to be squeezed out of his stomach. "God, I studied so hard. I loved my friends in religion so much. I paid for their board and lodging, I gave my all. With my whole body, my whole spirit, I did my best giving Bible lectures, but there's nothing more I can do. My wife is sick in bed, our children are crying for food . . . , I have lost all my energy. God, I can no longer do mission work."

When I heard Master Teshima's broken voice, in my mind I didn't understand what happened, but suddenly deep within me I was moved, and I was crying on the floor. All of us were crying.

Facing the Master's final, all-out confession of faith, our stubborn hearts and our worldly thoughts turned into a lamentation of intense repentance. Our Bibles and hymnals were wet with our tears.

I was surprised at the transformation of my mind—I had seen him as such a frightening Master, but now I looked up to him with an emotion of love I never knew before. I was filled with intense love. And I sensed a feeling of unity with my brothers and sisters. This was the first spiritual experience in my whole life. I said to myself, "This is the rebirth of my soul. This is without doubt the 'love of the Holy Spirit.'" My soul became in tune with this, and I kept repeating "Amen" endlessly.

Master Teshima described his frame of mind at the time, as follows:

My lectures failed completely. The logic broke down. The ideas were incoherent. But I finished the lectures by speaking out with all my soul. And I ended it by just lying on the floor and praying before the cross of the Lord. . . . When I finished the prayer and raised my head to look around, everyone's exalted faces were filled with deep emotion; these friends in religion had remarkably shining eyes, smiling with their taut brows expressing their confidence. Without thinking about it, somehow all of them were filled with the love of the Holy Spirit, and we all felt that Christ, who is still living, was standing right before us.

Altogether, like a dam had burst, triumphant hymns of faith spilled out of our mouths. Those who had much experience in the faith, as well as those new to the faith, altogether were enfolded in the love of the one Holy Spirit, in one peace, in one life. And after that some were blessed with the gift of speaking in tongues, and the spiritual power of faith healing. Everyone advanced remarkably in their faith and joy.

Now I understood the emptiness of the years of my Bible lectures. I realized fully how I had wasted so much passionate time and effort on the rationale of the cross and the theological commentaries on redemption, as well as on explanation of Greek phrases [of the Bible], and I cried in regret. I also saw that encouraging the people to have "faith in faith alone" would not save us.

However, God—in spite of our lack of faith and discouragement and failures, in spite of our weakness and sin and ignorance—is good enough to lead us all to salvation. This is just the grace of God, this is just the love of the Holy Spirit.

We return glory and praise to the God of Christ who was crucified on the cross so that he might grant a glorious spirit to humans created out of clods of earth, who forgives us, and loves us, and granted us a life (or love) that even though we die we may be reborn.

UNDER KUMAMOTO SKIES

AN UPSTAIRS MAKUYA ROOM IN KYOTO, BY ZAITSU MASAYA

Unexpectedly, someone had entered my room.

It seemed like I had heard my wife cry out, "Oh," in a small voice, showing her surprise. Soon after that, I heard heavy footsteps making a creaky sound climbing the stairs to my second-floor room. I was sitting in a tiny study room at the end of the hallway from the stairs, with my back to the door, when I sensed someone approaching from behind. Without any warning the person opened the door and came in, looking down at my back without saying a word. After a while I turned around and looked, and it was Master Teshima standing there in a black, double-breasted suit. I was so surprised that I thought it was a dream.

It was not a dream but something that actually happened in the late fall of 1961 when I was doing mission work in Kyoto. It was vividly burned into my brain, an unforgettable scene. That incident happened on the day of our meeting, when I was in my room all alone preparing for the meeting.

At that time we had a serious problem facing the unhappy ending of a couple's marriage. I was desperate, not knowing how we should handle that evening's meeting. In this situation I was in a frame of mind that I didn't care who might come in, so I just directed my vacant gaze behind me. It was Master Teshima. Seeing him was like Jesus Christ appearing all of a sudden to his disciples who were about to be swallowed by stormy lake waters on a dark night. Master Teshima came to me when I was just about to collapse. Since the room was so small, when he sat down his knees touched my kneecaps numb with cold. For a while Master Teshima was lost in thought with a stern face; after a while he opened his eyes and talked to me, looking me straight in the eyes. He said, "You know," which were the first words he always used in formal talks to us—his "you know" was so pleasant that it will never leave my ears.

"You know, if you are a missionary, you must learn to live listening to the Lord more. You are too concerned about other people, so you fail. You always exert yourself too much so as not to lose to others. For you, the Lord has prepared a road just for you. In order for you to fulfill the special career planned for you, you do not have to compete with others or be concerned about immediate success. You seem to be impatient. And you are not yourself."

What Master Teshima said was exactly right. Every word Master Teshima said sank into my soul, and I looked up at him, wondering how I could escape my predicament. Then Master Teshima glanced around my meager book shelf and spoke to me in easily understood phrases.

"You—Rome wasn't built in a day, you know. And it's not too late to start now. You can begin reading the Bible in earnest. In the original. You can't do anything unless you learn Greek, anyway. You do not have to be a scholar, but it is impossible to talk about the Bible if you don't go back to the original. Read it steadfastly each day, appreciate it fully, and when you discover something special, or receive some inspiration, write notes in the Bible. The New Testament has only twenty-seven books, so if you really want to, you can do it."

Although I had eagerly read scholarly books and literature, I was ashamed that I had never earnestly read the Bible in the original, and while listening to the Master, I was filled with the passionate idea: "I'll do it!"

Master Teshima said, "You need at least three years to start something new, they say. Why not try it steadfastly for three years. Without anyone knowing it you'll reach some level. And then in five years people around you will come to recognize you more. Do this for ten years and see. You'll be an expert in the field you chose to specialize in."

He continued, "Now the marriage problem has you down, but whether or not you amount to something, it's all up to you, it all depends on how you live the next ten years. Well, you must do it, Zaitsu."

Suddenly Master Teshima's warm, soft hand reached out, took hold of my cold hand, and squeezed it. As my body shuddered within, hot life flowed into it. By the time I became aware of what happened, Master Teshima had stood up and was going down the stairs. I jumped up and ran after him, but I just saw his back swaying to and fro going down the stairs, and my tears blocked the view of him. For me, the person we call Master Teshima was this kind of person. Just by his coming, the Master breathed a warm, warm breath of new life into my spirit that was trembling and crying in loneliness.

> Everyone will cry for the Master Teshima's love for us,
> If only they have a trace of what the Master engraved.

RETURN TO YOUR HOME!, BY MITSUNAGA KUNIKO

In my youth, after I was stigmatized as having spondylolysis [loosening of vertebrae], I was leading a discontented life with no hope at all for the future. It was a November day in 1956 when I was introduced to Master Teshima by my "angel" friend: my whole life was changed, and I was rescued from gloom to a bright world. Through that one meeting, that one laying on of hands by the Master Teshima, I had met the Lord our father, and I cried for joy to come across the one I for so long had been seeking.

Because my soul was saved, I thought I needed nothing other than this Christ. Even if my body did not get better it was all right, I was so filled with joy that I thought it was all right if I didn't get better. Shortly after our first meeting, I lived and worked in Master Teshima's house for ten months—this was the best time in my life, when I laid the foundation of my faith in the Lord for my whole life, and I was blessed.

At that time, when I was nineteen, I was sincerely loved by Master Teshima and his wife Chiyo as their daughter, the same as their three other children. Because I had lost my father when I was six years old, every day was happy for me, like being brought out of a lonely desert to an oasis.

Although I had converted [to Christianity], I did not understand the faith, and all I could say was "Yes, yes," and just follow them. I believed that absolute trust in Master Teshima was absolute trust in God, and that everything started from there.

Master Teshima, who knew my heart well, one time said, "Kuniko, you obey whatever I tell you, right?"

"Yes," I replied.

"Well, then, return to your own home!" he said.

"Oh, I don't want to, Master!"

Master Teshima sometimes pressed me with difficult questions.

Master Teshima could not eat hot food, and when served hot food, right away he was in a bad mood. What bothered me was when to serve him the noon meal. At the time he was editing "Light of Life" on the second floor, and I did not know when he would come down to eat. When he came down early I was confused and served up a bowl of the hot rice I had just cooked, and cooled it with a fan. Because if it wasn't ready at once, he would go back up to the second floor and not come down.

Times when I thought I had made a mistake, I apologized beforehand: "I am sorry, Master, today I did not cook very well," or "I'm sorry, I was late calling you."

Then Master Teshima's sharp tongue, having no one to blame, would just disappear.

The Aso Bible Meeting in the summer of 1957 was the first Bible meeting I attended.

Up to this time, my mother and relatives urged me to return to my home in Fukuoka. I think that when you are trying to live by faith, the love of your own parents is what stands in the way most of all. Just like the phrase in the Bible: "Do not think that I have come to bring peace on Earth. I have not come to bring peace, but a sword. For I have come to set a man against his father, and a daughter against her mother" [Matthew 10:34–35, cited here from Revised Standard Version].

I was standing at a crossroads: should I return home or should I stay in

Kumamoto? Master Teshima, who knew I was anxious about the matter, would not advise me. I told my family, "I want you to wait until I attend the [Aso Summer] Bible meeting. When it has ended I will come home." And for one month I was praying and praying, "God, what shall I do, what is best for me to do?" After I left it up to the Bible meeting and prayed under a waterfall, when I was soaking in a hot bath, suddenly an inner voice rose up from the bottom of my stomach, and at the same time I decided clearly: "Even if I am disowned, I will remain in Kumamoto and study the [Christian] faith."

When the [Aso Summer] Bible Meeting was over I told Master Teshima my decision, and he just said, "Well, that's good." But I could tell, behind that short reply, how much he had been praying for me and watching over me, and I was filled with a flood of emotions. If I had merely followed the advice and guidance of Master Teshima, then I would only have trusted in a person called "master." And if things had not gone well, then I might have blamed this person. Master Teshima taught us to learn for ourselves—that we should not trust in people (that is to say, not to make arbitrary decisions), but listen to Christ and live with trust in Christ.

Several days after I made that one step forward, in a living room in Karashima-chō, I had a spiritual dream and my spondylolysis was completely healed. It was a strange dream: in a room of the Shibata Inn where the Aso Bible Meeting was held, everyone left the room to attend the evening prayer called Sekiyōkai. I was left alone, so I hurried to leave the inn and follow the members. Then there was someone standing beside me.

I wondered who it was, and when I looked up that person was the late wife of Master Teshima, Teruyo. I had not known Teruyo at all, and had not even seen a photograph of her, but somehow I clearly understood it was her. Without saying a word Teruyo laid her hand on my head. When she did this my whole body was gripped by a spirit, like being shocked with electricity.

At that time, I knew intuitively that "my back is healed!" It was such a vivid event that I woke up, but my body was so numb that I still could not move.

The late Mrs. Teruyo Teshima, before she ascended to heaven, said, "Something good will surely happen to the members of Makuya after I die," and just as she said, through the working of the power of Heaven I was healed. I took off the stiff corset I had worn up to that time, and I began to live more freely both physically and spiritually. Although I had been told I was unable to have any children, the Lord made it possible for me to have three children. And that was not all, as part of this blessing, my mother (Mrs. Yugeta) and my brother and sister joined Makuya. In August 1989, on my mother's eighty-eighth birthday, her children, grandchildren, and great grandchildren—some thirty Christians altogether—gathered and gave thanks to the Lord Jesus Christ.

THE LORD'S CROWN OF LOVE, BY KAWASAKI SHIMEI

On June 4, 1962, three days after I collapsed from a serious case of tuberculosis, I received the Holy Spirit and experienced a dramatic conversion. Every night praise to the Lord like in the Psalms kept welling up in me, just like a dream. I dearly loved Master Teshima, and about every two days I wrote the Master, who at that time was in Kumamoto. Under these conditions my husband was given a melody from Heaven, and he used it to compose a hymn, "Until Exalted With the Blood of the Lord."

Although my physical condition was such that I was ordered by the doctor to follow strict bed rest, with the joy welling up in me I could not remain still, and because it was already planned, on June 16 I held a piano recital for my students. In those days Master Teshima came to Osaka from Kumamoto once a month to give a series of ten lectures on the Bible, and the night of the recital fell on the day of the tenth lecture.

Master Teshima arrived in Osaka during the day and happened to hear about the recital, so he looked around all the major concert halls in Osaka until he found this Asahi Seimei Hall.

That night I attended Master Teshima's meeting for the first time, and during the lecture the Master said, "Today I went to the piano recital for Mrs. Kawasaki's students, visiting one hall after another until I finally found it. The reason I went to a concert for students I didn't even know was to pray for the Lord's crown of love to be placed on Mr. and Mrs. Kawasaki." He wrote on the blackboard in large letters, "The Lord's crown of love."

While listening to him, how happy the Master was over the salvation of one soul; his love was so great I could not stop crying.

After the meeting Master Teshima said, "Medicine will ruin your body." That night, as he suggested, I decided to give up all medicine, and from that point the battle for faith began.

I was anxious about throwing away medicine and beset by fear, and there were times when I almost lost my faith.

About that time a letter came from Master Teshima. It said: "My dearest Mrs. Kawasaki. Remain quiet until a rainstorm has passed. Your heart's peace is faith. Sleep as if you are dead, without consciousness. Soon you will be healed by the power of the Lord's hand. Noah was victorious in his test of forty days and forty nights. You too will be victorious. Take care of yourself. Amen."

Clasping the Master's letter to my chest, I slept for ten days just as if I were dead.

And I was completely healed by the power of Christ's holy hand. I told the Master that by looking at the x-ray I could tell I was completely healed.

He scolded me severely: "The person who believes without looking is blessed—but being happy or sad from looking at an x-ray is not faith." After that he took a lot of pictures of me and was very happy.

ORTHOPRAXIS AND ORTHODOXY

— 38 —

Mujū Ichien's Shintō-Buddhist Syncretism

Robert E. Morrell

Mujū Ichien (1226–1312) is better known to us today as a literary figure—
perhaps the last major representative of the "tale literature" (*setsuwa*) tradition—
than as a Buddhist theoretician. But his place in this volume rests on his practical
application of wide-ranging theoretical interests.

He is generally identified in standard biographies as a disciple of the Rinzai
Zen pioneer and first abbot of Kyoto's Tōfukuji, Enni Ben'en (Shōichi Kokushi,
1202–1280), whom he met somewhat briefly late in life. But Mujū's religious
world was dominated by the Tendai sect, which had been established four centuries earlier at the Enryakuji on Mount Hiei by Saichō (Dengyō Daishi, 767–
822). In Mujū's day Tendai was still the secure center of the Buddhist establishment, providing the ground rules, the vocabulary, and the schedule of issues by
which the game was to be played. Today we see Kamakura Buddhism largely
through the eyes of the heirs of the reformers, now become the establishment.
The popular movements did in time overwhelm Heian Tendai and Shingon, but
we must remind ourselves that this did not take place overnight. In Mujū's day
the concerns, issues, and scriptures of Tendai were a given. But we also have
reason to believe that early on he was also associated with the disciplinary revival
of Eison (Shiembō, 1201–1290), and that toward the end of his long life his
interests took a turn toward Shingon.

Tendai's basic scripture was the *Lotus Sutra*, which states that the Eternal Buddha employs a variety of provisional teachings, accommodations (*hōben*) to human
needs and biases. "Truth" was not a term confined to the proper progression of
steps in a logical argument, nor the economy of a hypothesis to explain the
operations of certain physical phenomena. Religious "truth" is a matter of immediate experience ultimately beyond the grasp of all conceptual formulations.
Mythologies, metaphors, and other word-games might be more or less helpful
(but they could also be a hindrance) in bringing us to the threshhold of this
awareness; and their relative usefulness to the devotee to attain this goal was their
"empirical verification." Doctrinal variety was not only possible but inevitable.

Dogmatic exclusiveness was a fundamental error and became the common issue of the Tendai establishment against the new sects that arose in the Kamakura era. Tendai did not deny that the new methods or, rather, the new emphases could lead the devotee to enlightenment; it only objected to claims that a specific method was the only road to salvation. Curiously, it was not the establishment that opposed its entrenched dogma against new interpretations of scripture; rather, it was the establishment that defended the possibility of innovative plurality against the single-minded dogmatists. The concepts and literary images of the *Lotus Sutra* pervaded the thought of Heian and Kamakura Japan, and their influence on Heian life and thought can hardly be exaggerated. During the Kamakura period the *Lotus Sutra* gradually had to share its popularity with the scriptures of the Zen and Pure Land movements. But for Mujū and his contemporaries, it was still a work of enormous authority.

The doctrine of accommodation permitted Tendai a wide diversity of doctrine and practice, and Tendai provided the theoretical framework within which each of the emerging sects defined itself. Not only did the leaders of the new movements—Hōnen, Shinran, Nichiren, Eisai, Dōgen, Enni—all begin their careers either on Mount Hiei or at Miidera (Onjōji), the two main centers of Tendai Buddhism, but the Tendai synthesis contained within itself the seeds of their religious emphases: a program for meditation, devotion to Amida, and reliance on the *Lotus Sutra*—all held together by the doctrine of accommodation. It was necessary for Hōnen and Shinran to demonstrate that their new Pure Land movement was an improvement on the Amidism promoted by Tendai's Genshin (942–1017) in his *Essentials of Salvation* (*Ōjōyōshū*). Nichiren was to show that he had taken from the complexities of Tendai all that was useful for the degenerate times in which he lived: simple faith in the *Lotus Sutra*. And the proponents of Zen were to reassert their methods of meditation in full awareness of those elaborated in the *Great Calming and Insight* (an issue that their Chinese predecessors had resolved centuries earlier), and also to decide whether they would accommodate or reject other practices.

For Mujū doctrinal diversity was an expression of the Buddha's compassion. Each method had its special purpose, and all were approaches to the same experiential truth that in the end transcended every particular formulation. Some might be more or less useful, but all were possible. And the new movements of his age were entirely compatible with the tolerant Mahāyāna attitude toward the word games of philosophy and myth-making of religion. The spiritual life might be rationalized in a variety of ways. As Mujū would say: "There is not just one method for entering the Way, the causes and conditions for enlightenment being many." His syncretism, his conviction that truth not only can, but must, assume a variety of forms, is reflected throughout his life and writings. The gods of the native Japanese Shintō pantheon "soften their light to identify with the dust of human affairs (*wakō dōjin*)." The buddhas and bodhisattvas in their essential nature (*honji*) are ineffable, inaccessible to ordinary human understanding; accordingly, they assume familiar, local guises, "manifesting their traces" (*suijaku*) as a means of leading sentient beings to enlightenment. They assume the forms of Shintō gods, Confucian sages, Taoist immortals, or any other shapes appropriate to the expectations of the devotee, because the underlying Reality transcends all particular manifestations. And yet it is through these particular forms that we, symbolizing animals, are led to the ineffable. As Kūkai remarked with respect to all expedients: "The Dharma is beyond speech, but without speech it cannot be revealed. Suchness transcends forms, but without depending on forms it cannot be realized. Though one may at times err by taking the finger pointing at the moon to be the moon itself, the Buddha's teachings which guide people are limitless" (Hakeda 1972, 145). All forms point to the same experiential goal beyond all words, all concepts, all symbols.

Common to every Buddhist teaching is the recognition that all conditioned beings are in flux, evanescent, impermanent (mujō); and because each exists only interdependently with all other beings, it is intrinsically selfless (muga). To strive for one's own enlightenment is, in effect, to deny this basic principle of selflessness. So the Mahāyānists proposed as their spiritual model the bodhisattva, "a being compounded of the two contradictory forces of wisdom and compassion. In his wisdom he sees no persons; in his compassion he is resolved to save them" (Conze 1959, 130). This compassion arises neither from any desire for profit nor from a sense of altruism—without an alter, an "other," the word itself has no meaning. It springs rather from an awareness of the underlying identity between what is conventionally distinguished as "self" and "other."

The compassion of the Buddha is revealed in the manifold accommodations (hōben) he makes to human frailties, expedients, and "skillful means," which include not only the varieties of Buddhist teaching but the mythology of Shintō as well. The importance of the syncretism theme in Mujū's thought is to be seen in the fact that when, fairly late in life, he began to write, this was the first subject that he chose to elaborate. Most of his arguments and illustrations of this topic are conveniently concentrated in the ten chapters of the first book of Sand and Pebbles (Shasekishū, 1279–1283). After the preface and opening chapter, in which Mujū sets forth the general argument for the identity of the gods and buddhas as applied to the Ise shrines, is a series of anecdotes interspersed with doctrinal digressions.

Conventional morality held that "wild words and specious phrases" (kyōgen kigo) were to be avoided as impediments to enlightenment: hence the condemnation of literature as so much distraction from right views. But if nirvāna were to be realized within the world of everyday affairs, then these same "wild words and specious phrases" could be cause for praising the vehicle of the Buddha and condition for turning the Wheel of the Law. The concept was rooted in Indian Buddhism, but the phrase itself originated with the Chinese poet Po Chü-i (772–846), from whom it was borrowed by Japanese Buddhists as a catch phrase to express the concept of the noumenal realized through the phenomenal. It appears throughout Mujū's works, beginning with the preface to Sand and Pebbles: "Through the wanton sport of wild words and specious phrases I wish to bring people into the marvelous Way of the Buddha's Teaching." Still, the tension in the paradox remained: delusions of word and thought were certainly to be eschewed (and, strictly speaking, even the most "sacred" words and thoughts were ultimately impediments to enlightenment); but on the other hand, they might be utilized as expedients, accommodations. "Those who search for gold extract it from sand; those who take pleasure in jewels gather pebbles and polish them." Truth was a middle way between the poles of morality as conventionally (but necessarily) fixed, and morality as ultimately indeterminate. Literature was to serve the needs of society—the ultimate goal of both individual and society, in Mujū's view, being the enlightenment of all sentient beings.

In her famous defense of the novel in *The Tale of Genji*, Murasaki Shikibu also appeals to the doctrine of accommodation as the rationale for finding the sacred in the profane. Mujū starts from the same premise but, as a well-educated cleric, could be expected to carry the argument a step further, for better or worse.

The translation is based on Mujū Ichien, *Shasekishū*, in *Nihon koten bungaku taikei*, vol. 85, ed. Watanabe Tsunaya (Tokyo: Iwanami Shoten , 1976).

Further Reading

Edward Conge, *Buddhism: Its Essence and Development* (New York: Harper & Row, 1959); Yoshito Hakeda, tr., *Kūkai: Major Works* (New York: Columbia University Press, 1972); Alicia Matsunaga, *The Buddhist Philosophy of Assimilation: The Historical Development of the Honji-Suijaku Theory* (Tokyo and Rutland, Vt.: Charles E. Tuttle, 1969); Robert E. Morrell, *Sand and Pebbles (Shasekishū): The Tales of Mujū Ichien, a Voice for Pluralism in Kamakura Buddhism* (Albany: State University of New York Press, 1985); Hartmut O. Rotermund, *Collection de sable et de pierres: Shasekishū par Ichien Mujū* (Paris: Gallimard, 1979).

Sand and Pebbles

PROLOGUE

Coarse words and refined expressions both proceed from the Unconditioned, nor are the everyday affairs of life at variance with the True Reality. Through the wanton sport of wild words and specious phrases, I wish to bring people into the marvelous Way of the Buddha's teaching; and with unpretentious examples taken from the common ordinary affairs of life I should like to illustrate the profound significance of this splendid doctrine. So I rouse myself from the drowsiness of old age, and with an idle hand I have assembled at random that which I have seen and heard. I have recorded incidents just as they have come to mind, without selecting the good from the bad.

At a time when he should be aware of the things of impermanence that thought-by-thought obstruct his apprehension of Reality, and when he should be concerned over his step-by-step approach to the nether world, piling up provisions for the long journey to the subterranean regions and preparing the boat to carry him over the deep currents of the troubled seas of life, this old priest is writing down incidents that strike his fancy and recording frivolous worldly anecdotes. He is not concerned about how he wastes his time in the present, nor does he feel shame at what the wise and learned may say of him later on. But though it may seem useless, for the sake of those foolish people who are not aware of the great benefits of Buddhism, who do not know the profound intent of the gods who "soften their light and identify with the dust" (*wakō dōjin*; cf. *Tao Te Ching* 4), who do not discriminate between wise and foolish, and who do not believe that the operation of moral causality is determined and fixed, he has selected clear passages from the sutras and commentaries and set down the admonitions left by the wise of former times.

There is not just one method for entering the Way, the causes and conditions for enlightenment being many. Once a person understands their general significance, he will see that the purport of the various teachings does not vary. And when he puts them into practice, he will find that the goal of the myriad religious exercises is the same. So from among casual digressions this old monk extracts the sacred teaching, and among humorous anecdotes he points out the theory and practice of Buddhism. May those who have occasion to see it not despise this poorly written work by means of which they may come to comprehend the significance of Buddhism; nor should they blame the inclusion of extraneous material through which they may come to understand the operation of moral causality. May they use this work as a means by which to leave this village of birth-and-death and as a signpost to reach the great city of Nirvāna— such is the hope of this foolish old man.

Those who search for gold extract it from sand; those who take pleasure in jewels gather pebbles and polish them. So I call this book the *Collection of Sand and Pebbles*. It consists of ten chapters and includes over a hundred items.

Collected in midsummer in the second year of Kōan [1279] by a humble monk in the grove of letters, Mujū.

1:1. THE GREAT SHRINE AT ISE

While I was on a pilgrimage to the Great Shrine during the Kōchō era [1261–1264], an official explained to me why words associated with the Three Treasures of Buddhism [the Buddha, the Law, and the Order] were forbidden at the shrine, and why monks could not closely approach the sacred buildings.

In antiquity, when this country did not yet exist, the deity of the Great Shrine [the Sun Goddess, Amaterasu], guided by a seal of the Great Sun Buddha inscribed on the ocean floor, thrust down her august spear. Brine from the spear coagulated like drops of dew, and this was seen from afar by Māra, the Evil One, in the Sixth Heaven of Desire [Takejizai]. "It appears that these drops are forming into a land where Buddhism will be propagated and people will escape from the round of birth-and-death," he said, and he came down to prevent it.

Then the deity of the Great Shrine met with the demon king. "I promise not to utter the names of the Three Treasures, nor will I permit them near my person. So return quickly back to the heavens." Being thus mollified, he withdrew.

Monks to this very day, not wishing to violate that august promise, do not approach the sacred shrine, and the sutras are not carried openly in its precincts. Things associated with the Three Treasures are referred to obliquely: Buddha is called "The Cramp-Legged One" [*tachisukumi*]; the sutras, "colored paper" [*somegami*]; monks, "longhairs" [*kaminaga*]; and temples, "incense burners" [*koritaki*], etc. Outwardly the deity is estranged from the Law, but inwardly she profoundly supports the Three Treasures. Thus, Japanese Buddhism is under the special protection of the deity of the Great Shrine.

This shrine is father and mother to all the gods of this land. When Amaterasu closed the Rock Door of Heaven and dwelt in seclusion, disgusted by the heavenly improprieties committed by Susa-no-o, all the world was plunged in darkness. In their distress the eight hundred myriad deities built a ceremonial fire and performed the sacred dance [*kagura*], that they might coax her forth. When the Sun Goddess, curious at the sport of the divine maidens, narrowly opened the Rock Door and looked out, the world was illuminated. As everyone was thus enabled to distinguish the faces of others once more, they exclaimed: "Ara omoshiroshi!" ["How delightful it is again to see each other's faces."] This was the origin of the expression.

Then the god Tajikara-no-o carried her forth and drew a sacred rope across the Rock Door, asking her not to enter again into the cave. On being brought forth, she immediately became sun and moon and illumined the earth. Thus, even our now being affected by the light of the sun and moon is through the benevolent virtue of this deity. Since all of this arose by virtue of the seal of the Great Sun Buddha on the ocean floor, we have come to identify the deities of the Inner and Outer Shrines [Amaterasu and Toyoukehime] with the Great Sun Buddha of the Two-Part Mandala [Mahāvairocana (Dainichi Nyorai), the central Buddha in both the Matrix (*taizōkai*) and Diamond (*kongōkai*) assemblies]; and that which is called the Rock Door of Heaven is the Tusita Heaven [of the future Buddha Maitreya], also known as the High Plain of Heaven (*takama ga hara*).

Events that took place during the Age of the Gods all have their Buddhist interpretation. In the Shingon view the Tusita Heaven, indeed, is spoken of as the Great Sun Buddha's World-of-Dharma Palace of Inner Realization, his Land of Esoteric Grandeur. The Great Sun Buddha came forth from this capital of Inner Realization to assume local manifestations in the land of the sun [Japan]. Thus, the deity of the Inner Shrine at Ise is the Great Sun of the Matrix World; and patterned after the Four-Enclosure Mandala are the several shrine fences: *tamagaki, mizugaki, aragaki,* etc.

Likewise, there are nine logs on the roof of the main hall of the Inner Shrine symbolizing the nine Holy Ones of the Matrix World [Mandala]. We are accustomed to identify the deity of the Outer Shrine with the Great Sun Buddha of the Diamond World; and also with Amida. It is doubtless to symbolize the Five Wisdoms of the Diamond World that its design consists of five moon-circles. When the Two-Part Matrix-Diamond Mandala is viewed in the light of the yin-yang teaching, wherein the yin is female and the yang male, the eight petals of the Matrix parallel the shrine's Eight Maidens; and it is because the Five Wisdoms of the Diamond World are represented by male divinities that there is a group of five male shrine dancers.

Moreover, out of consideration of its burden on the people and its expense to the country, the shrine sanctuaries are thatched simply with miscanthus and it uses ceremonial offerings of thrice-pounded unpolished rice. The crosspieces are straight and the roof beams uncurved—so that the hearts of men may be rectified. Thus, those who with upright hearts consider the effect of their actions on the plight of the people and its expense to the country conform to the will of the gods. One who serves at this shrine quite naturally refrains from the Ten Grave Offenses proscribed by the *Net of Brahma Sutra* (*Bommōkyō*). If he murders, he is exiled from his clan for a long period of time, just as a monk is no longer counted among the sons of the Buddha if he commits one of the Ten Grave Offenses. Having struck a man and drawn blood, a Shintō priest is expelled from his office, just as if he had been charged with one of the Lesser Offenses prescribed for the Buddhist clergy.

The tabus observed at Ise differ somewhat from those of other shrines. Childbirth is spoken of as "bearing spirit," and those involved are under a fifty-day pollution; likewise, death is spoken of as "death-spirit" and also creates a fifty-day pollution.

Death proceeds from life, and life is the beginning of death. The shrine official informed me that this was handed down as the reason for birth-and-death both to be tabu.

Now the Great Sun Buddha is not subject to birth-and-death; and the original purpose for his coming forth from the Inner Realization of the Law Body and manifesting his traces in order to save the ignorant and deluded masses produced through the four forms of birth [i.e., from womb, egg, moisture, or by metamorphosis] was to put a stop to the round of birth-and-death, and to lead people to the Buddha's Path of eternal life. Thus, to speak of placing both birth-and-death under a tabu is the same as saying that we do not foolishly create the karma of delusive conduct which causes the painful cycle of birth-and-death. It is to say that we wisely practice the marvelous Law of the Buddha, and that we aspire to birth in a Pure Land (*jōdo*) paradise and to enlightenment. While it is entirely in conformity with the will of the deity of the Great Shrine that we believe in and practice the Way of the Buddha, it is contrary to the divine will for us to concern ourselves with the glories of this life, to pray for prosperity and longevity, to observe the tabus with a heart still deeply attached to the things of the world, and to be devoid of any sense of religious aspiration.

The august forms of the Traces Manifest by the Original Ground may vary, but their purpose is assuredly the same. To propagate Buddhism in China, the three bodhisattvas Mānava, Kāśyapa, and Dīpamkara—appearing as Confucius, Lao-tzu, and Yen Hui (Gankai)—first softened the people's hearts by means of non-Buddhist teachings. Later, when Buddhism was propagated, everyone believed in it.

In Japan the illustrious native deities who soften their light first manifested their traces—the Buddha using this as a skillful means to soften the rough disposition of the people and to lead them to belief in the Dharma. If we rely on the profound efficacy of the Original Ground while believing in the skillful means, close to hand, of gods who soften their light, we will realize our hope for peace and the end of calamities in this life, and attain eternal enlightenment, not subject to birth-and-death, in the next. Those born in our land should be thoroughly aware of this fact.

— 39 —

Contested Orthodoxies in Five Mountains
Zen Buddhism

Joseph D. Parker

Zen Buddhism has taken many forms in different centuries and locations in Japanese history. In the fourteenth through sixteenth centuries one group of government-sponsored temples, those belonging to the Gosan or Five Mountains temple system, played a role approaching in certain respects that of a state religion. Monks and nuns from these Zen temples were inevitably very much involved in a variety of socioeconomic and political relations in the world. In these and other ways, Five Mountains Zen joins other forms of Zen religious practice in questioning stereotypical associations current today of essential or "true" Zen Buddhism as a form of private, individual meditation practiced somewhere outside of social convention and of competition for power, wealth, and prestige.

The Five Mountains temple system took as its early foundation the major temples founded during the thirteenth century in the rival capitals of Kamakura and Kyoto with support from the Hōjō regents in Kamakura and the imperial family in Kyoto. Temples such as Kenchōji and Engakuji in Kamakura or Tōfukuji and Nanzenji in Kyoto were (and still are) imposing complexes of buildings modeled generally on important Chinese Zen temple compounds. The largest monasteries were populated by hundreds of men of various ages with a wide range of religious, social, economic, artistic, and other skills and social roles. Historians are just beginning to uncover evidence of a parallel system of nunneries also nascent at this time, which would by the late fifteenth century grow into a Five Mountains system of nunneries where women wielded significant power and influence comparable perhaps to that of the monasteries. In following continental practice, the teachers in the Japanese Five Mountains temples often freely combined different schools of Zen with other schools of Buddhism and relied on canonical Mahāyāna Buddhist texts; followed the Zen style of the important Chinese master Ta-hui Tsung-kao (Daie Sōkō, 1089–1163), which by the fourteenth century was growing influential throughout China, Korea, Japan, and Vietnam; and integrated many texts and cultural practices now associated with Chinese elite culture, including poetry, calligraphy, prose, and the teachings of the Neo-Confucian, Taoist, Ancient Civilization (kobun), and literati (bunjin) traditions.

The formal designation of a Five Mountains temple system seems to have first taken form initially during the Kemmu Imperial Restoration (1333–1336) under Emperor Go-Daigo (1288–1339; r. 1318–1339) and then, after the failure of the Restoration, in more enduring fashion under the Ashikaga shoguns in the early decades of the Muromachi period (1336–1568). Perhaps the most important early competition for Five Mountains orthodoxy occured in the mid-1320s between the monk Shūhō Myōchō (National Teacher Daitō, 1282–1337) and the monk Musō Soseki (1275–1351), who both rose to prominence in the capital of Kyoto and began to compete for imperial patronage. Compared exclusively in doctrinal terms, the two teachers show many similarities. When both monks received recognition by authorities as abbots of important temples, they seemed to have achieved parity. Yet the fortunes of Daitō's line of Zen soon took a sharp turn for the worse when Emperor Go-Daigo's restoration failed and Ashikaga generals took control of the government. This change in the political landscape led to a scramble among the most powerful lords in the new shogunate for alliances with prestigious cultural and religious leaders that could reinforce their prestige and claims to authority, as well as to intense competition among Buddhist leaders for powerful patrons.

In this upheaval Musō was most successful and Daitō seems to have fared poorly, for Daitokuji, which had held a position of great prestige, dropped completely out of the important hierarchical rankings of the Five Mountains temples by 1341 when the newly powerful Ashikaga shoguns rewrote the Five Mountains system. Musō and his disciples went on to dominate the abbacies of Nanzenji and the other major Five Mountains temples in both the capital Kyoto and the former capital Kamakura, dominance that would last until the sixteenth century. This achievement opened the door for Musō to claim the authority to speak in the name of the collectivity, that is, to define the "essential" truth of Zen as it was being institutionalized by the Ashikaga rulers and as it spread with their support through the Five Mountains temple system. Musō's claim to authority for his "true" Zen over that of Daitō was the result of an unequal struggle for power and patronage, rather than of a smooth, "natural" evolution of the single, higher-quality, or more "true" conception of Zen defined in strictly doctrinal terms. As sociologists of knowledge and historians of religion have shown, this process is typical not just of Five Mountains Zen but of religious and intellectual history generally.

Of course the fall of the Kamakura regents and the failure of Go-Daigo's restoration in 1336 did not mean the end of struggles to define Zen orthodoxy, only that the participants and their bases of power in these struggles shifted. The efforts of the Ashikaga shoguns to consolidate their power continued throughout the fourteenth century, and the Zen temples of the Five Mountains system were important players in this process. The decades around the turn of the fifteenth century are known as the Kitayama or Northern Hills period, after the villa built by the third Muromachi shogun Ashikaga Yoshimitsu (1358–1408) in the hills to the north of the capital. Yoshimitsu had considerable success at centralizing Ashikaga power in the 1390s and was even able to reunite in 1392 the divided Northern and Southern imperial courts. The period of relative stability continued through the rule of Yoshimitsu's successor, Ashikaga Yoshimochi (1386–1428; r. 1394–1423 and 1425–1428), who is referred to with Yoshimitsu in some of the translated passages below. The Northern Hills period has been given an authoritative position by both pre- and postwar twentieth-century academic historians and Japanese cultural nationalists as "representative" of Muromachi culture. While this designation serves those who feel that centralized governmental power produces great culture, we will see in our translations that even during a period when Ashikaga power was most successfully centralized, competition continued apace between rival conceptions of orthodox Zen.

A recurring theme in Ashikaga efforts to centralize power was their attempt to negotiate between and play off of the interests of the more powerful military governors (*shugo daimyō*), who often played key roles in shogunal court administrative, political, socioeconomic, and cultural events. Affiliating with different factions in the large metropolitan Five Mountains temples was one way in which the Ashikaga shoguns and their military governors worked at legitimation and enhancement of their authority on formal and informal social and cultural occasions. We can see such deployment of Five Mountains cultural practices through their relations with military governors in the Kiyō Hōshū (1360–1424) passage on "Enjoying the Way" translated below, and also more directly in the Kiyō passage titled "Manifesting the Mountain." Kiyō was one of the most influential Zen monks of the early fifteenth century and abbot of several of the most important Five Mountains temples, whose lectures and commentaries on such important documents as the Chinese Zen *kōan* anthology *The Blue Cliff Record* (Pi-yen lu, Hekiganroku; T 2003) were most highly respected and studied, and who in his lifetime taught the influential No dramatist Zeami Motokiyo (1363–1443) and the important political figure, cultural patron, and Shinto-Buddhist-Confucian syncretist Ichijō Kanera (1402–1481).

A newly developing institutional base for divergent conceptions of "true" Zen in this period was the rapidly proliferating number of subtemples, retreats, and hermitages that were being built in and around the major Five Mountains temples. Retired abbots and other senior monks such as Kiyō used them as gathering places for their disciples and students for religious training, textual and cultural study, and other activities integral to life in the Five Mountains Zen temples. We can see the high level of social interaction provided by the subtemples from the frequent mention of exchanges between friends, such as the more than twenty individuals who participated in the painting described by Gidō Shūshin (1325–1388) in the passage below. Gidō was one of the two most influential Japanese Zen monks of the second half of the fourteenth century and served as adviser to the shogun Yoshimitsu and as tutor and teacher to an impressive array of thinkers, poets, political leaders, and Zen monks. Many of the subtemples and retreats were funded by wealthy and influential military governors, in addition to members of the imperial court and the aristocracy. The shogunate made repeated efforts through the fourteenth and fifteenth centuries to limit the numbers of these subtemples, since they were a drain on the financial and other resources of the main monasteries and were not always responsive to centralized regulation and monastic codes. In this sense the subtemples provided the monks within the state-patronized, hierarchically organized Five Mountains temple system an independently funded locus of cultural and intellectual production, which also provided a site of resistance to centralized state control.

The proliferation of these subtemples inspired a reconsideration of the best site for Zen practice in the Five Mountains Zen temples, discussions found in the passages translated below by Gidō and his student, the important monk and aesthetic theorist Taihaku Shingen (1357–1415). Both of these short selections are from prefaces to paintings written in Chinese showing an idealized hermitage deep in mountain isolation, which, Taihaku's preface tells us, is not actually located far from the capital but quite near the Five Mountains monasteries in the capital city to which monks have retired. The controversial character of these subtemples is explicitly discussed in the first two translations below: in both passages an unidentified visitor drops by to challenge the cultural or spiritual values of the activities being carried out in the subtemple. The informal character of these documents retains the lively quality of debate that must have been part of the intellectual atmosphere of the Five Mountains temples, replete with red-faced embarrassment and applause for insightful responses. While in some respects these exchanges resemble the "question-and-answer" (mondō) texts of classical T'ang and Sung period Chinese Zen, they center around subjects and issues more relevant to Chinese classical literature than to question-and-answer texts.

In these documents we find at work the social mechanisms that functioned to regulate religious thinking as well as critical and artistic standards, experience, and practice. In the embarrassed withdrawal of the loser of the argument in Gidō's preface, and also in the humility of Kiyō Hōshū in his discussion of poetic interpretation related to Sekidō Mountain, we see the social consequences of straying from the path of orthodox, "true" Zen thinking as it was constructed in Five Mountains Zen during the Northern Hills era. Of course the discussion is not phrased in terms of orthodox and heterodox, of two equally valid if differing viewpoints; rather, the participants on both sides make claims to universal validity through such time-honored rhetorical techniques as the marshalling of quotes from accepted authorities or counterattacking with charges of "narrowness." Yet when we encounter this embarrassment at the level of informal exchange presented below, we as readers many centuries later are made uncomfortable, for we know we are seeing the losers in struggles between diverse views: we are meeting the excluded among the participants in contested relations and are confronted not with members of more powerful groups but with nameless individuals from groups with less power in late-fourteenth- and early-fifteenth-century Japanese elite, male society. While Gidō, Taihaku, and Kiyō described the views of the embarrassed guests as inferior Buddhism, "uncultivated," or simply untrue, they also present us with valuable information about the rejected alternatives of Five Mountains Zen: alternative forms of coherence and heterogeneous, nonorthodox methods of interpretation of Zen "truth."

The second period in Ashikaga culture that has been characterized as a "high point" by modern cultural nationalists and historians is the Eastern Hills or Higashiyama period in the last decades of the fifteenth century. During this period centralized Ashikaga control deteriorated, seen most vividly with the Ōnin Wars of 1467–1477, which heralded a period of decline in the decline of Ashikaga power, wealth, and patronage; a weakened authority for the Musō school and of the Five Mountains Zen, both affiliated with the Ashikaga shoguns; and ultimately the beginning of a new historical era. It is this decline in Ashikaga power that demonstrates to us the historical significance of Daitō's loss in fourteenth-century struggles for orthodoxy: that loss meant that the monks at Daitokuji, including the well-known eccentric monk-poet Ikkyū Sōjun (1394–1481), were forced to search for new patrons. The successful ending of their search eventually guaranteed the preeminence of Daitō's line of Zen after the sixteenth century, for by finding a patronage source in the newly forming merchant class, the Daitokuji monks largely freed their temple from dependence on the fluctuations in the power and wealth of the Ashikaga shogunate. This served them quite well when the fortunes of the Ashikaga shoguns declined in the late fifteenth century, so that by the sixteenth and seventeenth centuries Daitokuji held considerable influence both in the capital and in important regional centers. This influence was solidified by the incresing prestige and wealth circulating around a new cultural form associated with Daitokuji and popular among the merchants, the tea ceremony, particularly when the shogun Toyotomi Hideyoshi (1537–1598) used his prestige to establish the temple as a center for the ceremony shortly before his death. Through the enormously influential teaching of an eighteenth-century descendant in this line of Zen, Hakuin Ekaku (1685–1768), the Daitokuji style spread throughout the Five Mountains temples and has come to dominate Japanese Rinzai Zen into the twentieth century.

In the end these fourteenth-century political and institutional developments led ultimately to a position of prominence for Daitō's teachings in twentieth-century struggles over the authority to define "true" or orthodox Japanese Zen practice, and a corresponding decline in the authority and legitimacy of the teachings and practice of the Musō and other Five Mountains schools of Zen. The Five Mountains temples are now seen primarily as representatives of Zen culture and have capitalized on this commodified form of Zen through domestic Japanese and global tourism. Yet when questions about Zen "philosophy" arise, scholars and practicing masters turn not to the Muromachi era Five Mountains monks but to Daitō or to the more recently resurrected Sōtō school Zen master Dōgen Kigen (1200–1253).

Different religious conceptions, sacred texts, ritual practices, and symbols come to prominence or fall into disregard through their affiliations with individuals, groups, and institutions that are more or less successful in contested relations between different groups. By examining these linkages, we can understand how "orthodoxy" or "truth" is determined in each era of Japanese religious history. While the late-twentieth-century Japanese formation of these linkages and "truths" seems deeply entrenched due to the relative success of the postwar Japanese state at centralizing and regulating Japanese society, as does fascination with the Daitō and Dōgen lines of Zen both in Japan and abroad, alliances will shift and this orthodoxy too may be lost over the next centuries. In a similar manner to the struggle between Daitō and Musō, the passages below by Gidō, Taihaku, and Kiyō show us the contests between divergent views on which are founded in each age the edifice of a seemingly uncontested consensus. Just such a silencing of divergent views invariably underlies representations of the "essential" or "characteristic" teachings of a religious tradition. Such an apparent consensus on "truth" in the abstract or "essential" Zen Buddhism is interrupted by the multivocal character of historical struggle in which heterogeneous views are persistently and unavoidably present. Encountering those views as you do in the passages below destabilizes constructions of consensus, legitimation, and authority, constructions that can be preserved only by silencing divergent voices through various means and present us only with a struggle that has been erased. What is presented in these first three passages below, however, is precisely the voices of those who have since been silenced, voices we can hear speaking at precisely the time of Northern Hills culture when consensus and centralized unity are often said by twentieth-century historians to have been at their peak in Ashikaga period religion and culture. Since most twentieth-century Japanese and Euro-American historians of Zen Buddhism, who themselves live under highly centralized governmental systems, would emphasize medieval Japanese culture and history at its most centralized, we can see from these passages that even these periods are multivocal and contested in character.

The translations are from Kanimura Kankō, ed., *Gozan bungaku zenshū* (Tokyo: Shokabō Shoten, 1906) as follows: Gidō Shūshin's *Preface*, 2:1713; Taihaku Shingen's *Preface*, 3:2233; Kiyō Hōshū's *Inscription*, 3:2889–90; Kiyō Hōshū's *Explanation*, 3:2995–96; and Kiyo Hoshu's *Discussion*, 3:2994–95.

Further Reading

Martin Collcutt, *Five Mountains: The Rinzai Zen Monastic Institution in Medieval Japan*, Harvard East Asian Monographs 85 (Cambridge: Council on East Asian Studies, Harvard University, 1981); Andrew Goble, "Truth, Contradiction and Harmony in Medieval Japan: Emperor Hanazono (1297–1348) and Buddhism," *Journal of the International Association of Buddhist Studies* 12, 1 (1989): 21–61; John Whitney Hall and Toyoda Takeshi, eds., *Japan in the Muromachi Age* (Berkeley: University of California Press, 1977); Kenneth Kraft, *Eloquent Zen: Daitō and Early Japanese Zen* (Honolulu: University of Hawaii Press, 1992); W. S. Merwin and Sōiku Shigematsu, tr., *Sun at Midnight: Poems and Sermons by Musō Soseki* (San Francisco: North Point Press, 1989); Joseph Parker, *Zen Buddhist Landscape Arts of Early*

Muromachi Japan, 1336–1573 (Albany: State University of New York Press, 1998); David Pollack, *Zen Poems of the Five Mountains*, American Academy of Religion Studies in Religion 37 (Decauter: Scholars Press, 1985); Marian Ury, *Poems of the Five Mountains*, 2d rev. ed., Michigan Monograph Series in Japanese Studies 10 (Ann Arbor: Center for Japanese Studies, University of Michigan, 1992); H. Paul Varley, *Imperial Restoration in Medieval Japan* (New York: Columbia University Press, 1971).

Preface to Poems and a Painting on "White Clouds and Cinnabar Canyons" by Gidō Shūshin

"White Clouds and Cinnabar Canyons" is what the venerable Sung dynasty Chinese Zen monk Ch'i-sung (Kaisū, 1007–72) inscribed on the dwelling place of the Buddhist sage Hui-yüan (Eon, 334–417) of Mount Lu. There is a man, Ichū Tsūjo (d. 1429), who admired from afar the Way of Mount Lu and so took this as the name of his residence in the Eigen-an subtemple of Kenninji Temple. Once he asked the accomplished painter Zui (date unknown) to give this form in a painting, entitled it, "Painting of White Clouds and Cinnabar Canyons," and hung it on the wall of his room for his enjoyment. So Hui-yüan's dwelling has come completely into his own hands. Thereafter many gentlemen heard of it and clamored to write inscriptions to enrich it.

Afterwards, I was asked to write the preface. Unrolling it, I inspected the painting. Both the poems and the painting were extraordinary, and both clouds and canyons showed the other to their best advantage. Jade trees and fragrant grasses shone brilliantly; excellent words and outstanding lines gleamed brightly. Both my mind and my eyes were refreshed: I almost did not realize that they were mere poetry and painting.

Somebody said, "'Clouds and Canyons' are only the traces of Hui-yüan, and not the Way. If with poems and painting in brush and ink they have traced their traces, then are they not far from the Way?" I replied, "Not so. If one has communed spiritually (C. *shen-hui*) and attained Hui-yüan's way in one's mind, then one perceives the Buddhist teaching of 'the three realms of past, present, and future in an instant' and 'the three thousand worlds of the cosmos in a single tiny hair.' Outside of the Way there are no traces; other than traces there is no Way. Clouds! Canyons! Poetry or painting! All are of my Way. Where is there any distance?" The questioner then blushed and withdrew.

Altogether there were a number of poems: twenty-two by Zen monks of the mountain forests and two by high officials. I mention the Zen monks first because we have been exclusively [discussing] matters of the wilderness. That's all.

Preface to a [Painting of a] Place Surrounded by Halcyon Screens
by Taihaku Shingen

Among the mountains east of the capital, the luxuriantly towering one is called Mount Clearwater (Kiyomizu). Down below, the springwater is sweet and the

earth fertile, flourishing with a thousand dwellings crowded into just a prospering few yards area. My younger brother in the Buddhist Order Murō Yūshō
(active ca. 1415–1450) retired to live there, and being one taken with the
mountains, he hung a plaque under the eaves that said, "Place Surrounded by
Halcyon Screens."

A guest came by and said, "How poor is this dwelling's name. Now the
'Halcyon Mountain' is indeed nearby, but if it is not something you possess,
how can you call it 'Screens'? Outside your gate there are the jeweled halls of
the aristocrats, strollers wandering over the Fifth Ward bridge, and the dust
from the carts and the tracks of the horses in confused array. And to the left
and right villagers' gates cover the ground, while here is a pavilion and over
there is a tower, their halcyon curved eaves like winged birds soaring high, so
numerous they cannot be counted. So you should not take this as the residence
of a man of the mountains. Now as I see it, are you not stealing the name of a
recluse?"

Murō's reply said, "What you see are only its traces; what I have just named
is only its mind. Whether using the idea of retirement to South Mountain to
take a shortcut to official office as did Lu Ts'ang-yung (Ro Zōyō; active ca.
701–705), or coveting a hermit's headband as a pretense to being a recluse on
North Mountain as did Kung Chi-kuei (Kō Chikei; active late fifth century),
these are traces. And both having 'a gate busy as the marketplace but a mind
clear as water' of Imperial Minister Yeh Sung's (Tei Sū; early first century)
seclusion and the 'living in the city but naming it a mountain' of Shen Tso-
pin's (Shin Sakuhin; active ca. 1200) reclusion are the mind. Why do you
neglect my mind and only take up my traces?

"I was born in Shinano [modern Nagano Prefecture], grew up in the central
country, and then wandered to west of the barrier for study. The meanderings
of my blue straw sandals and wisteria staff reached nearly two thousand miles,
and the blue peaks and cinnabar canyons, the smoky trees and misty forests
now dwell in my eyes, and all are mine to possess. I have attained them in the
mind and externalized them as traces: still more tiny Clear Mountain! Where
is there any stealing? These mica clouds and shining stones, halcyon kingfish-
ers and peacocks on the paintings provide marvel upon marvel. But they are
merely to be used to surround the palatial banquet and to be displayed at an
elegant party, and I have nothing to do with such things. Again, where is the
coveting?

"There is only what the mind has attained, taking from the creator's inexhaustible treasury without prohibition, as did the Chinese poet-official Su Shih
(So Shoku, 1036–1101): just these halcyon screens. During free time from the
meditation mat, when I sit silently under the eaves, the evening sun lights up
half the peaks and the rich halcyon mountain slopes are lined up like screens,
so that the mountains of Shinano and the clouds of the mountain pass become
screen paintings and surround my desk. I do not realize that I am near the
jeweled halls and the Fifth Avenue bridge, and the dust of the carts and horses

and the myriad pavilions and towers are all at once annihilated and do not become sensory afflictions causing suffering and delusion and leading me astray in my Buddhist practice. If there were something to separate me from my surroundings, it would be my screens of verdure."

I, Taihaku Shingen of East of the River, heard these words and, applauding his accomplished cultivation of the mind, wrote a preface and gave it to him.

Inscription on a Painting of Sekidō Mountain
by Kiyō Hōshū

One day Genmyō (date unknown) brought a painting of Sekidō Mountain when here to visit and asked me to write a preface at its head. Now Sekidō Mountain lies between Noto and Etchū [in modern Ishikawa and Toyama prefectures], and looking out over the Hokuriku Highway there is a most beautiful view of temples, shrines, and monks' lodgings.

Certainly it has already been honored in verse exchanges by many gentlemen. During the Tempyō Shōhō period (749–756), the Holy One Chitoku (date unknown) cut thatch to make his home there, and the traces of his practice of the Way can still be seen in detail in his poetry. I was born later, and I reside in aristocrat-sponsored temples. The capital is separated by five hundred leagues of land from Noto and Etchū, and I live more than seven hundred years after the virtuous Chitoku. Whether speaking of the region or of the person, I have never set foot there or set eyes on him. If you were to have me speak well of this mountain, how can I write a preface without straying into speculation and fiction?

Genmyō replied, "How narrow your argument is! Didn't the Zen and Hua yen patriarch Ch'eng-kuan (Chōkan, 738–ca. 820 or 839) say, 'In the realm of boundlessness, self and other are separated by less than the tiniest tip of a fine autumn hair. In all realms of past and present, beginning and end diverge by less than the duration of an instant of thought.' So what need is there to get involved in that which obstructs past and present, region and boundary?"

I replied, "In recent years I have run to the east and gone to the west, and no spirit has been troubled on the road. What Ch'eng-kuan meant I have also forgotten. I am embarrassed to say that I was beating my earthen drum of pride to join in with the many court nobles' reed organs and great mirrors of court ceremonials."

Explanation of "Enjoying the Way"
by Kiyō Hōshū

Layman Hingetsu (date unknown), whose Buddhist name is Jōkan, is a Minamoto lord and master of the right sector of the capital and is from an aristocratic family at the imperial court. Having once served as a member of the highest of court ranks, he was favored by the deceased wife of Yoshimitsu, Hino Yasuko (1368–1419), for over ten years. In judgment he is broad-minded, and everybody expects him to rise to the rank of an imperial minister. In the summer of 1408, when the outstanding, great Minister of State Ashikaga Yoshimochi (1386–1428) reigned as a member of the Council of State, he also trusted this gentleman more than anyone else. The minister of state wrote the two characters "Enjoying the Way," and Hingetsu took them as his pen name. The brushwork is powerful, its movement soaring. When Hingetsu received the piece of calligraphy he treated it carefully and with great discretion, and he asked Nondualism Hōshū to explain its meaning.

Now our Buddhist sages have the Way of nondualism of the ultimate and the provisional. The ultimate is not the provisional, yet it cannot endure; the provisional is not the ultimate, yet it cannot be eliminated. Perpetuated or diminished: when they have been fused with each other, then we call this the realm of unfathomable Buddhist liberation. Penetrating heaven and earth, we cannot know its expansiveness; encompassing past and present, we cannot know its duration. Buddhas and sentient beings both have this Way, differing only in whether they are joyful or not. If we have a root of faith in our hearts and truly put it into practice and really carry it out, progressing more and more without rest, suddenly doubts will melt away. Then self-affirmation and self-contentment will be achieved. However, we are unable to talk of this with others, because we are in the midst of the utmost in happiness and joy, which gushes forth, and even the joys of tasting a feast or of hearing stringed and wind instruments will still be insufficient to describe it. Those who treat the ultimate and provisional as strictly opposed definitely cannot speak of this with us. Then extending and fulfilling this Buddhist Way brings all under heaven and later generations to enjoy this Way. Then while roaming at ease in a world of peaceful reign and roving at leisure in a realm of benevolent longevity, self and other have exactly the same essence. Sacred and mundane! Happiness and joy! These are what is called "the marvelousness of making oneself happy and making other people happy." The reason the minister of state wrote these characters out and gave them to you is found in this.

Signed: Kiyō Hōshū of the Room of Nonduality at Shōjuji Temple north of the capital,
summer of the year 1408

Discussion of "Manifesting the Mountain"
by Kiyō Hōshū

In the three years since succeeding to office, the outstanding, great Minister of State Ashikaga Yoshimochi (1386–1428) has practiced the Confucian virtues of benevolence and good government, and men were unable to keep their mouths from speaking of this. All under heaven is at peace, and conditions are not less than even the splendid civilization of the ideal Japanese ages of Engi (901–922) and Tenryaku (947–956). How fortunate are the peoples of all the lands.

He also takes the Buddha as his mind like the great Chinese patron of Buddhism, Emperor Wu (r. 502–549), greatly assisting our Buddhist Teachings, and in particular supporting the followers of Zen. So he commanded men who knew the Buddhist Way and were skilled in belles lettres each to write on the meaning of his pen name, 'Manifesting the Mountain' (Kenzan). Some adorned it in Buddhist verse, some praised it in prose, reaching its ultimate and exhausting it, and nothing can be added to what they said.

One day the minister of state's command was sent down to Nondualism Hōshū also to write an explanation. But with my rough and trifling words, how could I make manifest one ten-thousandth of Yoshimochi's virtue in order to join the teachers' ranks? But the minister of state's strict order would not allow me to refuse. I respectfully wrote out its meaning, saying, 'Manifesting' is 'luminosity' and 'mountain' is the image of 'bringing to rest,' as in the neo-Confucian Classic *The Great Learning* (*Ta-hsüeh*). Now as the founder of neo-Confucianism Chu Hsi (Shuki, 1130–1200) has written, the reason that people cannot conform to this Way is obfuscation and restlessness.

"Illuminating the obfuscated is called the luminous, and ceasing to be restless is called 'coming to rest.' Coming to rest and luminosity are like the two wheels of a cart or the two wings of a bird and cannot be separated for a moment, as described in the neo-Confucian Classic *Doctrine of the Mean* (*Chung-yung*). If at first there is not obfuscation, how can there be luminosity? If at first there is not restlessness, how can there be coming to rest? Both coming to rest and luminosity are established only after each movement and each obfuscation, so as The *Doctrine of the Mean* says, one who studies this Way should not be separated from them for an instant.

"Therefore, as the Buddhists would suggest, inwardly illumine the mind and outwardly bring the objective world to rest. If you bring the objective world to rest externally, then the mind will be without delusions; if you illumine the mind internally, then the objective world will be without passions. When the mind and its objects are united into one, then luminosity and bringing to rest will be merged. Then it becomes apparent that this Way resides in the darkest and obscurest places without ever being imperceptible and is found in the smallest and slightest without ever being diminished.

"How bright (and wise)! How lofty (and sagelike)! But mental grasping cannot attain to it. What the Great Teacher of Zen and Hua-yen, Ch'eng-kuan calls 'destroying the passions with great wisdom' (*hawaku daichi*), this is called 'luminosity' (*mei*); being without thoughts in pure Zen, this is called 'mountain': we can refer to it in this way. The minister of state has already learned of the marvelousness of this Way, and by means of his longevity he will live as long as the mountains and be manifest after ten thousand years, and by enjoying his blessings he will have a mountain of fortunes and be manifest beyond the good fortune of having a hundred fiefs.

"Then finally you will loftily manifest a mountain of all pervasive Buddhist wisdom in the realm of unfathomable liberation. Who can doubt this? How can the way of luminescence and bringing to rest be all that is completed? It also brings the lord to be above the Chinese sage emperors Yao and Shun and raises the people up into the highest realm of Taoist nonaction as easily as pointing to one's own palm, as it says in *The Doctrine of the Mean*. Then would not the minister of state's glorious great virtuous deeds illuminate a thousand years?

"The venerable teacher Jōtoku (dating unknown) has offered up this name to honor the minister of state for his encouraging people in this Way. The above-mentioned people between the four seas speaking of his benevolence and good government also have the same root. Looking on he whose benevolence and good government is spoken of everywhere between the four seas, he must have based the name on these traits."

*Signed: Written in the summer of the year of gathering dragons 1410 by Kiyō Hōshū,
formerly of the retreat of nonduality at Fumonji Temple*

Motoori Norinaga on the Two Shrines at Ise

Mark Teeuwen

Motoori Norinaga (1730–1801) wrote *The Two Shrines of Ise: An Essay of Split Bamboo* (*Ise nikū sakitake no ben*) in early 1798. At this time he was a leading scholar with more than four hundred students and a position as an adviser to the Tokugawa Lord of Kii. He had all but finished his life work and main claim to fame, the *Tradition of the Record of Ancient Matters* (*Kojiki-den*), which he had begun in 1764 and finally completed in the sixth month of 1798. He had in fact already published the first seventeen chapters of this work, in three portions appearing in 1790, 1792, and 1797. During the last period in his life, in which our text was written, Norinaga concentrated on spreading his ideas, rather than new research. *The Two Shrines of Ise* was one outcome of this. As indicated by its title, the text discusses theological matters pertaining to the Inner Shrine (*Naikū*) and the Outer Shrine (*Gekū*) of Ise, concentrating on the identities and characteristics of their deities—Amaterasu at the Inner, and Toyouke (or Toyuke) at the Outer Shrine. Most of the points argued in the text draw on Norinaga's polemic works (such as *Arrowroot Flowers*, Kuzubana, 1780, and *Scolding [Ueda Akinari] from Osaka*, Kagaika, c. 1787–1790) for the discussion of Amaterasu, and on chapter 15 of the *Tradition of the Record of Ancient Matters* on the subject of Toyouke.

Many of the themes that pervade Norinaga's oeuvre also make their appearance in the first part of *The Two Shrines of Ise*. The text stresses that the Japanese of "high antiquity" had had a sincere faith in the ancient tradition, and that this faith was lost when the "Chinese way of thinking" gained a foothold in Japan. Much emphasis is further given to the notion that Japan is the "land of origin," the land in which the gods were born, and from which they spread their beneficence throughout the world. As prime examples of this beneficence, the text mentions the light of the sun and the growth of grains. Both of these prerequisites to life, Norinaga argues, are gifts from Japanese deities—namely, Amaterasu and Toyouke, who reside in the Two Shrines of Ise. Therefore, Norinaga concludes, these deities should be revered at these shrines by all human beings throughout the world.

The text further demonstrates some of the sophisticated philological methods Norinaga had at his disposal. He employs two important analytical "tools" in this particular piece. First, he distinguishes between "ordinary logic" (*jōri*), which is within the grasp of human intelligence, and a higher "mysterious logic" (*myōri*). If the world were ruled by "ordinary logic" alone, it would be impossible for Amaterasu to be at the same time the sun that illuminates the world, and an imperial ancestor with a female human body, as the tradition in the *Record of Ancient Matters* seems to imply. Therefore, Norinaga argues, we can only surmise the existence of an unfathomable "mysterious logic," and he urges us to be sincere and have faith in the ancient tradition as it has been handed down to us. Secondly, there is the distinction between deities who are "physical bodies" (*utsushimimi*) and deities who are "spirits" (*mitama*). This distinction makes it possible to introduce yet another Amaterasu: the spirit that resides in the Inner Shrine.

Both these distinctions were essential to Norinaga's effort to come to terms with an ancient tradition that describes Amaterasu alternatively as the sun, a being with a human body, and a spirit. The fact that Norinaga developed such interpretative tools is revealing in itself: it shows his determination to treat the National Histories, including the chapters recounting the Age of the Gods, as factual history. It is this aspect of his thought that gives it its "fundamentalist" character. For Norinaga, there was only one truth, and that was the historical truth handed down by the ancient Japanese tradition. This approach was not entirely novel, but it was certainly against the mainstream of Japanese religious thought, which tended to recognize different levels of truth, and which disregarded the factual and the historical as "exoteric" and "shallow," and always probed for a metaphorical, "deeper" layer of "esoteric" meaning.

As mentioned above, the ideas expressed in *The Two Shrines of Ise* were not new. The text is a restatement of conclusions reached in Norinaga's research on the *Record of Ancient Matters*, and it contains very little that had not already been published when Norinaga wrote the work. Why then did he write it? This question becomes all the more pressing when we learn that Norinaga went to considerable trouble to have the work published. Fearing problems with the authorities, he went to great lengths to gain some insight into the probable reaction of the Outer Shrine, and the work was not published until the eighth month of 1801, a mere month before Norinaga's death.

The Two Shrines of Ise differs from any other work by Norinaga in that it constitutes his first and last attempt to translate his ideas about Shintō into concrete innovations in the political and juridical reality of the Shintō world. The work was an attempt at diplomacy. Its aim was to persuade the Outer Shrine priesthood to abandon its "medieval" theory about Toyouke and accept the "ancient truth" about this deity, as unearthed from the *Record of Ancient Matters* and other sources by Norinaga.

Norinaga's original intention was to ask the Outer Shrine's first priest to write a preface for *The Two Shrines of Ise*, adopting it as the shrine's official position. However, it soon became clear that official acceptance by the Outer Shrine was out of the question, and the shrine refused to assent even to publication of the work. The Outer Shrine did not take legal action when the work was eventually published, but it did file complaints with the *Yamada bugyō* against two of Norinaga's students at the Inner Shrine (in 1798 and 1803). These students had distributed printed pamphlets in the provinces, propagating their views on the relation between the gods of the Inner and the Outer Shrine. The first complaint resulted in a strict censorship imposed on all publications in Ise, and the second in the conviction of the accused, Masuya Suehogi (1764–1828), who was punished with a prohibition against his leaving the district of Uji (the town that served the Inner Shrine)—a kind of extended house arrest. The views of these two students were not necessarily the same as Norinaga's; in fact, they ranked Toyouke as a "servant" of Amaterasu, and as inferior, while Norinaga insisted that these two deities simply "cannot be compared." But the fact that the first of these complaints was being considered by the *Yamada bugyō* when Norinaga sent *The Two Shrines of Ise* to the Outer Shrine did not help his attempt at diplomacy.

What, then, were the theories of the Inner and the Outer Shrine on the subject of the deities of these shrines and the relation between them? The Inner Shrine argued that Amaterasu alone is the highest deity in the realm, and that Toyouke is a servant of Amaterasu with the task of preparing the food offered to her. This theory was put forward among others by the Inner Shrine priest Inomo Morikazu (1705–1773) in his *Record of Mount Kamiji* (Kamijiki, 1730), and it was adopted by Yoshimi Yukikazu (1673–1761), for example, in his *Essays on the Theories of the Five Books* (*Gobusho setsuben*, 1736). The Outer Shrine, however, propagated the radically different theory that Toyouke is another name for Ame no Minakanushi or Kuni no Tokotachi, the first deity to come into existence at the time of the beginning of the universe (according to different versions of the cosmogony, as recorded in the National Histories). According to the Outer Shrine, this deity was Ninigi's maternal great-grandfather, and thus an imperial ancestor on a par with Amaterasu. What is more, he was in fact "ultimately one" with Amaterasu. In the version of Outer Shrine theology that was current in the Edo period, Ame no Minakanushi/Kuni no Tokotachi was identified with the Confucian concept of *li*, the "principle" underlying the existence of the universe, and the Outer Shrine stated that this deity was the "essence" (*tai*), and Amaterasu the "working" (*yō*) of the primeval unity of the "Great Ultimate" (which Chu Hsi identified as *li*) that lies at the root of all existence. In other words, the gods of the Inner and the Outer Shrine are merely two aspects of the same entity. This theory was propagated by Deguchi Nobuyoshi (1615–1690) and many others at the Outer Shrine. Moreover, it was adopted by many scholars of Yamazaki Ansai's school of Suika Shintō, which dominated Shintō scholarship until the 1760s.

These conflicting views on the nature of the relationship between the Two Ise Shrines had a long history, extending back to the Kamakura period when (a less Confucian version of) the Outer Shrine's theory was first formulated in a series of so-called Secret Books (*hisho*). These books were attributed to ancient ancestors of the Outer Shrine priests, and it was claimed that they predated even the *Record*

of Ancient Matters and the *Chronicles of Japan*. In the Edo period Deguchi Nobuyoshi established a sacred corpus of texts, selected from these books, which he
called the "Five Books of Shintō" (*Shintō gobusho*), and defined them as Shintō
Classics on a par with the National Histories. The theories about Toyouke expounded in these books were of crucial importance to priests of the Outer Shrine
in their competition with the Inner Shrine for the favors of both the various
shogunates and private benefactors. One can imagine that if the public were to
view the god of the Outer Shrine as a mere servant of Amaterasu, donations would
decrease dramatically. This kind of competition did not arise before the early
Kamakura period, since until that time the shrines had been able to depend on
funding from the imperial court.

If anything, the competition between the Outer and the Inner Shrine was even
more severe in the Edo period than in preceding centuries. By the early seventeenth century, a considerable proportion of the inhabitants of Yamada and Uji
(the towns that served the Outer and the Inner Shrine, respectively) were so-
called pilgrim masters (*onshi*), self-professed "priests" who made a living selling
services to pilgrims. By this time, nearly every locality in Japan had its contract
with a pilgrim master in Ise, granting him the monopoly over all services to
pilgrims from that particular "parish" (*dansho*). Pilgrims were sold deity tablets
(*oharai* or *taima*), amulets, and other souvenirs of Ise, and they were required to
stay at the mansion of their pilgrim master when they went on a pilgrimage. Even
official priests of the Two Shrines doubled as pilgrim masters, and it is no exaggeration to state that the "pilgrimage business" was of fundamental importance
both in the economic and the political life of Ise.

The theological question of Toyouke's identity was of great importance to those
who depended on this "pilgrimage business." As noted above, the Outer Shrine
argued that the Two Shrines represent two aspects of a single sacred entity. From
this argument, priests drew the conclusion that the pilgrim masters of the Outer
Shrine communicated pilgrims' prayers to the gods of both shrines, rather than
to the god of the Outer Shrine alone. The Inner Shrine, however, insisted that
the Two Shrines are two separate religious institutions and stated that the prayers
handled by the pilgrim masters of the Outer Shrine were prayers to Toyouke only
and did not reach the ears of the famous Amaterasu. The Inner Shrine claimed
that therefore all pilgrims should have two prayer masters, one at each of the Two
Shrines. Needless to say, the Outer Shrine regarded the signing of contracts with
two pilgrim masters as completely illegal and said that this argument was simply
an excuse for stealing *dansho* from pilgrim masters of the Outer Shrine.

There was no unambiguous legislation on the subject of the relation between
the prayer masters of the Two Shrines. Until the early seventeenth century, the
Outer Shrine had the upper hand in the numerous conflicts between pilgrim
masters that were the inevitable result of this legal ambiguity. On a number of
occasions, the road to the Inner Shrine was simply blockaded, and pilgrims with
Inner Shrine contracts were denied access. This practice was forbidden by the
bakufu only in 1635. This proved to be a turning point, and the Inner Shrine's
viewpoint carried the day in two conflicts that were brought before the Edo Su-

preme Court (Hyōjōsho) in 1668 and 1671. However, even after this, the question of whether the Two Shrines are separate or "one" was not settled until 1826, when a *Yamada bugyō* solved yet another conflict between two pilgrim masters over this matter (that had been going on since 1814!) by announcing that the 1671 verdict "implied" that the shrines are separate.

Although Norinaga had many students at the Inner Shrine, and some (though very few) at the Outer Shrine, he seems to have been unaware of the juridical implications of the various theories about the deities of these shrines. His own theory includes some elements from the theory of the Outer Shrine, such as the idea that Toyouke and Amaterasu are like "a god and an emperor," and the notion that Amaterasu reveres Toyouke. Other ideas can be traced back to the Inner Shrine's views, for example, the identification of Toyouke as Toyouke-bime. However, the crux of the matter, the question whether the Two Shrines are separate or not, is not addressed by Norinaga. *The Two Shrines of Ise* would seem to imply that they are. This fact alone made a positive reaction from the Outer Shrine unlikely. When we moreover find that Norinaga's Inner Shrine students were highly indignant at the few "compromises" Norinaga had made to Outer Shrine theology, it becomes clear that Norinaga's attempt to put his ideas into practice at Ise was a complete failure. *The Two Shrines of Ise* stands as a monument to his naivete and serves as a stark reminder of the fact that theological arguments are reflections not only of the intellectual and religious trends of their age, but also of social and economic circumstances that may either inspire or inhibit theological innovation.

The following extracts were taken from my complete, annotated translation, *Motoori Norinaga's The Two Shrines of Ise, an Essay of Split Bamboo*, Izumi series 3, Wiesbaden: Harrassowitz Verlag, 1995.

Further Reading

H. D. Harootunian, "The Consciousness of Archaic Form from the New Realism of Kokugaku," in *Japanese Thought in the Tokugawa Period 1600–1868: Methods and Metaphors*, ed. T. Najita and I. Scheiner (Chicago: University of Chicago Press, 1978); Sey Nishimura, tr., "First Steps in the Mountains: Motoori Norinaga's *Uiyamabumi*," *Monumenta Nipponica* 42, 4 (Winter 1987); Sey Nishimura, tr., "The Way of the Gods: Motoori Norinaga's *Naobi no mitama*," *Monumenta Nipponica* 46, 1 (Spring 1991); Peter Nosco, *Remembering Paradise: Nativism and Nostalgia in Eighteenth Century Japan* (Cambridge: Harvard University Press, 1990); Mark Teeuwen, *Watarai Shintō, An Intellectual History of the Outer Shrine in Ise* (Leiden: CNWS Publications, 1996); B. M. Young, *Ueda Akinari* (New York: Columbia University Press, 1982).

The Two Shrines of Ise: An Essay of Split Bamboo

Of the Two Shrines of Ise, the Inner Shrine is the shrine of Amaterasu Ōmikami, the very august divine ancestress of the emperors, the Great Sun God of the Heavens, who rules the Plain of High Heaven and who for all eternity, as at this very moment, illuminates the world; and the Outer Shrine is the shrine of Toyuke no Ōkami, the originating spirit of grains and food, who bears the name of Toyouke-bime no Mikoto; she is the great god of the divine food (*mike-tsu-Ōkami*), whom Amaterasu Ōmikami deeply reveres on the Plain of High Heaven. That Amaterasu Ōmikami resides in the Inner Shrine is well known to the people, and of old there were no aberrant arguments about this fact, but lately there have been aberrant theories concerning Amaterasu Ōmikami herself, and one must beware not to fall into error. These aberrant theories say that, since Amaterasu Ōmikami is the great ancestress of the emperors, it is impossible that she should be the sun in the heavens, and they maintain that she is a god who has lived in this country in the form of an ordinary person, who in the Age of the Gods lived in the country of Yamato, and who has since died. This is the purport of these theories, and it is a most shocking, sacrilegious heresy. If you ask how it is possible that people in such a manner misconstrue the fact that [Amaterasu] Ōmikami is the sun in the heavens that to this day illuminates the world we see around us—a fact concerning which there were of old no aberrant theories because the purport of the holy classics is very clear and not in the least misleading—the reason is that the savants who nowadays expound the holy classics, being conceited and full of Confucian cleverness, cling only to the Chinese texts and are unable to believe the old traditions. Because they attempt to evaluate even the facts of the Age of the Gods through logical principles of the Chinese sort, they assume, for example, that the Plain of High Heaven stands for the imperial capital, or decide that Amaterasu Ōmikami is called "the god of the sun" because her virtue is being compared to the brightness of the sun. To measure everything in this way by Chinese logical principles, and to think that there is nothing beyond these principles, is the narrow-minded way of thinking of those who cannot understand that beyond ordinary logic there is also a mysterious logic. This is a serious error. How can one doubt that Amaterasu Ōmikami is the great ancestress of the emperors, as well as the sun in the heavens that illuminates this world? This principle is one that knows no bounds, that is difficult to fathom and mysterious.

Now then, the Plain of High Heaven, as can be seen in the holy classics, is the sky; and since the sky, over our empire as well as over China and India and other lands, forms but one whole and is not divided, Amaterasu Ōmikami is not only the sun god of our empire, but the all-embracing sun god that illuminates China, India, and all other lands as well. In the theories of Shintō scholars nowadays, however, she seems to be a sun god that is limited to our empire only. They greatly belittle her immeasurable blessings and beneficence, they speak about them as if they were something small and futile, and this is most lamentable. Even worse, they take Amaterasu Ōmikami to be a god who has long since died in the Age of the Gods—a gross sacrilege and the extreme of horror. Can the four seas and the myriad lands of the world continue to exist for even one day without the clear beneficence of this great god? In the

Age of the Gods, when the Imperial Grandson Ninigi no Mikoto was about to descend from the Plain of High Heaven to our country, Amaterasu Ōmikami from her own hands gave him a holy mirror with the command: "Regard this mirror as my spirit, and revere it as you revere me!" What is revered as the Divine Object in the Inner Shrine is this mirror, the very one to which Amaterasu Ōmikami, who illuminates this world, has committed her spirit. Therefore the god of this Inner Shrine of Ise is a god whom not only the people of our empire, but also the people of China, India, and other lands, all the people in the countless lands of the world, in all the lands upon which the sun confers her beneficence—she is a god whom all kings and vassals and common people alike must revere and worship for her blessings and beneficence. It is pitiful indeed that in other lands the true traditions of the Age of the Gods have all these years gone unknown, and that to this day naught is known of them; but who in the empire, where this knowledge has been passed down correctly in the holy classics and is clear, will not feel respect for these blessings and this beneficence? Here and now I need not discuss further how august is the fact that she is the divine ancestress of the emperors; however, to think only of this august fact, forgetting that now, at this very moment, all the people in the myriad lands of the world enjoy her beneficence, is lamentable indeed. Do not let this misconception delude you, scorn not this beneficence! How frightful, alas, how frightful!

As I mentioned above, in the Outer Shrine resides Mike-tsu-Ōmikami, a god whom Amaterasu Ōmikami deeply reveres on the Plain of High Heaven. Let me elaborate a bit upon the fact that this Mike-tsu-Ōmikami is a very, very august god, and that Amaterasu Ōmikami reveres her so deeply.

In the world there are countless treasures, but the highest, the ultimate treasure, without which we cannot do even for a day, is food. For all things in this world that pertain to humans presuppose life. Confucianists and Buddhists expound all manner of exalted arguments, but they can neither perform humanity or fidelity, nor practice austerities or study if they do not have life. However extraordinary, however great a matter it may be, one can only accomplish it if one has life. Without life all is futile. And if in the human world life is of such overriding importance, what then is it that allows humans to maintain life? It is food. Money is indeed august, but it cannot help to maintain life even for one day, and that is why I say that the highest and ultimate treasure in the world is food. This principle is well known to everyone; but why then do people regard it only superficially; why does no one take it carefully to heart; why has no one a deep regard for its truth? Moreover the gratitude that we owe our superiors and our parents is extraordinarily vast and great indeed, but, since this gratitude cannot exist if we do not have life, is not the gratitude we owe our food vast and great as well? It is well that we reflect seriously upon this matter.

Thus it is that in the beginning of the world this food that is so august arose from the spirit of Toyouke no Ōkami, and that this food will eternally, as long as heaven and earth exist, continue to grow year after year—all of this we owe to the blessings and the beneficence of this great god. Since there is not one among the people of the world, whether high or low, who does not depend upon food for the continuation of life, we should not forget even for one moment how extraordinary our indebtedness to this great god is; but, as with everything that we grow accustomed to and that comes to seem ordinary, we hardly notice it anymore; we forget how august her beneficence is and fail to appreciate it, and that is most frightful! When every once in a while there is a crop failure and there is little rice and grain, the poor suffer terribly and many die of starvation, and even if it does not go that far, is it not poignant how they can think of nothing but eating when mealtime passes by and their bellies grow empty? Reflecting well upon this, one must always be aware of how important and august is food, and how august is the blessing of this great god, and not forget it.

Now then, since the fact that humans maintain life with the help of food holds not only for the people of our empire but is the same for all people in the myriad lands, there are no people in these lands who do not share in the blessings of this great god. The empire is the land of origin, the ancestral land of the myriad lands, and all the countless things that have appeared and become known all have their origin in our empire; just as the sun and the moon in the Age of the Gods were born in the empire and thereafter spread their beneficence over the four seas and the myriad lands, so it is with the beneficence of Toyouke no Ōkami; the food in the myriad lands with which the people there maintain their lives originates from the spirit of this great god as well. The source of all those stories, that in China a king Shen Nung, and someone called Hou Chi, ancestor of the Chou, taught agriculture to the people and thus were meritorious rulers, lies in the spirit of Toyouke no Ōkami; but because this is a foreign country, people there have not the slightest notion of this truth, and so they just produce any explanation that has an impressive ring to it. Since there is no correct tradition in any of the foreign lands, it is inevitable that people there know nothing of such matters, but in the empire, to our great good fortune, the tradition is clear, and thus one should not take it lightly.

Moreover, the empire is a happy and abundant land where the rice and the grain are better than in any of the myriad lands, and the name by which it is called, the "Land of Fresh Ears," shows that the rice-ears in our country are especially abundant and auspicious. Because people since the Age of the Gods have treated the rice-ears with special reverence, the matter of the "god of the divine food" or *mike-tsu-kami* is of extraordinary importance. Also, as I mentioned above, there are at the court many great ceremonies relating to food. There are, thus, many deep reasons for the fact that Amaterasu Ōmikami particularly reveres Toyouke no Ōkami.

Well then, since this god is a god whom Amaterasu Ōmikami reveres so deeply, it is self-evident that she is boundlessly high and prominent. Yet although in High Antiquity everyone believed everything pertaining to the old traditions, never doubting it, and there were no aberrant theories, in the course of time all manner of theories from other countries intermingled with our own, and there came to be people who thought that this was good and who believed them; this habit spread as the generations succeeded each other, until finally everyone believed only those foreign theories, so that the significance of the correct tradition from the Age of the Gods was lost altogether, and there was no one left who knew it, and the hearts of all the people grew insincere, clever, and distorted. In all things people relied upon Chinese ways of thinking, so that they started to doubt even the tradition from the Age of the Gods. Aberrant theories arose, and they even began to practice deceit in these matters as well. Since Middle Antiquity aberrant theories started to arise about the god of the Outer Shrine, too, and because since that time there have been many aberrant arguments, matters have gone so far that the people can no longer discern what is correct and what is incorrect, and they have become confused as to what kind of a god she is.

It must have been five or six hundred years ago that in Middle Antiquity aberrant theories began to arise about the god of the Outer Shrine. The Five Books, named the "Five Secret Records," came into being, and in these books the name *mike-tsu-kami* is explained as a virtue of the element water. They say: "The element water transforms itself and becomes heaven and earth. . . , the name of this is Ame no Minakanushi no Kami; thus a thousand changes and ten thousand transformations respond to the virtue of the element water and give rise to the skill of the continuation of life; therefore it is also called *mike-tsu-kami*." They state that the *mike-tsu-kami* is Ame no Minakanushi no Mikoto, or they say: "Yorozuhatatoyoakizu-hime no Mikoto is the daughter of Takami-musubi no Kami, who is the crown prince of Toyuke Sumeōkami, she is the mother of Sumemima no Mikoto, therefore the two great gods Amaterasu Sumeōkami and Toyuke Sumeōkami are called the Great Parents of Ninigi no Mikoto." There are many matters about which they expound similar arguments, and if you open these books and read them you will see. They put Amaterasu Ōmikami and Toyuke no Ōkami on a par by saying: "They are equal in brightness and virtue," or "They are the sun and the moon." They regard both the Inner and the Outer Shrine as Great Parents, and they describe them as gods equal in rank and prominence; such is the essence of these books. Moreover, a theory arose recently that would place the Outer Shrine in a higher position than the Inner Shrine. Those people say that the god of the Outer Shrine is Kuni no Tokotachi no Mikoto. Furthermore, there are those who try to degrade the Outer Shrine and make of it an insignificant god. Their theory is that the god of the Outer Shrine, because she is called a "god of the divine food," is a god who prepares meals. In the course of these disputes over the rank and prominence of the Two Shrines, all manner of mistakes and lies have arisen; and as these theories proliferate, everyone becomes more and more confused and no one can determine what sort of a god the god of the Outer Shrine is.

It is a very, very sad and lamentable affair that the true august beneficence of Toyuke no Ōkami has become hidden and difficult to discern. Therefore I, Norinaga, will now try to distinguish and correct these aberrant theories and arguments, awesome though the task is, and to make manifest the august, true beneficence of this great god. The reason I name this work an "essay of split bamboo" is that, in the spirit of the common expression "as straight as split bamboo," I wish to indicate that I state the case correctly and sincerely without evasion or distortion.

The claim that these Five Books are much older than the *Record of Ancient Matters* (*Kojiki*, 712) and the *Chronicles of Japan* (*Nihon shoki*, 720), and the fact that they have given names to all of the authors that make them seem to be people of ancient times—all of this is the deceit of people of later ages, the purpose of which was only to claim that the Inner and the Outer Shrine are both great ancestors of the imperial line, and that they are gods of equal rank and prominence. These theories are exactly as described, point for point, in the books *Record of Mount Kamiji* (*Kamijiki*, 1730) and *Essays on the Theories of the Five Books* (*Gobusho setsuben*, 1736), to which I shall return later and thus shall not now discuss further. There is, however, something that must be said about them. First of all, of these Five Books, all of them forgeries, only the *Record of Yamato-hime no Mikoto* (*Yamato-hime no mikoto seiki*) does contain some passages that could never have been written by anyone of later ages and thus cannot be dismissed. One must, here and there, distinguish the true from the false. The other four books are vulgar, inferior works that are not worth looking at.

To begin with, [the writers of the Five Books] have, among all the many gods, decided upon Ame no Minakanushi no Kami [as the god of the Outer Shrine], because they thought that this god, being the first born in the beginning of heaven and earth, is a Great Parent who comes before Amaterasu Ōmikami, and that there is no god more prominent than he. This, however, is a most foolish, vulgar notion of later ages. It is not at all true that a god of later birth is less significant. If one decides the prominence of gods on the basis of the order of their birth, does that then mean that one regards all the gods that were born before Amaterasu Omikami as more prominent than she?

The god that among all the gods must be called the Great Ancestor of the emperors is Amaterasu Ōmikami. As for relations between lord and servant, this distinction exists only since Amaterasu Ōmikami has reigned in the Plain of High Heaven as its lord; before that there was no such thing as lords and servants. The relations of husband and wife and father and son, too, came into being only when Izanagi and Izanami no Ōkami had sexual intercourse and gave birth to the land and many gods; before that neither the relation of husband and wife nor the relation of father and son existed, so how could Kuni no Tokotachi no Mikoto be a Great Parent of the imperial line?

If one reflects upon the meaning of the aforementioned facts, one will surely realize that Kuni no Tokotachi no Mikoto is neither the first god in the beginning of heaven and earth, nor a heavenly god, nor a Great Parent of the emperors. The reason I elaborate upon this matter so extensively is that I, from the bottom of my heart, long to make the people who think that there is no god more prominent than Kuni no Tokotachi no Mikoto recognize their error, to correct immediately the old theory that this god resides in the Outer Shrine, and to make apparent the true, most august beneficence of Toyouke no Ōkami. Not to recognize the truth even now that I have explained it so extensively would indeed be the extreme of stupidity. There are also those who, even though in their hearts they do recognize the truth, find it hard to change their opinion now, and who continue to add ever more perversions and distortions in order to rescue this old theory; but this, with every word they speak, brings only the more shame of stupidity and deceitfulness upon them and will make them the laughingstock of later generations throughout the world. Since nowadays the Way of learning has been greatly developed, and especially since the advent of the school of Ancient Learning, [that is, National Learning, as developed by Keichū and Kamo no Mabuchi,] matters of the past are very clear; there is hardly anyone left who accepts the old theory on Kuni no Tokotachi no Mikoto. To persist in advocating that theory is like gluing together, again and again, an already shattered teacup that is quite useless, trying to continue using it as a teacup. Is not that the extreme of absurdity?

Further, one may object that these theories on Ame no Minakanushi no Kami and Kuni no Tokotachi no Mikoto are theories of our predecessors, and that one should avoid rejecting them now because they are of long standing and everyone, high and low, knows them well. Even though this at first sight seems entirely reasonable and correct, one must give the matter further thought. If we fail to correct such foolish, blind theories at the right time and continue to expound them, so that we are laughed at by later generations throughout the world, we perpetuate the shame of our predecessors endlessly; and is not that even more to the detriment of our predecessors? Moreover, we should have no little fear for this great god, should we allege that this most august god is some other god to whom she has no relation whatsoever, and should we obscure for long the great beneficence of the most important divine food and fail to make it known.

For all these reasons I want to correct and purify this old theory quickly. It is a fundamental law from High Antiquity that everytime one commits a blunder, one must reveal and purify it, and if one executes such a purification, all will be corrected and washed clean. In foreign countries, too, one finds in the Way of the Confucianists that one must quickly correct one's mistakes, and in the Buddhist teachings there is confession; therefore, whatever Way one follows, it will be in accordance with the intentions of [Amaterasu] Ōmikami, and likewise an act of loyalty and filial piety toward our predecessors, quickly to revise this unfounded old theory and to accept the correct theory, in which the truth is clear.

In the *Record of Ancient Matters*, in the passage where Sumemima no Mikoto descends from heaven to this country, it says:

> Then [Amaterasu Ōmikami] added [to the entourage of Sumemima no Mikoto] Ame no Koyane no Mikoto, Futodama no Mikoto, Ame no Uzume no Mikoto, Ishikoridome no Mikoto, and Tama no Ya no Mikoto, in all five chiefs of workers' groups, and they descended together with him.

The passage continues:

> Thereupon she added to this entourage the eight-foot-long curved jewels and the mirror that had lured her [from the Rock Cave of Heaven], the Herb Quelling sword, and the gods Tokoyo no Omoikane no Kami, Tajikara-wo no Kami, and Ame no Iwatowake no Kami, and she said: "Regard this mirror as my spirit, and revere it as you revere me!" and next she said: "Let Omoikane no Kami take charge of my affairs, and execute my worship." These two gods are worshipped in the shrine at Isuzu. Further, Toyouke no Kami, this is the god who resides in Watarai of the Outer Shrine. Further, Ame no Iwatowake no Kami, who is also called Kushi-iwamato no Kami or Toyo-iwamato no Kami, this god is the god of the gates. Further, Tajikara-wo no Kami, resides in Sanagata.

Then it says:

> Ame no Koyane no Mikoto is the ancestor of the *muraji* of the Nakatomi, Futodama no Mikoto is the ancestor of the *obito* of the Inbe, Ame no Uzume no Mikoto is the ancestor of the *kimi* of the Sarume, Ishikoridome no Mikoto is the ancestor of the *muraji* of the Kagamitsukuri, and Tama no Ya no Mikoto is the ancestor of the *muraji* of the Tamanoya.

On this passage we must reflect well. The five gods who are chiefs of workers' groups, Ame no Koyane no Mikoto and the others, who are mentioned at the beginning, are physical bodies serving Sumemima no Mikoto. The four gods Omoikane no Kami, Tajikara-wo no Kami, Ame no Iwatowake no Kami, and Toyouke no Kami mentioned next to these are not gods who are physical bodies, they are the *mitamashiro*, "spirit containers" of these gods, and [Amaterasu Ōmikami] added them to the mirror and the other objects and then handed them over [to Sumemima no Mikoto]. Everytime the words "(. . .) no Kami" appear in the ancient texts, we must distinguish between physical bodies and spirits. "Physical body" means the actual body of the god; "spirit" means his divine spirit. A *mitamashiro* is a mirror or some other object to which this spirit is committed; in everyday language, a Divine Object. Both physical bodies and *mitamashiro* are referred to as "(. . .) no Kami." In the *Chronicles of Japan*, in the section on Emperor Sujin, it says: "The emperor handed Amaterasu Ōmikami over to Toyosuki Iri-bime no Mikoto, and Yamato no Ōkunimitama no Kami to Nunaki Iri-bime no Mikoto." Since the physical bodies of these two gods were not in the palace at this time, it is beyond doubt that this refers to their *mitamashiro*, and from this we can learn that these, just like their physical bodies, were called "Amaterasu Ōmikami" and "Yamato no Ōkunimitama no Kami" as well. Further, this same section says: "The emperor hereupon proceeded to the plain of Kami-asachi, where he assembled the eighty myriads of gods and inquired of them by means of divination." Since these eighty myriads of gods could not, as in the Age of the Gods on the Plain of High Heaven, be assembled as physical bodies, it is clear that the meaning is that the emperor called up the spirits of these gods. On the basis of these facts we know that, when we find the words "(. . .) no Kami," we must distinguish between physical bodies and spirits.

This distinction exists as well for the gods in the passage from the *Record of Ancient Matters* just quoted; and if one asks how this distinction can be recognized, it is that the gods who are serving physical bodies and the gods who are *mitamashiro* are each mentioned separately, and that, because the five chiefs of workers' groups, Ama no Koyane no Mikoto and the others, mentioned in the beginning, are serving physical bodies, the houses that descend from them are given in the latter part of the above quotation. Also Ame no Oshihi no Mikoto, Ama-tsu-kume no Mikoto, and the other gods who figure in the passage following the one quoted are all physical bodies and have descendants because they came down from heaven to this country. Further, Omoikane no Kami and the other three gods have been recorded separately from those five chiefs of workers' groups, starting anew with the word "Thereupon," and grouping them with the curved jewels, the mirror and the sword. The words "These two gods," refer to the mirror, the *mitamashiro* of Amaterasu Ōmikami, and Omoikane no Kami. From the fact that one of these two gods is a mirror, we know that the other god, Omoikane no Kami, is a *mitamashiro* as well. Accordingly, this means that also Toyouke no Kami, who is mentioned next, is a *mitamashiro*, and that this *mitamashiro* resides in the Outer Shrine. And it also says that Omoikane no Kami is worshipped in the shrine of Isuzu, and that Tajikara-wo no Kami resides in Sanagata; that is what is recorded in the List of Deities [in the *Institutes of the Engi Period*] as "Province of Ise, district Taki, shrine of Sana." That Ame no Iwatowake no Kami is "the god of the gates" is recorded in the List of Deities as "Gods worshipped by the Sacred Maidens of the Gates in the Ministry of Worship, Kushi-iwamato no Kami and Toyo-iwamato no Kami (both major, Tsukinami and Niiname)," and as "Province of Tanba, district Taki, shrine of Kushi-iwamato, two gods (both principal deities, major)." Thus, for these gods only the place of residence is recorded, and nowhere is it mentioned that they are the ancestors of a house. Of the five chiefs of workers' groups, Ame no Koyane no Mikoto and the others, the houses that have descended from them are given, and not their places of residence, and so we can determine that there is indeed a distinction between gods who are physical bodies and gods who are *mitamashiro*.

Now then, the reason that in the passage in the *Chronicles of Japan* relating this descent from heaven these four gods, Toyouke no Kami, Omoikane no

Kami, and the others, are not mentioned is likewise that they are not physical bodies. This work lists only the gods who are serving physical bodies and describes the mirror, the curved jewels, and the sword as the regalia of Sumemima no Mikoto, omitting altogether the other gods who are *mitamashiro*. Thus it at last becomes clear that Toyouke no Kami is not a serving physical body, and for the very reason that she is not mentioned in the *Chronicles of Japan*! That Mr. Yoshimi [Yukikazu, the author of *Essays on the Theories of the Five Books*] did not understand this, and, ignorant of the distinction between physical bodies and *mitamashiro*, wrote that this god is a servant from the entourage, is again to be attributed to the well-known thoughtlessness of the Chinese way of thinking. How is it possible that all the Shintō scholars in the world expatiate on useless Sinifications like "heart transformations" and "matter transformations" but do not know that there is a distinction between physical bodies and spirits? Also his idea that Toyouke no Ōkami is an insignificant god because she does not figure in the section on the Age of the Gods in the *Chronicles of Japan* originates in his ignorance of this distinction. To state that she is not a prominent god because the fact that she resides in the Outer Shrine is not to be found in the National Histories is a gross distortion. The fact that Sumemima no Mikoto is worshipped in the Shared Hall at the Outer Shrine cannot be found in the National Histories either, and although Emperor Ōjin is worshipped in Usa in Tsukushi, the fact that this is his place of residence is not to be seen in the National Histories. Moreover we are not told that Emperor Jimmu's spirit is worshipped at all, nor even the shrine where he resides. Are these all to be disposed of as "insignificant"? In the *Chronicles of Japan* and in all the other National Histories, one finds that important matters that definitely should have been recorded are omitted, and also that rather insignificant matters are recorded. One cannot determine the importance of a matter by looking to see whether it is found in the National Histories!

Someone asks: If Toyouke no Ōkami is a god whom Amaterasu Ōmikami reveres, is then the Outer Shrine even more prominent than the Inner Shrine?

I answer: In all the universe there is no god as prominent as Amaterasu Ōmikami. That there are gods whom she reveres may, for example, be compared to the fact that in this country the emperor reveres the countless gods. On the Plain of High Heaven Amaterasu Ōmikami is an emperor with a physical body. Toyouke no Ōkami, whom she reveres, is a god who is a spirit; she has no physical body. Although in this country no one is more prominent than the emperor, he in turn reveres the gods; thus it will not do to say that these gods, for the reason that they are gods whom the emperor reveres, are all more prominent than the emperor. But neither can we say that these gods, for the reason that they are gods whom the emperor reveres, are all less prominent than the emperor; and likewise is it not right to say that the god of the Outer Shrine is less prominent than the god of the Inner Shrine. In the ceremonies of both shrines we worship a god who is a spirit, in the Inner as well as in the

Outer Shrine, and in that respect there is no difference between the Two Shrines. As things stand at present, the gods of both shrines appear to be on a par with each other and equal; but they differ from each other as emperor and god differ and are not equal. It is a frightful, vulgar notion that, even though they cannot be compared and designated more and less prominent, people still continue to dispute their prominence.

Again someone asks: Concerning the ceremonial homage they are paid by the court, and a myriad other matters besides, the Two Shrines of Ise differ in prominence and are not equal. In most matters the Inner Shrine is superior and the Outer Shrine inferior. Why then may we not say that [the god of the Outer Shrine] is less prominent than the god of the Inner Shrine, even though the Outer Shrine, in view of these differences, does appear less prominent than the Inner Shrine?

I answer: Because the Inner Shrine is the shrine where we worship the divine ancestress of the emperors, and in particular the mirror of her spirit, which is a most extraordinary imperial mandate, the ceremonies and myriad other matters concerning this shrine naturally are unequaled under heaven, and therefore the shrine of Toyouke no Ōkami, however prominent she herself may be, can never be its equal. That the Outer Shrine must be surpassed by the Inner Shrine is a matter of course. We should, however, not without reason determine the prominence of shrines on the basis of their ceremonies and the like. Therein lies the significance of the comparison of emperor and god that I made above. Now let me make another comparison. We have the Palace of the Emperor (ōmiya) and the shrine of a god (kami no miya): the shrine of this god is called the Great Shrine (ōkamumiya or daijingū) of Ise, but the construction of its buildings, for one thing, is not as spacious and magnificent as that of the palace of the emperors, and the deity is far less well off than the imperial court as far as officials, the myriad ceremonies, or the goods she is served are concerned. Would one for that reason say that Amaterasu Ōmikami is less prominent than the emperor? The reason for this difference is that one is an emperor with a physical body, and the other a god who is a spirit. You must realize that this same distinction exists between the gods of the Two Shrines.

In the matter of the great gods of these Two Shrines, proponents of the Outer Shrine dwell only upon the prominence of the Outer Shrine, concealing the fact that it is surpassed by the Inner Shrine, while people who want to denigrate the Outer Shrine dwell only upon its inferiority to the Inner Shrine, concealing the prominence of the Outer Shrine. Determined as they are to combat each other, their discourses are neither upright nor balanced; they are invariably one-sided. In general it is a law of nature in the world, that whenever something is divided into two parts, and these are placed in alignment, there arise automatically feelings of mutual envy and malice, and people begin to fight over which is superior and which inferior, which is higher and which lower. This is a practice that would be difficult indeed to prevent; but, as in the case of the

Two Shrines of Ise, where there can be no disputing which is "more prominent" or "less prominent," it is not merely downright common but positively frightful. Though the god of the Outer Shrine is a god whom Amaterasu Ōmikami reveres so deeply, they try to denigrate her with no scruples, and they insist that she is an insignificant god. Would that really make Amaterasu Ōmikami happy? They deliberately conceal the beneficence of the *mike-tsu-kami*, the peerlessly prominent spirit of the divine food, and equate her with gods entirely unrelated to her, arguing that she is Ame no Minakanushi no Mikoto or Kuni no Tokotachi no Mikoto. Would this sort of slander really make Toyouke no Ōkami happy? In the august presence of the physical bodies of these two great gods they would never dare to utter such idle, foolish lies; they do so only because they think superficially and do not fear the divine will of the gods; this because they do not show themselves before our eyes and speak to us. How frightful, alas, how frightful!

— 41 —

Shintō in the History of Japanese Religion:
An Essay by Kuroda Toshio

James C. Dobbins and Suzanne Gay

In modern times Shintō has commonly been portrayed as the indigenous religion of Japan. As such, it supposedly embodies Japan's unique identity and preserves its original essence. Though Japan has changed over the centuries, absorbing diverse social and cultural elements from the outside, its essential character can still be discerned, it is claimed, in Shintō's outlook and ways. This view has inspired many Japanese to look upon themselves as distinct from other people and has fostered a sense of cultural distance despite Japan's extensive appropriation of foreign elements. To a certain extent, this view is the product of the nineteenth- and twentieth-century political ideology that led to the ultranationalism of World War II. Though this ideology has been repudiated in the postwar period, its portrayal of Shintō, along with its rhetoric of uniqueness, remains dominant both inside and outside Japan.

In this article Kuroda Toshio, a postwar scholar of medieval Japanese history, criticizes this view of Shintō. He sees it as a modern construction of Shintō's identity that has been projected back in time and legitimated with evidence drawn selectively from various historical periods. Kuroda's own view is that Shintō did not exist as an independent religion until modern times. He argues that the term Shintō itself has had a variety of meanings throughout history, but in virtually no instances prior to the modern period has it referred to an independent religion. Rather, the beliefs and practices typically associated with Shintō were previously submerged in a broader religious worldview that Kuroda calls *kenmitsu* Buddhism. This worldview comprises not only the Exoteric doctrines (*ken*) and Esoteric rituals (*mitsu*) of Buddhism but also beliefs, customs, and traditions surrounding the kami, or Shintō deities. The components of kami culture came as much from outside Japan as from within, he contends, and they were ultimately grounded in the *kenmitsu* worldview through the identification of the kami as protective deities or as partners to or extensions of Buddhas and Bodhisattvas. Kuroda considers *kenmitsu* Buddhism, not some primordial essence preserved in an independent religion known as Shintō, to be Japan's primary cultural persona. But the *kenmitsu* worldview fell victim to attacks by Japanese modernists and was replaced by a new contruction of Japan's religious heritage, defined as two parallel traditions: an imported religion, Buddhism, and an indigenous one, Shintō. Kuroda's claim is that to understand Japan's culture one must first set aside this modern construction. Shintō will then be seen as facets and aspects of a larger, more inclusive religious worldview that does not privilege the indigenous over the imported.

Kuroda Toshio died in 1993 at the age of sixty-seven, but only after exerting a profound influence on the field of Japanese history. He is best known in Japan for his theory that the ruling elites (*kenmon*) of the medieval period consisted not only of the samurai warriors (*buke*) but also of the imperial aristocracy (*kuge*) and the large religious institutions (*jike*). This theory is a revision of the previous view that the medieval period was dominated by the samurai, a veritable age of the samurai. In the United States, Kuroda is better known for his ideas about Buddhism and Shintō, which are largely corollaries to his theory of the ruling elites.

The translation of this article first appeared in *The Journal of Japanese Studies* 7, 1 (Winter 1981): 1–21, and helped alert Western scholars to problems in the popular portrayal of Shintō. Kuroda's references to Japanese sources have been eliminated in the version below, and readers are referred to the *The Journal of Japanese Studies* for full documentation.

Further Reading

James C. Dobbins, ed., "The Legacy of Kuroda Toshio," special issue of *Japanese Journal of Religious Studies* 23, 3–4 (Fall 1996); Allan G. Grapard, *The Protocol of the Gods: A Study of the Kasuga Cult in Japanese History* (Berkeley: University of California Press, 1992); Helen Hardacre, *Shintō and the State, 1868–1988* (Princeton: Princeton University Press, 1989).

Shintō in the History of Japanese Religion

Shintō has long been regarded as a crucial element in Japanese religion that gives it distinctiveness and individuality. The common person's view of Shintō usually includes the following assumptions: Shintō bears the unmistakable characteristics of a primitive religion, including nature worship and taboos against *kegare* (impurities), but it has no system of doctrine; it exists in diverse forms as folk belief but at the same time possesses certain features of organized religion—for example, rituals and institutions such as shrines; it also plays an important role in Japan's ancient mythology and provides a basis for ancestor and emperor worship. In short, Shintō is viewed as the indigenous religion of

Japan, continuing in an unbroken line from prehistoric times down to the present.

Many people have discussed the role of Shintō in Japanese history and culture, but depending on the person there are slight differences in interpretation. These can be divided into two general categories. The first includes those who believe that, despite the dissemination of Buddhism and Confucianism, the religion called Shintō has existed without interruption throughout Japanese history. This has become the common person's view, and it is the conviction of Shintō scholars and priests particularly. The second includes those who think that, aside from whether it existed under the name Shintō, throughout history there have always been Shintōlike beliefs and customs (*shinkō*). This kind of interpretation is frequently found in studies of Japanese culture or intellectual history. This view can be traced back to the National Learning (*kokugaku*) scholar Motoori Norinaga in the eighteenth century, and it is reflected more recently in Yanagida Kunio's work on Japanese folklore. The same trend is discernible in the writings of Hori Ichirō, who claims an opinion similar to Robert Bellah's and Sir Charles Eliot's. Hori defines Shintō and "Shintōness" as "the underlying will of Japanese culture." He argues that Shintō has been the crucial element bringing the "great mix" of religions and rituals absorbed by the Japanese people into coexistence. Moreover, it has forced them to become Japanese in character. Maruyama Masao, speaking as an intellectual historian on the historical consciousness of the Japanese people, is also of this school. He maintains that the thought processes found in the myths of the *Kojiki* and the *Nihon shoki* continue to exist as an "ancient stratum," even though other layers of thought have been superimposed in subsequent ages. Maruyama is somewhat sympathetic to "Shintō thinkers of the Edo period"— including of course Motoori Norinaga—"down to the nationalistic moralists of the 1930s," and he even construes their assertions to be "a truth born of a certain kind of intuition."

Of these two groups, the views of the second demand special attention, but they should not be looked upon separately from those of the first. The two represent in a sense the external and the internal aspects of the same phenomenon. The views of the second group can be summarized as follows:

1. Shintō, with the Japanese people, is enduring. It is "the underlying will of Japanese culture," to borrow Hori Ichirō's phrase, an underlying autonomy that transforms and assimilates diverse cultural elements imported from outside. In the words of Motoori, any cultural element of any period (even Buddhism and Confucianism) is, "broadly speaking, the Shintō of that period."

2. Even though one can speak of Shintō as a religion along with Buddhism and Taoism, "Shintōness" is something deeper. It is the cultural will or energy of the Japanese people, embodied in conventions that precede or transcend religion. Here, the "secularity of Shintō" is stressed. Whether

people who maintain this position like it or not, what they advocate is akin to the Meiji Constitution, which did not regard State Shintō as a religion and on that basis placed restraints upon the thought and beliefs of Japanese citizens. It is also similar to the rationale adopted by certain movements today that seek to revive State Shintō.

3. Based on this line of thought, "the miscellaneous nature of Japanese religion," whereby a person may be Buddhist and Shintō at the same time, is taken as an unchanging characteristic of Japanese culture. When such a formula is applied to all cultural phenomena in history, then a miscellaneous, expedient, irrational, and nonintellectual frame of mind, more than any effort at a logical, unified, and integrated worldview, is extolled as that which is most Japanese.

The views of the second group when compared to those of the first differ in conception and central argument, but insofar as they both regard Shintō as a unique religion existing independently throughout history, the two share a common premise and reinforce one another. This view, however, is not only an incorrect perception of the facts but also a one-sided interpretation of Japanese history and culture. It is hoped that this article will demonstrate that before modern times Shintō did not exist as an independent religion. The main points of my argument will be as follows:

1. It is generally held that an indigenous self-consciousness is embodied in the word Shintō. I would argue that the original meaning of the word differs from how it is understood today.
2. The ceremonies of Ise Shrine, as well as those of the imperial court and the early provincial government, are said to have been forms of "pure Shintō." I would like to show that they actually became one component of a unique system of Buddhism that emerged in Japan and were perceived as an extension of Buddhism.
3. It is said that Shintō played a secular role in society and existed in a completely different sphere from Buddhism. I would maintain that this very secularity was permeated with Buddhist concepts and was itself religious in nature. The greater part of this paper will examine this question and the preceding two in their ancient and medieval contexts.
4. Finally, I would like to trace the historical stages and the rationale whereby the term Shintō came to mean the indigenous religion or national faith of Japan and to clarify how and when Shintō came to be viewed as an independent religion.

SHINTŌ IN THE *NIHON SHOKI*

The word Shintō is commonly taken to mean Japan's indigenous religion and to have had that meaning from fairly early times. It is difficult, however, to find a clear-cut example of the word Shintō used in such a way in early writings.

The intellectual historian Tsuda Sōkichi has studied the occurrences of the word Shintō in early Japanese literature and has divided its meaning into the following six categories: (1) "religious beliefs found in indigenous customs passed down in Japan, including superstitious beliefs"; (2) "the authority, power, activity, or deeds of a kami, the status of kami, being kami, or the kami itself"; (3) concepts and teachings concerning kami; (4) the teachings propagated by a particular shrine; (5) "the way of the kami" as a political or moral norm; and (6) sectarian Shintō as found in new religions. From these it is clear that the word Shintō has been used in a great variety of ways. Tsuda maintains that in the *Nihon shoki* Shintō means "the religious beliefs found in indigenous customs in Japan," the first definition, and that it was used from that time to distinguish "Japan's indigenous religion from Buddhism." He also claims that this basic definition underlies the meaning of Shintō in the other five categories.

It is far from conclusive, however, that the word Shintō was used in early times to denote Japan's indigenous religion, and for that reason Tsuda's analysis of examples in the *Nihon shoki* should be reexamined. The following three sentences are the only instances of the word Shintō in the *Nihon shoki*:

1. The emperor believed in the teachings of the Buddha (*Buppō* or *Hotoke no minori*) and revered Shintō (or *kami no michi*). (Prologue on Emperor Yōmei)
2. The emperor revered the teachings of the Buddha but scorned Shintō. He cut down the trees at Ikukunitama Shrine. (Prologue on Emperor Kōtoku)
3. The expression "as a kami would" (*kamunagara*) means to conform to Shintō. It also means in essence to possess one's self of Shintō. (Entry for Taika 3/4/26)

In examples 1 and 2 it is possible to interpret Shintō as distinguishing "Japan's indigenous religion from Buddhism," but that need not be the only interpretation. Tsuda himself indicates that in China the word Shintō originally meant various folk religions, or Taoism, or sometimes Buddhism, or even religion in general. Therefore, the word Shintō is actually a generic term for popular beliefs, whether of China, Korea, or Japan, even though in examples 1 and 2 it refers specifically to Japan's ancient customs, rituals, and beliefs, regardless of whether they were Japanese in origin. Since the *Nihon shoki* was compiled with a knowledge of China in mind, it is hard to imagine that its author used the Chinese word Shintō solely to mean Japan's indigenous religion. Though there may be some validity in what Tsuda says, the word Shintō by itself probably means popular beliefs in general.

In examples 1 and 2 Shintō is used in contrast to the word *Buppō*, the teachings of the Buddha. Tsuda takes this to mean "Japan's indigenous religion," but there are other possible interpretations of this without construing it to be the name of a religion. For example, it could mean "the authority, power, activity, or deeds of a kami, the status of kami, being a kami, or the kami itself," Tsuda's second definition of Shintō. In fact, during this period the character *dō* or *tō*, which is found in the word Shintō, meant not so much road or path but rather conduct or right action. Hence, Shintō could easily refer to the conduct or action of the kami.

In example 3 there are two instances of the word Shintō. While it is not unthinkable to interpret them as "popular beliefs in general," Tsuda's second definition, "the authority, power, activity, or deeds of a kami," is perhaps more appropriate, since the word *kamunagara* in the quotation means "in the nature of a kami" or "in the state of being a kami." The sentences in example 3 were originally a note explaining the word *kamunagara* as it appeared in the emperor's decree issued on the day of this entry, and according to Edo period scholars it was added sometime after the ninth century when the work was transcribed. Therefore, it is not reliable as evidence for what Shintō meant at the time the *Nihon shoki* was compiled. Even if it were, it is more likely that the compiler did not use the same word in two different ways but rather applied the same definition, "the authority, power, activity, or deeds of a kami," in all three examples.

Another possible interpretation of Shintō in the *Nihon shoki* is Taoism. Based on recent studies, it is clear that Shintō was another term for Taoism in China during the same period. Moreover, as Taoist concepts and practices steadily passed into Japan between the first century A.D. and the period when the *Nihon shoki* was compiled, they no doubt exerted a considerable influence on the ceremonies and the beliefs of communal groups bound by blood ties or geographical proximity and on those that emerged around imperial authority. Among the many elements of Taoist origin transmitted to Japan are the following: veneration of swords and mirrors as religious symbols; titles such as *mahito* or *shinjin* (Taoist meaning—perfected man, Japanese meaning—the highest of eight court ranks in ancient times which the emperor bestowed on his descendants), *hijiri* or *sen* (Taoist—immortal, Japanese—saint, emperor, or recluse), and *tennō* (Taoist—lord of the universe, Japanese—emperor); the cults of Polaris and the Big Dipper; terms associated with Ise Shrine such as *jingū* (Taoist—a hall enshrining a deity, Japanese—Ise Shrine), *naikū* (Chinese—inner palace, Japanese—Inner Shrine at Ise), *gekū* (Chinese—detached palace, Japanese—Outer Shrine at Ise), and *taiichi* (Taoist—the undifferentiated origin of all things, Japanese—no longer in general use, except at Ise Shrine where it has been used since ancient times on flags signifying Amaterasu Ōmikami); the concept of *daiwa* (meaning a state of ideal peace, but in Japan used to refer to Yamato, the center of the country); and the Taoist concept of immortality. Early Japanese perhaps regarded their ceremonies and beliefs as Taoist, even though they may have differed from those in China. Hence, it is possible to view these teachings, rituals, and even the concepts of imperial authority and of nation as remnants of an attempt to establish a Taoist tradition in Japan. If that is so, Japan's ancient popular beliefs were not so much an indigenous religion but merely a local brand of Taoism, and the word Shintō simply meant

Taoism. The accepted theory today is that a systematic form of Taoism did not enter Japan in ancient times, but it is not unreasonable to think that over a long period of time Taoism gradually pervaded Japan's religious milieu until medieval times when Buddhism dominated it completely.

Three possible interpretations of the word Shintō in the *Nihon shoki* have been presented above. It is not yet possible to say which of these is correct, but that should not preclude certain conclusions about Shintō. What is common to all three is that none views Japan's ancient popular beliefs as an independent religion and none uses the word Shintō as a specific term for such a religion. Also, there is no evidence that any other specific term existed. Moreover, when Buddhism was introduced into Japan there was a controversy over whether or not to accept it, but there is no indication that these popular beliefs were extolled as an indigenous tradition. Hence, Shintō need not imply a formal religion per se, and it need not indicate something that is uniquely Japanese.

THE SIGNIFICANCE OF SHINTŌ DEITIES IN THE ANCIENT PERIOD

In the previous section the word Shintō was analyzed to show how it was used and what it meant in ancient times. Now it is necessary to consider the institutional significance and place of kami in Japan during that period, especially as evidenced in the *jingiryō* laws and in Shintō-Buddhist syncretism.

The *jingiryō* is a set of laws of ancient Japan that instituted ceremonies to the kami. Needless to say, these laws include only those rites that had state sponsorship, but they nonetheless represent a fair sampling of the ceremonies current at that time. In brief the *jingiryō* laws cover the following topics: (1) the season, title, and content of official annual ceremonies; (2) imperial succession ceremonies and *imi* (seclusion to avoid things tabooed); (3) the supervision and administration of ceremonies; (4) *ōharai* (an official ceremony to exorcise evils and offenses from people); and (5) the administration of government shrines.

It is well known that the *jingiryō* law code of ancient Japan was modeled on the codes of Sui and T'ang China. Many scholars have already pointed out that the *jingiryō*, one section of the *ritsuryō*, was based on the Chinese *shiryō* or *tz'u-ling* code, which has been reconstructed in forty-six articles. When compared with the T'ang *shiryō*, the *jingiryō* is seen to occupy an identical position in the overall order of the law code and to correspond to the *shiryō* in topic and sentence structure. The official ceremonies described in the *shiryō* include: (1) *shi* or, in Chinese, *ssu* (veneration of kami of heaven); (2) *sai* or *chi* (veneration of kami of earth); (3) *kō* or *heng* (deification of the spirits of the dead); and (4) *sekiten* or *shih-tien* (deification of ancient sages and masters). From these the *jingiryō* of Japan incorporated only the first two and then added imperial succession ceremonies and *ōharai* ceremonies, not found in the *shiryō*. These changes probably reflect differences in the use of ceremonies in Japan and China, which the compilers of the *ritsuryō* code took into account. Not-

withstanding these differences, both codes are alike in that they record popular
ceremonies of society at that time, even though they include only those ceremonies that had official or political significance. The importance that Japan's
ritsuryō code placed on kami derived ultimately from such ceremonies. Originally, kami were popular local deities connected to communal groups bound
by blood ties or geographical proximity, and later to the imperial concept of
state as well. The kami associated with ancestor worship are one example of
such local deities. As the section following the *jingiryō* in the *ritsuryō*, the
government drew up the *sōniryō*, laws for Buddhist institutions, to regulate
priests and nuns. By compiling the *sōniryō* separately from the *jingiryō*, the
government placed ceremonies for kami in a different dimension from religions
such as Buddhism, which exerted a special influence on society through its
high doctrines.

In subsequent centuries the significance of kami changed somewhat from
what it had been under the original *ritsuyō* system. During the eighth century
the state enthusiastically embraced Buddhism, and the Empress Shōtoku, in
collusion with the priest Dōkyō, established a policy that was pro-Buddhist in
the extreme. Recent scholars have shown how this policy met with opposition
in aristocratic and court circles, and they claim that in conjunction with political reforms at the beginning of the ninth century there emerged the concept
of Shintō as an independent, indigenous religion. Certainly, it was during these
ninth-century reforms that court Shintō ceremonies and Ise Shrine's organization were formalized. Nonetheless, it is highly unlikely that Shintō was perceived as an independent religion in opposition to Buddhism at this time.

As is already well known, between the late eighth century and the eleventh
century, Shintō and Buddhism gradually coalesced with one another (*shimbutsu
shūgō*)—or, more precisely, veneration of the kami was absorbed into Buddhism through a variety of doctrinal innovations and new religious forms.
Among the doctrinal explanations of the kami were the following: (1) the kami
realize that they themselves are trapped in this world of samsara and transmigration and they also seek liberation through the Buddhist teachings; (2) the
kami are benevolent deities who protect Buddhism; (3) the kami are transformations of the Buddhas manifested in Japan to save all sentient beings (*honji
suijaku*); and (4) the kami are the pure spirits of the Buddhas (*hongaku*).
Among new religious forms were the *jingūji* (a combination shrine and temple)
and Sōgyō Hachiman (the kami Hachiman in the guise of a Buddhist monk).
Such religious forms are exemplary of ceremonies and objects of worship that
could not be distinguished specifically as Shintō or as Buddhist. The first stage
in this process of Shintō-Buddhist syncretization covered the late eighth and
early ninth century. During that period the first two doctrinal explanations of
kami, mentioned above, became current.

It is only natural that at this stage people became more cognizant of the
kami, especially in relation to the Buddhas. Examples of this are found in the
Shoku Nihongi. The entry there for 782/7/29 states that Shintō cannot be de-

ceived and that numerous recent calamities are retribution meted out by the great kami of Ise and all the other kami in return for the negligent use of mourning garb widespread among men. Such disrespect for decorum, and by extension for the kami, indicates implicitly the popularity of the Buddhas over the kami. Another example from the *Shoku Nihongi* is an imperial edict of 836/11, which states that there is nothing superior to Mahāyāna Buddhism in defending Shintō and that one should rely on the efficacy of Buddhist practices to transform calamity into good. This passage indicates that it is the Buddhas who guarantee the authority of the kami.

These examples reflect a heightened awareness of kami during this period, but they by no means imply that Shintō was looked upon as an independent and inviolable entity. On the contrary, there was more of a sense that Shintō occupied a subordinate position and role within the broader scheme of Buddhism.

THE MEANING OF THE WORD SHINTŌ IN MEDIEVAL TIMES

The *Konjaku monogatarishū*, composed around the eleventh century, contains the following two references. First, an old woman in China was possessed with heretical views: she served Shintō and did not believe in Buddhism. Second, there was an outlying province in India that was a land of kami, and to this day the words of Buddhism have not been transmitted there. Here "Shintō" and "land of kami" have nothing to do with Japan but clearly indicate "local deities" and "a land devoted to its local deities." Although these references are from a collection of Buddhist tales, they show that even in this period the word Shintō was used in its classical sense, as it was in China and in the *Nihon shoki*.

In medieval times the word Shintō generally meant the authority, power, or activity of a kami, being a kami, or, in short, the state or attributes of a kami. For example, the *Nakatomi no harai kunge* [see Chapter 21 in this volume], a work on Ryōbu Shintō of Shingon Buddhism, discusses the relationship of kami and Buddha in the following way: "The Buddha assumes a state in which kami and Buddha are not two different things but are absolutely identical. The Buddha constantly confers his mark (*suijaku*) on Shintō." Here Shintō must mean kami or the state of being a kami. The word Shintō is used in the same way in the *Shintōshū*, a collection of tales from the Sannō Shintō tradition of Tendai Buddhism:

Q: For what reason do the Buddhas and the bodhisattvas manifest themselves in the form of Shintō?

A: The Buddhas and the bodhisattvas manifest themselves in various forms out of compassion for and to save all living beings.

Besides these there are numerous other examples of Shintō used to mean kami. A saying in common parlance in medieval times was, "Shintō is a difficult thing

to speculate about." This example, if any, is representative of what Shintō ordinarily indicated in that period. It does not mean that one cannot conjecture
about the religion or doctrines of the kami, but rather that it is difficult to
fathom the conduct, the intentions, and the existence of the kami by human
intellect. Such a definition of Shintō was current throughout the medieval period, and even the *Japanese Portuguese Dictionary* of 1603 contains the following entry: "Xinto (*camino michi*). Kami [*camis* in the original] or matters pertaining to kami." The *camino michi* recorded here is the Japanese reading of
the Chinese characters for Shintō. It is clear that this word *michi* likewise does
not mean doctrine. *Michi* in the medieval period, just as in ancient times,
indicated conduct or ideal state like the *michi* in *mononofu no michi* or *yumiya
no michi* (the way of the warrior). Hence *kami no michi* means the state of being
a kami or the conduct of a kami. Even when *michi* is compounded with another
character and read *tō* or *dō* as in Shintō, the compound can have the meaning
of the other character alone. An example of this is found in the *Gishi wajinden*,
which states in reference to Himiko that "she served the *kidō* (demons)." The
same can be said of the *dō* and *tō* of *myōdō* (deities of the world of the dead)
and *tentō* (deities such as Bonten and Taishakuten), words that appear in *kishōmon*, medieval documents containing oaths sworn before kami and Buddhas.

The next question that must be dealt with is what religious content this
word Shintō was said to have contained. As pointed out earlier, during medieval
times Shintō was generally interpreted as one part of Buddhism. This was possible because the concepts contained in Mahāyāna Buddhism provided a rationale for absorbing folk beliefs. Just as a unique form of Buddhism evolved in
Tibet, so in medieval Japan Buddhism developed a distinctive logic and system
of its own.

Nominally, medieval Buddhism comprised eight sects, but it was not unusual
for individuals to study the teachings and rituals of all the sects. The reason is
that the eight held a single doctrinal system in common, that of *mikkyō* or
Esoteric Buddhism (Skt. Vajrayāna). The Buddhist teachings that were recognized as orthodox during the medieval period had *mikkyō* as their base, combined with the Exoteric teachings or *kengyō* (Buddhist and other teachings
outside of *mikkyō*) of each of the eight schools—Tendai, Kegon, Yuishiki
(Hossō), Ritsu, and so forth. These eight sects, sometimes called *kenmitsu* or
Exoteric-Esoteric Buddhism, acknowledged their interdependence with state
authority, and together they dominated the religious sector. This entire order
constituted the fundamental religious system of medieval Japan. Shintō was
drawn into this Buddhist system as one segment of it, and its religious content
was replaced with Buddhist doctrine, particularly *mikkyō* and Tendai philosophy. The term *kenmitsu* used here refers to this kind of system. At the end of
the twelfth century, various reform movements arose in opposition to this
system, and there even appeared heretical sects that stressed exclusive religious
practices—the chanting of the nembutsu, *zen* meditation, and so forth. Nonetheless, the *kenmitsu* system maintained its status as the orthodox religion until
the beginning of the sixteenth century.

In *kenmitsu* Buddhism, the most widespread interpretation of the religious content of Shintō was the *honji suijaku* theory, based on Tendai doctrine. According to this theory, the kami are simply another form of the Buddha, and their form, condition, authority, and activity are nothing but the form and the acts by which the Buddha teaches, guides, and saves human beings. Shintō, therefore, was independent neither in existence nor in system of thought. It was merely one means among many by which the Buddha guides (*kedō*) and converts (*kegi*) sentient beings. The *Shintōshū* cited earlier contains about fifty tales in which the Buddha takes on the form of a kami and saves human beings. The word Shintō in its title presupposes this meaning—that is, conversion by the Buddha. With Shintō interpreted in this way and with people's beliefs based on this kind of interpretation, individual Shintō shrines sought to emphasize the distinctive capacities and lineage of their own kami as a manifestation (*suijaku*) of the Buddha, as well as the unique teachings and practices passed down in their shrine or school. These claims were expanded through complicated doctrines and tortuous theories in a class of teachings now called sectarian or *shake* Shintō (Tsuda's fourth definition of the word Shintō, "the teachings propagated by a particular shrine"). Ryōbu Shintō of the Shingon tradition and Sannō Shintō of the Tendai tradition are typical examples of such teachings. Individual shrines in different areas adapted these teachings in such a way that during the medieval period countless theories of Shintō arose.

The theory of Shintō propounded by the Ise Shrine tradition, sometimes called Ise or Watarai Shinto, is of decisive importance in a consideration of medieval Shintō. Modern intellectual and Shintō historians have generally regarded Ise Shintō, which became active in the thirteenth century, as evidence of Shintō's tenacious, though hidden, existence as "Japan's indigenous religion" throughout medieval times. Moreover, they see it as the starting point for subsequent medieval theories of Shintō as they began to break away from Buddhism.

It is well known that even during Buddhism's apex in the medieval period Ise Shrine maintained ancient rites—whether uniquely Japanese or Taoist in origin—and upheld proscriptions against Buddhist terminology, practices, and garb. But it is equally important to realize that Ise Shrine did not completely reject Buddhism, for Buddhist priests would visit the shrine and Ise priests themselves possessed considerable knowledge of Buddhism. In this light, the proscription against anything Buddhist was probably regarded as a peculiar and mysterious practice, incomprehensible to society in general and even to the Shintō priests at Ise. This proscription, for example, is treated as strange in Mujū's *Shasekishū* and Tsūkai's *Daijingū sankeiki*, works closely associated with Ise Shrine, and in treatises by outstanding priests of Ise, such as the *Daijingū ryōgū no onkoto* by Watarai Tsunemasa. For the medieval mind this was only a natural response. The problem that arises here is how to explain in Buddhist terms what was a truly peculiar practice for the times, or even more so, how to advocate it in all good conscience as a praiseworthy feature of the shrine. The works mentioned above actually begin with this kind of question and end up expounding the immeasurable virtues of the kami at Ise. Also in Ise Shintō there is the expression "not to breathe a word about Buddhism." This in fact does not imply a rejection of Buddhism but rather indicates a special attitude or etiquette assumed in the presence of the kami. As stated previously in another article, this view draws on the philosophy of innate Buddhahood (*hongaku shisō*) found in Esoteric Buddhism that was popular at that time, the thirteenth century. In the final analysis, Ise Shintō was nothing more than one form of sectarian Shintō, which took for granted the existence of the Buddhas.

In the *Hieisha eizan gyōkōki* of the early fourteenth century, it states:

> There are identical as well as differing aspects in the method of conversion used by the *shinmei* (*kami*) in other lands and that used by Shintō in our own land. Our land, which is a land of the kami, is superior in that human beings are benefited by "the light of the Buddha melded to become one with our world of dust" (*wakō dōjin*, i.e., the power of the Buddha harmonized with our mundane world and manifested as kami).

This passage is indicative of how the word Shintō was interpreted in medieval times. It was used not to distinguish popular beliefs from Buddhism but rather to signify the form in which the Buddha converts and saves human beings.

SHINTŌ'S SECULAR ROLE

If Shintō is a manifestation of the Buddha and one form in which he converts and saves human beings, there arises the question of whether kami play precisely the same role as the Buddha. Here it is important to note the secular character of Shintō in medieval times. Many of the representations of kami familiar to people in the medieval period were secular in form. Admittedly, there were also numerous examples of syncretism with Buddhism, for instance, Sanskrit letters used to symbolize invisible kami or a Buddhist image enshrined in the inner sanctuary (*shinden*) of a shrine, or again Hachimanshin portrayed as a Buddhist monk, or Zaō Gongen as the Buddhist deity Myōō (Skt. Vidyārāja). Nevertheless, in many of the Shintō statues, portraits, and narrative drawings that survive today, kami were depicted in such secular guises as noblemen, ladies, old men, young boys, Chinese gentlemen, travelers, and hunters. A number of these became formalized iconographically during the thirteenth century.

The same can also be said of how the word *suijaku* (manifestation) was comprehended. *Suijaku*, as understood by the common people in medieval times, was not the abstract or philosophical idea found in the doctrines of Mahāyāna Buddhism but was mythological in nature or perhaps associated with concrete places or events. The term *suijaku* literally meant to descend from heaven to a given spot and to become the local or guardian kami of that spot. Hence, at that spot there would arise a legend of the mysterious relationship between men and kami, and the very area enshrining the kami would be looked upon as sacred ground where profound doctrinal principles lay concealed. The history of this manifestation—that is, its development over time—was related in the form of an *engi* (a historical narrative), and the positioning of its enshrinement—that is, its location in space—was depicted in the form of a mandala (a rational layout). This indicates that the legends, the architectural form of early shrines, and the rituals of worship were interpreted as mysterious principles expressing Buddhist philosophy. In short, secular representations in Shintō actually expressed an essence that was strongly Buddhist. The link between Buddhism and Shintō in medieval times is exemplified by the Kike school at Enryakuji. This school, which specialized in chronicles, concentrated on mysterious legends, especially Shintō legends, as a means of plumbing the depths of Buddhism.

Also in the medieval period Shintō was associated with numerous secular functions and duties. Shintō observances at court, such as the Daijō-e (a rite performed by the emperor upon his succession) and the Jinkonjiki (a biannual offering to the kami by the emperor) had no other purpose than to enshroud in mystery secular authority. Nonetheless, they derived their meaning from the fact that secular mystery lay within a world encompassed by Buddhist law. Eventually, the worship of kami became inseparable from secular authority, but at the same time it was incorporated into the multi-leveled *kenmitsu* system with its unique logic and structure resulting from Buddhism's development in Japan. Secular though it was, Shintō did not coexist aloof from Buddhism, nor did it constitute a non-Buddhist stronghold within the Buddhist sphere. Rather, its secularity functioned, in the final analysis, within a Buddhist world.

Because shrines were Buddhism's secular face, their upkeep was the responsibility of the secular authority, even though they themselves were integrated into Buddhism's system of control. For that reason, the imperial court made regular offerings to twenty-two specially designated shrines, and the provincial government bore the responsibility for ceremonies and maintenance at major shrines (*sōsha*, *ichinomiya*, and *ninomiya*) in the provinces. In the Kamakura period the bakufu stipulated in article 1 of the *Goseibai shikimoku*, the Jōei law code, that "efforts must be made to keep shrines in repair and not to neglect their ceremonies," thereby stressing the importance of maintaining shrines in the provinces and on *shōen* under bakufu supervision. In article 2 it dealt with Buddhist temples and their functions. These indicate not only the responsibilities that the bakufu inherited from the provincial government of the previous period, but also the obligations that secular administrative authority had to fulfill to religion.

As stated earlier, Shintō was looked upon as a skillful means by which the

Buddha, in his compassion, might lead people to enlightenment or deliver them to his Pure Land. Nonetheless, it is important to note that in actuality Shintō played an important role in the administrative power upholding the secular order. As pointed out in the previous section, the ability of "the light of the Buddha to meld and to become one with our world of dust" (*wakō dōjin*) was constantly stressed in medieval times, but that expression reflects an understanding of Shintō's ultimate significance or its final objective. On an everyday level, people felt a strong sense of fear toward the kami. For example, in many medieval oaths (*kishōmon*), it is recorded, "If I violate this pledge, may the punishments of Bonten and Taishakuten, of the kami of the provinces, and especially of the guardian kami of this *shōen* be visited upon this body of mine." It goes without saying that what was sworn in such oaths was, without exception, actions of worldly significance or things relating to the preservation of the secular order, rather than anything to do with religious affairs. It is true that in Buddhism also people would petition the Buddha for "peace in this world and good fortune in the next" (*genze annon gose zenshō*), but as a general rule matters of this world were addressed to the kami and those of the coming world to the Buddha. In times of worldly difficulty one might pray for the protection of the kami and the Buddha, but first and foremost for that of the kami. Or, when heading into battle, one would beseech the kami for good fortune in war. Concerning the kami and their power, it was generally said that they were strict in both reward and punishment. Such views simply highlight the influence and control that religion exerted over secular life.

Though there is not enough space to deal with it adequately here, the belief that "Japan is the land of the kami," with both its political and religious implications, was based on the secular role of Shintō described above. The secularity of Shintō and the political applicability of the concept of "the land of the kami" does not indicate that Shintō was without any religious character but rather shows that the Buddhist system that lay behind it pervaded all aspects of everyday life. The present-day illusion that Shintō is not a religion derives historically from a misunderstanding of this point.

THE EMERGENCE OF THE CONCEPT OF SHINTŌ AS AN INDIGENOUS RELIGION

The following two sentences are found in the *Shintōshū*:

1. Question: On what basis do we know that Shintō reveres the Buddha's teachings?
2. Question: How are we to understand the statement that the Buddha's realm and Shintō differ in their respective forms but are one and the same in essence?

Both of these questions pose kami and Buddha against one another. In the first Shintō clearly indicates the kami themselves, whereas in the second Shintō may be interpreted as the deeds, state, or authority of the kami, but it also conveys the idea of a realm of the kami by contrasting it to the Buddha's realm. A similar passage is found in the *Daijingū sankeiki* by Tsūkai:

> Amaterasu Ōmikami is paramount in Shintō and the Tathāgata Dainichi is paramount in Buddhist teachings. Hence in both *suijaku* (manifestation) and *honji* (origin or source) there is the supreme and the incomparable.

In this case Shintō may be understood as the ideal state of being a kami, but it is also important that, as a concept juxtaposed to "Buddhist teachings," it assumes a sphere of its own, meaning "the realm of *suijaku*," teaching and converting in the form of a kami. This is especially true of the Ise school's theory of Shintō. For example, in the *Hōki hongi* Shintō is contrasted to the "three jewels" (the three basic components of Buddhism—the Buddha, the Buddhist teachings, and the Buddhist order), or in the *Ruishū jingi hongen* it is juxtaposed to *bukke* (Buddhist schools). These imply that Shintō and Buddhism belong to separate spheres in the phenomenal world even though they are identical in essence. Examples that transfer emphasis to the word Shintō in this way are quite conspicuous in Ise Shintō. This was a natural tendency, since the Ise school's theory of Shintō had to stress the efficacy of Shintō above all, even more than other schools of sectarian Shintō.

The word Shintō, when set up as an object of contrast in this way, emerged with a sectarian meaning or with a special sphere of its own, even though fundamentally it meant the authority of the kami or the condition of being a kami. This is not to say that it immediately assumed the meaning of a separate teaching or religion liberated from the framework of Buddhism. Rather, what Ise Shintō tried to do was to cast the realm of Shintō in a resplendent light. This was attempted by reducing the terms contrasted with Shintō to purely Buddhist phenomena and forms—namely, Buddhist teachings, "three jewels," Buddhist schools, and so forth—and by defining Shintō relative to them. All the while, Buddhism, the overarching principle that embraced and unified both, was left intact as the ultimate basis. The Ise school also attempted to aggrandize Shintō by diverse embellishments and additions to Shintō that were non-Buddhist and by cloaking it in a dignity similar to that of the Buddhist scriptures. Nonetheless, in this case also the principles that Shintō held in common with Buddhism were likewise stressed.

In this way the word Shintō came to refer to a Japanese phenomenon, school, or sphere of Buddhism qua religious truth. This meaning of the word paved the way for later stages in which Shintō became a term for Japan's indigenous religion. The writings of the priests at Ise as well as the theories of fourteenth-century Shintō thinkers such as Kitabatake Chikafusa, Jihen, and Ichijō Kanera (corresponding to Tsuda's third definition of Shintō, "concepts and teachings concerning kami") played a particularly important role in this process. Nevertheless, it was not because these thinkers were critical of *kenmitsu* Buddhism, which was the orthodox religion of the medieval period. Rather, they were all adherents of the orthodox teachings, so that any statements they made, which might at first seem to oppose those teachings, were nothing more than an attempt, extreme though it may have been, to enshroud in mystery the authority of the governing system at a time when it was isolated and in decline. With the rise of the Shintō-only school (Yuiitsu or Yoshida Shintō) at the end of the fifteenth century, the word Shintō became more and more identified as an indigenous form of religion. It was even interpreted as the highest religion, though identical in essence with Buddhism and Confucianism. At this point the meaning of the word began to depart from the orthodox teachings of *kenmitsu* Buddhism. It just so happened that during this period the power of the orthodox religious order was in a state of decline because of the strength of various heretical movements of so-called new Buddhism, particularly of Shinshū uprisings (*ikkō ikki*). The Shintō-only school, which was one branch of sectarian Shintō, simply took advantage of this situation for its own unfettered development.

Beginning in the seventeenth century a Confucian theory of Shintō, with much the same structure as medieval theories, was formulated by Hayashi Razan and other Edo period scholars. Based on this interpretation of Shintō, the definition of Shintō as the indigenous religion of Japan, as opposed to Taoism, Buddhism, or Confucianism, became firmly fixed. Moreover, the Confucian concept of *dō*, the way, also influenced the word Shintō, imbuing it with the meaning of "the way, as a political or moral norm" (Tsuda's fifth definition of Shintō). Of course, Confucian Shintō amounted to nothing more than theories of the educated class subordinating Shintō's true nature to Confucianism. Actual belief in the kami, however, as found among the common people at that time, remained subsumed under Buddhism.

The notion of Shintō as Japan's indigenous religion finally emerged complete both in name and in fact with the rise of modern nationalism, which evolved from the National Learning school of Motoori Norinaga and the Restoration Shintō movement of the Edo period down to the establishment of State Shintō in the Meiji period. The Meiji separation of Shintō and Buddhism (*shinbutsu bunri*) and its concomitant suppression of Buddhism (*haibutsu kishaku*) were coercive and destructive "correctives" pressed forward by the hand of government. With them Shintō achieved for the first time the status of an independent religion, distorted though it was. During this period the "historical consciousness" of an indigenous religion called Shintō, existing in Japan since ancient times, clearly took shape for the first time. This has remained the basis for defining the word Shintō down to the present. Scholars have yielded to this use of the word, and the population at large has been educated in this vein.

There is one further thing that should be pointed out. That is that separating Shintō from Buddhism cut Shintō off from the highest level of religious philosophy achieved by the Japanese up to that time and inevitably, moreover artificially, gave it the features of a primitive religion. Hence, while acquiring independence, Shintō declined to the state of a religion that disavowed being a religion.

CONCLUSION

This article is an attempt to trace Shintō throughout Japan's entire religious history by extracting samples dealing only with Shintō from each period. The reader may be left with the impression, contrary to the assertion at the beginning of this essay, that Shintō has indeed existed without interruption throughout Japanese history. This is only natural considering the sampling method used. Moreover, it is undeniable that there is a certain continuity to it all. Therein lies the problem. Up to now all studies of Shintō history have emphasized this continuity by means of such a sampling process. In doing so they have applied to all periods of history a sort of surgical separation of Shintō from Buddhism and thus from Japanese religion as a whole. By such reasoning, anything other than Shintō becomes simply a superficial overlay, a passing thing.

The meanings of the word Shintō, as well as changes over time in customs and beliefs, would indicate that Shintō emerged as an independent religion only in modern times, and then only as a result of political policy. If that is so, can this continuity be regarded as a true picture of history? Or could it be that what is perceived as indigenous, or as existing continuously from earliest times, is nothing more than a ghost image produced by a word linking together unrelated phenomenon? Up to just one hundred years ago, what constituted the religion and thought of the Japanese people in most periods of history was something historical—that is, something assimilated or formulated or fabricated by the people, whether it was native or foreign in origin. This thing was something truly indigenous. In concrete terms, this was the *kenmitsu* Buddhist system including its components, such as Shintō and the yin-yang tradition, and its various branches, both reformist and heretical. It, rather than Shintō, was the comprehensive, unified, and self-defined system of religious thought produced by Japan in premodern times. Even today it is perpetuated latently in everyday conventions as the subconscious of the Japanese people.

Throughout East Asia, Mahāyāna Buddhism generally embraced native beliefs in a loose manner, without harsh repression and without absorbing them to the point of obliteration. The question here is how Japan should be interpreted. While acknowledging Japan as an example of this East Asian pattern, should one consider the separation of Shintō and Buddhism to be an inevitable development and, in line with Meiji nationalism, perceive Shintō as the basis of Japan's cultural history? Or should one view *kenmitsu* Buddhism's unique system of thought, which evolved historically from diverse elements, including foreign ones, as the distinguishing feature of Japanese culture?

Considering the magnitude of the problem, this article leaves much to be desired. It is hoped, however, that it has served to dispel fictitious notions about Japan's religious history and religious consciousness, and about Japanese culture in general.

— 42 —

Sasaki Shōten: Toward a Postmodern
Shinshū Theology

Jan Van Bragt

Sasaki Shōten, born in 1939, is a priest of the Nishi Hongan-ji branch of Shinshū. After graduating from Ryūkoku University (Kyoto) and being ordained as a priest, he continued his studies in religion at the State University of Kyoto. Soon after, he became a member of the Dendō-in (Pastoral Institute) of Nishi Hongan-ji, where he is still active today. It was in the 1984 issue of the *Bulletin* of this Dendō-in that Sasaki broached for the first time the problematics of the present article, in the form of a report of the results of a research program on the practices of Shinshū believers, which he had jointly undertaken with two sociologists, Omura Eishō and Kaneko Satoru. The strong reaction among the scholars of the sect to this report prompted the three scholars to enlarge on their findings in a jointly authored book, *Posuto-modan no Shinran* (The Postmodern Shinran) (Kyoto: Dō-bōsha, 1990).

The term "Shinshū" refers to the adherents of the school of Pure Land Buddhism or Amidism founded by Shinran (1173–1262). By the sixteenth century the Honganji branch of this school, which was organized after Shinran's death around his direct descendants and his tomb in Kyoto, had succeeded in bringing most of Shinran's disciples into its fold. In the beginning of the seventeenth century, however, a succession dispute led to the split of the Honganji into two "sects," commonly known as the Nishi (West or Honganji) branch and the Higashi (East or Ōtani) branch. As part of their official teachings, both branches reject the use of amulets, talismans, votive tablets and other devices and rituals for securing this-worldly benefits (*genze riyaku*) such as health, wealth, and longevity. While these beliefs are officially condemned as magical folk superstitions, what Sasaki and his colleagues confirmed through their field studies is that large numbers of Shinshū adherents engaged in these practices. In proposing a "postmodern Shinshū theology," Sasaki criticizes the "modern" rationalist stance that rejects such superstitions, and the attempts to account for and even embrace folk practices without violating official teaching.

The present article, based on a special lecture delivered at the Center for Religious Education of the Sōtō branch of Zen Buddhism, October 1986, was originally published in the February 12, 15, and 17, 1988, issues of the religious newspaper *Chūgai nippō*. The following considerably abridged translation of that text first appeared in *Nanzan Bulletin* 12 (1988): 13–35.

Further Reading

James C. Dobbins, *Jōdo Shinshū: Shin Buddhism in Medieval Japan* (Bloomington: Indianapolis: Indiana University Press, 1989); James Ketelaar, *Of Heretics and Martyrs in Meiji Japan: Buddhism and Its Persecution* (Princeton: Princeton University Press, 1990); Suzuki Daisetz, tr., *The Kyōgyōshinshō: The Collection of Passages Expounding the True Teaching, Living, Faith, and Realizing of the Pure Land* (Kyoto: Shinshū Ōtaniha, 1973).

Toward a Postmodern Shinshū Theology

We no longer belong to the "modern world." In many areas of culture and in popular religiosity, fundamentally new trends have come to the fore, leading us to conclude that we have entered a "postmodern" period, which naturally requires a postmodern "theology."

It is my contention here that tragedy awaits our sect in the future if we continue to absolutize a modernistic theology and refuse to face the many inadequacies of that theology attested by recent events. In this fin de siècle we must build a postmodern theology able to correct the aberrations of our modernistic theology.

THE DOCTRINE OF THE NISHI HONGANJI

During the three hundred years of the Edo period, the doctrine of our sect had been built up to such a degree of scholastic minuteness that it is no exaggeration to say that our theologians since the Meiji Restoration have had their hands full just with systematizing and cataloging the Edo legacy. That Edo doctrine may seem to be purely theological, but in fact it is intimately tied up with the political situation under the bakufu regime and bears the traces of many clashes with the other branches of the Pure Land School and with various other Buddhist sects. In sum, it shows a history of polemics against the "Path of the Sages" (*shōdō*) and the Pure Land school (Jōdoshū) [founded by Hōnen].

Another legacy of the Edo period are the aftereffects of the great doctrinal dispute that split our sect into two theological camps: the so-called Confusion about the Three Acts (*sangō wakuran*), the eighteenth-century dispute concerning the conditions for assurance in faith (*anjin*). The theologians of the "Forest of Learning" (*gakurin*), who came to be known as the "Progressives" (*shingiha*), demanded that trust in Amida be expressed in the "three kinds of acts" (*sangō*), namely, thought, word, and deed. There was a strong reaction against this from scholars in the field—the so-called Traditionalists (*kogiha*)—and the ensuing polemics were so disruptive and sometimes even violent that the feudal government had to intervene in 1804 and declare orthodoxy to be on the side of the Traditonalists. As a result of this dispute over "assurance in faith," our theology up to the present has been oversensitive to the point of being centered on a nitpicking definition of *anjin* that does not leave room for the slightest jot or tittle of deviation.

Against the background of that theological history, our theology considers the question of folk religious practices to have been solved once and for all; there is no room for further questioning. The whole question is caught in the net of the critical classification of teachings (*kyōhan*) or the "discrimination of true-provisional-false" (*shikegi han*). Jōdo Shinshū is, of course, true; all other Buddhist schools are provisional; and all doctrines outside of Buddhism are false. It is clear that folk beliefs belong to the third category and must be rejected together with everything provisional and false.

In the troubled period of the Meiji Restoration, our Nishi Hongan-ji had the good fortune of clearly siding with the emperor against the feudal lords but was of course caught together with all other Buddhist sects in the movement to "abolish Buddhism and demolish Shakyamuni" (*haibutsu kishaku*), the anti-Buddhist campaign of the beginning of the Meiji era [see Ketelaar 1990], and later in the policy of the Meiji government to make Shintō the state religion. For a time our theologians had their hands full with these things. During the Second World War our sect put up a "headquarters for wartime doctrine," where indeed a wartime theology was developed. It was only with the establishment of the Pastoral Institute (Dendō-in) that a beginning was made with the liquidation of that wartime doctrine. However, in November 1985, this Pastoral Institute was abolished by the senate of the sect and in its stead a "doctrinal headquarters" (*kyōgaku honbu*) established anew.

As for the postwar course of Shinshū doctrine, wherein Ryūkoku University plays a central role, I can say in summary that the influence of the democratization of Japan is certainly felt there, at least to the degree that a Conference of Indian Philosophy and Buddhist Studies was established, and that a modern kind of Shinran and Shinshū studies developed, not only within the sect this time but also among thinkers, literati, and historians at large. All this, of course, caused our theologians their share of headaches. There is at present some *Auseinandersetzung* of our theologians with scientific Buddhist studies, social sciences, humanism, Marxism, existentialism, and Christian theology. But since Meiji, folk beliefs and practices do not appear on the theological agenda; they have been barred from the theological precincts.

THE SHINSHŪ TRADITION AS A RELIGIOUS ORGANIZATION THAT FREED ITSELF OF MAGIC

There is one more important reason why folk belief has not become a topic in Shinshū doctrine. I refer here to the original life-style of Shinshū people: their particular way of relating to folk practices, which has been ridiculed by people of other sects in the saying, "Shinshū believers are ignoramuses" (*Monto mono shirazu*)—meaning that they ignore taboos, unlucky days, and so forth. Folklorists have been saying that "Shinshū destroys local usages and beliefs, so that regions with a strong Shinshū influence are barren ground for folklorists." Max Weber declared that while Buddhism, Taoism, and Confucianism have by and large played the role of fixing people in a "magical garden," only Shinshū has greatly contributed to the breaking of the magical circle (*Entzauberung*), and he gives Shinshū high marks for it. Already in the Edo period there were authors, like Dazai Shundai (1680–1747) and Buyō Inshi (fl. ca. 1816), who expressed their amazement about the fact that there was this tradition of radical adherence to a single Buddha, Amida, without indulging in incantations, magical spells, the use of magical water, and so forth. Professor Kojima of Maritime University observes that even today, on an island off Yamaguchi Prefecture, Shinshū is still called "the does-not-care sect" (Kannanshū). This points, for example, to the fact that even in the postwar period the Shinshū people there, at the cremation of their deceased, simply left the remaining bones in the crematorium (except for a small part that was consigned to the local temple) without minding the taboos surrounding people's bones; and also the fact that they had no memorial tablets, death registers, or god shelves, did not put up any Jizō images, and even had no graves. In other words, in that region the original shape of a Shinshū community, which had done away with all these popular usages, had been preserved. Seen from this kind of tradition, it is perhaps natural that folk practices appeared in theology only as things to be rejected.

And so, when we took up this problem again in *Bulletin 29* of the Pastoral Institute, as a sect for whom the question of folk practices had long since been solved, we were roundly criticized by many learned people for being faithless, for taking the easy path of giving in to actual conditions without regard for Shinran's position, for being promoters of non-Shinshū ways, and for being insolent people throwing sand on the fire of the modernization movement of the sect. But the collective and interdisciplinary study of folk practices within our sect had not simply been undertaken from the standpoint of Shinshū doctrine. It has its origins in a scientific study of the religious consciousness of people in the field and in a resolve of taking the actual situation fully into consideration.

THE ACTUAL RELIGIOUS CONSCIOUSNESS OF SHINSHŪ BELIEVERS

In 1961, on the occasion of the 700th anniversary of Shinran Shōnin's death, our sect launched the "Believers Movement" (*monshinto undō*), a movement aiming at the transformation of the sect from a religion of the household (*ie*) into a religion of the individual. In 1971 the "Assimilation Movement" (*dōbō undō*) was started, attempting to promote among members of our sect, which serves more than half of the discriminated villages (*buraku*) but did not work for their emancipation, a better attitude toward these victims of discrimination. Both movements continue today.

In the meantime, roundtable discussions (*hōza*) were organized to listen to the voice of the lay believers. There were also meetings of the believers on the occasion of the pastoral visitation of the Monshu (head of the sect) to all the districts. On these and similar occasions it became clear that our sect is on the point of losing its character of—in Weberian terms—a community of people freed from magic. These findings were confirmed by scientific research, and we came to the conviction that we are facing here an important and urgent problem.

The data on which our present position is based are mainly those assembled by a psychology professor of Osaka Municipal University, Kaneko Satoru (a Shinshū believer and member of our team), through surveys conducted among temple priests and faithful over more than ten years. It became clear from these data that the religiosity of our people, far from being of the "does-not-care" type, exhibits a primitive mentality with Shintōism as its core. This religiosity is intimately bound up with ancestor worship—which Kaneko calls a factor of animism—and also shows a level of conservative "authority cult," represented by the emperor ideology. One more important outcome of this research is that there exists a great difference in faith structure between the temple priests and the lay people—a real split or polarization of consciousness.

This constitutes, of course, a big problem for our sect, but the situation is further aggravated by demographic differences in the faith of the lay people according to locality, sex, profession, income bracket, education, and so forth. The "faith type" of our faithful can thus be characterized as one colored by a multilayered and this-worldly-benefit-oriented folk religiosity, and tied up with not necessarily desirable strands of social consciousness such as conservatism, blind faith in authority, and social (especially political) indifferentism. Among the male believers, who in general appear to be rather weak in their faith (and are, for example, rather passive when it comes to attending religious services), the data point to a desire to see our sect become more of a "character building organization" (more directed at moral and spiritual training).

These data shook us terribly. But however much we might wish to flee the facts, the reality is there and we cannot ultimately afford to ignore it. We are thus driven to the conclusion that unless we shoulder this situation as a pastoral and doctrinal challenge and come to a critical appraisal of these facts, there is no hope of a concrete revival of our religion. For some reason, however, this judgment of our team appears to win very little understanding within our sect.

A FLEXIBLE, TWO-PRONGED POSTMODERN THEOLOGY

First of all, why do we speak, in this context, of a "postmodern" theology? We certainly do not want to deny that many premodern elements survive in the makeup of our sect, and even in its theology. But when it comes to the attitude toward folk beliefs, the thinking in our sect has fallen in step with a theology that aims at a kind of *Aufklärung* or "modernism." Our call for a postmodern theology is being criticized as if it were a call for an affirmation of the status quo or for a return to premodern times. The reason for its being judged that way must lie in the fact that we have deliberately chosen antimodern terminology, because we felt that, in the question of folk practices, the current theology shows an all too strong modernistic trend. I thought I made my meaning clear enough in my report in the *Bulletin*, but few people seem to have read it carefully. In fact we do not claim at all that premodern things are good and modern things bad. Nor do we say that all postmodern things are ipso facto good. All we said was that, because we recognized serious problems in both the premodern and the modern, we wanted to look for a flexible, two-pronged postmodern theology. We also expressed the hope that, in the present intellectual and religious situation of Japan, a postmodern approach might provide a road for the different Buddhist schools to the spirit of their respective founders.

A THEOLOGY WITHOUT GRASS ROOTS ("THE FIELD")

To characterize the present situation of our theology we have used the expression "a theology without grass roots" (*genba naki kyōgaku*). This expression was eagerly taken up by journalists and has become a kind of fashion word. We meant by it that there is an all too big gap between what the priests are doing in the "field" of our religion and what theologians are talking about in their discourses. We then claimed that the filling up of this gap between actual field conditions and theology is a primary requirement for the revival of our religion and called for a move from a "theology without field" and a "field without theology" to a "theology rooted in the field" and a "theologizing field."

The problem lies not so much on the side of the field, since the priests there all had some kind of training in theology, but rather on the side of the theological establishment, where practically no theological reflection is done on what actually happens in the field. The widespread idea, however, that only the theologians would be faithful followers of Dōgen or Shinran, and the priests in the field simply religious figures serving a religious system of funeral services and folk practices, is little more than the self-conceited prejudice of an elite without an understanding of what religion is all about. One of our lay people, an assistant professor at the Osaka National Ethnological Museum and a participant in our research, had the following to say: "There is no other solution but that the religious establishment and each priest in the field shoulder both the respectable and the 'dirty' elements in a balanced way. Hōnen, Shinran, and all the eminent religious figures have, after all, done exactly that."

Our local temples and the religious life therein are not merely "localities." We have chosen to call them "fields" because we do not consider these local forms of our religion, shaped by historical processes, to be places without theological relevance or sites where Shinran would be absent. On the contrary, we see them as fields of theological sublimation of local folk beliefs and rites, where the question of how to make our Founder present to the present age is at stake. In a word, we see them as fields of bodhisattva activity by Shinran and the temple priests. It is this sense we wanted to restore to them by using the term "field." We have thus proposed to consider the local temple not merely as an administrative unit or as a place where the Buddha Dharma is for sale, but rather as a place for a concrete and realizable revitalization of our sect and a field of return to Shinran Shōnin.

We have, therefore, criticized the traditional theology that ignores or looks down on folk practices, ritual, religious community, and we have advocated instead a "field theology" (genba no kyōgaku), which, within its system, would embrace these three elements. Postwar theology has done well in the question of its compatibility with science, but it accords no place to a theology of folk practice, a theology of ritual, and a theology of religious community (ecclesiology). The position of these theologians appears to be that these things are not essential to our doctrine, and every temple priest can freely decide for himself about them. Modernistic theology even tends to say that these elements are alien or adverse to Shinran and should therefore be suppressed. Opposition to folk practice, to ritual, and to community are then treated as if they were self-evident characteristics of Shinran's religion. Folk practice, ritual, and community then are called alien to the spirit of Shinran, products of compromise with folk religion and secularized society, disreputable elements that it is better not to have. In that line one comes finally to advocating the dissolution of the head temple of the sect (honzan) as if this were the height of the Shinranesque.

In this view, the only thing that counts is for every individual to possess his faith as an autonomous subject. Therein would then lie the only path for a return to Shinran. That is truly a modern existentialist theology of unassailable respectability! It is the kind of theology which, during the forty years since the war the temple priests, this silent majority carrying the weight of temples and faithful, have been made to listen to. And since they were scolded by the professors with the words "All your doings go against the spirit of Shinran," they have been listening with a feeling of guilt and loss of self-confidence. It is this trend we have challenged by calling for a postmodern theology. Indeed, there is something in what the professors are saying, but would their view really be the only concrete means for a revival of our sect? Would it not be good to have a theology that takes the actual situation of our religion, with all its accretions, really into account?

To say it somewhat differently, with the anthropologists, we wanted to stress that each culture has a system of thought and behavior with regard to the world and the human, and that this system comprises, besides the two complementary elements, science and religion, a third domain, which usually carries the labels of "folk belief," "superstition," "magic." Modern theology has had eyes only for the area where science and religion overlap and has constantly ignored that third domain. We, on the other hand, wish to stress that the factual situation of our sect imposes on us the task of investigating the composite realm where religion and this third domain overlap. The profile not of pure theology but of the concrete faith of our believers in the field can only be drawn against the backdrop of this third domain, and precisely in the overlap of religion and this third domain lies the key to interpret the practices, rituals, and forms of community life of our sect.

Current theology considers that third domain as a kind of "low life" far beneath the level of religion and bound to disappear once people have real faith. Feeling themselves to be the real nembutsu practitioners, they have despised and ridiculed people involved in that domain. Considering themselves to be graduates from that realm of human frailty, they are unable, from that Buddha seat, to see the people as anything but recipients of their enlightening activity. Still, this third domain forms the basic religiosity of the Japanese people and is not likely to disappear merely because scholars in their theories condemn and reject it. It must be given due consideration when thinking of Japanese religion in the future.

We have then tried to catch this basic belief of the Japanese people under the categories of "by your grace" (okagesama) and "curse" (tatari). The first one being an animistic trend and the second a shamanistic one, the religious mentality of the Japanese can then be characterized as an "animist-shamanist complex." The element of "by your grace" suits very well the requirements of the field and has been adopted there as "by the grace of Amida" and "thanks to Shinran." The element of "curse," however, is something of an embarrassment. One does then, as if one does not see it, say that such things do not exist in Buddhism. That, however, is a little too arbitrary. We have therefore claimed that it is extremely important and urgent to give full attention to the whole "animist-shamanist complex," and we have proposed this as a key for the interpretation of the folk practices, rituals, and forms of community in our sect. For there certainly exist in the field typical Shinshū folk practices, for example, in the way of preaching, in all kinds of ritual, in the organizational patterns, and so forth. And, as appears in the research of the above-mentioned professor Kaneko, one can certainly discern in the collective psychology of our faithful the spirit of okagesama, the fear of curses and, moreover, the consciousness of "living together with the dead" (or the belief that communication with the dead is possible).

Next we must refer to the fact that in the actual faith of our believers "Amida belief," "founder belief" (in Shinran), and "ancestor worship" form a trinity. The problems concerning this triune structure of the faith of the Shinshū adherents will surely emerge as extremely important themes—if not as the problem of problems—for the policy-making bodies of our sect. For that, we absolutely need a theology that does not run away from the actual mentality of our people. If our theology remains a solo flight of theory only, it is to be feared that in the future the Buddha Dharma will be found only in the study rooms of our universities—these "Naga palaces." Religious practices, rituals, and community must become the tripod supporting the theories of our theology. A solo flight of theory without this threefold support can possibly be interesting for a part of the elite as a kind of religious construct or philosophy of religion, but history sufficiently proves that it cannot be the religion of the people.

The meeting with the transcendent beyond the secular and the dialogue with the infinite cannot be expressed by the sole one-track logic of theory or, buddhistically speaking, "discriminatory knowledge," and it is very well possible that they are more accessible to our people via the above tripod. The idea that everything can be solved by a merely theoretical doctrine, and that through it we could have direct access to our Founder, is certainly not very Buddhist. For, when it comes to looking through the illusions of the subject and the barrenness of logic only, Buddhism may have no rival.

In sum, our theology from now on must develop a doctrine of folk practice, a doctrine of ritual, and a doctrine of community; and clarify the realm where these three interpenetrate. I am convinced that, in so doing, a sketch-map can be drawn for the overcoming of the gap between our theology and the field, and for bringing our sect to a new life wherein our Founder is present.

A PLEA FOR SHINSHŪ CATHOLICISM ("SHINSHŪ C")

It is time now to come to our central theme. The proposal that our collective research on Shinshū doctrine and folk practices popular beliefs has come up with was baptized by us as "Shinshū Catholicism." The history of the religions of the world tells us that all world religions face the problem of the relationship of their doctrine with folk practices and thus of a theological interpretation of these practices. The case of Christianity with its two poles of Puritanism and Catholicism has struck us as typical, and so we have come to speak of Shinshū Puritanism (Shinshū P) over against Shinshū Catholicism (Shinshū C). Since this P-C polarity can be found in all religions, we have even thought of the possibility of this becoming a theme of common research for the theologies of different religions and sects.

In *Bulletin 30* of the Pastoral Institute, Ōmura Eishō, a professor of sociology at Osaka University, clarifies what we mean when we advocate a Shinshū Catholicism:

> In Christian circles it has become common sense to regard Puritanism and Catholicism both as ambivalent, each having positive and negative aspects. Puritanism has the positive aspect of maintaining the purity of the doctrine

with rejection of all compromise, but the negative aspect of falling into a hardened and exclusivistic sectarianism. Catholicism, on the other hand, tends to nestle uncritically in the given situation, disguising its compromise under the label of the "universally human." But when we propose that we should learn from the Catholic Church, we are thinking of its flexible, two-pronged attitude which, on the one hand, promotes puritanism in its monastic orders and, on the other, tries to adopt even the Japanese ancestor cult. In other words, the Roman Catholics appear to be aiming at a meta-Catholicism wherein both Puritanism and Catholicism are *aufgehoben*. For that reason we think that there is much to be learned from them.

When we advocate a Shinshū Catholicism, it is certainly not in the sense of promoting more compromises with folk religion. On the contrary, we maintain that Shinshū has become infected with folk religion precisely because in our theology Shinshū Catholicism has not been thematized. We also have the expectation that a way back to our Founder can be opened by such a thematization.

FUNERAL SERVICES AND THEOLOGY

I have been asked to give special attention to funeral and memorial services, which play such a big role in Japanese religion. And indeed, it is in connection with them that we find in our sect, right from the beginning, the problematics of folk practices and the two trends of Shinshū P and Shinshū C. On the side of Shinshū P we find Kakunyo (1270–1325), the great-grandson of Shinran, and on the side of Shinshū C there is Zonkaku (1290–1373). Although father and son, these two were at loggerheads all their lives precisely on account of their difference in opinion on folk practices. Kakunyo even called Zonkaku a heretic and twice excommunicated him. We can thus say that our Shinshū theology comprises this tension right from its beginning and that our present problem must be seen against this background.

To begin then with Shinshū P, in his *Notes Rectifying Heresy* (*Gaijashō*), Kakunyo writes:

> Shinran has said: "When I shut my eyes for good, you must throw my body into the Kamo River as food for the fish." What he meant was that we must despise our bodies and see faith in the Buddha Dharma as the only thing that counts. On reflection, it follows that we should not consider services for the dead as all-important but rather put an end to them.

Kakunyo thus appears as an abolitionist with regard to folk practices and an advocate of a "no-funeral-ism." His theology is ideological and rigoristic; he is typical of a Shinshū P for which faith is so supreme as to exclude everything else.

On the side of Shinshū C, Zonkaku treats the question in three of his treatises, *On Gratitude* (*Hōonki*), *Things Seen and Heard on the Pure Land* (*Jōdo kenmonshū*), and *On the Highest Path* (*Shidōshō*). He provides a theological underpinning for the Shinshū practice of funerals and memorial services, the monthly sūtra readings for the deceased, the memorial day in the month of death, and the yearly anniversary service. He writes, for example:

> Since the Buddha is uniquely worthy of reverence among all beings past, present, and future, and the guide of the four classes of living beings, there is nobody above him in rank. Still, to show his piety to his father, and his reverence for the king, he raised his body into the air and, attending the funeral of his father, helped carry the coffin. He did that as an example to be followed by the sentient beings of the future.

(The reference is to the early *Sutra of Grouped Records* [*Zōichiagongyō, T* 125]). And again:

> In life, one must admonish to zeal in self-cultivation, giving priority to filial piety; after somebody's death, one must fulfill one's duty of gratitude, giving priority to working good deeds for the deceased. . . . One must not neglect the monthly services for the deceased, and certainly not the yearly observances on the anniversary of the death. Even after many years have passed, on these anniversaries one must absolutely lay aside one's worldly affairs to pray for the peace of these souls.

There is certainly something here that not only Kakunyo but also present-day theologians cannot but see as folk religion, which is un-Shinshū, un-Shinran, and even un-Buddhist. Thus, since the Meiji era these folk religious texts by Zonkaku have been taboo in our sect and have received no attention at all from the theology professors. However, when looking at the life in our temples, it is clear enough that the greater half of that life consists of funeral rites, memorial services in the temple and monthly sūtra readings in the houses of the faithful. Therefore, it is precisely Zonkaku's theology that takes these practices seriously as theological topics and is a "theology of the field" totally incomprehensible to people engaged in "pure theology only." It is a theology for the temple priests whose life goes up in keeping our temples going, taking care of our faithful, and performing funeral rites and memorial services; a theology imbued with the sadness of not being understood by people who never toiled in tears to lead people to Shinran in the midst of all this.

How would Kakunyo and Zonkaku, while living by the same Amida-given faith, have come to such diametrically opposed theological positions with regard to funeral practices? Present-day theologians have nothing but praise for the Shinshū P of Kakunyo and consider it to be a faithful expression of Shinran's true intentions. Zonkaku's Shinshū C, on the other hand, is judged negatively as a theology that came to betray true faith through compromise with folk religion, and consider it therefore as inadmissible. But is this the true state of affairs? The crux of the matter might lie in a correct understanding of Zonkaku's texts. For Zonkaku knew very well that Shinshū is not a kind of Confucianism or ancestor cult and is not built on the performance by us of good works whose merits would be transferred to the deceased; he understood better than anyone else the centrality in Shinshū of Other-Power nembutsu. Still he wrote kindly that funerals, memorial services, and so forth are important—while adding sometimes that he did not like writing these things. What is the secret here? We think that we found the key to this mystery in Zonkaku's "give-and-take logic."

Dōgen, Shinran, and still Zonkaku lived in an age that presented an extremely vivid picture of hell (which is all but lost to the modern imagination), permeated with magic, folk beliefs, evil spirits, and wherein the powers of man were absolutely helpless before disease and natural disasters. It is then only natural that people had recourse to superstition and magic in order to ward off the ills that befell them one after the other. Up to a point that is still true today, of course, and we are all inclined to look down on people who run to "new new" religions, magic, fortune-tellers, and what have you, and to see ourselves as the true Buddhists. However, rather than looking at these superstitions themselves, we should pay attention to the fact that the people who have recourse to them have good reasons to do so. And there are plenty of reasons: incurable diseases, anguishes one cannot tell anybody about, the loneliness so typical of our age, and so on and so forth. Scolding people for their foolish superstitious behavior in self-righteous sermons without any appreciation of these woes in the background is an exercise in self-satisfaction unworthy of a religionist. In the face of the one hundred million Japanese who indulge in superstition, we should rather reflect on our lamentable failure as guides of the people, and come to the conviction that it is high time that we make folk practice and popular belief a topic of our theology.

GIVE-AND-TAKE LOGIC AS SHINSHŪ C

A "give-and-take logic" (*yodatsu no ronri*) was the outcome of Zonkaku's serious consideration of the question how the people of his time, beset as they were by all kinds of ills and relying on folk beliefs and magical practices to relieve them, could be set free from magic and brought to lead a life of true nembutsu. It consists in looking hard at the sufferings that induce people to indulge in magical practices, in understanding that psychology, and from there, with great sensitivity for the intricacies of human feelings, in sharply analyzing these superstitions. This then becomes a way to "jump into the inner castle of the enemy and to make what one grasps there into one's own medicine." Contrary to theology P, which cuts down superstition by logic and rejects it forthwith, one does not directly negate it here, but looks for salvation by way of empathy. One spares and embraces the popular practices to turn them into something Shinshū-like; one gives in to them in order to take them back to one's own side. Rather than drawing one's sword against the sword of the enemy, one grasps the other's sword to remold it into the shape of the nembutsu and give it back as a nembutsu sword that cuts through all superstition. This is ultra-C supreme swordsmanship!

In the eyes of the puritanists, this expedient means appears only as heresy, wishy-washiness, an unwarranted detour, or even as a way of suicide, in that the possibility exists of being cut down by the other's sword; or again as un-Shinranlike logic. It has thus drawn the concentrated fire of the purists. I myself, who have gone through a period of existentialist faith, can very well imagine how I would be on the side of that firing squad if I were an armchair theologian without contact with the field of temple life. Indeed, this give-and-take logic is a pitiful logic one cannot really feel for if one is not a temple priest in the true sense, for whom the relationship of Shinshū doctrine and folk belief is a *kōan* that besets one twenty-four hours a day in one's care for temple and believers. When advocating this logic as a characteristic of Shinshū C, we are well aware that nearly all theology of the Edo period and since Meiji as well, and also the studies on Shinshū and the Shinshū community by the modernists, are of the Shinshū P type, and that this theology has made very valuable contributions to our doctrine. But this does not mean as such that this theology is the only viable one. When the P people say that there are principles that cannot be tampered with if one wants to return to Shinran, I am completely with them, but on the point of folk beliefs I beg to disagree with much of what they say.

According to Shinshū P people, faith was everything for Shinran, and religious organizations and priests were superfluous. Nor is there any need for temples, temple ornaments, funerals, memorial services, tombs, rituals, Buddha images, sūtra readings, priestly robes, . . . Even *danka* (people belonging to a temple and supporting it) are not necessary. Those things did not exist in Shinran's time and Shinran would have proscribed them. A truly no-no theology of faith only! In this view, temple priests become parasites in the body of the lion, feasting on a Dharma that leads to hell!

However, although funerals and memorial services may be unnecessary according to Shinshū P people, it remains a historical fact that they have been practiced from the beginning in our sect. Shinshū P theology is then obliged to say that these Shinshū practices and rituals are all "praise to the Buddha's virtues," "thanksgiving for Amida's benefits," "savoring the taste of the Dharma," or "inducement to faith." Beautiful phrases those, but while we were caught up in that melody, the alienation of the people and the temple priests from official doctrine went on apace.

According to P theology, Shinshū consists only in this: At the moment of attainment of faith one enters the state of nonretrogression, and at the moment of death one enters great nirvana. Birth in the Pure Land is attainment of Buddhahood and enlightenment, identical with that of Amida. One then immediately becomes a bodhisattva of returning transference, that is, one returns to this world to work for the salvation of all sentient beings. In this scheme, of course, the memorial services for the dead, about which Zonkaku had been racking his brains in his essays, do not come into the picture and are absolutely meaningless. But, of course, Zonkaku himself was well aware of that. He also wrote the *Notes on the Essentials of the the Six Fascicles* (Rokuyōshō), a commentary on Shinran's main work, *The True Teaching, Practice, and Realization of the Pure Land Way* (Kyōgyōshinshō, 1224; see Suzuki 1973), which is considered by theologians as the most authoritative commentary on the magnum opus of Shinran. This should be sufficient proof of Zonkaku's theological acumen. Our P theologians gladly accept his *Notes on the Essentials* but want nothing to do with his thought on folk practices as expressed in the other works.

Zonkaku used the memorial services in question as means to bring the ordinary people of his day to the practice of the nembutsu. For these people in distress over the parting with their beloved ones, in great fear of curses worked by the spirits of the dead, and irresistibly inclined to offer prayers and good works for the salvation of their deceased, Zonkaku adopted the whole range of memorial services, found in the sūtras and even some not found there, as "usages of our land." This can be compared with the current tendency among Catholics to adopt the ancestor cult as a beautiful usage of the Japanese people. While observing these memorial services and anniversaries, he endeavored to assuage the pain of parting, to allay the fear of curses, and most of all to make people into true nembutsu practitioners, with the help of beautiful funeral rites, which he sought to imbue with the spirit of the nembutsu, according to which the deceased is first of all a bodhisattva who comes to save me, and it is first of all the people who sincerely revere the Buddha who are set free from the defilements and curses of the dead. In that sense, the *Things Seen and Heard* (Jōdo kenmonshū) begins indeed with a quotation from the (apocryphal and popular) *Ten Kings Sutra* (Jūōhyō; late T'ang, 10th c.) but ends with a quote from Shinran's *Kyōgyōshinshō*.

There are, thus, in our sect, two trends as to the theology of funeral services. On the point of pure doctrine, P theology is clear-cut, but from the viewpoint of the field with its C practice, there must be found a way to realize a community of nembutsu practitioners as envisaged by Shinran, in trying to liberate the people from their animist-shamanist complex and to transform this into true Shinshū belief, by observing the funeral rites with heart and soul. That is certainly what we are looking for and, therefore, our endeavor to establish a theology that articulates Shinshū C must not evoke the fear that we would be going away from Shinran. Would this not also apply to the Sōtō Zen school? I believe that also in Sōtō, where for seven hundred years the temple priests have elaborated Sōtō practices, Sōtō rituals, and Sōtō patterns of community life, the introduction of a theology C, which evaluates these elements, could prove to be a way of returning to Dōgen and could well reveal aspects of Dōgen and of Zen for which the theologians up to now have had no eye.

All of our faithful have the spirit of "love for the sect and defense of the Dharma." Therefore, freedom to express their faith should be guaranteed to them. If not, we cannot really speak of a sangha, a religious community. If we have trust in the Buddha and in our Founder, there is nothing to fear. The Shinshū P people are admirable in their absolutizing of faith. They may be the bodhisattvas of the era of the final law, and our Founder may have been like them. I, however, am not the Founder, and I can live only a Shinshū C.

Over against the simple negation of the existence in our sect of a Founder cult, of this-worldly benefits, and of prayers and good works for the dead, we have advocated a "theology of the Founder cult," a "theology of this-worldly benefits," and a "theology of ancestor cult." This has upset the P people and brought some turmoil in our sect, but the majority of the temple priests to whom we talked showed appreciation for what we are trying to do and start feeling that theology is an important affair of theirs and that the establishment of a "field theology" would be an unhoped for blessing.

PRAYING FOR THE DEAD AND CURSES

As already said above, prayers for the dead and fear of curses worked by the dead certainly belong to the deepest layers of Japanese religiosity. If we simply keep on rejecting these elements, the result will only be that our believers will stray away from our religion. We have therefore opted for a Shinshū C–type theology with a give-and-take logic.

For example, a believer who feels threatened by a curse is not saved if we simply tell him that curses do not exist. He will then most probably start drifting from one religion or folk belief to another in search of salvation. That is not a solution, and it has become clear from the data of field research on new religions, new new religions, Mount Ikoma, and so forth, that among the people frequenting them surprisingly many are Shinshū believers. One of the motivations behind our movement is the conviction that this is not right, that all the sufferings of the believers must be taken up at our temples by the temple priest and his consort, and that we want our sect to become such that the faithful can come to the temple with whatever concerns or ails them, with the certainty that they will be listened to, even if their feelings are not precisely Shinshūlike. If all our people could be helped by Shinshū P there would be no need for a Shinshū C. In fact, however, there are probably more C people than P people among our faithful.

When someone in fear of a curse comes to the temple, we try first of all to empathize with that person's feelings. And once we have grasped the content of the curse and the suffering lying in its background, we do not directly force Shinshū dogma on that person but try to instill Shinshū doctrine within that content and background of the supposed curse. Only when we are sure that the power of that injected nembutsu has done its work can we finally say: for one embraced by Amida's Primal Vow and living the nembutsu, there are no curses; fear no longer. "Let the curse do what it wants, I am protected by Namu Amida Butsu!" The difference between P and C on this point might be that P proclaims that there are no curses, while C assures that curses cannot touch the faithful. Our believers in the field are very sensitive to the grateful feeling that the nembutsu protects them from curses.

As for the transference of the merits of one's prayers and good works to the dead, would it not be good if there were a give-and-take kind of theology here too, which does not directly say that such transference does not exist but rather gradually leads to the awareness that it is the nembutsu transferred to us by the Other-Power of Amida that is the true help for the dead.

THEOLOGY AS FOLK PRACTICES: A PROBLEM FOR ALL BUDDHIST SCHOOLS

Our research and publications are animated by the hope of seeing our sect transformed into a community that does not run away from what is actually happening in the field, but takes it all upon itself and knows how to transform it into something wherein our Founder is present.

In the theology of folk practices, the Shinshū P line, running back from Rennyo to Shinran via Kakunyo, has been the mainstream. We are now advocating a line running back from Rennyo to Shinran via Zonkaku. Our fundamental position is that, in a big sect like ours, which is like a smaller-scale map of the pluriform society, the existence of a pluriform theology is a good thing. We believe then that Shinshū C is one of the concrete and realizable roads of a return to Shinran.

We further believe that the theme of theology and folk beliefs is practical not only for our sect but equally so for all Japanese Buddhist sects, since it appears to be the case everywhere that theology is dominated by a Buddhist Puritanism, and the practices of the faithful are left without theological reflection. It is therefore necessary that, among the theologians of every sect, there emerge people who specialize in the theology of folk beliefs and practices, the theology of rituals, and the theology of community. We are also convinced that the time has come for the different sects as such to establish research institutes to study these problems on a continual basis. It is true that each sect has already institutes for the study of its theology, but research into folk practice, ritual, and community cannot be done by theologians alone. It requires postmodern, avant-garde theory and can be brought to a good end only by an interdisciplinary approach with the collaboration of folklorists, anthropologists, scientists of religion, and so forth.

I have not limited my proposal to folk belief and practice, but also involved ritual and community, for the simple reason that these too are not treated by traditional theology. It will finally be a question, not of theology and folk practices, and so on, but of theology = folk practice, theology = ritual, theology = community. If not, our communities will always appear as betrayals of our founders, necessary evils, or something to be left to the sociologists. The time has come to consider the community as the doctrine of the sect. Funeral rites—this center of our talk today—are not merely folk practice and ritual.

Praise of the Buddha and thanksgiving for his benefits are not enough by themselves. There is Zen and nembutsu in the funeral rites. We intend the identification: funeral rites = Zen = Dōgen Zenji; or again, funeral rites = nembutsu = Shinran Shōnin.

SPIRIT BELIEF AS POSTMODERN RELIGION

Up to now, I have given you a rather free rendering of what was written up as
the report of our research in the Pastoral Institute *Bulletins* 29 and 30 (1984
and 1985), under the general title of "Shinshū Doctrine and Folk Practices."
To round off my talk, I now want to add a few words on some points that
transpired since then and use this to put into clearer relief some themes that I
have left rather vague.

I consider as very relevant for our problematics, and in a sense epoch-mak-
ing, a paper delivered by Professor Shimazono Susumu of Tokyo University at
the 1986 convention of the Kantō Sociological Conference. In that paper, Shimazono divides Japan's "new religions" into two categories. The first are religious organizations, like Tenrikyō and Konkōkyō, that originated among the
rural population around the time of the Meiji Restoration. These represent a
belief in a single saving deity and have much in common with the Amida belief
of the Pure Land school. It is the "entrusting, relying type." The second category
are those new religions that, like Ōmotokyō, Reiyūkai, and Seichō no Ie, originated in urban centers in the Taishō era and the beginning of the Shōwa era.
They are of the "spirit belief" type. They stress the existence of spirits, see them
as the causes of all the ills of human life, and promote communication with
the spirits in magic saving rituals. The so-called new new religions, like Mahikari and Agonshū, which have come into existence since 1970, still belong
to this second type.

Shimazono asks himself, then, why this kind of religion flourishes in modern
urban society, and comes up with a startling answer. In contrast with belief in
a saving deity, wherein one sees the will of the deity behind all events and aims
at an I-thou relationship with that deity, this spirit belief perfectly matches the
way of thinking and the manipulative attitude of modern technique. Each spirit
is one factor in the environment, which can be captured and manipulated by
the proper techniques. Spirit belief thus presents itself as experimental and
functional and exudes a feeling of certainty and efficacy. We could call this a
"manipulative" type of belief. This can be seen as a simple discovery, somewhat
like the egg of Columbus, but still comes as quite a shock. We, who had been
looking down on the new religions as premodern, even primitive, and have
made great efforts to show that our Buddhism can coexist with science, now
are confronted with the idea that the true match for a scientific-technical world
is spirit belief, the magical, pseudo-scientific, manipulative type of religion.

Our team is of the opinion that we must take this shocking idea into account
in our further research but did not come to any clear conclusions yet.

FERVENT SHINSHŪ BELIEVERS AND FOLK PRACTICES

Around the same time, also one of the researchers of our team, the above-mentioned Kaneko, divulged some surprising results of his research. The idea of Shinshū P is that folk belief diminishes where Shinshū belief deepens and, conversely, folk belief grows rampant where Shinshū belief declines. However, from the field research on the belief structure of average lay believers and of lay representatives of our temples, the following picture emerges. First, among the majority of ordinary lay believers, folk belief is strong and, in general, the stronger specific Shinshū belief the stronger also the belief in folk religious elements. However, when it comes to the temple representatives, this syncretistic trend breaks down. With them, indeed, folk belief appears to be swept away by deep Shinshū faith.

But, in fact, things are a bit more complicated. Among these leaders of our communities, shamanistic folk belief (belief in curses) is beautifully overcome but, at the same time, the deeper their Shinshū faith, the deeper also their faith in two other elements of folk belief, namely, ancestor cult and founder belief, become. For example, as to regular visits to the graves of the ancestors, polls among the general Japanese public of the same age group may register 76 percent yes, while among the said representatives 94 percent answer in the affirmative. Similarly, "founder belief," the veneration of our Founder Shinran as a Buddha, tends to become very strong.

It is not easy to say which conclusions should be drawn from this, but one thing seems clear enough. A theology of folk belief cannot simply carry on with the presupposition of Shinshū P that all folk belief is a minus and to be rejected. For the moment it seems as if our Shinshū practice makes a distinction between the animist (*okagesama*) element and the shamanistic (curse) element of the Japanese religious complex. The shamanistic level of Japan's folk belief, which is rejected by our temples, has vicariously been taken care of by the new religions, like Reiyūkai, Mahikari, and so on. These new religions do not ask our believers to reject Shinshū; they rather say that since the temples take care of the services for the bones of the dead, you must respect them, but we shall take care of your ancestor's spirits and of all your anguishes and distresses. In fact, as I pointed out before, the number of our faithful who run to the new religions with their difficulties is very high.

THE LACK OF A "DOCTRINE FOR EMERGENCIES"

It looks thus as if we have built up a theodicy for the happy days by adopting the animistic *okagesama* mentality but have nothing to offer when misfortune visits our believers. We may then have to say that we have no theodicy for unhappy days, no doctrine for the emergencies of life.

I myself have come to know how necessary such a doctrine is through the unutterable anguish I experienced when my second son drowned in the temple pond. For years afterward, my nembutsu was interspersed with the cry: "Why? Why?" Religionists who tend to despise the practices of folk belief would do good to visit one of these places, say, for example, the Kamikiri Jinja on Mount Ikoma, where people go to pray for beloved ones who are incurably sick, and have a good look at the faces of the people there. . . .

THE LACK OF A THEOLOGY OF ANCESTOR VENERATION

Recently, first-class authorities on Japanese religion, like Yanagawa Keiichi and Yamaori Tetsuo, have again highlighted the important place of the ancestor cult in Japanese religiosity. They have also stressed the stability that this vertical dimension imparts on the family system—a stability not assured by the sole horizontal relationships of husband and wife. And we have already said a few words on how deeply this ancestor cult has penetrated the life in the field of our sect.

In view of these facts and the challenge they present for our sect, it is extremely regrettable that we do not have a "theology of ancestor cult." This reminds me again of the fact that our promotion of Shinshū Catholicism was originally triggered by the publication of the *Guidelines Concerning Ancestors and the Deceased for Catholic Believers* (*Sosen to shisha ni tsuite no katorikku shinja no tebiki*). Therein the Japanese usages are boldly admitted into the lives of Catholics, and there is no shade of fear that this would corrupt Catholic faith. It is admirable in its trust in the strength of the faith of one's own religion.

THE LACK OF A THEOLOGY OF THIS-WORLDLY BENEFITS

Would our believers be running to New Religions in times of need, if we truly had a theology of this-worldly benefits (*genze riyaku*)? It is probably true that Shinran speaks much more about this-worldly benefits than Dōgen, and Kaneko Daiei (1881–1976), one of our most famous theologians of the former generation, has expressed the opinion that we have to rethink fundamentally our doctrine on "nonretrogression in this life" and "this-worldly benefits." In a conference he said, for example: "I want you to study carefully what is meant exactly by earthly benefits. We must come to understand why there is no contradiction between, on the one hand, maintaining that there is no true worldly benefit outside of the Jōdo School and, on the other, rejecting all religion that seeks worldly benefits."

Bandō Shōjun, the priest of the famous Hōon-ji Temple in Tokyo, once said: "The nembutsu at times deigns to enter into the midst of folk practice and magic belief, from there to turn people to a true Buddhist life." May I finally express the heartfelt wish that you, who shoulder the future of Sōtō Zen, may elaborate a theology, not merely of folk practice, but of Zen folk practice, a theology of the true folk practice of Sōtō Zen.

— 43 —

Contemporary Zen Buddhist Tracts for the Laity:
Grassroots Buddhism in Japan

Ian Reader

The translations in this section are samples of the popular literature such as leaflets and pamphlets distributed by Buddhist sects in Japan to their followers. All of the items given here have been produced by one major established Buddhist sect, the Sōtō Zen sect, in the 1980s, but their style and the themes they express can be regarded as typical and representative of the contemporary popular literature of Japanese Buddhism in general. All were published by the sect's head office and governing body in Tokyo, and they reflect the messages that the sect leaders wish to impart to people affiliated to temples of the sect, as well as the basic orientations of Buddhist followers at the grass roots in Japan. Visually attractive and often containing bright photographs and colorful illustrations, such pamphlets and other sect literature are sent (as were numerous other pamphlets and booklets) to the sect's fifteen thousand or so temples throughout Japan, where they are, at least in theory, distributed to sect members and to temple visitors. In practice, whether they are widely distributed depends on the temple priest; it is a reasonable supposition to say that only a small number of those produced actually are read by members of the sect.

Although these pamphlets may not be widely read, and although in terms of content they can hardly be said to offer influential new contributions to Japanese religious understanding, they are important documents because they clearly express, in simple and atmospheric language designed to capture the emotional attention of their Japanese readers, the concerns, nature and orientations of established Buddhism in late-twentieth-century Japan, and which have, indeed, been crucial and central to Buddhism's development and the ways in which it has been assimilated by and permeated into the lives of the Japanese populace over the centuries. Written in language that will be readily understood by ordinary Japanese, and eschewing the use of complex Buddhist terms or philosophical speculation, such pamphlets seek to convey messages and impart emotional feelings that create an empathy between the reader and Buddhism, and that will make him or her feel the need and desire to remain loyal to the sect and (a vital element in the economic and social structure of Japanese Buddhism) to continue to hold the memorial services for their ancestors at sect temples. To some extent this use of plain, direct language and of easily understood pamphlets and other forms of popular media to convey messages (among which, in recent years, can also be included the use of videos, glossy magazines, and even music and song) has been assimilated from the new religions that have been extraordinarily successful in Japan, not just in terms of recruitment but in putting their teachings across to large numbers of people through extensive use of the media and popular tracts, and through their use of straightforward language and images.

Though the translations all come from one sect, they reflect many of the basic concerns of Buddhism in general in Japan. As will be discussed further below, these revolve particularly around the salvific powers of the Buddhas, the virtue of faith, the need to venerate one's ancestors, and the importance of maintaining the bonds and relationships that have historically developed in Japan among the Japanese people, their ancestors, and the Buddhist temples. As these translations demonstrate, such concerns are as important in Zen Buddhism as in any other Buddhist sect in Japan. Although Zen, in doctrinal terms at least, holds that meditation is at the core of Buddhism and emphasizes "self-power" (jiriki) and its importance in the quest for enlightenment (in contrast to the faith-based concepts of salvation through "other-power" (tariki) as expressed in the Pure Land sects), such teachings aimed at the ordinary members of the sect make virtually no mention of meditation or enlightenment, instead emphasizing the salvific powers of the Buddha(s) and the ethical duties and practices concerned with venerating the ancestors and maintaining right relations with them through the medium of Buddhism. What these contemporary Zen Buddhist publications show, then, is that, whatever Buddhism might appear to be doctrinally and in terms of goals and spiritual practice, and although Buddhism has developed numerous schools of thought and spiritual practice in Japan, it is as a religion concerned with the concerns, needs, and worries of ordinary people, particularly in the realms of faith, intercession, and the relationship between the living and the spirits of the dead, that it has made its mark upon the lives of the Japanese.

The first translation provided here, *Trust and Dependence* (*Kie*), affirms the importance of faith in the Buddhas as a means of enabling one to lead a happy and peaceful life and tells people to "entrust everything to the Buddhas." It was published by the sect as part of its gesture of worship (*gasshō*) campaign in the 1980s: the *gasshō* gesture is a prayerful one in which the two hands are held with palms together, fingers pointing directly upward. It signifies both veneration and greeting, and in Sōtō Zen literature and contemporary teaching the gesture and posture are considered to have immense symbolic meaning, representing purity of heart and mind, correctness of form, and right behavior. These themes are reflected in the pamphlet translated here, whose comment that followers should express their faith by vowing to say that "I shall live from now on as the child of Buddha" reflects a general understanding, shared by priests and laity alike, that

Buddhism and the Buddhas venerated in it serve most clearly as a means of emotional support that provides "peace of mind" and happiness. As such, the basic preoccupations of the Japanese with regard to Buddhism are squarely focused in this world and in personal happiness: concepts such as enlightenment are barely mentioned. The pamphlet also emphasizes the importance of causal or karmic relations (*en*), a term that affirms the notion of interdependence. This is especially important in Japanese terms, suggesting among other things the karmic bonds that tie the living and their ancestors together—a bond that, as will be discussed further below, is vital to Buddhist temples and rituals, and to the involvement of the Japanese with Buddhism. Underlying the emphasis on causal or karmic relationships, then, is the implicit affirmation of the relationship that has arisen between the Japanese and Buddhism and which this and the other translations given here seek to maintain and continue.

Besides its focus on faith, grace, and happiness, Buddhism has become most deeply ingrained in the lives of the Japanese through its role in providing a framework of interpretation and practice through which to deal with death and with the spirits of the dead. From the seventh and eighth centuries onward, Buddhism became the medium through which the processes and problems of death were dealt with: Buddhist funerals and memorial services came to be used as the ritual means whereby the spirits of the dead have been transformed into benevolent ancestors guarding over the living members of its household and kin. In taking on this role, Buddhism in Japan thus assimilated basic Japanese concepts about the soul after death, namely, that it continued to exist as an entity that had a potential influence in this world. As a result, Buddhist philosophical concerns about the nonexistence of a fixed soul or permanent self, or about rebirth, have been of little importance in Japan. The Japanese words for dead person and Buddha are the same (*hotoke*), reflecting a commonly accepted gloss between the two states, and it is fair to suggest that, for the large majority of people, concerns about the attainment of Buddhahood have largely been transposed from the world of the living to that of the dead, and are closely connected to the Buddhist rites that transform the soul into a peaceful and benevolent ancestor.

One of the most central and pervasive elements in the social, cultural, and religious lives of the Japanese, namely, venerating and paying homage to their ancestors, thus became expressed through the ritual medium, and became the preserve, of Buddhism. This close relationship between the Japanese and Buddhism developed over centuries but was formally established in the Tokugawa era (1600–1868) when laws were enacted to mandate that everyone become Buddhist and be affiliated with a Buddhist temple, which in turn provided them with their sectarian affiliation. Belonging to a sect thus was often more a matter of convenience or circumstance, dependent on the sectarian affiliation of the temple nearest to one's home, than it was to any particular volition on the members' part, and this factor remains much the same today. People are members of a sect not so much because they prefer a particular form of sectarian teaching but because tradition and historical and family circumstances have made them so.

Although the laws enacted by the Tokugawa were subsequently repealed, Buddhism has continued, at least in the eyes of most Japanese, to be closely associated with the extended series of mortuary rites and practices that follow death and with the veneration of ancestors. Calendrical Buddhist festivals, such as the summer Obon Festival, when the living members of the family gather to make offerings to their ancestors and to have memorial services said for them at the family temple, continue to be among the most widely attended of all religious events in Japan. Many households have a family Buddhist altar (*butsudan*) at which the ancestors are enshrined, and large numbers of Japanese grow up accustomed to the practice of making offerings to the ancestors, visiting Buddhist temples and reciting Buddhist prayers for their souls.

This deeply ingrained social relationship has long been a mainstay of Buddhism in Japan. Indeed, many Japanese, even while openly stating that they have no religious faith, despite not knowing much if anything about Buddhism, and despite eschewing any interest in other Buddhist practices, consider that they will "die Buddhist" and that, should a death occur in their family, they would naturally become involved in Buddhist rites and call for the services of a Buddhist priest.

This deep relationship has had profound effects on the shape and nature of Japanese Buddhism and has conditioned the perspectives of the Japanese and of the Buddhist sects active in Japan. Buddhism for most Japanese is a religion of death and the ancestors, and what ritual and spiritual practices it espouses, and moral and ethical teachings it professes, are intimately bound up with these aspects. Neither philosophical concerns nor the desire to undertake meditational or similar spiritual practices have conditioned the reasons why most people belong to their sect, and consequently they are barely touched upon in the popular literature of Buddhist sects. In contrast, the importance of rites concerning the ancestors, and ritual behavior before the family Buddhist altar, are very important and figure prominently in Buddhist publications such as those translated here, and in the religious practice that they advocate.

The second translation, the *Ten Articles of Faith* (*Shinkō jūkun*), a one-page text that has appeared in many Sōtō publications over the years, shows how central such issues are to Sōtō Zen Buddhism. Faith here, as indeed in the first translation, is closely equated with practice and with the performance of actions connected with the ancestors, and with the bonds that tie people to Buddhist temples. Such bonds are strengthened through the ritual calendar, with various festivals marked out as days when the obligation to attend the temple is stressed. Observances of the ritual and festive calendar are a central feature of Japanese religion, and much of the activity at Buddhist temples is linked to this cycle. The Obon Festival and other occasions (such as the spring and autumn equinoxes, when people visit their ancestors' graves) concerned with the memorialization of the dead are probably the most commonly performed religious activities in Japan, in which (according to contemporary statistics) close to 90 percent of the Japanese participate either regularly or occasionally. Indeed, for most people such ritual and festive times are the only occasions when they might visit a temple. Buddhist organizations such as Sōtō are thus acutely aware of the importance of this calendrical cycle of religious events within the life patterns of the people, and their publications dwell very much on encouraging the observance of such events. Indeed, as the third translation also shows, they may well focus almost entirely on the emotional and cultural significance of such calendrical events for the well-being and continued happiness of the people.

The articles of faith do not, save in the final article, mention meditation; even here it is only brought in as something to be done twice a year. What they emphasize are the importance of the correct observance of etiquette (in bowing to the temple, making a gesture of worship before eating, telling the ancestors the family news) and of paying homage to the ancestors. In this there is a basic morality that centers on paying homage and showing gratitude to the ancestors for what the life they have bestowed on the living, and of recognizing that such benevolence creates obligations that have to be repaid through observing the correct rituals for the ancestors—a theme that is emphasized in the last translation. One could say that in this respect the Buddhist notion of "right action" has, in Japanese Buddhism, been well and truly transformed into and interpreted as "the correct ways of memorializing the dead, and of venerating the ancestors."

This concern with form and with the way in which things are done is endemic in much Japanese social behavior, and in the contemporary teachings of the Sōtō sect this concern can be seen most clearly in the constant references made to the gesture of worship (*gasshō*) that occur in these, and numerous other, Sōtō publications. Most of the people who are affiliated, through their parish temple, with the Sōtō Zen sect have never taken part in meditation. Meditation, indeed, is, in the eyes of the laity, regarded as something for religious specialists, while the priesthood and leading lights within the sect recognize that the sect's growth has historically been a result not of its meditational practices but of the rites it has conducted for the ancestors. Instead of emphasizing meditation, then, one finds other physical forms of posture that can be performed easily and in everyday life emphasized, almost, one might suggest, as alternatives. As the first translation affirms, the gesture of worship allows one to become peaceful and to express a simple but strong faith. Faith is thus expressed through form. Though the shorter *Heart Sūtra* (*Hannya shingyō*), widely recited in Japanese Buddhism and highly popular in Sōtō rituals, states that "form is no other than emptiness" (*shiki soku ze kū*), it is clear from the perspective of the religious etiquette and ritual symbolism illustrated in these texts that form has a specific significance of its own, regardless of any philosophical equation with emptiness.

The third translation, *Peace of Mind in Human Life* (*Jinsei no yasuragi*), provides a further insight into the perspectives and needs of contemporary Buddhism. The circumstances that lie behind the nostalgic imagery brought out in such publications are that in the contemporary era numerous encroachments have been made into the grass-roots support structures of established Buddhism. The growth of the new religions has helped to transfer the allegiance of large numbers of individuals and at times whole families away from the established Buddhist sects, while the processes of secularization and urbanization have contributed to weakening the hold of established and traditional religions such as Buddhism on their followers. For sects such as Sōtō, whose traditional base of support has been more in rural and agricultural areas than in urban areas, demographic change has weakened its base further.

All this has caused Buddhist sects such as Sōtō to do what it can, not so much to gather new converts as to retain the loyalties of its current adherents, many of whom have little or no doctrinal involvement in the sect, and whose affiliations are centered on the ancestors. Thus great emphasis is placed on the importance of the traditions that bind families to particular temples, and on the deep connections between the temple and the ancestors. This often is expressed through the use of powerful nostalgic imagery that seeks to play on the emotional feelings of, and to create a sense of empathy in, the reader that will cause him or her to withstand the social pressures of change and the lure of the new religions that offer the individual a path to salvation. Often these are tied into important festive events in the yearly calendar. This pamphlet, for instance, relates to and was issued prior to the summer Obon Festival.

Such literature often, as here, makes use of idealized images of the past, identifying Buddhism with such images while simultaneously criticizing the modern world, which is depicted as materially rich yet spiritually poor. In contrast to the turmoil of the modern world, Buddhism, its temples, and its deep connections with the ancestors represent a "Japanese spiritual homeland" (kokoro no furusato), in which the Japanese can feel at home with themselves and make contact with their culture. Within this nostalgic imagery, too, a strong emphasis on morality is maintained through the concepts of gratitude (to the ancestors) and obligation, which requires one to repay their favors by performing memorial services and attending the temple.

These three short translations, then, indicate much about the actual nature of Japanese Buddhism today and about what it means for the Japanese people: the relationship between the living and the dead, the importance of the correct ritual procedures and postures, the importance of performing memorial services for the ancestors, the importance of faith and of the supportive and sustaining power of the Buddhas that enable people to live happily. These, rather than the philosophical constructs or even the monastic practices such as meditation and teachings focused on the nature and attainment of enlightenment, are the things that dominate the relationship between the Japanese and Buddhism, and these are the themes that have driven and sustained Buddhism through the centuries, and that remain at the heart of its action in contemporary Japan.

Further Reading

William M. Bodiford, "Sōtō Zen in a Japanese Town: Notes on a Once-Every-Thirty-Three-Years Kannon Festival," *Japanese Journal of Religious Studies* 21, 1 (1994): 3–36; Kawahashi Noriko, "*Jizoku* (Priests' Wives) in Sōtō Zen Buddhism: An Ambiguous Category," *Japanese Journal of Religious Studies*

22, 1–2 (1995): 161–183; Kenneth Marcure, "The Danka System," *Monumenta Nipponica* 40, 1 (1985): 39–67; Ian Reader, "Transformations and Changes in the Teachings of the Sōtō Zen Buddhist Sect," *Japanese Religions* 14, 1 (1985): 28–48; Ian Reader, "Zazenless Zen?: The Position of Zazen in Institutional Zen Buddhism," *Japanese Religions* 14, 3 (1986): 7–27; Ian Reader, *Religion in Contemporary Japan* (Honolulu: University of Hawaii Press, 1991), esp. 77–106; Ian Reader, "Buddhism as a Religion of the Family" in *Religion and Society in Modern Japan*, ed. Mark Mullins, Shimazono Susumu, and Paul Swanson (Berkeley: Asian Humanities Press, 1993): 139–156; Robert J. Smith, *Ancestor Worship in Contemporary Japan* (Stanford: Stanford University Press, 1974).

Trust and Dependence: For the Sake of a Correct Foundation for Your Life

WHY IS THE WORLD FULL OF UNEASE?

The scientific civilization of the current age has in many ways greatly fulfilled our expectations. Our homes are full of electrical appliances, and thanks to air conditioners we can enjoy cool summers and warm winters. Communications have developed so that we can get to distant places quickly and in comfort. The audiovisual world of televisions and videos relays information and entertainment to us, while in our stores and supermarkets, foodstuffs and clothing from all over the world are widely available. The development of medical knowledge and techniques has had an immense effect on our lives, extending life expectancy greatly.

From such perspectives, the present world has satisfied human expectations and appears to be extremely rosy. However, one has to ask the question: have we become really happy?

In fact, it could be said that, to the extent that our material desires have been fulfilled, people's minds in the present world have slid into an extraordinarily famished state. Human desires have no limit. As soon as one desire is fulfilled, the next one rises up in our heads. Thus, however much we progress materially, we are never satisfied but are caught up in a trap of unsatisfied desires.

If, in all of this, we happen to look into the depths of our minds, we are liable to be stricken with an indescribable isolation and unease and become aware of the vacuity of just satiating our material desires.

WHAT ARE THE UNDERLYING PRINCIPLES BY WHICH WE LIVE AT PRESENT?

On a daily basis we uphold our spirits by thinking about various things, such as our position in our company, our academic record, money, our house, or our family and friends. There may also be those who say that having a good healthy body is foundation enough for a satisfied life.

But please think a little about this. All these things are ephemeral. One has to leave one's company when one reaches retirement age. However good one's academic record is, if one does not have a suitable job to go with it, it is of little use. Money, too, can rapidly disappear and lose its value in times of economic crisis and inflation. There is always the fear that the home that one has striven so hard for may disappear in a fire. We cannot even rely on our families. The number of cases of people who want to get divorced from their wives as soon as they retire is growing. Although living a long, healthy life is a good thing, there are many people who end up having to spend the last years of their lives alone and without sufficient support and protection. . . . This is contemporary reality.

You are probably aware of all this. In truth, everything is impermanent. And so you come to the terrible realization that all the things you thought would sustain you in reality have no foundation. What, then, are the things that we ought to have as our correct spiritual foundations?

THE PRAYERFUL GESTURE (GASSHŌ) OF FAITH: A BEAUTIFUL AND PEACEFUL FORM

Trust is something immense that unites body and mind and allows us to live in peace. We usually think we live our lives under our own strength, and everyone lives seeking their own personal happiness. However, if we are asked, "Are you really happy?" why is it that so few people are able to answer, "Yes, I am"? Most people are living in anguish, enveloped in all sorts of problems, forms of unease, and situations that are not what they wished. How, then, can one become happy?

One of the most important teachings of Buddhism is that of karmic relations (*en*). This word expresses the underlying reality that all things, from human beings to animals, minerals, water, and the air we breathe, exist in a state of mutual interconnection and interdependence. One never lives by one's strength alone. Even if you do not recognize this, and think you will be able to act solely on your own, doing just what you want, if the karmic connections (*en*) around you are not properly ordered, you will not be able to achieve any of your wishes. Being aware of this interconnectedness and thinking not just of yourself, but of the happiness of all around you at the same time, and nurturing good relations . . . that is the way to happiness.

Humans are foolish and it is totally impossible for them—even with computers or the advances of science—to control all the infinite and spreading threads of karma. Therefore we, as followers of Buddhism, even while striving with all our might to cooperate and maintain good karmic relations, have to trust in and leave the results up to the Buddhas [*omakase suru*, "to leave the results up to, entrust someone with a task," a term that is widely used in Japanese religious contexts (especially by religious practitioners and people praying at religious centers) to indicate acceptance of fate and of human dependence on spiritual beings such as deities and Buddhas].

In this life, true peace of mind is attained by receiving and accepting the "fate" that the Buddhas give to us. Is this not the true spirit of trust?

THE GESTURE OF WORSHIP (GASSHŌ)

This is the form that manifests one's deep trust [in the Buddhas]. Moreover, for human beings it is the most beautiful and indispensable form of action. The gesture of worship is not just a posture to adopt when performing acts of worship and faith before the family Buddhist altar or in front of the Buddha image at a temple. It is also the gesture one uses to pay homage to the Buddha nature that lies within each and every one of us. This includes respecting and acknowledging with this gesture of worship your own Buddha nature, for, as the *Dhammapada* states, "you yourself are your own friend; if you spurn yourself, you are the friend of no one; if you do not regulate and put yourself in order, it is truly difficult to be friends with someone else." Making this gesture of worship is the basic form and way of putting ourselves in order. Therefore, whenever and wherever our minds are seized with unease or suffering, or at any time of crisis or trouble, let us first quietly join our hands together and make the correct form of the gesture of worship.

This is truly marvelous. When your spirit is enveloped in this gesture of worship, don't you feel that all the vexations that have bothered up till this point start to dissolve? As soon as one makes this gesture of worship clearly, a soothing wind can be felt blowing through one's mind.

THE IMPORTANCE OF VENERATING THE THREE JEWELS

There are three elements necessary for the development of Buddhism. One is Śākyamuni, the Buddha, who attained the highest form of human nature and perceived the truth (enlightenment). The second is the Law that Buddha taught. The third consists of those people who seek to follow the true path established by that teaching. In Japanese the word used for such people (*sō*) is nowadays considered to refer to priests, but in the original Indian language it signified the *sangha*, a word referring to the whole community of Buddhist followers who performed Buddhist practices together. In this sangha there were not just people who had become monks, but also lay people as well.

These three basic elements from which Buddhism was formed (Buddha, Law, sangha) are known as the "Three Jewels." And for we followers of Buddhism these "Three Jewels" provide the greatest foundation of all. The first step for followers of Buddhism is to have trust in, and pledge oneself, to the Three Jewels; this is not just in Japan, but among all those who have faith in Buddhism, in India, Sri Lanka, Thailand, Tibet, and elsewhere. In these different countries, the words used to recite this item of faith vary, but they all mean the same:

> I pledge my trust in the Buddha.
> I pledge my trust in the Buddhist Law.
> I pledge my trust in the sangha.

Zen Master Dōgen [the principal founder of Sōtō Zen in Japan and the sect's main textual authority] exhorted all people to venerate the Three Jewels, and he said the following:

> I place my trust in the Buddha because he is a great teacher. I place my trust in the Law because it is good medicine. I place my trust in the sangha because it is an unsurpassable friend. You should know the great virtues of the Three Jewels, which are the most unsurpassable, deepest, and wonderful." (From the *Shushōgi* [The Principle of Practice and Enlightenment].) [This text was edited, compiled, and published by the sect in 1890, using sections from many of Dōgen's writings, and has ever since been used in the sect as a cardinal text and basis of faith and sect teachings.]

These are the correct principles to enable each of us to spend this human life, which does not come to us twice, without regret and with a rich spirit.

To express one's trust and dependence in the Three Jewels is none other than to vow that "I shall live from now on as the child of Buddha." That alone is sufficient. Whoever we are, we are all children of Buddha, and if, while expressing our trust in the Three Jewels, and if we mutually respect and greet each other with a gesture of prayer and worship, we shall be able to walk strongly forward along the road to Buddhahood together.

The Ten Articles of Faith

1. Let us always clean the family Buddhist altar (*butsudan*) every morning, and, by making a gesture of worship (*gasshō*) and venerating them, let us give thanks to our ancestors.
2. At the dining table, let us make a gesture of worship before eating.
3. At the temple, as we stand before its Main Hall, we should without fail make a gesture of worship and bow.
4. Let us enshrine our household mortuary tablets (*ihai*) at the temple and without fail visit it on the various death anniversaries [of our ancestors]. [These tablets have the posthumous name of the ancestor engraved on them and represent the ancestor's presence. It is normal for one tablet to be placed in the family altar, but a second may also be placed at the Buddhist temple as well. The Buddhist sects exhort their followers to do this as it makes the bond between family members and the temple stronger and encourages them to visit the temple more often.]
5. On the first morning of every month, let us all go to the temple to pray for the safety of the family.
6. When our children are born, let us have them named at the temple, and on the one hundredth day [after the birth] visit the temple and report this news to our ancestors. [While it is most common for parents to take their newborn babies to Shintō shrines to place them under the protection

of the Shintō gods, there has also been a tradition of asking the Buddhist priest to bestow a name on the child. This is a practice that still may be found today, and one that Sōtō encourages as it is believed to foster a particularly strong karmic connection among the child, family, and temple.]

7. When our children enter school and come of age, let us without fail visit the temple and report this to our ancestors.

8. Let us celebrate weddings [more commonly celebrated at Shinto shrines or, in recent years, at specialized wedding halls] before our ancestors at the temple. On occasions when this is not possible, let us visit the temple afterward and report the news to our ancestors. [It is customary to report family events to the ancestors at the family Buddhist altar. This injunction, and the injunctions in the previous articles, to report family events to the ancestors also at the temple, thus seeks to further affirm and cement the bonds of loyalty and karmic relationship between the temple and its members.]

9. On Buddha's birthday (*Hanamatsuri*) [in Japan celebrated on April 8, an important date in the Sōtō calendar], let us visit the temple together with our children and commemorate this by drinking sweet sake [*amazake*, which on this occasion is usually a nonalcoholic beverage, or a sweetened tea (*amacha*) given out to those who visit temples].

10. On Enlightenment day [*Jōdō-e*, December 8 in Japan, the most widely celebrated observance in the Zen sects] and on the day of the commemoration of the Buddha's death [*Nehan-e*, February 15 in Japan], let us all gather at the temple and, listening to talks about Buddhism and doing Zen meditation, remember the Buddha.

Peace of Mind in Human Life

Whenever the time of the Obon Festival [which commemorates the ancestors and takes place in most parts of Japan in August] comes around, I think of the way of life of the countryside. I am enlivened by memories of this enjoyable festival, memories of visiting the graves together with one's family and doing the Bon dances and then eating delicious watermelon cooled in the well. When I see melons, eggplants, and deep red tomatoes in the same fields that my ancestors tilled, I instinctively want to offer them to the ancestors. In recent times, one has been able to eat cucumbers and tomatoes at all times of the year, and one can gaze through the windows of flower shops at all sorts of flowers and plants that bloom throughout the four seasons. This is convenient, but, on the other hand, I feel that thoughts of a seasonal nature, in which one felt the texture of things seen by the eye and tasted by the tongue, are gradually becoming less and less. Even for someone who lives in a city, however, seeing the vegetables and fruits arranged outside the greengrocer's shop is a reminder of one's dead ancestors [and the gratitude that is owed to them].

It is often said that forgetting to express gratitude is a normal human trait, but gratitude is an essential part of recognizing where we come from. As you know, the ideogram used to express the term gratitude (*on*) is made up of the ideogram for mind (*shin*) beneath the ideogram for cause (*in*) of origin or source (*gen'in*). If one asks the questions how have I come to be born here and how have I continued to live so far, one will see that this whole process is one that involves one in debts of gratitude. Such debts are not, of course, contractual or materially fixed; rather, they are debts that should lead us to recognize a sense of obligation that one has toward one's parents and ancestors, and that should be recalled whenever one thinks of them. This is I consider a natural human emotion, and Buddhism enables us to reflect on such things by paying homage to and thinking about the dead at the Obon Festival. Not only the dead, however: in the sūtras it is taught that one should also venerate one's living parents. The Obon Festival is a time for respecting one's living parents and one's ancestors. By doing this at the Obon Festival one expresses the wish to be peaceful, to return to one's original self, to think of one's own past and future, and to think of one's ancestors and also one's parents.

This is what in Buddhism we call attaining peace of mind. True peace of mind will never come from worrying or from not being satisfied with anything. When one sees a Buddha statue, one naturally becomes calm, and the turbulence of the mind subsides. At such times we should quietly calm our minds and join our hands together in a gesture of worship (*gasshō*). Without fuss, one should sit quietly and still: this is the mind and form of Zen meditation. The Obon Festival is an important event that occurs once a year to allow us to get such peace of mind.

Peace of mind is one of the greatest blessings of life. For a husband and wife, the real issue is not whether their characters are compatible, or whether they have the same character. Is it not, rather, the question of whether they can be relaxed with each other and can live together in a peaceful state of mind? The problem is that in contemporary society we have lost sight of this peace of mind that enables us to live in true happiness.

This celebration of the Obon Festival has in fact continued for almost 2,500 years according to the teachings of Buddha. Through this festival, which is a vital spiritual home (*kokoro no furusato*) of the Japanese people, we wish to restore our peace of mind and, especially among young people, to cultivate satisfied minds.

SPECIAL PLACES

44

Keizan's Dream History

William M. Bodiford

Keizan Jōkin (1264–1325), the author of the selections translated below, usually is remembered only as a revered patriarch of the Sōtō Zen tradition and as the founder of Sōjiji, one of the Sōtō Zen school's dual headquarter temples. Keizan, however, can also be viewed as an ordinary, indeed average, rural Buddhist monk of medieval times. He was not a great innovator, original thinker, or gifted writer. Although lacking in literary merit and philosophical profundity, Keizan's writings remain significant precisely because of their routine content. They provide a day-to-day record of rural Zen monastic life that reveals four important aspects of Japanese religiosity that all too often are overlooked: history, dreams, ritual, and women.

Keizan wrote primarily to provide himself a place in history. By recording his own history and that of the newly established Soto Zen lineage, Keizan sought to direct the future. Keizan knew that the precedents he recorded would dictate who gained control over which temples, which Buddhas and gods were worshipped, the calendar of ritual observances, and the mutual obligations of the temples and local lay patrons. Most major temples and shrines in Japan possess comparable historical records in which generations of worshippers found similar guidelines. Because these other records usually lack clear authorship and describe miraculous events, modern readers tend to view them as more mythological than historical. Keizan knew no such distinction. He did not wait for pious tradition to invest his life with the miraculous but recorded his own miracles. He believed that publicizing these miracles would enhance the status of his new monastery, which he named Yōkōji on Tōkoku Mountain, as a sacred center of the nascent Japanese Zen lineage.

Records of Japanese temples and shrines inevitably include dream episodes. Keizan recorded more than twenty-three of his dreams and wrote: "In all matters I have relied upon the interpretation of my dreams." Temples and shrines must be located where ordinary human beings can contact the Buddhas and gods. Dream visions recorded by the religious patriarchs such as Keizan testify that such is the case. Subsequent generations of pilgrims visit the same sacred sites to experience the same dreams of the Buddhas and gods. These dream visions, therefore, became shared public documents that advertised the spiritual power of the site and confirmed the correctness of ritual, social, and economic arrangements.

Participation in its cycle of ceremonial observances helps monks, nuns, wealthy patrons, and local people establish connections to the sacred history and spiritual power of religious sites. Keizan's Zen tradition stressed monastic ritual. Dōgen (1200–1253), the first Sōtō Zen patriarch in Japan, wrote extensively on the style of ceremony that he had observed in Song China. Keizan's teacher Gikai (1219–1309), who had studied under Dōgen, also journeyed to the major monasteries of China for the sole purpose of mastering Song-style Zen ceremonies. Keizan wrote detailed descriptions of the rites he learned from Gikai, occasionally including both instructions for the ritual and accounts of his own ceremonial performance. These rituals usually identify Keizan with the Buddha, with the lineage of Zen ancestors, with Zen awakening, and with his local monastic community and its lay patrons.

Keizan's most important patron was a woman, Lady Taira Sonin. In 1212 she and her husband donated land for what eventually became Keizan's main temple, Tōkokusan Yōkōji. Sonin eventually became a nun with her own chapel. Keizan compared the closeness of their relationship to a magnet and steel. Keizan's dependence on a female patron was not at all unusual. When Dōgen founded his first temple, Kōshōji at Fukakusa near Kyoto, an aristocratic woman named Shōgaku donated the Lecture Hall. Dōgen taught a number of laywomen and nuns, including Keizan's grandmother Myōchi. Other Sōtō monks who studied with Keizan as well as his disciples founded temples that were sponsored by women patrons. Women outnumber men by a significant margin in the records of early donations preserved at Tōkokusan Yōkōji. Fifteenth- and sixteenth-century records of Sōtō funeral sermons similarly reveal that the vast majority of lay funerals conducted by rural Zen teachers were for women. Clearly, without the support and religious devotion of countless women, Japanese Zen institutions (and perhaps most other Buddhist institutions as well) could never have succeeded on such a wide scale. Yet today we know the names of only a few of these vital female patrons. None of their biographies have survived. Keizan's descriptions of Sonin, his grandmother, and his mother therefore provide rare glimpses into the essential role played by women in the propagation of Buddhism in Japan.

During his lifetime Keizan never bothered to compile or edit his writings. After his death his records became scattered among his various disciples and their temples. Although a few original documents exist, for the most part scholars have read only late editions of uncertain reliability. The standard edition of Keizan's *Records of Tōkoku Temple* (*Tōkokuki*), selections from which appear below, for example, was first published in 1929 based on a manuscript version compiled in 1718, almost four hundred years after Keizan's death. We now know that it contained many later additions and the order of its entries had been rearranged. To remain as close to Keizan's own words as possible, the selections from *Records of Tōkoku Temple* translated below are based on an unedited 1432 manuscript. Unlike the standard published text, the entries in the manuscript are not arranged in chronological order. To aid the reader, section titles as well as dates and full names (when known) for people mentioned in the text have been added.

The text used for the translation is published in Ōtani Teppu, "Daijōji hihon Tōkokuki," *Shūgaku kenkyū* 16 (1974): 231–248.

Further Readings

Akamatsu Toshihide and Philip Yampolsky, "Muromachi Zen and the Gozan System," in *Japan in the Muromachi Age*, ed. John Whitney Hall and Toyoda Takeshi (Berkeley: University of California Press, 1977): 65–86; William Bodiford, *Sōtō Zen in Medieval Japan* (Honolulu: University of Hawaii Press, 1993); Martin Collcutt, "The Early Ch'an Monastic Rule: Ch'ing kuei and the Shaping of Ch'an Community Life," in *Early Ch'an in China and Tibet*, ed. Whalen Lai and Lewis R. Lancaster (Berkeley: Asian Humanities Press, 1983): 165–184; Martin Collcut, *Five Mountains: The Rinzai Monastic Institution in Medieval Japan* (Cambridge: Harvard University Press, 1981); Martin Collcutt, "The Zen Monastery in Kamakura Society," in *Court and Bakufu in Japan: Essays in Kamakura History*, ed. Jeffery P. Mass (New Haven: Yale University Press, 1982): 191–220; Bernard Faure, *Visions of Power: Imagining Medieval Japanese Buddhism* (Princeton: Princeton University Press, 1996).

Records of Tōkoku

CONSTRUCTION OF YŌKŌJI'S DHARMA HALL

1324: GENKŌ 4, SENIOR WOOD YEAR OF THE RAT

3d Moon, 3d Day: Dharma Seat (*hōza*, i.e., lecture platform) erected. Today is Junior Earth Day of the Ox, the day when the stars meet, one of my six corresponding days (*rikugō nichi*). On this day the Buddha first turned the wheel of the Dharma in the Deer Park. The day when the Buddha, in his former life as Prince Kalyāṇakārī (Zenji), went to the Dragon Palace to seek the fabulous wish-fulfilling pearl corresponds to Shōwa 3 [1314], 5th Moon, Junior Earth Day of the Ox. According to the *Constellations and Stars Sūtra* [*Shukuyōkyō, T* 1299], when this day occurs during the second moon before entering into the third moon, then it is a day of infinitely good fortune. Everyone in this temple, therefore, gathered for the scripture recitation. We chanted the Śūraṅgama *dhāraṇī* (Ryōgonshu) once. At the sound of the first gong, the carpenter Zenshin erected the Dharma Seat.

2d Moon, 9th Day: Select days with good stars, like the Demon Constellation, Puśya (Fusha), one of my six corresponding days, Junior Wood of the Ox, the infinitely lucky days of the second moon, as lucky days for disturbing the earth with construction projects. When we started the foundations of the Dharma

Hall, everyone's participation was requested. We recited the Disaster-Averting *dhāraṇī* (Shōsaiju), thereby following the splendid example of my teacher, Gi-kai of Daijōji, who thus performed prayer (*kitō*) rituals for construction projects. Three hundred workers cleared the land, and numerous monks participated. A temporary hallway was built from the Monks' Hall (*sōdō*) to the Abbot's Square (*hōjō*).

DEDICATION OF YŌKŌJI'S DHARMA HALL

Format

4th Moon, 8th Day: Performed the dedication ceremony for the new Dharma Hall.

On the previous day the following announcement had been posted on the east wall of the Dharma Hall:

In the Land of Japan, on the 8th day, 4th moon, of the first year of Shōchū [1324], the Head Master Keizan Jōkin will come to this temple and dedicate the Dharma Hall according to the following schedule of events.

[1] Hour of the Dragon [ca. 8:00 A.M.]: Decorate the hall. Hang red curtains (omit this time); next to the Dharma seat erect a turning-the-Dharma-wheel banner, as well as banners of the eight dragon king gods, octagonal mirrors, and two white lions. Place the staff in a bag and lean it on the floor. Place the whisk in a bag to the left of the incense burner. Erect side stairs. The elder who sounds the clapper enters from the right stairs, and the attendant who holds the incense enters from the left stairs. To the left of the Dharma seat place a small chair for presenting orations, and place another small chair to the right. The elder who sounds the clappers is positioned there. On the left set a reading stand on which to place the texts of the orations. Place a seating chair at the rank ahead of the temple administrators. The patron Fujiwara Togashi Iekata is positioned there. Below the Dharma seat erect a table on which to place the incense burner. In front of it place the bowing cushion. That is where the patron bows. Erect a table on which to place the patron's donations. Erect a table on which to place flower vases and incense burners. That is where the patron offers incense.

[2] Next, a light snack is served in the Abbot's Square, Myōgon'in.

[3] Next, sound the drum for the monks to assemble as usual. The only difference is that the ceremonial instruments are sounded as the master enters the hall. The brocade banners, umbrella, etc., are omitted.

[4] The elder who sounds the clappers enters first and stands at the rank ahead of the temple leaders. When he takes his seat, he passes to the right of the Dharma seat. Next the patron enters. The temple receptionist leads the patron to the rank ahead of the temple administrators.

[5] Next, the opening orations are presented. The master stands in front of the small chair. The patron passes the texts of the orations to the teacher

and the teacher responds. Incense is given to the attendant who passes it to the temple supervisor. The receptionist passes the oration texts of both ranks to the teacher to be read.

[6] When the teacher's responses are finished, the attendant passes the texts to the Group Leader to be read.

[7] Next, pointing to the Dharma seat, the teacher makes a Dharma statement. Next, he gets down from his chair. The master stands at the center stairs. (The abbot of Jōjūji, Mugai Chikō [d. 1351], stands at the right stairs, and the attendant holding the incense burners stands at the left stairs.)

[8] Next, the teacher offers incense. (Incense is offered first on behalf of the emperor, then the patron, then the Buddha, then one's Dharma lineage.) When incense is being offered on behalf of the patron, the patron will bow three times.

[9] Next, the attendant who is positioned at the chair, offers incense, gets down from his seat, and performs a formal bow. Both ranks of monks perform formal bows as usual, except that ceremonial instruments are sounded for each bow. Last, the abbot of Jōjūji performs formal bows.

[10] Next, at the sound of the clapper, the abbot of Jōjūji takes the bell from out of his sleeve and, sounding it once, calls out: "Exalted dragons and elephants assembled at this Dharma site, see now the first meaning!"

[11] Then, there is a session of questions and answers, which will be followed by a formal Dharma talk.

[12] Dharma talk.

[13] When the Dharma talk has ended, the abbot of Jōjūji again sounds his bell and calls out: "See clearly the Dharma of the Dharma King. The Dharma of the Dharma King is thus." Sounding his bell again, he gets down from his seat and bows to the patron.

[14] Next, monks bow as in the sequence of formal greetings, sounding the bell at the head and end. The abbot of Jōjūji performs the abbreviated threefold kowtow. The leaders and assembled monks do likewise. The former leaders and retired officers do likewise. The attendants perform the full threefold kowtow. The nuns and female assistants bow three times. The novices and young boys bow nine times. The carpenters bow twice.

Respectfully posted by the attendant Genshō Chinzan. Dated.

Opening Orations

Text of the oration submitted by Sondō and Meihō Sotetsu (1277–1350), representing both the East and West Ranks of Officers, and by Sokei and Kōan Shikan (d. 1341), representing all the assembled monks, of Tōkoku Mountain, Noto Province:

In celebration of the Buddha's birthday we invite you to dedicate this hall by turning the wheel of the Dharma. Thus, the waters of Dong (*tōsui*) reverse their flow; the branch streams of our lineage overflow the Realm of the River and Lake. The great solaris (*taiyō*) illuminates everywhere; its rays radiate universally throughout the Land of the Sun. The raging waves that cover the globe ask to know the fountainhead. The lamp of enlightenment transmitted at Yōkō [Eternally Radiant Temple] requests that the right livelihood be demystified, so that now, during the Latter Five Hundred Years, we might once again see the Buddha preaching to his assembly at Vulture Peak.

Head of the hall, please accept our oration with compassion.

As witnessed by all the generations of Buddhas and ancestors.

Respectfully submitted by Sondō and Meihō Sotetsu, etc., on behalf of both ranks. Genkō 4 [1324], 4th moon, 8th day

Text of the oration submitted by Fujiwara Togashi Iekata, the great patron of Tōkokusan Yōkōji in the Sakai Estate, Kashima District, Noto Province, Country of Japan, Southern Hemisphere of Jambudvīpa (Nan Enbu):

On the 8th day of this moon we ceremoniously observe the auspicious anniversary of the Tathāgata Śākyamuni's birth. I respectfully request our teacher, the head of the hall, to assume his newly crafted treasure throne and dedicate this hall for the sake of mankind.

I've heard that teaching has a foundation. It's called transmitting the flame, and it originates in the revelation of Dharma succession. This is termed "Dedicating the Hall." Conveyed in secret without outward sign, the black and white of Dharma succession must be forcibly requested. Humbly, I do so request.

Great Monk, Dear Teacher, Head of the Hall: Please take the incense from your breast. Fill the heavens with its burning scent.

Great Zen Teacher, Abbot of Jōjūji: Please strike your bell. Evidence its sound to the ends of the earth.

Head of the hall, please accept my humble oration with compassion.

As witnessed by the full assembly of Zen teachers of every rank and the abbot of Jōjūji.

Respectfully submitted by Fujiwara Togashi Iekata, the great patron.

Genkō 4 [1324], 4th moon, 8th day

Keizan's Responses

Remarks by the founding monk, Keizan Jōkin of Tōkoku Mountain, on arriving at this temple to dedicate the hall:

Taking up the text of the patron's oration, he replied: Donating this temple to me resembles coughing up spit bubbles. As for requesting me to teach, to inaugurate this splendid seat, by the perfectly penetrating hands and eyes of these tattered monks, by your solid faith that protects the precious Dharma, even before I took up the text of your oration, not a person could have doubted it. I ask the supervisor to explain, so all gods and men will know in detail.

Taking up the text of the oration by the two ranks, he replied: O' phoenixes, O' dragons! You are such auspicious signs, such good omens: like stars above the heavens, like waters below the earth. These syllables are as obvious as your eyes and feet. Group leader, inform the assembly of all particulars.

Pointing at the Dharma seat, he said: This seat is so tall and wide. Neither the holy ones nor ordinary beings can cope with it. Yet the Buddhas and ancestors soar over it, fanning the winds of true religion.

Remarks delivered while presenting incense: This first stick of incense is humbly to wish the emperor a reign of ten thousand years (*banzai*) and a long life without undue effort. May he equal the heavens in expanse and the earth in dependability. May the multitudes of subjects who rely on him multiply like yin and yang. This second stick of incense is presented on behalf of this temple's great patron, his descendants, and his clan. May all patrons who contribute to these halls and who support this assembly enjoy long lives like the pine and the oak, which endure repeated new years without losing their greenery. By their generosity to the Dharma and to the Saṅgha, by their continual bountiful gifts to this assembly, may they cultivate good roots from generation to generation and ride in this vehicle from generation to generation. This third stick of incense is offered to He who was born today, our true teacher, Śākyamuni, the Tathāgata, as well as to all the generations of Zen ancestors who are his direct descendants and to good Zen masters everywhere. Through the eons they have performed the major and minor Buddhist ceremonies, assisting all assemblies to realize Buddha by debates and by resolving doubts. This [fourth] stick of incense was already offered long ago, even prior to the seven Buddhas of the past. Neither ordinary beings nor the holy ones know its name. Even before this commonplace (*heijō*), unborn (*fushō*) tribute has been spoken, it cannot be kept secret. Dearly departed teacher, Reverend Gikai, Master Tettsū, founding abbot of Shōjurin Daijōji in Kaga Province, third abbot of Eiheiji, fifty-third Dharma-generation descendant of Śākyamuni Buddha, the scent of your incense appears before us, wafts over your Dharma descendants, burns across the heavens, and settles over the sprouts in the fields. Thus I express my debt of gratitude to you for nursing me in the Dharma. Keizan took his seat.

The abbot of Jōjūji sounded his bell once and called out: "Exalted dragons and elephants assembled at this Dharma site, see now the first meaning!" He sounded his bell once and sat down.

Keizan said: "To expound the first meaning is to be the mother of wisdom for all Buddhas, to be a pundit for all the holy ones. Throughout the ages no person has doubted this. In this assembly isn't there a tattered monk who can demonstrate his understanding in debate?"

A monk asked: "A beautiful phoenix comes to perch in a jeweled tree in the garden. The Uḍumbara plant blossoms filling the world with its scent. These events are what kind of good omens?"

Keizan replied: "People's noses originally have no doubts."

A monk asked: "Lions roared, winds stirred. Dragons droned, clouds arose. The five positions separated, the ways of guest and host joined. At that very moment the Lord Śākyamuni assumed birth at Lumbinī. The master glowed with an all-pervading radiance. The Lord Śākyamuni pointed one hand to the heavens and one hand to the earth and said, 'Above the Heavens and below the heavens, only I am to be revered.' Master, the first words of today's all-pervading radiance are what?"

Keizan replied: "The Dharma seat is so marvelously high, its girth must permeate the earth."

The monk said: "Your howl at once rattles the nine continents. All Zen men within the four oceans heard completely."

Keizan replied: "Where they hear there is no echo. Their ears are within the sound."

A monk said: "It is recorded that when Muzhou Daoming (Bokushū Dōmyō, n.d.) ascended the Dharma seat in a Hall Dedication Ceremony, he asked the Prior, 'Is the superintendent present?' The Prior replied, 'Present.' Muzhou asked, 'Is the supervisor present?' The Prior replied, 'Present.' Muzhou asked, 'Is the group leader present?' The Prior replied, 'Present.' Muzhou said, 'The three sections are not the same. Taken together, they all conclude with the first point. The additional text is too long. I will deliver it another day.' Then Muzhou vacated the Dharma seat. What does it mean?"

Keizan replied: "Clouds gather, clinging to the mountains. Rivers flow, expanding the oceans. A design of elegant warp and woof. Please appear identically."

A monk asked: "The old Buddha, Hongzhi Zhengjue (Wanshi Shōgaku, 1091–1157) commented by saying, 'Master Muzhou expounded with ten letters, directing with both hands.' How do you understand this?"

Keizan replied: "The infinite universe cannot conceal it. The entire body reflects no image."

The monk asked: "Does what the old Buddha said and what you said have the same meaning or a different meaning?"

Keizan replied: "This old monk never rests among sameness and difference."

A monk said: "Chisel a vein of royal jade and every chip is a jewel. Smash sandalwood and every splinter is fragrant."

Keizan said: "In heaven above the stars all glitter. In earth below the trees all thrive."

A monk said: "This mountain monastery has ten scenic spots. I will mention each one and ask you before this assembly of monks from all quarters to think of a song of praise for each. Do you permit it?"

Keizan replied: "Mountains are high; valleys are low. Who can doubt it?"

The monk said [1]: "Sitting with one's entire body until it cuts through the solitary peak. The astrological phases cut off all voices, so one can hardly ask. Isn't this Squatting Monkey Ridge (Kyoenryō)?"

Keizan replied: "Sit through a thousand peaks and ten thousand peaks. Take in the four seas and five lakes in a single glance."

The monk said [2]: "Its pines in the wind surely brush the bright moon. There is no convenient occasion for handing down instructions. Isn't Cloud Gathering Peak (Shūunpō) like this?"

Keizan replied: "Dragon pines stir up clouds. Tiger rocks howl out the wind."

The monk said [3]: "Hauling firewood and transporting via water are miraculous. Entering the hollows, climbing the peaks is the wind of *prajñā* (Perfect Wisdom). But as for Circuitous Stream Peak (Unsuipō), what is it?"

Keizan replied: "Washing the clear sky, making it clearer. A single drop from the fountain of Caoxi (Sōkei) fills the Realm of the River and Lake."

The monk said [4]: "Gold and grain are the Tathāgata's one attachment. This vast field holds the future. Millet Sprout Field (Aohara) is of what variety?"

Keizan replied: "Golden grain, the Tathāgata, and the great field convert the living."

The monk said in reference to Inari Peak (Inarimine) [5]: "Inari marvelously appears in Jambudvīpa. Surely since long before there must have been doubts. As for the marvelous response of Inari, what then?"

Keizan replied: "In front of the mountain there is a strip of unused field. So many times it has been sold. So many times it has been bought."

The monk said [6]: "Transcending all eons, the rice from the monastery's fragrant kitchen builds mountains and builds tombstones, terminating all feelings of hunger. Facing Rice Abundant Tomb (Iimorizuka), how will you get a word in edgewise?"

Keizan replied: "One bowl of rice from the monastery's fragrant kitchen; ten thousand men use it without using it up."

The monk said [7]: "In death there is life. Six gates open. The five elders thusly continue their cool sitting. What about Buried Corpse Hollow (Umeshitani)?"

Keizan replied: "One flower blossoms with five petals. The fruit it produced ripens naturally."

The monk said [8]: "One trunk pillar standing amidst the rivers and clouds. Its branches sweep the earth with their shadows as it supports the heavens. How do you understand Shoe-Hanging Hackberry (Kakikutsu Enoki)?"

Keizan replied: "Traversing oceans and scaling mountains, none of the practitioners who come will ever be able to repay the cost of their straw sandals."

The monk said in reference to Crow Rock Peak (Usekimine) [9]: "Stone crows understand a language no man hears. Speaking and listening simultaneously, nodding their heads. The language that stone crows understand: Who knows its sound?"

Keizan replied: "The country-viewing pavilion and Crow Rock Peak watch one another from early morning to evening rest."

The monk said [10]: "The stone women flutter their sleeves without thought or feeling. The wooden men meld to their spot without life. But what about Shaman Witch Field (Mikohara)?"

Keizan replied: "The stone woman sings and dances. The wooden man claps his hands. Such idiots and fools resemble a master among masters (*shuchūshu*)."

The monk said: "Each one of the ten scenic spots has received your comments. The one drop of Tōzan [i.e., Dongshan Liangjie (Tōzan Ryōkai, 807–869)], the clan of Taiyō [i.e., Dayang Jingxuan (Taiyō Kyōgen, 942–1027)], flow to all ten scenic spots, pulsating through them. This sacred monastery pierces the clouds beyond the dark greenery. Its jeweled towers and vermilion buildings hang in the empty sky. Is this the scenery of the whole mountain?"

Keizan replied: "The ten scenic spots radiate universally (fukō) throughout Tōkokusan [Grotto Valley Mountain]. The great solaris (taiyō) that fills the eyes appears today the same as in olden days."

Keizan's Dharma Talk

Keizan then lectured: "Wondrous spirituality pervading unrestrained; universal radiance sparkling bright; perfectly illuminated without defect. Who can doubt it? Seeing and hearing both perceive without mistake and function without obstructions. All people possess this bright wisdom. One's entire body cannot contain its outstanding magnitude. Don't wait for the stony turtles to understand language. Don't hesitate to sit in the treetops listening to their realization. From the first, one is not restricted to knowing or not knowing. Who says 'Ordinary Mind is the Way'? The ancestors and masters extend their hands and transmit their minds. All the Buddhas certify the bestowal of this mystical realization. Don't seize hold of appearances. Don't seek after affairs. Only when the mind realizes this spiritual communion will the religious lifeblood of the Buddhas and ancestors flow through. Transcend mundane calculations of the facades of being and emptiness. Become the only one to be revered, attaining the status of the ancestors. Become the marvelous virtuous reverence within the universe. Become the highest illumination within the vast emptiness. Know of every single place that it is one's own self. Every single place is one's radiant wisdom. Every single place is one's wayfaring chapel (dōjō). Every single place is one's practice of Buddha activity. When you return home and sit, how will you understand this?"

Keizan put down his fly whisk (hosso) and remained quiet for awhile. His subsequent expressions of thanks to the invited guests were not recorded. Then, he continued: "Earlier a monk asked about this story. When Muzhou Daoming ascended the Dharma seat in a Hall Dedication Ceremony, he asked the prior, 'Is the superintendent present?' The prior replied, 'Present.' Muzhou again asked, 'Is the supervisor present?' The prior replied, 'Present.' Muzhou again asked, 'Is the group leader present?' The prior replied, 'Present.' Muzhou said, 'The three sections are not the same. Taken together, they all conclude with the first point. The additional text is too long. I will deliver it another day.' One day while the ancient Buddha Hongzhi Zhengjue was residing on Yuantong Peak of Mount Lu, he went to Donglinsi [Eastern Grove Monastery] to perform a Hall Dedication Ceremony. Hongzhi cited the story of Muzhou and commented as follows: 'Master Muzhou expounded with ten letters, directing with both hands. Muzhou's Hall Dedication has been carefully investigated for you people on Yuantong. Now consider the Yuantong Hall Dedication. What will you people say? Ultimately, what do you make of it? Meeting together the sound of knowing is known. Why must the clear wind move heaven and earth?' As for Muzhou and Hongzhi: seven highways, eight advancements. This is my verse summary: All doubts naturally vanish. Now that I have performed this Tōkoku Hall Dedication for you, what will you make of it? 'Above the mountains [i.e., heaven] and the round earth both know themselves; the fine jade and rough stone entirely in hundreds of tiny shards.'"

The abbot of Jōjūji sounded his bell and called out: "See clearly the Dharma of the Dharma King. The Dharma of the Dharma King is thus." He came down from his seat and sounded his bell again.

YŌKŌJI'S BUILDINGS

1324: GENKŌ 4, SENIOR WOOD YEAR OF THE RAT

7th Moon, 6th Day, Senior Metal Day of the Dragon: Yōkōji's name plaques for the buildings arrived. They read: Fukōdō [Universal Radiance (Dharma Hall)], Saishōden [Highest Victory (Buddha Hall)], Yōkōji [Eternally Radiant Temple (Main Gate)], Kōsekiin [Wafting Scent (Kitchen)], Senbutsujō [Buddha Selecting (Monks' Hall)], Myōgon'in [Marvelously Strict (Abbot's Square)], Tōkokusan [Grotto Valley Mountain (Gate)]. Two plaques did not arrive. All the calligraphy was by the noted master Fujiwara Yukifusa, a descendant of the famous calligrapher Fujiwara Tsunetomo who was miraculously fathered by Yukiyoshi. It is a rare miracle that all the name plaques of the entire temple are written by the same brush. Even the ruling court never commands more than one or two name plaques at a time. It is a blessing for this temple. On the very day the plaques arrived at the temple there were auspicious events. Noichi Tōjirō of Kaga Province donated a Nirvana Image to the temple. Its depiction of the four transcendent virtues of Permanence, Bliss, Self, and Purity was unbelievably perfect. On the seventh day of the plaques' arrival (i.e., the 12th day of that moon), Keizan returned to Yōkōji. On the ninth day (i.e., the 14th day of that moon), Keizan ordained two new monks (named Meijō and Unshō) who enrolled as residents of Yōkōji and performed ritual offerings to the Nirvana Image for nine consecutive days. Each of these occurrences is an auspicious sign of the plaques' arrival.

LIFE AT YŌKŌJI

1325: SHŌCHŪ 2, JUNIOR WOOD YEAR OF THE OX

4th Moon, 11th day: Permitted the nun Myōshō Enkan [Keizan's cousin on his mother's side] to receive initiation in Precept Rituals. I asked her: "How do you understand the story (kōan) of Linqi (Rinzai) raising his fly whisk?" Myōshō Enkan remained silent. I said: "Your remarks cannot be expressed with paper and ink." Myōshō Enkan bowed and departed. Thus I permitted the precept initiation.

12th day: Bid farewell to Sonin, the abbess of Enzūin Chapel, as well as her attendant and group leader as they left the temple gate to visit Myōshō Enkan, the abbess of Hōōji Convent in Kaga Province.

15th day (full moon): Began Summer Training Retreat. After three days installed the image of the Sacred Monk. (Invited the abbot of Jōjūji, Mugai Chikō [d. 1351], to perform the consecration.)

14th day: Kohō Kakumyō (1271–1361) brought bamboo tallies for use in the Precept Recitation Ceremony (fusatsu) and said that they were from bamboo groves at Kōmyōzanji Temple in Tōtōmi Province. They will become permanent property of Yōkōji. I've heard it said that Eiheiji's bamboo tallies are from the bamboo groves of Mount Suzuka in Ise Province. I appreciated his kindness in bringing a gift from Tōtōmi and immediately arranged for these tallies to be used in the Precept Recitation Ceremony.

5th moon, 23d day: Made two vows. For life after life, existence after existence, I will convert all living beings and lead them to supreme awakening. I will regard all sins from the distant past that cannot be eliminated as my rare treasures. No other vows shall interfere with the proper endeavor to fulfill these two vows. These two vows were made not for my own self. One of the vows was made [in 1282] when in this present lifetime I awakened my bodhi-seeking mind under the guidance of master Jakuen (1207–1299) of Hōkyōji Temple. I vowed with the bodhisattva Mañjuśri (Monju) as my witness to disregard my own life on behalf of fulfilling this vow from life to life, existence to existence. The other vow was made in accordance with my compassionate mother Ekan's final instructions to become a bodhisattva dedicated to saving women. She could not be denied. I must follow her instructions and fulfill her command. May the Buddhas of the past, present, and future, the Śūraṇgama Sūtra and all the Buddhist scriptures maintain and protect my adamantine resolve. If these vows accord with the intentions of the Buddhas, then I must certainly experience a mystical dream. While thinking those thoughts I fell asleep. Just as dawn broke I had the following dream: There was my old tattered robe that I had not worn in a long time. Wanting to put it on, I unfolded it and discovered rat nests. It was defiled with cow dung and horse dung, horse tails and human hair, and every kind of impure filth. I shook all the filth out and put it on. Truly it was a marvelous dream! It was an auspicious sign that my vows had been renewed. The Buddhas and ancestors had responded to aspirations and witnessed my two vows.

24th day: The anniversary of my former teacher Ejō's death. After performing the scripture recitation ceremony in his memory, I returned and wrote this entry.

The subsequent abbots of Yōkōji first should be selected from among Keizan's Dharma heirs and should serve as abbots in order of seniority. I have four main disciples. And there is perhaps one more as well as the disciple of a disciple [i.e., six in all]. If Yōkōji's abbotship should ever become vacant, these six heirs should cooperate in selecting someone to propagate Buddhism and benefit the living [i.e., serve as abbot]. Everyone associated with this mountain monk Keizan and all future generations of my lineage must know that each one has a responsibility to propagate Buddhism and benefit the living. All I want is for each generation of my lineage to teach on behalf of the Buddha, to save others, and to prevent the Dharma from disappearing. Dated Shōchū 2, Junior Wood Year of the Ox [1325], beginning of autumn, 7th moon, 2d day.

The six disciples: Meihō Sotetsu (1277–1350), Mugai Chikō (d. 1351), Gasan Jōseki (1276–1366), Koan Shikan (d. 1341), Kohō Kakumyō (1271–1361), Genshō Chinzan (n.d.).

7th moon, 28th day: Initiated Supervisor Sokei and Supervisor Sondō in precept rituals.

Same day, midnight: Transmitted Dharma lineage to Kohō Kakumyō. Also presented him with my meditation mat. He was my last Dharma heir. The very next morning he left Yōkōji and went to Izumo Province.

7th moon, 16th day: Experience following auspicious dream: A person held a box about a foot deep full of clear water. On the surface of the clear water floated a gold key that formed words that read "room," "rock house," and "dipper grotto." After I awoke I understood what it said. "Room" (shitsu) is Mount Shōshitsu, the residence of Bodhidharma. "Rock House" is Mount Stonehead (Sekitō), the residence of Sekitō Kisen (Shitou Xiqian, 700–790). "Dipper Grotto" is Grotto Valley (Tōkoku), my residence. It means that there is no difference in our understanding. We share the same clear flow. What a marvelous sign!

5th moon, 20th day: Daichi (1290–1366) arrived from distant Kyushu to study. He presented me with copies of Second Revised Tōzan's Five Positions Occult Secrets Revealed (Jūhen Tōzan goi kenketsu), Sayings of Tōsu Gisei (Tōsu Gi go), and Sayings of Shinketsu Seiryō (Shinketsu-ryō go). The Second Revised Occult Secrets has not even been circulated in China, much less Japan. This is the first time anyone has seen it. It should be kept as a secret treasure and should not be shown to anyone except the most highly qualified. It will be our lineage's most precious asset. The Sayings of Tōsu and Sayings of Shinketsu have been published and already circulate widely.

YŌKŌJI'S ORIGINS

1320: GEN'Ō 2, SENIOR METAL YEAR OF THE MONKEY

Last Night of the Year, Evening Meeting: Keizan explained the origins of this temple. He said:

It is recorded that Dōgen, the abbot of Eiheiji, once said, "Hundreds of thousands of millions of worlds are revealed in each moment. The Buddhas and ancestors appear to teach you this topic. If I face this issue and attempt to give you a hint, I would say, the thousand mountains and the million valleys: how high, how low." His great-grandchild, Keizan Jōkin, holding his breath in reverence, will continue the discourse. Assembled monks, do you want to hear?

Keizan paused for awhile and then said:

Such words of no thought, of no awakening, and of no birth! Your nostrils themselves and the clarity of your eyes are the real topic. No matter how much I talk, I could only add that emptiness, in the end, cannot be divided into high or low. Do not analyze yourselves by grasping hold of "yes" or "no." Piercing intellectual investigations of this floating world are unimportant. This mountain monk Keizan sits in meditation within a training hall like the moon reflected in the water, instructing students like reflections in a mirror, and enters the samādhi of the chimerical to perform Buddhist rituals that resemble dreams.

Lady Sonin, our landlord, invited me here because she wanted to support a monastery. On my first visit, her husband Unno Nobunao helped me search out a site to build a hermitage in the mountains. At that time, I divined this valley as the place for my meditation cushion. We returned to the patron's residence to stay the night.

That night I dreamed that I was squatting on the innermost summit of this mountain. Looking into the distance below, I saw that this spot rose above the peaceful mountains below. In between the sky and the ground, within the valley gardens, suddenly a temple materialized. The several buildings, their roofs lined up in all directions, filled the valley. To the right of where the gate would be, there stood a great hackberry tree, the tips of its branches lushly intertwined. Monks gathered from all directions to hang numerous wornout straw sandals there.

Divining that dream, I understood it as an omen of a superior site that meant if I resided here the tattered monks arriving from all directions certainly would pay back the cost of their straw sandals [i.e., would become worthy students].

Moreover, the following year when I went back to the overlook where I had been in my dream, there was a wild hackberry tree, its growing branches in full leaf. This means that the monastery will certainly flourish. The clouds gathered together like congregations of monks. When we dug a well, the water gushed out to fill the Realm of the River and the Lake. How fantastic. How fantastic. Asleep or with open eyes, dreaming or awake, I saw the same thing.

In the Zen tradition itinerant monks are referred to as cloud-flowing monks. To visit teachers, to inquire of the Way, monks scale mountains and transverse oceans. Be it east or west, traveling north or south, they have no fixed abode. Walking their meandering route, higher and higher they come up or little by little go down. Like clouds and flowing streams, they travel beyond the farthest mountain, beyond the ends of the seas. They wear straw sandals and shoulder pilgrimage staffs. If one of them meets a good Zen master to whom he can respond, he will immediately open his bright Eye of the Correct Teaching (shōbōgen). That is how he would repay the cost of his straw sandals and break his pilgrimage staff. This is the rule for Zen monks.

I remember when [in 1313] I first returned to this mountain to build a hut. Venerable Vajraputra (Bajarahottara), the eighth of the sixteen major arhats, came to this mountain and entered my dream. He examined the mountain and said: "Elder Jōkin, although this is a small mountain, it is a superior location. There are no spots to obstruct the gods. Your propagation of Buddhism and teaching of students will succeed as desired."

Therefore, I built the hut and began teaching students from all quarters. For tea, I boiled pine needles. For a tea bowl, I used oak leaves. When I first received donations, I used a small pot to measure the rice——not having any standard measure.

[In 1317] when Sonin donated the Abbot's Square, I formally named this monastery. Because I admired Dongshan Liangjie (Tōzan Ryōkai, 807–869, who lived on Grotto Mountain) from the distant past and also valued the insight of dreams in the present, I named this monastery Tōkoku Daikapō Yōkōji (i.e., Grotto Valley, Great Hackberry Peak, Eternally Shinning Monastery) and named the Abbot's Square Myōshōgon'in (Marvelously Adorned Building).

For food I relied upon the two holy bodhisattvas Avalokiteśvara and Ākāśagarbha (Kokūzō), and on the two gods Vaiśravaṇa (Bishamon) and Mahākāla (Karaten). The three treasures (the Buddha, His Teachings, and His Community), the two holy ones, and the two gods were our patrons. And Inari, the god of this mountain, the protective spirits of the land, and Shōhō Shichirō (a guardian god) were our servants. That summer [1318] we conducted the first ninety-day training period here. Our comptroller and my attendant obtained bucketfuls of wild rice from Elder Wetlands (Chōja-ga-sawa), located in this province. We stored that rice for three full years.

On the night of the 8th day of the last moon, the anniversary of the Buddha's awakening, as I slept in the seated posture, one of those buckets entered my dream. It stood right in front of this old monk. I purified it for use. That same dawn the temple patron also dreamed the same dream. A man presented me with a great serving of rice. I ate some rice and then presented the rice to him. That bucket of rice when used as this old monk's eating bowl shrunk to only two-thirds its size. It automatically became the appropriate amount of food for a disciple of the Buddha. Thus a monk's eating bowl can contain the vastness of the sky while at the same time any single thing can fill the entire bowl. Each person receives in accordance with his needs. There is no fixed allotment.

Tonight is the last night of the old year. Tomorrow is the first day of the new year, the beginning of spring. Your eating bowls partake of the endless nourishment of joy in the Dharma as each receives the rice treasures that sprout from Elder Wetlands. For this reason, sometimes a bucketful of this treasure rice is equivalent to one bushel, while other times a single bowlful donated to gods and men fills one bucketful. The extremely large equals the minute. The extremely small equals the immense.

All the Buddha's disciples receive the nourishing light of food to eat from his ūrṇa (tuft of hair between his eyebrows). Each person eats the food as the food consumes people. The gruel suffices. The steamed rice suffices. If you embody the fortitude not to squander a single grain of rice then a scoopful fills a bucket while a bucketful fills one cup. When a small amount is needed, use a small amount. When a large amount is needed, use a large amount.

The Buddhist Way certainly transcends opulence and frugality. Therefore, administrators are to receive large portions. Moreover, approximately one bushel of rice, divided into thirds, should be used for the daily meals. Two-thirds are to be offered to the revered Three Treasures and one-third allotted for feeding the compassionate underlings. Whether serving many or a few, the managing monks should follow the same procedures. Abundance or scarcity depends on the offerings received from men and gods and Heaven's blessings. If the community of monks is limitless, then they certainly will beckon limitless fortune. The community, whether large or small, will have rations appropriate for each day's meals. If there is enough for steamed rice, cook steamed rice. If there is not enough for steamed rice, cook rice gruel. If there is not enough for rice gruel, cook rice broth. This has been the family teaching of the Sōtō lineage since the time of Furong Daokai (Fuyō Dōkai, 1043–1118).

Monastic administrators must serve all monks with a large heart. The monastic cook is to balance the three virtues of cooked food and to cultivate the two fields of merit. Even the entire great earth could never exhaust the twenty years lifespan of limitless blessings bequeathed by Śākyamuni Buddha.

Now, I ask you assembled monks, as for the activities of endless merit, what then?

Keizan paused for awhile and then said: In the dark grotto valley [i.e., Yō-kōji], coming and going regardless of the locked barrier, walk the two-headed men.

The text above address clarifies the history of this monastery. I have written down the details for future reference.

SONIN'S PLEDGE

1321: GEN'Ō 3, JUNIOR METAL YEAR OF THE COCK

New spring (1st moon), the following was recorded:

This monastery is located within the Sakai Estate, in the district of Kashima. Its property boundaries are listed in its deed. Lady Taira Sonin is the daughter of Sakō Hachirō Yorichika and is the wife of Unno Saburō Shigeno Nobunao. The two of them, Sonin and Unno Nobunao, donated this land as an act of faith.

They declared: "We donate this small mountain. We desire only that Master Keizan reside here for awhile. We will take absolutely no notice whether the temple thrives or decays. Also, we are not concerned whether the master observes or violates the Buddhist precepts. Likewise, if the master gives the land to a wife, child or relative, or even to outcasts (*hinin*) and beggars, we will not interfere. We will donate the land to the master once and for all with no intention of ever resuming control. We have long awakened to the mind of no attachments and dare not harbor any material desires."

I was moved by the patrons' pure intentions. I decided this would be my final resting place and would be the pure site at which to intern the remains and writings of our successive patriarchs.

FIRST DREAMS OF YŌKŌJI

1312: SHŌWA 2 [1313], SENIOR WATER YEAR OF THE RAT [1312]

Spring: Sonin awakened her *bodhi*-seeking mind and donated the land. On that night I lodged at the patron's house at Nakakawa. In my dreams I saw the temple buildings appear and in front of the main gate stood a hackberry tree with straw sandals hanging on it. From this, I knew that it would be a superior site where monks would repay the cost of their straw sandals. It was the peaceful, quiet place where I wanted to live out my life in seclusion.

1317: BUNPŌ 1, JUNIOR FIRE YEAR OF THE SNAKE

In response to the desires of Sonin, the patron, and in accord with the dying wishes of Sakō Hachirō Yorimoto, her brother who was the land steward (*jitō*) of Nakakawa, the former residence of their father, Yorichika, was donated to Keizan as an offering for his karmic benefit and for the fulfillment of their prayers. That residence was converted into the Abbot's Square.

8th Moon, Autumn: Moved the residence and rebuilt it as an Abbot's Square.

10th Moon, 2d Day: Moved disciples. Performed formal inauguration ceremony.

1313: SHŌWA 2, JUNIOR WATER YEAR OF THE OX

8th Moon: When I first built a hut to serve as a makeshift kitchen-office (*kuin*), Vajraputra (Bajarahottara), the eighth arhat, came here. After looking over the mountain landscape, he told me: "Although this is a small mountain, it is a superior location. It is superior to Eiheiji. At Eiheiji, the abbot's building sits in a hollow. That is where the obstructing gods reside. All of Eiheiji's past obstructions have resulted from poor location. This mountain monastery, however, has no obstructions. Your propagation of Buddhism and teaching of monks and nuns will succeed as desired." It is true. In the nine years since erecting that hut, there have been no obstructions. Doing nothing special, I practice Buddhism and the monastery flourishes more every year.

1317: Bunpō 1, Junior Fire Year of the Snake

Winter Training Period: Koan Shikan (d. 1341), the comptroller, Genka Tek-kyō (d. 1321), the supervisor of the Monks' Hall, and Kakunichi, the sanitation officer, dreamed the same dream: Inari, the mountain god of this monastery, gave them a favorable announcement. Inari said, "I am the former master of this mountain. I support Buddhism in this province. I will offer salted pickles (etc.)." His spiritual arrow pacifies the mountains to the west. Just one shot pacifies both the mountains in front and in back.

I also had a dream. The guardian god of this province came and reported: "This is a message from the First Shrine of the province. I will supply vegetables." Thus we receive the mystical blessings and protection of the First Shrine.

Also, to protect the temple, I carved a piece of camphor wood into an image of a seated Vaiśravaṇa. His left hand holds a wish-fulfilling jewel and his right hand forms the mudrā of offering. He is the main image in the kitchen. I can feel his protection in my dreams.

Winter: Mahākāla also came. One of the workers observed him.

1318: Bunpō 2, Senior Earth Year of the Horse

Spring: Getsuan Kōei dreamed that the guardian god Shōhō Shichirō came to this mountain to announce: "Enshrine me in the Abbot's Square and I will guard over this lineage and protect this monastery." According to these omens, the mountain god, the First Shrine, and Shōhō Shichirō protect this temple and provide offerings.

Avalokiteśvara used to be the main object of worship in this temple. Therefore, Avalokiteśvara stands alongside the new central image [of Śākyamuni Buddha]. Because Ākāśagarbha rains treasures down to the monks, his image also stands on the other side. Therefore, the three treasures of the Buddha, His Teachings, and His Disciples, the two holy ones (Avalokiteśvara and Ākāśa-garbha), and the two gods (Vaiśravaṇa and Mahākāla) all are patrons who support this monastic community.

1319: Gen'ō 1, Junior Earth Year of the Ram

9th moon, 15th day (full moon): First performed service for arhats. Should be performed every 25th day of each moon. That is what the venerable arhats expect.

I am a sixteenth-generation Dharma descendant of the high patriarch Dong-shan Liangjie [Tōzan Ryōkai, 807–869], who lived on Grotto Mountain. Because I admire his teachings, I named this mountain "Tōkoku" (Grotto Valley). My changing "mountain" to "valley" is based on the precedent of Dongshan's disciple Caoshan Benji [Sōzan Honjaku, 840–901], who named his monastery Caoshan (Sōzan) Mountain in honor of the sixth patriarch's Caoxi Valley.

I am an eleventh-generation Dharma descendant of the high patriarch Dayang, "Great Sun" [Dayang Jingxuan, Taiyō Kyōgen, 943–1027]. Because I admire the Great Shining Sun that fills my eyes, I have named this temple "Yōkōji" (Eternally Shining Temple).

The Buddha Hall is named Highest Victory Hall (Saishōden) because when the Buddha preached the *Highest Victory King Sutra* [*Saishōōkyō*, T 665], the two bodhisattvas Avalokiteśvara and Ākāśagarbha stood by his side.

The Monks' Hall is named Buddha Selecting Site (Senbutsujō) because mental emptiness extends to each.

The Kitchen is named Wafting Scent Hermitage (Kōsekiin) because eating food gives strength.

The Bath is named Source of Enlightening Water (Myōsuiin) because washing away impurities is awakening.

Lady Taira Sonin is the second coming of my grandmother, the laywoman Myōchi, who had been Dōgen's disciple since the time he was at Kenninji Temple in Kyoto. The Lady Sonin and I stick together like steel and a magnet. As teacher and patron, or teacher and disciple, we are inseparable.

1321: Gen'ō 3, Junior Metal Year of the Cock

1st moon, 28th day: Genka Tekkyō passed away. He was one of the first five people I ever ordained, just like the venerable Kaundinya (Chinnyo) who was one of the first five disciples ordained by the Buddha. He had served as Jōmanji Temple's first supervisor and served as supervisor for my master Jakuen (1207–1299) at Hōkyōji Temple. Here at Yōkōji he was assistant abbot. Forever hereafter he should be revered as the supervisor of this temple.

KEIZAN'S AUTOBIOGRAPHY

During the time of the Buddha Vipaśyin (Bibashi Butsu), the first of the Seven Buddhas of the Past:

After having attained the awakening of an arhat I resided in the Himalaya Mountains north of Mount Sumeru, the central axis of the world. At that time there existed a Kokila Bird tree spirit, a four-legged beast with a dog's head, a bird's body and the belly and tail of a reptile. That tree spirit instantly attained enlightenment and to this day, together with venerable Subinda (Sohinda), the fourth arhat, continues to reside among the snowy Himalaya Mountains of Uttara Kuru (Hotsu Kuroshu), the Northern Continent. Likewise, in this present existence I have been born here in northern Japan. I have prior karmic links to the Northern Continent and am a child of Hakusan, the White Mountain.

My eighth year of life [i.e., seven years old, 1271]: Shaving my head as a novice, I joined the community of Master Gikai, then abbot of Eiheiji.

My thirteenth year [1276]: I became a fully ordained monk, the last disciple ordained by Master Ejō, formerly the second abbot of Eiheiji.

My eighteenth year [1281]: I resolved to attain the Way.

My nineteenth year [1282]: While studying under Prior Jakuen I awakened to the *bodhi*-seeking mind and attained the stage of nonretrogression.

My twenty-second year [1285]: Upon hearing a stray sound I attained awakening.

My twenty-fifth year [1288]: Like Avalokiteśvara, I pronounced the universal vow (to save all beings) of the supremely compassionate *icchantika*, who never enter Nirvana.

My twenty-eighth year [1291]: I served as abbot of Jōmanji in Kaifu, Awa Province, Shikoku Island.

My twenty-ninth year [1292]: Elder Gien of Eiheiji authorized me to perform precept ordinations. In early winter of that year, I administered the precepts for the first time, ordaining five people. By my thirty-first year [1294], I had ordained more than seventy people.

My thirty-second year [1295]: I realized the teaching of Master Gikai, the founding abbot of Daijōji, Kaga Province. I inherited Gikai's Dharma line, becoming his foremost disciple and Daijōji's first assistant abbot. Attaining the honor of shared abbotship was Gikai's attestation that I had attained the fortitude to surpass my teacher.

My thirty-third year [1297]: The ceremony for appointing me chief monk was conducted in the abbot's building.

My thirty-fifth year [1298]: I assumed full office by becoming Daijōji's second abbot. For nineteen years I instructed students at Daijōji, until [in 1317] I moved to this monastery (Yōkōji) as its founding abbot.

Ever since having realized the fruit of awakening, throughout five hundred rebirths I have appeared in bodily form in order to propagate the Dharma and benefit the living.

Bodhidharma appeared in a dream and ordered me to bathe in the pure water flowing out of the rocks at the base of his seat. Bathing in the icy pool, I was naked. He presented me with a *kaṣāya* robe. Placing it on, I awakened to the *bodhi*-seeking mind.

The future Buddha Maitreya appeared in a dream and presented me with a blue lotus throne. It transported me through three rebirths. He led me flying across the sky. Celestial beings performed music to send off Maitreya. As he led me to the inner palace in Tuṣita heaven, I attained the stage of nonretrogression.

Śākyamuni appeared in a dream and manifested his bodily form of preaching the *Ratnakūṭa Sūtra* (*Hōshakukyō, T* 310). He explained the three methods of liberation, namely, liberation through opportunity, liberation through mind, and liberation through objects.

My fifty-eighth year [1321]: On this first night of the beginning of spring, in the third year of the Gen'ō era, I have sat in meditation, neither dreaming nor awake, testifying to the seal of awakening.

KEIZAN'S MOTHER

1322: Genkō 2, Senior Water Year of the Dog

6th moon, 18th day: Established the Universally Pervading (Enzūin) Avalokiteśvara Hermitage at Supreme Lotus Peak (Shōrenpō) and appointed as its first abbess Sister Sonin, the main patron of Yōkōji Temple. Its main object of worship is the image of an eleven-headed Avalokiteśvara that my compassionate mother of this rebirth had kept and worshipped throughout her life.

The history of this image of Avalokiteśvara began during my compassionate mother's eighteenth year [ca. 1244–1245]. She had become separated from my grandmother and did not know where grandmother had gone. For seven or eight years my mother suffered distress over this. Finally, she went to the Avalokiteśvara Worship Hall of the Kiyomizudera to perform seven days of worship. On the sixth day, along the road to the temple she purchased the head of this image of Avalokiteśvara. She thereupon made the following declaration and prayer. "While traveling to the Kiyomizu in order to pray for knowledge of my mother's whereabouts, I have obtained the head of this image and thereby will establish a karmic connection. If this connection is true, then show me some of your compassion. If you help me find my mother, then I will complete your body and worship you my whole life."

The next day, on the road, she met a woman. The following day, on the way to worship at Kiyomizu, they met again and the woman informed my mother of her mother's whereabouts. She immediately went to a Buddhist artisan and ordered a body carved for this image of Avalokiteśvara. Thereafter she continued her devotions to it all of her life.

One morning when my compassionate mother was in her thirty-seventh year [ca. 1263–1264], she dreamed that she had swallowed the warmth of the morning sunlight. She had a sensation in her womb and realized that she had become pregnant. At that point she prayed to this image, saying, "If this unborn child is to become a holy man, is to become a great religious master and is to become of benefit to gods and men, then let me have an easy delivery. However, if these are not to be, then, Avalokiteśvara, use your spiritual powers to wither it dead while still in my womb."

Every day she made 3,333 prostrations and recitations of the *Avalokiteśvara Sūtra* (*Kannongyō*). After seven months, while traveling on the road to the birthing room, she calmly gave birth to me. She named me Yukio (Traveling Birth). I was born in the Avalokiteśvara Worship Hall in Tane Village, Echizen. After that, in all affairs and concerns, she would pray to this image.

My career has been without difficulty. All the good things that I have accomplished—my becoming a monk, my study of literature, my Buddhist training, my attainment of knowledge, as well as my Dharma succession, my abbotship and my teaching gods and men—occurred because of the power of my mother's prayers to this image.

And that is not all. When I was young, I was hateful and would pass by people as if they were my inferiors. Therefore, my mother again prayed to this image, saying, "Keizan, in spite of his ability, his cleverness, his wisdom, and his being better than the rest, will never be of benefit to gods and people as long as his hatefulness continues to increase. With the power of prayer, put an end to his hatefulness."

By that time, in the winter of my eighteenth year [1281], I had awakened to the Way-seeking mind, and in the autumn of my nineteenth year [1282] I strengthened my resolve to pursue the Way. Finally, I began serving as group leader, managing Hōkyōji Temple's affairs at the head of the other monks. Everyone was happy for me. Then, one person spoke ill of me. My hatefulness flared up. I was ready to commit a major transgression. Yet, while planning my revenge, I repented my anger. I thought, "Since youth I have tried to better myself and surpass others. Now, I have awakened my *bodhi*-seeking mind and serve in this monastic office. My goal is to master Buddhism and to teach gods and men. That is my vow. If I commit an evil act, then the way will be closed to me. From now on I will not be hateful." Since then, I have gradually developed compassion and compliancy. And now, I have become a great master.

All of this is due to the power of my mother's prayers. Therefore, in her eighty-seventh year [ca.1313–1314] when my compassionate mother passed away, she bequeathed this image to me.

[In 1317] when I entered this mountain as abbot of Yōkōji, I designated one hill, named Supreme Lotus Peak (located next to Circuitous Stream Peak and Millet Sprout Field). I have built a retreat there, named Universally Pervading Avalokiteśvara Hermitage, and appointed as its first abbess Sister Sonin, the main patron of Yōkōji Temple. I also have presented her with clippings of my hair and my preserved umbilical cord along with my compassionate mother's image of Avalokiteśvara. It is now the main object of worship at this hermitage. Because Sonin is unequaled in her faith and her purity and has awakened her *bodhi*-seeking mind, I have given this image to her. The hair clippings and umbilical cord are to be placed to the right of the image. They should be kept in a pewter box.

I have written this for future reference. Henceforth Universally Pervading Avalokiteśvara Hermitage will offer prayers to protect Yōkōji Temple, prayers to fulfill my mother's vow to save all women, and prayers for Keizan's promotion of the Buddhist Dharma that benefits the living. This is the history of the Universally Pervading Avalokiteśvara Hermitage.

The geomancy of this land indicates that a hermitage should be located at Supreme Lotus Peak. That is why the monk Myōshinbō occasionally has heard the mystical sounds like an assembly of monks reciting scriptures there. I spoke of this while preparing the site this spring. There can be no doubt that those sounds were good omens for the hermitage. Yōkōji's Buddha Hall and the Universally Pervading Avalokiteśvara Hermitage were constructed the same year.

—45—

Tōkeiji: Kamakura's "Divorce Temple"
in Edo Popular Verse

Sachiko Kaneko and Robert E. Morrell

Many Japanese today have heard echoes of popular Edo accounts of the unhappily married woman who, if she could manage to toss a single clog over the walls of Kamakura's "Divorce Temple" (Enkiridera), would be protected from her pursuers and could eventually arrange a separation from her husband. Predictably, historical records tell a less dramatic story, but one that touches issues basic to our understanding of interactions between church and state, convents in Japan, and Buddhist attitudes toward women.

The convent was founded in 1285 by Kakusan Shidō (1252–1305), widow of Hōjō Tokimune (1251–1284), the Kamakura military ruler who repelled the Mongol invasions in 1274 and 1281. Tokimune and his wife, Lady Horiuchi—Kakusan was her religious name—were both students of Zen practice under the Chinese abbot Wu-hsüeh Tsu-yüan (Mugaku Sogen, 1226–1286), who was installed as founding abbot of Kamakura's Temple of Perfect Enlightenment (Engakuji) in 1282. When Tokimune suddenly became ill and died two years later, Kakusan and her son, Sadatoki, who succeeded his father as Hōjō regent, collaborated to establish the Eastern Temple of Rejoicing (Tōkeiji), within a stone's throw of the Engakuji.

Kakusan and Tokimune shared common interests, and we have every reason to believe that they enjoyed a happily married life. For four centuries after its founding, Tōkeiji's reputation was as a "Temple into which One Runs for Refuge" (*kakekomidera*), the specific association of "refuge" with "divorce" (*enkiri*) appearing quite late in its history. In the so-called November Incident in 1285, Sadatoki, suspecting political intrigue, ordered the extermination of many members of the Adachi clan, to whom Kakusan was related. It is probable that Kakusan would have liked to have seen her convent as a temple of refuge, of sanctuary for the innocent from political harassment. But were there any precedents?

We experience the world both as social creatures and as individuals. Our institutions and our philosophies attempt to reconcile group commitments to personal needs and aspirations, for any imbalance jeopardizes the quality of our lives. Without effective social controls, selfish interests infringe on the common good and the strong dominate the weak. Conversely, when an individual is not given adequate institutional and philosophical means to evade the tyranny of majority opinion, his or her frustration may be resolved by madness or suicide. Or, if one's lot is endurable, one may protest by attempting social change, or one may escape into dissipation. People of both sexes have often found themselves victims of this tyranny, in both Japan and the West; and in both parts of the world, the convent and the monastery have been available, at least until the secularization of modern society, as an alternative to the more extreme solutions of the problem of social alienation. They have provided a way out, sanctuary, asylum, for those whom society would break. Until as late as the French Revolution, the Christian Church was able to exercise the right of sanctuary, as popularized in Victor Hugo's *Hunchback of Notre Dame.*

After the fall of imperial Rome in 476, the Christian Church, widely accepted as the sole guardian of God's revelation to mankind, had strong centers of ecclesiastical authority in the West as the nations of modern Europe took shape from the ruins of the old coalition. Tensions between church and state, revealed in the confrontations of Frederick I (Redbeard) with Pope Alexander III, England's Henry II with Thomas Becket, and Henry VIII with Clement VII, occurred as secular nationalism challenged the power of the well-established institutions of the church. As a dominant institution reshaping the post-Roman world, the Western monasticism of St. Benedict (ca. 480–ca. 547) and his successors was often comfortably beyond the reach of secular interference. Such great abbeys as Cluny and Westminster, their allegiance being primarily to Rome, could for centuries maintain autonomy in the face of kings and princes. This competition was healthy for society as a whole, since each side provided a check on the other's excesses. An echo of these ancient rivalries can doubtless be found in the principle of a balance of power incorporated in our modern legal institutions: a state that succeeds in suppressing internal dissent from official policy enjoys only a pyrrhic victory by deactivating a self-correcting mechanism for its own health and safety.

Buddhism was never so autonomous in the countries of East Asia as the Christian Church was in the West. From its inception there was little doctrinal incentive to establish a single center of authority. The first Three Councils in India, through the period of Aśoka (r. 269–237 B.C.E.), did attempt to establish a common scriptural canon and general principles of belief and behavior; but the spirit of the movement was centrifugal, and the Mahāyāna even rationalized theoretical diversity with its doctrine of skillful means (Skt. *upāya*, J. *hōben*). When Buddhism finally made its appearance in China and Japan, it was as an association of administratively independent sects often competing with one another while recognizing a common commitment to the Buddha's teachings. Politically they were too disorganized to present a strong common front against secular authority. The eminent Chinese monk Hui-yüan (Eon, 334–416), pioneer of Amida pietism, might argue persuasively during a period of political disunity that "A Monk Does Not Bow Down Before a King" (*Sha-men pu-ching wang-che lun*), but Buddhism was eventually subordinated to the state by three major persecutions, and a monolithic Confucian political ideology. Ironically, by successfully eliminating its competition, Confucianism removed the very challenge that might have kept it from stagnating.

The Buddhist sects in Japan fared somewhat better than they did in China, at least until Nobunaga's destruction of Tendai's Enryakuji on Mount Hiei in 1571, the decentralization of the powerful Honganji Pure Land sect, and the establishment of Neo-Confucianism as the official ideology of the Tokugawa military regime. Unfortunately, they never enjoyed the independence of their Western counterparts—to the detriment of both church and state.

But Buddhism in both China and Japan could provide the individual with a moral defense against the overwhelming claims of secular authority. It could give Nichiren (1222–1282) and Dōgen (1200–1253), for example, grounds for appeal to principles of human behavior beyond the authority of the bakufu: they could dare to defy the military establishment because of their primary allegiance to the Buddha's Teaching. During the Jōkyū Disturbance in 1221, when Myōe (Kōben, 1173–1232) was brought before the leader of the Kamakura military government and Tokimune's great-grandfather, Hōjō Yasutoki (1183–1242), on charges of having given shelter to the defeated enemies of the state at his Kozanji Temple in the hills northwest of Kyoto, he replied by appealing to a higher authority:

> There is a report that I have given refuge to a large number of stragglers, and this is indeed true. . . . Because this mountain temple is a site dedicated to the Three Treasures of Buddhism, it is a place where taking life is forbidden. Birds pursued by falcons, and animals fleeing from hunters, all conceal themselves here just to survive. Thus I accept the responsibility for the fact that soldiers fleeing from their enemies— their only thought being to save their lives—conceal themselves here among the roots of trees and the clefts of rocks. . . . If I could, I would hide these stragglers in my sleeves or under my surplice. . . . If this is in violation of the way of good government, then you should without delay sever this foolish monk's head. (Kubota and Yamaguchi, eds., *Togano-o Myōe Shōnin denki*, 163–165)

Deeply moved, Yasutoki dismissed all charges. Myōe, a dedicated monk who shunned political maneuvering, was revered in his time by people of every sect as the model cleric. For Kakusan, the notion of a convent as sanctuary may have been inspired by Myōe's example.

During the Edo period (1615–1867), the Tōkeiji became popularly known as the "Divorce Temple" (Enkiridera) when it was a center for a relative handful of disaffected wives of the commoner, but not of the samurai, class. As family relationships became increasingly oppressive over time, principally as the result of official government support of male-oriented Neo-Confucianism, the number of women seeking divorce at the Tōkeiji correspondingly increased. Tōkeiji and one other convent, the Mantokuji northwest of Edo, became widely known as "divorce temples." For those who served in the convent for a specified period of time—two to three years—the Tōkeiji arranged for a divorce to be given them by their husbands. Not being an arm of the government, it could not itself issue a divorce; but it was able to exert sufficient social pressures to effect the same result. A few of the fugitives stayed on to take the tonsure, but they were by far the exception.

By some estimates more than 2,000 divorces were arranged through the Tōkeiji during the last century and a half of the Edo period. Records for only 380 cases survive, represented by over 800 documents, none of which was executed before 1738. When we consider the entire population of Japan over a period of 150 years, 2,000 cases of divorce must represent a minuscule fraction of unhappily married women; and the geographical locations of Tōkeiji and Mantokuji limited their influence to a few adjacent areas around Edo. Although they were not an effective practical solution to this social problem, they were at least able to stand as symbols that a woman's rights could be protected by appeal to principles beyond the demands of a rigid social structure.

In our age of concern for women's rights, we should be careful not to generalize from the social behavior in Edo Japan to earlier periods of Japanese history. Let us first of all remember the prominent role in mythological and early historical periods of women as Himiko, Jingū, Suiko, Gemmei, and (Empress) Shōtoku, and that the main deity of the Shintō pantheon is female. Then we note the great flowering of Japanese literature during the Heian period dominated by women. And when we come to Kakusan in the Kamakura period, we find no delicate, pampered court lady; but neither do we find a disenfranchised wretch like Kane, whose story will be told below. Kakusan grew up in harsh times dominated by the spartan ideals of the newly risen samurai class, in the tradition of Kiyomori's wife, Nii-dono, who sank beneath the waves with the child Emperor Antoku at the Battle of Dannoura; of Yoshitsune's mistress, Shizuka Gozen; of Yoshinaka's wife, the warrior Tomoe; of Yoritomo's wife, Masako, the "Nun Shogun"; of Horiuchi's aunt, Matsushita Zenni, whose thrifty patching of *shōji* is extolled in Kenkō's *Essays in Idleness*; and of the aristocratic but forceful wife of Fujiwara Teika's son, Tameie, the nun Abutsu (d. 1283). Even making allowance for differences in social class, there is a great falling off by the time we get to Kane in the Tokugawa period. Unfortunately, our modern stereotype of the traditional Japanese woman as forever docile and exploited, like many of our other commonplace notions about Japan, is largely the product of a period spanning only about two and a half centuries—although without question a most important period for an understanding of modern Japan. It does not tell us the whole story; but, willy-nilly, it is where we find the Tōkeiji as "Divorce Temple."

On entering the convent a woman might submit a statement of grievances, as we see in the following case from Kaei 3 (1850):

> Eight years ago when I was fourteen, I was adopted by the landlord, Shichibei, of 2-chōme, Kanda, [Edo]. Four years later I became Kanjirō's wife, through the help of Kanematsu, a tenant of Tauemon of Renjakuchō and we moved to the house owned

by Tauemon. Kanjirō, my husband, would frequent houses of prostitution and seldom came home. Our household became so destitute that I appealed to my own father, Kimbei, of 4-chōme, Hongō, who kindly gave me some rice. I pawned my clothes. When my husband ordered me to ask my father for more money and I objected, he became furious and struck me on the head with a *geta* until I was badly hurt. I knew that he was short-tempered, so I endured these abuses.

Then Kanjirō wanted me to become a prostitute, but I told him it was out of the question. He became very disagreeable, refused to earn a livelihood, and often would not come home for three days.

Having become helpless, I left Kanjirō this year in the fifth month. With only the summer dress I had on, I went to my mother's native home to live with Uncle Sōemon at Neriki-mura in Kazusa Province. In the hope of leaving Kanjirō, I sent Kanematsu an envelope containing a lock of my hair and combs for my husband, together with a letter requesting that a divorce be arranged. But Kanjirō only caused trouble.

Finally I have decided to seek refuge in your honorable temple. I have not violated my integrity as a woman. But there is little left for me except to throw myself into the sea or a river if my plea is not heard. I beg you to graciously arrange a divorce for me.

Kaei 3 (1850), the twenty-first day of the tenth month
4-chōme, Hongō
Landlord Kimbei
Daughter Kane (Seal)

Kane also notified the convent that her personal property consisted of seven items: two kimonos in a striped pattern, two sashes, two hair ornaments, and a mirror. She stated that these were taken by Kanjirō to a pawn shop, and she testified that she took neither money nor any other goods from Kanjirō's household.

Tōkeiji then issued a summons to Kanjirō and to Kane's family. But Kanjirō had already filed a petition with the town magistrate, Toyama Saemon, to recover his wife. So he and Kane's father sent an acknowledgment to the Tōkeiji for the summons and indicated that they would come to the temple after they received instructions from the town magistrate. When Kanjirō subsequently instituted a countersuit for divorce, the statement from Kane's father confirmed his daughter's list of grievances to the temple. Although the later documents have not survived, it is believed that Kane served her term of service at the Tōkeiji and was granted the divorce.

Such social problems provided rich subject matter for a popular entertainment of the eighteenth-century Edo townsman, the new verse form called *senryū*, after the pen name of its most prominent promoter, Karai Hachiemon (Senryū, 1718–1790). Like haiku it consisted of seventeen syllables, usually in groups of 5-7-5. But it required no seasonal reference (*kigo*) or "cutting words" (*kireji*) to indicate a pause or stop and it tended to focus on the curiosities of human entanglements rather than on the aesthetics of the human condition. The great Matsuo Bashō (1644–1694) might well argue that his haiku was high art (*ga*), but no one could make the claim for *senryū*. Still, its deft sketching of the townsman's attitudes and moods make vivid for us times and social circumstances long gone. Among its stanzas available in modern printings are some five hundred composed with reference to the divorce temple at Pine Grove (Matsugaoka).

Senryū arose from the practice of stanza-linking (*tsukeai*) in linked verse (*renga*), a popular diversion known as "connecting with a preceding stanza" (*maekuzuke*). A foundation stanza (*maeku*), usually the 7-7 portion of the *tanka*-like unit of thirty-one syllables, was provided to a second player who added a "joined stanza" (*tsukeku*) of 5-7-5. The townsman "poet," with few artistic pretensions, would submit his "joined stanza" to a judge together with a small fee, perhaps sixteen *mon* (about twenty *yen* in today's currency). In ten-thousand-stanza competitions (*mankuawase*) the total of these fees would make a tidy sum. In the popular competitions of the Genroku period (1688–1703), small prizes were awarded for the best verses, competition was intense, and the entertainment degenerated into a kind of gambling. During the Kōō period (1716–1735) the authorities prohibited its practice, but as restrictions relaxed, stanza connecting made a strong comeback. It is from this time that we have the first written records of such competitions. The first major collection of stanza-connecting is *Mutama River* (Mutamagawa) by the competition judge Kei Kiitsu (1695–1762), compiled in 1750 and published in 1774. Some stanzas follow the standard linking, but others have as their foundation stanza the 5-7-5 phrase and a joined stanza of 7-7. Several of its verses pertaining to the Tōkeiji are to be found among the translations below.

But in the history of *senryū* Kei Kiitsu gives way to his younger contemporary, Karai Hachiemon, whose very pen name, Senryū, has become synonymous with the genre. He was the most popular judge of ten-thousand-stanza competitions between 1757 and 1789, the year before his death. His decisions, published annually in short pamphlets, are known collectively as *Ten-Thousand-Stanza Competitions Judged by Senryū* (*Senryūhyō mankuawase*). It is estimated that the 80,000 items selected for inclusion in these pamphlets represent perhaps 3 percent of 2,300,000 stanzas submitted for his decision.

From this literary pool the editor Gorōken Arubeshi (Momen) culled a group of 756 stanzas for the first book of *The Willow Barrel [of Poems in the Haikai Style]* (*[Haifū] Yanagidaru*), published in 1765. Gorōken published twenty-two more annual publications between 1767 and 1789. With the twenty-fourth book, compiled by Karakuan Hitokuchi and published in 1791, the year after Senryū's death, the core of the Yanagidaru collection was complete. But subsequent additions until 1840 brought the number of volumes issued under this title to 167. Most of the Matsugaoka-related *senryū* appear either in the *Ten-Thousand-Stanza Competitions Judged by Senryū* or in the derivative *Willow Barrel*.

Senryū continues to be written even today, but the late eighteenth century was its golden age. Karai's selection of verses was also compiled in the *Gleanings after the Willow Barrel* (*Yanagidaru shūi*), known originally as the *Collection of Ancient and Modern Connected Verse* (*Kokonmaekushū*) published posthumously in ten books between 1796 and 1798. The editor is unknown, but it is sometimes credited to Santō Kyōden (1761–1816), famous as a writer of "Yellow-covered Books" (*kibyōshibon*) and as an artist.

Divorce under any circumstances in Edo Japan was rare, at least by modern standards. But for the woman to initiate the process was considered by many to strike at the roots of a stable Confucian society. The writers often, but not always, appear to sympathize with the unhappy woman. Sometimes their lack of familiarity with the customs of the Tōkeiji lead them to make statements which are in error; and at other times they unintentionally throw light on an area perhaps otherwise obscure. Early Western observers of Japan, for example, sometimes claimed that the convent was little more than a brothel. Were this indeed the case, we can be sure that it would not have passed unnoticed by the Edo townsman in his often caustic satirical verse. Perhaps surprisingly, the *senryū* poets never so much as hint about any improprieties at the Tōkeiji.

Although the following *senryū* were composed independently by a number of individuals over a span of years, they are grouped into a sequence beginning with stanzas on the general nature of the Tōkeiji, and then following the refugee from her home, typically from Edo, down the Eastern Sea Route (*Tōkaidō*) to Kamakura. We then see her life at the Tōkeiji and her departure after three years with the letter of separation.

The translations are from texts found in Hozumi Shigetō, *Rikon seido no kenkyū* (Tokyo: Kaizōsha, 1924); Nakanishi Kenji, *Nihon shiden senryū kyōka* (Tokyo: Koten Bunko, 1972–1981); Yamazawa Hideo, ed., (*Haifū*) *Yanagidaru* (Tokyo: Iwanami Shoten, 1950–1956); Yamazawa Hideo, ed., (*Haifū*) *Yanagidaru shūi* (Tokyo: Iwanami Shoten, 1966); and Yoshida Seiichi and Hamada Giichirō, eds., *Senryūshū kyōkashū*, Koten Nihon bungaku zenshū 33 (Tokyo: Chikuma Shobō, 1967). Comments in brackets are those of the translators.

Further Reading

R. H. Blyth, *Edo Satirical Verse Anthologies* (Tokyo: Hokuseido Press, 1961), and any number of other works by this ebullient, prolific (and sometimes controversial) writer who is buried at the Tōkeiji; Kaneko Sachiko and Robert E. Morrell, "Sanctuary: Kamakura's Tōkeiji Convent," *Japanese Journal of Religious Studies* 10, 2–3 (1983): 195–228; Kubota Jun and Yamaguchi Akihō, *Myōe Shōnin shū* (Tokyo: Iwanami Shoten, 1981); Haruyo Lieteau, "The Yasutoki-Myōe Discussion," *Monumenta Nipponica* 30, 2 (1975): 203–210.

Matsugaoka Tōkeiji as Divorce Temple

endan wa	for joining together
Izumo hadan wa	Izumo; for breaking asunder,
Matsugaoka	Matsugaoka

Izumo nite	joined together
musubi Kamakura	at Izumo, separated
nite hodoki	in Kamakura
hikikaramu	untangling
en wo kakikiru	tangled relationships:
kama no tera	Temple of the Sickle

[The Great Shrine at Izumo, dedicated to the Great Land-Rule Deity (Ōkuni-nushi), is the oldest shrine in Japan. It has been a traditional symbol of auspicious marriages, just as the Tōkeiji at Sickle Warehouse (Kama-kura) has been associated with divorce, at least since the middle of the Edo period.]

enoki de	if not at the nettle tree,
torinu sarijō wo	get your letter of separation
matsu de tori	at the pine
mazu enoki	first the nettle-tree—
sore de ikanu to	if this won't cut [the marriage tie],
matsu de kiri	then try the pine.

[Prayer before a certain Chinese nettle-tree in Edo's Itabashi district was thought to help one get a quick divorce. The pine refers, of course, to Matsugaoka (Pine Grove), i.e., Tōkeiji.]

Kamakura e	come to Kamakura
gozare amazake	and "we will give you
shinjō nari	sweet wine"

[The stanza makes a siren's song of a set phrase from the Edo period to the present used to tease or entice children:]

koko made oide	"come here, and sweet
amazake shinjō	rice wine I'll give you."
kuyashiku wa	"if you are upset,
tazune kite miyo	come here and inquire"—
Matsugaoka	Matsugaoka
Matsugaoka	in topsy-turvy fashion,
ama sakasama ni	at Matsugaoka it is the nuns
hima wo toru	who take their leave

[. . . of their husbands, who alone normally had the right to initiate divorce, and most other, proceedings. Our poet does not approve.]

Matsugaoka	Matsugaoka:
hantetsu mono no	a meeting place
yoridokoro	for misfits

Matsugaoka	Matsugaoka:
onnadatera no	a club just for
kaisho nari	women

[And that would never do!]

Matsugaoka	at Matsugaoka—
nyōbō ni natta	only those who were
hito bakari	once wives

[Except, of course, the small contingent of full-fledged permanent nuns.]

te irazu to	those never handled
iu wa jūshoku	by men consist of only
hitori nari	the resident abbess

[At the time this stanza was composed, the Tōkeiji had not, in fact, had a resident abbess since the tenure of Gyokuen from 1728 to 1737. An acting head nun administered the convent until the Meiji period.]

jūjisama	[among all the women]
bakari otoko wo	only the Mother Superior
motte mizu	has not known men

[. . . and yet the Tōkeiji opens its doors to women with marital problems.]

kanzoku wo	having disciples
suru deshi wo motsu	destined to return to the world:
Matsugaoka	Matsugaoka

[Elsewhere those who enter the religious life come with the intention of staying, whether or not they do. But not at the Tōkeiji, where most of the residents can be expected to leave in two to three years.]

hana chiru	we should call it
sato to iubeki wo	"Village of Fallen Flowers"—
Matsugaoka	Matsugaoka

[Or, as composed earlier:]

Matsugaoka	why not call it
hana chiru sato to	"Village of Fallen Flowers"?
naze iwanu	Matsugaoka

[Critics are quick to lament the years of wasted youth but can propose no viable alternative for the exploited. Some are even hostile.]

Kamakura e	going to Kamakura
yuku hazu fudan	is only appropriate for one
ama yobari	always called an "*ama*"

[*Ama* can mean "nun" but also, and perhaps derivatively, "hussy, slut" (Kenkyūsha), a term of denigration for women, especially young women.]

tonda yome	the impossible wife
otera de toshi wo	opts for three years
mittsu tori	at a convent
jō no kowasō	those who enter seem
no ga hairu	to have frightful dispositions:
Matsugaoka	Matsugaoka
doku nyōbō	the vicious wife
ura made mo kuru	returns for a second round
Matsugaoka	to Matsugaoka
mada ibiri-	still trying
takuba Kamakura	to torment him, she goes
made oide	to Kamakura
Kamakura no	what stubbornness:
sabaki wo ukeru	to receive a judgment
ki no tsuyosa	from Kamakura

[While "strength of spirit" (*ki no tsuyosa*) might be applauded today as "will power" or "self-determination," for the writer of this stanza it was simply "intractability, stubbornness."]

kakekomi soshō	at Matsugaoka
bakari aru	nothing but runaway
Matsugaoka	litigation

[To this outside observer, at least, there appears to be no serious religious activity at the Tōkeiji—just divorce proceedings.]

Kamakura de	at Kamakura
hanahada warui	they steer the women
kaji wo toru	way off course

[The nautical imagery—"take the rudder" (*kaji wo toru*), i.e., "steer a course"— is also used for the management of household affairs: *ikka no kaji wo toru*, to "manage household affairs" (Kenkyūsha).]

Matsugaoka	Matsugaoka:
otoko no tame no	an uninviting place
mazui toko	for men
amadera wa	the convent:
otoko no iji wo	where a man's will
tsubusu toko	is crushed

[Another version of this stanza replaces the first line with "Matsugaoka," but the meaning is only slightly changed.]

inu wo sute	leaving the dog,
saru no kakekomu	the monkey takes refuge
Matsugaoka	at Matsugaoka

[The monkey and the dog are known to be incompatible models for the estranged husband and wife. Note the use of the verb "*kakekomu*," cognate with *kakekomi-dera* (Temple of Refuge).]

kuyashisa wa	frustrations
zai Kamakura e	described and sent to those
kaite yari	at Kamakura

[A preliminary inquiry is sent but there is no reply. One must apply in person.]

sōishita	at such a place
toko e amadera	as this they had to build
tate mo oki	a convent!

[Convenient enough for Kakusan, no doubt, but not for those who had to travel thirty-two miles (thirteen *ri*) from Edo. Another possibility turns on the term "woman of Sagami Province" (*Sagami onna*), which in the Edo period could mean "amorous female." Thus, the stanza could be interpreted as: "How strange to establish, in a hotbed of licentiousness, a convent where sex is prohibited for three years."]

THE DECISION TO LEAVE HER HUSBAND, AND THE JOURNEY TO MATSUGAOKA

Kamakura e	before setting off
yuku mae kawa e	for Kamakura is the leap
sude no koto	into the river

[It took considerable determination to apply to the Tōkeiji for refuge and to remain there for three years. Some first attempted suicide by drowning.]

Kamakura no	before Kamakura,
mae ni nisando	she flees two or three times
sato e nige	to her parents' house

Takasago ni	abused by [the pines]
ibirare yome wa	of Takasago, the young wife flees
matsu ni nige	to the pines [of Tōkeiji]

[The old pines of Takasago, ancient symbols of longevity, here refer to her husband's parents. And so the woman takes refuge among other pines, at Matsugaoka (Pine Grove).]

abumi kara	from [Musashi] stirrups
kura made yome no	to [Kamakura] saddle, the wife
ikkiochi	rides down alone

[Musashi Province, in which Edo was located, was known for manufacturing a variety of stirrups called *Musashi abumi*: as spoken (or written in *kana*), the *kura* of Kamakura could be understood as "saddle," although the proper characters mean "warehouse." The interest of the verse turns on its horse-related items. According to Tōkeiji documents, most of the refugees came from Sagami and Musashi provinces, the modern prefectures of Kanagawa, Saitama, and Tokyo. There were also some from Kazusa and Shimōsa provinces (Chiba Prefecture), but these were of less interest to the Edo-based *senryū* poets.]

kotchi e wa	from her parents' house
konu to sato kara	they come out all upset, saying:
sawagidashi	"she didn't come back here."

[The wife is missing. Has she returned home, gone to a friend's house, committed suicide, or perhaps started on her way to Matsugaoka?]

sato kara mo	also from her parents' house,
so-shiranu kao de	coming out to inquire and pretending
tazune ni de	that they don't know

kakioki no	a note left behind
koto namu san to	"good heavens!" he exclaims—
jūsan ri	thirteen *ri*

[. . . from Edo's Nihombashi to the Tōkeiji.]

Matsugaoka	Matsugaoka:
Edo no uchi kara	here she came having heard of it
kikite iki	at her house in Edo

Matsugaoka	to Matsugaoka
surikogi kizu wo	she goes with bruises received
ukete yuki	from the wooden pestle

[In a comparable Western situation the poet would doubtless speak of a rolling pin rather than a pestle.]

Matsugaoka	Matsugaoka
onna no hitori	is one place to which women
yuku tokoro	travel alone

[Usually when she makes a journey, the wife is accompanied by family, relatives, and friends. And so also is she likely to be on her return.]

shinkon ni	with grim
tesshite yome wa	determination the wife travels
jūsan ri	the thirteen *ri*

[. . . from Edo's Nihombashi to the Tōkeiji. A *ri* is 2.44 miles/3.93 kilometers.]

Kamakura e	to Kamakura
yome aruite mo	the young wife walks,
aruite mo	and walks

[So, if she could afford it, she is more likely to have hired a four-strut palanquin [*yotsude kago*], a small light conveyance named for the four struts of bamboo on each corner of the cabin. A single pole through the top was supported on the shoulders of runners in front and behind.]

Kamakura e	"to Kamakura"—
mese to yotsude wa	and the palanquin bearers
sore to miru	get the idea
ikuji naki	timidly inquiring
nari de kiki kiki	time and time again:
jūsan ri	thirteen *ri*
hakkuri itte	"go eight or nine *ri*
kikasshare to	down the road and ask someone"—
watashimori	the ferryboat captain

[The crossing of Rokugō River separating Edo and Kawasaki was the major hurdle of the journey. Rokugō is a special name for the lower portion of the Tamagawa River, especially where the stream now flows down from Rokugō Bridge at the intersection of Kawasaki City and Tokyo's Ōta Ward. In the early Edo period there also seems to have been a bridge spanning the river, but by the late eighteenth century it had to be crossed by ferry. Beyond the river the fugitive would have to travel through Tsurumi, Kanagawa (Yokohama), Hodogaya, and Totsuka, where a spur off the great Tōkaidō road led to Kamakura.]

kuri aru yo	nine *ri* to go!
isogasshai to	"you'd better hurry," exhorts
watashimori	the ferryman
onna no	eloping,
kakeochi Rokugō	the woman runs toward
sashite yuki	Rokugō

[Here is a switch. Usually it is the abused wife, not the eloping lover, who races toward Rokugō.]

sono fune	"come over here,"
koko e to iu uchi	she calls to the ferryboat—
otte kuru	the family in hot pursuit
mae ni wa	before her,
ōkawa ushiro kara	a large river behind her,
teishu kuru	the pursuing husband

[But having crossed the Rokugō River, the runaway feels a bit more relaxed and may decide to stop at Kawasaki's well-known Mannenya for tea or perhaps at the Tsuruya (Crane Shop), or Kameya (Turtle Shop), famous for their bean cakes in the shapes of cranes and turtles. The average traveler would walk about ten *ri* (roughly twenty-five miles/forty kilometers) a day. So if she started in the morning, this would mark the halfway point.]

Matsugaoka	to Matsugaoka—
made ni manjū	but along the way she samples
futatsu kui	two pieces of bean cake

Matsugaoka	"she's going to Matsugaoka"—
da to manjūya	the proprietor of the sweet-bean shop
minuitari	is most observant

Hanareyama	"Here is Separation Hill"—
to wa kisō na	a good omen for those on their way
Matsugaoka	to Matsugaoka

[A short distance before arriving at the city along the Kamakura Road, the traveler passes this small hill on the right, followed by Koshiyama and Jiōyama.]

Yakimochizaka	at Jealousy Hill
amadera no	she inquires about the road
michi wo kiki	to the convent

un no nasa	bad luck:
Yakimochizaka de	at Jealousy Hill
ottsukare	apprehended

[Yakimochizaka (Jealousy Hill) is in Totsuka, north of and close to, Kamakura.]

sekikonde	"where is the temple
sarijō no deru	that serves separation papers?"
tera to kiki	she inquires hastily

amadera wo	how pitiful
tazuneru kao no	the face of one inquiring
kinodoku sa	about the convent!

yatsu shichigō	lost among
magotsuite	[Kamakura's] Seven Valleys
yome aruki	wanders the young wife

urotaeta	in a dither
onna gosan wo	the woman races here and there
atchi kotchi	among the Five Mountains

urotaeta	Kenchōji:
kakeiri mo aru	here too are runaways,
Kenchōji	in a dither

[The runaway has almost reached her goal. Kenchōji is just down the road, south of the Engakuji and its neighboring Tōkeiji.]

Engakuji	just in front of
mae nite yome wo	Engakuji he apprehends
tokamaeru	his wife

[The Tōkeiji, and freeedom, was just a stone's throw away from the Engakuji. But others are more fortunate.]

jūsan ri	after a solo trip
dokukō wo shite	of thirteen ri, cutting
en wo kiri	the marriage tie

rōcha	in she runs,
kite wa tobikomu	dressed in Rō brown—
Matsugaoka	Matsugaoka

["Rō brown" was the name of a color made fashionable by the Kabuki actor, Segawa Kiku no ō II (1741–1773), also known as Rō. Was Matsugaoka just another frivolous diversion for the current runaway, or did she have her reasons?]

Matsugaoka	Matsugaoka:
niko niko dereba	while one leaves all smiles,
beso beso ki	another arrives weeping

Kamakura no	you cannot enter
rō wa daitete	the prison at Kamakura
irerarezu	carrying a child

[If a woman was confined in a civil prison, her children would be sent to live with relatives. So the poet suggests that the convent is also a kind of prison, where children are not permitted.]

Matsugaoka	Matsugaoka:
me wo sasu hodo wa	enough [milk left in her breasts]
mada nokori	to squirt as far as her eye

[Some of the refugees might still be nursing mothers. And in Edo Japan as today, the new burdens of caring for a baby may have aggravated existing tensions with her husband. Some may have come as far as the Tōkeiji, only to decide that three years of separation from their child was too long.]

midorigo ni	pining
hikarete Omatsu	for her baby, Omatsu
tachikaeri	returns home

[The stanza trades on several puns: Omatsu (Miss Pine) as a woman's name, and Matsu-gaoka (Pine Grove), whose trees are green (*midori*). Written with a different character, *midori* is also the first element of *midorigo*, "child."]

[Meanwhile, the runaway's family and neighbors are out looking for her.]

jūsan ri	thirteen *ri*:
giri de tabidatsu	neighbors on either side come along
ryōdonari	out of obligation

[. . . but it's a bother.]

kinjo no shū	the neighbors
mazu kawasuji wo	first of all check out
kokorogake	the river bank

[. . . before committing themselves to a boat crossing and a lengthy expedition to find the runaway.]

tashika ni	certainly this road
michi yome no ato	will put him on his wife's trail —
jūsan ri	thirteen *ri*

jūsan ri	thirteen *ri*
saki da ni tatta	away, but he inquires
yo ri tazune	for only four

[The husband only looks for his wife for four of the thirteen *ri* to Kamakura because he is searching in an area with a radius of four *ri* from Nihombashi. There are other alternatives to her having gone to the Tōkeiji.]

uranai e	to a fortune-teller
hitori Rokugō e	goes one, while two or three
nisannin	head for Rokugō

ido ya kawa	checking wells
nozoki Rokugō	and rivers along the way,
sashite yuki	they move toward Rokugō

[Has the woman committed suicide, or has she gone to the Tōkeiji? But Rokugō is a bottleneck, and sometimes they find her.]

uranatte	"a fortune teller
kita to Rokugō	told me I'd find you here"—
de oitsuki	caught at Rokugō

Rokugō de	at Rokugō
yōyō yome wo	they finally apprehend
toramaeru	the young wife

[But if they don't, the pursuers still have a good distance to travel to Kamakura, with no guarantee of success. And if they arrive at the ferry too late, they may have to spend the night before crossing.]

Rokugō no	the pursuers
ichiban fune ni	take passage on Rokugō's
oite nori	first boat of the day
Kamakura da	she is already in Kamakura,
no ni maigo no	but still they call out: "Oaki,
Oaki yai	poor lost child!"
Kamakura no	her palanquin
modoru yotsude ni	returning from Kamakura is passed
otte ai	by the pursuers

[. . . who are probably not aware that it was the one she hired. And suppose the wife has not fled to Matsugaoka after all?]

Kamakura ni	"she is not
inai to koto ga	at Kamakura," they say—
muzukashii	a difficult situation

[Or perhaps the family arrives just as she slips into the Tōkeiji, where her pursuers may not enter.]

oitsuita	having finally
tokoro ga kao wo	caught up with her, they only
mita bakari	glimpse her face
karakago de	the pursuers return
otte no modoru	with an empty palanquin
Matsugaoka	from Matsugaoka

LIFE AT THE CONVENT

[For the regulars the daily routine is occasionally broken by the news that a new candidate for divorce has arrived, but soon everyone is back to her daily chores, including tidying up the temple grounds.]

ima yoi	"a good runaway
kakekomi ga atta	has just arrived"—
haite iru	sweeping as usual

[The newcomer has successfully made it to the Tōkeiji. Now she must present a convincing case, and, if accepted into the convent, adjust to an unfamiliar lifestyle.]

Matsugaoka	at Matsugaoka:
Naracha no mama to	"All I had was some Nara tea,"
gatsu gatsu shi	gobbling down her food
kurumaza no	seated within
bikuni no naka e	a circle of nuns—
hazukashisa	shyness
Matsugaoka	At Matsugaoka
guchi de nai no wa	those who don't complain
irenu tokoro	don't get in

[The meaning of the stanza is somewhat ambiguous since *guchi* can mean either "stupid" or "complaining." One interpretation cites the old phrase, "women are foolish creatures" (*onna wa guchi na mono*) and argues that the negation, *guchi de nai*, therefore refers to "men." Hence, those not "foolish" (i.e., men) cannot enter the Tōkeiji."]

Kamakura ni	would that
nebaru makura no	there were greasy pillows
araba koso	in Kamakura!

[Pillows soiled by heavy hair oil, such as that of the camellia, are unpleasant enough, but the writer of the stanza suggests that they are preferable to the sexless pillows at Matsugaoka.]

kokoro nai	all those many
makura no ōi	loveless pillows:
Matsugaoka	Matsugaoka
Kamakura de	At Kamakura
tawara no yō na	the pillows look like
makura wo shi	rice bags

[Tōkeiji evidently used *kukurimakura*, pillows made of straw stuffed with batting or husks. No doubt they were more comfortable than "box pillows" (*hako-*

makura), used to keep the hair from getting ruffled, but they were harder on one's vanity— part of the price to be paid for the separation paper.]

sannen wa	"for three years
zai Kamakura to	I will reside in Kamakura"—
kakugo suru	she is resigned
Kamakura no	for three years
matsu ni sannen	among the pines of Kamakura
mi wo kakushi	she secludes herself
ii musume	a fine girl
hotokegakushi ni	in seclusion with Buddha
mitose nari	for three years

[The worldly writer of this stanza—no Bashō—apparently considered the religious life inappropriate for the young and attractive.]

nakōdo wa	for three years,
mitose uramiru	bitterness toward the go-between—
tsurai koto	what a pain!
nakōdo wa	the go-between
sennichi amari	for more than a thousand days
uramirare	is resented

[. . . by the husband's family, which no doubt feels that she made a poor choice. But the new arrivals at the Tōkeiji could not care less, and have new friends to meet.]

omae mo ka	"you, too?
watashi mo ku sa to	I am also nineteen"—
Matsugaoka	Matsugaoka

[Literally, "nine" (*ku*), but "nineteen" is implied. This was considered to be an unlucky age, since *jū* ("ten") could be construed, with a different character, as "heavy," or "double"; *ku*, also with a different character, can mean "pain." The two young women commiserate.]

Matsugaoka	Matsugaoka:
aimitagai no	sharing each other's
shaku wo oshi	discontents
Matsugaoka	at Matsugaoka
nita koto bakari	they talk to each other
hanashiai	about similar things

kore yue to	"here's the culprit,"
ekubo tsukiau	tweaking each other's dimples:
Matsugaoka	Matsugaoka

[Trouble with the husband frequently arose from his affair with another woman.]

watchi ga mo	"so does my husband
yuku to butsusa to	go out to gamble and whore"—
Matsugaoka	Matsugaoka

oyako shite	"parents and son
ibirimashita to	all tormented me to death"—
Matsugaoka	Matsugaoka

minna shite	"everyone
ibirimashita to	did something to abuse me"—
Matsugaoka	Matsugaoka

nureta sode	the young wife
yome Kamakura no	dries her wet sleeves on the pines
matsu de hoshi	of Kamakura

[Sleeves wet by tears of distress (a standard image in courtly poetry), or sleeves wet because of an unsuccessful attempt at drowning? Perhaps both.]

matsukaze wo	hearing the wind
uhatsu no ama de	in the pines for three years
mitose kiki	as an unshorn nun

[Only the very few who pledged to become lifetime nuns had to take the tonsure. But the Edo townsmen who composed these stanzas sometimes misunderstood the convent procedures, or perhaps conveniently ignored them for the sake of the verse. The birds of passage did, however, have their hair cut short.]

momiage no	they compliment each other
ato wo homeau	on what is left at the sideburns:
Matsugaoka	Matsugaoka

niatta to	"it is becoming," they say,
beso beso homeru	plying her with compliments—
Matsugaoka	Matsugaoka

Matsugaoka	at Matsugaoka
wara de yuute mo	fastening hair even with straw
koishigari	betrays attachment

Matsugaoka	at Matsugaoka
wara de mo tabane	one does not make a chignon
sasenu tokoro	even with straw

fundoshi mo	"if even your shorts
kinu nara tore to	are silk, get rid of them"—
Matsugaoka	Matsugaoka

[No frills were permitted, not even a silk loincloth.]

Kamakura ni	at Kamakura
katsuo mo kuwazu	three years without
sannen i	even a bonito

[The fare was strictly vegetarian.]

tachimono wa	among the items
otoko to soshite	for abstention are: men,
gyorui nari	and all kinds of fish

muzukashisa	how difficult!
shōjin wo shite	breaking off the relationship,
en wo kiri	with vegetarian food

zange shina	"repent,
zange shina yo to	repent of your evil ways!"
Matsugaoka	Matsugaoka

[Rites of repentance are a common feature of the Buddhist religious life. But our poet suggests that the runaway wives had all the more need for self-examination.]

amadera e	on her way
Enoshima kakete	to Enoshima a mother
haha wa yori	visits the convent

[Before the persecution of Buddhism (*haibutsu kishaku*) and its forced separation from Shintō (*shimbutsu bunri*) in the early Meiji period, Enoshima had been a popular site of Shintō-Buddhist syncretic worship. It was especially known for the temple to Ben(zai)ten (Sarasvatī) built by Mongaku in 1182 with Yoritomo's support. A mother making a pilgrimage to Enoshima now has another reason to visit Kamakura.]

> *Kamakura de*　　　　at Kamakura
> *ima dōshin wo*　　　the mother now seeks
> *haha tazune*　　　　religion

[So it might appear. But of course she is simply visiting (*tazunu*) her daughter at Matsugaoka.]

> *hidoi koto*　　　　　good grief!
> *Matsugaoka e no*　　travelling companions
> *tsure ga deki*　　　　to Matsugaoka

[Parents visiting their daughter at the Tōkeiji feel that they have enough problems and now they are joined by another group going to the same destination. . . . Or does the stanza perhaps refer to the feelings of a runaway who is in too much of a hurry for idle chatter?]

> *Enoshima e*　　　　　the second time
> *nidome no toki wa*　she visited Enoshima she wore
> *koromo de ki*　　　　a nun's robe

[Our poet to the contrary, it is unlikely that refugees staying at Matsugaoka would have been permitted out of the compound for casual excursions.]

> *geka nado ni*　　　　there were also those
> *kakattamo aru*　　　needing a surgeon's help:
> *Matsugaoka*　　　　Matsugaoka

[The abuse might be physical as well as psychological, as we are reminded by the "bruises received from a wooden pestle."]

> *Matsugaoka*　　　　　Matsugaoka:
> *chitto hajiku ga*　　with some skill at the calculator,
> *nasshobun*　　　　　the business office

[Many of the refugees doubtless had only household skills. But there were records to be kept at the Tōkeiji, and one able to use the *soroban* (abacus) calculator might be assigned special chores.]

> *jionna no*　　　　　waiting out the term
> *nen'ake wo matsu*　to make her an honest woman:
> *Matsugaoka*　　　　Matsugaoka

Kamakura mo	even in Kamakura,
sanjū made wa	until you're thirty
oshiku nashi	it's all right

[For the young there is always a tomorrow—well, perhaps not always.]

ichinichi mo	never to remarry,
sowazu sennichi	she dies in the convent
tera de shinu	of a thousand days
sannen no	within three years
aida ni gei mo	one's artistic accomplishments
gutto nuke	fall off considerably

[Short hair, no ornaments, spartan fare, and, of course, no playing of musical instruments.]

Enoshima mo	at Kamakura
yome Kamakura ni	the wife even forgets
ite wasure	"Enoshima"

[Since the island of Enoshima is only a short distance from Kamakura, it would be hard for a Matsugaoka resident not to be aware of it. But here "Enoshima" refers to a well-known *koto* piece.]
[The services of men were sometimes required, as guards or carpenters. But care had to be observed.]

Matsugaoka	At Matsugaoka
daiku ni ban wo	the guard keeps his eye
tsukete oki	on the carpenter
otoko mite	the dogs there
hoeru inu ari	howl at seeing a man:
Matsugaoka	Matsugaoka
koko ni ketsu-	"she's holed up here,"
-karu to mite yuku	looking up as he passes by
Matsugaoka	Matsugaoka

[Chance brings her husband to Kamakura.]

Kamakura no	separation:
gemmei ni	following strict orders
shitagai rien	from Kamakura

[Only a husband could grant a divorce. But if a woman fulfilled the requirements set by the Tōkeiji, the civil government in Edo could easily enough "persuade" him that it was in his best interest to do so.]

enkiru ni ya	with the Kamakura
Kamakura-dono ga	authorities pressing, no doubt
ushirodate	he will grant the divorce
sarijō ga	arriving by courier,
hikyaku de todoku	the letter of separation—
Matsugaoka	Matsugaoka

[Matsugaoka provided the forms, but the husband had to sign statements to the effect that he accepted the convent's judgment (jiō rien sōmon) and that he would not interfere with his wife's remarriage (rienjō). They were then returned to the wife at the convent and she would be free to leave.]

amadera e	poorly written,
kite akuhitsu wo	it comes to the convent—
hittakuri	and she grabs it

[Elegant penmanship would be the last thing on the woman's mind after waiting three years for her letter of separation.]

shōjin	cleansed in body
kessai shite	and mind she receives
sarijō wo	the letter of separation
senguri ni	one after another
sarijō no kuru	she sees the letters of separation
Matsugaoka	arrive at Matsugaoka

[And sooner or later it will be her turn.]

sarijō wo	getting her
uhatsu no ama ni	letter of separation
natte tori	as an unshorn nun

Foundation stanza (maeku):

morai koso sure	she really got it!
morai koso sure	she really got it!

Joined stanza (tsukeku):

sarijō wo	along with getting

| *toru uchi toshi ga* | the letter of separation— |
| *mittsu fuke* | three years of aging |

[In this "foundation stanza" we see something of the origins of *senryū* in "stanza connecting" (*maekuzuke*) in the earlier standard linked verse (*renga*), and in its less-constrained cousin, *haikai*.]

sannen no	for three years
furukizu uzuku	the pain of old scars—
Matsugaoka	Matsugaoka

Kamakura de	at Kamakura
tsuie no toshi wa	the expenditure in aging
mittsu yori	is three years

[The cost of the separation is not to be counted in terms of money, but in terms of time lost.]

sarijō ga	the letter of separation—
oshō no te kara	returned from the hand
modotte ki	of the abbess

[Usually the abbess must dun the reluctant husband to sign the letter of separation, but occasionally she can mediate a reconciliation.]

nyōbō to	after just
sōdan wo shite	consulting with his wife,
tsuma wo saru	he lets her go

[This stanza seems to ridicule the man who gives his wife a divorce after the two discuss their differences, very likely under the auspices of the Tōkeiji. The law was clearly on the husband's side, but public opinion was ambivalent.]

hoshizukiyo	after gazing wearily
akiru hodo mite	so long during star-lit nights,
en wo kiri	the separation

[The tranquility of the mountain convent was not to every townsman's taste.]

THE RETURN HOME AND AFTERMATH

shōgatsu wo	she returns
mitsu shite kite	after three New Years Days,
wakaku naru	young again

[. . . at least to the extent that she is now unmarried and can begin a new life.]

amadera ni	returning,
itte waga mi ni	having gone to the convent
shite kaeri	to assert herself

[There is a kind of contradiction in asserting oneself to take refuge in a convent, whose teaching and practice is directed toward selflessness.]

matsuyani de	after three years
sannen migaki	of brushing with pine resin,
mata shiraha	white teeth again

[Blackened teeth had long been an ornament of the married woman, so white teeth were an indication that the woman was free to marry again. "Pine Resin" is used in this stanza to suggest "Pine Grove" (Matsugaoka), of course, but the substance hardly seems suitable as a tooth powder.]

sannen sugiru	three years later
to hitori wa	she cannot return
kaere-ezu	on her own

[When she first came alone to Matsugaoka, fear and dissatisfaction helped the woman to surmount all obstacles. Now on her return home she is accompanied by family and friends.]

mononofu wa	the warrior
higaeri yome wa	returns in a day—the wife,
sannen me	after three years!

[The life of the warrior may be dangerous, but if he survives the battle, he returns home in a short time. For the wife who escapes to Matsugaoka it takes considerably longer and three years in a period of relatively short life expectancy was not to be dismissed lightly.]

michi michi mo	street after street
iken de modoru	returning home with much discussion:
Matsugaoka	Matsugaoka

[Is she returning with her parents and the letter of separation, or has she decided to return to her husband? In either case, the way home is paved with opinions.]

jūsan ri	with thirteen *ri*
saki de otoko wo	ahead of them,
soshitteru	they criticize men

[The runaways usually arrived alone at Matsugaoka, but they return to Edo with their parents or perhaps another companion from the convent. The husband may be divorced, but he is not completely exorcized.]

Kamakura wo	when they return
modoreba momo ya	from Kamakura, peaches
kuri mo nari	and chestnuts

[It is commonly said that peach and chestnut trees bear their first fruits after three years, the same period required at the Tōkeiji.]

Rokugō wa	Now calmly
shizuka ni koeru	crossing the Rokugō—
sannenme	the third year
koko wo kuru	"how great my fear
toki no kowasa to	at the time I first came here"—
sannenme	and now the third year
sennichi no-	a thousand days
-gare no koto yome	of freedom—the wife
omoidashi	reminisces

[Having returned to Edo's world of Confucian responsibility, the woman, perhaps unmarried, looks back nostalgically.]

yume bakari	in Kamakura
naru Kamakura ni	two or three years—
ni-sannen	now all a dream

[While the woman was at Matsugaoka, the time seemed to pass slowly. But now that she is again immersed in worldly affairs, the events of those days appear far away.]

hiroi mi ni	horizons broadened,
natte Kamakura	she now comes sightseeing
made mo miru	even to Kamakura

[Soon after her stay at Matsugaoka, perhaps the memory of her marriage and divorce would be too vivid to permit a visit. But time mellows us all.]

APPENDIX

Chinese Romanization Conversion Tables

For the nonspecialist, the inevitable problems of accommodating to a new vocabulary of names, titles, places, and dates can only be aggravated by the variety, and often the intuitively unfriendly nature, of systems for romanizing Asian scripts. For readers of *Religions of Japan in Practice,* a major difficulty is likely to be the use today in the English-speaking world of two major competing systems for the romanization of Chinese: Wade-Giles and pinyin.

The Wade-Giles system originated in the romanization devised by Thomas Francis Wade (1818–1859) as set forth in his *Book of Experiments* (Hong Kong, 1859), and *A Progressive Course Designed to Assist the Student of Colloquial Chinese* (London, 1867). This was adopted and somewhat modified by Herbert Allen Giles (1854–1935) in his *Chinese-English Dictionary* (1892), with still later emendations. The following conversion tables use a more or less "standard version" of the Wade-Giles system. It should be noted, however, that in the current "modified" Wade-Giles system, the circumflex (ˆ) is generally omitted where formerly used over e, as ê. Moreover, the umlaut u (ü) is preserved only in yü, nü, and lü, to distinguish them from yu, nu, and lu.

The Pinyin romanization system was promulgated in 1957 as an aid in teaching standard pronunciation. It replaced the Wade-Giles system in China, and, to some extent in Western language writings, during the 1980s. For additional information, see *A Chinese-English Dictionary* (Beijing, 1978–1979), 956–959; *Reform of the Chinese Written Language* (Peking: Foreign Language Press, 1965 rev. tr.); and Jerry Norman, *Chinese* (Cambridge: Cambridge University Press, 1988), pp. 257–264.

Tone marks can be indicated in both systems, either by the superscripts (Wade-Giles) or by marks over vowels (pinyin), e.g., Tao[4]-hsüan[1] or Dào-xuan:

Wade-Giles	Pinyin	
(superscript)[1]	(over vowel)	ˉ
(superscript)[2]	(over vowel)	´
(superscript)[3]	(over vowel)	˅
(superscript)[4]	(over vowel)	`

Whether one system ultimately replaces the other will be decided in time. Meanwhile, we must at present learn to live with the confusion of two romanizations, with authors and publishers rarely willing to provide us with an easy transition between them. The student of Japanese must also remember the Japanese pronunciation of the characters together with the Hepburn romanization if he or she plans to use a Japanese biographical dictionary or even an index in English romanization. Hence the following tables.

TABLE 1
Wade-Giles to Pinyin

Wade-Giles	Pinyin	Wade-Giles	Pinyin	Wade-Giles	Pinyin
a	a	ch'ui	chui	chūn	jun
ai	ai	ch'un	chun	chung	jiong
an	an	ch'ūn	qun	chung	zhong
ang	ang	ch'ung	chong		
ao	ao	cha	zha	ê	e
		chai	zhai	ên	en
ch'a	cha	chan	zhan	êng	eng
ch'ai	chai	chang	zhang	êrh	er
ch'an	chan	chao	zhao		
ch'ang	chang	chê	zhe	fa	fa
ch'ao	chao	chên	zhen	fan	fan
ch'ê	che	chêng	zheng	fang	fang
ch'ên	chen	chi	ji	fei	fei
ch'êng	cheng	chia	jia	fên	fen
ch'i	qi	chiang	jiang	fêng	feng
ch'ia	qia	chiao	jiao	fo	fo
ch'iang	qiang	chieh	jie	fou	fou
ch'iao	qiao	chien	jian	fu	fu
ch'ieh	qie	chih	zhi		
ch'ien	qian	chin	jin	ha	ha
ch'ih	chi	ching	jing	hai	hai
ch'in	qin	chiu	jiu	han	han
ch'ing	qing	chiung	jiong	hang	hang
ch'iu	qiu	cho	zhuo	hao	hao
ch'iung	qiong	chou	zhou	hei	hei
ch'o	chuo	chu	zhu	hên	hen
ch'ou	chou	chū	ju	hêng	heng
ch'u	chu	chua	zhua	ho	he
ch'ū	qu	chuai	zhuai	hou	hou
ch'ua	chua	chuan	zhuan	hsi	xi
ch'uai	chuai	chūan	juan	hsia	xia
ch'uan	chuan	chuang	zhuang	hsiang	xiang
ch'ūan	quan	chüeh	jue	hsiao	xiao
ch'uang	chuang	chui	zhui	hsieh	xie
ch'üeh	que	chun	zhun	hsien	xian

Wade-Giles	Pinyin	Wade-Giles	Pinyin	Wade-Giles	Pinyin
hsin	xin	k'uang	kuang	lüan	lüan
hsing	xing	k'ui	kui	lüeh	lüe
hsiu	xiu	k'un	kun	lun	lun
hsü	xu	k'uo	kuo	lung	long
hsüan	xuan	ka	ga		
hsüeh	xue	kai	gai	ma	ma
hsün	xun	kan	gan	mai	mai
hu	hu	kang	gang	man	man
gua	hua	kao	gao	mang	mang
huai	huai	kê	ge	mao	mao
huan	huan	kei	gei	mê	me
huang	huang	kên	gen	mei	mei
hui	hui	kêng	geng	mên	men
hun	hun	kou	gou	mêng	meng
hung	hong	ku	gu	mi	mi
huo	huo	kua	gua	miao	miao
		kuai	guai	mien	mian
i	yi	kuan	guan	mieh	mie
		kuang	guang	min	min
jan	ran	kui	gui	ming	ming
jang	rang	kun	gun	miu	miu
jao	rao	kung	kong	mo	mo
jê	re	kung	gong	mou	mou
jên	ren	kuo	guo	mu	mu
jêng	reng				
jih	ri	la	la	na	na
jo	ruo	lai	lai	nai	nai
jou	rou	lan	lan	nan	nan
ju	ru	lang	lang	nang	nang
juan	ruan	lao	lao	nao	nao
jui	rui	lê	le	nê	ne
jun	run	lei	lei	nên	nen
jung	rong	lêng	leng	nei	nei
		li	li	nêng	neng
k'a	ka	lia	lia	ni	ni
k'ai	kai	liang	liang	niang	niang
k'an	kan	liao	liao	niao	niao
k'ang	kang	lieh	lie	nieh	nie
k'ao	kao	lien	lian	nien	nian
k'ê	ke	lin	lin	nin	nin
k'ên	ken	ling	ling	ning	ning
k'êng	keng	liu	liu	niu	niu
k'ou	kou	lo	luo	no	nuo
k'u	ku	lou	lou	nou	nou
k'ua	kua	lu	lu	nu	nu
k'uai	kuai	lü	lü	nü	nü
k'uan	kuan	luan	luan	nuan	nuan

Wade-Giles	Pinyin	Wade-Giles	Pinyin	Wade-Giles	Pinyin
nüeh	nüe	sêng	seng	ta	da
nung	nong	sha	sha	tai	dai
		shai	shai	tan	dan
o	o	shan	shan	tang	dang
ou	ou	shang	shang	tao	dao
		shao	shao	tê	de
p'a	pa	shê	she	tei	dei
p'ai	pai	shei	shei	têng	deng
p'an	pan	shên	shen	ti	di
p'ang	pang	shêng	sheng	tiao	diao
p'ao	pao	shih	shi	tieh	die
p'ei	pei	shou	shou	tien	dian
p'ên	pen	shu	shu	ting	ding
p'êng	peng	shua	shua	tiu	diu
p'i	pi	shuai	shuai	to	duo
p'iao	piao	shuan	shuan	tou	dou
p'ieh	pie	shui	shui	ts'a	ca
p'ien	pian	shun	shun	ts'ai	cai
p'in	pin	shuo	shuo	ts'an	can
p'ing	ping	so	suo	ts'ang	cang
p'o	po	sou	sou	ts'ao	cao
p'ou	pou	ssu	si	ts'ê	ce
p'u	pu	su	su	ts'ên	cen
pa	ba	suan	suan	ts'êng	ceng
pai	bai	sui	sui	ts'o	cuo
pan	ban	sun	sun	ts'ou	cou
pang	bang	sung	song	ts'u	cu
pao	bao			ts'uan	cuan
pei	bei	t'a	ta	ts'ui	cui
pên	ben	t'ai	tai	ts'un	cun
pêng	beng	t'an	tan	ts'ung	cong
pi	bi	t'ang	tang	tsa	za
piao	biao	t'ao	tao	tsai	zai
pieh	bie	t'ê	te	tsan	zan
pien	bian	t'êng	teng	tsang	zang
pin	bin	t'i	ti	tsao	zao
ping	bing	t'iao	tiao	tsê	ze
po	bo	t'ieh	tie	tsei	zei
pu	bu	t'ien	tian	tsên	zen
		t'ing	ting	tsêng	zeng
sa	sa	t'o	tuo	tso	zuo
sai	sai	t'ou	tou	tsou	zou
san	san	t'u	tu	tsu	zu
sang	sang	t'uan	tuan	tsuan	zuan
sao	sao	t'ui	tui	tsui	zui
sê	se	t'un	tun	tsun	zun
sên	sen	t'ung	tong	tsung	zong

Wade-Giles	Pinyin	Wade-Giles	Pinyin	Wade-Giles	Pinyin
tu	du	wang	wang	yeh	ye
tuan	duan	wei	wei	yen	yan
tui	dui	wên	wen	yin	yin
tun	dun	wêng	weng	ying	ying
tung	dong	wo	wo	yo	yo
tz'u	ci	wu	wu	yu	you
tzu	zi			yü	yu
		ya	ya	yüan	yuan
wa	wa	yai	yai	yüeh	yue
wai	wai	yang	yang	yün	yun
wan	wan	yao	yao	yung	yong

TABLE 2
Pinyin to Wade-Giles

Pinyin	Wade-Giles	Pinyin	Wade-Giles	Pinyin	Wade-Giles
a	a	cha	ch'a	dang	tang
ai	ai	chai	ch'ai	dao	tao
an	an	chan	ch'an	de	tê
ang	ang	chang	ch'ang	dei	tei
ao	ao	chao	ch'ao	deng	têng
		che	ch'ê	di	ti
ba	pa	chen	ch'ên	dian	tien
bai	pai	cheng	ch'êng	diao	tiao
ban	pan	chi	ch'ih	die	tieh
bang	pang	chong	ch'ung	ding	ting
bao	pao	chou	ch'ou	diu	tiu
bei	pei	chu	ch'u	dong	tung
ben	pên	chua	ch'ua	dou	tou
beng	pêng	chuai	ch'uai	du	tu
bi	pi	chuan	ch'uan	duan	tuan
bian	pien	chuang	ch'uang	dui	tui
biao	piao	chui	ch'ui	dun	tun
bie	pieh	chun	ch'un	duo	to
bin	pin	chuo	ch'o		
bing	ping	ci	tz'u	e	ê
bo	po	cong	ts'ung	en	ên
bu	pu	cou	ts'ou	eng	êng
		cu	ts'u	er	êrh
ca	ts'a	cuan	ts'uan		
cai	ts'ai	cui	ts'ui	fa	fa
can	ts'an	cun	ts'un	fan	fan
cang	ts'ang	cuo	ts'o	fang	fang
cao	ts'ao			fei	fei
ce	ts'ê	da	ta	fen	fên
cen	ts'ên	dai	tai	feng	fêng
ceng	ts'êng	dan	tan	fo	fo

Pinyin	Wade-Giles	Pinyin	Wade-Giles	Pinyin	Wade-Giles
fou	fou	jiao	chiao	long	lung
fu	fu	jie	chieh	lou	lou
		jin	chin	lu	lu
ga	ka	jing	ching	luan	luan
gai	kai	jiong	chiung	lun	lun
gan	kan	jiu	chiu	luo	lo
gang	kang	ju	chü	lü	lü
gao	kao	juan	chüan	lüan	lüan
ge	kê	jue	chüeh	lüe	lüeh
gei	kei	jun	chün		
gen	kên			ma	ma
geng	kêng	ka	k'a	mai	mai
gong	kung	kai	k'ai	man	man
gou	kou	kan	k'an	mang	mang
gu	ku	kang	k'ang	mao	mao
gua	kua	kao	k'ao	me	mê
guai	kuai	ke	k'ê	mei	mei
guan	kuan	ken	k'ên	men	mên
guang	kuang	keng	k'êng	meng	mêng
gui	kui	kong	kung	mi	mi
gun	kun	kou	k'ou	mian	mien
guo	kuo	ku	k'u	miao	miao
		kua	k'ua	mie	mieh
ha	ha	kuai	k'uai	min	min
hai	hai	kuan	k'uan	ming	ming
han	han	kuang	k'uang	miu	miu
hang	hang	kui	k'ui	mo	mo
hao	hao	kun	k'un	mou	mou
he	ho	kuo	k'uo	mu	mu
hei	hei				
hen	hên	la	la	na	na
heng	hêng	lai	lai	nai	nai
hong	hung	lan	lan	nan	nan
hou	hou	lang	lang	nang	nang
hu	hu	lao	lao	nao	nao
gua	hua	le	lê	ne	nê
huai	huai	lei	lei	nei	nei
huan	huan	leng	lêng	nen	nên
huang	huang	li	li	neng	nêng
hui	hui	lia	lia	ni	ni
hun	hun	lian	lien	nian	nien
huo	huo	liang	liang	niang	niang
		liao	liao	niao	niao
ji	chi	lie	lieh	nie	nieh
jia	chia	lin	lin	nin	nin
jian	chien	ling	ling	ning	ning
jiang	chiang	liu	liu	niu	niu

Pinyin	Wade-Giles	Pinyin	Wade-Giles	Pinyin	Wade-Giles
nong	nung	re	jê	ta	t'a
nou	nou	ren	jên	tai	t'ai
nu	nu	reng	jêng	tan	t'an
nuan	nuan	ri	jih	tang	t'ang
nuo	no	rong	jung	tao	t'ao
nü	nü	rou	jou	te	t'ê
nüe	nüeh	ru	ju	teng	t'êng
		ruan	juan	ti	t'i
o	o	rui	jui	tian	t'ien
ou	ou	run	jun	tiao	t'iao
		ruo	jo	tie	t'ieh
pa	p'a			ting	t'ing
pai	p'ai	sa	sa	tong	t'ung
pan	p'an	sai	sai	tou	t'ou
pang	p'ang	san	san	tu	t'u
pao	p'ao	sang	sang	tuan	t'uan
pei	p'ei	sao	sao	tui	t'ui
pen	p'ên	se	sê	tun	t'un
peng	p'êng	sen	sên	tuo	t'o
pi	p'i	seng	sêng		
pian	p'ien	sha	sha	wa	wa
piao	p'iao	shai	shai	wai	wai
pie	p'ieh	shan	shan	wan	wan
pin	p'in	shang	shang	wang	wang
ping	p'ing	shao	shao	wei	wei
po	p'o	she	shê	wen	wên
pou	p'ou	shei	shei	weng	wêng
pu	p'u	shen	shên	wo	wo
		sheng	shêng	wu	wu
qi	ch'i	shi	shih		
qia	ch'ia	shou	shou	xi	hsi
qian	ch'ien	shu	shu	xia	hsia
qiang	ch'iang	shua	shua	xian	hsien
qiao	ch'iao	shuai	shuai	xiang	hsiang
qie	ch'ieh	shuan	shuan	xiao	hsiao
qin	ch'in	shui	shui	xie	hsieh
qing	ch'ing	shun	shun	xin	hsin
qiong	ch'iung	shuo	shuo	xing	hsing
qiu	ch'iu	si	ssu	xiu	hsiu
qu	ch'ü	song	sung	xu	hsü
quan	ch'üan	sou	sou	xuan	hsüan
que	chüeh	su	su	xue	hsüeh
qun	ch'ün	suan	suan	xun	hsün
		sui	sui		
ran	jan	sun	sun	ya	ya
rang	jang	suo	so	yai	yai
rao	jao			yan	yen

Pinyin	Wade-Giles	Pinyin	Wade-Giles	Pinyin	Wade-Giles
yang	yang	zang	tsang	zhu	chu
yao	yao	zao	tsao	zhua	chua
ye	yeh	ze	tsê	zhuai	chuai
yi	i	zei	tsei	zhuan	chuan
yin	yin	zen	tsên	zhuang	chuang
ying	ying	zeng	tsêng	zhui	chui
yo	yo	zha	cha	zhun	chun
yong	yung	zhai	chai	zhuo	cho
you	yu	zhan	chan	zi	tzu
yu	yü	zhang	chang	zong	tsung
yuan	yüan	zhao	chao	zou	tsou
yue	yüeh	zhe	chê	zu	tsu
yun	yün	zhen	chên	zuan	tsuan
		zheng	chêng	zui	tsui
za	tsa	zhi	chih	zun	tsun
zai	tsai	zhong	chung	zuo	tso
zan	tsan	zhou	chou		

INDEX
